THE COMPLETE BOOK OF
BUILDING
AND
COLLECTING
MODEL
AUTOMOBILES

A 1/4-inch-scale model of an automobile museum with roof removed to reveal a varied display of miniatures of cars of various types and ages. Some of these models were built from kits of plastic parts; others are cast-metal miniatures available in completely assembled and painted form. For other views of the museum building, see Fig. 148.

"Model Racing Buyers' Guide"

THE COMPLETE BOOK OF
BUILDING
AND
COLLECTING
MODEL
AUTOMOBILES

LOUIS H. HERTZ

CROWN PUBLISHERS, INC., NEW YORK

OTHER BOOKS BY LOUIS H. HERTZ
THE COMPLETE BOOK OF MODEL RACEWAYS AND ROADWAYS
THE COMPLETE BOOK OF MODEL AIRCRAFT, SPACECRAFT AND ROCKETS
THE COMPLETE BOOK OF MODEL RAILROADING
ANTIQUE COLLECTING FOR MEN
THE TOY COLLECTOR
NEW ROADS TO ADVENTURE IN MODEL RAILROADING
ADVANCED MODEL RAILROADING
COLLECTING MODEL TRAINS
MESSRS. IVES OF BRIDGEPORT
RIDING THE TINPLATE RAILS
THE HANDBOOK OF OLD AMERICAN TOYS
MAKING YOUR MODEL RAILROAD
MECHANICAL TOY BANKS
MODEL RAILROAD CONVERSION MANUAL
MINIATURE RAILROAD SERVICE AND REPAIR MANUAL

TO A. J. (TONY) KOVELESKI

An old friend and the man who, more than any other,
sparkplugged today's model automobile enthusiasm.

CONTENTS

INTRODUCTION

The purpose of the writer's *The Complete Book of* series, each dealing with a separate category of models, of which the present volume is the fourth, has been to provide books that are at once comprehensive, informative, and practical. They have been intended to be both of immediate assistance and of enduring reference value to the beginner and experienced hobbyist alike. Thus have followed in turn *The Complete Book of Model Railroading, The Complete Book of Model Raceways and Roadways, The Complete Book of Model Aircraft, Spacecraft and Rockets,* and, now, *The Complete Book of Building and Collecting Model Automobiles.*

The history of any group of models has been found to be of enormous interest to all participants in the hobby related to them, and separate historical chapters were included in the three previous books. In the present book an alteration in this arrangement has been called for by the fact that the collecting side of the hobby already bulks so large in the overall model automobile picture—as evidenced by its inclusion in the title as well as by the sheer magnitude of historical material uncovered during the course of research for the book. Accordingly, the reader will find no distinct section devoted to history as such, but rather a very substantial amount of such material included in Chapter 5 at such points as it applies to or demonstrates certain specific points of model automobile collecting. The telling of "The Story of the Model Automobile" as such must consequently await publication as a separate and complete book in itself.

Cumulative experience indicates that several cautionary or explanatory notes are called for here: First, the fact that a particular model or series of models is mentioned in the text or pictured does not necessarily mean that it therefore is particularly desirable, rare, or valuable. On the other hand, some readers have been known to assume the opposite and to take it that something perforce is unduly rare because it is not specifically cited in a book! These are fallacious assumptions, but they are known to have arisen on a number of occasions. Second, the fact that some models or catalog pages happen to have been reproduced larger than others on the pages of a book sometimes but not often has any bearing on the relative actual importance of the subjects of the pictures in question. If any clue to such things is to be found, it will be found in the accompanying captions. Third, there is, of course, a vast gulf between a reading list and a bibliography. Because a work is regarded as holding sufficient interest and usefulness to be included in a list of books suggested for further reading, it does not follow that the writer who so mentions such a book agrees with each and every statement or opinion expressed therein.

Having attempted to clarify these matters, the most important portion of a proper introduction remains, wherein are enumerated the names of all those who in one manner or another—information, pictures, suggestions, and opinions—have been of assistance in the preparation of the book at hand. At this point the present writer always fervently trusts that no such names have inadvertently been overlooked. If there are any, it is most emphatically unintentional, although it must be pointed out that, particularly in the preliminary stages of work on a book or even prior to the development of the book idea itself, there are usually many brief anonymous exchanges of ideas during encounters with enthusiasts at hobby shops and other meeting places, the results of which may well eventually blend into the final pattern and fabric of a book. To all such contributors the writer can only say that he is as sincerely grateful as to all those specifically recorded on the following list of names of those to whom the writer wishes to express his profound appreciation:

To G. William Holland, that skilled cameraman and himself a model automobile collector, who, once again, as in the case of several of the writer's recent books, journeyed widely in order to provide many superb special photographs. The form of the captions makes clear which of the models illustrated are specimens in Mr. Holland's own collection.

To Anthony and Doris Koveleski; George S. Indig; Helen C. Harris; Charles A. Stenman; Mark Haber; Ward Kimball; Adam Pellicot, Jr.; Walter Dreyer; Lloyd W. Ralston; Robert A. Ahlers; Joseph N. Imler; William A. Hall; Gates Willard; Joseph G. Gollins; C. W. Frey; Thomas W. Sefton; A. E. Moredock; L. C. and Gertrude Hegarty; John F. Marron; Dr. G. A. Robinson; B. J. Donnelly; William H. and Lillian B. Gottschalk; Leon Perelman; Dr. Clinton B. Seeley; Rev. Richard E. Matera; Thomas Matera; Dr. James Nixon; George H. Hartman; Diane Pudlo; Arthur B. Lundahl; Ethel K. Goldberg, Maurice G. Gherman, Geoffrey Wheeler, Bud Hollzer, and William H. Van Precht of *Craft, Model & Hobby Industry;* Irwin, Nathan, and Lewis Polk, Robert L. Colandro, Marguerite Hubert, Lee Fox, and Anne D. Podell of Polk's Model Craft Hobbies, Inc.; Gilbert Rose of Aristo-Craft Distinctive Miniatures; Ace Products; Raymond L. Spong; Henry Kuell; John L. Davis; I. Warshaw of the Warshaw Collection of Business Americana; George N. and Miriam W. Lawson; Paul H. Schmidt; Marcelle W. Peterka; William Miller; Charles Woodland; Herb Leavy and Joseph Daffron of *Model Racing Buyers' Guide;* Ken Wootton; Dr. Cecil Gibson; Donald Lichtenberger; Charles R. Kudolla; Clare Donzé; Suzanne Donzé; Peter Foss; and David K. Bausch.

To Myron B. Shure, Richard M. Shure, Joseph N. Shure, John E. Schutz, Jim McAfee, Mike Eckstein, Warren Schmidt, William O'Brien,

Alf Christiansen, John Oltyan, Robert Douglas, Lillian Sang, R. R. Ballenger, George L. Strobel, Harry Brown, and James Squillacioti of the Strombecker Corp.; Katherine Hargrave Dowst; W. S. Hicks of F. W. Woolworth Co.; S. R. Lewis; L. S. Bixler; Henry J. Cole; William D. Perry of Perry Promotions; A. M. Koveleski of Auto World; Karl F. Landgraf; G. M. Pooley of B. T. Batsford Ltd.; Ralph Bertini; David C. Byrd; F. Brian Jewell; Robert Matthews; Jerome Silverman; Stanley Goldsmith, Harry Urban, and Sally Newman of the Barclay Mfg. Co.; Sanford D. Bogaty; R. N. MacLeod, Phil Cameron, and José Rodriguez, Jr., of *Car Model;* Abe Linick; George H. Tissen; Jean Zeiler of Walter Kidde & Co., Inc.; Robert Bostoff; Maurice H. Romer; Douglas Bell of the Vintage Chevrolet Club of Ameirca, Inc.; Charles C. Merzbach of Charles C. Merzbach Co., Inc.; W. E. Letroadec of the American Society of Mechanical Engineers; Gary Moore of the National Biscuit Co.; C. Hahn; F. R. Eckford of the Illinois Institute of Technology; Roland H. Baker, Jr.; Fred C. Ziesenheim; John Ziesenheim; Joseph R. Ziesenheim; Harvey W. Lepselter of Louis Marx & Co., Inc.; Henry Katz, Richard L. Keats, George H. Fink, and Nathan Cohen of the Buddy L. Corp.; W. van Roosbroeck; R. Carleton Estes; Robert Grew; Frank Grew; William Politis; Edward Force; Nelson Adams; George Frost; Don La Spaluto; P. N. Conner; G. W. B. Lacey and T. E. Lillywhite of the Science Museum, South Kensington, London; Ben McCready, W. Voorhees, Ted Erickson, Robert F. Williamson, R. A. Berger, and the entire office staff of *Playthings.*

To Karl H. Kuebler; Stephen J. Olin; Robert Olin; H. Fred Gade; Michael F. Spielman of *Toys and Novelties;* Ray Swain of R. S. Publicity Service; A. J. Degan of the Riemann, Seabrey Co., Inc.; E. W. Spear of Armour and Co.; Arthur E. Anderson; Lynn Becker; A. M. Donofrio and Don Robbins of the Craft Master Corp.; Lou and Jay Kramer of Life-Like Products, Inc.; Donald Lefft, Chris Jelley, Mike Rickett, H. J. Fallmann and Charles Baxter of Lines Brothers, Ltd.; Mel Miller of the Ringling Museum of the Circus; Melvin R. Roberts; Vance Bell of *Steel;* Paul L. Kohnstamm and Justin Pulver of H. Kohnstamm & Co., Inc.; John R. Cuomo, John Tillotson, and Richard Schwarzchild of the Aurora Plastics Corp.; Arthur Barnett of the Hubley Division, Gabriel Industries, Inc.; H. G. Michael and John R. Blazer of the Industro-Motive Corp.; Phil Thompson of the Hawk Model Co.; Dave Nelson of Lindberg Products, Inc.; George Toteff and Len Bolton of Model Products Corp.; Anthony P. Iati of the Model Rectifier Corp.; Jack M. Besser, Joe Belanger, and Wade Newman of Monogram Models, Inc.;

Howard E. Rieder, Joel K. Rubenstein, and Bert Post of Revell, Inc.; C. W. McClellan of the Fisher Body Craft Craftsman's Guild; J. E. Petit of the Testor Corp.; R. Clover of Auto-Models Ltd.; Stuart John Meyers of *American Bicyclist;* James B. Russell of the American Russkit Co.; Grover C. Schaible of the Pyro Plastics Corp.; A. L. Davenport, Jr., of the Pactra Chemical Co., Inc.; Charles J. Ulrich of the C. J. Ulrich Co., Inc.; J. George Silverstein; J. Noel Martin, Town Clerk of the Royal Borough of Kingston upon Thames; Nancy F. Chudacoff of the Chicago Public Library; John D. Frisoli of Scientific Models, Inc. Fred E. Dickey; J. Wheeldon of Peco Publications and Publicity Ltd.; Steve Curry; and Kohnstamm-Wolfe, Inc.

To Anne Adams of *The Lamp;* R. G. Whitelaw of the New Jersey Zinc Co.; Clyde and Vera C. Austin of Austin Craft; S. D. Toon and Heath Ltd.; Eric Kahn and Joseph Steinberg of the Schuco Toy Co., Inc.; Gerald Fisher and Rhoda S. Miller of Reeves International Inc.; Mark Goroff, Eric Schulbach, Ruth Sherman, and Roberta J. Wolfson of the Fred Bronner Corp.; Walter Caddell and Milt Grey of the Hobby Industry Association of America, Inc.; Henry Blankfort of the Blankfort Group; Louis S. Wetzel, Arthur Rosenbloom, Ruth Cohn, and John Donoghue of Renwal Products, Inc.; Ralph M. Titcomb; H. Hudson Dobson; H. Hudson Dobson, Jr.; Lynne Pressman and Micky Graubard of the Pressman Toy Corp.; Ralph Leonardson of Sears, Roebuck and Co.; Edward Schutz of the Fisher-Price Co.; J. Edward Jones; Jerome Smith of the Lead Industry Association; the Zinc Institution; Frederick Strauss and Arthur Davis of the F. J. Strauss Co., Inc.; Arthur Henriques; Elizabeth Thompson; Roger Arcara; the International Silver Co.; Paul F. Runge of Ace R/C, Inc.; Mike Baltus; Ben Millspauch; Andrew Wittenborn; Michael Brook of the Minnesota Historical Society; Margaret A. Kately, Virginia K. Christopher, Marcella B. Chretien, and Virginia Napier of the Scarsdale, New York, Public Library; Juanita Doares and Bodhan Melnyk of the New York Public Library, Astor, Lenox, and Tilden Foundations; the Jersey City, New Jersey, Public Library; the Connecticut State Library; the New York State Library; Guy Harrison; L. D. Morgison; W. H. Young; Harold H. Carstens, Naomi Drake, and Steven Ahlstadt of of Carstens Publications; Clyve Hall and P. H. Franic of Bell Toys Ltd.; the Smithsonian Institution; the Secretary of the Citroën Car Club; the Citroën Co.; the Ford Motor Co.; Americana Archives; Bentalls Ltd.; A. H. Redles of Bachmann Brothers, Inc.

Louis H. Hertz

PART I

Building
Model
Automobiles

Getting Acquainted

Man apparently is basically a widely traveling creature. The inordinate attraction to, or even the need of intelligent man for, miniatures of the artifacts by the aid of which he or his fellows were better able to indulge these instincts to move, to explore, and to observe evidently is something that is inherent in the very blood or the total collective subconscious of the human race. For much of man's recorded span on earth, this need was necessarily one that could largely be fulfilled only with miniatures of ships. Thus, through many centuries, we find evidence of model shipbuilding. Then, with the dawn of the Machine Age, at first fitfully in the years prior to 1801 and then full blown in the nineteenth century, the potentials for satisfying this need expanded wondrously. Today, in addition to the enduring hobby of model ships and boats, multitudes of all ages devote substantial portions of their sparetime activities to hobbies involving the construction, operation, and accumulation of model railroads and train equipment; model aircraft, spacecraft, and rockets; model raceways and roadways, both of which involve model automobiles; and, last but not least, model automobiles and related vehicles of land transportation.

The omnipresence of the miniature automobile as a subject of construction and collecting in the model hobby world of the second half of the twentieth century can be a matter of surprise only to those who do not pause to consider the position

that the real automobile has today come to occupy in our lives. The automobile is everywhere; it is the form of transportation with which most individuals personally are acquainted and the only form of transportation most individuals ever are likely personally to own; a majority may today in fact ride in no other during their lifetime if buses, trucks, and other related forms are to be accounted, as they usually are, under the single inclusive heading of automobiles. A good case can be made out for the claim that the automobile now has become the number-one subject of modeling interest in the United States, Canada, Great Britain, France, and all other countries from which current information is available. To set this picture forth candidly is certainly not to denigrate other forms of transportation or their enthusiastic mirroring in model form, but simply to paint an accurate picture in a world and, indeed, in an economy that admittedly have become increasingly geared to road transportation in the shape of the self-propelled vehicle that is steered by its driver.

The model automobile hobby is thus no surprise. The forms and directions that it has taken are, however, in a number of ways somewhat startling and unprecedented, particularly to those who have long been familiar with modelmaking hobbies and trends. The two most noteworthy of these characteristics of the model automobile hobby are its gravitation to static, nonoperating miniature replicas and the amazingly heavy em-

Fig. 1.   Three 1/2-inch-scale, 1/24th-size models of automobiles of enduring beauty of the 1930's, constructed from easily assembled kits of plastic parts. The cars are, left rear, 1934 Duesenberg SJ Torpedo Phaeton; left front, 1937 Mercedes-Benz 540-K Cabriolet; and, right, a 1931 Rolls-Royce Phantom II Henley convertible.

Monogram Models, Inc.

phasis on the collecting aspects. It may well be that the first of these points is in turn to a substantial extent responsible for the second, for if a hobbyist is to build or acquire models that are not intended for operation, it logically follows that the end result will be the formation of a collection, although this is by far from being the sole explanation for the phenomenon of present-day model-car collecting. Nor is model-car construction by any means not an end in itself for a great many enthusiasts, carrying with it the same pleasures of creative craftsmanship that does any model-building hobby.

STATIC MODEL AUTOMOBILES

So pronounced has become the trend of interest toward nonoperating model automobiles that many people simply refer to this type of miniature as "static models." The meaning of this term is universally understood; such models do not possess any means of self-propulsion, whether in the form of an electric motor, clockwork, or other device. In effect, this term cleanly separates them from the powered model automobiles employed on operating model raceways and roadways—primarily today the electrically powered slot car—from model automobiles fitted with internal-combustion reciprocating engines and usually operated on a tether attached to a center post, and from radio-controlled model automobiles, whether powered electrically or by other means, which are operated and controlled entirely independently of any guiding slot or tether. These comprise all the popular forms of operating model automobiles today, and they properly form an entirely separate hobby of their own and one that is covered at length in another volume in this series, *The Complete Book of Model Raceways and Roadways.* This is not to say that these powered forms of model automobiles may not involve at times considerable and important elements of model building to prototype or free-lance designs, and of customizing and decoration and other things that are also involved in the creation of static models; but the two hobbies, although both involve miniature automobiles, manifestly are completely separate and distinct ones.

Conversely, although the specific designation "static model" obviously connotes that the given model is nonpowered, it would be erroneous to assume that without exception all the models that fall within the ken of interest of the builder and collector of model automobiles are without propulsion. Static model merely refers to one category of such models, although from the standpoint of present-day production in the form both of kits of parts and models sold in completely assembled form it is by far the predominant one. Many of the old model automobiles today so avidly sought and collected were fitted with means of propulsion, whether electric, steam, clockwork, friction, or other; the collector may even seek and find and treasure early examples of electric slot cars or internal-combustion reciprocating engine racing cars. Many such old model cars were not powered; they are equally sought. Even today, in current production, there are some models fitted with various forms of power that may properly fall within the province of the model automobile collector, although his interest is seldom primarily based on the factor of the presence of the power, but rather on the comparative merits of the unit as an overall miniature automobile.

Another highly developed factor in the model automobile hobby that affects the enthusiast who is interested in construction, the man who primarily is simply a collector, and the hobbyist who combines both interests with equal zeal is the historical factor. Probably no hobby has seized upon and developed this more strongly, and certainly not in a shorter time, than that of model automobiles. Furthermore, this is distinctly a twofold historical interest. In one form it involves the history and development of the real or prototype automobile as such. In the second form it is chiefly concerned with the history and development of the toy and model automobile manufacturing industry itself. Both approaches may well overlap and combine in the individual hobby patterns of many individuals, but the model automobile hobby cannot properly be understood unless this division of historical interest is fully understood and kept in mind.

IMPORTANT AND UNIMPORTANT DISTINCTIONS

Failing to understand this distinction can lead to much confusion and to an enthusiast's failing to derive all the enjoyment that the hobby potentially holds. Whether to retain one or the other outlook, or to combine both, is of course a matter for each individual to determine for himself. Being unable to appreciate the distinction, or, grasping it, and nevertheless exhibiting an intolerant attitude to those who have chosen to adopt an outlook somewhat different from one's own, is a different matter altogether and one that in the end inevitably is self-defeating. Another possible pitfall concerns excessive concern over the supposed niceties of the usage of the terms "toy" and "model" or their combination in the form employed in the preceding paragraph.

If one wants to become petty or to insist on analyzing every nuance to the infinite degree, a hobbyist can allow himself to become immeasurably miserable over this matter. "Toy" was once a bad word in the eyes of any serious model hobby-

Fig. 2.   Probably the all-time favorite miniature automotive design. This fire engine and its numerous variations, as manufactured by Wilkins and its successor, Kingsbury, between the early 1900's and the 1940's was doubtlessly owned by more boys than any other clockwork automobile model of any substance. The Wilkins and Kingsbury vehicles remain prime favorites among model automobile collectors.

Ward Kimball

Fig. 3. Top, two views of a portion of the model automobile collection of Arthur Yeckes, including both cast-metal miniatures and larger models (*Arthur Yeckes*). Below, a selection of old model automobiles, mainly cast-iron models of the 1920's and early 1930's in the collection of Adam Pellicot, Jr. (*Adam Pellicot, Jr.; William Dreyer photograph*).

ist. In the 1930's, and even somewhat later, a great many model hobbyists, regardless of their category of interest, regarded it as a matter of extreme importance that they make it crystal clear to all who would listen that they were not playing with toys but were serious, mature hobbyists who were dealing in models—something utterly and entirely different. "Model" is still obviously the proper and desirable description, but the day now is long far in the past where there is any need for anyone to work himself up over any real or imagined distinctions between "toy" and "model," and this is most particularly true as concerns miniature automobiles. The history of the model automobile prior to World War II is essentially that of the toy automobile, and many of these toys were in fact fine models in every sense of the word, although a number of them must of course be taken in the context of their time and the materials and manufacturing methods then available or favored. Today what the hobbyist and the distributors of hobby goods may look upon as a model may well at the same time be equally properly rated as a toy by youngsters and purveyors of toys. If there is any difference at all that might be worthy of notice—and even this

distinction has relatively little meaning as far as classifying the miniatures themselves—it is one of outlook and use, not one of the character of the given article itself. There are boys who are playing with toy automobiles who in a short time may well come to look at them, not as playthings, but as the objects of a serious model building or collecting hobby; there are other youngsters of perhaps the same age who already look upon the same miniatures as do many teen-agers and adults, as models. And to bring the matter full circle, there also are many adults who collect and study them, particularly the older models, unabashedly calling them by the name "toy," and looking at them primarily as such. As regards the hobby as a whole, these distinctions really are no longer of any material importance in any event, and no thoughtful individual need be particularly concerned over them.*

---

* However, in Chapter VIII of the writer's book *Antique Collecting for Men,* will be found what is felt to be a prudent and acceptable exposition of the usually accepted differentiation between miniatures, samples, models, and toys that may prove of interest to those who wish to pursue the point in greater depth.

Fig. 4. A 1-inch-scale motorized custom chassis built from a kit, with fully detailed engine and suspension system. A battery-powered electric motor is concealed inside the engine, and drives the chassis through the driveshaft and differential. Any type of body desired can be built and mounted on this chassis by the individual hobbyist.
Lindberg Products, Inc.

There is on the other hand one very important distinction that broadly enters into the hobby of model automobiles. Model automobile enthusiasts frequently speak of "old model cars" when what they actually mean are "models of old cars." A moment's consideration will reveal that there is a world of difference between the two and that the two phrases can never properly be used interchangeably. In the former case the model itself is old; in the latter instance the model is of recent or even contemporary construction, whether originating as a finished miniature or in the form of a kit of parts that are assembled by a hobbyist, and it is the prototype or original automobile on which the model is based that is old, not the model itself. A miniature of, say, a Model-A Ford, that was manufactured in 1928 is an old model car; a miniature of the same Model-A Ford built in 1968 is a model of an old car. The hobbyist who is collecting with his interest centering on the history of the miniature automobile industry as such will without question be interested in the 1928 production; his interest is likely to be considerably less in the 1968 one. On the other hand, the enthusiast whose collecting is based on the history of the real automobile, while the 1928 production may still be of some interest, is likely to find the model made in 1968 far more suitable for his purpose not only because of its ready availability but also because as a model itself it is very likely to be considerably more accurate and detailed a rendering of the prototype than the miniature made several decades earlier.

DEFINITIONS OF TIME

All this obviously brings the model-automobile enthusiast to another important point: Just where does one draw the distinction in time between what properly is and what is not an old model? This is not easy, because as in any collecting enterprise definitions of "old" always vary with the age of the individual hobbyist himself and in any event invariably must keep advancing. Even the latest

Fig. 5. Two types of widely collected models are illustrated by these miniature aerial ladder trucks, their relative interest to a given hobbyist depending on his personal collecting pattern. Top left, a 20-inch-long friction-powered model manufactured by Dayton Friction about 1912 (*Ward Kimball*). Bottom left and right, an 11-inch-long 7-mm.-scale (1/43rd-size) cast-metal miniature, introduced in the late 1960's. Its ladder extends to a height of 17 inches, representing a 65-foot ladder (*Corgi—Reeves International, Inc.*).

model of today must in time become an old model as the years pass. For some time the most widely accepted dividing line among collectors of all types of toys and models has been World War II. This is not only because the cataclysms of the great wars inevitably provide bench marks in our thinking about time but in addition because in the United States the manufacture of metal toys and models was prohibited and discontinued for approximately three years after June 1942. To both the collector and the historian, World War II provides a clear-cut distinguishing point between the old and what many consider the new or at least the recent. It is true that some models that went out of production in 1942 reappeared in 1945 or 1946; therefore the distinction is not absolutely definitive. However, in most cases there were some minor differences between the postwar models and those made until 1942, even though the same basic dies and molds were employed, and it usually is possible for the specialist clearly to distinguish between the postwar productions and the earlier models.

However, it is obvious that World War II is no longer a completely satisfactory and acceptable barrier to many, and will become ever less acceptable with each succeeding year. For some time to come, it may well remain the most suitable point of marking what may be considered the truly historical period of models. Nevertheless, there are many kits and models made after the war that already are popularly accounted "old" and are collected as such. Thus, while the hobbyist must ever be careful to distinguish between old model cars and models of old cars, it should be kept in mind that the former is by no means necessarily an absolute in terms of specific dating. Possibly someday an acceptable formula will be worked out and acknowledged by most collectors whereby an "old

model car" will be defined as a model that last was manufactured a certain number of years prior to the date at the time—perhaps ten years or fifteen years before. On the other hand, there will probably always be a certain number of hobbyists who will argue for the point that "old" and "obsolete" are synonymous terms and that a model car or kit becomes "old" as soon as it is no longer in current production. To many, however, this will no doubt seem a rather opposite extreme than endeavoring to hold indefinitely to using World War II as a line of demarcation.

The hobbyist may also not infrequently hear use being made of the term "contemporary model" among model-automobile builders and collectors. This arose in a well-intentioned effort to attempt further to clarify some of the problems of dating and terminology discussed in the preceding paragraphs. Originally, the term "contemporary model" was evidently intended to refer to a model manufactured at the same time as was the real automobile on which it was based, or at least at approximately the same time. Thus, a miniature of a Model-A Ford that was constructed in the late 1920's or early 1930's, or a miniature of a Cord 810 that was built in the late 1930's, would be referred to as a "contemporary model." The idea was not without considerable merit, but was rendered somewhat less effective than was hoped by various intangibles, and most importantly by the fact that many hobbyists did not understand or would not accept the usage intended; no doubt there was an area for considerable misunderstanding. As a result a substantial body of model-automobile enthusiasts began to accept and use the term in the exactly opposite sense than that which had been intended. They spoke of a contemporary model as one currently manufactured and sold at any given time; in 1965, say, a miniature of a 1928

Fig. 6.   The word "classic" is applied so frequently and loosely to old actual automobiles and to some extent to models that many hesitate to use it at all. Here, however, are two collectors' turn-of-the-century favorites that justly deserve the designation if anything does: left, a Hafner clockwork runabout *(G. William Holland Collection)* and, right, a Clark friction hansom cab *(G. William Holland photograph)*.

Fig. 7. Nine 1/2-inch-scale (1/24th-size) models built from kits of metal parts that assemble without requiring soldering. In order the models are: 1962/63 BRM Formula 1 car, 1963 Lotus 25 Formula 1 car, 1961 Ferrari Formula 1 car, 1927 Bugatti Type 35B sports/racing car, 1932 Alfa Romeo P3 racing car, Lotus Super-seven sports car, Porsche 904 Grand Touring car, 1929 M type M.G. sports car, and 1927 Delage Grand Prix 1.5-liter car.

Auto-Models Ltd.

Model-A Ford that was being manufactured in 1965 was to them a contemporary model. This naturally led to an enormous amount of confusion and misunderstanding over the usage of the term, and the two diametrically opposed usages virtually canceled each other out and at the present time has rendered the term meaningless. This is unfortunate because, given a single universally accepted meaning, it could have been a valuable addition to model-automobile nomenclature.

THE DIVISIONS OF THE HOBBY

The model-automobile hobby as such readily divides into the two principal divisions indicated by the title of this book, "building" and "collecting," although the same hobbyist may and often does pursue both branches, to some extent at least. Each can be and often is an entirely separate and distinct hobby, however, and certain definite popular divisions can readily be discerned within each of the two major branches.

Model-automobile building is in many ways similar to any other sort of model-building hobby. On the other hand it carries within it such enormously strong aspects of individual design and creativity as to make it unique among model-building hobbies. In the main, although he may at times undertake some free-lancing along accepted lines of real locomotive construction, the model railroader buys or builds his equipment following strictly prototype designs. So, too, to a very considerable extent does the model-aircraft or model-ship enthusiast follow prototype designs, especially insofar as his static models are concerned; such modifications or designs originating purely as models as he may undertake are almost invariably on operating models, and are brought into being entirely in the interest of securing better operating performance in a boat intended to be sailed or in a flying model airplane. Essentially only in the field of model automobiles has the static model become a widespread

subject of individual creativity, whether in the form of modifying or customizing models of specific prototypes, or in unusual forms of painting and decoration, or in the all-out creation of miniature automobiles that are literally evocations of their builders' concepts of what an automobile should be.

At this point many hobbyists are prone to raise the point as to whether the latter truly can be classed as models. This is another one of those rather pointless debates in which some modelmakers seem to delight. One school holds that a model, to be properly so designated, must be a recognizable miniature of an actual prototype; that one can go just so far in customizing or changing or decorating a model automobile and that beyond a definite point—not everyone necessarily agrees on when this point is reached—it ceases to be a model and enters such a never-never land of fantasy that the term "model" simply can no longer be applied. The other school maintains that no matter how unusual in appearance, how far removed from any specific prototype or even from accepted automobile design as a whole, a miniature may be, so long as it embraces reasonably practical or even possible elements of present or even futuristic automotive mechanical or visual design, the unit in question most certainly properly is a model automobile. Both sides can and do cite chapter, verse, and modeling text and dictionary definition to substantiate their viewpoints. If the matter is considered objectively, it must be granted that there is much that can be said for both sides if one feels that the matter is one that is worthy of deep and serious consideration. Essentially, as in the case of the matter of the meaning of the words "toy" and "model," it is an argument that serves little practical purpose, nor does it really have much validity in today's modeling picture. The average person is prone to arrive at certain practical conclusions in matters of these sorts and to accept as broad and inclusive a definition of the word "model" as the present overall climate of the hobby may require. Such certainly is the practical purpose and intent of this book.

It must also be noted and admitted that in this argument concerning what may or may not properly be classified as a model automobile, there is the important, even overwhelming, factor of the generation gap. Older enthusiasts are likely to be much more conservative in their model-building activities, to lean toward reproducing ordinary automobile prototypes. Younger hobbyists are at the opposite end of the spectrum: they are more likely to lean to what their elders regard as extreme or even grotesque models; more likely to experiment with new ideas and design concepts; more likely

Fig. 8. A .48-inch-scale (1/25th-size) model Chevrolet 1956 two-door sedan, with opening doors, hood, and trunk. Built of molded plastic components from a kit that offers optional trim for reproducing several different prototype series. See also the customized version pictured in Fig. 56.
Revell, Inc.

Fig. 9. Another comparison of types of model automobiles. The giant 3-inch-scale model of a 1907 Rolls-Royce at the left is an individually handmade replica of evidently contemporary or near contemporary date (*The Smithsonian Institution*). At the right is a modern cast-metal miniature of the 1907 Rolls-Royce Silver Ghost (*"Matchbox"—Fred Bronner Corp.*).

to customize; in short, more likely to allow their creative impulses to take full sway. All this exuberance, which certainly should be far from unexpected, is in the main only for the good. We are told, and it is no doubt in a number of instances true, that automobile manufacturers have spotted potential real automobile designing talent by examining the model cars entered in various contests by teen-agers and that as a result some of these model builders have gone on to training and eventual positions in the automotive industry. The practical assessment of such talent is not easy, and many older modelmakers are simply not qualified to judge whether a younger enthusiast's highly customized or entirely individually created model is a portent of real ability (and this may be of an artistic nature by no means necessarily limited to the automotive world) or is simply a youthful grotesque. Most of us, therefore, simply have no right to sit in judgment or to attempt to say what is or what is not properly a model as such. It is only when younger hobbyists, simply because they are young, go to the point of creating designs or decorations that the older enthusiasts must inevitably find offensive, that one can justly object to certain aberrative extremes. It is in fact probable that many younger hobbyists deliberately evoke these themes simply because they know they will prove annoying to more mature individuals. In the natural fullness of time most of these younger enthusiasts will come to appreciate why hot-rod hearses and Iron Cross decorations really are neither humorous nor attractive.

A SUMMARY OF THE HOBBY TODAY

As with most model-building hobbies, model automobiles present so many possible cross-hatchings and overlappings that it would be almost impossible to construct a chart that would clearly show all its ramifications. The model-automobile builder may construct a model from a kit, exactly as the model is intended to be put together to one set design; he may work from a customizing kit that provides him with two or more basic options, plus many possible combinations of extra customizing parts; he may combine two or more kits; he may employ a kit in combination with a substantial number of separately purchased customizing parts; or he may build a model using both some parts and some raw materials, or he may build a model up virtually from scratch, using few or perhaps no commercial parts whatsoever.

He may build models of old automobiles, models of contemporary automobiles in stock form; he may build models of hot rods, drag racers, funny cars, or various others that are to the average automobile enthusiast rather unusual or even weird types; he may customize his models to varying degrees, from a few added chrome details to a complete restyling of the body, or he may free-lance and branch out and create in model form his own conception of the ideal automobile either of today or of the future. He may indulge in all sorts of fancy painting and decorating, again either following more or less actual real automobile usage, or he may lean toward the rather extreme, innovative, and often unprototypical. (The average somewhat staid individual whose acquaintanceship with automobiles is more or less limited to the types displayed in dealers' showrooms must be somewhat cautious as to what he defines as the unprototypical; there are some wondrously unusual automobiles in existence and in use among hot-rod and custom-car afficionados, the sight of which the average automobilist in most parts of the country

Fig. 10. A group of six highly individualistically customized 1/2-inch-scale (1/24th-size) or .48-inch-scale (1/25th-size) model automobiles, representing some rather novel and in some cases extreme concepts of automotive design. Although often changed almost beyond recognition, in most cases the starting point was a standard commercial kit of plastic parts.

Revell, Inc., and Testor Corp.

may in a lifetime of driving never encounter.* Many may feel that this is in fact just as well, because at least some of them appear so far out to older enthusiasts as possibly to suggest the advisability of opening fire upon them under the impression that they are invading interplanetary vehicles!)

On the other hand there is the ever-growing army of old-car enthusiasts whose love of obsolete automobiles, with its accompanying loving preservation, use, and display of antique vehicles, is to a considerable extent at least somewhat incomprehensible or ludicrous to the younger generation. This increasing interest in and enthusiasm for old automobiles continually is reflected in the model cars currently available and in the choice of pro-

____

* Some model-car kit manufacturers actually have had built to their order full-size working replicas of automobile designs that originated as the subjects of unusual model kits, or have commissioned custom-car designers to create and build previously nonexistent types so that they could subsequently be offered in kit form as miniatures of existing prototypes.

totypes reproduced in miniature form by today's model builders. In turn the availability of models and kits for these old-timers unquestionably has stirred in many younger hobbyists an appreciation of and interest in old cars and their history that they otherwise might not have developed until they were many years older.

Insofar as the collecting side of the model automobile hobby is concerned, it, too, has several distinct aspects. Though this matter is gone into at considerable length in Part II, it should be summarized here: Model-car collecting may simply be the retention, accumulation, and display of model automobiles and other vehicles built by an individual enthusiast—in other words, a collection recording his interests, skills, and workmanship, regardless of whether his main hobby interest is reflected in models of ordinary cars, highly customized models, unusual finishes, individualistic designs, or whatever. In another phase, model-car collecting can be based on the history of the real automobile itself, as already noted and as will be returned to before the conclusion of this chapter. A third form of model-car collecting is based on a primary interest in the history and development of model cars themselves; and here the miniatures and the history of the manufacturers of the miniatures are the predominant interest, rather than the prototypes and the history of the manufacturers of the prototypes, as is the case in the preceding form of collecting. Still another form of model-car collecting has developed recently, fitting somewhere loosely between the second and third types and embracing some of the interest and nature of both. In this latter form of collecting, the hobbyist usually collects the current products of one or more favored modern manufacturers, purchasing as many new models as possible as they become available. This is a type of collecting that is a creation of the model-automobile field and almost entirely confined to it; its promotion by the model-car manufacturers themselves is a unique contribution of the model-automobile hobby.

All these types of model-automobile collecting may be limited, combined, overlapped, or expanded by the individual hobbyist according to his personal program. There are no rigid rules or patterns, and the possibilities for an enthusiast following what seems to him the most interesting and rewarding plan of collecting are virtually unlimited.

There is still another aspect to the model-automobile hobby that should be included in this summary, and that is the obvious connections and relationships with other model hobbies. Wherever a hobby calls for the creation of a complete scene, at least one reproducing a segment of the world as it has been since the turn of the century, then there must almost always be present the model automobile. The more recent in time the scene to be modeled, the greater the emphasis on automobiles is likely to be. For many decades the usual model-railroad layout has made use of considerable numbers of miniature automobiles; more recently, so too has the model raceway and even more so the model-roadway system. Even the builder of static model airplanes who seeks to arrange some of his models in realistic scenic displays often makes use of static model automobiles. As a result there is an enormous number of model hobbyists who build and collect model automobiles who do not think of themselves as model-automobile hobbyists, but rather as model railroaders, operators of model raceways and roadways, and so on. Nevertheless, the interests, activities, and aspirations of these hobbyists play a considerable part in the overall model-automobile hobby. So, too, do the interests, activities, and aspirations of collectors of military miniatures, who may not only collect military vehicles as such—and this is a distinct facet of interest in the model-automobile hobby itself—but who often also employ more conventional types of automobiles, perhaps modified or painted in army styles and colors, as integral parts of their miniature scenes and displays.

TYPES OF AUTOMOBILES

Interest in model automobiles may limit itself to one or more or embrace a considerable number of types of automobiles and related vehicles. Among these may be counted ordinary or stock automobiles, racing cars (a category particularly favored, and most especially so in Great Britain), buses, trucks, specialized service vehicles (especially fire engines), military vehicles, including such equipment as self-propelled gun carriers and mobile rocket launchers; construction equipment, including bulldozers and road rollers, tractors and related farm equipment; mobile showmen's engines, customized automobiles, hot rods, dragsters, the recently popular so-called "funny cars," early self-propelled road carriages, and so on. Most of these categories are self-explanatory. However, something should be said concerning the groupings and terminology that have been set up and accepted, at least to a certain extent, in the United States and Great Britain concerning old automobiles, and, by extension, some other types of early or obsolete vehicles, because the matter touches upon a really important point.

First, the so-called categories. The beginner, and often the fairly well-established model-automobile hobbyist is likely to find himself confused and sometimes repelled by hearing all sorts of terms—"veteran," "antique," "classic," "special interest," and so on—bandied about and their precise definitions argued and debated, often with great heat. The matter is confused by the fact that some states have set up a legal definition for antique automobiles for licensing purposes and will issue a special type of license and license plate— usually restricting the use of the car in certain ways; this will be issued to but not necessarily required by a car of over a certain but highly variable number of years of age. Furthermore, in the United States, three major clubs define "antique" in three different ways: as a car made before 1916, as a car made before 1930, and as a car thirty-five years or more of age. (Some states define an antique car as one twenty or more years of age; some require the vehicle be as much as forty years of age.) Then there is the so-called "classic" car category, which is not based on age alone—a classic may or may not be an antique—but on

certain nebulous standards of design or construction, or both. To expand and confuse things still further, there are the so-called "special-interest" cars, another somewhat nebulous category.

In Great Britain there is somewhat less confusion and area of debate among enthusiasts, particularly in the ceaseless arguments heard in the United States as to whether a particular car properly is or is not a classic or a special-interest car, for the British standards are logically founded on date alone. In Great Britain an automobile made before the end of 1904 is designated a "veteran" car; one made between the beginning of 1905 and the end of 1916 is called an Edwardian car—more in token to a feeling for an era than in strict historical accuracy, for Edward VII, the

Fig. 11.   The range of available present-day miniature cast-metal automobiles and trucks, which in some cases may incorporate plastic components and which are often offered at surprisingly moderate prices, seems almost endless, as suggested by these examples. Substantially, this is but a sampling of what is available and is added to or varied annually.

Tootsietoy—Strombecker Corp.

monarch for whom the period is named, reigned from 1901 to 1910; and a car made after 1916 is termed a "vintage" car, with a seeming general consensus that the "vintage" period ended in the middle 1930's and that anything later should be called a "post-vintage" car. Note, however, that these definitions are based on date alone, and there is no need to argue as to whether a specific make of car or a specific year of a make or even a specific model and body type of a specific make and year is to be accorded the accolade of classic or special-interest car. In short it appears, though the thought may shock many Americans, that the British are as a whole more logical and less snobbish concerning old automobiles than are many citizens of the Republic.

AFFECTION AND AFFECTATION

In according or denying recognition under certain labels to old cars in the United States, it must certainly strike many less restrictive-minded individuals that such divisions and limitations are for the most part arbitrary and capricious. The situation is not dissimilar to that obtaining in many other fields of antiquarian and collectors' interest, although with certain special overtones in the case of the automobile, and in these other areas the supposed classifications are as often disputed or ignored by most less rigid and more progressive minds. The average hobbyist, the average proverbial man in the street, even one with no particularized interest in old automobiles, usually has a very clear and

instinctive grasp of such things, and more often than not his instincts are correct.

The situation was summed up by the present writer in the introductory paragraphs of an article called "Classics: Golden Days Recalled," that appeared in the Fall–Winter, 1966, issue of *Model Racing Buyers' Guide:*

"People's outlook on the old automobile as an historical artifact are a combination of affection and affectation. We have no sympathy for the latter view; to us all old cars are beautiful, interesting and important. There may be varying degrees of these qualities attributable to different cars, but we dislike attempts to categorize them and accept or reject certain makes and models because of such questionable groupings as classic, vintage, antique, and so on. To us all old cars are classic in the truest and most practical sense of the term: they played their parts in their time in satisfying a contemporary need for better transportation.

"This is not to say that we cannot see basic differences in the cars of a bygone era. Some were designed as racers; some to provide low-cost transportation; some to attain opulence and performance; some were noteworthy for new design concepts. However, such specific attributes are not the sole factors that determine whether a car deserves to be commemorated. From the viewpoint of the practical model fan, what is most important is availability, either assembled or in kit form."

In short, for all practical purposes an antique car is an old car and a classic is any old car possessing beauty or historical importance in the continuing march of automotive history. It would seem wise for the model-automobile hobbyist to adopt this viewpoint, and most of them certainly do so. By the same token the majority of model-automobile enthusiasts shun the not infrequently proffered theory that a major attraction of the model-automobile hobby is that it permits a man to have automobiles of great cost or great rarity by owning them in miniature form, when he would probably never possess the prototype. This concept obviously borders on the absurd, and is not taken seriously by thoughtful hobbyists. Only to one extent could this line of thought possess any validity. That might occur when a hobbyist builds or collects models of former (and fondly remembered) automobiles once owned or driven by him or his family, or other makes of cars recalled as noteworthy or desired in former days.

It is more than a little pertinent to note at this time that a great many enthusiasts of automobiles, both real and model, unwittingly make themselves ridiculous in the eyes of their fellowmen by their use of words that convey an attitude of affectation and condescension. Such a hobbyist often adopts certain mannerisms in the erroneous belief that he thereby makes himself readily recognizable as a true automobile buff.

For example, there is the practice of substituting the French word *marque* for the good old established American word "make." This is especially annoying because, in the usage of such enthusiasts, Hupmobile or Saxon may be referred to as makes of cars, while Cord or Pierce-Arrow are *marques*. The snobbish implications are obvious and annoying to the average man, and do much to prejudice him against automobile hobbies and hobbyists, both real and model. It is quite true that many automotive terms coined in France during the great experimental period in the 1890's came directly into the English language and have long been an integral part of it, including the word automobile itself—despite early efforts to impose "motor vehicle" in the United States—and such other words as "carburetor" and "chauffeur" (which in French means "stoker"). Some of the automotive terms we adopted from the French have for some time become virtually obsolete, such as "chauffeuse" (a woman who drives an automobile) and "tonneau." * However, recent adaptation of foreign words such as *marque* as substitutes for long-established words in the common speech is of

---

* An article in *The New York Times* of April 4, 1968, relates how the Stratemayer Syndicate is revising and updating its long-popular series of children's books, including the removal of references to running boards on automobiles. Presumably "tonneau" also is being eliminated.

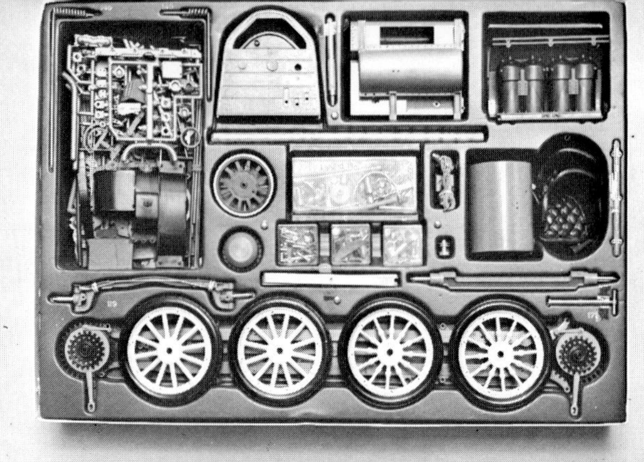

Fig. 12.   For the model automobile kit there appears to be virtually no limits of intricacy and opulence. This kit contains almost 400 parts of brass, copper, steel, plastic, and other materials, and builds a 1 1/2-inch-scale (1/8th-size) superdetailed model of a 1907 Fiat F-2 race car measuring 20 inches in length.

G. William Holland Collection

Fig. 13. Factories in an ever-increasing number of countries are actively producing detailed cast-metal miniature automobiles sold in finished form. Pictured here are 7-mm.-scale models of a 1924 Isotta Fraschini made in Italy, a 1912 Rolls-Royce, and a 1927 Bentley made in Great Britain, and another Rolls-Royce made in Spain.

Auto World

course a different matter altogether. So, too, for that matter is the affectation in the United States of British substitutes for American terms, such as "windscreen" for "windshield." "Windscreen," "petrol," "spanner," and so on, are perfectly proper and natural in Great Britain; in the United States their use more than savors of affectation. Whether in relation to models or to full-size automobiles, such usages in the United States are deplorable, and serve only to harm the hobby by seeming to set it apart from the common ken; this practice is found only in regard to model automobiles of all popular American modelmaking hobbies and has repelled many who would otherwise take great pleasure in participating in the building and collecting of model automobiles.

In the United States the building and use of the automobile has long been in the mainstream of life as in no other country in the world; to do anything that in any way tends to remove it from that mainstream is the height of folly!

THE STORY OF THE AUTOMOBILE AS TOLD IN MODELS

While it is not possible here to give a complete history of the automobile as such, the assembling of a collection of model automobiles illustrating the history of the real automobile is one of the most popular forms of model-car collecting. Therefore, some succinct summary is desirable in order to put the matter into some kind of focus for the reader who is not as familiar as he might want to be with the subject. The pictures of models of old automobiles that accompany this particular portion of the chapter and that will be found elsewhere in this volume will serve somewhat to illustrate this story, although no effort has been made to tie the story and pictures together into anything approaching a fully integrated whole. To do so would of necessity involve pictures of many individually hand-built miniatures not readily available either as current or collectors' kits and models. Rather, the purpose here, in addition to telling the story, is to inspire the hobbyist who is so inclined to set forth and, within the limits of his own constructional or collecting talents, lay out and activate a suitable collecting program of his own.

How is the automobile to be defined? If it is only to be considered in the sense of what generally is thought of today as an automobile, particularly if it is to be limited to machines powered by internal-combustion reciprocating engines, then much automotive history is to be ignored. Even more narrow would be definitions that insisted—as sometimes is done for particularized special-interest reasons—that the true automobile must not only be internal-combustion powered but also that the form of supplying the fuel and the method of ignition must be substantially identical with that employed in the present-day internal-combustion-powered automobile. Again the definitions can be narrowed by specifying that the automobile must have a differential, that is to say, an arrangement of gearing that permits one driven wheel to rotate at a different speed than the opposing driven wheel when the vehicle is driven around a turn.

Thus, depending on self-imposed limitations of definition, there are several recognized "inventors" of the automobile powered by the internal-combustion engine. The Frenchman Jean-Joseph Étienne Lenoir generally is credited with perfecting the first practical gas engine in 1860, although he had many predecessors in the field. In 1862 Lenoir fitted one of his engines to a wagon and drove it a sufficient distance over the roads around Paris to prove the soundness of the idea. Lenoir's engine had an electric-spark ignition, but his vehicle had no differential and his fuel was illuminating gas that was always in a gaseous state from the moment it was loaded into the vehicle until the moment of ignition. Lenoir would appear to deserve unstinting credit as the inventor of the practical internal-combustion-powered automobile. Nevertheless many cavil over the matter of the form of the fuel because it was not loaded onto the vehicle in liquid form and then vaporized into a gaseous state just prior to ignition, as is the case with the modern automobile powered by an internal-combustion engine.

The next claimant is Siegfried Marcus of Austria. Marcus ran his first car in 1865. It employed a liquid fuel—gasoline—and an electric-spark ignition, but had no differential and, in fact, no provision for steering. The latter omission was corrected on a larger and more prepossessing vehicle Marcus demonstrated in 1875, but, like Lenoir, he never did very much to follow up his ideas. Gottlieb Daimler of Germany built a motorcycle powered by an internal-combustion engine—a Daimler improvement on the then widely popular Otto engine—in 1885 and a four-wheeled vehicle in 1887, but the early Daimler engines were not electrically ignited, and the 1887 Daimler had no differential. In 1886, however, another German whose name was later to be linked with that of Daimler through a merger of the companies that grew out of their early efforts, Karl Benz, built and ran a four-wheel automobile powered with an internal-combustion engine, using spark ignition, and fitted with a differential. Thus, as you prefer, you may take Lenoir, Marcus, or Benz as the inventor of the automobile powered by an internal-combustion engine, depending on whether you demand liquid fuel or a differential in your definition of an automobile. Daimler would appear to be quite out of the picture, except for the later commercial coupling of his name with that of Benz, although a number of early accounts credited Daimler as being the inventor of the internal-combustion-powered automobile.

However, two other names should enter this picture, the Americans George B. Brayton and George B. Selden. Brayton began manufacturing gas engines of his own design in the early 1870's, and in 1874 he introduced an even more successful oil engine that he evidently applied to a road ve-

Fig. 14.   Examples of four important collectors' categories of old model automobiles are pictured here: a World War I period friction racer made by Dayton; a Buddy "L" steel moving van of the 1920's (*Lloyd W. Ralston*); a Strauss clockwork lithographed bus of the 1920's (*Robert A. Ahlers*); and an Arcade cast-iron bus of the 1930's (*Joseph N. Imler*).

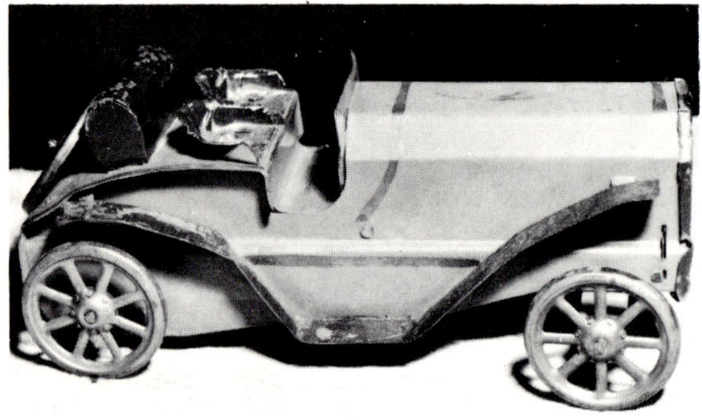

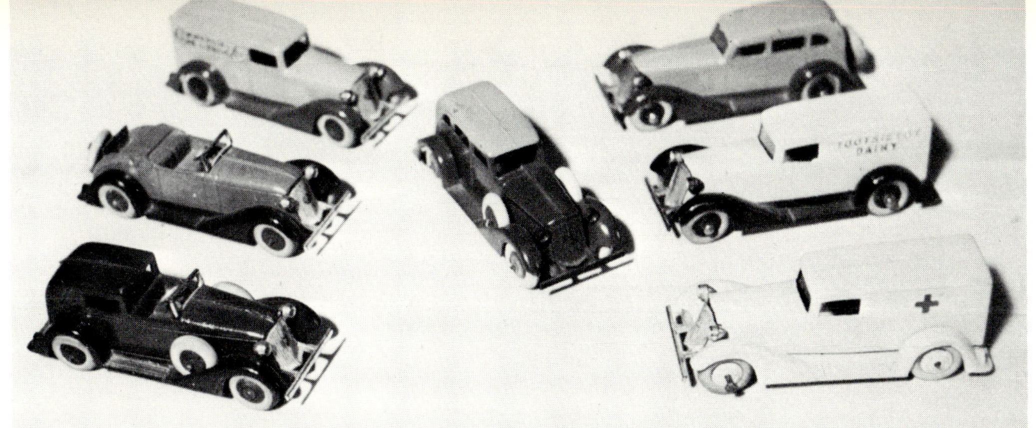

Fig. 15.   Old cast-metal miniature-car collectors' favorites, seven examples of the famous Tootsie-toy Graham-Paige series of the 1930's. The first of these was introduced in 1933, and a version of the ambulance (lower right) was made until 1942. The vehicle at the left rear is the tire truck; that behind the ambulance, the milk truck.

William A. Hall

hicle. The original drawings for the controversial Selden patent, applied for in 1877 but not issued until 1895, include a small three-cylinder Brayton engine. Selden has been the subject of so much discussion, litigation, and acrimony that almost everyone interested in automobile history has definite ideas concerning him, usually polarizing at one of the two extremes that he was an abused and cheated pioneer or that he was some sort of charlatan. Yet there is no doubt that Selden designed

Fig. 16.   Illustrating a very important distinction, that between an old model car and a model of an old car. The second full-dimensioned cast-metal miniature automobile made by Dowst and later incorporated in the Tootsietoy line was the Ford Model-T touring car put into production in 1914. It is shown at the top as originally manufactured with spoked wheels and also with the solid wheels that replaced them in the early 1920's. It is an *old model car (Adam Pellicot, Jr.; William Breyer photograph)*. Below is a cast-metal miniature Ford Model-T touring car put into production in the late 1960's. It is a *model of an old car (Corgi— Reeves International, Inc.)*.

an essentially practical internal-combustion-powered automobile in 1877 or earlier, which would give him priority over Benz but not over Lenoir or Marcus. It is also true that, although Selden built a model and submitted it with his patent application, he did not build an actual full-size vehicle according to his design until the patent was involved in the famous litigation in the early 1900's. The 1/2-inch-scale kit-built model Selden car at the right of Fig. 18 is a replica of this later prototype, not of a car actually built in 1877, although it resembles the original patent drawings closely. Most early American automobile manufacturers accepted the fact that the Selden patent was valid, and paid royalties; Ford and a few others did not. Contrary to popular belief, and often repeated in supposedly authoritative books, the courts never declared the Selden patent invalid. The final decision on appeal in 1911 was that the Selden patent was valid but not basic or broad enough to be applicable to the types of automobiles then being manufactured. The Selden matter is a most curious and complicated one, and by no means as clear cut as various writers, especially biographers of Henry Ford, have presented it. There is no doubt that regardless of subsequent ramifications, Selden's name should stand as one of the great pioneers and inventors of the automobile powered by an internal-combustion engine.

THE REAL PIONEER AUTOMOBILES

Discounting the theory that the history of the automobile must begin with the pioneers of the vehicle as it chiefly exists today, as a machine powered by an internal-combustion reciprocating engine, the story carries back approximately a century before Lenoir's wagon, for steam was the first great practical activating force. Somewhat curiously, both the automobile and the locomotive trace back to the same common ancestors, for although the railroad itself was in existence long before the advent of the locomotive, there were steam carriages for ordinary roads in operation prior to the partial transferral of the idea to that of a machine to run on rails. Historians usually trace the first practical application of a self-propelled vehicle back to the three-wheel steam carriage built by Nicholas Joseph Cugnot in 1769 and operated in Paris, and there were several other steam-powered road vehicles constructed in France and in Great Britain during the later years of the eighteenth century. During the first decades of the nineteenth century, at approximately the same time the steam locomotive was being brought to practical fruition, the steam carriage was also highly perfected in Great Britain, and many public coaches powered by steam, or what we would today call buses, were in regular and popular service. In the 1830's, however, this most promising beginning was stifled when the operators of the old horse-drawn coach lines were able to have laws enacted that so restricted the speed and usefulness of the steam carriages as to render their further commercial operation rather pointless.

Although some experimentation did continue in Great Britain throughout the remainder of the century, these laws, some of which remained in force until the early 1900's, seriously inhibited continuing development in this field, and the main-

streams of automobile invention turned elsewhere, especially to France. One result was the already mentioned use of so many words of French origin in association with the automobile. Substantial progress was made in France in developing steam-powered cars, often of tricycle design, in the 1870's and 1880's. In the 1890's automobiling interest rose to great heights in France, with races being organized and steam, gasoline, and electrically powered vehicles competing. These three forms of power have remained the three chief classifications into one of which most automobiles fall, although other forms of power were experimented with in the early days, including compressed and liquid air, as well as other fuels for cars powered by internal-combustion reciprocating engines. (Our own times have seen many automobiles in war-torn or occupied countries operated by various forms of gas when gasoline was not available.) Generally speaking, internal-combustion engines have become the almost universal standard for automobiles in recent decades, although both electricity and steam have continued to have their advocates. While it generally is felt that, except in the eyes of a rather limited group of enthusiasts, steam power presents little potential for a return, the same is not true of electricity. Experiments in the latter field are in continual progress, seeking to overcome the one great drawback to this form of power, the necessity for recharging the batteries at

Fig. 17.   A substantial amount of detail and working features can be and now often is incorporated into cast-metal miniatures, as exemplified by these four, models respectively of a Holmes wrecker and a Lincoln Continental executive limousine *(Corgi—Reeves International, Inc.)*, and a Rolls-Royce Phantom V limousine and a Ford Mustang fastback *(Dinky Toys—Meccano Ltd., Lines Bros.)*.

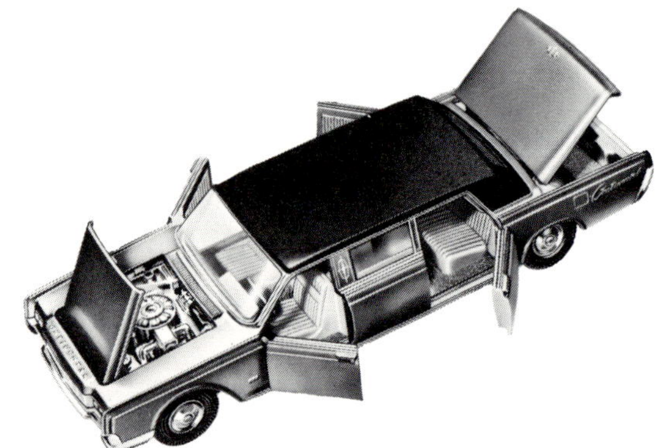

Fig. 18. Left, the original patent model of the controversial Selden patent, applied for in 1877 but not issued until 1895 (*The Smithsonian Institution*). Right, a 1/2-inch-scale model of the Selden, built from a Mod-Ac kit of wooden parts of the early 1950's, the dimensions being determined by scaling down a full-sized Selden car constructed in the early 1900's. (*Polk's Model Craft Hobbies, Inc.*).

frequent intervals, and there are many who predict a resurrection of the electric automobile, at least for local driving, within the near future.

The great years of late-nineteenth-century automobile development in France brought to fame a great many inventors and builders, but the names of many of them remained virtually unknown in the United States for almost two-thirds of a century except to a relatively few specialists in automobile history. Had it not been for the burgeoning model automobile hobby in the late 1950's and 1960's, such names as Bollée, Bouton, de Dion, and Serpollet would still probably be essentially unheralded in America. However, the increasing interest in building and even far more greatly in collecting models of their automobiles are at last bringing them a considerable measure of belated fame in the New World.

THE AUTOMOBILE IN THE UNITED STATES

As for the history of the automobile in America, it, too, can be traced back in the United States to the late eighteenth and early nineteenth centuries, with the names of John Fitch and Oliver Evans most prominent. Evans's combination steamboat, dredge, and self-propelled land vehicle of 1804 may be regarded as the first automobile in the United States; but it is only from 1852, when Moses Latta delivered his self-propelled steam fire engine, the *Joe Ross,* to the City of Cincinnati, Ohio, that the practical use of the automobile in the Western Hemisphere can be dated. Although there also were many steamrollers and steam tractors, until the 1890's the most noteworthy use of the automobile in the United States was in the shape of the great self-propelled steam fire engines that developed into machines of substantial size, caliber, and beauty—some were equipped with differentials—that have been vir-

tually ignored by most who have purported to relate the history of the automobile. Even though as automobiles the early Latta and the Lee and Larned self-propellers of the 1850's * may be regarded by some, especially when compared to later models, as somewhat cumbersome and unconventional, the self-propellers built starting in 1872 by the Amoskeag Manufacturing Company of Manchester, New Hampshire,† and their subsequent proprietors, the Manchester Locomotive Works, were fully developed practical automobiles in every sense and by every reasonable criterion unless one is to consign them to limbo simply because they were powered by steam engines rather than by internal-combustion engines.

The self-propelled steam fire engines, the early British road carriages, and the French cars

---

* It is sometimes believed by those who have made only a cursory examination of the usual illustration that the first fire engine built by the Silsby Manufacturing Company of Seneca Falls, New York, in 1856 was a self-propeller. This is not correct. The gearing that can be seen on one of the rear wheels did not drive the wheel. Rather, the wheel drove the gearing and thereby operated an air blower in the firebox.

† The Amoskeag steam fire engines are probably the best known, and are considered by most as atypical of the breed—a conclusion not completely justified, as there were many builders of fine steam fire engines. In recent years some curious folktales have come into circulation concerning the Amoskeag engines, both self-propelled and horse-drawn. The most diverting is that there was no great factory that manufactured hundreds of engines, but, instead, a humble, pious individual workman named Amos Keag who lovingly made them by hand. This story may originate with a typographical error in *The Index of American Design,* or it may predate the book and in turn be responsible for the typo. Its ready popular acceptance is in any case lamentably typical of the theme favored by a substantial number of people that repudiates any connection between art, beauty, craftsmanship, and the machine, and insists that every creation of merit must be the handwork of the proverbial "humble, pious workman."

Fig. 19. A segment of the history of the automobile illustrated by 3/4-inch-scale (1/18th-size) models assembled from kits of plastic parts: 1903 Rambler, 1904 Oldsmobile, 1909 Stanley Steamer, 1911 Mercer Raceabout, 1911 Buick "Bug," and 1914 Stutz Bearcat. These plastic kits were developed from some of the wooden kits of the early 1950's illustrated in Figs. 129, 130, and 131.

Aurora Plastics Corp.

of the 1890's all figure importantly in the history of the model automobile, and their replicas in miniature, continue to engross the model-automobile enthusiast.

As in France, the automobile became a matter of great interest and experimentation in the United States in the 1890's. In France there may have been somewhat greater proportionate general interest in the automobile as a device for sport and racing. While automobile racing played an important part in developing and publicizing the automobile in the United States, it is proper to say that in the United States the main trend, almost from the start of the decade, was toward effecting mass-production manufacture of the automobile. In fact, the story of the automobile in America actually is primarily one of ever larger factories and ever greater productivity and the resulting lowering of prices and ever wider popular appeal and usage. Despite the fact that there always were a few American makes of automobiles that aimed at a very limited and high-priced market, this was the theme from the start, long before Ford, despite the way in which some have attempted to picture

Fig. 20. A 3/4-inch-scale model of a 1910 Maxwell built from a kit of parts of various materials, including wood chassis and body, and metal fenders, hood, radiator, and fittings.

Scientific Models, Inc.

the early manufacturers as largely a set of inept bunglers who saw the automobile only as a luxury for the wealthy. There were, both by the standards of the times and even of today, large factories devoted to the manufacture of automobiles in the United States prior to the turn of the century. Progressively the output grew larger, bringing acclaim in turn to many of the early names: Duryea, Haynes, Locomobile, Olds, Willys. It was in fact John N. Willys whom the early American automobile industry regarded as its great production genius. Originally Willys was not a manufacturer but a highly successful automobile salesman. In 1908, wondering why he could not get delivery on Overland cars as fast as he could sell them, he visited the factory in Indianapolis, Indiana, found the company in financial difficulties, bailed them out, and soon afterward took charge. By 1911 the Willys-Overland * plant in Toledo, Ohio, was the largest automobile factory in the world.

Automotive history has tended to credit the Duryea brothers, Charles and Frank, with having built the first successful automobile powered by an internal-combustion reciprocating engine in the United States, and with having opened America's first automobile factory in 1893. This was hotly disputed by Elwood Haynes, and there are still proponents of the Haynes claim for priority, which cannot be dismissed as specious.

In the approximately seventy-five years since the start of the Duryea and Haynes enterprises, more than two thousand makes of automobiles have been manufactured in the United States,

an amazing number, especially when the comparatively small number in production today is considered. Some of more than two thousand never made more than a mere handful of cars; some were simply assembled from standard components readily obtainable from various independent manufacturers of automobile parts; some merely represented a change in nameplate for the benefit of a distributor, but a great many were substantial and worthy enterprises for their time. Some very wonderful cars have fallen by the wayside over the years for one reason or another. Today the Auburn, for example, is but a vague memory to most, except for those who commemorate it in model form, and it is difficult to realize that in the early 1930's Auburn ranked about thirteenth in American car sales. The Maxwell in the early 1920's was not merely the subject of the running joke by Jack Benny that it became in later days, but one of the most popular of American automobiles. The make disappeared because Walter P. Chrysler, who acquired the company in 1921, preferred to promote an automobile bearing his own name. The most unusual sequence of transitions undoubtedly is found in the case of the Rambler. The Rambler became the Jeffrey. In turn the Jeffrey became the Nash, and, within recent memory, the Nash became the Rambler again. However, most of the more than two thousand makes have vanished without trace or successors, although in some instances the companies that made them still flourish, as in the case of Franklin, Hupp, and Studebaker. A few manufacturers who once made passenger cars still exist as truck manufacturers.

Obviously it is impossible to chronicle the histories of even a handful of these magnificent cars. Here, however, is a list of the dates at which some of the most famous or popular makes of American automobiles came into being: Auburn, 1900; Cadillac, 1903; Chevrolet, 1912; Chrysler, 1925; Cord, 1929; Dodge, 1914; Duesenberg, 1920; Ford, 1903; Franklin, 1902; International, 1907; Lincoln, 1921; Oldsmobile (originally sim-

---

* In 1913 there appeared the Willys-Knight, the latter name usually conjuring up a vision of a mounted medieval warrior in armor, and today many assume this to have been the intended purpose of the name. Actually, it indicated a Willys car with an engine employing Knight sleeve valves. In these engines, which were built under license from the inventor, Knight, by several automobile manufacturers, there were no conventional valves, springs, or camshaft—simply two sleeves on each cylinder that moved up and down on a film of oil.

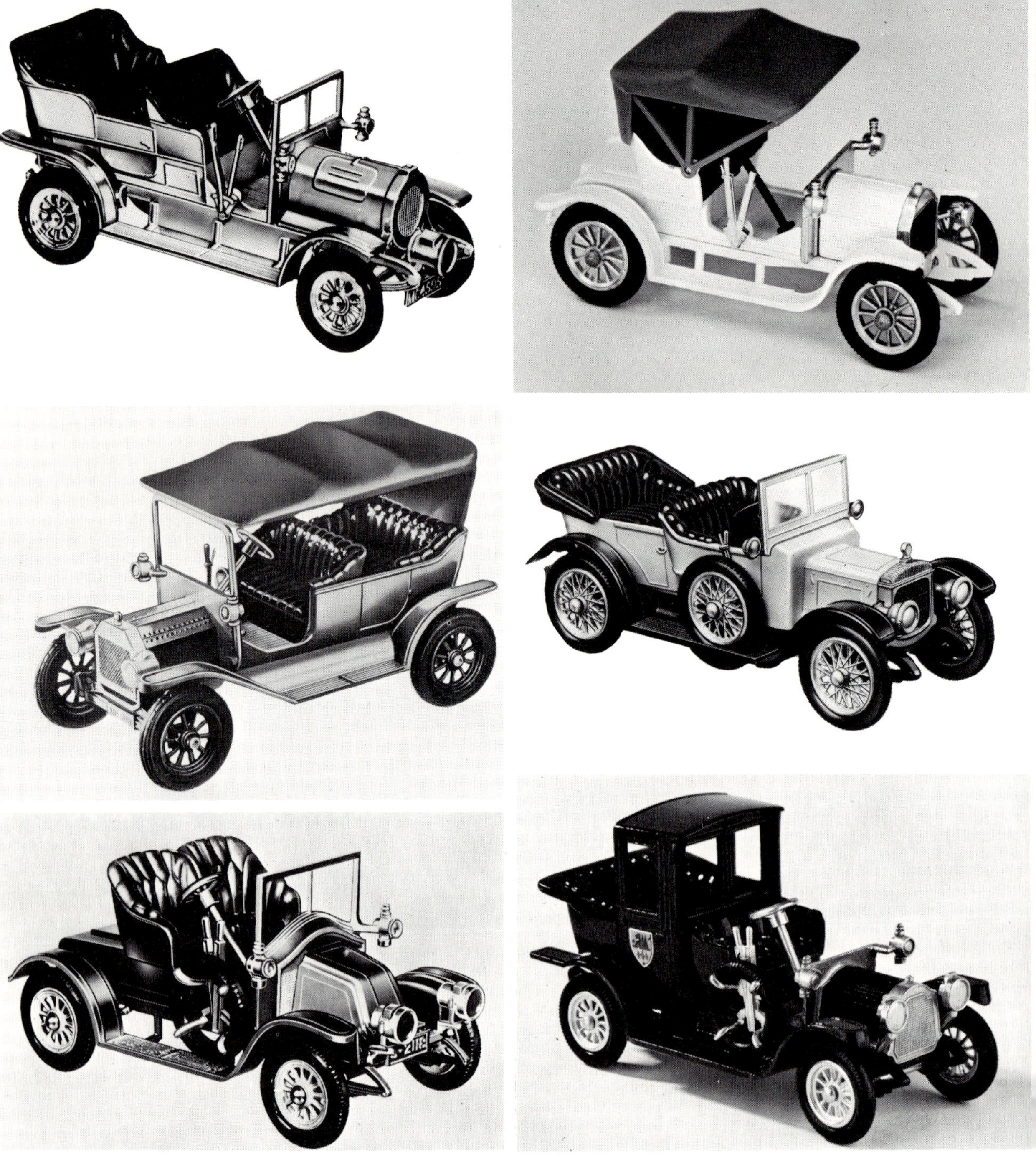

Fig. 21.   Another segment of the history of the automobile, this time illustrated by means of cast-metal miniature cars available in completely assembled and painted form: 1904 Spyker, 1909 Opel, 1911 Ford Model T, 1911 Daimler, 1911 Renault, and 1912 Packard Landaulet.

"Matchbox"—Fred Bronner Corp.

ply the Olds), 1897; Packard, 1899; * Pierce-Arrow, 1901; Rambler, 1902; Reo, 1904; Stanley, 1897; † Studebaker, 1902; Stutz, 1911; White, 1900, and Willys (originally the Willys-Overland), 1908. Yet this list, glamorous as may be many of its names, may pale beside even a limited and somewhat wraithlike list of some of the other more than two thousand makes. Who, for instance, aside from the industrial historian, the dyed-in-the-wool automobile fan, and perhaps some model builders will find more than a few names even vaguely familiar in a compendium that embraces all but one letter of the alphabet: Alsace, Baker, Carter-car, Dort, Elmore, Fox, Gadabout, Holsman, Imp, Jackson, Kissel Kar, Lenox, Mohawk, Northern, Omar, Pope, Quick, Rocket, Simplex, Trumbull, Upton, Velie, Walworth, Yale, and Zip? Diligent research has as yet failed to establish the existence of an automobile whose name begins with the letter *X* having been manufactured in the United States. However, as even now still previously unrecorded makes are being discovered, there is still hope.

Until comparatively recently, most of the models of old cars built or collected by hobbyists were of prototypes dating from after the turn of the century, machines admirably early but still immediately recognizable as automobiles. It is only of late that there has been much interest in the true horseless carriages of before 1901. As a result, most of the models pictured immediately adjacent to this survey are miniatures of real vehicles of the early twentieth century. However, this outlook is now rapidly changing, with an ever-increasing interest being shown by model-automobile enthusiasts in models of cars of the 1890's and even earlier.

---

* Several different dates and versions of the birth of the Packard are given by automotive historians. Part of the confusion is due to the fact that the car built by the Packard brothers, James and William, was not originally named the Packard but, rather, the Ohio, and the Packards sold out their interest in the business in 1904.

Fig. 22. Two more cast-metal miniatures representing steps in the historical progression of the automobile. These are 7-mm.-scale (1/43rd-size) models of a 1910 Renault (top) and a 1927 Bentley Le Mans. These pictures present an interesting example of the results obtained by posing model cars in front of photographs of real scenes.
Corgi—Reeves International, Inc.

---

† In 1899 or 1900, F. E. and F. O. Stanley sold out their automobile business to the Mobile Company of America, Inc., the original Stanley thereby becoming the Locomobile. In 1901 the Stanleys returned to the manufacture of automobiles under their own name, thereby creating another of the not uncommon problems of this type in automotive dating; should the Stanley steamers properly be dated from 1897 or 1901?

The Basics of
Model Automobiles

The model automobile enthusiast will be concerned with five things: scale and size, fidelity, detail, workmanship, and historical background. Depending on individual outlook, the hobbyist's proportionate interest in each of these may vary considerably, or he may have no particular interest in one or more. The first four relate entirely to the models themselves. The fifth, historical background, may relate to either (but in some cases to both) the prototype vehicle that is the subject of the reproduction in miniature or to the model itself.

Powered model automobiles, while they are of considerable historical importance, are somewhat apart from the mainstream of the present-day automobile hobby. Still, a few words should be said about them here, especially concerning the constructing of larger scale models of automobile engines, chassis and engine combinations, or complete cars wherein small electric motors are introduced to demonstrate the working of the engine and other components, and at times to demonstrate the entire model automobile itself in motion. This interest may extend to incorporating such things as a complete and working suspension system into a model car. Of course, the powering of model automobiles may be accomplished by means other than electricity, although this is the mode customarily employed at the present time. A small concealed electric motor and battery is at once the most unobtrusive and practical method currently available, and almost invariably employed when

the purpose is that of serious demonstration rather than an intent merely to make a model automobile capable of motion for motion's sake alone. For the latter purpose anything from rubber bands to miniature jet-propulsion units may be and are employed.

The more skillful modelmaker may wish to construct a working model automobile that is powered by means of a miniature steam engine or a miniature internal-combustion engine. Such models would prove most interesting construction projects, and would be widely admired by all who saw them as outstanding examples of the model builders' art; but, again, this is something of a departure from the mainstream. It might be noted that it would be somewhat easier to construct a working model steam-powered automobile, wherein a single-cylinder engine would suffice for prototype authenticity, than a model automobile with a working miniature of even a four-cylinder internal-combustion reciprocating engine, much less a six or an eight, although anything is possible for a good modelmaker who is willing to expend sufficient time in the planning and execution of a project. Most model automobiles powered by internal-combustion engines, whether commercially manufactured or individually built by hobbyists, achieve working fidelity to power method but not scale reproductions of prototype power plants by using a single-cylinder model airplane engine or an adaptation of one to power their model cars. As for

Fig. 23. Relative model sizes in different scales. All four specimens are based on prototypes of approximately the same length. However, the second model from the left is built to 7 mm. scale (1/43rd size) and is 4 1/16 inch in length. The model at the right is built to .48 inch scale (1/25th size) and measures 7 15/16 inches over the same dimensions.

G. William Holland Photograph

live steam power, even today it is possible to purchase ready-to-run working model steamrollers and steam tractors, and they are indeed fascinating miniatures to operate and demonstrate. There probably are few men of any age with souls so dead that they cannot derive great pleasure from seeing any steam-operated miniature in operation, or from working one themselves.

The collector of old model automobiles is, of course, acutely interested in the type and details of the power form of his models that are provided with means of self-propulsion, both from a tech-

Fig. 24. A group of 3/8-inch-scale (1/32nd-size) models built from kits of plastic parts. Top and second row, American prototypes: Cougar GT-E, Camero SS350, Firebird "400," and Mustang fastback 2 + 2; bottom rows, British sports cars: Sunbeam Alpine, MGB, Austin Healey 3000, and Triumph TR-4.

Revell, Inc.

Fig. 25. Actual working steam-powered tractors and steamrollers represent a unique specialty of enduring interest. Top row, old model steam tractors, left to right, Weeden (*Joseph G. Collins*) and Bing and Doll (*C. W. Frey*). Below, modern 10-inch-long steamroller and tractor (*Schuco Toy Co., Inc., and S. D. Toon & Heath, Ltd.*).

nical and a historical angle. However, virtually without exception, such collectors are little concerned with whether their models operate or not, or in actually operating them if they are in working order.

So much, then, for the operating aspects of the model automobile hobby, except to point out that the powering and movement of the entire automobile as such, discussed here, should not be equated with the potential for manual movement of components of the static model automobile, such as doors, trunk lids, and hoods that are capable of being opened and closed. Such detailing can and does play an important role in the building and detailing of static model cars.

THE FUNCTION OF THE MODEL AUTOMOBILE

If propulsion and movement are not of great import to the model automobile hobby, except historically both as concerns prototype and model, what, then, is the purpose and function of the model automobile? If the answer had to be summed up in one word, that word would be *display*. Naturally, to the builder, detailer, and customizer of model automobiles, there is ever the importance of the pleasure derived from construction, and this facet of the picture certainly should never be played down, anymore than should the thrills of the chase to the enthusiast who primarily is a col-

Fig. 26. An assortment of modern inexpensive cast-metal miniature vehicles. Some interesting points on production methods can be observed by studying these models and observing how the same basic unit may be varied by different paint and lettering. The models of this type are all too often overlooked by collectors until the colors or designs are changed and it suddenly becomes very difficult to secure specific specimens.

Barclay Mfg. Co., Inc.

lector. Nor should the element of the possibility of entering a miniature model in model automobile contests and seeing a customized miniature car secure an award for its meritorious construction, design, or finish be overlooked when calculating the overall purpose and rewards of the model-automobile hobby. Yet, in essence, the end result and goal for both the model-automobile builder and the model-automobile collector is possession of the model.

Possession, too, is not quite the same as display. In the long run, however, as models either built or secured in completed form tend to pile up, it often becomes impractical for a hobbyist to keep every piece shelved where it may readily be seen. There are model automobile enthusiasts who have accumulated in one way or another thousands of miniature automobiles. Collections numbering in the hundreds of specimens are by no means uncommon. Eventually sheer lack of available display space and a need to protect models from overcrowding may necessitate some being carefully packed away.

As far as it is practical, no models should deliberately be discarded, even if they seem to represent one's rather crude early attempts when compared with examples of more recent and ex-perienced workmanship. From an individualistic standpoint, such models may be desirable for demonstrating this very factor of constantly enhanced skills. They may also eventually possess some historical interest and value themselves for latecomers to the hobby, or they may be found fertile sources of desirable parts for subsequent model building or customizing activities. To many the vital point is that while the cost of the original materials or kit is likely to have been quite nominal, the transformation of these components into a finished model often represents a fair amount of working time to complete, paint, and decorate the model. The value of this effort, even though it is not something that can readily be measured in dollars and cents, is nonetheless inherent in the resulting miniature automobile.

WHAT IS AVAILABLE

There are three main ways in which model automobiles can come into the hands of the hobbyist or be created by him:

1. Building (or having them built) from scratch, that is to say constructing them from various raw materials such as wood, metal, or plastic.

Fig. 27. A large model—1-inch scale (1/12th size)—superdetailed model of a Honda Formula 1 racing car built from a kit. It features such details as fully operating rear-wheel universal joints and working suspension, is equipped with actual semipneumatic tires, and is powered by means of an electric motor.

Model Rectifier Corp.

2. Building from kits, or at least using a standard kit as a starting point for a final model that is modified to a varying degree from the standard model normally built from a given kit. Some kits provide extra parts so that one of two or more versions of the same car may be constructed, as for example, a convertible with the top optionally up or down, or a stock or souped-up version of the same car. Some kits also include a variety of customizing parts that can be applied as the individual model builder sees fit.

3. Securing model automobiles in completely assembled and finished form.

Methods 1 and 2 are customarily used by builders of model automobiles, with those making use of commercially available kits being by far in the overwhelming majority. Some model-automobile collectors who buy and assemble kits make use of the talents of an expert model builder to assemble and complete the model. This is sometimes due to lack of faith in one's own skill, but more often it is intended to secure a really fine and professional-looking paint job worthy of a model to be displayed in a permanent collection, since a good painted finish is by far the more difficult part of the operation. In the main, however, hobbyists desiring models built from kits do all the work themselves.

Method 3 for the most part refers to the type of model automobile that is completely assembled and finished in a factory and is sold only in such form. By far the great bulk of these models are sold to model-automobile collectors who want to place them in their collections of model cars. Some quantities of such assembled models are of course also sold to operators of model-raceway layouts, model-railroad layouts, and the like, who use them as part of their overall scenic picture.

HOW MODEL AUTOMOBILES COME INTO BEING

While serious hobbyists almost invariably come to feel that their model automobiles, in kit or finished form, are created especially for their benefit, by far the bulk of miniature automobiles are made essentially for a mass toy market making miniature cars as playthings. Indeed, despite manufacturers' endeavors to promote and capture as much as possible of a serious hobby and collectors' market, in most cases it would simply be impossible for the models that are the object of this hobbyists' and collectors' interest to be manufactured in the form in which they are made and sold at current prices if it were not for their reliance on this great toy market. The individual hobbyist all too often finds the manufacturers' selection of subjects for new models, or the forms and sizes in which new models are offered, somewhat inexplicable, and often waxes quite critical over such affairs, either among his fellows or in letters to magazines and to the manufacturers themselves. Another frequently heard matter of wonderment among model-car hobbyists is that so often two or more manufacturers will bring out models of the same prototype at about the same time, and the question is asked why the supposedly purely altruistic model-car manufacturers, who in the eyes of the hobbyist presumably exist solely to make the greatest range of different models available for the serious enthusiast, cannot genially get together, discuss their plans in advance with one another, and mutually agree that each will produce replicas of different prototypes!

The hobbyist who thus questions and wonders, and frequently makes a pest of himself with letters to manufacturers, must realize that the in-

Fig. 28. Miniature trucks have maintained an abiding popularity among model-automobile fans for many years. Pictured at the top are two big steel models of the 1920's, a Buddy "L" ice truck (*Thomas W. Sefton*) and a Steelcraft tank truck, with detail photograph showing the GMC insignia on the radiator (*G. William Holland photographs*). Center, a 3/8-inch-scale 1962 Chevrolet hot rod (*Aurora Plastics Corp.*) and a .48-inch-scale Dodge (*Industro-Motive Corp.*), both built from kits of plastic parts. At the bottom are two cast-metal miniatures (*"Matchbox"—Fred Bronner Corp.*).

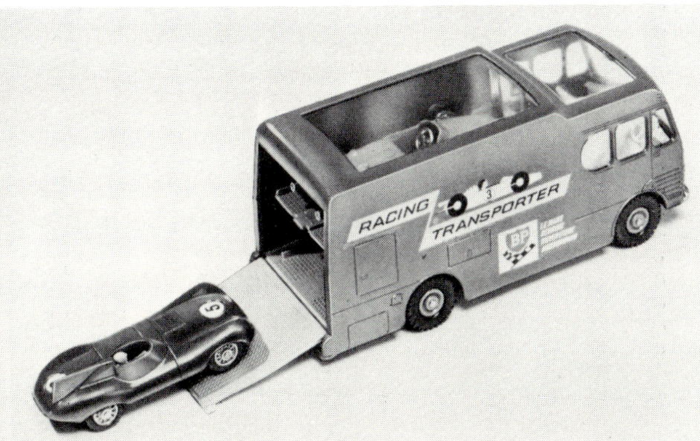

dustry simply does not exist primarily for his benefit, but rather that he is the incidental recipient of benefits. Not only is the model-automobile industry geared to vast quantities for the toy trade, but, as with most successful industries, it is a highly competitive one. Accordingly, when a prototype appears likely to be particularly popular, it is only natural for more than one manufacturer to include it in his line. This on the one hand makes more ma-

terial available for the model builder or collector who happens to be specializing in some particular category that embraces the models in question. On the other hand it draws groans of protest from other hobbyists who do not understand the basic situation and would prefer to have other models available.

There is, in fact, no doubt that from the standpoint of the serious builder or collector of

Fig. 29. Regardless of what sort of prototype a model-car enthusiast is interested in, it is possible to find kits of plastic parts available today for building miniatures. Pictured here are six examples in 1/2-inch scale, a dragster with parachute, two fun cars, an oval track car, and two customized units.

Monogram Models, Inc.

model automobiles the overall situation is improving. The sheer weight of increasing mass and buying power in the model automobile hobby naturally tends to make more and more manufacturers anxious to cater to and sell to this rapidly growing market. Nevertheless, the model-automobile hobbyist remains and probably for the most part always will remain the tail that cannot expect to wag the dog. An understanding and appreciation of this situation on the part of model automobile enthusiasts will inevitably save a great deal of useless aggravation and frustration.

SCALE AND PROPORTION

With model automobiles, as with all model hobbies, a matter of predominant interest to most enthusiasts is that of scale and proportion—that is, the relation of the size of any given model to the size of the actual vehicle that it reproduces in miniature. For reasons that will be noted in a moment, this subject is likely to be considerably more complex and confusing to beginners in the model automobile hobby than to enthusiasts whose interest is confined to other types of models. If the newcomer to model automobiles has had previous experience in other model-building hobbies, such as model railroading for example, he is likely to be startled to find that a term he has been accustomed to using, and whose meaning he supposes he readily understands, often seems to take on an entirely new interpretation in the model-automobile hobby: the word "scale." Actually, the meaning of the word does not change, but it is often loosely and improperly used when applied to model

Fig. 30. Two highly detailed cast-metal miniature trucks. Left, a car transporter with operable upper deck. This model is built to 9/32-inch scale. Right, a model of a British fire engine with working doors, interior details, and removable equipment.

Dinky Toys—Meccano Ltd., Lines Bros.

automobiles. In fact, the term has now become so widely misused in the realm of miniature automobiles that even specialized magazines and dealers, who once retained the correct meaning, now appear to feel it is fruitless to attempt to continue to insist upon proper usage.

Scale is always properly expressed in terms of a dimension on the model that equals a dimension—usually 1 foot—on the prototype. Thus scale is stated as, for example, a scale of 1/2 inch to the foot. In common usage, however, hobbyists would refer to it simply as 1/2-inch scale, it being automatically understood that this refers to 1/2 inch to the foot. A model of an actual automobile 16 feet long that is built to 1/2-inch scale would be 8 inches long. If the actual or prototype automobile had wheels 2 feet in diameter, the wheels on a 1/2-inch-scale model would be 1 inch in diameter. If the prototype had 15-inch-diameter wheels, the wheels on the 1/2-inch-scale model would be 5/8 inches in diameter. Similarly a model of the same 16-foot-long prototype automobile built to 1-inch scale would be 16 inches long; a model built to 3/4-inch scale would be 12 inches long, a model built to 3/8-inch scale would be 6 inches long, a model built to 1/4-inch scale would be 4 inches long, and so on. Every other dimension of the real car would similarly be reduced according to the scale being used. On a 3/8-inch-scale model a wheel 2 feet in diameter on the prototype would come out 3/4 inches in diameter; the same prototype wheel size would come to 1/2-inch diameter in 1/4-inch scale. All this has long been established and is readily understood. Given a plan for building a specific automobile in any scale, a modelmaker can readily take the dimensions, whether given in the measures of the prototype or a model built to a specific scale, and readily transfer them to the proper sizes for any other scale desired. Obviously, the easiest scales with which to work are based on the more common divisions of English linear measurement, 1 inch, 3/4 inch, 1/2 inch, 3/8 inch, 1/4 inch, and so on. Of course, if it is desired to build a larger size model, the

hobbyist can exceed 1-inch scale and use a larger size, such as 1 1/2-inch or 2-inch scale.

Most of the scales from 1/2 inch down are identical with some of the most common model railroad scales, such as 3/8-inch scale and 1/4-inch scale. This is not so much because the model-automobile scales were taken from model railroad scales but because initially virtually all popular modelmaking scales originated by taking the fractions easiest to work with, or multiples of an inch. Scales of 1 inch, 3/4 inch, 1/2 inch, 3/8 inch, and 1/4 inch, for instance, will be found widely used not only in model railroading but also in model-airplane and model-ship construction.

There are, however, a few scales extensively used for model automobiles that are departures from this general principle and do derive directly from model railroad usage. The most common of these are 7 mm. and 3.5 mm. scale. Although the scale itself is expressed in millimeters, a unit of the metric system, they still relate to the usual English linear measurement of 1 foot on the prototype: a scale of 7 mm. to the foot; a scale of 3.5 mm. to the foot. The 7-mm. scale is close to the widely used model automobile scale of 1/4 inch to the foot. These represent the most commonly used scales for O-gauge model trains in Europe and America respectively. A scale of 1/8 inch, however, seldom is employed for model automobile construction, although it is widely used by builders of model airplanes and boats. Instead the 3.5-mm. scale, which is slightly larger than 1/8 inch, is most commonly employed on both sides of the Atlantic, the 3.5-mm. scale being the scale of both American and European HO-gauge model railroads. (However, in Europe, the OO gauge [which uses the same track gauge as HO but a 4-mm. scale], is infinitely more common than HO gauge 3.5-mm. scale.)

All this is quite readily understood, and these scales are extremely easy ones with which anyone desiring to build a model of an automobile or anything else to work. When the scales are expressed in fractions of English linear measurement, various dimensions can be calculated by using an ordinary ruler. When the scales are expressed in millimeters, special rulers, originally made for model-railroad use, that provide dimensions in millimeters for prototype feet are readily available in hobby shops. In all cases there may be certain unavoidable difficulties in converting very small prototype dimensions to the desired modeling scale, but even in such cases this system is extremely easy to employ.

It will immediately be seen that a model built to a scale of 1 inch to the foot will be 1/12th the size of the prototype; a model built to 1/2-inch scale will be 1/24th the size of the prototype, and so on. These fractions properly represent "proportion" or "size," never scale. If you know the scale to which a model is built, or to which you intend to build a model, it is very simple to determine the proportion or size. Simply divide the scale into 12.00 (representing the 12 inches that make up a foot), first converting the fraction into its decimal equivalent. For example, 1/2-inch scale is converted to .5 inch for this purpose. Dividing .5 inch into 12.00 gives us 24, which checks out to 1/24th size. Similarly, 1/4-inch scale converts to .025, which when divided into 12.00 comes to 48— 1/48th scale. Here, as in other instances, the 12.00 must be carried out to further decimal places; you actually are dividing .025 into 12.000 in this case.

If a metric scale is involved, the same procedure is followed, except that to secure the size or proportion you convert 12.00—one foot—into its metric equivalent—304.8 mm.—before dividing. Then you proceed and divide, say, 7 mm. into 304.8 mm. The answer is 43.54. The 7-mm. scale usually is given as being 1/43rd size; as can be seen, this is not accurate, and the 7-mm. scale does not divide evenly into the metric equivalent of one foot. If anything, it would be more correct to refer to the 7-mm. scale as representing 2/87th size, but even this is not precisely accurate; it is really a little larger than 2/87th size. The 3.5-mm. scale customarily is stated to be 1/87th size. This is almost but not quite on the button, for 304.8 divided by 3.5 mm. is 87.08—in any event it is not the 1/86th size that occasionally is given for the 3.5-mm. scale. However, a scale of 4 mm. to the foot, which is occasionally used for model automobiles because it matches the scale of OO gauge trains, when divided into 304.8, gives us 76.2, usually rendered as 1/76th size, and this is a little farther from the fraction customarily cited than 3.5 mm. scale is from 1/87th size. Another metric scale that sometimes is advocated or used for model automobiles is 10-mm. scale, a little larger than 3/8-inch scale. The proportion for 10-mm. scale is usually given as 1/30th. Actually dividing 10 into 304.8 gives a result of 30.48, a little more than 1/30th; or, in terms of actual size, a model built to 10-mm. scale actually would be a little less than 1/30th size, almost midway between 1/30th and 1/31st size, in fact. (The larger the denominator in the fraction indicating proportion or size, the smaller the model; but the larger the

Fig. 31. Buses are another distinct collectors' category. Pictured here are two old cast-iron models, a Kenton double-deck bus of the World War I era (*G. William Holland photograph*) and an Arcade of the 1920's and 1930's (*Lloyd W. Ralston*), and, below, their modern cast-metal miniature counterparts (*"Matchbox"—Fred Bronner Corp.*).

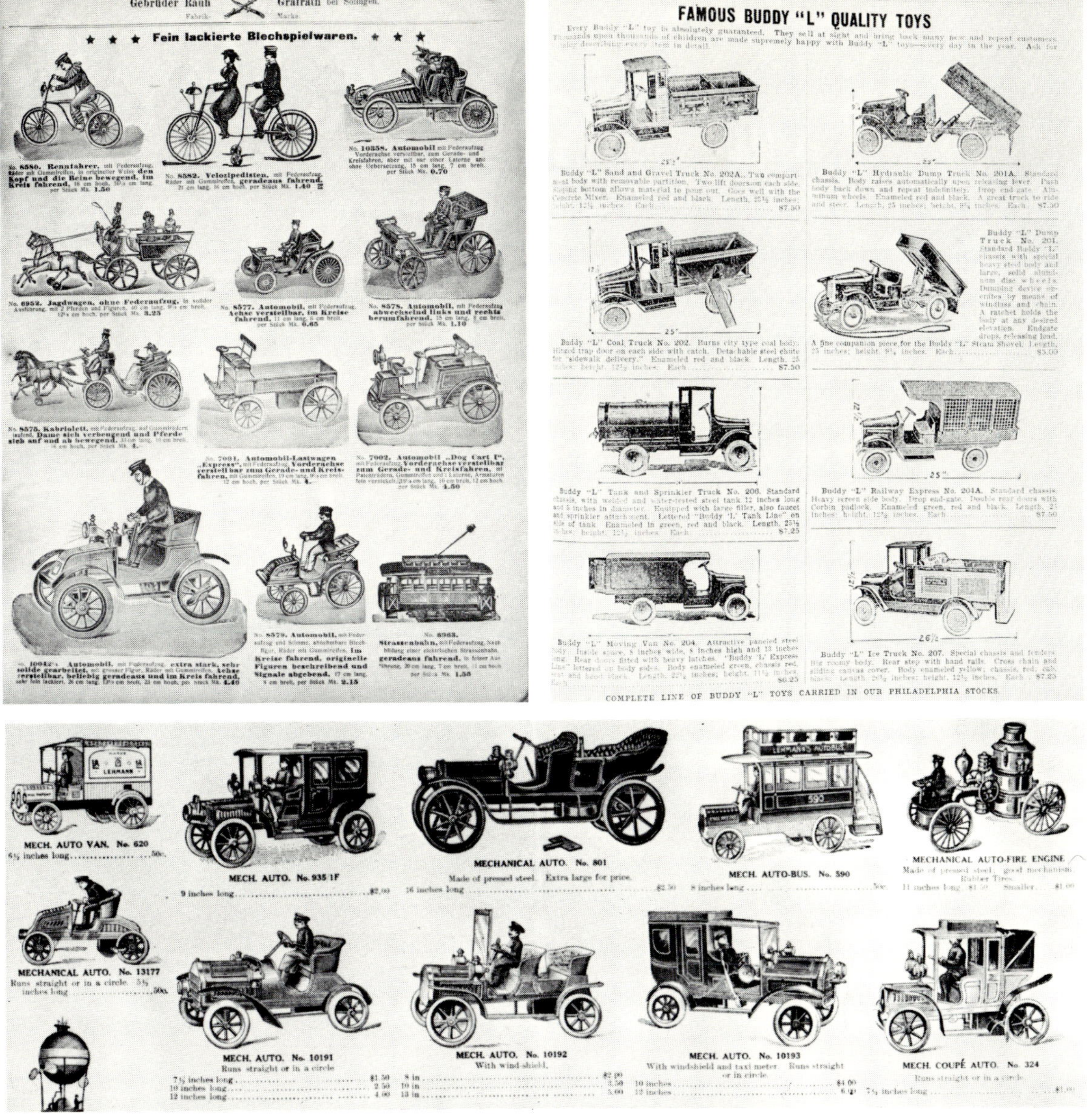

Fig. 32. All old catalogs of miniature automobiles are of considerable interest to collectors. Shown here are a page from a German catalog of 1906 (*A. E. Moretock*) and an American catalog of 1927 (*A. J. Koveleski*). Below is a segment of a page from a 1910 catalog. The cars illustrated are, left to right, top row: Lehmann, Carette, Converse, Lehmann, and Wilkins; lower row: unidentified, three Bings (note that the third Bing is a taxicab with meter), and a Gunthermann.

actual scale in terms of fractions of an inch, the larger the model.)

It will also be readily observed that if you know the proportion to which a model is built, it is equally easy to determine the scale used by dividing the proportion into 12.00 inches or 304.8 mm. Thus, taking a 1/24th-size model, the scale would be determined by dividing 24 into 12.00. The result is .5 inches, or 1/2 inch. Assuming a proportion of, say, 1/64th and dividing 64 into 12.00, we get .1875 inch, that is, 3/16 inch, and accordingly 1/64th size is 3/16-inch scale. Actually, this is a scale that very seldom is employed for building

model automobiles although a few operators of H1- (S-) gauge model railroads have employed it in an endeavor to secure miniature automobiles built to the same scale as their trains for purposes of scenic accompaniment.

It should also be noted that size or proportion, while usually expressed as a fraction, such as 1/24th size, can also properly be given as a ratio, such as 1 to 24, or 1:24. In fact, size and proportion are also sometimes referred to as ratio instead, it being understood that the ratio concerned is that of the model to the prototype, and this method of denoting what is meant as ratio,

Fig. 33. An example of a kit that offers the hobbyist his choice of assembling any one of three substantially different models. These are all highly customized cars, based on the Ford Model T, that can be optionally assembled from the same kit. Each model measures more than 16 inches in length, 1-inch scale being employed.

Lindberg Products, Inc.

while not so often used as size or proportion, also is technically correct. The important thing always to remember is that scale is one thing; size, proportion, or ratio—by whatever name it is called—is something entirely different, and in proper usage never is scale.

THE GREAT POINT OF CONFUSION

The fact that the usual metric scales such as 3.5 mm. and 7 mm. do not work out evenly in terms of size or proportion does not mean that they are not good and valid scales for the model builder. Any hobbyist with ordinary model-building skills can easily build models of automobiles or anything else to scales of 3.5 mm., 4 mm., and so on. *However, if we take size or proportion as a starting point and work from the other direction, it will be found that not all the commonly used sizes will work out to practical scales,* that is, scales that can easily be used by an individual hobbyist building models from scratch. Yet we find a number of these sizes either already well established or rapidly being established in the model automobile field. How and why has this come about? This is particularly pertinent, for it is a matter that tends to cause endless confusion to beginners, and it would seem only fair for them to be entitled

to an explanation of something that upon consideration often seems supremely illogical and impractical. Why, then, have model automobiles departed so widely from accepted modelmaking scales and practices?

There are actually several answers to this question, but the first step that set the trend and that overall, once taken, probably played the widest part stems uniquely from the relationship between the real automobile industry itself and the manufacture of model automobiles. As is generally known, especially in the years since World War I and even more particularly since the later 1920's when styling and color began to play an increasingly important role in real automobile design, the automobile industry itself has made very extensive use of models in their design and styling departments. In many instances numerous models are made of proposed renovated or entirely new designs before full-size mockups of the finally selected or most likely treatments are constructed. Almost invariably, these models have been built to one-half or one-quarter the size of the proposed actual automobile. They are relatively big models, as usually is found desirable for this purpose; a 1/2-size model is, of course, a model built to a scale of 6 inches to the foot; a 1/4-size model is a model built to a scale of 3 inches to the foot. These

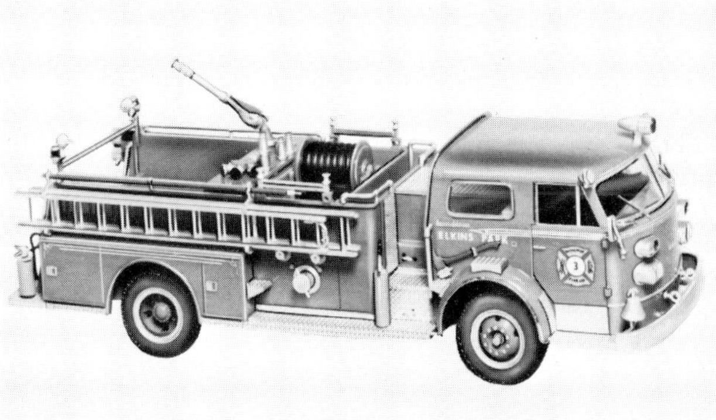

Fig. 34.   Another extremely popular category is fire engines. Top, three old models, a large steel Buddy "L" (*Thomas W. Sefton*), and cast-iron Hubley and Williams units (*Ward Kimball*). Center, two modern cast-metal miniatures ("*Matchbox*"—*Fred Bronner Corp.*). Bottom, two built from kits of plastic parts, a 3/8-inch-scale 1930 Ford engine as a "surf buggy," a kit with much appeal as the basis for assembling it as a straight 1930 fire-engine model, and an .48-inch-scale modern pumper (*Aurora Plastics Corp.*)

large scales are extremely easy to work with. For example, in a scale of 3 inches to the foot, 1/4 inch equals one inch of the prototype, 1/8 inch equals 1/2 inch of the prototype, 1/16 inch equals 1/4 inch of the prototype, and so on. They are good scales and they work out into perfect scale and proportion combinations, whichever way one chooses to look at them. For the most part the real automobile designers tend to look at them in terms of size, and refer to them as 1/2-size and 1/4-size models; not infrequently making the error of calling them 1/2 scale and 1/4 scale.

Following World War II, the automobile industry became extremely conscious of the hobby interest in model automobiles and the potential for publicity and goodwill, both in general and in reference to specific makes of automobiles, by encouraging model-automobile building and by using models themselves for promotional purposes. Plans for real cars readily were furnished to model manufacturers; in some cases the tools for making models and kits were subsidized directly, or perhaps indirectly by real automobile manufacturers contracting to take large quantities of models themselves. The model manufacturers were working closely with the real automobile firms who were used to thinking of models in terms of ratio to the prototype over and above reference to a specific working scale. What size should the new models be? Somewhere at some perhaps now never to be determined place and date someone stretched out his two hands to indicate an approximate "good" size—that is, prepossessing in appearance but not too large for economical manufacture—and said, "Oh, about so big; say, 1/25th the size of the real car." The automobile men involved were accustomed to thinking in terms of what seemed round numbers for model size, and 25 does sound like a much more nicely rounded number than 24.

The result was a proliferation of 1/25th-size models and kits to build 1/25th-size models. Large manufacturing concerns with expert engineering and drafting staffs can readily draw up plans for models and for the tools and molds for making models accurately computed to be 1/25th the size of the prototype, and this was and continues to be done. The only difficulty is that when an individual hobbyist desires to build a model himself to the same proportion he finds that the scale for a 1/25th-size model works out to .48 inch to the foot, a most difficult scale with which to work. Similarly, viewed offhand without considering all the implications, 1/50th sounds much more like a nice round number than 1/48th. However, while the scale for a 1/48th-size model is the even, long-established, and easy-to-work-with 1/4-inch scale, the scale for 1/50th size is .24 inches per foot. Or take 1/64th size and 1/65th size. The former comes to an even 3/16-inch scale; the latter can be run out almost indefinitely; at seven decimal places it is .1846015 inch to the

foot. Again, a factory can readily produce a model based on any size selected, but an individual model builder is very severely handicapped, even if he has available scale rulers that give him actual dimensions in fractions of an inch or millimeter for corresponding prototype dimensions—and such scale rulers are not always readily available anyway for any but the most widely used scales.

Another occasional cause for seemingly odd sizes and scales is an actual desire to correct insofar as possible an already existing error, as in the case of 1/42nd size. Contemplating entering the model-automobile field following World War II, some European manufacturers took note of the fact, already mentioned, that although usually accepted as such, 7-mm, scale does not really represent a model 1/43rd the size of the prototype. Actually a 7-mm.-scale model is a little more than halfway between 1/43rd size and 1/44th size, 7 divided into 304.8 (the number of millimeters in a foot) gives an answer of 43.54, not an even 43. Accordingly, 1/42nd-size models were introduced, built to a supposed scale of 7.2 mm. to the foot. This is much closer to an even scale-size relationship, but still not an exact one, as can be determined by dividing 7.2 into 304.8—the answer is 42.1943 when carried out to the fourth decimal point. Of course, one is speaking in terms of microscopic sizes here; nevertheless the point is still accuracy and precision, which are so important to modelmakers.

A third and important reason for many of the odd sizes is simply that of a manufacturer seeking a practical size. At one extreme, the smaller models, it is well known that one of the major ideas and promotional points behind one popular line of miniature cast-metal model automobiles is that each is packed in a standard-size container simulating the container for a common article of use. Accordingly, the aim was that all models in the series fit the container and more or less fully.

Fig. 35.   Military vehicles can form a very extensive specialized category. These are models assembled from kits of plastic parts. In the group at the left are a 3/8-inch-scale personnel carrier, a Patton tank, an amphibious Weasel, Jeep and gun, cargo truck, and armored half-track (*Monogram Models, Inc.*). At the right is a 3/8-inch-scale Lacrosse missile-launching truck (*Renewal Products, Inc.*).

Fig. 36. Relatively large-scale models constructed from kits containing mainly die-cast metal parts, supplemented by some detail and trim components of molded plastic. Top, 3/5-inch-scale, 1/20th-size 1932 Chevrolet coupe and touring car. Below, .5454-inch-scale, 1/22nd-size 1930 Packard roadster and Dietrich victoria.

Hubley Division, Gabriel Industries, Inc.

As a result the models in this range are made to a variety of scales, some of them standard or close to a standard scale, others quite unusual. Hence you may find models in this series, all very close in actual physical size, ranging from about 1/70th to 1/100th proportion. Much the same thing will be found in some other lines of very small models, for somewhat similar if not absolutely identical reasons. Although a number of manufacturers have endeavored to stabilize on one fixed scale, many have had to approach the field for one reason or another with the thought that a given model should be approximately a certain size, and varied their scales accordingly. Some see a trend today toward greater stabilization and standardization in general obtaining throughout the field; others do not agree that this is something that truly can be now or that possibly can at any time be designated a trend. This is something concerning which it is not possible to be dogmatic because practical production and sales considerations from the standpoint of the manufacturer must of necessity often dictate such things. A similar variation in scales to that of the so-called miniature cars may also be found at the opposite extreme in some of the larger models. One line, for example, consists of kits ranging in size from 1/22nd to 1/18th size. The 1/22nd size represents a scale of .545 inch to the foot; the 1/18th size is a scale of .666 inch to the foot.

THE POPULAR SCALES

It might appear at first glance that a scale of exactly .666 inch to the foot—two-thirds of an inch to the foot—would be a very easy scale to work with. However, this is not the case, although it would be if the standard divisions of English linear measurement were in thirds, sixths, and so forth. If this were true, a scale of 1/6 inch to the foot would also be an easy scale for model builders—it frequently is used for model aircraft and occasionally for model automobiles, and figures out to models built to 1/72nd size. This scale can also be expressed as 1 inch to 6 feet, although in the more customary terminology of scales it is 1/6 inch to the foot. To avoid confusion, it appears best always to retain the rather standard prototype measurement of 1 foot and translate the model building scales into their ratio to the prototype 1 foot. Regardless of the availability of scale rulers or not, the easiest scales for a modelmaker to work with will always be found to be those based on the usual system of dividing English linear measurement into 1/2, 1/4, 1/8, 1/16, 1/32, and so on, of an inch.

A device sometimes employed by model-automobile builders for model building in various scales, including some that do not evenly match up with their relative model proportions, is known as a proportion wheel. The outer rim of the wheel is set to the prototype dimension, and the corresponding actual dimension in various scales is then read through small windows cut in the wheel.

For ease of working and the attainment of ultimate accuracy and proper relationship between scale and proportion, the following scales and sizes are recommended to those who wish to build model automobiles from scratch: In the 1/24th- and 1/25th-size range, the 1/24th size with its scale of 1/2 inch to the foot. This is suggested with full awareness that when the .48-inch scale of the 1/25th size is translated into the nearest octonal fraction, 15/32 inch, the scale thus arrived at is only a few thousands of an inch off. Nevertheless, it still is off. In the next popular size downward, there is little competition for the 3/8-inch scale, 1/32nd size, save possibly from a very few who prefer the 10-mm. scale. The 3/8-inch scale is unquestionably advocated. Next down, we come to the possibility of building to the so-called 1/42nd size, with 7.2-mm. scale; to the so-called 1/43rd size, with 7-mm. scale, or to a true 1/48th size with 1/4-inch scale. Here a combination of logic, accuracy, and ease of handling plans and actual construction work indicates favoring the 1/4-inch scale, 1/48th size, and this in spite of the fact that there are those who like today to think of 1/43rd size or in some cases of the 1/42nd size as a sort of universally accepted standard collectors' size, and the fact that a model of any given automobile when built to a scale of 7.2 mm. or 7 mm. will be perceptibly larger (though the actual difference in size will be quite minute) than a model of the same car built to 1/4-inch scale. Anyone building a model from scratch will find 1/4-inch scale much easier to employ than either of the metric scales, and it provides an exact relationship between scale and proportion; although, as will be appreciated from the preceding discussion, this is in no sense a really vital factor unless one has to approach the subject from the standpoint of a preselected proportion and then work out the proper or the closest scale for that proportion.

It will be observed, if only by some older model-building enthusiasts, that at no time has the advocacy of one scale or another in a general size area been introduced on the basis of one choice being that of an "American" or "British" scale because it is measured in units of English linear measurement, and the metric scales being "foreign." This was a rather pointless and ridiculous viewpoint frequently argued with considerable popular acceptance in the 1930's and even sometimes later. The English linear measurement scales are advocated where there is a choice because they

are easier for the average model builder to work with, using the ordinary measuring tools ready at hand and because they work out to precisely correct scale and proportional relationships. In regard to the choice between 7.2-mm., 7-mm., and 1/4-inch scales, it is, of course, fairly easy to build to 7-mm. scale using an easily obtainable HO-gauge model railroad scale ruler based on 3.5-mm. scale and simply doubling each dimension. A few model-automobile builders also have advocated using 17/64-inch scale when working in this general size range. This is an American purist's O-gauge model railroad scale, and works out to what is always considered 1/45th size, although the actual decimal equivalent is .2666 inch. While 17/64-inch scale provides O-gauge model railroad equipment with a truer gauge-to-scale relationship based on an actual railroad track standard gauge of 4 feet, 8 1/2 inches, there is surely no point in employing it for model automobiles where the factor of the gauge and scale relationship—gauge being the width between the inside edges of the running rails of real or model railroad track—does not enter into the picture.

In the smallest widely popular size, the builder of model automobiles has a choice of 4-mm. scale, 1/76th size; 3.5-mm. scale, 1/87th size; and 1/8-inch scale, 1/96th size. The 3.5-mm. scale is well established and matches that of HO-gauge model railroads, while the 4-mm. scale is equally well established in Europe and matches that of OO-gauge model trains.* As noted, HO-gauge model railroad rulers that translate prototype feet into 3.5-mm. scale are easily accessible. On the other hand, although virtually no model railroad equipment is now built to 1/8-inch scale, this scale is and long has been extremely popular and accepted among builders of model airplanes and of model ships. Unless the model builder's aim is precisely to duplicate the scale employed on an HO- or OO-gauge model raceway or model railroad system in his model-automobile construction, the 1/8-inch scale must be recommended for the model-automobile builder. On the other hand, it should be admitted that at the present time relatively little scratch building of model automobiles as such is done in a size smaller than 1/4-inch scale, 1/48th size.

---

* American HO-gauge and European OO-gauge model trains use the same gauge of track, 16.5 mm., although the scales are different; American OO-gauge employs 19-mm. gauge track but the same 4-mm. scale and cited 1/76th proportion as European OO, which, as already noted in the text, is not exactly correct either.

Fig. 37. Still another specialized category is made up of motorcycles. Shown here are four old Hubley models, three conventional types (*L. C. Hegerty, G. William Holland photograph*), and a 9-inch-long model ridden by Popeye (*Lloyd W. Ralston*). Below are four modern cast-metal miniatures, a Lambretta, Triumph Speed Twin, Triumph Thunderbird, and Honda Benly (*Britains—Reeves International, Inc.*).

MORE SCALE FACTS AND TERMINOLOGY

Nothing that has been said here should be construed as in any way disparaging the scales other than those recommended above that are commonly used by many manufacturers of finished model automobiles or kits. The approach has been in terms of what is best for the hobbyist who desires to build model automobiles from scratch. The enthusiast who purchases assembled model cars or who builds them from kits will naturally accept what is offered in any size generally satisfactory, as far as the final physical dimensions of the model go, and make use of whatever appeals to him, unless he is determined to be an absolute purist. All too often the role of the purist will be found to be somewhat uncomfortable and unrewarding, and liable to detract substantially from the pure and unadulterated enjoyment that an individual rightly should expect to derive from any hobby. The matter of assorting scales in a model-building program or in a collection will be dealt with shortly. Here, however, is a table giving the most widely used model automobile scales and their commonly accepted respective proportions, although, as has been demonstrated, the usually cited proportions are not always necessarily absolutely accurate:

SCALE	PROPORTION	MATCHING MODEL RAILROAD GAUGE
1/8 in.	1/96th	E
3.5 mm.	1/87th	HO
4 mm.	1/76th	OO
3/16 in.	1/64th	H1 (S)
1/4 in.	1/48th	O
7. mm.	1/43rd	O
7.2 mm.	1/42nd	O
3/8 in.	1/32nd	No. 1 or Standard
10 mm.	1/30th	No. 1 or Standard
.48 in.	1/25th	—
1/2 in.	1/24th	No. 3
3/5 in.	1/20th	—
3/4 in.	1/16th	—
1 in.	1/12th	—
1 1/4 in.	1/10th	—
1 1/2 in.	1/8th	—
2 in.	1/6th	—
3 in.	1/4th	—
6 in.	1/2	—

The relative model-railroad gauge names are provided essentially merely to provide a ready cross-check. It is incorrect usage to refer to any scale merely by a model-railroad gauge name, as, for example, to call 3.5-mm. scale "HO scale," or 1/4-inch scale "O scale." The model-railroad gauge-name designations actually refer only to the measurement of the model track gauge, and some model-railroad gauges such as O or Standard may have more than one fairly well-accepted scale. Regardless of this, in describing any scale in terms of its model-railroad application, the word "gauge" should always properly be included, thus; HO-gauge scale, not HO scale.

The model automobile hobbyist probably will at other times encounter a number of other terms and designations referring to scale, some relating to general conceptions and some seemingly to specific scales, although none are couched in the form of definite measurements in inches or millimeters but entirely in words. "Scale to size," "scale to price," "constant scale," and "collectors' scale" and variants of the latter are the most likely to be met with. Some enthusiasts deplore the use of many of these designations, and feel that they tend only to confuse things, particularly for the beginner. This may partially be correct, but any potential confusion can immediately be removed simply by explaining what these generally understood terms do—and do not—mean.

"Scaled to size" and "scaled to price" from the practical standpoint mean the same thing, namely, that the exact scale and proportion employed on a manufactured model or kit has been determined by a desire or a necessity that the finished product work out to fit a predetermined actual physical size. This required size may be dictated by the need to fit the model vehicle into a standard-size container or by a need to sell it at a certain price or perhaps to be accommodated on the manufacturer's established tooling. Instances have already been cited where one of these factors is operative. In any event there is certainly nothing derogatory to be read into either of these expressions except perhaps by those who would like to force all model cars into the confines of a particular scale. These two terms are in fact more of the trade and industry than of the hobbyist. However, model-automobile enthusiasts have a considerable measure of sophistication, and in recent years these two expressions have been increas-

Fig. 38.   Four more 7-mm.-scale (1/43rd-size) cast-metal miniatures: a working dump truck, a snorkel fire engine, a truck used as a camera van, and a rear-entrance double-decked bus. The fire engine measures 9 7/8 inches in length, and the elevating booms extend to a height of 14 5/8 inches.

Corgi—Reeves International, Inc.

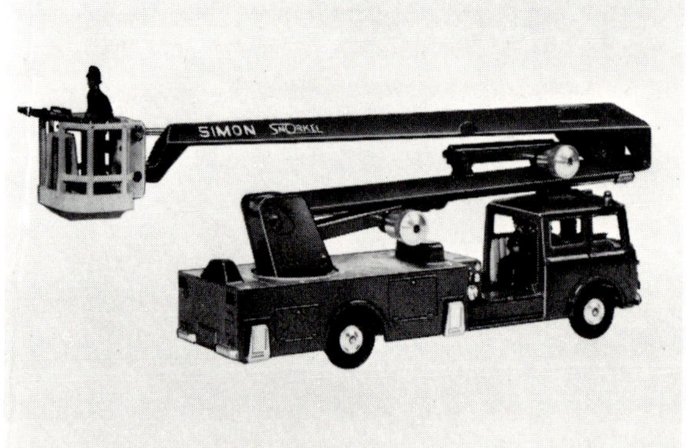

ingly heard being used among hobbyists themselves.

"Constant scale," on the other hand, is largely a manufacturers' public-relations locution, and is found in advertising, in catalogs, and on packaging. It usually is employed by a manufacturer to indicate that all the models in a product line, or at least all the units in a given series of models or kits, are built to the same scale. In effect, it is the precise opposite of "scaled to size." Because it originally was widely used in connection with 1/6-inch scale, 1/72nd-size models—and airplane models at that, although 1/6-inch-scale model vehicles were manufactured as far back as the late 1920's at least—a number of hobbyists have been given the impression that "constant scale" actually is a specific and definite scale of 1/6 inch. This is far from true, for while more than one manufacturer conceivably could use the same "constant scale," various manufacturers have their own and frequently greatly varying "constant scales," whether they make use of this particular designation or not.

"Collectors' scale" is a designation coined to indicate vehicles of small size, approximating the overall sizes found in various series of miniature cars widely favored for collecting purposes, but actually built to a number of different scales. In short, "collectors' scale" means the same as "scaled to size" or "scaled to price." The term "collectors' scale" might be said to have been created in defense against those who would insist on only one scale being valid for model-car collectors—usually 7-mm. scale—and such arbitrary names for such a one particular scale—again usually 7-mm. scale—as "true collectors' scale" or "standard collectors' scale."

At this point, it is logical to include both for model-automobile collectors and for builders some of the common variations in scale in terms of physical measurements. A model of a prototype vehicle that is 16 feet long will measure 8 inches in 1/2-inch scale, 1/24th size, and 7.68 inches in .48-inch scale, 1/25th size. The total difference in length will be about 1/3 inch, with smaller but corresponding differences in height and width. A difference of 1/3 inch in length is certainly noticeable, particularly when two models built to different scales are placed side by side, or even to the acute automotive fan, when models of different prototypes built to different scales are displayed together. On the other hand, in the view of most enthusiasts the difference is really not sufficiently great to become exercised over.

Dropping down to smaller scales, the 16-foot prototype will work out to 4 inches in a 1/4-inch-scale, 1/48th-size model, and to 112 mm. in a 7-mm.-scale, 1/43rd-size model. If the models are compared in terms of inches, the 7-mm.-scale model will be found to measure 4.409 inches in length; if compared in millimeters the 1/4-inch-scale model will be found to measure 101.6 mm. in length. The actual difference is that the 7-mm.-scale model will be 10.4 mm., or about 2/5 inch longer than the 1/4-inch-scale model. It will be noted that there actually is a greater proportionate difference between the two small scales used as examples than between the two large scales. Obviously, even if the difference was the same, it would be much more noticeable when comparing two models built to smaller scales than two models built to larger scales. In either case, the differences are admittedly present. It certainly is up to each hobbyist to determine for himself, as he plans his own hobby program, just how important these differences may be to him. There always is a certain satisfaction for many enthusiasts when dealing with scale models to adopt an outlook of purism and perfection. On the other hand, experience has shown by now that the less attention hobbyists pay to such matters, the less rigid their outlook, and the greater will be their overall enjoyment in participating in the hobby.

VARIATIONS IN MODELS

There is another factor that enters into this, too, although it seldom is realized by most model builders until they attempt to combine components from two models or two kits into a single miniature automobile of their own construction. This is that models and kits may not be entirely accurate, either in their overall design or in the scaling of individual components. Unintentional errors and conscious compromises do creep into the design of models and kits. This is primarily due to the fact that many dimensions that must be taken from the prototype do not work out evenly in the small dimensions that are employed on models. It is easy enough in, say, 1/2-inch scale to determine that a prototype measurement that is 3 feet should come out an exact 1 1/2 inches in the model. However, there invariably will be found to be prototype measurements in inches and fractions of inches that do not convert to model dimensions so easily. With such measurements the designer of a model often must make compromises, perhaps making one part a little larger than true scale and perhaps another part a little smaller. As a model in itself, everything is made so as to fit together perfectly. Nevertheless, in many cases parts that seemingly should be identical in two models, particularly two of different makes, will be found to be noticeably different

Fig. 39.   A group of interesting and varied models constructed from kits of easily assembled plastic parts. Pictured here are, reading downward, left side, a 1933 Chevrolet panel truck, 1928 Ford pickup truck, and 1932 Chevrolet roadster; on the right side are a 1928 Ford station wagon, and two custom show cars, the lower one based on a Ford Model T.

Model Products Corp.

even though the miniatures are replicas built to identical scales of the same prototype. For example, in the case of two 3/8-inch-scale models of a given popular prototype, it might logically be assumed that both being to the same scale, the radiator assembly from one kit would interchange perfectly with the radiator assembly from the second kit. Yet, even eliminating differences in the particular assemblies that may be molded by the two manufacturers, it may be found that the radiators are not only not interchangeable but that when carefully compared these replicas of the same prototype component differ perceptibly in size—and possibly also in exact detail and appearance! Yet individually as a totality, each of the two kits may be considered an equally valid and exact scale model of the same prototype. These differences do arise, as anyone who has tried to "cross kits" knows.

In the course of preparing his book *Model Car Collecting,* F. Brian Jewell very carefully measured one popular model-car kit that was designated as a 1/25th-size model. He found that it was, overall, closer to a 1/27th-size replica than 1/25th, but even more tellingly he found that merely in the length, width, height, wheelbase, and track alone the dimensions worked out when compared to those of the prototype to no less than four different scales or proportions, none of them ex-

actly .48-inch scale, 1/25th size! Yet, withal, as a unit most hobbyists would consider this an excellent scale model. Nevertheless, there undoubtedly would have been even more variations in scale found if Jewell had carried his investigations even further. In fact, Jewell worked out a very complicated point system for analyzing and grading any given car model in terms of scale fidelity, detail and features, and general appearance.

In view of all these things, it will seem apparent to most that it is not only difficult but perhaps even a little foolish for the hobbyist who wishes to retain a practical outlook to be too finicky on matters concerning his acceptance of scale or comparative scale between two models of generally similar size.

There is, however, yet another and not unimportant factor that enters into this picture. This is the indisputable fact that it often is necessary for a model-automobile designer, whether an individual hobbyist constructing a model from scratch or an engineer preparing designs for the commercial mass production of a model or a kit, deliberately to hedge or cheat on scale and fidelity to prototype in order to make the resulting model look "right." To accomplish this, it may be necessary to exaggerate one or more features or lines or dimensions of the prototype and to soft-pedal or reduce others. This is a highly variable and al-

Fig. 40. Models based on old and new internal-combustion reciprocating engine road equipment. Top, a Hubley cast-iron road roller (*Joseph G. Collins*) and a Williams road scraper (*G. William Holland photograph*). Bottom, modern cast-metal miniatures of a diesel road roller and a snow tractor ("*Matchbox*"—*Fred Bronner Corp.*).

most imponderable matter but its employment and necessity are well known to most experienced model builders. It may sound paradoxical and even ridiculous, but at times an exact scale model does not look like an exact scale replica, whereas a model with which compromises with absolute fidelity to scale have been taken does appear to be a precise scale miniature of the prototype.

Various explanations for this situation have been offered, but it is an extremely difficult affair to set down in words. It is one of those chiefly intuitive matters, both in need and in execution, that must be felt more than studied. One reasonable explanation—although it is probably far from the whole story—is that one views a model almost in its totality at a glance, whereas an observer usually can take in only a portion of so large an object as a full-size automobile from one viewpoint. A contributing factor may also be that many people are so accustomed to seeing photographs and drawings that are deliberately exaggerated to give an appearance of greater dimensions in advertisements of automobiles that our concept of the overall appearance of many automobiles is conditioned

by this rather than by the actual cars themselves. In any event, most automobiles are viewed either in repose, close up where the observer can view only a side or end at once, or in motion, at a distance. To obtain the same view of a real automobile as is usually had of a model, the observer would probably have to stand at an elevation of two or three stories and a hundred or so feet away from the prototype. It is therefore really not so strange that exact scale models at times do not give the exact impression of the prototype that we carry in our minds and that some exaggerations sometimes are necessary in the model in order to make it look "right." Of course, it may be argued that in this case right is wrong and that if a model is truly built to exact scale throughout, it will be a true scale model and that this is the paramount consideration. There is much to be said for this line of thinking, but it is not universally accepted even by experienced builders of models from scratch. In the case of a model or a kit for constructing a model that is designed for mass appeal and sales, practical considerations of overall appearance must often of necessity take precedence.

Fig. 41. Four .48-inch-scale (1/25th-size) model cars constructed from kits of plastic parts. Top left, an imaginative design; lower left, the transparently molded Ford "J" car (see Fig. 53) in painted form; top right, the Mako Shark, and, lower right, 1967 Corvette.

Model Products Corp.

SOME FINAL POINTS

Of the factors other than scale and size that generally concern the model-automobile enthusiast as enumerated in the opening sentence of this chapter, some already also have been touched upon, if only incidentally. The matter of fidelity is also obviously under consideration, with the question raised—and perhaps not entirely satisfactorily answered—as to whether fidelity to prototype, indeed, even fidelity to the spirit of the prototype, is always identical with fidelity to scale.

The matter of workmanship as such is a matter that essentially belongs to the chapter following. So, too, is the theme of detail, except that it is proper to remark here that most model-automobile hobbyists, including both the builder of models and the collector of modern models to a considerable extent appear continuously to feel that more and ever more detail is desirable. The day now is long past when it was an uncommon and really extraordinary thing to find a model whose hood can be opened to reveal to view a detailed miniature engine. Fidelity, of course, pertains to many things, fidelity to scale—although

there has just been noted the necessity or the desirability of exceptions to this at times—and fidelity to prototype detail and finish. Anyone can, if he so desires, build or decorate a model in any manner he sees fit. To a large extent, however, the model-automobile builder desires models that follow the prototype in proportions, in correctness of detail, and even in the color or colors of the paint. The collector of old model cars is little concerned with these things except occasionally and even then at a very subsidiary level and substantially by way merely of curiosity value. At the other extreme, the ardent model-automobile customizer frequently is totally unconcerned with fidelity to a prototype or even—because there often is no prototype involved—with practicality as an automobile design. (Although at times his aspirations and activities may be somewhat inhibited by the insistence of contest officials that any model to be judged bear at least a rational resemblance to a practical full-size automobile.)

In short, the collector of old model cars may be said to deal in Christmas Past, the modern builder and collector in Christmas Present, and the all-out custom-model car buff in Christmas Yet to Come.

Construction and Customizing

By far the vast majority of model automobiles that are built today are assembled from relatively inexpensive kits of molded plastic parts. In many cases these kits have been simplified and prefabricated to such a degree that a great many enthusiasts have come to look upon them as representing what might be called "instant automobiles." This is not literally true, of course, and the simpler kits are an undeniable boon to younger hobbyists and to all those who are just beginning, as well as to those who are more interested in displaying and collecting a finished model rather than constructing one. While most model automobile kits still require the use of an adhesive to bond the various parts into a completed model, simplification has now reached a point where a number of kits now available are designed so that the various components simply snap and lock together into the finished model, thus eliminating entirely the need for using cement in the assembly process. Some fans, however, still employ it, at least at certain points in the building of models of this type, in the belief that its use assures a sturdier and more permanent construction.

Another point of simplification lies in the fact that molded plastic parts can be and invariably are molded in color. As a result, a creditable-appearing model automobile usually can be attained from a kit simply by assembling the parts without the need to paint them, unless, of course, the builder wants a different color finish. It is not too much to say that the real art and enjoyment of model-car building as such has to a large extent now moved from merely assembling the model from a kit to enhancing or making more realistic its appearance through specialized painting and decorating techniques, or through extensive super-detailing and customizing endeavors.

Invariably, every action produces its own reaction. Inasmuch as there are great numbers of hobbyists whose main delight is in the construction of a model and to whom the possession of the finished model is of little interest other than as graphic evidence of their skill as model builders, the simplification of many kits led to a demand for the availability of more complicated kits or kits involving materials that required more skill in finishing and assembling than the majority of those generally available. As a result, there is an increasing number of kits available, often for the fabrication of larger scale models, that require considerable more time and skill for their basic assembly. Some of these kits, or superkits as some have dubbed them, still provide essentially plastic parts. Others combine plastic components with those of other materials. One such kit, which at the moment undoubtedly holds the crown not only for detail and elaboration but also for cost, builds a 1 1/2-inch scale replica of a 1907 Fiat racing car. The finished model measures 17 inches in length, and includes such features as working springs, working steering, working timing gears, working chain drive, and working transmission.

Fig. 42. Four more .48-inch-scale (1/25th size) models that can readily be assembled from kits of plastic parts. Top, two American prototypes, the Ford GT and the Studebaker Avanti. Bottom, two British prototypes, an Aston Martin and a Jaguar XKE convertible. The kit for the latter may also be assembled as a hardtop model if desired.

Aurora Plastics Corp.

Despite all these movable parts it is not, however, a working model as such, but a superdisplay miniature. To provide all this detail the kit provides no less than 823 different parts, of which 144 are molded in plastic of five different colors, including simulated wood; 173 are of polished brass; and the remaining 506 are fabricated of aluminum, copper, iron, leather, rubber, and steel.

This is a fairly expensive kit, and one that is somewhat complicated to assemble. When it is considered that there are available almost numberless kits of plastic parts for building comparatively detailed models in smaller scales selling for a dollar or less, the price that many enthusiasts willingly pay for a kit of this magnitude may appear even more startling. But the main point is that this particular superkit is likely soon to be equaled or even surpassed both in number and caliber of parts and in price by other such superkits. Kits of this type may involve a combination of a number of methods of assembly. In the case of the 1907 Fiat, for example, some parts are cemented but others are secured by means of press fits, self-tapping screws, and miniature nuts and bolts.

Between the extremes of kits of this type and the greater number that sell for a few dimes or a few shillings, there are available model-automobile kits costing varying amounts in between, mostly in the lower price bracket. For those who prefer materials other than plastic, there also are available kits whose primary material is metal, both in the form of castings and of components fabricated from sheet material, as well as kits reminiscent of the earliest miniature automobile construction kits furnishing mainly wooden parts. As

the model-automobile hobby grows apace, the type of kit and the variety of materials employed in kits now appears to be ever broadening the choice available to enthusiasts.

PLASTIC KITS

In his book *Plastic Model Cars*—an excellent guide for superdetailing models built from kits with especial emphasis on racing cars—Dr. Cecil Gibson observes that what is at once the most difficult and the most important point in building a model automobile from a kit of plastic parts is to eliminate all telltale signs that the model has been built from a kit. This is not often easy, especially when there is no intention of embellishing the model with added detailing and when its accomplishment obviously calls for a great deal of skill and patience. Before leaving the matter of patience, it might be well to make the final observation that patience in itself often is in practice a very workable substitute for skill or experience. The average beginner often can make up in patience much of what he may lack in skill. Obviously, it is much easier to take off too much material than to add it back on, whether the material in which a fan is working is plastic, metal, or wood.

In the case of plastics it is literally possible to weld back some of the plastic material when too much has been removed, but it is at best a ticklish job and often not worth the effort. This brings up the question of what sort of kit is best for the beginner. The best advice unqualifiably is to start with inexpensive and simple kits. This is not to say that the novice may not be capable of constructing an excellent model from, say, a ten-dollar kit or even a fifty-dollar kit, but it is far wiser and more prudent to play the odds and not take the first, or even the second or the third, plunge into deep water. The obvious advantage of the less costly kits at this point is that they provide the newcomer to the hobby with an inexpensive means of learning the ropes as regards the cutting, finishing, and assembling of plastic components. If a part is spoiled, a duplicate kit can be bought for very little.

While manufacturers always will replace a part that is supplied in defective form or that was missing from a kit—this can happen on occasion, despite the care exercised at the factories to prevent it—the very nature of the process by which inexpensive kits of plastic parts are mass-produced precludes the stocking and sale of separate replacement parts in most cases. In the case of the average inexpensive kit, when the hobbyist has spoiled vital parts the best and indeed in most instances the only solution is to purchase a duplicate kit in order to secure these components.

WORKING WITH PLASTIC PARTS

However, it should not be implied that the assembling of any kit of molded plastic parts into a commendable finished model automobile is in any sense an extremely difficult or unduly delicate matter. An essential step is to separate and trim the various parts that, especially in the case of the smaller units, customarily are molded in groups and furnished in kits in the form of groups, or "trees" as they are called. In the molding process, a considerable number of parts are molded in a single shot from the injection molding machine. The resemblance of these "trees"—and hence their name—to a real tree is manifest, the parts themselves being as it were the fruit that is connected to the branches by thin stems, and the branches in turn to what might be considered larger branches, and these, in turn, to the trunk. All of them represent openings in the mold that are filled with plastic during the molding process. In the case of groups of very small parts, there may be far more surplus plastic involved in filling these connections to the parts than in the parts themselves. The actual points at which the parts join the runners usually are molded very thinly, and it is often easily possible to break small parts away at the stems by hand without actually having to cut them with a knife. However, breaking is somewhat uncertain, and even when it appears possible it is

Fig. 43. Two beautifully handmade ¼-inch-scale (1/48th-size) model cars constructed from scratch by C. W. Frey: a 1910 Locomobile roadster and a 1910 Packard Landaulet. The chassis of the Packard also is pictured. These models were built up entirely of brass except for the rubber tires. See also Fig. 44.

C. W. Frey

best to use a knife to cut the part off. In any case it will be necessary to trim the part carefully with a modelmaker's knife once it is separated so as to remove all excess plastic at the point where the component that is to be used was connected to the main body of plastic.

It may also be necessary to remove excess plastic in the form of "flash" around or at one or more sides of the part. "Flash" is the very thin layer of surplus plastic that may be forced out of the engraved cavities in the mold and between the two halves of the mold by the great pressure involved when the molding machine forces the plastic into the mold. While the modelmaker's knife is the basic tool in cutting parts from the "trees," trimming away excess plastic at the point of jointure, and removing "flash," very fine sandpaper often may be used beneficially in the final stages of preparing a part. Some model builders find it

Fig. 44. In order to build the two 1/4-inch-scale models pictured in Fig. 43, C. W. Frey had first to research and draw up his own plans, making use of various contemporary sources, including the illustrations from old automobile magazines shown here with the 1910 Locomobile and 1910 Packard chassis posed before them.

C. W. Frey

very helpful to glue small pieces of fine sandpaper to blocks of wood of various shapes, including curved surfaces, for ease of manipulation during this process. It should be noted that fine sandpaper (or "glasspaper," as it is known in Great Britain) to the modelmaker is infinitely finer than what usually is considered the finest of ordinary household or carpenters' sandpaper. Builders of model automobiles should obtain and use the special fine grades of sandpaper sold in hobby shops or by mail-order supply houses specializing in supplies for hobbyists. Very fine files of the type known as jewelers', needle, or Swiss files may also at times be used to advantage in removing excess plastic and finishing parts. Of course, they cut much more coarsely than the fine sandpaper, and the latter usually is still employed for the final finishing.

In all of these cleaning-up and finishing processes, whether using a knife, a file, or sandpaper, the great danger is removing too much material, with the result that parts fit loosely. In such cases a completed model automobile probably still can be assembled, for the cement that bonds the parts together will compensate for lack of fit in most cases, but the appearance of the fin-

ished model, especially upon close examination, will suffer. Actually, most plastic components now are so well molded that a knife alone will be sufficient for the average hobbyist to employ in cleaning up the parts, and the novice would probably be well advised, in this respect, to confine himself to this tool, at least on his first kit assembly projects. Even so, it is necessary to guard carefully against removing too much plastic or trimming and smoothing surfaces unevenly—the latter being an ever-present danger with all cutting tools and materials.

The writer is aware that the foregoing advice is contrary to that sometimes given beginners by many experienced modelers who suggest that once the parts have been separated from the "trees" with a knife, all further trimming be done with the slowest cutting material, fine sandpaper. The theory is that the retardation of speed in the work imposed by the sandpaper acts to prevent the beginner from making mistakes or removing too much material. It is a logical theory, but those who advance it forget their own early zeal and the time it has taken them to accept the advantages of patience. In the writer's experience, novices are too understandably anxious to see something completed as a result of their efforts to follow this mode of construction, and even when they attempt to do so, are prone to attempt to speed up the job by exerting too much pressure on the sandpaper in an effort to make it cut faster, and frequently break delicate or unsupported parts.

There is another point that all workers with plastic components should constantly keep in mind. In itself, the plastic employed in present-day kits is a very strong material, and will stand a great deal of abuse. However, highly detailed model automobile kits must of necessity contain many small and delicate parts that all too readily snap when pressure is ill-advisedly applied, and great care must be exercised in cutting, finishing, and handling such components. Of course, if, say, a steering-wheel shaft or a torsion bar is accidentally snapped in two, the parts can be cemented together, but this in itself is a delicate process, the part may break again during the process of cleaning up the bond, and will probably never look as good upon close examination as the unit in its originally molded form. Therefore, the watchword in working with any sort of delicate plastic unit or subassembly incorporating such units must ever be caution and not audacity!

A further word of warning: Do not separate and trim all the parts in a kit before starting the assembly process. Most manufacturers' step-by-step instructions advocate removing the parts

Fig. 45. Two more beautifully detailed and individually crafted models, in this case, trucks built to the relatively large scale of 1-inch to the foot. Both are models of the 1921 Autocar Type XXVIB, a cabless dump truck and a stake truck with cab. These models were built by the Autocar Company for promotional purposes.

The Smithsonian Institution

from the "trees" and trimming them only as each part is needed as the model car is put together. Some modelers ignore this advice and cut and trim all the parts before starting any assembly work. It has been observed that of all modelmaking hobbies, model-automobile enthusiasts are by far the most prone to do this, and in general to ignore prepared instructions or deliberately to attempt the exact opposite of that which is advocated. Obviously, instructions are prepared for good purpose, yet a number of people seem to feel that instructions no longer are necessary. There are several very good reasons why the parts should be removed from the "trees" and trimmed only as they are required. Manifestly, there is always a substantial danger of losing small parts if they are all detached and stored. Furthermore, most parts are marked with an identifying number that corresponds to the number used in the instruction drawings and text. In the case of some odd-shaped or delicate parts it is impossible to place the number on the part itself, and it is therefore placed adjoining the component on excess plastic that will be trimmed away, and the identity of the part may be difficult to ascertain if the trimming has been done at a somewhat earlier period of time. Lastly, in some cases parts can properly be given their final trim and cleaning only when they can be related to other parts that will adjoin them in the final finished model.

MORE ABOUT THE TRIMMING PROCESS

There have even been cases where model builders who acted too hastily have confused excess plastic from the trees with actual parts once everything was cut apart! In any case, the surplus plastic should never be discarded until the model automobile has been completed. There are two reasons for this. One is that it is possible for small parts to be overlooked at times and the seemingly excess plastic thrown away with such units still attached.

The second reason is that it can furnish the model builder with a supply of identically colored plastic. Although it is a very ticklish thing to accomplish satisfactorily, at times serious overcuts in plastic components can be corrected by in effect welding a small piece of surplus plastic to the damaged unit by applying the heat of a match to the adjoining surfaces, and then reshaping and trimming the part. This has been satisfactorily accomplished by experienced model builders, but it is an extremely difficult and delicate operation owing to the danger of overheating and melting the original part out of all semblance to its original form, thus making a bad matter worse. However, to some deft hobbyists it is one of the tricks of the trade, and its possibilities should be kept in mind. Novices might well experiment by using scrap plastic, as it is an extremely handy trick if one wishes to undertake extensive detailing and customizing operations.

Another favorite material of the advanced model builder and customizer, model-automobile body putty, can also be used to rectify mistakes in cutting and trimming, although its main value is in extensive recontouring and fill-in operations at the hands of the dyed-in-the-wood model-car customizer.

So far reference to cutting, trimming, and finishing operations have been confined to hand tools and hand-manipulated materials: knives, files, and sandpaper. A substantial number of model-car builders also make use of small-size hand-held power tools, hand grinders powered either from a household outlet or, what is less expensive and just as satisfactory, if not even more so for light work with plastics, battery-powered tools of this type. These are quite acceptable for use on plastic and wood, although generally not suitable for metals except possibly of the very lightest and softest kinds. Various sizes and types of bits and grinders can be fitted as desired in the chucks of such units, and a great variety of useful work can be performed in the form of cutting, grinding, shaping, smoothing, and polishing of plastic components particularly. Their only drawback is that in the hands of a somewhat unskilled user a power tool of necessity provides a strong temptation to remove too much material or to work too hastily.

TOOLS

Actually, very few special tools are required by the average hobbyist engaged in model-automobile building or kit assembly, although a great variety of very enticing special tools for modelmakers is available. The fan who goes in for more advanced forms of model building will find many of them extremely useful. As a matter of fact, as every model enthusiast is aware, tools have a sort of mystique of their own, and there is always a certain amount of pleasure to be derived in acquiring and employing additional types, even if there remains some question as to the actual necessity of making use of an inordinate variety if the hobbyist is to confine his activities to assembling conventional kits. Good tools are desirable and the very act of owning them is enjoyable, but they will not alone suffice to enhance a hobbyist's individual skill or provide in themselves a magic and automatic road to super modelmaking.

As far as the general run of model automobile kits containing plastic components goes, one tool alone actually is basic and essential, a good knife. Almost anything in this line can be accomplished with a good knife and fine sandpaper, and even the latter is not regarded as an absolute requisite by many experienced enthusiasts. The knife, in fact, can be a good ordinary sharp pocket knife or a razor blade, although the latter definitely is not to be recommended unless you wish to make the bandage business prosper. The tool that has become known as the modelmaker's knife, a handle designed to receive interchangeable blades of different shapes, has become more or less the accepted standard among workers with plastic model components. It is inexpensive, and the blades can readily be changed when a different shape is required or when it is desirable to replace a dull

blade with a new one. A knife handle with the basic small straight blade will suffice in most instances. If the hobbyist finds himself using alternate blade shapes a good deal, it will probably pay to acquire several handles and keep each one equipped with a different frequently used type of blade. This will not only save time in changing blades but also allay a temptation to employ a perhaps less suitable type of blade for a given cut rather than bother changing the blade to a special type and then replacing the basic blade.

Aside from the knife itself, the builder of kits or the hobbyist otherwise working with plastic materials will find it useful to supply himself with a few other aids, some of which can easily be made at home. The most useful will be clamping devices to hold parts in position while the cement is drying. These may include ordinary rubber bands, which are useful in many instances for this purpose, spring clothespins, and all sorts of homemade gadgets for applying a moderate pressure to hold together components being bonded. Also useful will be toothpicks, pins, and cotton-tipped swabs for applying model cement in varying amounts, and pins or tweezers for use in lifting and positioning small components during the cementing process.

Fine sandpaper and small files will also be found useful in trimming and finishing plastic components, as already mentioned, and a pair of long-nosed or needle-nosed pliers can be a tool of a thousand uses, including forming specially shaped cementing clamps out of wire.

The aforementioned tools and oddments should provide the hobbyist with virtually everything he will require in the way of tools and equipment for constructing model automobiles from kits of plastic parts. However, not only these but some additional equipment will be found useful for more adventuresome model building from scratch or for extensive superdetailing and customizing activities involving plastic or wooden models and components.

Saws are particularly valuable to the model-car customizer. There are two basic kinds especially suitable for fine work in plastics and wood

Fig. 46.   An example of models constructed from a kit of plastic parts that can be assembled in two different forms. These are 1941 Lincoln Continentals in 1/2-inch scale (1/24th size). One has been put together to represent the car with the top up, the other to show it with the top down.
Monogram Models, Inc.

Fig. 47. Three .48-inch-scale (1/25th-size) Fords built from kits of plastic components, a GT, shown with doors and deck lids open; a Cougar II and a Mustang II. Note the reflected underbody detail on the latter. Kits of this type often come with optional parts to permit several variations to be constructed.

Industro-Motive Corp.

that are readily available from hobby supply houses. One is the razor saw, a fine-toothed stiff saw permanently set in a handle, which is ideal for making straight cuts. Also available is a key-hole-saw version of this tool that has many applications when work in close quarters is concerned. Care must be exercised not to bend the blades of these saws by applying too great a pressure or by using them on materials for which they are not suitable; they are not intended as substitutes for hacksaws in cutting heavier metals. The second basic type of saw favored by model-automobile builders is the jewelers' saw, which comprises a saw handle and a separate, thin, replaceable blade, and provides greater flexibility and sensitivity in model work. The jewelers' saw is essentially a smaller version of what is usually known as a coping saw or jigsaw in America and as a fretsaw in Great Britain. In general it may be said that the razor saw is ideal for straight cuts and heavier materials, while the jewelers' saw is especially suitable both for light straight cuts and for intricate and rounded cuts, the fine blade allowing sharp turns to be made during the cutting process. In addition to these types of saws, some hobbyists also find conventional-size coping saws suitable for some model-car work. Also available are small saw blades that can be fitted to the handles of model-maker's knives.

It goes almost without saying that a good assortment of pliers is of substantial help to anyone engaged in extensive model-building efforts in any field. Many, however, assume that the variety of the assortment should be limited to types and that once one has a basic set of the various kinds of noses—long, needle, flat, and round—this is sufficient. This is not really so, for the experienced hobby workman knows that there is a considerable variation in effect in using pliers of different lengths on materials of various compositions and shapes. The imponderable that can only be termed "feel" is also very important in selecting and using pliers; after a while the hobbyist with a fairly adequate assortment of pliers will instinctively know for which tool to reach for a given operation. If you feel in a position to build up your modelmaker's tool kit extensively, try getting pliers in several lengths; you will often find that this will actually give a greater flexibility in work than merely having several different nose types in the same length, although this is not to say that the variation in noses should be disregarded. Some advanced modelmakers have a dozen pair of pliers on their benches, and they continually switch them in use. A pair of good wire cutters or diagonal cutting pliers should also be included in any fairly comprehensive assortment of modelers' tools. However, if you are going to try to use them for purposes other than cutting the relatively fine wire used in most model work, such as bolt cutters or sub-

Fig. 48. Seven body styles of Ford Model A's built to 3/5-inch scale (1/20th-size) from kits of die-cast metal parts: roadster, coupe, phaeton, victoria, four-door sedan, pickup truck, and station wagon (*Hubley Division, Gabriel Industries, Inc.*). The eighth model is a 1/2-inch-scale Model-A station wagon with a Chevrolet engine built from a kit of plastic parts (*Monogram Models, Inc.*).

stitutes for shears in cutting light brass or tin, they will not last long as the true and precise instruments they should be.

Many hobbyists are unaware of the usefulness of the pin vise, probably because its name is so complete a misnomer. A pin vise actually is a small hand-manipulated chuck that will take the smallest of drills (and taps). The hobbyist turns the pin vise with a motion of his fingers, while exerting just sufficient pressure to keep the bit going into the material to be drilled without snapping the delicate drill, as so often happens when attempts are made to drill tiny holes with even the smallest of conventional-style drills. The pin vise will be found a real boon to any model builder whose activities carry him into model-automobile construction above and beyond assembling kits without additional detailing or modifications.

One other tool, and that one especially created for working with plastic model automobiles, deserves special mention. This tool is known as the auto-cutter. It consists of a sharp blade similar to those used in regular modelmaker's knives, but in this case set into a bit that can be used in an electric soldering pencil. The result is a heated knife blade that effortlessly cuts through plastic with a combination softening and cutting action. Inasmuch as this tool cuts "like sixty"—to use a good old Americanism that dates from a time when for any vehicle to go a mile a minute, or sixty miles an hour, was considered an extraordinarily fast speed—it requires a little practice on scrap pieces of plastic to get used to its action. Once the proper manipulation of the autocutter is learned, however, it will be found to be a most valuable and almost necessary addition to the plastic model builder and customizer's toolbox.

BONDING PLASTICS

The plastics customarily used in model-automobile kits are members of the styrene family, and require the use of a special type of adhesive to bond the parts together. The types of cements or glues usually used in home workshop work for wood and other materials cannot be employed; neither can another type of cement especially made for model use, "model airplane cement," as the latter is a cellulose adhesive especially compounded for balsa and other light woods and model-airplane covering materials.

What is known as a "solvent adhesive" must be employed when working with styrene. By this is meant an adhesive that actually dissolves a small portion of the surface of the two plastic

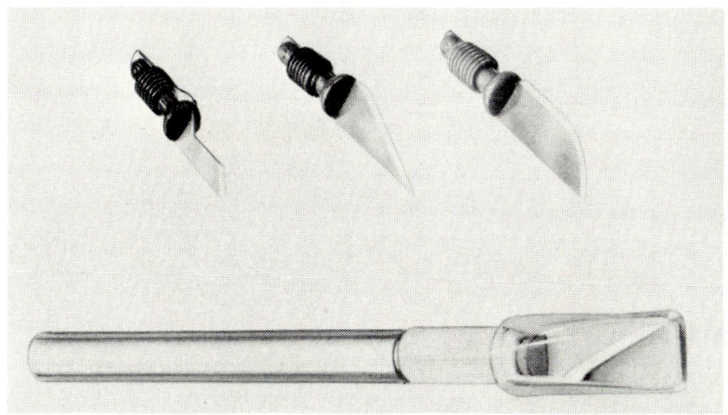

Fig. 49.   A modelmaker's knife with three types of interchangeable blades. Knives of this type have by now become standard and almost indispensable aids to hobbyists who work with wood or plastics, whether in straightforward kit assembly, customizing, or building models from scratch.

Strombecker Corp.

moldings at the point where they are to be joined. This adhesive is readily obtainable in hobby shops. It is put up under various names and by various manufacturers, and may be found designated as "plastic cement" or "styrene cement" or other, similar, names and is sold both in tubes and, in liquid form, in jars. Some modelers highly favor one particular brand, while others feel they are all pretty much alike; of course, the identical cement may be packaged and sold both by the manufacturer of the cement under his own label and under proprietary labels by manufacturers of model kits. Regardless of the brand, it is desirable that caution be observed at all times when using any of these solvent adhesives.* The special characteristic whereby they dissolve a little of the surface of the plastic components to be joined also means that if any amount, no matter how minute, is allowed to drop on a surface other than those to be joined, or if excess cement is squeezed out of a joint onto such a surface, the cement must be removed immediately or it will start to eat into and disfigure the surface. In their zeal, a great many model builders, and particularly beginners, apply more cement to joints than actually is necessary. It must be admitted that it is rather difficult to control the amount of cement deposited when it is squeezed directly from a tube or brushed or swabbed on from a jar. In point of fact, only comparatively

---

* The usual model cements, glues, solvents, paints, thinners, and similar materials are generally quite safe if used in a well-ventilated area. However, some are highly toxic if breathed or taken internally; some are highly inflammable. In all cases they should be used only in a properly ventilated area and away from any spark-producing equipment (including, obviously, any operating miniature electric or internal-combustion engines) or open flames or units with pilot lights, such as stoves or heating equipment. They should always be stored so as to be inaccessible to children.

large surfaces call for brushing or swabbing on the plastic cement. Most of the parts involved, and consequently the joints themselves, are relatively small, and the preferential mode of applying the cement is to place a drop or two from a toothpick that has been dipped into the cement.

Most kits are designed so that whenever possible the points at which two parts are to be cemented together will be internal joints, although manifestly it is extremely difficult to eliminate external joints altogether. The advantage of having internal joints is that it reduces the danger of excess cement reaching surfaces that will lie exposed in the finished model. Regardless of this, it is good to try to make every joint as neat as possible and unsullied by the effects of surplus cement, especially on external joints. If the hobbyist tries to make every joint as clean and neat as possible, this practice will in time become almost automatic.

Once a surface has become damaged by accidental contact with a solvent adhesive, it is extremely difficult ever to restore it to absolutely perfect condition. This is not to say that much cannot and should not be done in an effort to correct, insofar as is possible, the defect. If the pitting is very bad, occasionally some fresh matching plastic can be welded onto the damaged surface, and then the excess filed and sanded away, but it must be admitted that this seldom results in a completely satisfactory effect, and the possible greater damage that may result suggests that such attempts best be left to the hands of the really expert modeler. A number of hobbyists have found that when the surface damage is slight, fairly good results can be obtained by polishing the area in question with a very, very mild abrasive such as toothpaste, automobile rubbing compound, or silver polish. Such a polishing operation requires a great deal of patience, however, and is always accompanied by the danger that the physical pressure employed in the polishing, regardless of how slight it may be, may misalign or break delicate moldings.

One of the most common failings involved in cementing plastic components is for the hobbyist to proceed from one joint to another without allowing ample time to intervene to permit each joint to harden and set tightly. The inevitable result is that parts cemented previously will be moved out of proper alignment or break. It is true that plastic

Fig. 50.   Four views of a highly detailed model with removable hood. This is a 1/2-inch-scale (1/24th-size) replica of a 1929 Mercedes-Benz SSK, a famous speedster of its day, built from a kit of colored, clear, and chromium-plated plastic parts. A beautiful model from whatever angle you view it.

Lindberg Products, Inc.

cement will set superficially within a minute or two of application, but a joint may not truly be completely bonded for several hours. Naturally, the time that any given joint requires fully to set depends somewhat on the size of the area joined, the amount of cement needed, and on the relative degree of clamping and support that may have been required and employed by a particular joint. There is no hard-and-fast rule, and much at times must depend on the patience of the model builder. In practice, few if any hobbyists would be willing to wait any great length of time between every two cementing operations. All that can be said is to point out this condition and caution model-car builders to take into consideration the importance of letting joints get a proper set and above all to be careful of applying any pressure against a recently cemented joint while proceeding to further cementing. Partly because of this situation, some hobbyists like to assemble several different kits more or less simultaneously, working on one while the cement is drying on another.

While all ordinary plastic kit components readily bond together when plastic cement is applied to their surfaces, this does not hold true of chromium or otherwise plated parts, a number of which are used in model-automobile kits. In the case of these plated parts, the plating must carefully be scraped away at any point where a cemented joint is to be made so as to expose the plastic underneath the chromed surface. The plastic cement is then applied in the ordinary manner to the exposed plastic; it will not bond to a plated surface. To avoid disfiguring the completed model, care must be exercised not to scrape away any more of the plating than is absolutely necessary to make a good joint; in the completed model the exposed surface will of course be concealed by the joint.

WORKING WITH MATERIALS OTHER THAN PLASTICS

There are a number of adhesives available for bonding materials other than the styrene plastics and which commend themselves to hobbyists working in wood and metal. Model airplane cement is suitable for balsa construction, and may also be used with other light types of wood. However, in most cases greater satisfaction with the latter, and in fact with most types of wood—although pinewood and basswood are the materials most often employed in model building—may be had with one of the modern types of all-purpose household glues. In recent years the epoxy cements have become available, and these can be employed to join almost any materials, including many not previously easily glued, including metal-to-metal and metal-to-wood joints. The epoxy cements are very useful for repairing broken cast-metal model automobiles. In all cases it is important that the joint be

Fig. 51. Models built from .48-inch-scale (1/25th-size) kits each of which contains sufficient molded plastic parts to permit two complete, different but related, models to be constructed. Top, the 1922 Ford Model T in hot-rod and stock form; bottom, similar versions of the 1934 Ford.
Aurora Plastics Corp.

Fig. 52. A group of customized and superdetailed 1/2-inch-scale (1/24th-size) and .48-inch-scale (1/25th-size) model dragsters, as exhibited in competition at a recent model automobile customizing show. Some of the components used began life as parts of kits of plastic cars for rather conventional models, as, for example, the coupe body on "37".

Revell, Inc., and *Testor Corp.*

carefully aligned and properly held until the bonding agent has set. Epoxy cement has one disadvantage; in some cases it will damage painted surfaces and at least some plastics; it is not recommended that it be used in such cases, at least not until an actual experiment on scrap material indicates that it will not act deleteriously. A safe rule of thumb is not to attempt to use an epoxy bonding agent on plastic or on a painted surface but to confine its application to wood, metal, and rubber. If only by providing a safe, sure, and easily used adhesive for metal, the epoxy cements have more than won themselves an important and honored place on model enthusiasts' workbenches.

The materials other than plastic most often employed by model-automobile builders and customizers are of course wood and metal. Wood is still perhaps the most easy and satisfactory material to work, and with the exception of one special tip that will be offered in a moment, little need be said concerning it. Balsa wood, widely used for building model airplanes, is available in a variety of shapes and grades in virtually every establishment selling hobby goods. It is easy to work with, and, despite its extremely light weight, relatively sturdy. Basswood in various shapes also is fairly easily obtained, although not quite so widely offered as balsa. Basswood, while still a fairly light wood, is heavier and somewhat more substantial than balsa. It is easy to work with, although, not being so soft as balsa, a little more difficult to manipulate, a fact that many model builders feel is somewhat advantageous. This material is a favorite among all modelmakers, including builders and customizers of miniature automobiles.

There is a long-standing, if minor, difference of opinion among many model builders as to whether it is important that a model be built of substantially the same materials as the prototype. Aside from commercial vehicles and, of course, station wagons, most of the products of the automotive era have presented at least an external surface of metal, although wood often was extensively used in their internal framing. The pertinent fact

Fig. 53. Top and side view of a .48-inch-scale (1/25th-size) model of the Ford "J" car assembled from a kit of parts molded in clear plastic. This replica, which features many interesting details, may either be left as a clear "see-through" model, as shown here, or painted on the inside of the body, as was done with the example pictured in Fig. 41.

Model Products Corp.

here is that the working of wood is within the ability of almost any hobbyist, whereas extensive construction with metal, involving as it usually does extensive forming, soldering, drilling, and tapping operations, is something that—kits excepted —only a somewhat limited number of model craftsmen possess the skill satisfactorily to accomplish. An extraordinary number of beautiful model automobiles have been and still are being built of wood. The main difficulty presented by wood as far as the appearance of the finished model goes is in the securing of a satisfactory final finish, most particularly when the wood surface is intended to represent metal. However, this can be satis-

factorily accomplished with a little extra effort. The secret lies in priming the wood surfaces with some kind of filler or sanding sealer and then carefully rubbing it down by hand and sanding it with an extremely fine grade of sandpaper after it has dried. This process usually has to be repeated several times before painting. Alternately, after the first sealing, rubbing, and sanding, several thin coats of paint are applied over the original sealer, with each coat being allowed to dry, and are then carefully rubbed down and sanded before another thin coat of paint is applied and the process repeated.

By employing this method, wooden surfaces can readily be made to take on the texture and appearance of metal. Great care must be used throughout the process, especially on thin wooden surfaces such as automobile sides, not to apply too much pressure and crack or break the material. In the case of some wooden parts that were to take on the appearance of highly polished metal in the finished model, as many as fifteen or even more separate rubbing and sanding stages have been used, but the effort was well worth it, for the results were almost indistinguishable from metal even upon the closest examination by experienced model builders. It is worthy of note to observe that this method of finishing is not essentially different—at least in its technique if not in its purpose —from that employed on fine real automobiles before the advent of quick-drying lacquers in the 1920's, when a good finish usually was obtained by applying a great number of coats of paint, each being carefully rubbed down by hand after it had dried and before another coat was applied. In fact, this method still is often employed by enthusiasts of old real automobiles who are seeking to duplicate the original finish.

Fig. 54. Two .48-inch-scale (1/25th-size) model Fords built from a kit of plastic components. This particular kit supplies sufficient optional components to permit the miniature to be built as a 1946, 1947, or 1948 with top up or down, and in stock, racing, or custom versions, according to the selection of the hobbyist.

Industro-Motive Corp.

MODEL AUTOMOBILES OF METAL

The highly prefabricated kits of metal parts now available for building model automobiles should present no more problem to the average hobbyist than do those with plastic components. In most cases the metal parts are in the form of die castings, designed to key together when assembled with screws or with suitable adhesives such as epoxy cement, and usually requiring very little cleaning and finishing before assembly. This usually is easily accomplished by using small files and suitable abrasive paper. Cast-metal kits often present parts with some "flash" similar to that which may be found at times on plastic parts. As far as is known, none of the kits of metal parts for building model automobiles currently available in the United States, Canada, and Great Britain require the employment of soldering in their construction. The advent of epoxy adhesives has in general completely removed any necessity for soldering in connection with metal model kits of all types. Soldering has always been the great bugaboo of the average model builder, despite the readiness with which a comparatively limited number of experts employ the art. Soldering has always been extremely difficult, although not impossible, when zinc die castings are involved, and almost invariably disastrous with white-metal die castings, with the attempted operation as often as not melting some of the castings. It becomes more and more apparent that of all the fields in which the availability of epoxy adhesives has proved a great boon, modelmaking must have benefited as much as any. There is one point that should be brought out in connection with the painting of model cars built of metal, whether constructed from kits or from raw materials. To attain a truly satisfactory and lasting paint job, the metal should be purged of all traces of grease and oil, including the oils naturally acquired through handling during the process of construction, and should then be brushed with a coat of primer before any paint is applied. Failing to take the time and effort properly to accomplish these steps may result in the paint itself failing to bond properly to the metal surfaces, and eventually peeling and flaking.

Much praise is due those who work competently at model-automobile building in metal. Such models may even involve considerable machine work at times; certainly in any case a fair amount of skill in the art of metalworking is a requisite. Those who can accomplish such work will hardly require suggestions or information from me. However, for those who wish to attempt such projects without substantial previous experience, a few hints may be appropriate: If a great deal of metal cutting is involved, it will usually be found more efficient to employ a regulation hacksaw of small size than a modelmaker's saw. There is a somewhat widely accepted fallacy that because

Fig. 55. Four examples of interesting and often highly meticulous underbody detailing on 1/2-inch-scale (1/24th-size) or .48-inch-scale (1/25th-size) plastic models. Note, for instance, the brake fluid lines running to each of the four brake drums on the model at the upper right.
Testor Corp.

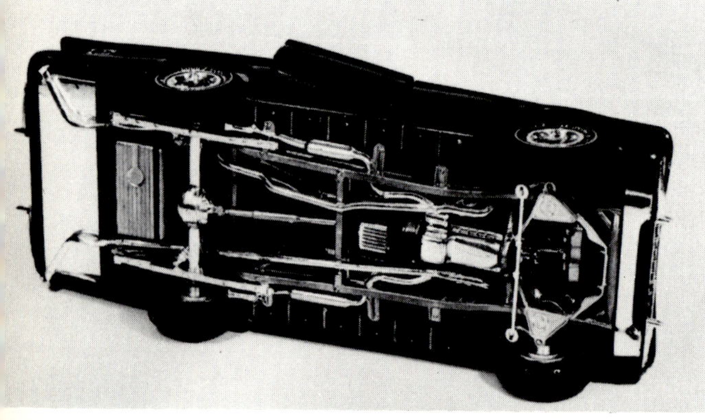
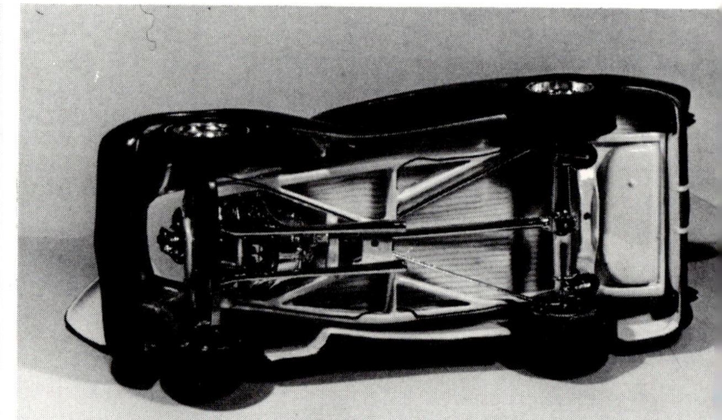
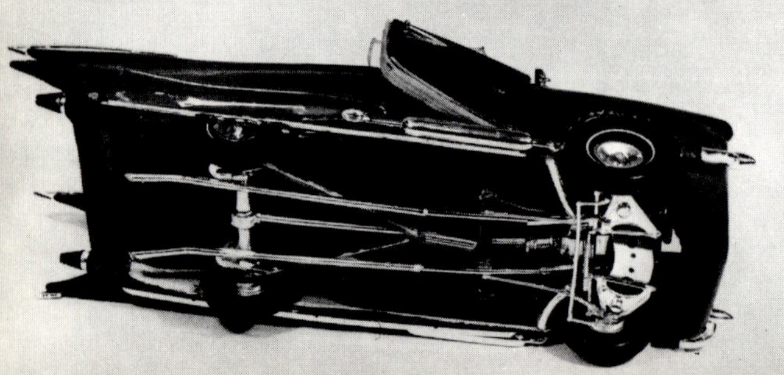

one is working on miniatures one should always use miniature tools. On the contrary, the smaller versions of regulation mechanics' and metalworkers' tools will often prove far more suitable for extensive model work in metal than the tools usually designated for modeling purposes, particularly the cutting and finishing tools, many of which are essentially suitable only for plastics and for limited use on very soft or thin metals or for delicate finishing work. On the other hand, when working with small drills and taps it is usually better to use the lightest tools available rather than the standard sizes. For instance, breakage of small taps and drills usually is due to too much torque being exerted by standard tap wrenches and hand drills. A pin vise makes a good tap wrench for very small taps. If a tap is too large for a pin vise, try using the smallest size tap wrench available, but remove or disregard the handle and employ a finger motion on the chuck itself to run the tap in, using plenty of oil and the conventional tapping action of running the tap in for a little way, reversing it, and then running it in a little deeper on the next turn.

PLANS AND DATA

Regardless of the materials with which he works, the hobbyist who desires to build a model automobile from scratch rather than a kit will find himself up against the problem of securing suitable plans and pictures. This presupposes that he will wish to build a model of some automobile that is not available in kit form, although this does not always necessarily follow. Some builders will want to construct a car of a type that is available as a kit, either for the pleasure of building everything themselves or because they feel they can build a better, more detailed, model than can be produced from a kit or because they wish to build a model in a scale different from that for which a kit, or kits, are available. If an accurate kit in any scale of the same car that an individual wishes to construct from scratch is available, then much of the would-be model builder's problem is solved. Few individuals care to scratch-build models of prototypes for which kits readily are available. In most cases, it is the lack of availability of a kit—at least as the basis of a superdetailed model—that impels a hobbyist to scratch-build a model automobile.

There is no model-building hobby for which suitable plans and data are less readily available than that of model automobiles. The reason is that of all popular model-building hobbies, model-automobile construction is by far the most recent to achieve widespread popularity. It came into being more or less full blown following World War II, with an almost concomitant availability of kits. The subsequent multiplicity of kits in the later 1950's and 1960's probably was the greatest factor in the amazing growth of the hobby in recent years. For the most part, model-automobile building did not undergo the early stages common to most other model-building hobbies when, few or no simple kits being available, most model builders had to work from scratch, and innumerable sets of plans

Fig. 56. Two interesting .48-inch-scale (1/25th-size) customized models. Top, a 1957 Chevrolet mounted on a display stand (compare with the standard model illustrated in Fig. 8 and built from the same kit of plastic parts). Bottom, a 1956 Ford pickup truck whose customizing includes a rather unusual top- and bottom-hinged split cab-door arrangement.

Revell, Inc.

Fig. 57. Three 3/8-inch-scale (1/32nd-size) dragsters based on popular prototypes making use of famous stock coupe body designs. Constructed from kits of plastic parts, the basis is, top left, a Willys, top right, a Ford, and lower left, a Fiat. The shallow windows on the Ford are the result of a "chopped" top.

Monogram Models, Inc.

were provided regularly in periodicals and books devoted to the subject. A survey of the famous pioneer American magazine *The Modelmaker* during its entire existence from 1924 to 1939 reveals perhaps half a dozen references to model automobiles, mainly fire engines, and no plans. An examination of *Model Craftsman* during the 1930's bespeaks an almost identical situation and limitation, although there are a few plans for fire engines. It is the writer's recollection that during the whole of the 1930's only two sets of drawings for model automobiles other than fire engines were published in the United States, for an early Oldsmobile in *Model Craftsman* and for a Packard in *The Cleveland Model News*. Yet during this period hundreds of plans were published for model airplanes, ships, and railroad equipment, and today the scratch builder in these fields has a veritable treasure trove to draw upon. A situation virtually identical to that in the United States appears to have obtained in British model periodicals.

Since World War II plans have appeared and continue to appear in American and British model-automobile magazines, but they are mainly of well-known racing cars, as are the plans included in Rex Hays's excellent guide to model-automobile building from scratch, *Motor Modelling*. It does not seem that anyone has ever estimated the total number of makes and models and body styles of automobiles that have been manufactured throughout the world since the dawn of the automotive era, and it may well be that it is impossible for anyone ever to make such an estimate with any degree of accuracy. For practical purposes it might be said to be an infinite number; and the odds are very high that the hobbyist who picks a specific car to model will not be able to find suitable plans in existence.

SECURING INFORMATION

In almost every case, then, the would-be model builder must undertake considerable research, assemble his data, and prepare his own drawings, a set of working drawings in the scale in which the builder is working being a virtual necessity, although some excellent models have been constructed without them by builders working only from one or more photographs of the prototype. In either case, a certain amount of intuition, based on a fair knowledge of automobile design and practice, is necessary. There are many fairly good sources for information on the appearance of obsolete automobiles, notably advertisements in general periodicals and illustrations published in old automotive magazines. At one time or another, a picture of almost every car (although far from every body style) was published somewhere. Most large libraries have files of old automobile magazines as well as general periodicals, although the researcher may find to his dismay that in magazines where the advertisements were published in blocks before or after the main body of the magazine, early library binding practice often removed and discarded these now-sought-after advertising pages when the periodicals were bound. Old automobile catalogs and sales brochures are another helpful source of pictures and information, but these are less readily obtainable when something specific is required. There exists, of course, a lively trade in old automobile magazines, advertisements, and sales literature, and they are all sought-after collectors' items in their own right.

Many of the earlier drawings and photographs of automobiles were pleasantly accurate and forthright, often of dead-side views that are very easy to translate into working drawings in any

Fig. 58. Four detailed and customized models deriving from kits of plastic parts for standard coupes. Most model automobile builders would classify these as "mild" customs, as contrasted with more extreme or "wild" customizing efforts. Also, compare these coupes with those illustrated in Fig. 57.

Revell, Inc., and *Testor Corp.*

scale, once any one dimension on the prototype can be ascertained and all the other dimensions worked out accordingly. As time went on, however, the desirability and the art of exaggeration in automobile renderings was discovered, with the result that many illustrations of later cars provide a great many problems—in translation, as it were. This is where intuition and deductive reasoning enter the picture, if they are not already present under the circumstances of having a good view of the side of a particular car but not the front and rear. Anyone who attempts to make drawings from any sort of an illustration that is not a dead-side or end view must have or acquire some knowledge of the principles of perspective. In many cases the work involved in researching and preparing a proper set of plans may be much greater than that of actually building the model once the plans are completed. Nevertheless, the hobbyist who is willing to spend the necessary time digging for data and who has the ability to analyze and coordinate this data usually will be rewarded by achieving an amazingly accurate set of plans and, eventually, a model.

When suitable side or end views are found, they often can be enlarged or reduced (usually it is a matter of enlargement) through the photo-

static process, although this may involve a certain amount of acrimonious discussion and explanation with the photostat people if they do not happen to be familiar with the requirements of the model-building fraternity. The work must be done absolutely accurately, and the operator should be made aware of this need. Furthermore, no matter how accurately the job is done, there is unfortunately an area for failure in the physical nature of the photostatic process and materials themselves in that during the drying process the paper, either for the negative or for the positive, or both, may shrink; moreover, it may shrink unevenly, with consequent distortion and inaccuracy. On the other hand, the frequently advocated method of copying pictures or plans in another scale by laying out a sheet of paper ruled with numerous evenly spaced horizontal and vertical lines so as to form a grid, and by making a completed drawing in the scale to which the model is to be built by reducing and laying out one element of the prototype at a time, is in actual practice liable to prove far less satisfactory. It is comparatively easy to start and reduce the wheels accurately to scale and draw them in with a compass, and even to follow up satisfactorily by measuring and drawing in the main

Fig. 59. Six futuristic car designs that were winners in a recent Fisher Body Craftsman's Guild Model Car Competition. Not only do these models, which represent 1-inch-scale (1/12th-size) replicas of proposed prototype designs reflect interesting styling concepts, they display meticulous model craftsmanship as well.

Fisher Body Craftsman's Guild

dimensions, but once one begins working in smaller dimensions, and most particularly in curved surfaces, it is almost impossible to avoid serious errors and distortions, which are usually substantially greater and more grievous than those caused by any possible shrinkage of the paper during the photostatic drying process.

Being aware of the disadvantages inherent in each of these two methods, the individual hobbyist who finds himself called upon to prepare a set of working drawings may decide which procedure to follow. Of course, if the model-automobile builder possesses some competence as a draftsman, even an amateur draftsman, he will probably be capable of making up a fairly satisfactory and accurate set of drawings without having to resort either to the photostatic or grid methods of reduction.

DESIGNING MODEL AUTOMOBILES

One element of the overall hobby of building model automobiles involves the designing of complete vehicles according to the hobbyist's taste. To some extent this is involved in the more extreme forms of customizing—customizing that in effect is substantially more the creation of an entirely new vehicle, or at least the creation of an entirely new body for an existing chassis. Customizing also involves the nostalgic creation and modeling of a modern version of some famous or cherished make of automobile of the past, incorporating elements of modern automotive design with a retention of certain recognizable classic features that served particularly to distinguish a particular make, such as hubcaps or hood lines. It must be admitted that often these points of resemblance are of necessity somewhat obscure and are readily recognized for what they are only by true initiates; once the average man has passed the point of the Packard hood and hubcaps or the Pierce-Arrow headlights set into the fenders, and perhaps the Cord 810 hood, he will have exhausted his stock of points of ready reference with distinctly individualistic design features of the automotive past.

The art of model-automobile designing as such also revolves around the annual competitions sponsored by the actual manufacturers of automobiles and bodies, of which those conducted by the Fisher Body Craftsman's Guild are perhaps the best known and longest established. Open to boys eleven to twenty years of age who live in the United States, these competitions (there actually are two, one for the eleven-to-fifteen-year age group and one for those fifteen to twenty) today award well over $100,000 in prizes and scholarships. One of the objects of the contests is, of course, to spot promising talent for actual automobile designing in the future, and it appears that in some instances these contests actually have brought to the attention of the automobile manufacturers designers who have gone on to important careers in the automotive industry, although there is naturally somewhat of a tendency to overemphasize this aspect of the situation.

With the possible exception of the extreme or ultra-"wild" model-car customizer, a summation of the principles of successful model-car design as enunciated by the Fisher Body Craftsman's Guild is of value. Presumably they reflect the basic thinking of modern-day real automobile designers and stylists, although not everyone—and particularly admirers of old automobiles—may necessarily agree with these principles or, even assuming their acceptance in toto, that modern automobile design practice always faithfully adheres to them. *Simplicity:* the design should feature clean basic shapes and lines that blend easily. *Proportion:* a balanced relationship of one part of the car to the rest, front to rear, upper roof to lower body. *Form:* the shape and external appearance should reflect the automobile's purpose; for example, sports cars should have an exciting fleet look; a station wagon should reflect comfortable transportation and versatility. *Unity:* every detail of the design should be related so that the design as an entity produces a single, harmonious effect.

It is also fair to note that there are those—recognized artists and art critics—who maintain that automotive design is truly at its best and most beautiful when it is utterly and essentially starkly functional to the purpose of the automobile: a high box (the body) with a smaller box (the hood) in front, mounted on four wheels.

In most cases the hobbyist who wishes to produce model automobiles of his own design will work in wood, perhaps using some metal trim, although some fans do build such models of metal or plastic or cast plaster. Many construct their models directly in the final material, but in this area of modelmaking a great many first work out the design in modeling clay until they achieve exactly the design and effects they seek to achieve, and then transform the clay design into a more permanent material. Starting with a clay model is, in fact, the usual procedure in producing the model automobiles used in designing in the real automobile factories.

Unless the finished model is to be cast in plaster from molds made directly from the clay original, the usual procedure is to lay out the clay design on a gridded board so that a series of cardboard templates can be produced for use as guides in accurately reproducing the original clay design in the final material. The clay employed should be a grease-base modeling clay, and it is usually formed around a wooden core or armature roughly cut to the basic form. Holes are bored in the armature so that the clay mass may be firmly footed and the armature coated with a sealer so that the wood will not absorb grease from the clay. The clay is worked into the design of the car body, at first roughly to the general size and contour and then very smoothly and carefully with finer tools to its final shape and smoothness. The cardboard

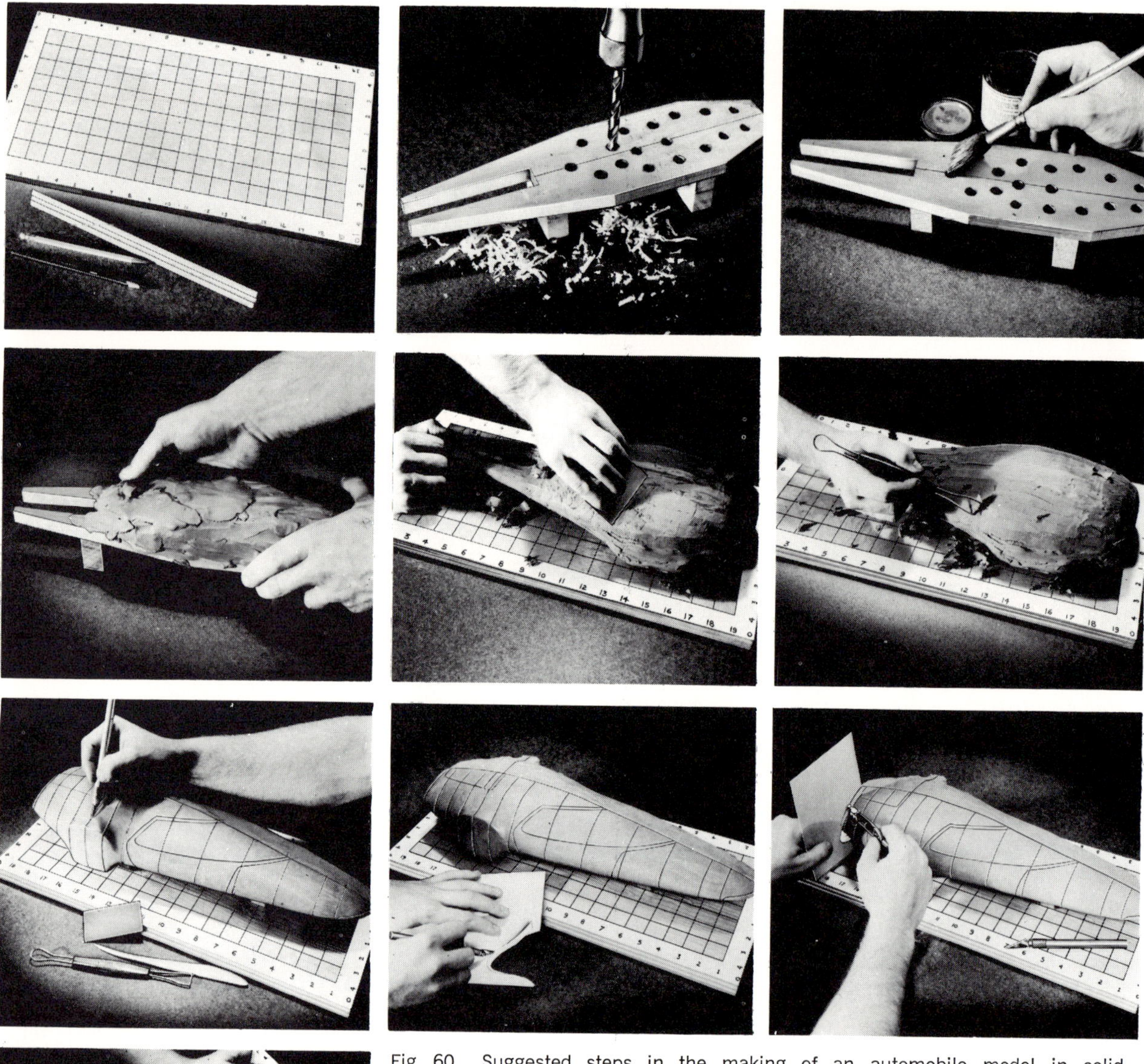

Fig. 60. Suggested steps in the making of an automobile model in solid clay built to 1-inch scale: setting up a layout board divided into one-inch squares, through making and sealing a wooden form, applying and shaping the clay, and preparing and using templates to assure that both sides of the model have identical contours.

Fisher Body Craftsman's Guild

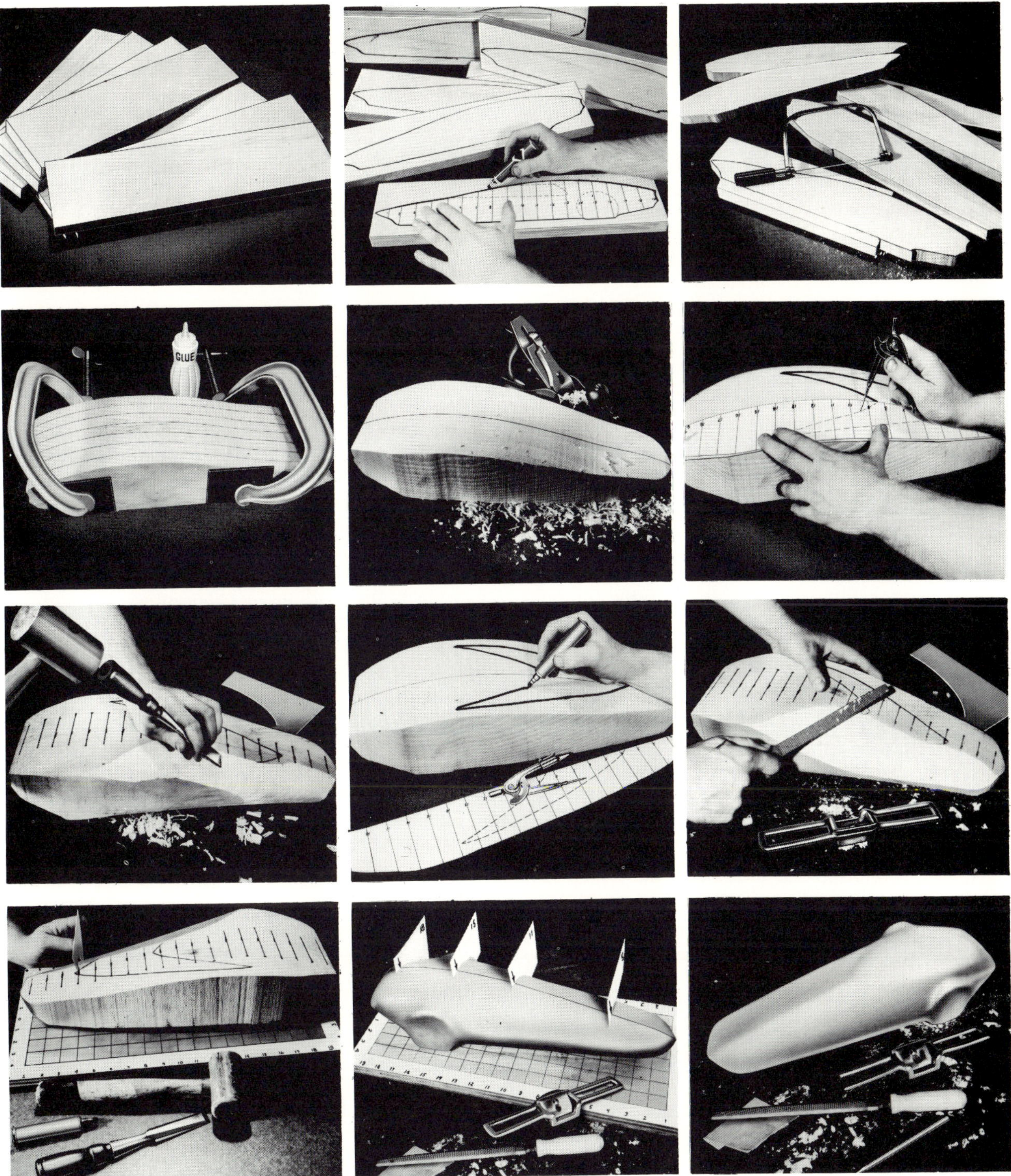

Fig. 61. Steps in constructing a 1-inch-scale solid wooden model automobile. If a solid wooden block of kiln-dried wood of sufficient size is not available, a block may be formed by gluing together a laminated block as shown in the first four photographs. The templates are made and used in a manner similar to that shown in Fig. 60.

Fisher Body Craftsman's Guild

templates are numbered for their stations as indicated by the markings that have been placed on the lines on the gridded board. Some hobbyists finish only one half of the clay model, one side, and then make templates. The templates in turn are used to contour the second side of the clay model so that it is identical with the first. If a hobbyist is going to reproduce the clay model in wood, rather than by making a plaster casting, it is not really necessary to complete the second half of the clay model unless it is felt desirable to view the clay model in its entirety to pass upon it as an entity before going on to making the wooden model, as the templates for one side of the clay model can as readily be used for both sides of the wooden model as for those of a clay model.

The wooden model may be carved from a solid block of wood or, in the case of larger models, several pieces of wood may be laminated together with glue to form the block. Usually the wooden model is worked on upon the same gridded board upon which the clay model was prepared, so that the readings on the board will provide the same station designations for the use of the cardboard templates. Cutting the wood down to the contours indicated by the patterns is a delicate and painstaking business. It must be remembered that the templates indicate the side cuts to the center line; a basic top template must also be prepared for the clay model and its outline transferred to the top of the block of wood. It is necessary to check continually with the templates to see that the proper amount of material is being removed and, even more important, that not too much is being cut away. Some builders using this method feel that a complete set of templates for each side is essential for satisfactory work, and prepare such a dual set; others find that the templates for one side only are sufficient for properly completing both sides of the wooden model. After the wooden block is cut to conform to the templates, there must follow a thorough fine finishing process, using progressively finer sandpaper. Finally, window, door, trunk, and hood lines are defined by scoring with a knife or file.

Obviously, the result of this process is a solid model, the body of the automobile formed from a solid block of wood. This is the type of model customarily used for visualizing new automobile designs; and of course when properly sealed, painted, and polished, and completed with wheels and other fittings, it presents a considerably more prepossessing appearance than might appear possible while the work is in progress of shaping the block of wood. However, if a full and hollow model is desired, of an appearance and caliber similar to that secured when a regular plastic kit is assembled, the work involved is much more complicated and delicate. The fact is that even the building of a solid model by this method is much more difficult than it sounds or looks when one examines the how-to-do-it photographs of an expert's work, and it is, in truth, another good example of those things so frequently met with in modelmaking: in the text, something is made to appear relatively easy, whereas, in practice, many who essay it will find this is not the case at all.

THE TERMINOLOGY OF CHANGE

At this point a discussion of terminology is in order. It is somewhat difficult today strictly to define some of the broader terms commonly used. "Conversion" and "free-lancing" were once relatively widely used and generally understood terms in model-building hobbies in general and most particularly in model railroading. The former of course referred to some change, usually of a major nature and presumably in the way of being an enhancement in working or appearance in some standard product; the latter meant the application of individual creativity in model designing and construction. There also entered into the matter of free-lancing a considerable and never completely resolved discussion of whether one was ever jusutified in departing in this area from that which was prototypically correct or at least practical. The same overtones are much heard today in reference to customizing, most particularly in model-automobile customizing. While "conversion" and "free-lancing" are terms still widely understood and used among those long engaged in general model work, there is an increasing tendency today in the model-automobile hobby, especially among newer or younger enthusiasts, to replace them with other and more particularized terms; most specifically, "detailing" and "superdetailing," which have largely replaced "conversion," and "customizing," a term that more or less has become a substitute for "free-lancing" where static model automobiles are concerned. As a matter of fact, "conversion" always carried with it a measure of connotation of improvements in mechanical working as well as an enhancement of appearance. Accordingly, while it is still often used in connection with slot cars, it never had much usage in its fullest and perhaps best-known meaning in connection with static model automobiles. It is interesting to observe, also, that "customizing" is a term almost exclusively met with and employed in connection with model automobiles, attempts to introduce it to

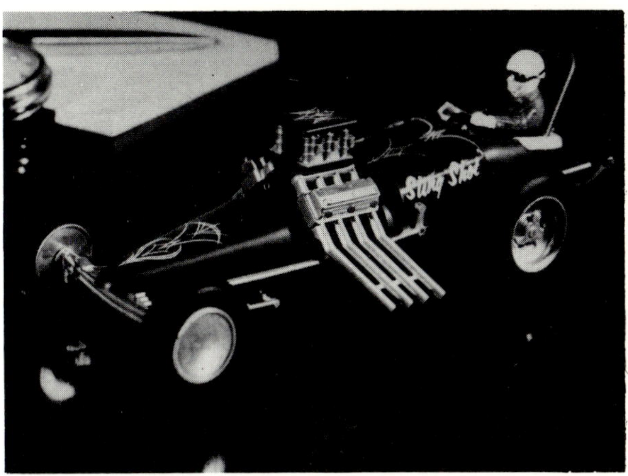

Fig. 62.   While most builders of model automobiles, as distinguished from builders of slot cars for use on model raceways and roadways, are not too interested in powered models, essentially static models sometimes are powered. Two methods are shown here: left, jet propulsion by the use of a CO_2 (carbon dioxide) cartridge (*Walter Kidde & Co., Inc.*), and, right, a concealed battery-powered electric motor (*Lindberg Products, Inc.*).

other types of models having been almost totally rebuffed.

"Detailing" and "superdetailing" were once both widely used as indicative of relative degrees of the same thing, although the line between them was always difficult to define and there was seldom general agreement on the matter. Continually advancing progress both in the detail regularly incorporated in model-automobile kits and in the amount of detail customarily added by individual hobbyists has rendered it ever more difficult to establish acceptable interpretations of the two terms. The fact is that today many model-automobile hobbyists use them more or less interchangeably to refer to the same thing. They may refer both to changes (such as making a trunk lid open) or to additions, such as installing a miniature jack within the trunk. Progress in detailing is rapid and amazing. Not too long ago such things as cutting out, hinging, and making operable such things as car doors and hood and trunk lids was considered an amazing achievement in detailing—or in superdetailing, if you prefer. Today a number of inexpensive commercial kits offer these things as a matter of course in the normal assembly of the stock kit. Making the glass in miniature car windows crank up and down was once regarded as an almost unbelievable ultimate in superdetailing. It is still a matter of great admiration for the hobbyist who attains it, and is certainly by no means a commonplace, but, having successfully been accomplished, it is no longer quite the absolute beyond which no one conceivably could go that it once was. Where can, where will, the superdetailers proceed next? There probably is no frontier they cannot attain if they so desire.

As for customizing terminology, some fans feel that all customizing can be subdivided into the rhyming categories of the "mild" and the "wild." These terms are more or less self-explanatory, and in view of what already has been said regarding extremes in car design and customizing, nothing more need be said here. There are, however, three terms frequently involved in the making of "wild" customized models, as well as in the so-called hot rods, that should be explained here: "chopping," "sectioning," and "channeling."

In the United States each of these terms has a very distinct meaning referring to a particular type of operation. "Chopping" involves lowering the roof line of a car by removing pieces of the window and door posts and superstructure. In short, the height of the car is reduced between the belt line and the roof. "Sectioning" is the act of lowering a car body by removing a piece all around the body of the car body below the belt line, that is, somewhere between the belt line and the rocker panels. "Channeling" means removing a section of the body from the lower edge upward. All three operations are favorites among model-car customizers, even as they are among customizers of real automobiles; the designation "custom car" now having lost much of its original meaning connotating a special opulence of finish and accouterments and all too often now conveying to many an implication of the despoiled and debauched.

The British, perhaps more forthrightly than many who use the term imagine, have applied a broader meaning to "chopping" and the "chopped car." In Great Britain any model car that has undergone such extreme or wild customizing is referred to as a "chopped car," and any of the

Fig. 63. Two models of especial interest for enthusiasts of high-speed prototypes. Left, a .48-inch-scale (1/25th-size) replica of the Indianapolis winning Lotus Ford (*Industro-Motive Corp.*). Right, a 1 1/2-inch-scale (1/8th-size) electrically motorized model dragster that is 24 inches long (*Lindberg Products, Inc.*). Both are built from kits of plastic parts.

attendant processes are known in a general way as "chopping." Whether it was the original intention or not of some wag who to his surprise was taken seriously at his tongue-in-cheek suggestion of the term, "chopping" now is considered a very fitting description for such mutilations by many fans who have automatically accepted the word as bearing the same connotation it has when mentioned in connection with Anne Boleyn. As a result, a number of model-car enthusiasts in the United States now automatically refer to any model that has been so transformed—whether based on a modern kit of plastic parts or, even far more horribly and ruinously, on an old collectors' item—as an "Anne Boleyn," or, somewhat more familiarly and less regally, simply as an "Annie." Some other aspects of this situation will be examined in Chapter 5; for the moment our concern is with the technical aspects of the act, and with the results.

Where chopping, sectioning, and channeling are concerned, the situation is once again that where the deed is made to look much simpler than

it actually proves to be in practice. It is no easy task for anyone accurately to measure off and then cut away an exactly equal portion of any part of a model-automobile body, whether near the roof, as in chopping; amidships, as in sectioning; or at the bottom, as in channeling, and then—at least in the cases of chopping and of sectioning—cementing the remaining portions back together again into a more or less whole car body. Obviously, in the case of older cars where all the posts are vertical, it is much easier to chop a body than with more recent prototypes with slanting windshields and roof lines. In fact, it is virtually impossible to chop many recent types of cars because once even a small section has been removed from all the posts the remaining upper and lower sections of the body simply will not again meet and align. When car sides are more or less vertical, sectioning, too, is fairly easy for the good workman, but with cars with rounded sides or tapered ends, the customizer is again in trouble, although usually not in quite so bad a situation as if he endeavored to chop the

Fig. 64. Two aids for those who wish to superdetail or customize model automobiles. Left, concealed hinges for hoods, doors, or trunks, with optional magnetic locks. Right, a sectioning kit with tape in various scale widths from 3 to 6 inches with which to mark a body accurately as a guide in evenly removing material in remodeling.

Auto World

Fig. 65. An excellent example of what an enthusiast can do in the way of creating a special model by using a commercial kit of plastic parts as a basis. The right hand photograph shows a 1/2-inch-scale (1/24th-size) 1928 Lincoln as assembled from the kit (*Lindberg Products, Inc.*). Left, a town car as built by William Dreyer, using the same kit as a starting point. (*William Dreyer photograph*).

upper parts of the bodies. A good workman can often manipulate his components so that with sufficient filing and puttying and fitting, a fairly competent body will emerge.

Channeling where one need only cut away material at the bottom of the model seems at first glance to be by far the easiest of the three operations to carry out successfully; actually it is likely to be as difficult, if not even more difficult, of accomplishment as chopping and sectioning, because once you start to channel a body you become involved with all the lower components of the car, the fenders or wheel wells, the chassis, the engine if the model incorporates a miniature engine, and so on.

A recent aid to customizers engaged in chopping and sectioning is the availability of scaled tapes for accurately laying out these operations. The tape widths represent various measurements on what would be a real car, say, three inches, four inches, and so on. Tape of the appropriate scale measurement for the dimension that is to be re-moved is carefully and evenly applied all around the model car body where the cuts are to be made, and is then used as a guide for making the cuts with a razor saw or with an auto-cutter.

As to the results? Often at the expense of interior room and comfort, our modern outlook has become somewhat attuned to the conception that the lower an automobile, real or model, may be, the sleeker and faster-looking it will appear. If we accept this thesis, even when sectioning or channeling operates against the desired unity of the overall car design the results may be not altogether displeasing when carried out by a hobbyist who is not only a good workman but who also possesses some talent for design. As far as the term "chopping" goes, it appears for the most part to be as well applied even when confined to its original American meaning of working between the roof and belt line. In almost every case the result is seen as an absurd disfigurement by most beholders, regardless of how it may look to the customizer. Most thoughtful hobbyists seem to agree that it

Fig. 66. A group of five 3/8-inch-scale (1/32nd-size) sports cars assembled from kits of plastic parts and here seen mounted on labeled display stands fashioned from box tops. Left to right, top row: Jaguar XK-120 and Ferrari America; center, Cunningham; bottom row: Ferrari Sportster and an M.G.

Aurora Plastics Corp.

Fig. 67. Another segment of automobile history as illustrated by model cars. These are 3/8-inch-scale (1/32nd-size) models built from kits of plastic components. Starting from the upper left, the cars are two 1906 Renaults; 1909 Lozier, Rolls-Royce, and Cadillac; two 1911 Stevens Duryeas; 1911 Packard, 1911 Mercer Toy Tonneau, 1914 Raceabout, 1915 Ford Couplet, and 1915 Ford delivery wagon.

Plyro Plastics Corp.

is virtually impossible to rebuild a car in this manner with really satisfying results from an esthetic standpoint. It is only fair to remark, however, that there may be exceptions and that such exceptions pass general notice simply because the work has been performed in such a satisfactory manner that a totally new unity of design has been created.

As far as chopping old cars goes, most minds simply boggle at what, if anything, anyone believes he can accomplish by lowering the roof and absurdly reducing and distorting the glass areas either of a real or model say, 1930 Ford Model A. Old cars as well as modern vehicles have their own proper overall unity of design, and once this is tampered with a very important element of their appearance inevitably is destroyed.

CONTOURING AND CUSTOMIZING

In all these cutting and contouring operations on plastic models, the enthusiast finds a most invaluable aid in the form of a material known as body putty. This is a paste material designed for filling in openings as well as raising new contours that can then be shaped as desired to conform to the requirement of a new or modified body design. When hard, the putty can be worked with facility. There are, however, two schools of thought regarding the best way to employ body putty to close in deep areas. One holds that if the area to be filled in is 1/8th inch or more in depth, the bulk of the space should be filled in with plastic wood, with the body putty used only to fill in the uppermost reaches of the space. The other school holds that the best procedure is to fill the area entirely with body putty, but by using a number of successive thin layers and allowing each layer a full twenty-four hours to dry and set properly before applying another. In all cases a relatively thin layer of body putty requires twenty-four hours to dry. If one deep layer of body putty is applied, it will take many days to set properly, hence at least one advantage in using plastic wood under the putty. Some model-automobile builders favor plastic wood over body putty for all filling and contouring jobs, but this obviously is a matter for personal preference to determine after an individual has experimented with both materials.

Many hobbyists apply a layer of plastic model cement to the section of the model automobile that is to receive body putty before applying the putty. The plastic model cement works on body putty in the same manner as it does on plastics, and helps to form a more permanent bond than

would be the case if the putty were applied directly to the plastic of the model-car body. Still another tip in working body putty is to sand down the putty, after it has fully set, to a fairly smooth finish, and apply a light coat of paint. The paint serves to show up the tiny pits and holes that might otherwise pass unnoted at this stage but would be revealed later—too late—in the final painting. The paint is sanded away, leaving paint in the pits that makes them even more visible; additional body putty is then applied to fill in the small pits. After the final putty has dried, the puttied areas are given their last very fine sanding. What is known as "wet" and "dry" sandpaper, here employed as wet paper, is recommended for all final fine sanding operations on body-putty contours or, indeed, wherever an extremely fine finish is desired. This is a form of very fine sandpaper available in several grades. It may be used dry, in the conventional manner in which sandpaper ordinarily is employed, or it may be dipped in water and used wet when an extra and superfine finish is desired. To repeat, here once again, as in so many instances of model-car work, an ample resource of patience is an absolute necessity in employing body putty in customizing.

The model-automobile customizing enthusiast will find a wealth of suggestions in the model-car magazines listed in Appendix II, as well as in the *Car Model Custom Annual, Building Customs from Wood and Scrap Parts,* and in the books already mentioned in this chapter and listed again in Appendix II.

It is impossible to enumerate all the ways in which model automobiles may be detailed or customized, and, as has been seen, detailing and customizing frequently overlap. Detailing grows more elaborate and ingenious with each passing year. It may take the form of inanimate detail, such as the addition of the correct wiring to a dummy miniature automobile engine, or it may be working detail, such as hinged doors and windows that can be rolled up and down. Or it may concern itself with such things as upholstering the seats in a car, using either actual upholstering materials or flocking sprayed on over wet paint to imitate upholstery and carpeting. The extent to which detailing may be carried today by great numbers of model-car enthusiasts is indicated by the fact that a booklet is now available that is entirely devoted to one aspect of detailing, *How to Wire and Detail a Model Car Engine,* by Mike Doughty. The publications referred to in the preceding paragraph as being of interest and value to customizers will prove equally useful in matters of detailing.

4

Painting and Decorating

Most of today's kits for static model automobiles come with the various parts molded in plastic of appropriate colors, and can be assembled into very attractive and commendable-looking miniatures without requiring any painting whatsoever. Painting is of course required if you wish to change the color of any components, or to provide a greater range of color variation. Most experienced model builders tend to paint some if not all of their models, for there is no doubt that in most cases a somewhat superior and more realistic finish can be obtained in this manner. For the hobbyist who is going in for extensive rebuilding, detailing, or customizing, painting virtually is a must. In numerous instances model automobiles are customized mainly or entirely by means of special painting and decorating techniques. In the case of kits comprising mainly metal parts, painting is a necessity, for such components are supplied in the bare, unpainted metal. Painting also is a requisite when wooden parts are employed; the touchstone of successful painting of wooden parts being the proper sealing and sanding of the relatively porous wood surfaces.

All in all, therefore, the acquisition of the techniques involved in painting is a requisite for most model-automobile enthusiasts. It is axiomatic that a model car can be made or unmade through its paint job. This literally is true. Some hobbyists can take a stock kit, assemble it without addition or change, and then by means of an especially careful and attractive paint and decorating job come up with a model that stands out above dozens or hundreds of others and may, purely because of its superb finish, prove a winner in a model-car contest. On the other hand, some hobbyists can spend almost endless hours putting meticulous craftsmanship into detailing or rebuilding a model that justly should be an acknowledged standout and that then is spoiled by a heavy, sloppy, amateurish paint job that grossly detracts from rather than enhances the work that has been put into the model. The moral obviously is: If your model-automobile-building activities are to be other than putting together stock kits and relying entirely on the color molded into the plastic parts, learn to paint and to paint well. Equally obviously, this can be achieved only through considerable experimentation and actual experience.

METHODS OF PAINTING

There are three possible basic methods by which model automobiles can be painted: brushed, dipped, and sprayed. One of these, dipping, however, need not concern us long here. Some very fine finishes have been produced by the dipping process, especially on metal model automobiles, but in general it must be considered beyond the province of the vast majority of hobbyists, if only because it requires too large a quantity of paint to warrant its use on a single miniature. Also, it usually is

72

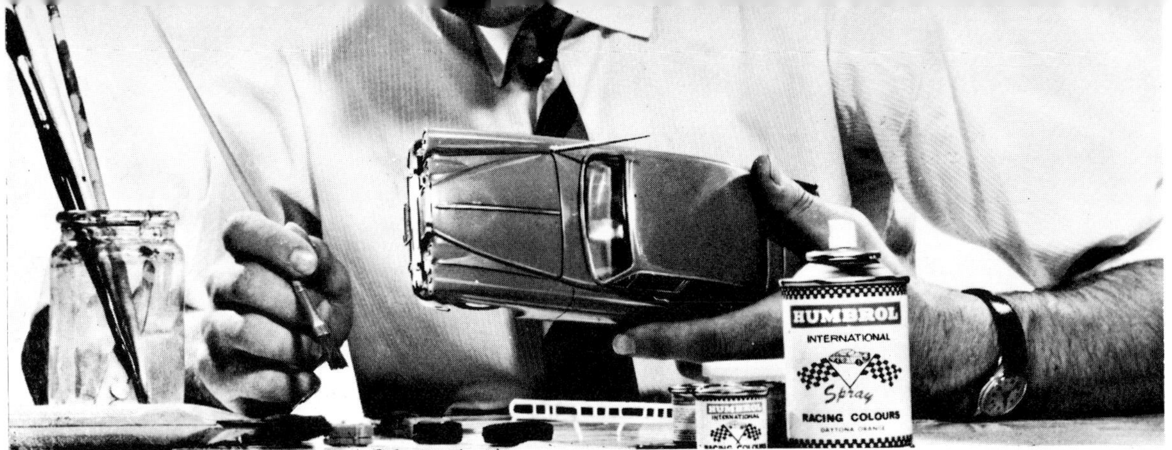

Fig. 68. Many model automobile builders attain excellent results with brush painting. It is far more important that the paint be thinned sufficiently so as to flow smoothly from the brush than that the first coat completely cover the model. Also, cheap brushes are almost invariably a false economy.

advisable only when a single color is to be applied to an entire body. It might well be noted, nonetheless, that dipping does serve readily to produce a smooth, even coat, free of any possibility of brush marks, although on the other hand there is a tendency for blobs of paint to coagulate at the edges or in corners.

There are several systems by which paint may be sprayed: spray cans containing both paint and propellant that are discarded when they are exhausted; small spray guns or airbrushes that spray by means of a separate replaceable can of propellant or air from a spare tire, and spray guns or airbrushes that are powered by means of small air compressors. The major difference between the second and third type of spraying is that while an air compressor always will provide an assured even pressure throughout the spraying operation, the use of a separate can of propellant or a spare tire involves a diminishing source of pressure that may run out during a critical spraying operation. The same thing applies, of course, to the use of spray cans; the prudent modeler learns quickly from experience just about how much paint he can get from a spray can. Spray cans provide a handy mode of applying paint, especially when several colors are to be used on a single model, and are today widely favored as being both convenient and relatively inexpensive. A compressor-operated spray gun or airbrush probably is the ultimate in model-car painting equipment. Such outfits are available today at a cost that is relatively inexpensive in terms of what such equipment formerly cost but that at the same time must appear somewhat substantial to the average model builder. A disadvantage of some importance to many model builders is that any spraying method other than spray cans requires that the gun or airbrush and paint jar must be thoroughly cleaned before each change of color. While it is possible to have several jars for different color paints in use at the same time, there always is a certain amount of bother and waste attached to their use.

SAFETY IN PAINTING

There should, regardless of the method of painting employed, always be plenty of ventilation in the area where painting is conducted. Some dust may come in through an open window, but better a little dust than inhaling paint vapors for an hour or more in an enclosed room. Too, paint can be highly combustible. This is especially true of spraying when, in effect, the spray can or gun or airbrush acts like the carburetor of an automobile and breaks the paint down into tiny fragments mixed with air—a highly volatile mixture. Therefore, *never paint near an open flame, and include in this classification the pilot light on a stove or in a furnace.*

The spray can itself is safe when properly used and highly dangerous when misused or abused. It is true that within sane limits, the warmer the area where the painting is undertaken, the better will be the results, and that if you paint in a cold area the paint will dry too slowly for good results. It is a common misconception that the warmer the spray-paint can, the better will be the paint job regardless of how cold it may be in the room where the painting is undertaken. Best results are obtained when both the spray can and the painting area are at a natural warm temperature. *Never try to warm the can artificially, much less try to heat it!* It is true that the paint will flow more freely when the can is warmed, but it is prudent practice never to warm a spray can, even in lukewarm water, in an attempt to improve performance. If the weather or the heating system do not provide enough warmth to allow the paint to spray freely, wait until it is warmer. It also goes without saying that it is not good practice to place spray

Fig. 69. It is always desirable if spray painting can be done in a booth, such as the one shown here that is provided with a turntable, or, if necessary, within a large carton. The conventional direct method of operating a spray can is shown at the left (*Pactra Chemical Co.*). At the right is an interchangeable pistol-grip handle that converts any spray can into a spray gun. (*Auto World*).

cans on or near a hot furnace or radiator in an effort to warm them. Spray cans are loaded with freon gas, the same gas used in refrigerators. Freon is a nontoxic gas, safe under normal conditions but highly explosive if sufficiently heated. Every spray can bears a safety warning that reads something like this: "Contents under pressure. Do not puncture, throw container into a fire, or store above 120 degrees Fahrenheit. Heat may cause bursting. Keep away from direct sunlight, windows, stoves, furnaces, etc. Use only in adequately ventilated areas. Avoid breathing vapors or prolonged skin contact. Keep away from children. Do not swallow." These admonitions should carefully be read and scrupulously followed.

BRUSH PAINTING

Painting with brushes can produce a fine, perfectly smooth job, free of brush marks, if care and the proper brush are used. Brush painting usually falters because cheap brushes are employed—a clasic example of false economy—or through failing to thin the paint when thinning is called for. Paint should be thin enough to flow smoothly from the brush, and this is far more important than that the first coat should completely cover the model. It will give far better results in most cases if you use two or three thin, flowing coats than to try to finish a surface in a single coat. Though red sable or camel's hair brushes will cost a little more than bargain brushes, they will enable you to cover a given area with fewer strokes and less chance of brush marks. Similarly, when very fine detail must be painted, there is nothing better than a red sable brush with an extra fine point.

Almost any of the modern modelmaker's paints for plastics seems to dry rapidly, but it is good practice to allow more time than appearances or even the manufacturer's instructions might indicate. Never touch a painted surface with your fingers to see if it is dry! If it is not, you will ruin the surface; even if it is dry but not yet fully hardened or "set," you may rub away paint. Most brush paints require a substantial period to set really hard. Always allow at least two hours before putting on a second brush coat over the first; better still, be patient and let the coat dry overnight. If the weather is humid, even an overnight wait may not be sufficient. In fact, it is best never to paint anything when the weather is damp.

Spray paint, when properly applied in mist-like coats, tends to dry much more rapidly than brushed paint, and a second spray coat usually can be applied within half an hour or even sooner; some paint manufacturers say within as little time as one to five minutes. Most spray paint seems to require that additional coats be applied in fairly rapid succession or else each coat be permitted to dry overnight before another coat is applied.

Regardless of whether you brush or spray your models, any plastic models or plastic parts require special paints formulated for use on plastics; many ordinary paints will eat away the plastic moldings! Play safe by using only one of the regular brands made and designated for plastic models, and always employ the compatible thinners, protective coats, and so on, produced by the same paint manufacturers. For a long time only enamels were available for use on plastic models. More recently, compatible lacquers have been placed on the market, so the hobbyist now has a choice of an extremely wide range of colors in special lacquers for plastics, as well as enamels. Metal models may be painted with either, and with special model paint or with any regular paint. However, there are advantages in sticking with

Fig. 70. Four 1/2-inch-scale (1/24th-size) or .48-inch-scale (1/25th-size) customized dragsters that not only show good structural workmanship and detailing but interesting and careful painting and decorating as well. Note the use of two body colors on the two top cars, and the blend paint effect on the front fenders of the car at the lower left.

Revell, Inc. and *Testor Corp.*

the special paints made for models regardless of the materials being painted: a wide variety of special colors compounded for automobile use are available as model paints in very small containers, and in many instances it is possible to obtain the same color both in the form of brushing paint and in spray cans.

A few model builders attempt to use real automobile paint, suitably thinned, on some of their models, feeling it provides somewhat greater authenticity. There may be some validity or at least measure of personal satisfaction to this in cases where a real automobile manufacturer has created a special tint for use on certain models. However, the validity often is mainly theoretical because paint, too, tends to "scale down" in appearance, and what may appear a very light shade when applied to the broad expanse of a real automobile often appears much darker and not at all a true rendition of the same color when applied on a six- or eight-inch miniature! The fact is that a particular real shade of paint often can be much more accurately rendered on a model by using a lighter shade of paint than the original. Thinned-down real automobile paint is satisfactory for metal models. In the case of plastic models the real automobile paint may eat into the plastic, as previously mentioned. In some cases this effect can be overcome by first suitably prime painting the model car, but the whole thing is a very touchy business, and the best advice that can be offered is that as far as plastic models are concerned it

is better all around to confine yourself to the wide range of special paints made for use on plastic models. With a little skill acquired through experience with these plastic paints, almost any real car color can satisfactorily be duplicated by blending paints if the desired shade is not available as a standard paint.

When brushes are used they should be thoroughly cleaned, using the thinner for the paint that has been employed. At the same time, with the paint job completed, the tops of the cans or jars should be tightly screwed and the containers inverted momentarily, so the paint itself will form a seal. After using a spray-paint can, the can likewise should be inverted and made to spray in this position for a few seconds in order to clear the nozzle. If the nozzle on a spray-paint can does become clogged, it should be cleaned and cleared with thinner.

UNDERSTANDING SPRAY PAINTS

If good results are to be obtained, it is important that the hobbyist understand how the spray can projects its pattern of paint. As already noted, the effect of a spray can is to vaporize the paint into extremely tiny particles. These particles issue from the nozzle in a cone pattern. The pattern should be kept in mind at all times during painting, as well as the fact that the size of the pattern, but not its comparative variation in density, will con-

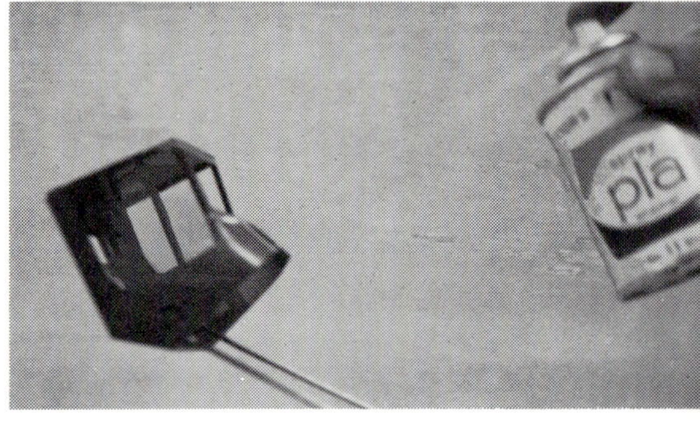

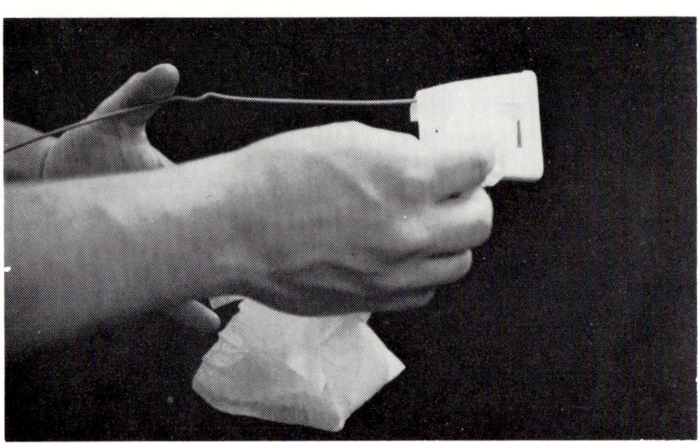

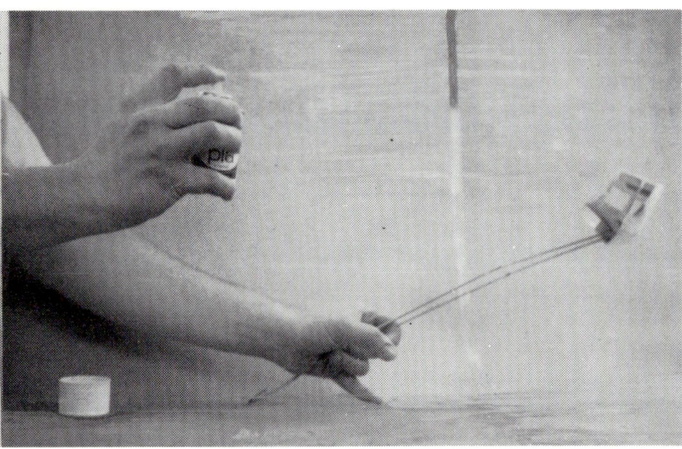

Fig. 71. Some tips on painting. In sequence: employing a bent wire coat hanger to hold a model while painting; cleaning dust and oil from model parts prior to painting; holding spray can at a distance from model for the first coats; attaining a high-gloss finish by close spraying of final coat, and hanging unit up to dry by using the coat-hanger holder.

Testor Corp.

Fig. 72.   Interesting paint variations and multicolor effects may be observed on these .666-inch-scale 1/18th-size) Duesenberg SJ's, two town cars and a phaeton assembled from kits of die-cast metal parts. Note the use of reverse colors on the two town cars. The phaeton is black with olive body trim, with a tan trunk with gray trim.

Hubley Division, Gabriel Industries, Inc.

tract as a spray can is used. It is always advisable to spray paint into a paint booth, whether a special one with a hand-manipulated turntable, as pictured in Fig. 69, or an ordinary large cardboard carton. The use of such a spray booth will not only prevent the spray mist from touching any surrounding objects but also, and equally important, the booth will serve to keep dust from settling on models once they have been cleaned just prior to painting. The turntable will be found very convenient in painting various areas of the model without having to touch it with the hand. If you use a homemade spray booth, you can easily build a similar turntable by using a piece of carboard carton or light wood, pivoted to turn freely on a nail run into a supporting block of wood. It is not really necessary that the turntable be cut in the form of a circle; a pivoted one-foot square piece of heavy cardboard will serve just as well.

Because the paint spray issues from the nozzle in small particles, and there actually is no point in the cone where the spray is substantially even over any pronounced area, virtually all successful amateur spray painting must be based on movement of the spray can on the object being painted. (Factory production methods often move the object being painted past a fixed spraying device; but, except for a few hobbyists who have made elaborate rigs to draw a car body past a fixed spray can for "blend" or "fade" paint jobs where one color is applied over another in a pattern that ranges in continuous gradation from light to dark, the fixed-spray method practically never is used by home hobbyists.) Whenever practical it is, of course, easier for the model builder to move the spray can rather than the model. The purpose of a turntable in a home paint-spray booth of course is not to move the model during actual spraying, but to allow it to be shifted so that all surfaces can conveniently be reached by a moving spray can. Basically, home spray painting should consist of

a series of steady, even passes of the spray can or other spraying device from one side to the other.

The beginner always tends to hurry and to overspray. It takes a certain amount of time to gain experience in manipulating spray cans. The expert often can apply a good but extremely light initial coat that will dry sufficiently in a few minutes to permit a second coat; but the novice's first coat of paint, no matter how careful he tries to be, is almost invariably heavier, and requires more drying time. At times it will be found desirable to hold the model or various component parts in a position not attainable by simply laying them on the turntable. It will usually be found that a satisfactory holding device for the car or major parts, either for use by holding and manipulating in the hand or for resting on the turntable, can be made by suitably bending an old wire coat hanger or a section of a hanger. In the case of cars that come in kit form, with separate pieces molded for such parts as hood and trunk lids and doors, these parts should temporarily be taped to the body in their closed position so that the entire body exterior can be painted at once and so that there will be no variation in the color and tone patterns of the various parts except where it may be especially desired by a customizer. In the latter case, it is especially desirable that the opening parts be taped in their closed positions so that the desired variations in the custom paint job will be absolutely consistent where called for, as, for example, around the entire lower portion of a model-car body.

PREPARING FOR PAINTING

The preparation of model automobiles and parts for painting can be as important as the painting itself. Techniques differ somewhat between various materials. A cardinal rule in painting all materials is to touch the surfaces as little as possible with your hands once they have been cleaned, for inevitably you will transfer some minute quantities of oil to the surface. This is particularly important in handling plastic surfaces. If possible it is well to handle a car body or other component only with a cloth, tweezers, or other holding device once it has been cleaned for painting. The final cleaning process should consist of carefully going over every surface with a slightly moistened, clean lint-free cloth to remove all dust, and then allowing the body to dry thoroughly before painting.

Masking tape, which should not be confused with the striping tape referred to later, is a handy aid in painting two-tone bodies. The use of the masking tape remains the same regardless of the material being painted. To produce a two-tone car, first paint the entire body with the color that will predominate. When that color is thoroughly dry, carefully cover the areas that are to remain that color with masking tape, and spray the second color onto the remaining exposed area. When the

second color in turn is thoroughly dry—better allow more than normal drying time for drying when using tape—the tape is removed and you have a two-tone body. The opposite approach could be employed, but this method is preferable since every part of the body will receive a coating of paint before any masking tape is applied. The reverse method runs the risk of slight portions of the body remaining without any paint at all, unless extreme care is taken in cutting and aligning the masking tape. However, the exact procedure used will to some extent have to depend on the colors involved. It is somewhat difficult to apply a light-color paint over a dark color without darkening the tone of the light paint, while putting a dark coat over a light one will not cause trouble.

Clear plastic bodies are seldom used for static model cars. Bodies molded in clear plastic are generally designed for use on electric model racing cars. However, from time to time builders of static model automobiles make use of the avail-

Fig. 73.   These photographs illustrate some of the techniques employed in painting clear bodies, such as that shown in Fig. 53. Bodies of this type may be painted either on the inside or on the outside. Parts to be left clear, such as windshields and headlights, are masked as at upper left, and the masking tape is removed after the paint is dry, as at lower left. The fourth photograph shows racing stripes being applied to a model by means of tape of the type pictured in Figs. 81 and 82.

"Model Racing Buyers' Guide"

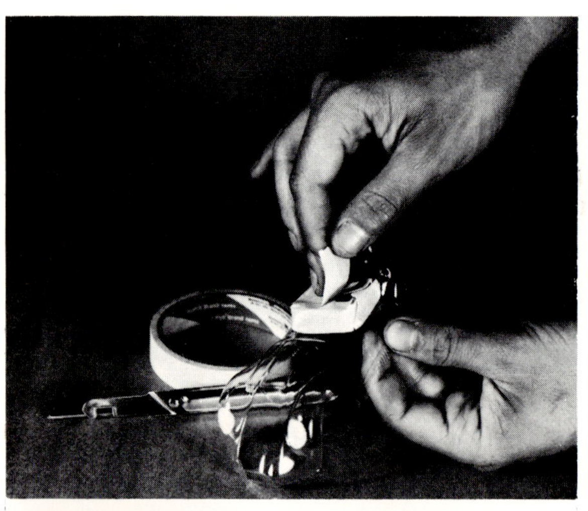

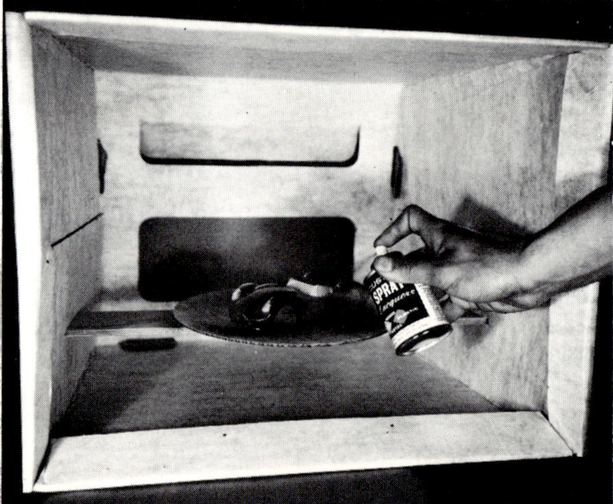

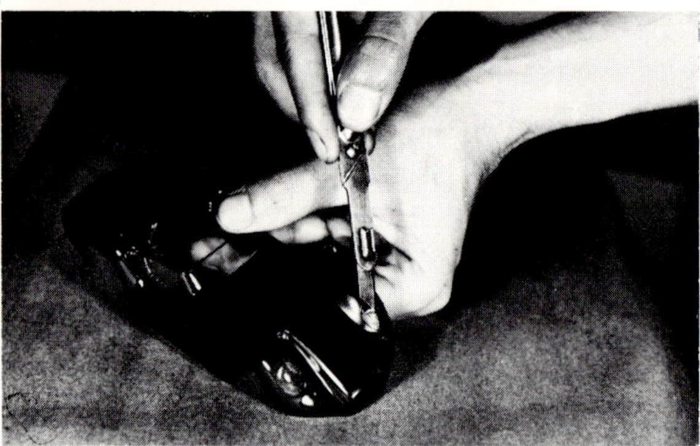

ability of such clear bodies in building models of cars for which commercial model bodies are not otherwise available. Clear bodies very often do not have the depth of molded detail usually desired by static-model automobile builders. They do have one advantage, however, that appeals to some model builders in that the window glass already is, as it were, molded in place, and it is only necessary to paint the remainder of the body, leaving the windows clear, to have a complete car body without further ado. Whether painting clear bodies on the outside or the inside, the windows (and the headlight lenses) will have to be carefully masked off first, so that they appear as clear glass in the finished model. This requires very precise cutting and alignment of the masking tape, and is especially difficult when the body is to be painted from the inside and the masking tape must be applied inside the car body. Originally the thinking in regard to clear slot-car bodies was that the painting was best done on the inside to prevent the paint from being nicked or chipped in an accident. In addition, the clear plastic body over the paint gave the impression of a very high gloss polish. More recently, however, the thinking appears to have shifted in favor of painting the outside of these bodies, the same as with any molded plastic body. The introduction of a protective antichipping clear spray to be applied over the final coat of paint lent further weight to the arguments of those

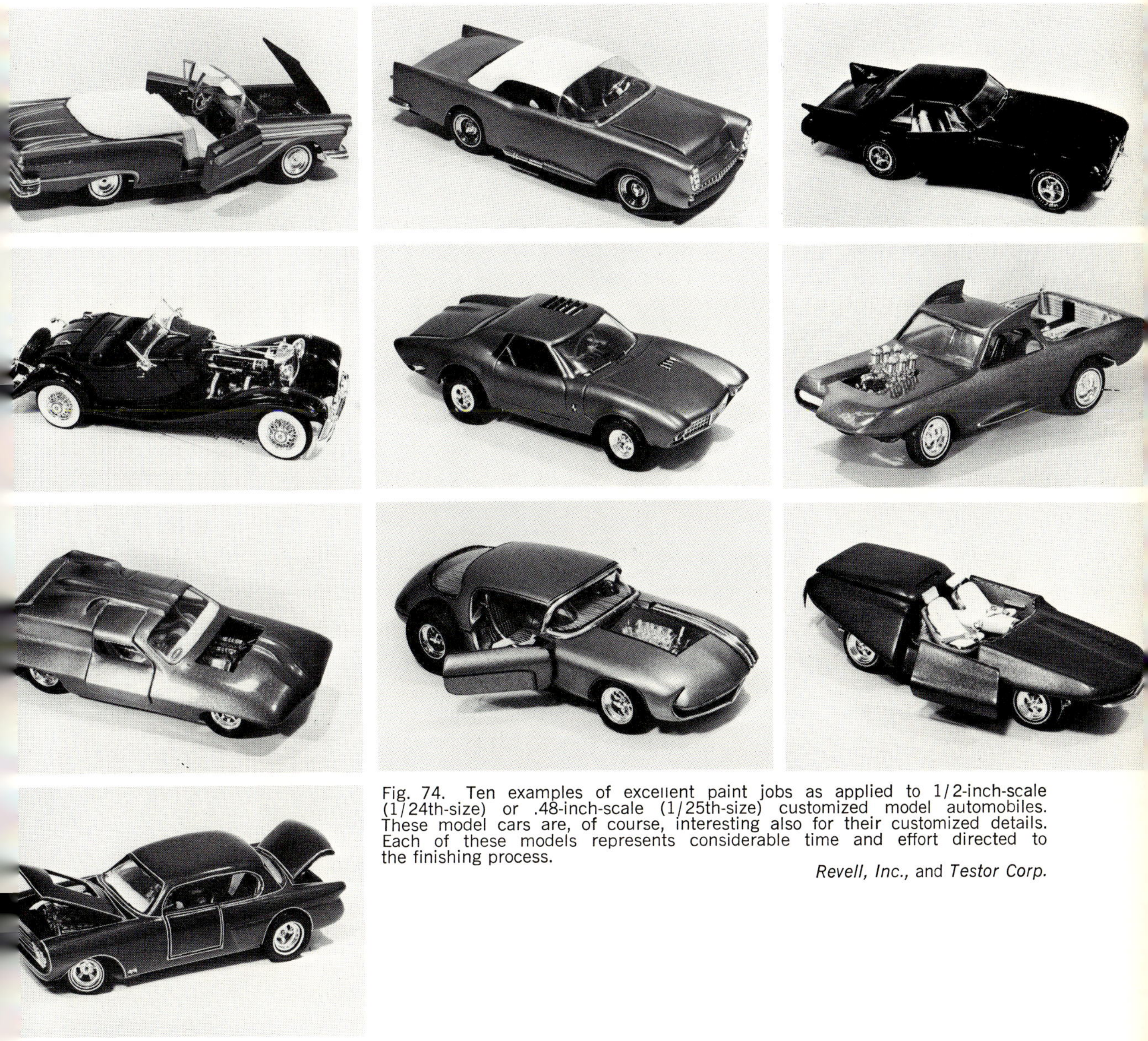

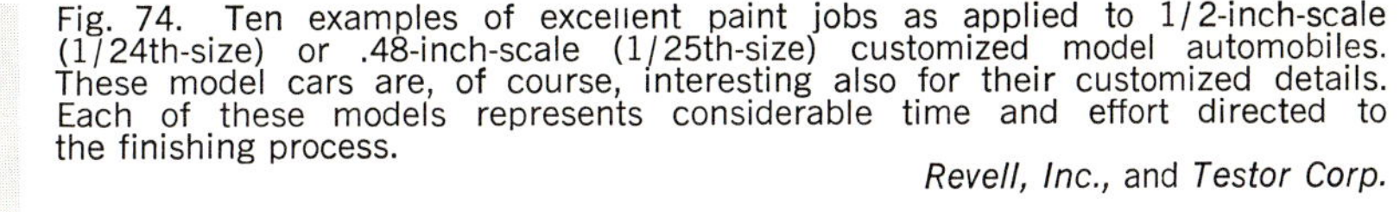

Fig. 74. Ten examples of excellent paint jobs as applied to 1/2-inch-scale (1/24th-size) or .48-inch-scale (1/25th-size) customized model automobiles. These model cars are, of course, interesting also for their customized details. Each of these models represents considerable time and effort directed to the finishing process.

Revell, Inc., and *Testor Corp.*

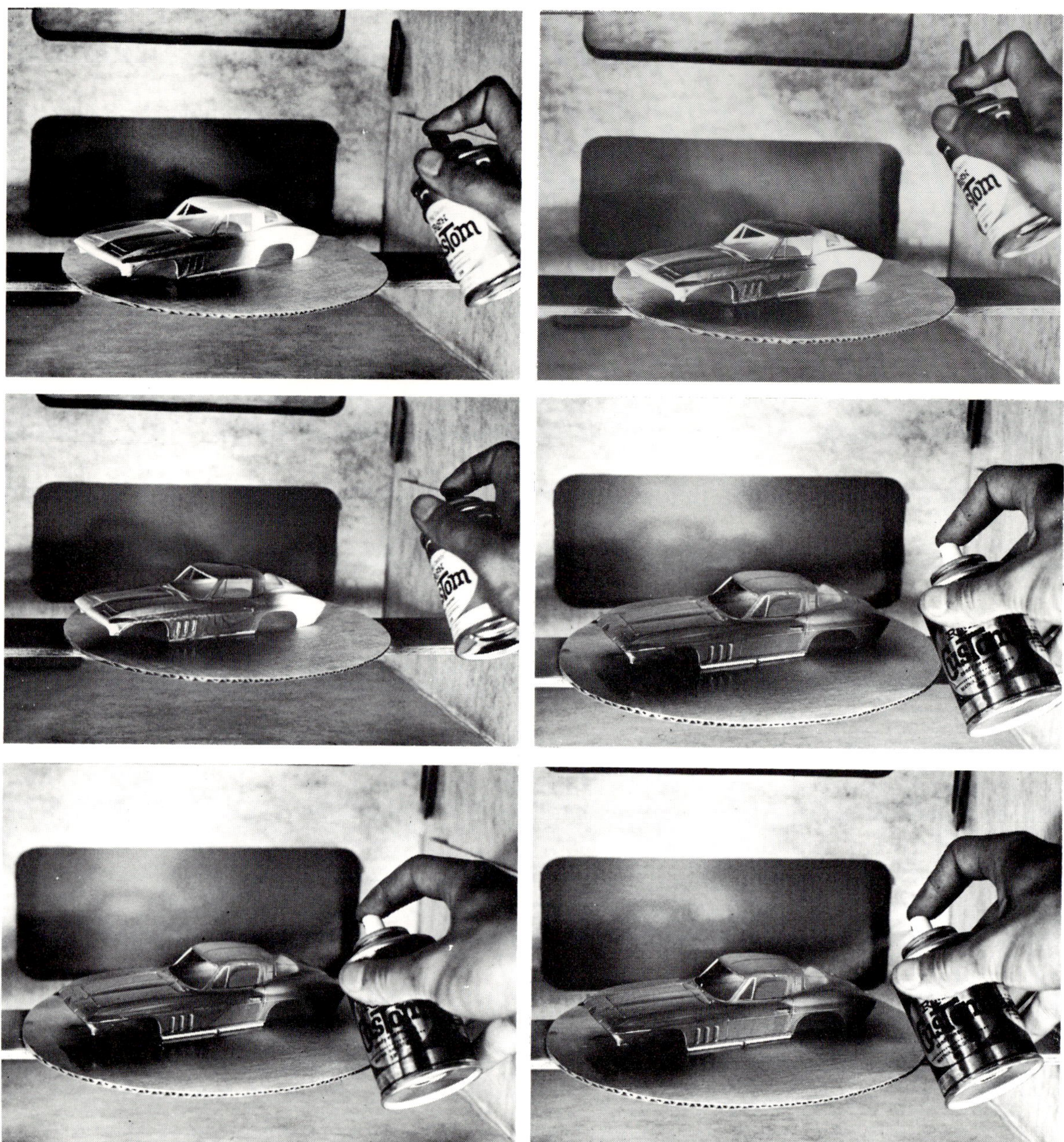

Fig. 75. This sequence illustrates the application of a so-called candy color to a model-automobile body molded in colored plastic. In the first three photographs a base coat, gold in this instance, is applied. The second three pictures show the translucent crimson candy coat being applied after the base coat has dried. Spraying is done in a series of steady, even passes, from left to right.

"Model Racing Buyers' Guide"

who advocated painting clear bodies on the outside. Of course, when a clear body is used for a static model automobile rather than a slot car, there is no need to worry about the matter of paint on the outside chipping in an accident on the model racetrack, and there never was any question but that the window masking always necessary on clear bodies was easier if the body were painted on the outside. Some clear bodies now are sold prepainted with metallicized colors, the glass areas being left free of paint. However, if any alternate or further painting is to be undertaken on such bodies, the glass areas must of course be masked anyway.

Fig. 76. Three .48-inch-scale (1/25th-size) model cars neatly finished in interesting and, in two cases, somewhat unconventional finishes. Top left, a 1968 Dodge Charger, top right, a customized version of the same car with a cantilevered roof, and bottom, a 1968 Plymouth Barracuda. *Model Products Corp.*

The clear bodies often come with considerable excess material left in the mold that must be trimmed off before they are ready for painting. After trimming, the edges should carefully be sandpapered. The entire surface to be painted, whether inside or outside the body, should be lightly scoured with steel wool or very fine sandpaper. This should be done after the headlights and windows have been masked, for these surfaces that are to be left to appear as clear glass must be free of any marks. Optionally, instead of rubbing the body with steel wool, clear plastic bodies may be primed with a special clear body primer. This primer does not discolor the body and can be used for painting clear bodies inside or outside. After scouring or priming, the clear body shell is then painted in the conventional manner.

PAINTING METAL CAR BODIES

While the larger metal model automobiles built from kits may be painted either with brush or spray, the painting—usually repainting—of small-scale metal models sold in assembled form generally is best done with brushes. Owing to their small size the painting of these models is a rather delicate job, and usually involves only brushes of the smallest size. The models usually are painted as a unit, no attempt being made to dismantle them so as to paint the parts individually. In many cases it would be extremely difficult to dismantle the factory assembly of the models of this type and then to reassemble them satisfactorily. If it can be done and the parts painted separately, either with brush or spray, the average hobbyist, who may not have the finest of artist's touches, may well find that a superior painting job results. A few hobbyists prefer to remove the old paint and apply their paint upon the bare metal. It should be borne in mind that in most cases almost a complete disassembly job will be required if this is done, because most of these models incorporate some rubber and plastic components (of which the tires are the most obvious), which would be deleteriously affected by the chemicals in paint-remover solutions should they happen to come in contact with them.

Generally the models of this type are sold already painted in appropriate colors, although the hobbyist may desire a model of a particular car in another color. In the main, however, the desire to repaint is due to the fact that the models often are made in Europe and that trucks and other commercial and service vehicles may bear unfamiliar names and markings. This is unimportant when the models are collected simply as models;

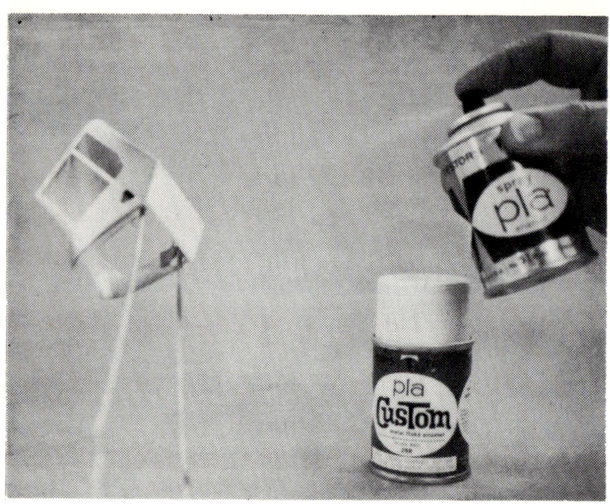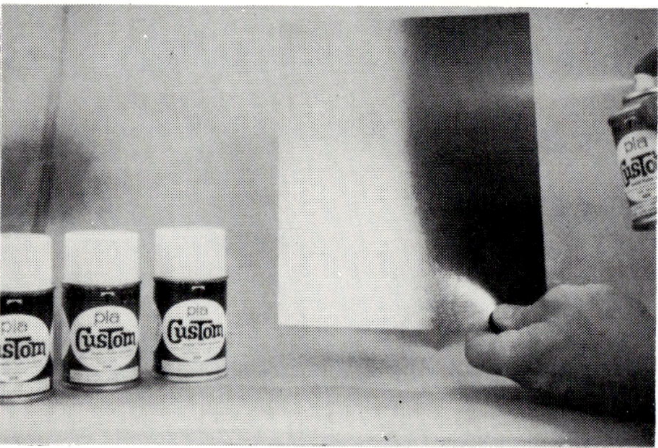

Fig. 77. Metal-flake paint effects. The first photograph shows a red metal flake with copper tint being obtained by spraying red metal-flake paint over a metallic copper base coat. The second photograph shows how the metal-flake effect varies greatly, depending on the base coat used. The same gold metal flake was sprayed on the sheet of paper previously half covered with a gold base and half with a glossy black base.

Testor Corp.

or, rather, the originality of such colors and markings is vitally important from the standpoint of the hobbyist who is collecting the models as such. However, when they are to be displayed as part of the scenic effects on an American model raceway or model railroad, it may be desirable that a vehicle be repainted and relettered, or at least that obviously foreign lettering be obliberated. Similarly, when American-made models are used for a similar purpose in Great Britain or elsewhere, it may well be preferred that the American coloring or lettering be replaced with something more authentic locally.

It should be kept in mind, however, that much of the interest in these small models lies in collecting them, and in collecting them in the variations of color and lettering in which they are manufactured; much if not all of the collectors' value depends on their being in the original factory finish. While this matter is dealt with in more detail in the next chapter, it is pertinent to note here that, bearing this situation in mind, many hobbyists who buy such a model with the intention of repainting it for some reason or another make it a practice to purchase a second specimen of the identical vehicle and put it away without alteration as part of their own present collection or as a token toward their collection of the future.

STATIC CAR MODEL PAINTING
TECHNIQUES

Having covered the variables and departures from the practices followed by most static car model builders, the remainder of this chapter may be devoted to the types of models and painting involved in the majority of instances where static model automobiles are concerned, that is to say, the painting of model cars built up or customized by using components molded of polystyrene.

Some modelers prefer to paint as many of the small parts as possible while they are still attached to the "trees" on which they are molded. This is not always practical. It is logical to paint all the parts that take a particular color at one time, so at least some of the small parts will probably have to be separated and divided into groups according to the color they are to receive. This always involves some danger of losing or misplacing parts. As already noted in the previous chapter, it is usually good practice not to detach small parts from the "trees" until they are actually required in the assembly process, but when a considerable amount of special painting is involved some modelmakers feel it is worth the risk of departing from this usage in order to obviate the necessity of separately spraying numerous small parts. If a group of parts is to be painted at once, great care must be exercised to see that some of the parts do not become lost. One way to accomplish this is to detach the parts, separate them into groups according to the color they are to be painted, and then mount each group in such a way that they can conveniently be painted. At times very small parts may be held in position for painting by setting one end, usually a section of the "tree" that is allowed to remain attached to the part, into clay or putty, or by taping the end to a board and then spraying the entire group as one unit. Care must be taken that the portion so held

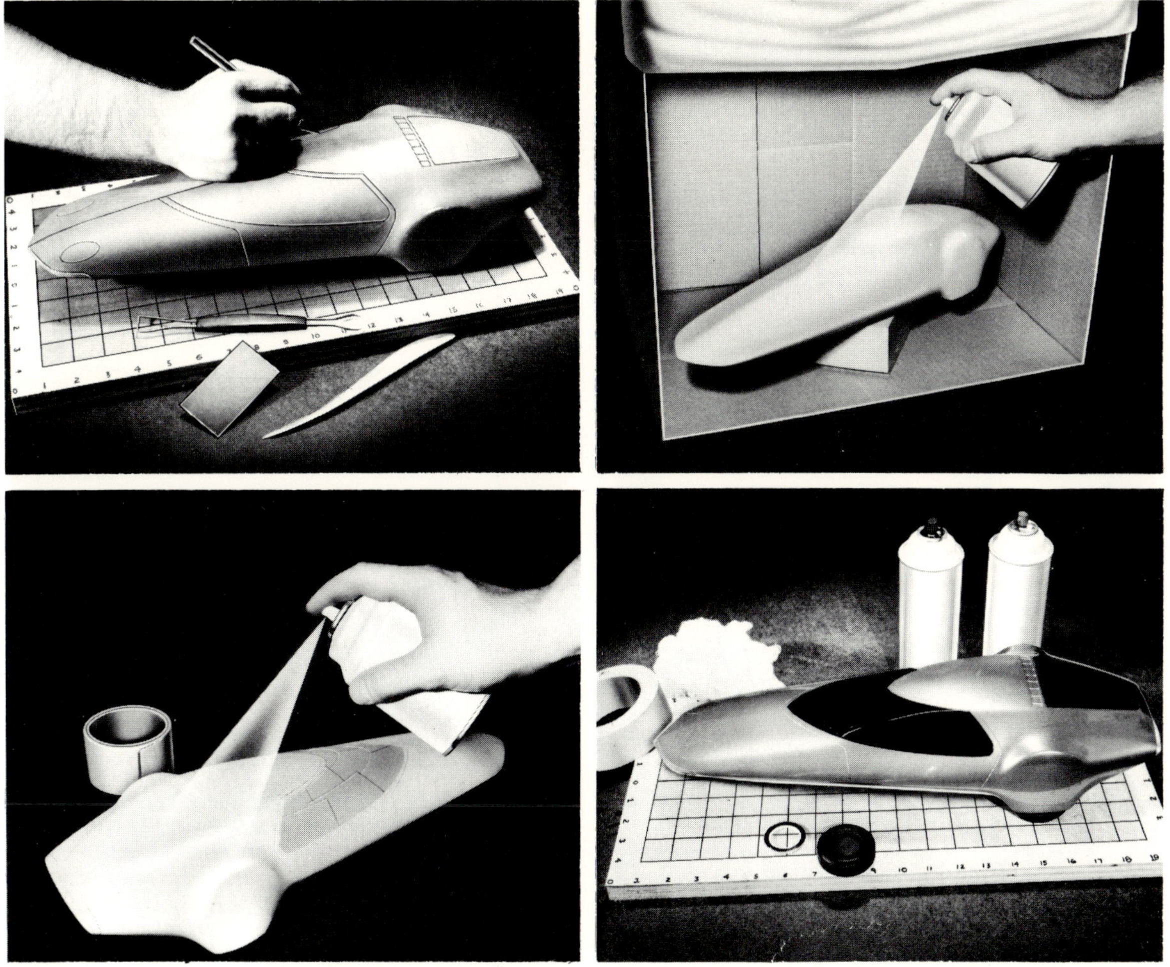

Fig. 78. These photographs illustrate the finishing of a solid-model automobile body. The steps shown here are: marking in body features; spraying the primer coats; window area masked with tape during spraying the final body coats; and the finished model with the "glass" areas filled in with black.

Fisher Body Craftsman's Guild

or covered is surplus plastic that does not require paint.

All parts that are to be painted should be cleaned prior to painting, and handled as little as possible. If body putty has been used in constructing a model or in repairing a defect, the part or assembly involved should be given a coat of special primer, since polystyrene moldings and body putty receive paint differently. To make sure that the finished coat of paint will be absolutely uniform throughout, some hobbyists prime all the parts in a given model if body putty has been applied to any of them.

The best results usually are obtained by using several thin coats of paint. Experienced modelmakers are not unduly concerned if the first pass with a spray can does not completely cover an area. Novices usually try to cover the surface completely at the first pass, keeping the spray can too long on a given area. This usually results in too much paint and in runs. The trick is always

to make steady, straight passes with the spray can, never lingering in any one spot. The first passes should be made about fifteen to twenty inches from the model, coming in to perhaps a foot away on subsequent passes, being sure to allow time for drying between passes. While not exactly a hard-and-fast rule, the closer the spray can is held to the model, the more rapidly the can should be passed along the model. To achieve a very high gloss finish, the final pass may come in as close as perhaps five or six inches from the model, with a relatively rapid pass. This will result in a rather wet coat of paint that will dry to a high gloss. However, if you come in this closely, but fail to move the spray can rapidly, the result will almost certainly be unsightly runs in the final coat of paint.

At this point, assuming you have achieved a desired high-gloss finish without runs, you will have to decide if you are satisfied with the finish resulting from the spraying or if you want to go

83

on and try to put a sort of superfinish on your model automobile with rubbing compound and wax. This process is not without its pitfalls, for once you undertake the process you must carry it through to its conclusion, and there always exists the danger of applying too much pressure and damaging a delicate part. In most cases it is desirable to let the paint job set for a considerable period of time—some hobbyists advocate waiting several weeks, especially with enamels—so that the paint is truly hard. Then the car is carefully rubbed down with a special model-automobile rubbing compound, and then just as carefully waxed. There are also variations in the process that result in differences in final appearances. Some enthusiasts prefer merely to rub down their cars with the rubbing compound but not to apply wax, resulting in a sort of soft velvet luster. Others first rub the car with especially fine sandpaper to attain a smooth finish, then apply the rubbing compound, and finally wax the model. These are matters for experimentation and personal preference. In any case, whether the hobbyist calls a halt after the painting or goes on through other finishing processes, it is always wise to handle the model with a cloth to avoid finger marks on the surface.

With static models that attempt authentically to duplicate older cars at the time they were current, select colors known to have been used on the particular car, or, if this information is not readily obtainable, at least use historically appropriate colors. This is, of course, an entirely different matter from the free-lance art of customizing cars, whether of old or modern prototypes. While there were always some brightly colored sports cars and roadsters, automobiles did not extensively blossom into rainbow hues until about the mid-1920's, and even then the more conservative colors long continued to lead in popularity. If in doubt about the authenticity of a color for an older prototype, bear in mind that black or a medium-to-dark blue is usually a safe bet for most cars; limousines and town cars were almost invariably black or very dark blue.

CUSTOM PAINT JOBS

Custom paint jobs have attained tremendous popularity in the world of model-car builders, and are the subject of frequent local and national contests, as well as being fascinating for their own sake. Regardless of whether the customizing process includes physical changes to a model or, as often happens, lies entirely in the painting, the finish of such models invariably plays a most important role. Almost anything goes, and the hob-

Fig. 79. The use of decalcomanias for decorating purposes is well illustrated in the variety of examples shown here as applied to 3/8-inch-scale (1/32nd-size) hot rods. The basic prototypes in these models built from kits of plastic parts are, respectively, 1921 Ford, 1924 Buick, 1929 Ford, and 1932 Ford.

Aurora Plastics Corp.

byist usually endeavors to produce a paint job that is not only meticulously applied but that will set a particular car apart by virtue of the uninhibited use of bright colors, often applied in unusual combinations or by using special paints—so-called candy colors, metallicized and metal-flake paints, pearlescent colors, translucent lacquers, and so on. Here the hobbyist is completely removed from the attempts at historical color duplication described above, and in the midst of what can justly be termed the wild, weird, and wonderful world of the model-car customizer.

This is not to say that literally *everything* goes, although some models of this type may indeed give such an impression at first glance. The truth is that color harmony, an appropriate color scheme, and plain good taste always of necessity must continue to play an important part in assessing the merits of such things, whether on a personal, individual basis, or during a formal competition. Very often a fortunately restraining and educational awakening as regards the wilder and weirder aspects comes during a contest when a paint scheme that does show thought and attention to the points outlined wins out over many purely wild designs. In contests of this type the judges usually look beyond such things as the first visual impact. They pay considerable attention to the harmony of the colors, as combined on the outside of a car, and the relation between the outside colors and the interior and unholstery colors. Other factors that can count for or against a model are the use of colors to point up features of body design or to accent minor parts. All this does not mean that customized paint jobs should be either casually observed or else judged with the same view that a conservative individual would employ in selecting a family car. Many of the customized paint jobs take a little getting used to for the average person before a full appreciation of their own particular beauty can be obtained. Nevertheless, certain basic rules of taste and esthetic appeal remain, although perhaps applied at a somewhat different overall level.

A further observation might well be made for those who are interested in competing in customizing contests. As far as the painting and decorating are concerned—and in many cases the handling of these matters is sufficient in itself to produce an outstanding custom—the judges generally tend to pay primary attention to the use of color itself, both in painting and in decorative striping or other embellishments. Loading down a car with fancy decalcomanias such as monster heads, snappy slogans, skulls and crossbones, iron crosses,

Fig. 80. Two painting aids for model-car customizing. Top, a metal-flake paint kit that provides finely ground metal-flake color in powdered form together with lacquer for mixing. Bottom, a new imitation chromium-plate finish that may be applied with a brush in the same manner as is paint.
Auto World

and so on, may have a certain appeal to some younger hobbyists. However, this type of thing seldom is regarded as adding to the merits of a model. Competent judges usually pass over such models quickly, and devote their attention to the cars that exhibit originality and beauty through the colors themselves.

By the time the model-automobile hobbyist is interested in going into the use of the specialized paints whose use is favored by many customizers, he probably will have already familiarized himself with the basic techniques of spray painting, particularly the art of gently misting a color during a single pass of the spray can. Many of the special paints depend on applying one color over another, not to cover the first color, but to supplement it. Often the final effect depends, both

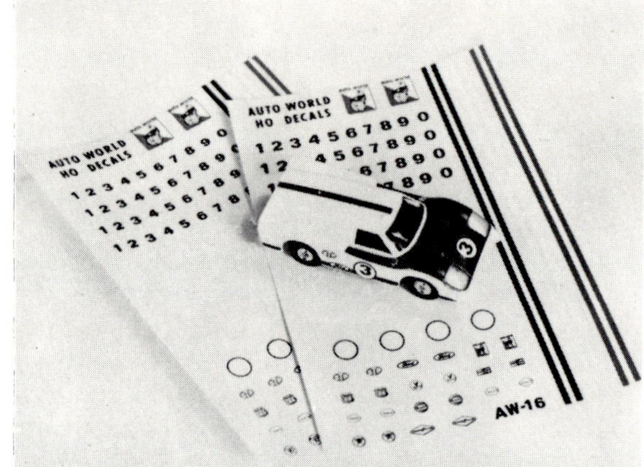

Fig. 81. Materials for decorating and lettering model automobiles. The upper two photographs show pressure-sensitive striping tape, as well as, to the right, numbering and insignia decalcomanias. The lower two photographs picture a relatively recently introduced new type of pressure-sensitive lettering material.

Auto World

in overall beauty and in the precise shade and effect attained, entirely on the ability of the modeler in spray painting. Candy colors, for instance, usually are applied in mists over a solid gold or silver base and are built up by successive passes about one minute apart, sometimes involving a dozen or more passes to attain precisely the effect desired. Or a candy color may be applied over a base other than gold or silver to secure a special effect. Or, again, at times two different base colors may be applied before the candy-color sprays. Metal-flake colors, on the other hand, require the use of no base color, and a finish can be entirely built up with passes of metal-flake paint, yet additional and totally different effects can be had when the metal-flake colors are applied over a base color. Metal-flake paints can be applied over bases of various colors,

and certainly nothing should be said here that might inhibit the ingenious and artistic customizer from creating special effects. However, it might be noted that there seems to be general agreement among many modelers that metal-flake colors appear more attractive when applied over a black base than over a lighter color base. It is relatively easy to experiment by coating pieces of paper with base colors and then spraying over them with metal-flake paint to contrast the varying effects of different color bases and overcoats.

The special paints either alone or in combination with ordinary colors provide an almost unlimited opportunity for the experimenter with special custom paint jobs. An enthusiast could experiment for years with different color combinations without exhausting the possibilities, for not only the choice of colors but the number of coats,

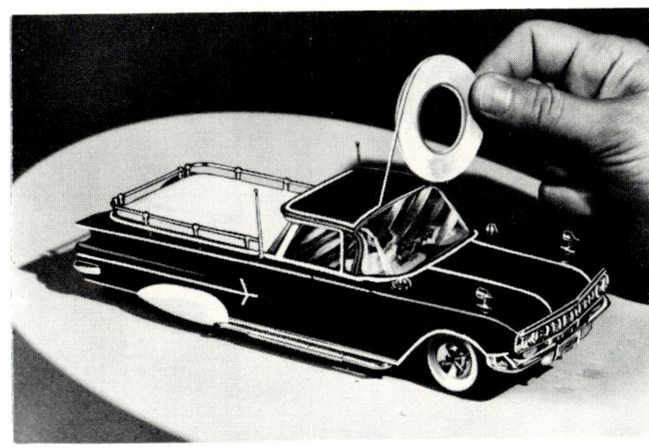

Fig. 82. More decorating aids, including scale self-sticking die-cut license plates for fifty states and ten Canadian provinces. The second view of the same customized model demonstrates the application of the type of striping tape shown in Fig. 81 *(Auto World)*. Also pictured is a kit, available in fabric or leather, for upholstering the interiors of model automobiles (*C. J. Ulrich Co., Inc.*).

the distance from which the spray is applied, and other factors enter the picture. One good point of all this is that even the beginner stands a good chance of achieving an outstanding color combination. One important suggestion is that the hobbyist who experiments in this direction keep a notebook record of all his experiments and actual paint jobs, noting the base color of the plastic, the colors used, and number of passes, and the distance of the passes for each color. It will then be possible accurately to duplicate any particularly pleasing and outstanding color combinations.

THE DECORATION OF MODEL AUTOMOBILES

Most experienced model-automobile builders probably would agree that the less decoration, the better. They would also agree that decoration really serves a valid purpose only when it duplicates actual decoration or necessary appurtenances on a specific prototype automobile, or is appropriate to a real or imagined prototype, such as racing numbers and stripes, or the insignia of sponsors, such as various tire or gasoline or spark-plug companies. Otherwise, it is difficult tastefully to add to the overall appearance of a model car simply by applying a multiplicity of decorations. While some very attractive effects have been achieved on model automobiles by the prudent and thoughtful use of scrolls and other purely decorative patterns, in the main it might be well to let the general feeling prevail, for more often than not attempts at decoration that depart from prototype practice tend to diminish rather than enhance the appearance of a model automobile.

There are several means by which racing numbers, lettering, and designs may be applied to model automobiles: decalcomanias or transfers, a relatively new type of lettering that transfers from its backing sheet by means of pressure and without the need of moistening, as is the case with decalcomanias, and removable pressure tape stickers, the usefulness of the latter usually being limited to racing numbers against a round background. Decalcomanias are still the most widely used form, and are available in the greatest number and variety of designs for various scale models. Decalcomanias are printed in color on transparent paper with an adhesive backing and a backing sheet. The desired decalcomania is cut out of the sheet, immersed briefly in warm water in order to loosen it from the backing sheet, and then carefully slid into the desired position on the model, where it is pressed firmly but gently in place, with any excess water being carefully dabbed away with a clean cloth. Some hobbyists also make use of a special decalcomania setting solution to make the decals snuggle down as it were over irregular surfaces and further to bond them to the surface

Fig. 83. The results of careful workmanship during all stages of construction. Here are two models built from kits of plastic parts. Top, a 1/2-inch-scale (1/24-size) 1937 Cord 812, in this case built with top and side windows up, and headlights retracted (*Monogram Models, Inc.*), and bottom, a .48-inch-scale (1/25th-size) 1923 Lincoln touring car artfully posed in a miniature rain-swept night scene (*Model Products Corp.*).

hobbyists have become accustomed to employing this method and achieve satisfactory results. Another method, in the form of narrow self-adhesive pressure tape in various widths and colors, and so thin as not to mitigate against the effect when applied, is now available, and is becoming very popular. The tape can be cut to any desired length and carefully laid down on the car body; when properly aligned, it is pressed into the desired position.

MODEL-CAR CONTESTS

Model-car styling or customizing contests have become an established part of the hobby and have proved to be events of substantial interest to model-automobile enthusiasts. In numerous instances they prove definite incentives toward which hobbyists direct their efforts, whether held on a local or national level. In many cases prizes of considerable worth are awarded. Aside from styling and Concours d'Elegance competitions that are conducted in conjunction with slot-car racing events, the contests usually are confined to static model cars and may be of one of two types. Some competitions are complete customizing events, in which painting and decorating are important in the overall picture but are by no means the sole subjects to be judged. The other type of contest is essentially a painting and decorating competition, with the emphasis of the judging directed primarily or entirely to these matters. In most cases the larger contests are divided into various classes, involving car types and degree of customizing and the ages of the contestants, and there may be various groupings and cross-groupings, as seem appropriate to the organizers of the contest.

In the overall contests the total number of possible points that may be awarded usually are divided into ten or fifteen different groups that may cover such things as appeal, modifications, workmanship, detailing, interiors, engines, and so on. Invariably there will be one classification devoted to paint and decoration, although painting skill may also apply toward points in some of the other groups, as well as engines and interiors. In the contests directed primarily to painting and decorating, these factors of course play the supreme role. Even in large overall contests, the classes set up for models as built-from-stock kits without additional detailing or customizing are, in effect, of necessity largely painting and decorat-

of the model. The variety of available decalcomanias is almost unlimited, and with a little practice most hobbyists become skilled in their use, although the application of a series of individual letters or numbers, or of striping, by this method is something that does require care and patience.

Much can often be accomplished in giving an attractive finish to a model automobile by means of striping, either of a purely decorative nature or, on racing cars, as part of the national color scheme each country is assigned. Probably the ideal way to apply any striping to a model car would be to do it by hand with a very fine brush, a process that calls for extreme skill and steadiness. There are individuals who can apply perfect striping in this manner, but they are few and far between; the average hobbyist should attempt hand striping only if he has supreme confidence in his ability. As mentioned, striping can be applied by means of decalcomanias, and many ing competitions, the only other factor being involved here being that of workmanship and how well a given kit has been assembled.

Personal enjoyment and satisfaction being the main goals of model-automobile building, few hobbyists build and customize cars simply with the idea of winning contests in mind. However, these competitions do add considerable zest and interest to the activities of many enthusiasts; and whether one competes or not, they do point up the relative importance of painting and decorating in the field of model-automobile building.

Fig. 84. Two 3.5-mm.-scale model trailer trucks built from kits of metal parts. Initially marketed primarily as accessory units for HO-gauge model railroads, such models are also of substantial interest to model-automobile enthusiasts. The van truck kits are supplied with prepainted and lettered bodies.

C. J. Ulrich Co., Inc.

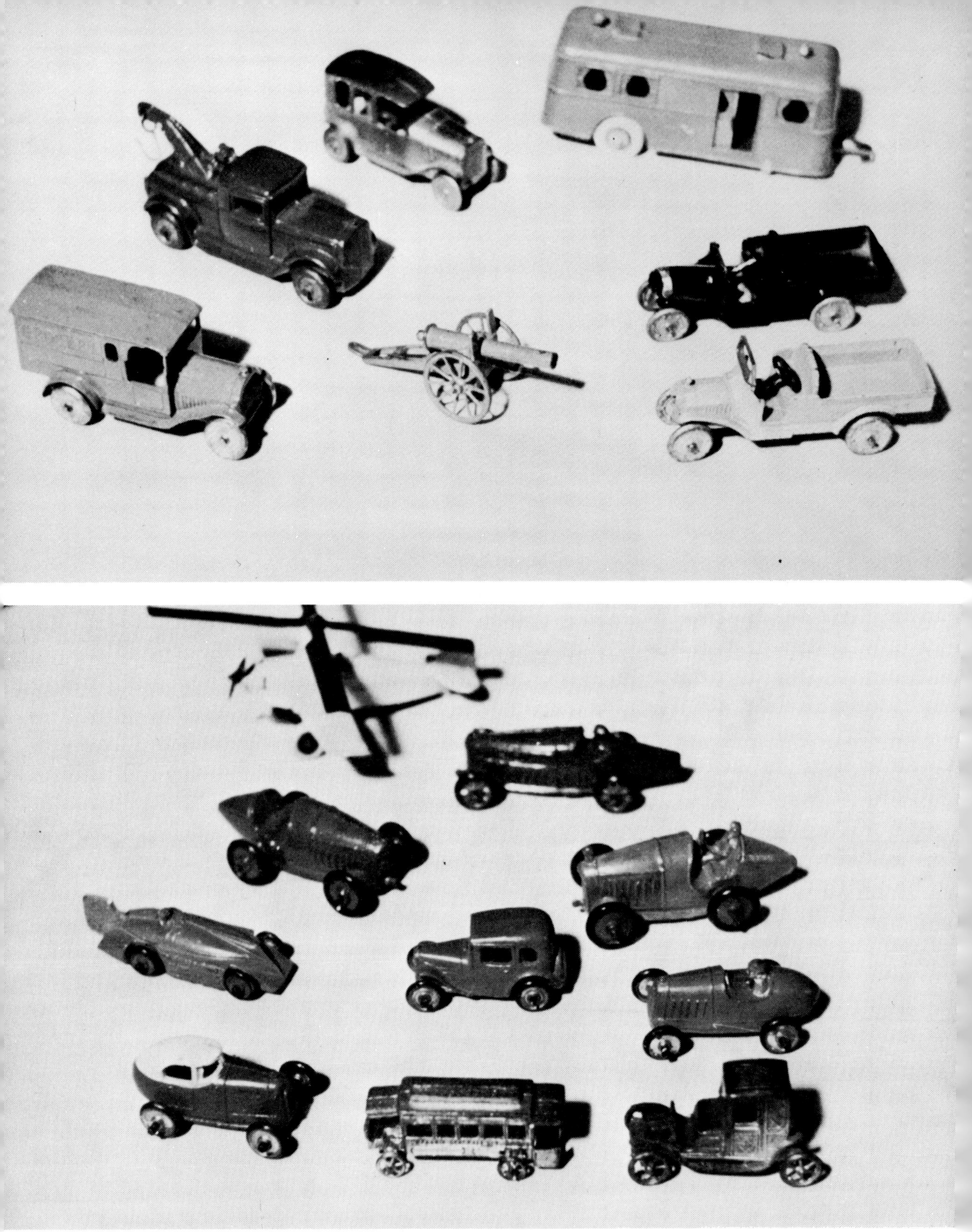

Fig. 85. Model-car collectors' delight: cast-metal miniature vehicles from the 1920's and 1930's. Several different makes are represented, including Tootsietoy, Barclay,
and Kansas Toy & Novelty, as well as three pieces manufactured in France.

William A. Hall

PART II

Collecting Model Automobiles

5

Collecting Model Automobiles

"Collecting" is a word of many usages and shadings. Many objects, including miniature automobiles, may "collect" dust—to the despair in many cases of those who must clean them or who, alternately, are the recipients of the strongest injunctions not to dare to touch them at any time and under any circumstances. There are people who meticulously "collect" string or tinfoil or empty thread spools against some possible likely or improbable future need. Virtually every human being has within him sufficient of what some regard as a commendable desire to preserve (and others look upon merely as a manifestation of the pack-rat instinct) to feel at some time or other that it is a worthy project to save something. The general appeal and hobby value of collecting such things as stamps or coins or books or ironwork or Indian arrowheads or minerals is today well recognized and accepted. Similarly, in our automotive age, it is not a matter of surprise or one requiring particular comment to find that someone pursues the hobby of collecting model automobiles. What is surprising to most is the great variety of levels and outlooks at which the miniature-automobile-collecting hobby is pursued.

It is, indeed, quite a task to attempt to classify and describe lucidly these variations of what usually appears to many at first glance to be a basically quite simple and monolithic avocation.

Many active enthusiasts of long standing are virtually unaware of the existence, much less the practices and nuances, of many popular types of model-car collecting other than their own. The man who collects on the basis of miniature replicas that are accurate and detailed models of specific prototype automobiles often is amazed to find other collectors seeking and treasuring what appears to him to be crude models bearing little resemblance to an automobile. Yet another collector will be equally aghast at the thought of collecting something merely because it is a good model and of ignoring or downgrading something that is undeniably an important part of the history of the model automobile industry simply because it is not an accurate rendition of a specific identifiable prototype. Ask the first half-dozen self-designated model-automobile collectors that you meet precisely what they collect and what standards they use, and you are very likely to receive a half a dozen totally different and often quite contradictory replies. In short, the possible and actively practiced ramifications of model-car collecting are comparatively far broader and more diverse than many other collecting hobbies. There are, of course, model-automobile collectors who do collect everything imaginable in miniature cars, and approach the subject with a completely catholic outlook.

Fig. 86. Early cast-iron pull-toy miniature automobiles, types originating in the first decade of the twentieth century, but carried over in production for some years thereafter. Left, a Dent No. 50; center, unidentified; right, Shimer No. 888.

Ward Kimball

THE DIVISIONS OF COLLECTING

There really is no way to condense even the most basic divisions of model-car collecting into a cut and dried formula. There are just too many potential overlappings. One way of simplification, however, is to set forth several sets of essentially fundamental pairings.

1. *Handwork* (whether in models built from scratch or from kits, or in the form of conversion, superdetailing, or customizing a model built from a kit or a model purchased in finished form) *versus the model obtained in completely finished form.* The latter approach may in fact also extend to the collecting of kits, preserving them, often in sealed, unopened condition, invariably in unassembled form in the original boxes. Handwork usually involves the craftsmanship of the collector himself. Some collectors do buy and preserve models built or assembled by others. Still others may buy kits, but then turn them over to someone else to assemble for them.* In the case of scarce obsolete kits, even the hobbyist who likes to build everything in his collection himself may find it necessary to obtain the desired model in already assembled form.

2. *Old car models versus models of old cars.* Sufficient already has been said concerning this obvious and basic distinction to render any further comment at this point unnecessary.

3. *The prototype automobile versus the model automobile itself* as the criterion of collectability. Or, to put this in an alternative way, the history of the real automobile and thereby of *the real automobile industry versus the history of the toy and model automobile and its industry.*

At no point in the model-automobile collecting hobby is there probably a greater and more antithetical gap between viewpoints than within this third pairing. This is not to say that an enormous number of collectors do not eventually find these two outlooks compatible. However, a great many do not—at least for some period of time—and are to varying degrees sorely troubled either by their inability to do so or by the situation itself. It must be admitted that the collector who approaches model automobiles from the standpoint of the prototype motor vehicle is usually less tolerant of the man who approaches the subject from the standpoint of the primacy of the history of the toy and model industry than is the latter in regard to understanding the outlook of his opposite number. The man who collects model automobiles from the standpoint of real automobile design and history is essentially interested only in how good a miniature rendition of a specific prototype may be a particular given model. He is not especially interested in the seemingly endless minutiæ of company histories, the lives and personal characteristics of the men involved in the design, manufacture, and merchandising of the product, details of methods of production, and all the other points that so fascinate hobbyists who are interested in toy and model-automobile history and who literally thrive on the uncovering, recording, and reading of these chronicles.

---

* A little complication arises here. Most manufacturers of kits for building model automobiles customarily supply finished models, known in the trade as "built-ups," of some or all of their line for store display use. Such models, if secured by the first type of collector in the pairing, simply represent good handwork. However, inasmuch as the assembly work was done at the factory as part of the manufacturers' production program, such built-ups also are often of considerable interest to those whose theme of collecting is based on the history of the model-automobile industry. If possible, the latter type of collector will also get the counter display sign or stand or shadowbox that usually is supplied with such built-ups, as part of said history.

DIFFERENCES OF APPROACH AND OUTLOOK

Another factor that enters into the overall picture is that the enthusiast whose interest primarily is based on real automobiles and the real automobile industry almost invariably is interested only in collecting model automobiles. Apart from even more limiting types of specialization that will be discussed later, he may well limit any considera-

Fig. 87.   The development of the real motor vehicle can be traced and illustrated by means of commercial toys as readily as by means of scale models, as demonstrated by these four Kingsbury pieces, dating from just after the turn of the century to the 1930's.

Lloyd W. Ralston; B. J. Donnelly;
Joseph N. Imler; G. William Holland

tion under this heading to passenger vehicles, thereby automatically eliminating trucks, fire engines, motorcycles, tractors, military vehicles, and other self-propelled land vehicles. However, even including these, it seldom occurs to the prototype-vehicle-oriented collector to go beyond these limits. Yet a substantial number of collectors of old model cars do collect other similar or related products in the same manufacturers' lines as the old model automobiles themselves. For example, the collector of old Tootsietoy or Dinky Toy miniature die-cast automobiles, trucks, tanks, and similar road vehicles will very often collect Tootsietoy or Dinky Toy miniature die-cast airplanes, boats, trains, and other articles. This is perhaps the most widespread expression of such extended interest. However, some enthusiasts carry this interest even further by collecting much more extensively in the overall product lines of one or a number of manufacturers of miniature automobiles. Some enthusiasts of old Tootsietoys, for instance, prize anything produced by the old Dowst Company that originated the line, including not only all sorts of small cast-metal toys, charms, and souvenirs but laundry supplies and periodicals and books dealing with the laundry industry as well. If a collector of old Dinky Toys were to pursue a similar broad-gauge pattern, it would involve a tremendous multiplicity of such things as Meccano sets, Hornby trains and accessories, and so on.

Obviously, long before any such stage as this is reached, prior in fact to even collecting nonautomotive die-cast toys made by the manufacturers of cast-metal miniature automobiles, the collector would, whether consciously or not, be involved in a species or outpost of the now far-flung, widely popular, and relatively stabilized hobby of toy collecting. As already observed in this book, far too many who like to think of themselves as engaging in a hobby involving models are somewhat foolishly and unnecessarily alarmed at references to the word "toy" and somewhat reluctant to apply it in connection with an activity of their own. The bare truth is, in essence, whatever one may at first choose to call it or how one may choose to look upon it, the great majority of model-car collectors are toy collectors. This is particularly true of those who have approached the hobby of model-automobile collecting from the viewpoint of old model cars and the industry that made them. It is possible to use the words "toy" and "model" conjointly, as if one modifies and explains the other, or as alternates; but in the hobby of model-automobile collecting, probably far more so than in any other model hobby, it is extremely difficult to separate the two terms, regardless of the fact that there are those who can and will proffer sometimes lengthy and involved explanations in an attempt to distinguish between the two. Sometimes these explanations are based on supposed physical points, sometimes on tenuous distinctions in ultimate use and in the outlook of the purchaser, collector, or user. It is in fact by no means difficult to assert a logical distinction between the same article when bought as a plaything for a youngster as a toy and when acquired by an adult for his hobby use as a model. In the end, where the history of the miniature automobile is concerned, it is impossible to escape the fact that it is simply ludicrous to attempt to establish by some form of ex post facto reasoning that the pioneer manufacturers of the articles that are so avidly collected today ever thought of themselves as anything but toymakers. In many cases the manufacturers of today still think of themselves by this time-honored title. The bridge and bond between model-automobile collecting and toy collecting is strong and enduring.

It is not without interest that it also is possible to comment on the relative prevalency of the differences in approach and outlook from various specific standpoints. While all generalities can, of course, at times be questioned and· disputed if desired, and there always may be exceptions—very often minor exceptions that merely serve to confirm the accuracy of the overall generalities—it would appear that the following comments more or less may be taken as in the main holding true, proportionately at least, if not in terms of pure raw figures:

Those who already are more or less developed automobile enthusiasts (as distinguished from those whose automotive interest is confined to the maintenance and use of a family car—sports-car enthusiasts, admirers and students of old automobiles, collectors of automobile books, catalogs, insignia, and other automotive memorabilia, and so forth) almost invariably approach the model automobile from the standpoint of real car usage and history, not that of old model cars and their history as such. Similarly, younger enthusiasts almost always come into the hobby with the same outlook. In fact, it usually is the younger

Fig. 88. Six more Kingsbury models. Kingsbury's paralleling of the development of the automobile, as indicated by this group of specimens from the era of World War I to the late 1930's, as well as the preceding figure, made them the preeminent manufacturer of clockwork toy automobiles.

William H. Gottschalk; G. William Holland photographs

hobbyist who understandably is most adamant in trying to find and hold to a distinction between models and toys and who most ardently insists that his is a model-, not a toy-, collecting hobby. These outlooks can and often do change later, although in many cases they do not. However, it is not at all uncommon for a hobbyist whose interest at first was confined simply to interest in model cars as related to the design and history of real automobiles gradually to fall under the spell of the old model car and history of the toy and model outlook. On the other hand, a greater proportion of adult enthusiasts are inclined to approach the hobby with more of a primary interest in the history of the miniature car than of the real one. Enthusiasts who already are collectors of other kinds of toys and models, such as toy trains, naturally enough usually enter the model-car hobby with an outlook almost totally oriented toward interest in the history of the miniature car as such.

There also is a rather interesting most definite geographic or national relationship of proportionate interest in the outlook on model-car collecting from the standpoint of the real automobile and its history as contrasted with the viewpoint of the history of the toy and model car. Every indication proclaims that the latter outlook is far more widespread and zealous in the United States and Canada than in Great Britain and Ireland, or anywhere else in the world. This concept and interest might almost be said to amount to a mania in America. As one such hobbyist put it, American model-car collectors will hardly be satisfied in their research until they ascertain what food the Dowst brothers most enjoyed at dinner! * Yet this is all relative, of course.

* This is really a replay, modified to suit the occasion, for the long-popular saying among toy and train collectors that their desire for details is so great that they would like to know what Mr. Ives liked for dinner.

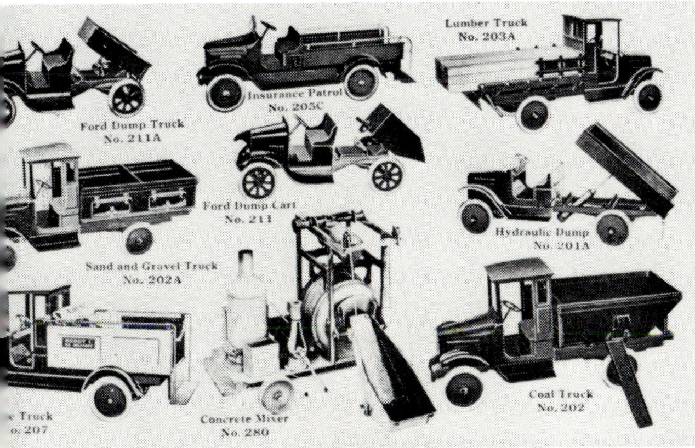

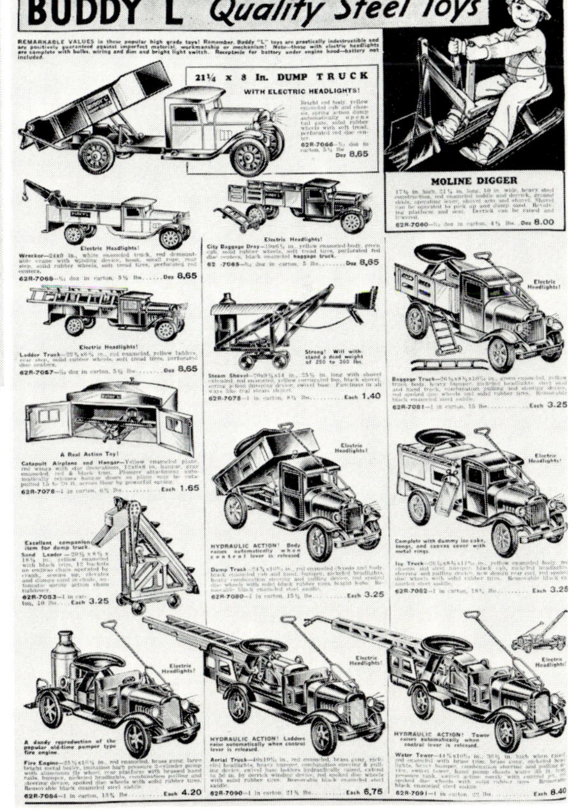

Fig. 89. The steel truck in all its glory and variations commands a very substantial amount of enthusiasm among collectors. Pictured here are catalog offerings of groups of Buddy "L" vehicles from the late 1920's and mid-1930's, respectively, as well as photographs of Corcoran (*G. William Holland Photograph*) and Structo trucks (*William A. Hall*).

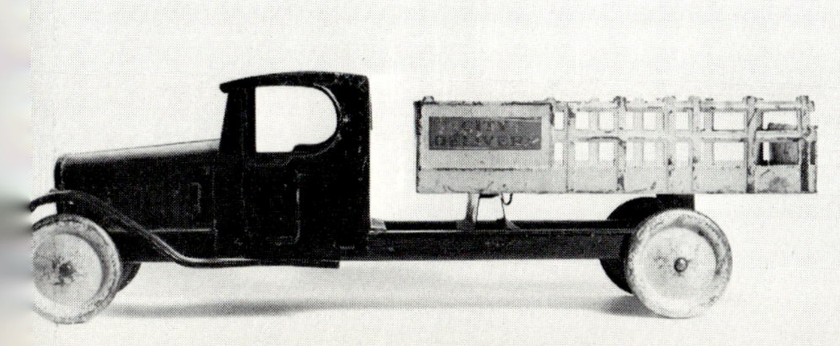

Fig. 90. Two all-time classics in the best sense of that often-abused term, both clockwork-powered: The Brown model of the Lee & Larned self-propelled fire engine, the first working-model automobile ever manufactured, produced from the late 1850's to the early 1870's (the front wheels on this specimen are replacements), and the turn-of-the-century Converse Hansom cab.

G. William Holland Collection
Leon Perelman; G. William Holland photograph

In Great Britain and Ireland there also is a very considerable and ardent enthusiasm for this outlook, yet proportionate to the overall spectrum of model-automobile collecting, it is noticeably less than in America. Yet as the investigator looks even farther eastward, to the European Continent itself, although there are some notable exceptions, it becomes evident that there is an almost inordinate diminution of this outlook, despite the fact that the concerted hobby of model-automobile collecting is enormously popular on the Continent.

One hesitates to speculate and attempt to draw conclusions as to the reasons for this geographic gradation that undeniably exists. It should be noted that to all intents and purposes the identical geographic situation obtains in regard to all forms and interests of toy and model collecting. One possible contributing reason that frequently is advanced is that for over thirty years now, Americans have been exposed to a considerable body of literature dealing with the history of models and toys and their manufacturers in general—and most especially relating to trains—and that when they started in great numbers to approach the specific collecting of model automobiles as such, it naturally followed that to a large extent they did so along the lines more or less widely and regularly established—lines that, it must be added, they generally tend to regard as by far the most sophisticated and mature approach to such hobbies.

However, it must be admitted that many Americans obviously are puzzled and not a little disturbed by this sequential diminution of acceptance of this outlook as one moves eastward, particularly inasmuch as model-car collecting as a really widespread hobby generally is regarded as having originated more in Great Britain and France than in the United States, and Americans have to a large extent accepted the, quite strange to them, European concept of collecting something as it is currently manufactured. Perhaps the disconcertion of Americans at the lesser appeal —at least so far—in Europe for what they feel certain is the more scientific and assured outlook is that they have so often been advised by Europeans that they are brash and young that it seems difficult for many of them to accept the fact that they have developed a somewhat more sophisticated approach, particularly vis-à-vis France, which to an American is traditionally the land of sophistication in wine, women, and automobiles.

COLLECTING CURRENT MODELS

Collecting something of *contemporary* manufacture has indeed been a rather strange idea to American hobbyists. It is true that the concept of currently manufactured small cast-metal model automobiles as being something suitable for collecting is not a new idea. As early as 1935 the Meccano catalogs listing Dinky Toys used the

Fig. 91.   Three interesting cast-iron models of the period between world wars I and II: a Kenton touring car, and, of the 1930's, a Hubley Bell telephone truck and an Arcade fire engine. The latter is extremely interesting as a model of a then-modern internal-combustion engine-powered pumper but still retaining the long-traditional boiler as a selling feature of the toy.

G. William Holland photographs

phrase "A charming collecting hobby" in a prominent position. At the time, this was regarded as rather grotesque and laughable. Indeed, the idea of collecting what generally was regarded as "a five-and-ten-cent-store toy" at the time they were being manufactured was looked upon as ludicrous. With the possible exception of new issues of coins or postage stamps, collecting hobbies were devoted to things that were old, obsolete, or difficult to obtain, not something that one could buy cheaply at any time a person wanted it. For the most part, when something was in current production it had no collectors' value, only an intrinsic value as a product for use. After it went out of manufacture, relatively few people had interest in acquiring it, and its value dropped sharply, perhaps to virtually nothing. Then, after a period of time the article might gradually take on some collectors' interest, and specimens might slowly acquire a correspondingly increasing value. It would, however, take a long, long time for this collectors' value ever to start to approach the original retail cost. In fact, it seemed extremely improbable in the 1930's that the majority of obsolete toys ever would attain a collectors' value equal to (much less surpassing) the original price.

Certainly it seemed highly unlikely that a most inexpensive miniature automobile currently being turned out in immense quantities would. The suggestion that a Tootsietoy or a Dinky Toy automobile might ever attain a collectors' value many times that of the original cost would have been regarded as sheer lunacy.

Then came a radical change. Soon after World War II, especially in Great Britain, substantial numbers of individuals started to purchase currently available miniature automobiles for collections. Many were not merely buying selected specimens representing particular cars of which they desired models, but actually were attempting to buy every model, and often every variation, of a specific line or lines of miniature cast-metal automobiles. To American hobbyists this appeared at first quite a reversal of accepted and well-established collecting principles, and most tended to look upon the matter as somewhat absurd, and in fact a throwback to the attempts to stimulate sales on this basis in the 1930's. But it was impossible either to disregard or attempt to curb this new phenomenon. To give further impetus to this movement, in many cases the manufacturers themselves were encouraging the scientific and purposeful collecting of a toy product—in this case miniature automobiles—on a serious and historical basis relating not only to the history of the prototype automobile but to the history of the model automobile and the toy and model industry. When this became apparent, even the most rigid old-line die-hard and upholder of the ancient principle that one does not collect current manufactured goods simply had to capitulate, and capitulate not only with good grace but with enthusiasm.

To understand how moving and revolutionary was the new outlook adopted by a number of manufacturers (not by any means necessarily all, but in the main those who were the largest and those who were the longest established) one really has to be old enough or experienced enough in other toy- and model-collecting hobbies to recall the traditional outlook of the other manufacturers. This attitude usually was, first, to ignore the situation in the belief that if this were done this absurdity would simply go away. When this failed, then the proper outlook was to cooperate as little as possible and, in fact, in some cases actually to try to discourage it. The reasoning usually involved a belief that (1) such collectors probably were crazy or, even worse, that anyone seeking information might well be a spy for a competitor; (2) that every dollar spent by a collector for old specimens was a dollar that he did not spend with the manufacturer through his retailers for current goods, and (3), regardless of the other two, it cost a great deal in unproductive effort and expense to answer the numerous letters from hobbyists that often sought extremely detailed information on extremely obscure points. Furthermore, rightly or wrongly, there was long a widely held belief, among certain collectors at least, that in certain instances manufacturers discouraged collecting because they covertly felt that comparisons between current goods and those made ten, twenty, or even more years earlier would tend to be rather disconcertingly favorable to the obsolete models in terms of design, quality of materials, workmanship, and value for a given price.

Be all this as it may, although this generally negative outlook to model collecting still obtains among some toy manufacturers, it has almost entirely vanished in the area of model automobiles, and the exact reverse is true. While still understandably for the most part not desiring to get involved in a great deal of detailed correspondence concerning the fine points of old models, most of the established manufacturers are aware that interest in and the collecting of their old models and the study of their historic past is of considerable current promotional and publicity value. This is precisely what so many collectors tried without much success to impress upon a number of manufacturers of other types of models in the 1930's, 1940's, and 1950's. Many recent entrants in the field of miniature-automobile manufacturer also are to a considerable extent aware of the value of encouraging the collecting not only of their current but also of their obsolete numbers.

True, the hobbyist who primarily is interested in the model automobile as a reflection of the

Fig. 92. Four more cast-iron models of beauty and desirability, these dating from the 1920's and 1930's: two Kenton Royal Circus trucks, a Vindex coupe, a 12-inch-long Hubley touring car, and a Hubley replica of an Ahrens-Fox fire engine.
Adam Pellicot, Jr.; William Dreyer photographs

real automobile and its history buys and collects somewhat selectively from this viewpoint. But there now is a tremendous amount of collecting of current or just recently discontinued models by both older hobbyists and extremely young ones on the basis of attempting to secure all the models, past and present, in a given series or of a given make or of a number of makes, which is to a considerable extent the result of many manufacturers' encouragement of serious model-car collecting. This in practical effect works out to mean collecting from the standpoint of the model car and of the model-car industry. In one notable instance a modern manufacturer actually lists not only his earlier models but their known variations in the bulletin published for his model-car-collectors' club. It is true that this helps to move what might otherwise be stale merchandise off dealers' shelves, and also

implies that it would be very wise to purchase each of their current models, but it still is a phenomenon that rather staggers the old-time collector while enlisting his support and goodwill. Another manufacturer has published articles describing and illustrating their older and comparatively long-obsolete miniature cars in their general model and hobby magazine. Such things would have been absolutely unheard of only a relatively short time ago.

THE LIMITS AND BOUNDS OF COLLECTING

This is now the place to delve more specifically into some of the popular forms and patterns of collecting. Any really clear-cut analysis is made extremely difficult by all the possible cross-hatch-

Fig. 93.   In the grand tradition. The steam fire engine was always a popular seller, as suggested by the vestigial boiler seen in the engine in Fig. 91. Pictured here are Hubley cast-iron models of the World War I era (*Ward Kimball*) and the mid-1930's (*G. William Holland photograph*), and a Schieble friction model (*Lloyd W. Ralston*).

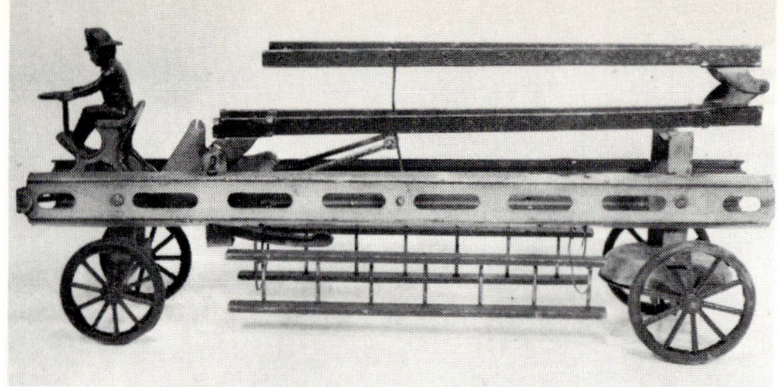

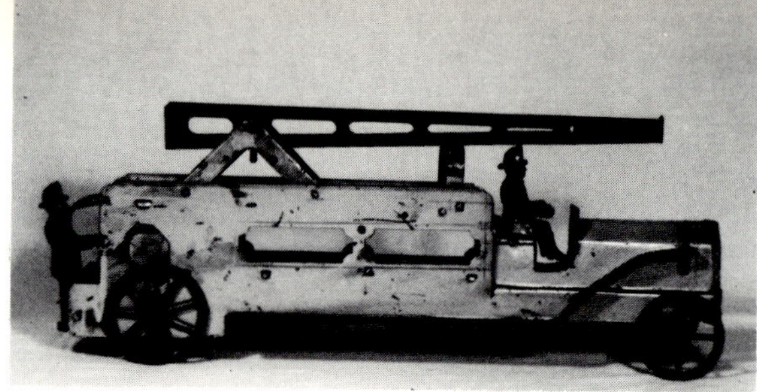

Fig. 94. Three more fire engines: a more or less standardized clockwork-powered design manufactured by Wilkins and their successor, Kingsbury, and two Dayton Friction models, a ladder truck and water tower, both friction-powered (*Lloyd W. Ralston*). Compare the Dayton trucks with that in Fig. 5.

ing of collecting practices. In short, the hobbyist may collect any type of model or combination of models he desires. He may collect everything ever made in the form of a toy or model automobile and related vehicle. This would undoubtedly involve a potential field of some tens of thousands of different models; the likelihood of obtaining more than a mere representation of many types and categories would, financial considerations aside, be very slim indeed. Although many collectors gladly accept anything that happens to come their way in the model-automobile line, the majority of model-car collectors limit their endeavors to more restricted fields.

Even within a more limited field the potential is enormous and beyond the practical scope of most hobbyists. There are, however, some collectors who have assembled collections numbering in the thousands of different models. To give some idea of the possible range of the field, it might be mentioned that a recent French catalog of model cars lists approximately 4,000 of what might be termed small models—mostly approximating 1/4-inch scale, 1/48th size—manufactured in completed form in various countries between World War I and 1967. This list does not include many of the early European models or the bulk of the models made in the United States. The latter alone would add substantially to the total. Not even taking into consideration that many additional models are being added continually, such a list could easily be expanded to over 5,000 models of this general type. The same catalog also lists, apparently somewhat more completely, about 3,000 models manufactured in kit form since World War II. Either of these totals appears rather forboding to the average active or would-be hobbyist. The only practical answer is some self-imposed form of limitation or specialization.

Such limitations may take the form of specializing according to countries (either of the origin of the prototype cars or of the actual manufacture of the models), car types, the materials of which the models are fabricated, range of scales or general sizes of the models, types of power or the total lack of power in the models, period (again, either of the prototypes or of the actual models), and makes (here, again, either prototype makes or the makes of the miniatures themselves). A hobbyist might collect only models of cars whose prototypes were made in the United States or Great Britain, for example. Or he might collect only those made in the United States, regardless of the countries from which the prototypes originate. He might collect every type of automotive vehicle imaginable —passenger cars, trucks, service vehicles, military vehicles, farm vehicles, and so on. On the other hand, a collector may well limit himself to styles of passenger cars or commercial vehicles, or even more rigidly, say, to sports cars or fire engines or perhaps limousines. Or he might collect models made of any materials, or confine himself to die-cast or cast-iron or plastic or stamped-metal models.

As far as types of power or the lack of power is concerned, a large proportion of the model automobiles of the types now widely collected were made as nonpowered models. On the other hand, particularly when ranging into some of the larger specimens, a collector might limit himself to clockwork-powered models or friction-powered models or electrically powered models. As to make, this could be to a specific make or a few preferred makes, or it could be to a family or families of cars such as General Motors or Chrysler cars. Make can even be reduced to terms of a specific model or models, such as only miniatures of the Ford Model T or Ford Model A. A collector who set out to

Fig. 95. The fire engine in cast-metal miniatures as made in three countries: six Tootsietoys of the 1920's and 1930's (*William A. Hall*); two Hill (British) engines of the 1930's—one full dimensional (left) and one a "flat"—and five German models tentatively ascribed to Ernst Plank (*Dr. Clinton B. Seeley*).

secure every model ever manufactured of the Ford Model T, regardless of size or materials or other limiting factors, for example, would have a far more extensive and difficult task than most hobbyists would imagine possible upon first contemplating the idea. To collect all Fords would, of course, be an even more difficult task. In connection with collecting by prototype make, there is a widespread tendency among model-car collectors to concentrate unduly on certain of the makes generally regarded as among the finer or most outstanding—not necessarily the most expensive—such as Bentley, Cord, Duesenberg, Packard, Pierce-Arrow, Rolls-Royce, Studebaker, and the like.

Except for the individuals who build the models in their collections from scratch, the choice of what prototype cars can readily be collected by make naturally is limited by what models were or are being manufactured. Although the collector who is involved in collecting from the standpoint of the history of the toy and model-automobile industry is not usually concerned with prototypes except as a sort of secondary or complementary matter of identification or interest, it is worth pointing out that a great many more prototype makes have been reproduced in model form at one time or another than generally is realized. As far as is known, no one has yet attempted to compute the total number of prototype makes that have been recognizably reproduced in manufactured miniature automobiles. It must certainly run into many hundreds. There is, however, a pitfall inherent in collecting by prototype make, especially when the hobbyist is involved in older models. This is that an overenthusiastic collector will at times read a specific prototype identification into a miniature when it did not exist at the time the model was designed and manufactured. Many early models were free-lance or composite designs, and it is all too easy for a hobbyist who is collecting a certain prototype make to look at a miniature, see some resemblance in the hood or fenders or trunk or some other feature to the make in question and eagerly accept the model as representing the wished-for make. There also are miniature cars that bore specific real automobile names but had no resemblance whatsoever to any actual car ever made under that name. The little die-cast racer pictured in Fig. 107 has the identifying name "Buick" cast in, for example. However, it bears not the faintest resemblance to any real Buick that ever existed. This particular tiny model is, in fact, a game marker (playing piece), and the identical casting was made bearing the names of other makes of cars. Nevertheless, a collector specializing in model Buicks might accept this particular model, even though the same model but with other names cast in would be equally appealing to collectors specializing in at least three other prototype makes.

COLLECTING BY MAKE OF MODELS

An equally valid but far less obvious instance of this sort of thing can be found in the Tootsietoy Raceway outfits No. 5081, with cars with all-metal wheels and tires made in 1932 (Fig. 108), and the otherwise identical set except for the cars having rubber tires, No. 05081, manufactured in 1933, 1935, and 1936. Each set contained eight identical racing cars differing only in color (white, red, yellow, gold, lavender, silver, green, and orange) and in an individual racing number cast into the tailfin of each car. These numbers were keyed to an identification chart (also containing the name of a noted real racing driver imagined for each car) on the accompanying cardboard racecourse, and the individual packing compartments in the

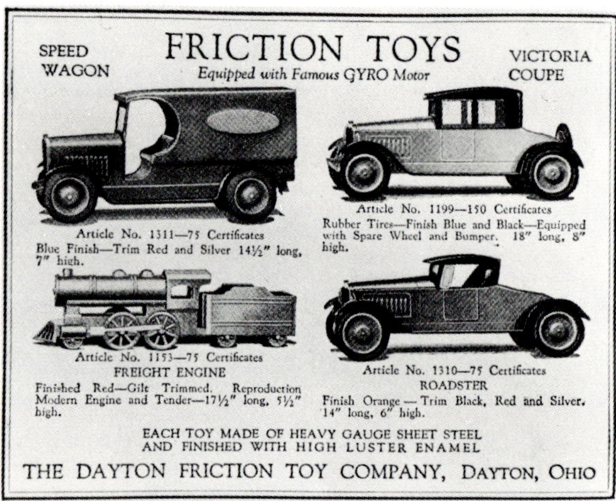

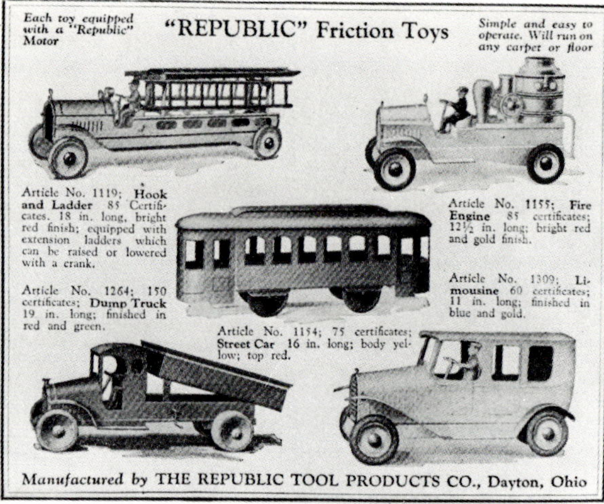

Fig. 96. The friction toy automobile in its last years of measurable popularity. These are advertisements of Dayton Friction and Republic vehicles from a 1926 catalog of premiums offered for United Cigar Store certificates (*Americana Archives*). The photograph shows a simple 7-inch Turner roadster. (*Ward Kimball*).

box also provide the tie-in data between numbers and makes. The eight cars were designated as follows: (1) Stutz Bearcat; (2) Duesenberg Special; (3) Marmon Special; (4) Packard Special; (5) Blitzen Benz; (6) Studebaker Champion; (7) Peugot (*sic*) Special, and (8) National. The present-day collector specializing in Duesenbergs, for instance, would thus insist on a specimen bearing the No. 2; a Packard specialist would require No. 4; a Studebaker specialist would find only No. 6 acceptable, and so on. The cars also were sold separately, but—given the usual exigencies of day-to-day factory usage—by no means necessarily without racing numbers cast into the tailfins. The first version with metal wheels and tires was No. 4666, and the rubber-tired model was No. 04666 from 1933 to 1936. In 1937, all Tootsietoy automobiles by then having rubber wheels or tires, the number of the separate racing car was dropped back to 4666, and remained in the line until World War II.

The hobbyist who collects from the standpoint of the real automobile would want only such of the numbered cars as might correspond to his specialized prototype or prototypes, although he might desire specimens with both types of wheels, and would have little use for the box or racecourse. The Tootsietoy collector, on the other hand, would not only regard the box and racecourse a real treasure, but would want one of each racing car bearing a number in both wheel styles, as well as specimens of the unnumbered cars. Furthermore, he would want all possible color variations that might exist within the set versions—and there is no way of knowing, barring actual specimens turning up, whether only the eight specified colors were used on the numbered cars and if the same color invariably was applied to the same number throughout the production run of the raceway outfit. The No. 4666 with metal wheels and tires is known to exist in red, blue, green, and yellow as sold separately, and the No. 04666 in red, white, green, and yellow. The avid Tootsietoy collector would, of course, want them all. Furthermore, it is not as yet known whether there is any sure and certain way of distinguishing a rubber-tired No. 4666 from a No. 04666. If such a means of distinguishing can be ascertained, Tootsietoy collectors would want complete color sets (probably but not necessarily four each) of the No. 04666 and the rubber-tired No. 4666. Seemingly the only effective clue that can be provided on this point up to the present time is that a No. 04666 or a rubber-tired No. 4666 could be red, white, green, or yellow, but that a rubber-tired racer of this model *without tailfin number* and painted silver definitely would be a rubber-tired No. 4666. There still is considerable question as to whether the change in number from 04666 back to 4666 again exactly coincides with a change from the die-cast metal wheel or hub with a separate rubber tire to the one-piece molded rubber combination wheel and tire, or not. Should this prove the case, the change in wheel would provide a sure means of distinguishing between the two numbers, but it seems improbable that this theory can be confirmed.

At any rate, the above actually touches on many bases in providing a thumbnail sketch involving many of the outlooks and points of which important notice is taken by collectors who approach the hobby from the standpoint of toy and model-automobile history. Many of them will be referred to again later in this chapter. The point is that the collector who is collecting according to the make of the miniatures themselves is completely and deeply committed to this outlook. Collecting by makes may involve one or two or a great number of makes. Tootsietoy undoubtedly is the most important and popular of makes of miniature cast-metal cars among collectors in the United States. Even in Great Britain where interest in the native Dinky Toys understandably probably ranks supreme, Tootsietoy runs a close second, at least among hobbyists who primarily are interested, not in models of old cars, but precisely and particularly

in old model cars. Naturally, among the great body of collectors with this viewpoint, the potential interest must be among the products of companies that were operating in this field a reasonable length of time ago. The usual line of demarcation is World War II.

Many collectors who have approached the hobby in terms of the history of the toy and model automobile have shown preference in their choices to products that could definitely or at least with some likelihood be identified as to make. Speaking here only of the miniature cast-metal cars, this has served further to make old Tootsietoys, Dinky Toys, Barclay, Erie, and Manoil the makes most usually thought of by potentially specializing collectors. The lines of the first three were very extensive and have survived and remained active in the miniature-automobile field down to the present day. Erie and Manoil actually made rather short lines of cars; nevertheless, most of their products were marked and readily identifiable.* Hence they

---

* Hubley also made die-cast models marked with their name for a few years prior to World War II, and of course again since the war, but for reasons that are not wholly clear Hubley never seems to have attracted much of a following as a specialty make among collectors of die-cast models made before the war. The main reason, however, probably is that so many hobbyists were collecting and to some extent specializing in their prewar cast-iron models that for some time their name was thought of mainly in this connection.

Fig. 97.   On occasion contemporary comic strips found a reflection in model automobiles as in the case of these miniatures. The models pictured are the six styles of the Tootsietoy "Funnies" of the early 1930's with, center rear, the regular No. 0807 delivery motorcycle manufactured only in 1933, which derived from the Smitty and Herbie motorcycle shown in front of it. For Andy Gump in his car, see Fig. 219.

Adam Pellicot, Jr.; William Dreyer photograph

Fig. 98. The drawing shows a Plank model automobile of about 1904, with the body forming a box for postage stamps. The clockwork-powered propeller-driven Aero-Mobile was a novelty of the early 1920's. Not by any means as unusual is the glass candy container in the shape of an automobile made by Victory in the early 1940's, for such containers in varying automotive forms had long been popular.

G. William Holland photographs

commended themselves to hobbyists who like to have all the answers at once with everything rather easy and cut and dried. By coincidence, all the Eries and many of the Manoils, like all the Tootsietoys and Dinky Toys and most of the later Barclays, were die-cast (pressure die-cast in British terminology). Actually, there were many other makes of miniature cast-metal cars prior to World War II, a fact that was known or at least suspected by a number of thoughtful and alert hobbyists, although the great extent of these operations was hardly known or appreciated. In regard to American slush-cast models, British collectors for the most part generally simply begged the issue by referring to everything of this type as "Barclays." The majority of American collectors were somewhat more discriminating, and, although they may have suspected the likely existence of only a handful of other makes, realized that by no means everything that turned up in slush-cast models could be Barclay. This meant that there were a great many models about that were unidentifiable and for this

reason rather looked down upon and scorned by many collectors with somewhat limited outlook. Now that they can be identified as to make, a number of other makes undoubtedly will move into the preferred or highly desirable category.

Yet it must also be observed that, on the other hand, there has always been a substantial body of collectors who were most fascinated by the variety and collecting potential of the unidentified models and who specialized in collecting by make in a reverse sort of way by limiting themselves to, or at least favoring, the specimens that could not be identified as to make!

SIZES, MATERIALS, AND PERIODS

As already emphasized earlier in this book, there is no such thing as any standard accepted collectors' size, in spite of all efforts to promote such a thing. The very idea is in itself a contradiction in terms, particularly when collecting by make of model rather than make of prototype and of col-

Fig. 99. Wooden model automobiles of the 1930's: a German miniature of a lumber truck, one of a series that frequently is predated (*G. William Holland photograph*); three American trucks (*Adam Pellicot, Jr.; William Dreyer photograph*), and a group of American vehicles from 1940.

lecting really old models are concerned. Notwithstanding, there is something to be said on the part of the collector whose interest is prototype-oriented for a collection of models all built to the same scale, if only to make comparisons between one design and another easier. However, there are so many other things that would enter the picture, such as the caliber of the models, including the actual fidelity to the specific proclaimed scale, and the amount of detailing, that the benefits would still fall far short of the effect desired. Overall, however, custom and sheer weight of numbers do have their inevitable effect. A great number of miniature automobiles are presently being manufactured and have for decades past been manufactured to exact or approximate scales in 1/4-inch scale, 1/48th size; 7-mm. scale, 1/43rd size; and 7.2-mm. scale, 1/42nd size. Today one or another of these scales is used for a substantial proportion of the model automobiles whose promotion is, in part at least, directly directed to the collectors' market. As a result, a great many collectors limit their collections to 1/4-inch to 7.2-mm. scale models, or, not infrequently, to one of the three specific scales within this range. Given their choice, most Americans, if forced to select one favorite among the three undoubtedly would prefer to see the dominance of the 1/4-inch scale. However, they realize that so great a proportion of the models in this general size range come from European countries where the metric scales prevail that this outlook is, from a practical standpoint, rather fruitless. In actual collecting usage the choice usually comes to settling on the 7-mm. or 7.2-mm. scales or both, and then determining whether or not to admit also 1/4-inch-scale models to the collection.

Similarly, the prevalence of plastic kits for building .48-inch scale, 1/25-size, and 1/2-inch scale, 1/24th-size models has served to create another more or less accepted size range for collectors' models when approached from the standpoint of the prototype automobile.

It should not, however, be assumed that all whose collections reflect this viewpoint select

and adhere to one or more particular scales, any more than they may adhere to limitations on materials or time periods. Many who collect by make of prototype automatically take in anything reflecting their chosen make or makes, from tiny castings of the type represented by the Buick in Fig. 107 to juvenile automobiles—cars large enough for children actually to ride in that were propelled by pedal power or other means.

When model-automobile collecting is approached from the standpoint of the make of the models themselves, considerations of size to some extent may still be present, but in most instances as a means of classification into series. In the realm of the miniature cast-metal models there are several commonly used designations of size, of which the great point of demarcation is again the word "standard." Curiously, here too, although in this context the word has a more definite and widely agreed upon meaning, the cars referred to by this designation approximate in size the 1/4-inch, 7-mm., and 7.2-mm.-scale models to which the word is applied by collectors with a different outlook. However, scale as such is of relatively little concern to collectors by makes of model cars, par-

ticularly as to old model cars, manufacturers being in most cases quite variable and unconcerned with whether models were built to the exact same scale as their series mates. They were, in fact, mainly interested in producing models of a certain general size that could be sold for a uniform price. Hence the expressions used to designate these sizes in a general way by collectors have for the most part the same meaning today, even if the words are not always identical (as in some cases they are), as they did in the historic past when the models themselves actually were being made.

In this context and usage—bearing in mind the subject at hand is that of the overall miniature cast-metal models—"standard" size means a model of the size that in the 1920's and 1930's could satisfactorily be retailed for ten cents. By and large this means a model of a passenger car or truck measuring from about 3 to 4 1/2 inches in length. "Small" size models were five-cent sellers, measuring less than 2 3/4 or perhaps 3 inches in length. "Large" size, or "jumbo," models usually ran 5 1/2 inches or more in length; they did not appear until the mid-1930's, and many also were at that time ten-cent sellers. "Midgets" are very

Fig. 100. Initially very inexpensive, many of the Lehmann clockwork lithographed sheet-metal cars are still fairly readily obtainable, but their cheap construction, frequently undignified outlook, and other factors militate against their popularity in the eyes of a great many hobbyists.

G. William Holland Collection

small models, almost invariably with the wheels cast integral and nonturnable, of the type pictured in Figs. 107 and 212, although some midgets ran up to almost 2 inches in length. Not all models with integrally cast wheels are considered midgets; the Cosmo No. 1703 (Fig. 111), for instance, is customarily considered a small-size model, having been copied from a five-cent Dowst limousine, although the Cosmo version retailed for substantially less. "Flats" are two-dimensional models with integral wheels of the charm and souvenir type. They actually do have a third dimension, but the models are obviously not full-bodied replicas with a width by any means proportionate to their length and height. The terms "midget" and "jumbo" come directly from Tootsietoy usage in the 1930's, and "flats" has come into the language of model-car collectors directly from military miniature terminology.

Although scale may to some extent roughly enter into this picture, the major factors obviously are price (as of the 1920's and 1930's, for today virtually all models of comparative sizes sell for respectively higher prices) and proportion. A standard-size (that is, ten-cent) steamroller may be built to a much smaller scale than a standard-size sedan, or a standard-size parcel delivery motorcycle (both shown in Fig. 112) may be built to a much larger scale than a standard-size sedan. Collectors soon become accustomed to having only to glance at a given model and being able to determine if it should be classed as a small, standard, or large-size item. Bear in mind that price and the general lengths refer to ordinary passenger cars or trucks (the latter almost always are built to a somewhat smaller scale than size-related pleasure cars). Standard-size trailer trucks, for instance, often are much longer than the corresponding-size passenger cars or regular trucks, or longer than the sizes indicated for large or jumbo models and may originally have been twenty-five-cent sellers. However, their general proportions immediately proclaim them as belonging to the standard-size models. Similarly, small-size trailer trucks may be as long as standard-size passenger cars, and originally have retailed for more than five cents. Again, their proportions immediately indicate that they are to be regarded as small size or, if the collector prefers the term, "small series," items. An interesting point to be borne in mind in such considera-

Fig. 101. Seven more Lehmann vehicles. Note the difference in name between "OHO" in the preceding figure and "ALSO" in this one, as well as the differences in the limousines. This and the preceding figure illustrate both run-of-the-mill Lehmanns and some comparatively desirable models.

C. W. Frey

tions is that in the case of automobile transport trailer trucks, standard-size trucks customarily carried small-size automobiles as their cargoes, and the small-size cars might well also be sold separately as five-cent toys.*

It may safely be assumed that in the somewhat instinctive division of cars into sizes or series, British collectors are as adept concerning their own products as are Americans regarding theirs. To relate the remarks concerning five-cent and ten-cent sellers to British pricing in the 1920's and 1930's, it should be recalled that in this period the rate of exchange was such that a British penny was worth two American pennies. That is, ten cents

in the United States was equivalent to fivepence.† Generally speaking, the British-made miniature cast-model automobiles and trucks (the latter known in Great Britain variously as lorries, vans, wagons—or, on occasion, trucks) were a little more expensive in Great Britain itself in the 1930's than their American counterparts were in the United States at the time. Prices of sixpence to ninepence were not uncommon for vehicles comparable to American ten-cent sellers. When the American automobiles and trucks were exported to Great Britain, the shipping costs and duties worked out to make the retail prices in Great Britain just about the same as for the British-made models. This was by no means the usual case with American toys exported at the time that customarily had to sell in Great Britain for noticeably higher prices than their British counterparts. American enthusiasts will no doubt choose to interpret the higher prices on British miniature cast-metal automobiles as evidence of superior production methods in the

---

* For example, the Tootsietoy small-sized Buick coupe No. 101, and sedan No. 103 that were carried on the three- and four-car Mack auto transport trucks 1932–1935. Actually, the small Buicks appeared in 1931 and were sold, with cardboard garages, as ten-cent toys (and again in 1932). It was not until 1932 that these cars were sold without garages, as part of an expanded series of five-cent toys, or used on the auto transport trucks. The chronology of the latter is as follows: No. 190 three-car transport (two sedans and a coupe), 1932–1933; No. 0190 three-car transport with rubber tires (on the tractor and semitrailer but not on the cargo), 1933; No. 190X four-car transport (two sedans and two coupes), 1933; No. 0190X, same but with rubber tires on the tractor and semitrailer, 1934–1935. Other auto transport trucks from 1935 on were assigned new numbers, had new and larger Mack tractors, and carried rubber-tired small-size Fords as cargo.

---

† For American enthusiasts who enjoy leafing through and studying old or current British catalogs (although in most cases the editions of the latter that most Americans are likely to see today have prices in dollars and cents), it should be noted that the symbol for the British penny is d.—6d. is sixpence. There are twelve British pennies to a shilling (s.) and a figure such as two shillings, sixpence is expressed as 2/6.

Fig. 102. Several somewhat more interesting and desirable German lithographed automobiles are illustrated here, all clockwork-powered except the Hess friction-driven "Flirt." The others are a Gunthermann model given as a Christmas gift in 1904; an inexpensive Guntka one-seater, and a Tipp delivery truck especialy lithographed for a Philadelphia department store.
G. William Holland Collection

United States; their British counterparts will unquestionably hold with equal fervor that this price situation proves that the British productions were of superior quality.

VARIATIONS IN NOMENCLATURE

It is proper at this point to comment regarding some common variations in nomenclature that may puzzle enthusiasts on both sides of the Atlantic who supposedly speak the same language. Most Americans who have given the matter any thought are under the impression that what is called a "truck" in the United States invariably is known as a "lorry" in Great Britain, and that "truck" or "van" is employed there only in reference to types of railroad cars. This is not the case. This American belief in the ubiquity of the name "lorry" for all types of British motor trucks probably stems from hearing the term used repeatedly in France in World War I and in subsequent motion pictures wherein British troops invariably refer to their vehicles as "lorries." In connection with this terminology, it is curious to note that while Americans

always speak of a coal truck, dump truck, ice truck, stake truck, tank truck, delivery truck, and so on, they invariably say "moving van," sometimes "delivery van." In the United States "truck" may also refer to the undercarriage of a railroad car, whether fixed or swivel (but never to the entire car itself), or to the leading or trailing wheels of a locomotive. Also, in the United States the word "tractor" may refer to a two-wheel power unit substituted for the front wheels of a formerly horse-drawn vehicle to convert it to self-propulsion, the conventional farm tractor, or the power unit that hauls trailers or semitrailers. In Great Britain the farm tractor is similarly a tractor, but the power unit for trailers is known as a "mechanical horse," and presumably the same designation applied to conversion units for horse-drawn vehicles. There is in fact a considerable difference of opinion in the United States itself regarding the proper nomenclature for trailer and semitrailer trucks. Many do not distinguish between the two, and call all such units "trailers." Others insist that a trailer properly is a unit with road wheels at both ends, while any unit with road wheels only at the rear and small wheels at the front that are let down only when the unit is stand-

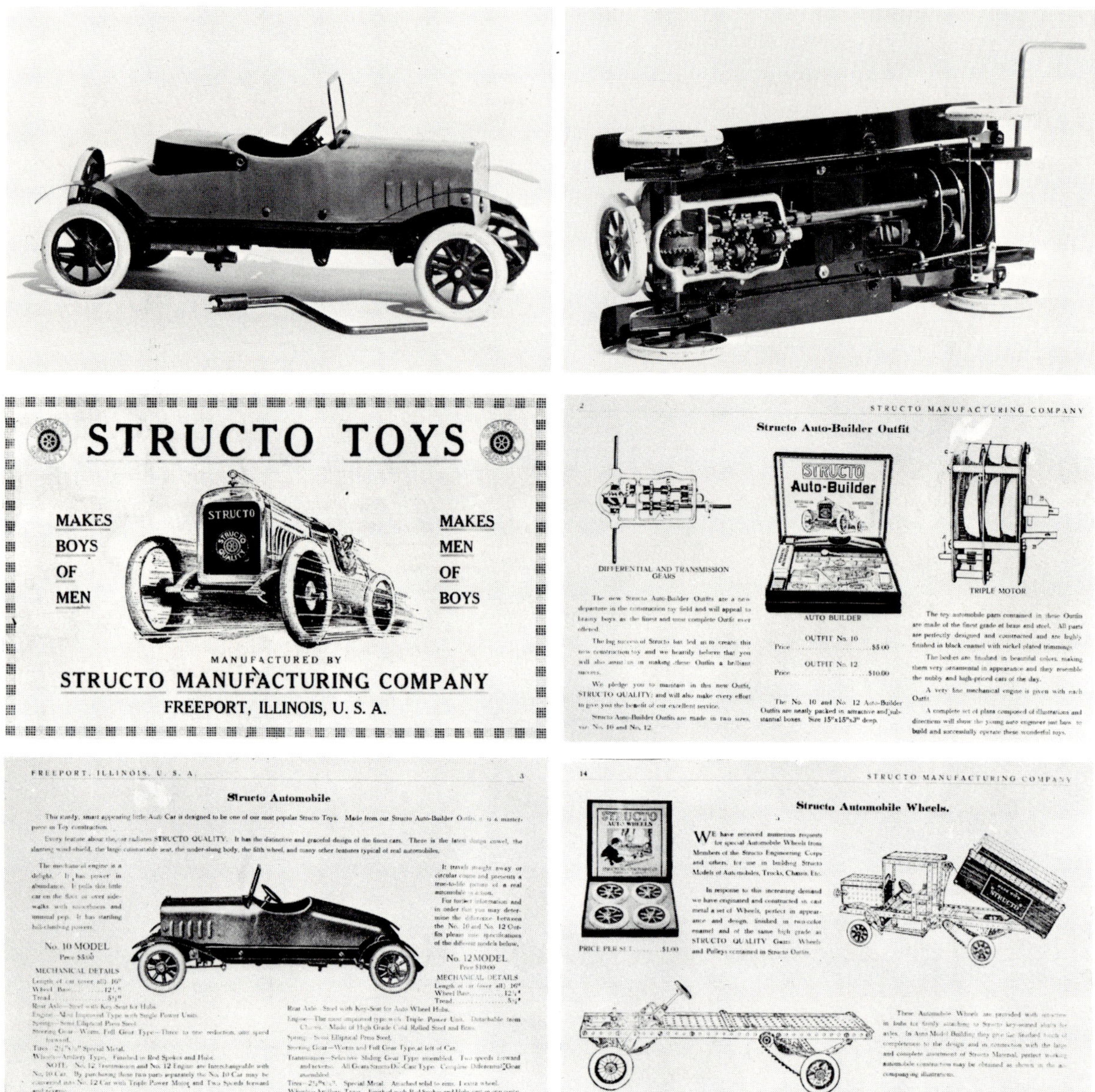

Fig. 103. The magnificent early Structo cars. A peak was reached in model-automobile production with the first Structo Auto-Builder outfits, from which youngsters could construct heavy steel, clockwork-powered models with working transmissions, of about 1917. Shown here are two views of the early form of the deluxe No. 12 roadster (*Ward Kimball*) and the cover and several pages from an early catalog describing the cars, kits and parts. (*A. J. Koveleski*).

ing detached from its tractor correctly is a semi-trailer. British usage appears to be to call all such units "trailers," but to designate pleasure and camping units of the mobile-home type not as trailers but as "caravans." In the United States, however, these are always known as "trailers," as are various other types of small baggage- or cargo-carrying carts that may be attached to pleasure cars.

All this can be somewhat confusing in international discussions among collectors and in trading negotiations. In fact, when the collector moves into the area of passenger-car types, confusion is even more confounded. This is so because to a great extent real car manufacturers were never able to agree particularly on standardized names for body types. It is particularly true in the United States where advertising policy and popular usage have combined to produce a strange combination of native and French terms, many deriving from horse-drawn vehicle types. To this day, for example, no one seems to have been able

Fig. 104. Further developments in the Structo line. These photographs show the later version of the No. 12 roadster, with solid wheels and lower windshield (*C. W. Frey*), and a tractor of the 1920's (*Joseph N. Imler*). By the early 1930's the clockwork models had been discontinued, and only steel pull toys were being made, as represented by this page from a catalog of 1935.

to come up with an acceptable standardized definition of what is a Berline or a Pullman automobile body style!

In the United States "touring car" originally referred to a large four-door open vehicle with a demountable top, but by the 1930's this class of car had become known by the somewhat classier name of "phaeton." In Great Britain at the same time, however, the word "tourer" was used to describe a fairly small two- or four-passenger open or convertible car of a type that would be called "roadster" in the United States. Today in international usage the "tourer" or "sports tourer" appears to have evolved into the touring car, a high-powered type frequently raced that bears no resemblance to the conventional American touring car of pre-1930 popularity. Coupe seems to have always held the same meaning in both countries, but what in America is a sedan usually is called "saloon" in Great Britain, except in the case of models of American prototypes where the original designation "sedan" usually is applied. In the United States today and for several decades past the word "saloon" generally conjures up only a wistful vision of a type of bygone establishment where huge glasses of beer were dispensed for a nickel adjacent to an opulent free-lunch counter. What was known formerly in the United States as a "town car" (and informally by its drivers, who are exposed to the elements, as the "go-to-hell-chauffeur car") appears to have usually been designated "town sedan" in Great Britain. However, the name "town sedan" was used in the 1930's by American automobile manufacturers to designate at times what appears to have been essentially a conventional four-door sedan, the only possible logical explanation for this cognomen being that it was somewhat more opulently appointed than might be thought necessary or desirable by a rural or farm dweller. If anyone wishes to muse on the vagaries and implications of automobile body styles, they need only be reminded that at this period Ford not only made a Model-A town sedan but also produced a veritable town-car body on their Model-A chassis! Presumably the reasoning behind offering this body style on an economy car

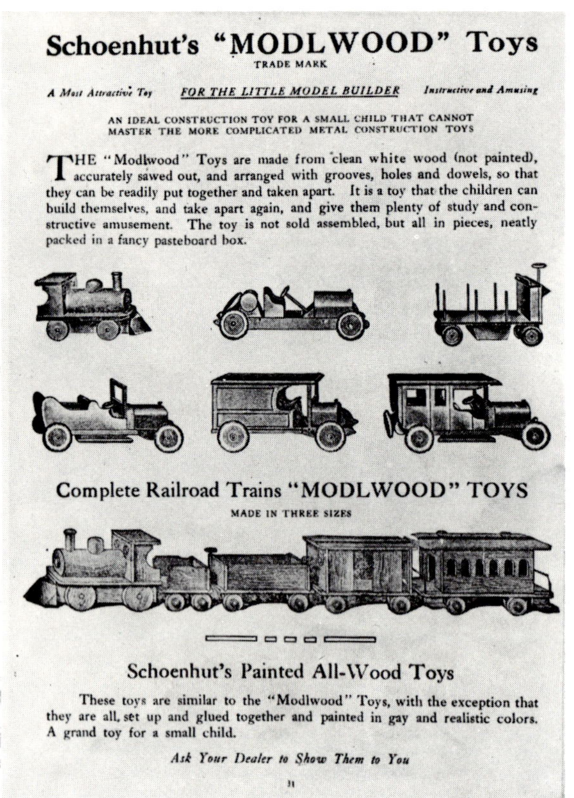

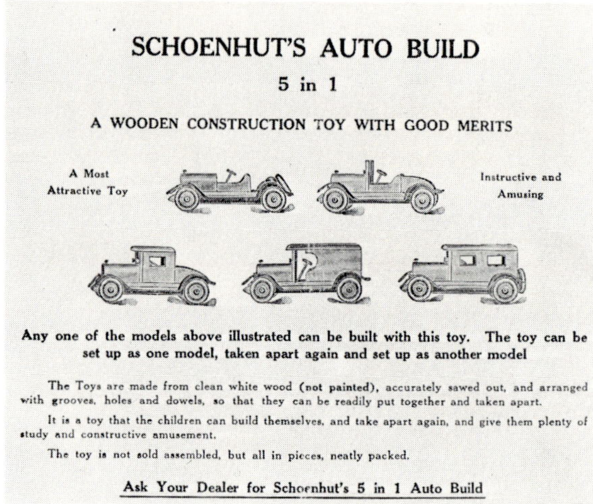

Fig. 105. The first model automobile kits ever marketed were introduced by Schoenhut in 1913, and five of the automobile body types of these "Modlwood" toys are shown at the left. Each was constructed from an individual kit that built only the one model. In a later version, right, five different models could be built up from a single set of parts.

A. J. Koveleski

during a depression was to enable millionaires to continue to ride in the style to which they had become accustomed, including to and from a run on their bank, for the price of a Ford. A limousine is a large four-door car, presumably with folding jump seats for additional passengers, and always with a retractable glass partition separating the driving and passenger compartments distinguishing it from essentially the same car as a seven-passenger sedan. It may be that originally the British saloon was similarly distinguished from what was simply called a "car" by the presence of this glass partition and the implication of being chauffeur-driven.

And what precisely then is a victoria and what a brougham? These body styles are not at all well defined except that all have in common the fact that greater privacy is assured the passengers in the back seat by the fact that all or a portion of the adjacent side window area is not provided with a full window * and usually is covered with imitation leather that often extends upward to cover the roof of the car. Essentially it appears that

such a car with only two doors is a victoria and with four doors a brougham. In the latter there sometimes are small side windows in the rear section, in which case the car may still be called a brougham or may be designated a brougham sedan. In most cases a victoria or brougham is equipped with inoperative and purely decorative "landau irons" or "S-irons" on the blank areas on each side of the rear seat. These irons also sometimes appear on other types of car bodies; for instance on the Model-A Ford coupes as shown in Fig. 106. Broughams built today still carry the landau irons, a curious vestigial throwback to horsedrawn carriage days. A landau originally was a carriage with a double top that could be thrown back or removed from both sides of the center door, and the horse-drawn landau accordingly was fitted with four landau irons, two facing backward and two facing forward at the rear. In automotive use only the latter pair are retained. There also was a small, single-seat horse-drawn vehicle known as the landaulet, and in the early days of the automobile there was a distinct automotive body style known by this name. It was similar to a town car and was in fact the forerunner of this style. Then at the other extreme in the pioneer period of the automobile there was the ubiquitous style known as the "runabout," usually representing the sim-

---

* The Ford Model-A victoria of the early 1930's retained this characteristic if only somewhat residually enough to justify the name but by the mid-1930's the Ford V8 "victoria" appears to have become simply a style name applied to a conventional two-door sedan.

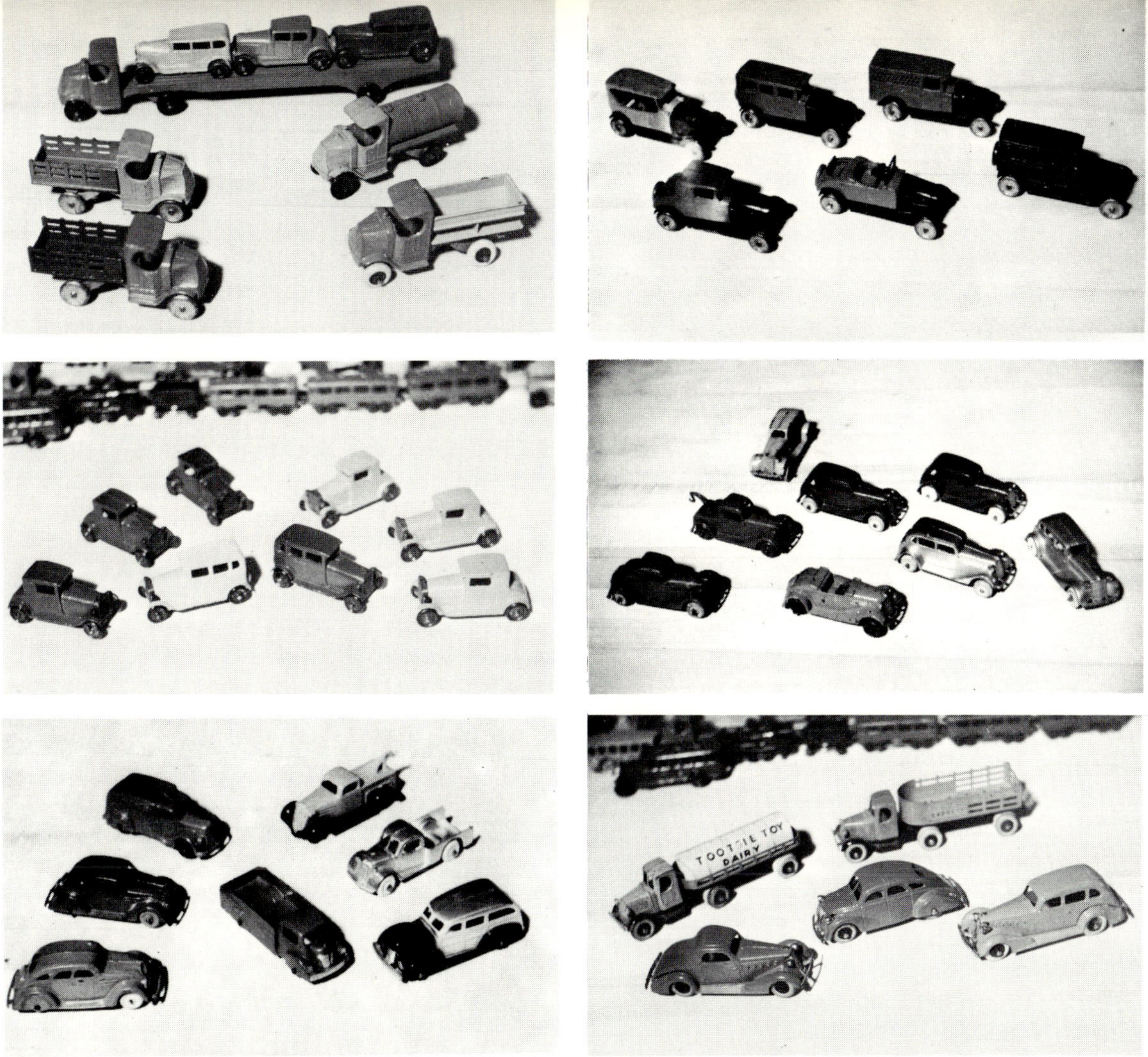

Fig. 106. An assortment of Tootsietoy cast-metal miniatures of the 1920's and 1930's, including some color and minor variations. The third, fourth, and fifth groups are made up entirely of models of Fords, but other types also are shown, including the six body styles of the General Motors series in its first year (1928) of production with black chassis.

William A. Hall

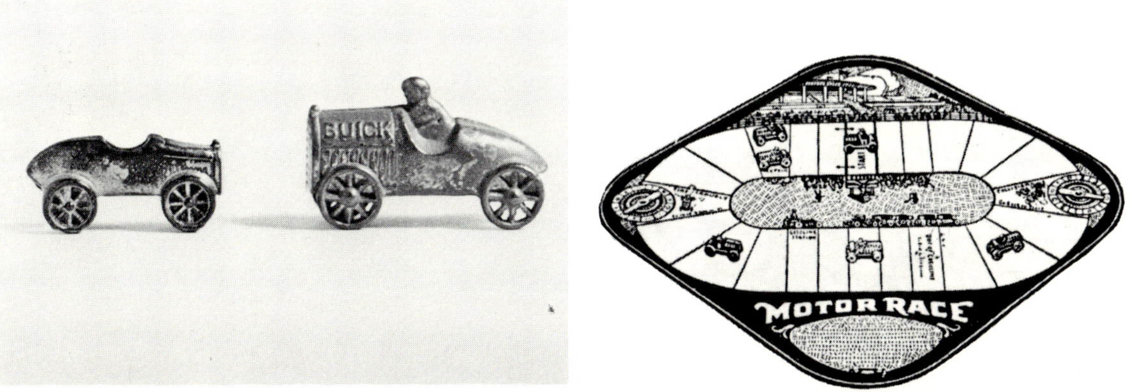

Fig. 107. Tiny cars with nonmoving wheels were usually party favors, souvenirs in boxes of confectionery, or game markers, although there were exceptions such as the Tootsietoy "Midgets" illustrated in Fig. 212. Painted cars with names cast in, such as the "Buick" at the right of the photograph, almost invariably were game markers, included in sets such as "Motor Race."

G. William Holland photographs

plest and cheapest type of self-propelled vehicle. In time it evolved into the roadster.

SPECIALIZATION

Certain specializations and limitations of interest are often determined according to the material or materials involved in the construction of the miniature vehicles. Others are determined on the basis of the means of power or the absence of power in the models. In the case of sheet-metal models, differences in the method by which the material is finished, whether lithographed or painted, also becomes a concomitant of material itself as a classification. For example, collectors specializing in clockwork-powered model automobiles are not overly concerned with the materials involved, although some may specialize in or at least favor painted sheet-metal models, while others favor lithographed miniatures. By and large, however, they are not concerned with material and finish as such. A cast-iron model that has a clockwork mechanism is automatically accepted for the collection; a nonpowered iron model is not. Much the same applies to collectors who specialize in friction-powered models. It is of little importance if the model is made mainly of wood with little more if anything aside from the wheels and power mechanism of metal, as holds true with many of the earliest American models, or if the model incorporates substantially more metal components in its construction, or if it is made almost entirely of metal. The interest here is primarily in the mode

of power, and the sequence of materials involved as outlined here is simply a matter of progression of design.

A great many collectors, however, base their specialization on the material or materials involved. Thus innumerable collectors favor model automobiles and models of other self-propelled vehicles made of cast iron. Cast iron is, in fact, one of the major material selections on which model-automobile collections are based. Usually included with the cast iron is the other material with which a certain number of miniature automobiles were similarly manufactured, by using nonpermanent molds of sand, cast aluminum. This is a definite case of collecting by material. Similarly, there are many collections built around the theme of stamped or pressed sheet-metal automobiles. This material sometimes is divided by collectors into further specialties of light metal, and then perhaps further subdivided into painted or lithographed models, and the heavy pressed-steel models of the Buddy "L" and similar types. The interest here is not for power type at all, although an awareness of its presence or lack of presence in given models may enter into the picture. Essentially the specialist of this type is interested in materials, however, although the collector of heavy-gauge-steel stamped-metal models may embrace pull toys, clockwork models, friction models, and perhaps others in his activities.

There is and always has been relatively little interest in specializing in wooden models, except on the part of such collectors who follow the very interesting and rewarding specialty of col-

Fig. 108. The "Tootsietoy Speedway" outfit of the early 1930's. The eight cars were identical except for numbers and colors. The cars themselves were not otherwise marked, but were identified not only as to make but also as to driver by means of the chart printed on the playing board.

Adam Pellicot, Jr.; William Dreyer photographs

Fig. 109. Pressure die-cast models. Top, the four Hubley Packards of the 1930's. Center, three Erie models of the 1930's, all three types were made in two sizes. Bottom, almost all of the Manoil body types; the models in the rear are post-World War II; those in the center row were made both before and after the war, and the four in front only prior to the war.

Dr. Clinton B. Seeley

lecting early model-automobile kits and models built from such kits. For the most part, however, wooden models are too close to the homemade or home-assembled ideal of things for them to have much interest for the average collector, who is usually oriented toward the metal-manufactured product, as are most who collect from the standpoint of toy and model history. On the other hand, there are a good many enthusiasts who specialize in glass miniature automobiles, which, in effect, means glass candy containers in the form of automobiles and other vehicles.

One region where cognizance of materials is particularly notable and widespread is in the collecting of the very small models, the models usually thought of as miniature cast-metal automobiles. The inclusion of the word "metal" in that description is a clue to the situation. Many collectors are interested in these models only if they are made entirely or substantially of cast metal, usually of zinc or lead alloys cast in permanent molds as contrasted with the nonpermanent sand molds in which iron and aluminum models are cast. However, many collectors of old model cars accept the small sand-cast models with enthusiasm equal to the collecting of die-cast or slush-cast miniatures. In point of fact, most collectors of models made prior to 1942 tend to collect the small model cars regardless of what material they are made, including not only cast metal but also the relatively few specimens made of wood, plaster and pulp compositions, plastic, and often the more extensive series of glass models as well. Plastic is the material that grates on some, and creates the divisions of concept that are becoming increasingly noticeable among collectors of contemporary models and in fact most of the models sold in completed form since World War II.

Some collectors insist on collecting only models made of cast metal; others accept models with some plastic components, but draw the line at models primarily constructed of plastic. It is not really a matter of whether or not plastic is either a good material or a traditional material for miniature automobiles. Obviously, regardless of the prejudices of some collectors, this material is going to be with us, and will play an increasingly important role in the manufacture of model automobiles for a long time to come. There is much to be said in favor of die-cast metal, and it is, in truth, the original and the long-traditional material for the smaller sizes of model automobiles, especially in the United States, Great Britain, and France. It has a pleasant feel and heft to it. Evidently the comparable weight-to-bulk relationship actually has a good deal to do with its popularity. At least one manufacturer already has established the validity of this point by finding greater acceptability for models built from his plastic kits among collectors by including weights that are inserted in the models so as to give the completed miniatures an overall weight approximating that of metal replicas of similar size. On the other hand, modern collectors are exposed to a certain amount of promotion on the part of manufacturers of and dealers in cast-metal miniature cars to the effect that only metal models should be regarded as truly collectible.

In short, while metal is traditional, plastic, either by itself or in combination with metal, is

Fig. 110. A galaxy of slush-cast models of the 1920's and 1930's. Five early Kansas Toy and Novelty vehicles; a group of Barclay models with metal wheels, and a second group with rubber tires, and, finally, a Savoye police patrol and stake truck (*Dr. Clinton B. Seeley*), and a Savoye coupe. (*G. William Holland photograph*).

here to stay. At one time in the 1950's it was freely and widely predicted by some that within ten years plastic would practically replace cast metal as a material for model automobiles. This has not happened, nor does it seem likely to at present. Obviously, this matter of whether or not to collect small-size model cars that are made of materials other than cast metal must in the final analysis rest with the personal outlook, preference, and decision of each collector.

Lastly, in the survey of the major potentials for limiting collections of model cars comes the matter of periods and dates, both as of the prototypes of the models to be collected and of the models themselves. Although there are many possible variations and personal preferences, the matter would appear to boil down to that of old model cars as opposed to models of old cars. Here to the latter must also be added the conceptions of all those who collect from the standpoint of the prototype automobile. In short, if a hobbyist is collecting old models, the only point to be determined is the dividing line that he is to establish and accept as dividing what is an old model from those that are not to be considered old. It is a rather ticklish point because a miniature that may well and properly seem to be an old model to an enthusiast who is twelve or fifteen years of age is not likely to seem an old model to a hobbyist of thirty or forty. One hobbyist might logically define an old model as "anything manufactured before I started collecting." Another, with equal justice, might unabashedly take the nostalgic approach and say "anything that was made when I was a boy." Others might cite specific and often varying dates as representing the absolute moment in time that establishes a specimen as being an old model in their eyes.

Nevertheless, if you were to question a number of collectors of old models, you would undoubtedly find that a substantial majority would reply "anything made before World War II," or, in the United States at least, more specifically "anything made up to June 30, 1942." That is the date beyond which the War Production Board prohibited the further manufacture of metal toys and models in the United States, including even the making up into completed salable units of parts already fabricated and on hand (because of the diversion of labor from the war effort that this assembly would involve).* Production of metal toys and novelties stopped in Great Britain in

---

* The Strombecker Corporation possesses in their collection the set of handmade samples for the new models designed but never put into production for the planned 1942 Tootsietoy line.

Fig. 111. The first three full-dimensioned Dowst vehicles with movable wheels. Left rear, the No. 4670 Model-T truck introduced in 1917; right rear, the No. 4570 Model-T touring car brought out in 1914. Center, the No. 4570 with the solid wheels used on both Model T's after the early 1920's. Right front, the Dowst No. 4528 limousine that appeared in 1911, and, left foreground, the Cosmo No. 1703 with nonmovable wheels that was derived from it about 1917.

Adam Pellicot, Jr.; William Dreyer photograph

1940. (In making use of the term "pre-World War II," collectors in the United States and Great Britain should bear in mind that the war started for these countries respectively in 1941 and 1939. Production officially resumed in both countries in the latter part of 1945. In most cases the first postwar models were substantially the same as those made prior to the war, although in virtually every case collectors are aware of points of difference that distinguish the prewar from the postwar productions of the same model. The most obvious of these on both the American and British lines that carried over from before to after the war is the change from white rubber to black rubber tires and wheels.*

Certainly the interruption of the continuity of production during World War II provides a clear-cut line of demarcation between that which may be generally considered old and that not, with a more or less ready means of identifying specimens as belonging to one era or the other. Furthermore, for similar reasons, World War II generally is accepted by collectors of all other types of models and toys as the most obvious and preferable division in time. Moreover, in the case of model automobiles, it takes on an added significance that makes it even more pertinent than in other col-

---

*Even allowing for possible private substitutions by uninformed collectors of reproduction white tires on postwar models that should carry black tires, the tire color is not an absolutely certain indication in every case. However, it is in most cases a substantially accurate guideline, and certainly far more than a mere rough rule of thumb.

Fig. 112. Although the actual sizes and scales of cast-metal miniatures may vary widely, most collectors are aware of what is meant by the terms "standard" and "small" sizes, and the relation of size to original price. Top, six of the small-size Tootsietoys of the early 1930's (five-cent sellers) compared with a standard size ten-cent limousine. Bottom, a Barclay parcel-delivery cycle and steamroller, both regarded as standard size (ten-cent retail items) although their scales are respectively substantially larger and smaller than the passenger vehicles in the same series.

G. William Holland photographs

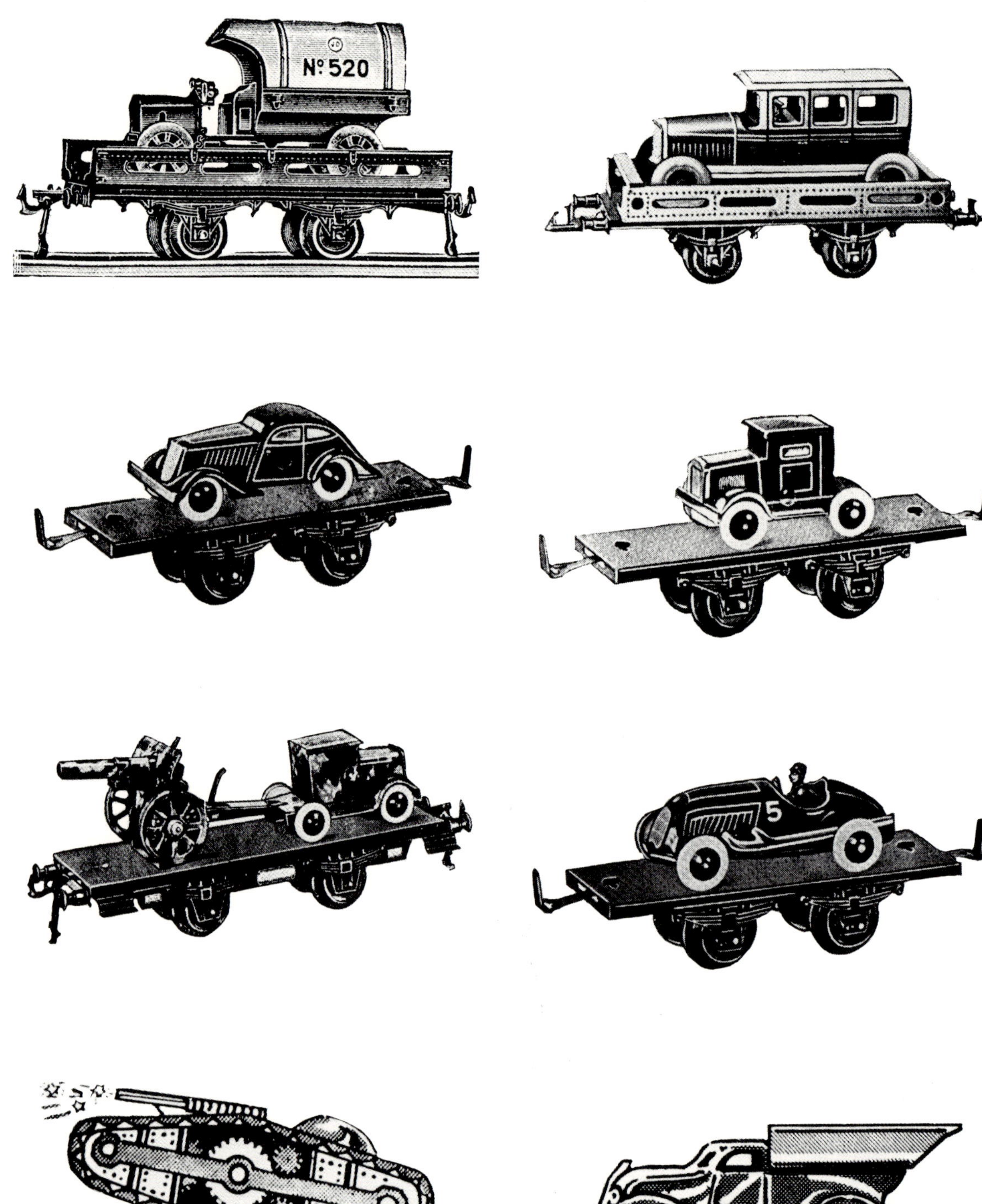

Fig. 113. The collecting of old model-railroad cars mounting miniature vehicles can be an interesting specialty in itself both for collectors of model automobiles and of model trains. O-gauge examples are shown here from about 1910 to 1940: first, two Bing; then four Distler, and, finally, two Marx models.

lecting hobbies, for it is widely recognized that despite various and often tentative prewar activities it was only following World War II that model-automobile enthusiasm and activity on a truly widespread scale quickly burst forth to claim its rightful recognition as a leading model-hobby activity, both in building and in collecting.

Yet it must at the same time in fairness be observed that as time passes and World War II recedes ever further into the past, there will be many who legitimately may feel that while the war always will provide a vital point of reference both because of the suspension of production and the marking of the great outburst of the hobby that followed, there may well come a time when it is both desirable and practical to modify somewhat this current thinking. A fair number who collect from the standpoint of the toy and model industry already are collecting in various postwar periods— up to ten years after the war, up to fifteen years, right down, in fact, to the present moment in their collections. On the other hand, for most serious collectors and students, World War II still remains the usual time stop if they desire to limit their collections as to period.

It also would be possible to collect on the basis of models made up to an even earlier date; to specialize, for instance, in cast-metal miniature automobiles made prior to, say, 1930, or even earlier. It would be an interesting limitation on a collection that would allow the practitioner really to concentrate his efforts and funds on a limited and difficult field. But most collectors would tend to find such a limitation in field too restrictive, and thus once again the commonly accepted mark of World War II has its appeal.

The hobbyist who collects from the standpoint of real automobile history does not find quite the same drawbacks in limiting his collection to models whose prototypes were made before World War II, or to any other arbitrary range of dates, for models of old cars have been and are being made in profusion. Thus the enthusiast who may decide to collect only models of prototypes made before World War II, or before 1930 or before World War I or before 1910 or between any two dates the collector arbitrarily determines to set for himself, such as models whose prototypes were made between 1910 and 1925, or some other time span, usually can find a fairly respectable number

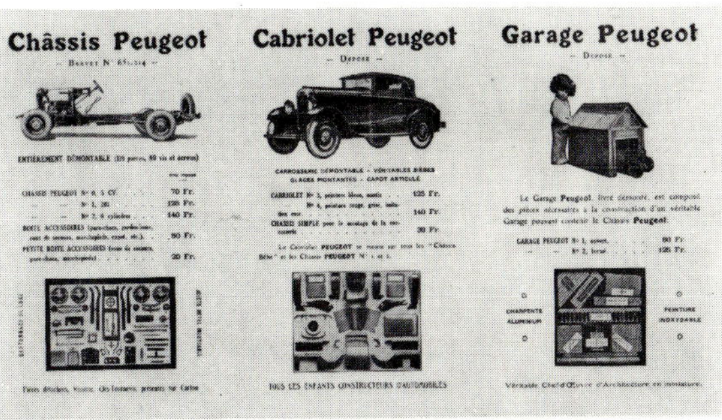

Fig. 114. An interesting French model of a Peugeot, put out about 1930 as a construction set somewhat similar to the earlier Structo sets. While in many ways cruder, it incorporated a few novel features of its own, such as a hinged hood and windows that could be lowered or raised. Also pictured is one side of the sales circular.

Ward Kimball

B-98—Body 13½x28 in. $4.50 ; B-99—body 14½x33 in. $5.00 ; B-100—body 15½x37 in. $6.00

B-100—Body 14x37 in. $7.50. Horn 50c. Lamps 50c each extra.

B-105—Special Body, 15x37 in., $10.00. Horn 50c; Lamps 50c. each extra.

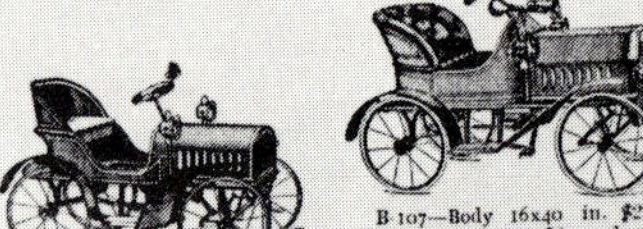

B-111—Body 16x40 in. $15. Horn 50c. Lamps 50c each, extra

B-107—Body 16x40 in. $22.50; Horn $1.50; Lamps 50c each extra

B-103—Body 16x40 in. Complete with Lamps, Horn and Clock, $40.00

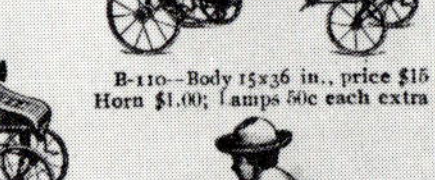

B-110—Body 15x36 in., price $15 Horn $1.00; Lamps 50c each extra

B-203—Body 15½x41 in., $7.50

B-200—Body 15½x51 in. $10.50. Horn, 50c, Lamps 50c each extra

BM-22—Glascock Racer $5.50

B-222—The "Irish Mail," $5.00

B-201—Body 16x56 in., complete with Lamps and Horn, $30

B-224—Auto Horn 50c

B-225—Auto Horn 75c

"Fairy" Ball-Bearing Tricycle
B-226—3-5 yrs., $10.25 ; B-227—4-6 yrs., $12.75 ; C-228—5-8 yrs., $15.00

B-108—Hand Car Body 14½x33 in., $7.50

"Fairy" Ball-Bearing Velocipede
B-229—For 3-5 years . . . . . $ 9.25
B-230—" 4-6 . . . . . 11.25
B-231—" 5-8 . . . . . 13.70

B

AUTOMOBILES

No. 7057—DODGE. American red body with yellow striping. Length over all 35 inches. Has nickel plated motometer, steel front radiator and bumper $6.00

No. 6057—STAR. Measures 31½ inches long. Cream colored with red and blue striping. For small children $6.00

No. 9057—DURANT. Bright orange finish, with black and yellow striping, red wheels. 10-inch rubber tired disc wheels, nickeled motometer, steel front radiator and seat. Gas control on steering wheel. Front bumper, and rear springs. Length over all, 35 inches. A real value $8.50

No. 7157—HUPMOBILE. Ozark blue finish with red striping, red wheels, 10 inch rubber tired disc wheels, nickeled motometer, adjustable windshield, rubber pedals, running board and fenders, bumpers, springs, head lights, license tag, steel front radiator and seat. Gas control on steering wheel. Length over all 41 inches $12.75

No. 6257—FRANKLIN. American red finish with yellow striping, red wheels. 10 inch rubber tired disc wheels, nickeled motometer, adjustable windshield, running board and fenders, bumper, springs, and upholstered seat. Gas control on steering wheel. Length over all 43 inches $14.85

No. 5257—JEWETT. Packard gray finish with Yale blue panel, red and yellow striping, red wheels, 10 inch rubber tired disc wheels, nickeled motometer, adjustable windshield, adjustable spot light, tool box, headlights, horn, instrument board, springs, running board and fenders, gear shift and upholstered seat. Gas control on steering wheel. Length over all 39 inches $15.75

AUTOMOBILES

No. 570. Fire Chief Finished in fire red, trimmed in yellow. Length over all, 34 inches. Has 10-inch disc steel wheels, rubber tired. Equipped with large bell, road lamps, bumper, and imitation gear shift with Onyx ball handle. Steel spring chassis. Pedals are adjustable to leg lengths of 12½ to 15½ inches. Price $8.45

No. 1572. Fire Chief—Finished in fire red, trimmed in yellow. Length over all, 42 inches. Has 10-inch new style auto wheels, rubber tired. Equipped with large bell, running board and fenders, road lamps, fire lanterns, bumper, instrument board, and imitation gear shift with Onyx ball handle. All steel frame, spring chassis. Worm gear type steering gear with adjustable steering post. Pedals are adjustable to leg reach of 16 to 19 inches........$14.95

AUTO DUMP TRUCKS

No. 1563. Dump Truck—Finished in bright green, trimmed in yellow. Black box. Length over all, 45 inches. Has 9-inch disc steel wheels, rubber tired. Lever operates dump feature and end gate and automatically opens when bed is dumped. All steel frame, spring chassis. Pedals are adjustable to leg reach of 14 to 17½ inches................$7.95

No. 1568. Dump Truck—Finished in bright green, trimmed in dark green and yellow. Length over all, 57 inches. Has 10-inch disc steel wheels, rubber tired. Lever operates dump feature and end gate automatically opens when bed is dumped. All steel frame, spring chassis. Equipped with bumper and horn. Pedals are adjustable to leg reach of 16 to 19 inches...$15.85

No. 1569. Dump Truck—Finished in bright red, trimmed in light blue and yellow. Length over all, 57 inches. Has 10-inch new style auto wheels, rubber tired. Equipped with bumper, horn, road lamps, running board and front fenders. Lever operates dump feature and end gate automatically opens when bed is dumped. All steel frame with heavy springs. Worm gear type steering gear with adjustable steering post. Pedals are adjustable to leg reach of 16 to 19 inches $19.85

AUTOMOBILES

No. 1521. Graham—Finished in brown with green panels and white stripe. Nickel plated radiator band. Length over all, 42 inches. Has 10-inch new style rolls auto wheels with 1-inch rubber tires. Equipped with adjustable windshield, rear view mirror, running board and fenders, instrument board, bumper, road lamps, parking lamps, spotlight, and horn. All steel spring chassis. Worm gear type steering gear with adjustable steering post. Pedals are adjustable to leg reach of 16 to 20 inches. $14.85

No. 1530. Hudson—Finished in blue with light green panel. Nickel plated radiator band. Length over all, 47 inches. Has 10-inch new style rolls auto wheels, rubber tired. Equipped with adjustable windshield, rear view mirror, running board and fenders, instrument board, bumper, road lamps, imitation gear shift with onyx ball handle, horn and spare wheel with cover. Upholstered seat and all steel spring chassis. Has worm gear type steering gear with adjustable steering post. Pedals are adjustable to leg reach of 17½ to 21½ inches........$19.50

No. 1542. Peerless—Finished in black, trimmed in red, cream and green. Chromium plated radiator shell. Length over all, 47 inches. Has 10-inch new style rolls auto wheels with 1-inch rubber tires. Equipped with adjustable windshield with wings, running board and fenders, instrument board, bumper, nickel plated road and parking lamps, imitation gear shift with onyx ball handle, bulb type horn, large composition steering wheel, and trunk on rear. All steel frame with spring chassis, upholstered seat, and worm gear type steering gear with adjustable steering post. Pedals are adjustable to leg reach of 18 to 21½ inches. Price $27.50

No. 562PB. Stutz Racer with Pneumatic Balloon Tires and Ball Bearing Wheels—The ball bearing wheels and pneumatic tires make this auto very easy to operate and at a greater speed than is possible in other autos. Finished in light blue, trimmed in dark green with red and yellow striping. Length over all, 65 inches. Has ball bearing heavy duty wire auto wheels with Federal Pneumatic balloon tires, non skid tread. Chromium plated hub caps. Tire size 2:50x12.75. Equipped with bumper, large steering wheel, upholstered seat and imitation gear shift with onyx ball handle. All steel spring chassis. Worm gear type steering wheel with adjustable steering post. Pedals are adjustable to leg lengths of 19 to 22 inches $33.75

of specimens readily available that fit within his selected dates. Of course, some hobbyists collect only models of comparatively recent or modern prototypes. A collector who so desires can set his guidelines to cover, say, models of cars whose prototypes were made from the end of World War II to 1960 or from 1950 or 1955 or some other date down to and continuing through the present time, or any other period desired. In fact, a collector might decide to start collecting with models of cars manufactured in the year he began collecting, and then carry the theme on forward with each succeeding year.

In short, any hobbyist may easily set up any highly personalized collecting scheme of things that happens to appeal to him. Within the overall possibilities of the hobby, there is an almost endless range of potentials for such patterns, whether the enthusiast limits himself to a rather tight and narrow specialty or a very broad one, or whether, as many do in the final analysis, he collects anything and everything in the way of miniature automobiles.

THE RISE OF MODEL-CAR COLLECTING

Virtually nothing was heard of model-car collecting as a valid and purposeful hobby in itself prior to World War II except for the references in the

Fig. 116. The headlights of Georges Carette. Of the better German clockwork automobiles of the years just prior to World War I, Carette models were among the most widely sold in the United States and among the most favored by collectors today. Many were sold with headlights and sidelights, but in many cases these were purchased as separate accessories by individual customers, resulting in a plethora of types and combinations today. Pictured here are a 13-inch touring car (*Dr. James Nixon; Ward Kimball photograph*), a 12-inch limousine (*Adam Pellicot, Jr.; William Dreyer photograph*), a 15 1/2-inch limousine (*Ward Kimball*), and the detail of another 15 1/2-inch limousine (*C. W. Frey*).

Fig. 117. Sharing equal stature with Carette as a collectors' favorite among German clock-work automobiles, and embracing post–World War I production as well, are the models manufactured by Bing. Photographs of four examples are shown here (*Ward Kimball*), as well as catalog drawings of a passenger car and a racing car of 1905.

Meccano catalogs; and the general reaction that greeted these has already been noted. Very probably there were a few persons who built individual model automobiles or who assembled models from the kits available between 1913 and the war, especially from the kits made by the Scientific Model Airplane Company in the 1930's, and who thereafter retained such models, thereby becoming in effect model-automobile collectors.

For the most part such conscious model-automobile collecting as actually was done prior to World War II was either as a subsidiary part of general toy collecting or, and on a somewhat more meaningful level, was a manifestation of an interest in certain particular models or makes on

the part of toy-train collectors. In the first instance the collecting was, if anything, rather accidental and without particular intent and purpose in most cases. Old model and toy automobiles were then usually looked upon as rather uninteresting and unimportant. Specimens that would be indeed highly prized today were of such comparatively recent production that they hardly seemed proper articles for the attention of the collector. It is true that in the 1930's numerous train collectors were seeking and prizing many of the miniature trains made even in the 1920's or early 1930's, but apart from this specialized activity, for the most part collectors of "old" toys usually thought in terms of things made prior to the start of the twentieth century.

Fig. 118. The front cover and two pages from the Tootsietoy consumer promotion booklet of 1932, "Let's Make Believe with Tootsietoys." The right-hand pages refer to the "Funnies" set, illustrated in Fig. 97. Unlike this booklet, most Tootsietoy catalogs and literature were directed to the trade.

George H. Hartman

In some cases, such as many horse-drawn cast-iron toys and mechanical banks, they managed to delude themselves nicely as to dating. Toy collectors for the most part, if they regarded old automobiles as collectible, believed that only those made before 1901 were worthy of their attentions. If later specimens were included, it usually was because of a lack of knowledge of prototype design or the inclination toward willing self-delusion that led them erroneously to ascribe far too early dates to their supposed pioneer "horseless carriage" toys. During this same collecting era, and until the cessation of metal toy production during World War II made almost every metal toy, no matter how old, salable as a current plaything, the shelves of toy stores and other outlets were loaded with dead stock. These included all sorts of old automobiles and trucks dating back to the 1920's, and even to World War I or earlier, that virtually could not be given away for use as toys and were usually ignored by most toy collectors. How these endless rows of obsolete Schieble, Buddy "L," Kingsbury, and other such model vehicles, not to mention the almost endless multitudes of specimens of the very inexpensive makes that were to be observed shelved and going begging in the late 1930's, would warm the heart of any collector of the present era!

A few alert collectors (most of whom were train collectors who were familiar with the potential desirability and collectibility of toys of fairly recent manufacture) acquired some toy automobiles and trucks that were remembered from childhood or that possessed some historical interest or that obviously had workmanship of outstandingly high caliber or beauty. The individuals who kept these items probably deserve to be rated as among the first true model-automobile collectors in a purposeful sense, but it seems safe to say that few if any of them ever really thought of themselves at the time as being model-automobile collectors as such. Neither did the train collectors, who were even less interested in the cars they acquired as automobiles, but rather merely as one type among a number of other products also made by the various toy-train manufacturers. As, in the later 1930's, toy-train collecting took on an increasingly scientific and sophisticated historical outlook, products other than trains gained in interest and appeal for a number of train collectors. Coming across old automobiles, boats, steam engines, and other toys made by the same companies that manufactured trains, such collectors might well take them in and preserve them as interesting but usually wholly subsidiary adjuncts to their main interest.

This interest in old toy automobiles from a purely historical point of view by train collectors should carefully be distinguished from the purchase—often by the same individuals, pursuing more than one facet of a broad overall hobby of miniature trains—of current or obsolete model automobiles for use as scenic adjuncts by operators of model-railroad systems. Such model railroaders were extensive purchasers of suitably sized model automobiles, the younger ones of course clamoring to have them bought for them.

COLLECTING MINIATURE CAST-METAL MODEL AUTOMOBILES

There is a now rather widespread legend that many boys in the 1920's and 1930's accumulated large quantities of Tootsietoy and miniature cast-metal automobiles and trucks of similar size for use with their toy-train layouts. This theory has been advanced in recent years to explain the great boom in this type of miniature automobile that took place

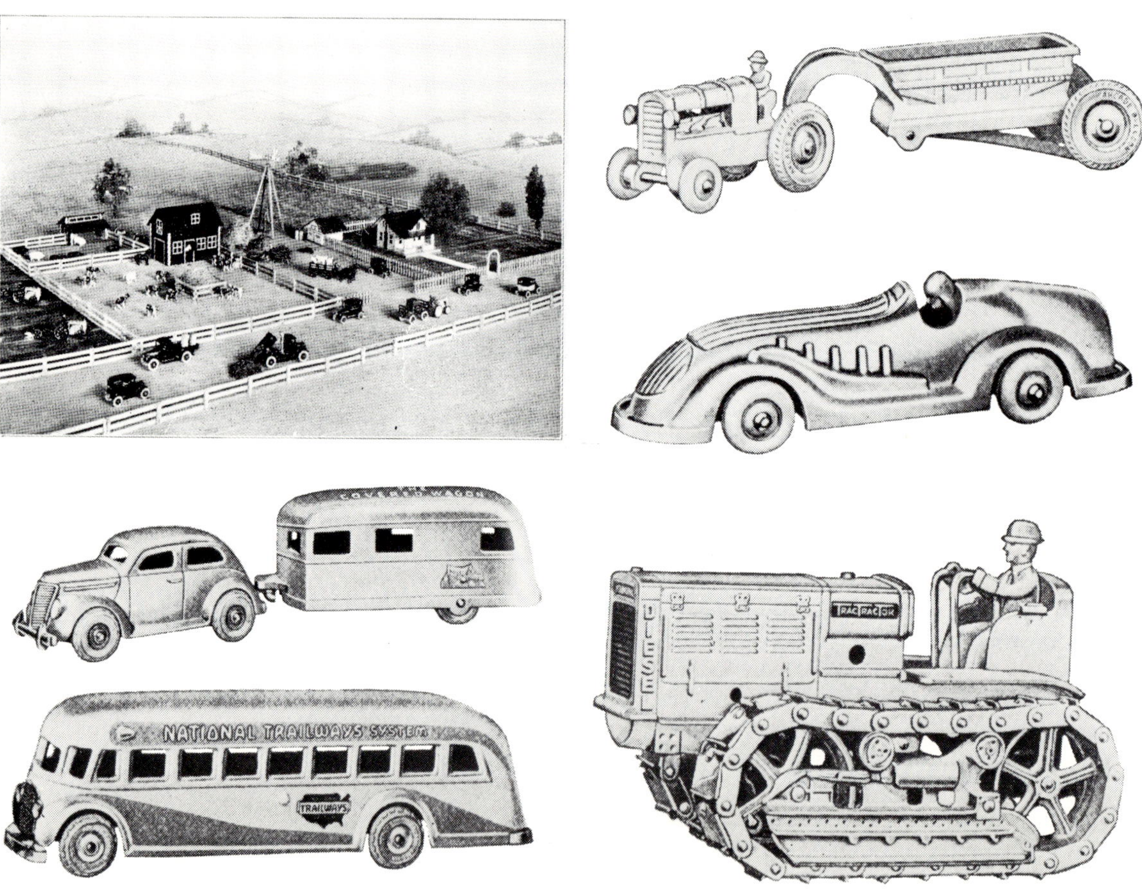

Fig. 119. An Arcade window display of the 1920's, including a number of their cast-iron automobiles, trucks, tractors, and farm accessories (*Lloyd W. Ralston*). Also pictured are five Arcade models of the late 1930's. In addition to cast-iron passenger cars, Arcade always went in fairly heavily for work vehicles.

in the middle and late 1920's, or, as some would have it, at various times in the 1930's.* Those who propound it link the date of the boom in the little automobiles with an imagined corresponding date marking a great boom in model trains. This theory, conveniently combining two largely unrelated things at a date usually tailored to suit the teller's convenience in order to wrap up everything seemingly neatly and logically,† not only is pure legend and nothing more, but unwittingly does a great disservice to the innate and independent attractions of these little automobiles and trucks themselves. If only for this reason it is worth examining and dismissing the legend. The germ of the legend usually is the realization that a substantial number of the early miniature cast-metal cars approximated 1/4-

inch scale and that 1/4-inch scale is the popular scale for O-gauge miniature trains in the United States. Hence the possibility arises for a very neat and superficially logical explanation arrived at entirely by means of tenuous ex post facto reasoning. If the theory were advanced by model railroaders intent on claiming credit unto themselves for the popularity of this type of model automobile, the reasons for promoting the legend, although somewhat less than completely admirable, would at least be understandable. However, as far as can be ascertained, model railroaders have not concerned themselves in the matter in the least, and the legend has entirely been planted and cultivated by model-automobile enthusiasts! Again, in so doing, they are strangely denigrating the intrinsic appeal of the subject of their own chief interest.

In advancing the concept that because the cars and O-gauge trains are seemingly of the same scale the popularity of the one must inevitably be linked to the other, they completely overlook two major realities. One is that the overwhelming majority of the miniature trains of the period, even of just the O-gauge trains, were simply toys, not built to scale. In terms of length or width or height the locomotives and cars usually fell far under scale, but in their specific proportions many of their elements were far over scale, and this was invariably true of the track. The second is that most youngsters have a definite and well-developed if sometimes personalized sense of size and proportion. This may not necessarily at all accord with that of an adult who is versed in building or observing scale models, but the sense possessed by a child almost always is clear and logical in its own

---

* There was a great boom in miniature cast-metal automobiles in the middle and late 1920's because at that time the leading manufacturer secured the financial backing needed properly to produce and promote a wide range. There also was a continuing rise in the business in the 1930's because such admirable five-and-ten-cent toys naturally were popular, and sold widely in a depression economy.

† Although the 1920's indubitably were the golden age of toy trains, they already were long-beloved staples, and there was no particular and sudden boom in toy trains in the middle and late 1920's comparable to the boom in miniature cast-metal automobiles. And, while sales of the latter toys continued to rise markedly in the early 1930's, overall sales of toy trains fell off badly in the first depression years. Nor can the theory be adapted to fit into a supposed distinction between toy trains and scale-model railroads and the rise of the latter hobby in the 1930's. The scale-model-railroad business, for all its contemporary and retrospective emblazonment, really was a quite negligible factor in the early and middle 1930's.

Fig. 120. The ten-cent cast-iron vehicle. In the late 1920's and 1930's the manufacturers of cast-iron models went in extensively for small-sized pieces, which could be retailed for a dime, in an effort to compete with the ten-cent zinc and white-metal alloy automobiles. Five examples are shown here that span the era, from the stake truck and fire engine with metal wheels through the wheel with rubber tire (as on the tank truck) to the all-rubber wheel and tire combination.
G. William Holland photographs

Fig. 121. The photograph shows the first of the Buddy "L" trucks, the No. 200, literally the first, this being the sample (along with that of the steam shovel and derrick) initially given to the real Buddy "L", Arthur B. Lundahl, by his father, who manufactured the toys. The folder pictured is the first catalog put out by the company, in 1922.

Arthur B. Lundahl

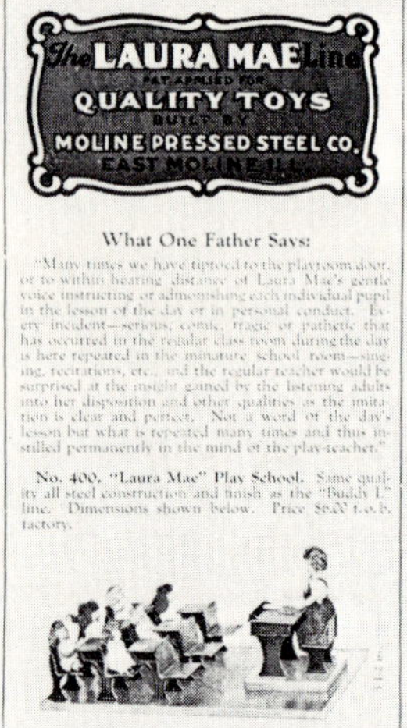

The LAURA MAE Line
PAT. APPLIED FOR
QUALITY TOYS
BUILT BY
MOLINE PRESSED STEEL CO.
EAST MOLINE, ILL.

What One Father Says:

"Many times we have tiptoed to the playroom door, or to within hearing distance of Laura Mae's gentle voice instructing or admonishing each individual pupil in the lesson of the day or in personal conduct. Every incident—serious, comic, tragic or pathetic that has occurred in the regular class room during the day is here repeated in the miniature school room—singing, recitations, etc., and the regular teacher would be surprised at the insight gained by the listening adults into her disposition and other qualities by the imitation so clear and perfect. Not a word of the day's lesson but what is repeated many times and thus instilled permanently in the mind of the play-teacher."

No. 400. "Laura Mae" Play School. Same quality all steel construction and finish as the "Buddy L" line. Dimensions shown below. Price $6.00 f.o.b. factory.

TAKE yourself back twenty, yes even thirty or more years, and live once more those vivid child dreams that were once your unchallenged path to realistic anticipations of the things you would do when you were "big like daddy and mother."

The playthings of your childhood days were the language of the future. With them you made *your dreams come true.* And the champions of your heart were the playthings you could actually do things with, those that *really worked.*

Crude then they were, but now made perfect through the fashioning of sheet steel, by master craftsmen, directed by a man who knows children, into exact working models of Motor Trucks, Steam Shovels, Hoists, etc. Today these beautiful, practical, educational playthings that *really work* and last for years, are the rightful heritage of every American child.

—FRED A. LUNDAHL.

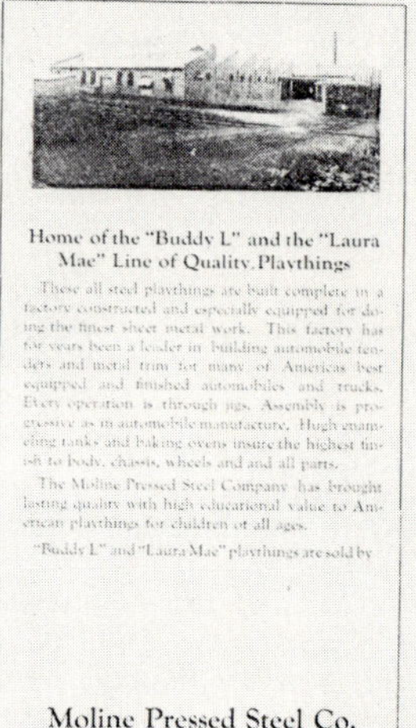

Home of the "Buddy L" and the "Laura Mae" Line of Quality Playthings

These all steel playthings are built complete in a factory constructed and especially equipped for doing the finest sheet metal work. This factory has for years been a leader in building automobile fenders and metal trim for many of America's best equipped and finished automobiles and trucks. Every operation is through jigs. Assembly is progressive as in automobile manufacture. Huge enameling tanks and baking ovens insure the highest finish to body, chassis, wheels and and all parts.

The Moline Pressed Steel Company has brought lasting quality with high educational value to American playthings for children of all ages.

"Buddy L" and "Laura Mae" playthings are sold by

Moline Pressed Steel Co.
East Moline, Illinois

All Steel Playthings—

The BUDDY L Line
PAT. APPLIED FOR
QUALITY TOYS
BUILT BY
MOLINE PRESSED STEEL CO.
EAST MOLINE, ILL.

thought impossible, a reality to-day

The Child's Dream come True

Realistic and sturdy playthings of true educational value; *all steel* construction throughout, spot welded and riveted at every point and given two coats of baked-on automobile enamel finish in colors.

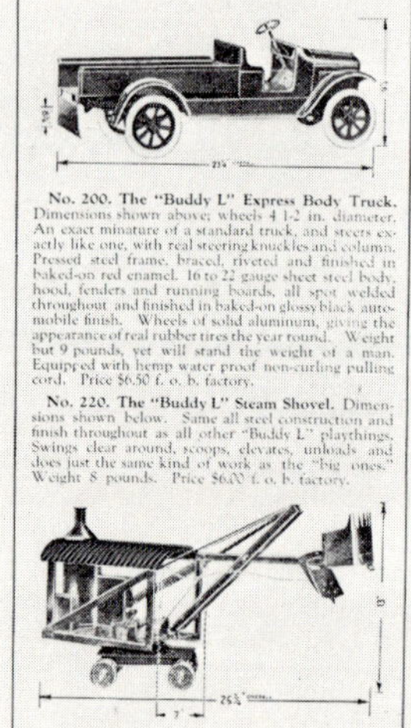

No. 200. The "Buddy L" Express Body Truck. Dimensions shown above; wheels 4 1-2 in. diameter. An exact miniature of a standard truck, and steers exactly like one, with real steering knuckles and column. Pressed steel frame, braced, riveted and finished in baked-on red enamel. 16 to 22 gauge sheet steel body, hood, fenders and running boards, all spot welded throughout and finished in baked-on glossy black automobile finish. Wheels of solid aluminum, giving the appearance of real rubber tires the year round. Weight but 9 pounds, yet will stand the weight of a man. Equipped with hemp water proof non-curling pulling cord. Price $6.50 f. o. b. factory.

No. 220. The "Buddy L" Steam Shovel. Dimensions shown below. Same all steel construction and finish throughout as all other "Buddy L" playthings. Swings clear around, scoops, elevates, unloads and does just the same kind of work as the "big ones." Weight 8 pounds. Price $6.00 f. o. b. factory.

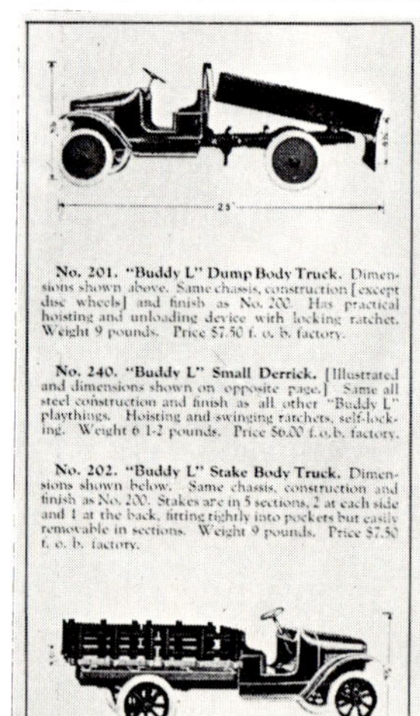

No. 201. "Buddy L" Dump Body Truck. Dimensions shown above. Same chassis, construction [except disc wheels] and finish as No. 200. Has practical hoisting and unloading device with locking ratchet. Weight 9 pounds. Price $7.50 f. o. b. factory.

No. 240. "Buddy L" Small Derrick. [Illustrated and dimensions shown on opposite page.] Same all steel construction and finish as all other "Buddy L" playthings. Hoisting and swinging ratchets, self-locking. Weight 6 1-2 pounds. Price $6.00 f.o.b. factory.

No. 202. "Buddy L" Stake Body Truck. Dimensions shown below. Same chassis, construction and finish as No. 200. Stakes are in 5 sections, 2 at each side and 1 at the back, fitting tightly into pockets but easily removable in sections. Weight 9 pounds. Price $7.50 f. o. b. factory.

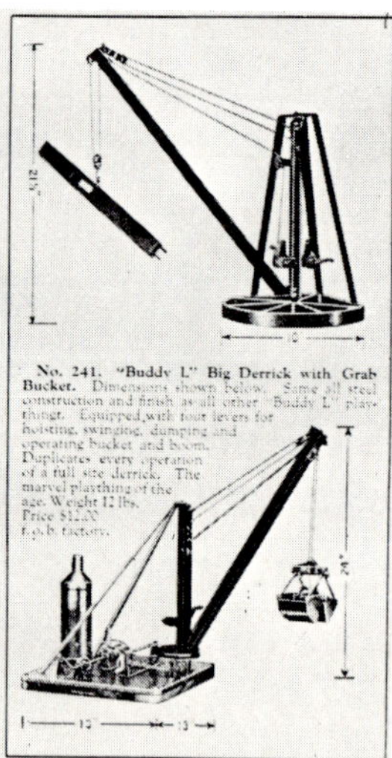

No. 241. "Buddy L" Big Derrick with Grab Bucket. Dimensions shown below. Same all steel construction and finish as all other "Buddy L" playthings. Equipped with foot levers for hoisting, swinging, dumping and operating bucket and boom. Duplicates every operation of a full size derrick. The marvel plaything of the age. Weight 12 lbs. Price $12.00 f.o.b. factory.

Fig. 122. A varied assortment of friction toys of the later years of the genus, reproduced from ➤ a 1920's jobber catalog, providing a good representation of the Dayton, Schieble, Turner, and Republic lines, and including some nonpowered models. The electrically illuminated fire alarm and gas pump were made by Gong Bell.

A. J. Koveleski

DAYTON FRICTION TOYS

Observation Bus
No. 2000. Disc wheels. Finish, Orange, black and red trimming. Size 26 [inches] long, 6½ inches wide, 7 inches [high]. Each $5.00

Victoria Coupe
No. 800. Finish, fawn top and body, red and black trimmings. Size, 19 [inches] long, 6 inches wide, 8 inches high. [Each] $2.25

Fire Engine
No. 730. Finish, red, black, gold. 14½ inches long, 5 inches wide, 8 [inches] high. Each $1.50

Racer
No. 430. Disc Wheels. Finish, red, gold trim. Size, 11 inches long, 3½ [inches] wide, 3¾ inches high. Each, $0.75

Monoplane
No. 700. Disc Wheels. Finish, silver trimmed in blue and red. Size, 13½ [inches] long, 13 inches wide, 5 inches high. $1.50

Delivery Truck
No. 705. Steel wheels, steel tire finish, grey and red. Size 14½ inches long, 5 inches wide, 7 inches high. Price, each $1.50

Five-Ton Truck
No. 920. Finish, grey body, burnt orange trimmings, steel tires. Size, 20½ inches long, 6½ inches wide, 5½ inches high. Each $2.50

Hook and Ladder Fire Truck
No. 1510. Finish, red and black. Size, 26 inches long, 6½ inches wide, 7½ inches high. Each $4.00

No. 745—Hook and Ladder. Disc Wheels. Finish, red and black. Size 18 inches long, 5 inches wide, 6 inches high. Each $1.50

No. 785—Two Ton Truck. Finish, green, red and burnt orange; size, length 14½ inches, width 4½ inches, height 5¾ inches. $1.50

Roadster
No. 720. Disc wheels, steel tire finish. Size 13½ inches long, 5 inches wide, 6 inches high. Each $1.50

Dump Truck
No. 1500. Finish, red bed, orange body. Size, 20½ inches long, 6½ inches high. Rubber tires. Each $3.50

No. 540—Dump Truck. With rubber tires. Finish, same as above. Size 14½ inches long, 4½ inches wide, 6½ inches high. Each $2.00

Electric Fire Alarm
No. 666—Electric Fire Alarm. Turn the bell; press the button handle and ring the bell and light the lamp. Complete, with binding posts and bulb for connecting with electric train. Each $1.25

Electric Gas Pump
No. 900—Electric Gas Pump is 13 [inches] high, made so that when the handle is turned a bell rings at every gallon and a lamp in the top flashes at every five gallons. A pointer shows on the dial the number of gallons pumped and changeable sign on front shows Price per day. This toy is complete in every detail including a Mazda lamp and a battery. Each .... $[illegible]

SCHIEBLE FRICTION POWER AND PULL TOYS

All Friction Power Toys are equipped with the new, powerful friction motor, silent rubber tires, new double bar bumpers, bright colors, and packed in individual cartons.

The Pull Toys are sturdily made of durable sheet steel, electrically welded and enameled in bright, attractive color combinations.

No. 110—Friction Power Inter-City Bus. Size 21¼ x 6¾ x 3¾ inches. Each $2.50
No. 10—Bus. Pull toy model, 21¼ x 6¾ x 5¾ inches. Each $1.00

No. 102—Friction Power Rapid Transit Trolley Car. Size 22 x 7¾ x 5¼ inches. Each $2.25
No. 12—Trolley. Pull toy model, 22 x 7¾ x 5¼ inches. Each $1.00

No. 109—Friction Power Ladder Truck. Size 20 x 7¾ x 5½ inches. Each $2.50
No. 19—Ladder Wagon. A pull toy, size 20 x 7¾ x 5½ inches. Each $1.00
No. 18—Hose Truck. Pull toy model, 20 x 7¾ x 5½ inches. Each $1.00

No. 3—Speedster. Pull toy model, 18¾ x 6½ x 5¾ inches. Each $1.00
No. 4—Runabout. Pull toy model, 17⅝ x 6⅝ x 5¾ inches. Each $1.00

No. 100—Friction Power Locomotive. Size 27½ x 6¾ x 5⅞ inches. Each $2.25
No. 8—Engine. Pull toy model, 21 x 5¾ x 4⅜ inches. Each $1.00

No. 9—Battleship. Pull toy model, 18¾ x 6¼ x 4½ inches. Each $1.00

No. 106—Friction Power Dump Truck. Size 18¾ x 7¼ x 3¼ inches. Each $2.25
No. 101—Friction Power Service Truck. Size 18¾ x 7¼ x 3¼ inches. Each $2.25
No. 6—Sand Truck. Pull toy model, 18¾ x 7¼ x 3¼ inches. Each $1.00

No. 113—Garage. Size 22 x 13½ x 16 inches. Each $2.50

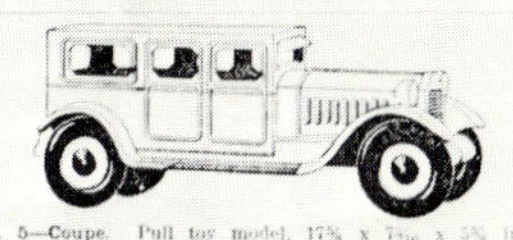

No. 5—Coupe. Pull toy model, 17⅝ x 7¾ x 5¾ inches. Each $1.00
No. 7—Sedan. Pull toy model, 17⅝ x 7½ x 5¾ inches. Each $1.00

TURNER FRICTION AND PULL TOYS

Turner Toys are made of heavy sheet auto steel, electric welded and securely cleated with heavy lugs; finished with high grade enamels.

No. 166—Packard Sport Pull Toy Model. Finish, Light Green and Gold. Size, [?] inches long, 7¾ inches wide, 9¼ inches high. Rubber tires. Each $2.50

No. 66F—Packard Racer with Turner Motor. Finish, Red and Gold. Size, 26¼ [inches] long, 7¼ inches wide, and 7 inches high. Rubber tires. Each $3.00

No. 566—Lincoln Sedan. Pull toy model, 27 inches long, 11 inches high, finished in red, fawn and tan. Rubber tires. Each $4.00

No. 266—Packard Dump Truck. Pull toy model, 27¼ inches long, 7¼ inches wide, 9¼ inches high, with rubber tires. Each $3.00

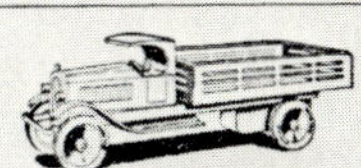

No. 99—Speed Truck with Turner Motor. Finish, Red and Tan. Size, 17½ inches long, 6 inches wide, 7 inches [high]. Rubber tires. Each $2.00
No. 33—Speed Truck. Pull toy model 16¼ inches long, 6 [inches] wide, 6 inches high. Finish: Red and light green with rubber tires. Each $1.00
No. 88—Speed Truck. Pull toy model 22 inches long, 7 inches, 9 inches high. Finish: Red, gold and blue. Each, $2.00

No. 277—Dump Truck. Equipped with Turner motor; finish red, gold and tawn; 22 inches long, 7 inches wide, 9 inches high. Rubber tires. Each $2.75
No. 299—Dump Truck with Turner Motor. Finish: Red, gold and light green. Size, 17½ inches long, 6 inches wide, [?] inches high. Rubber tires. Each $2.00
No. 288—Dump Truck. Same size and description as No. 277 but pull toy model. Rubber tires. Each $2.00
No. 233—Dump Truck. Pull toy model 16¼ inches long, [?] inches wide, 6 inches high. Finish: Red. Each $1.00

No. 433—Hook & Ladder. Pull toy model 16 inches long, 5 [inches] wide, 7 inches high. Finished in red and gold enamel. $1.00

No. 55—Garage Set. Garage 14 inches long, 8 inches wide, 7½ inches high, equipped with sedan pull toy. Finish: Red, gold, blue and cream colors. Each $1.75

No. 360—Fire Engine. Pull toy model 26¼ inches long, 7¼ [inches] wide, 11½ inches high. Finish: Red and gold. Rubber [tires]. Each $3.00
No. 388—Fire Engine. Pull toy model 22 inches long, 6 [inches] wide, 11 inches high. Finish: Red and gold. Each, $2.00

No. 455—Garage. Finished in attractive colors, 14 inches long, 8 inches wide and 7½ inches high. Each $1.25

TURNER FRICTION AND PULL TOYS

No. 399—Fire Engine. Equipped with Turner motor. Finish: red and gold. Rubber tires. Size, 15 inches long, 8 inches wide, 5 inches high. Each, $2.00
No. 333—Fire Engine. Pull toy model, 15½ inches long, 5 inches wide, 8 inches high. Red and gold finish. Each $1.00

No. 666—Locomotive & Tender. Pull toy model, 30 inches long, 5 inches wide, 8¼ inches high. Red and gold finish. Each $2.00

No. 499—Hook & Ladder. Equipped with Turner motor and bell. Finish: red and gold. Size, 16 inches long, 5 inches wide, 7 inches high. Rubber tires. Each $2.00

REPUBLIC SPECIAL FRICTION TOYS

No. 1060—Hook and Ladder with Power. Color, body in red, trimmed in green; striped in gold. Size, length, 18 inches; width, 5 inches; height, 6¼ inches; ladders extended 26 inches. Each $1.50

No. 1090—Roadster with Power. Color, body in Red; trimmed in Green and Gold. Length, 18½ inches; width, 6¾ inches; heigh, 7 inches. Each $1.50
No. 1170—Speedster. Body in Green trimmed in Gold. 11 inches long, 5 inches wide, 5¼ inches high. Each $1.00

No. 2000—Taxi Cab. Body in black and orange. Size, 11 inches long, 5 inches wide, 5½ inches high. Each $1.00

No. 550—Safety Coach with Power. Finish, light blue with red and black trimmings. Size, 29¼ inches long, 8¼ inches wide, 9½ inches high. Equipped with rubber balloon tires. Each $5.00

No. 360—Fire Engine with Power. Finish, red and gold. Size, 23⅞ inches long, 6⅛ inches wide, 9 inches high. Equipped with rubber balloon tires. Each $3.50

No. 375—Tower Truck without Power. Finish, red and gold. Size, 24 inches long, 7½ inches wide, 7½ inches high. Equipped with rubber balloon tires. Each $3.00

No. 385—Dump Truck without Power. Finish, red and green. Size, 24¼ inches long, 7½ inches wide, 8 inches high. Equipped with rubber balloon tires. Each $3.00

way. To the average youngster the miniature cast-metal automobiles usually looked far too small properly to go with even O-gauge trains. A child's tendency is always toward oversize proportions, and this is not necessarily incorrect reasoning. A child at play usually populates his trains, automobiles, houses, and so on with imaginary people, and these people must rationally fit into the various vehicles and buildings. A toy automobile whose imagined seated driver's line of vision rested below the rail top of toy train track or whose passengers would have to climb approximately their full height to board a railroad car to a child obviously were enormously undersized. The automobiles that a child sought for use with his trains or requisitioned from among his existing toys almost invariably were considerably oversize in relation to the supposed proper scale for miniature trains of a particular gauge, and even more mature model railroaders will be found to have almost always have selected matching automotive vehicles on the basis of these proportions. A few adult scale-model railroaders did obtain miniature automobiles correctly scaled to HO-, OO-, and O-gauge scale-model trains in the 1930's, but the odd thing is that the average adult viewing such layouts almost always felt that the automobiles were underscale! Even today this holds true, as anyone readily can establish for himself if he cares to question visitors to a scale-model railroad-club exhibition concerning this point.

Miniature automobiles were bought and used in profusion with miniature railroad systems. In the 1920's and 1930's they were almost always stamped-metal or cast-iron vehicles, and almost always from 50 percent to several hundred percent overscale! It was not, in fact, until HO- and OO-gauge model trains began to become popular in the middle and late 1930's that Tootsietoy and vehicles of similar size extensively were used by model railroaders, and then, in further evidence of what has been stated, they usually were the models actually approximating O-gauge scale that were used with the HO- and OO-gauge trains—again a case of model cars better than 50 percent oversize looking "right" to most hobbyists. It should also be noted that although in the middle and late 1930's Meccano made both O-gauge trains and miniature cast-metal automobiles, many of which were built to or close to the technically correct size for O-gauge, the company made relatively few attempts to tie the two lines together in their promotions because they realized that to the average user the cars simply looked too small to belong with the trains. Dinky Toy automobiles and trucks were shown in some pictures of train layouts, and

there were some attempts at articles tying in the two lines.* In the main, however, the sales approach was that of offering two entirely distinct classes of toys, although some of the articles by then incorporated in the Dinky Toy line, such as baggage and baggage trucks and figures of railroad personnel, initially offered in pre-Dinky Toy days specifically as accessories for Hornby trains, continued to be widely illustrated and purchased for this usage. It was not until Hornby brought out their line of British OO (Hornby "Dublo") gauge trains in 1938 that the Dinky Toy automobiles and trucks were again widely pictured and sold for model-railroad use. Most of the Dinky Toy vehicles were greatly overscale for OO but in spite of this, or rather because of it, they looked eminently "right" for this smaller gauge in the eyes of most model-train enthusiasts.

RECONSTRUCTION OF A PICTURE

With all this in mind, pertinent as it is to an understanding both of the popular use of these miniatures when they were made and to the rise of model-car collecting, it is equally vital to reconstruct the true picture of the basic appeal and use of these little cars and trucks in the 1920's and 1930's.

For the most part, Tootsietoys and similar miniature cast-metal automobiles and trucks were played with as essentially independent toy systems complete within themselves. They were usually played with on the floor, sometimes by younger or sick children in bed, occasionally on tables, and at times out of doors, but they were primarily indoor toys. They were far from without appeal to girls, especially when girls and boys played together, but they were of course basically boys' toys. Younger boys simply toyed with them, but usually highly imaginative adventures and traffic patterns were planned and acted out by older boys—say those around six to twelve years of age. A very common procedure was for boys who had seen

---

* For example, an article entitled "Road-Rail Services for Hornby Railways" in the February 1936 *Meccano Magazine,* begins on a hopeful note to the effect that the availability of the Dinky Toy vehicles have provided splendid opportunities for adding automotive traffic to Hornby layouts. The accompanying illustration, although in this case showing the No. 33 series mechanical horses and trailers that admittedly were scaled somewhat under the usual size for Dinky Toy automobiles, relates the vehicles to a Hornby station with station staff, baggage truck, and trunk, and makes manifest the incongruity of the combination that was all too obvious in the eyes of young enthusiasts.

Fig. 123.   Another interesting collectors' specialty or sidelight is comprised of collecting garages, gas stations, and accessories. Illustrated here are three lithographed metal gas stations, the first two Marx and the third one European, and three Arcade cast-iron cars (including a taxi rank) with accessory pieces.

C. W. Frey

motion pictures to reenact any automotive sequences with their cars when they returned home. That by the early 1930's the Tootsietoy people themselves were fully conversant with the usual mode of play in which their models were involved is made evident by the 1932 booklet, *Let's Make Believe with Tootsietoys,* which, unlike most of their literature relating to the toys was directed to the youngsters rather than to the trade,* and

wherein are found such descriptions of play as "When Bill drove up in his Racing Car, he was surprised to find the Tootsietoy Trucks just standing still. So he signalled Jack in his Monoplane to go down to the Beach and find the driver, who had gone in swimming."

Regardless of how many pieces an owner might have, usually each unit had a distinctly recognizable character and personality for him, as

* The writer has seen only a 1932 consumer booklet of this type. There may have been editions in other years as well. However, 1932 would be the year in which such an extra promotional effect would have appeared

most called for because in that year Tootsietoy sales slid off badly in the face of competitors introducing ten-cent automobiles with real rubber tires, a feature that did not appear on Tootsietoys until late in 1932.

often did the people he imagined driving and riding in them. (Boys themselves usually thought in terms of driving one of the snappier or more favored units, such as the "Racing Car" mentioned in the quotation above.*) Most boys customarily looked with the highest degree of regard on those units they had owned the longest, regardless of how worn or battered they had become. Also, in connection with this idealization of their oldest and therefore most familiar vehicles, boys mainly tended to look upon the automotive styles current at the time their first models were manufactured and acquired as the most desirable level of structural and esthetic perfection. This, of course, is entirely consistent with the usual outlook of very young children whom any change may make feel insecure, although it is contrary to some of the popular later-day legends among collectors, and particularly the englossed Tootsietoy Graham Legend which credits the appearance in 1932 of the rubber-tired three-piece Grahams with automatically turning a previous mere play interest on the part of innumerable miniature-car enthusiasts into a serious collecting hobby. The Grahams and other rubber-tired models played their own revolutionary role in the toy trade, and were extremely attractive to boys just starting their play with miniature cast-metal cars; but the truth is that they were regarded by many longer-established enthusiasts as rather curious interlopers with, to the older boys, rather unnecessary rubber tires. Of course, part of this outlook can be ascribed to the fact that the acceptance of the rubber-tired cars would somehow dis-

---

*There are some curious aspects of snobbery or lack of connection with reality in this depression-time 1932 booklet. The truck driver, it will be noted, is, unlike Bill and Jack, nameless, and evidently when recalled from his dereliction was supposed to drive, hopefully alternately and not simultaneously, more than one truck. On another page it is implied that in the summer the fathers of Tootsietoy owners would likely be out playing golf.

loyally imply that everything they had played with and cherished in previous years was somehow faulty and inadequate.

Tootsietoy and others in the 1920's and 1930's also made similar model airplanes, boats, and trains. The boats did not appear in any great numbers until the 1930's, but the airplanes and trains were widely available in the 1920's. Because of their obvious much smaller scale, the boats seldom entered into play combinations with the automobiles, but the trains, and even more frequently the airplanes, often were combined in play with the cars and trucks, although there were innumerable boys whose interest and activity with toys of this type was confined almost exclusively to the automotive vehicles or who almost always limited their play to one general type of unit at a time, play with trains or boats, for example, being independent of play with automobiles and with each other. On the other hand, as long as the size of the toys was fairly consistent, the boys usually combined cast-iron automobiles with the die-cast and slush-cast metal models in their play. Many, probably most, boys of the ages involved did not or could not detect any real difference in the two basic types of cast-metal cars and trucks, although a few undoubtedly were conscious that there was some distinction, if perhaps to them an intangible one, between the cast-iron and the lead- or zinc-based alloy vehicles. The really important differences in the eyes of the youngsters was of size and the relative proportion of one unit to another in a group of toys; and, as already emphasized, most children have a very well-developed sense of the practical interplay of these factors and of the principles involved, even if they are still far too young to be able verbally to enunciate these principles in a manner understandable to an adult.

Another point worth emphasizing in connection with the customary independent play with these little cars and trucks is that they were, in effect, instant toys. Their use did not require that

Fig. 124.   Two small lithographed sheet-metal garages and their accompanying clockwork lithographed automobiles. At the left is a Bing double garage with limousine and touring car (*G. William Holland Collection*). At the right is a Lehmann single garage with what, although not fully visible, must be a sedan, for it is lettered SEDAN on the hood (*Ward Kimball*).

special space be cleared or time involved in setting them up before they could be played with, as in the case, say, of a toy train that ran on tracks and might well include a number of accessory pieces—not that setting up such a model-railroad system took too long for the average boy. However, all that was necessary with the automobiles was to bring them out from wherever they were kept—usually a conveniently reached box—and full play could be started immediately. Of course, many children played with the automobiles in connection with other toys, such as blocks or toy animals and structures,* or even with homemade miniature buildings made from cardboard or boxes.† In particular there were always garages and fire houses to be built of blocks or cardboard or boxes to accompany the little automobiles.

WHEN DID THE COLLECTING START?

In his book *Model Car Collecting* F. Brian Jewell observes somewhat dubiously that some hobbyists assert that they were active as collectors of miniature cast-metal automobiles in the early 1920's. Presumably he refers primarily to British hobbyists. However, in the United States there are similarly collectors who trace their interest back to about 1925, about the time that the Tootsietoy automobiles became widely promoted and accepted. One can agree with Mr. Jewell that these early dates of active collecting interest may be

---

* In the later 1920's and 1930's, many of the stores in the United States handling miniature cast-metal automobiles also sold an extensive variety of usually British-made cast-metal farm animals, ponds, bridges, dovecotes, dog houses, fences, and similar articles. These, no doubt through a process of association of materials, price, and proximity on the counters, frequently were bought and played with as a logical part of the miniature cast-metal automobile picture.

† *The Jolly Book of Boxcraft,* by Patten Beard, published in New York in 1915, illustrates and extols this type of combined play of commercial miniature automobiles and homemade buildings. It appeared a little prior to the great blooming of the miniature cast-metal automobile, and the vehicles illustrated are slightly larger lithographed sheet-metal cars.

so, but must disagree with his reasoning for questioning the validity or importance of such claims, which is based on the theory that there is little meaning in collecting anything if the potential variety available at the time is very limited. In 1925 there were at least several dozen miniature cast-metal automobiles and related vehicles being manufactured or sold in the United States, France, and Great Britain, which would be far more than enough to inspire anyone so inclined to start collecting in earnest. Counting color variations, there must have been at least one hundred to two hundred, Tootsietoy alone at that date accounting for over sixty varieties. Nor is the matter to be properly questioned on the basis that it is impossible to recognize a collecting hobby as such unless there is a certain minimum participation therein. Actually, except for such ones as may artificially be created and stimulated for commercial ends, all collecting hobbies start in a limited and personal way but are nonetheless valid because there is a lack of awareness or communication among widely scattered participants. Even one isolated but sincere and enthusiastic individual can found a new collecting hobby that may one day sweep the world, although in many instances it will be found that several widely separated persons quite unknown to each other will have independently conceived the same idea at approximately the same time. In either case, the fact that the hobby does not become widely known or shared by many others until somewhat later would in no way detract from the achievement of such an individual or individuals.

The real touchstone for determining longevity in active collecting of miniature cast-metal automobiles, as it is for any other collecting hobby, is that of outlook. It is upon this point and this point alone that most claims for supposed very early activity in model-car collecting fall short. That is to say, there are many men who now are active model-automobile collectors who first accumulated specimens in the 1920's (or conceivably even earlier) or in the 1930's, and many of them still possess some or all of these early acquisitions, and have proudly incorporated them into their

Fig. 125. Small lithographed sheet-metal German automobiles of the type often erroneously referred to as "penny toys." Most of the cars of this type actually retailed for five and ten cents each in the United States. Still fairly widely sold in the 1920's, they were largely driven off the market by the American-made cast-metal miniatures.

C. W. Frey

Fig. 126. Two somewhat interesting but rather late model automobiles made during what might be described as a modern revival of the friction toy. Two views of a 12 1/2-inch-long tailfin Cadillac manufactured in Japan, and a 10-inch Porsche produced in Germany.

C. W. Frey

present-day collections. But the fact that a man today has in his collection some of the selfsame cars that he played with as a youngster some decades ago does not establish that he was a collector thirty or forty years ago or that he has been collecting ever since.

The truth is that many men who now are active model-car collectors have been fortunate enough to retain some or all of their boyhood specimens. In fact, many who are not even collectors similarly have kept their old miniature cast-metal automobiles—too many, say those collectors who like to think that many of the early models are excessively rare and have survived only in the most minute quantities. Most growing boys, especially in that era before adult model building and model-collecting hobbies became widespread and therefore respectable, were torn between renouncing an

interest in what they feared might be regarded by many of their contemporaries and elders as childish things, and a hankering to retain some of their toys in which they still felt an active interest, or at least an attachment. Thus a great deal of material, whose loss was later seriously regretted, usually passed from the ken of its original owner.

While the larger, more substantial, and more costly toys, such as steel trucks of the Buddy "L" type, all too obviously proclaimed both to boys and elders that they were outgrown and should be given away, miniature cast-metal automobiles often passed unnoticed because of their small size and low cost. Accordingly, many a boy simply packed his models of this type away in a corner of a bureau drawer or closet, and for years virtually forgot their very existence. A considerable number of present-day collectors have related that it was not until they returned from service in World War II that they thought of these miniatures for the first time in years, and congratulated themselves upon their foresight in retaining them.

A number of these gentlemen did thereafter become model car collectors, and if more or less haphazard childhood acquisition and subsequent fortuitous preservation of specimens in this manner constitutes collecting in any valid context, then there were tens of thousands of collectors of miniature cast-metal automobiles in the 1920's and 1930's. Logic, however, compels a rejection of the thesis that either or even both acquisition or preservation in themselves properly equates with collecting in the sense the term now is used by model automobile enthusiasts, albeit it might be possible for purists to cite dictionary definitions to establish a case for this in a wholly linguistic denotation.

However, every thoughtful hobbyist will agree that the term "collecting" implies a great deal more than mere accidental gathering of toys for play (the selection of the models in most cases being by the giver and not the recipient) and saving them. There must be, if the individual involved is truly to qualify as having been a collector in the 1920's or 1930's, at least some purposeful intention connected with the gathering of the specimens other than simply as objects of juvenile play. Such intention could be the deliberate seeking of varied specimens of replicas of real vehicles or of trying to establish or complete a series of available models. Or there must have been some purposeful preservation of the models in question, whether to retain what knowingly had been assembled in a deliberate effort at collecting or even merely because the owner somehow believed or sensed that the models would somehow, someday, take on true historical value and interest either from the standpoint of the prototype vehicles or of the manufacture of the miniatures themselves. It can be said that at least one of the foregoing factors or inclinations must have consciously been present somewhere along the line for an individual validly to claim a background of collecting miniature cast-metal automobiles that extends back some time before World War II. It might seem that, dealing as it does with matters of thought and outlook, it would be extremely difficult to determine whether what survives in the original owner's hands today actually represents a conscious collection or just a fortuitous survival. Actually, the nature of the assemblage of models itself usually settles the point. Are the models all of a certain general size, or are all models that represent good replicas of specific prototypes, or are the models gathered in an obvious pattern of color and other variations? If the answer to any of these is Yes, then it must be granted that the individual in question was a collector in the true sense. There are few collectors whose credentials in this direction are impeccable, but a sufficient number of collections have survived to establish beyond any doubt that there were, in the 1920's and 1930's, a limited number of pioneering individuals who took the hobby of collecting miniature cast-metal automobiles seriously. These few had the incentive, hardihood (for this surely must have been required in the face of those who would consider the practice an absurdity), and the means to purchase over a period of years every different model within the scope of their collecting pattern that appeared on the market, or at least that was offered at the points of sale that they frequented with regularity with this in mind. Some of them still are collecting, and justly merit the credit for their longevity in the hobby that they proudly claim.

COLLECTING AFTER WORLD WAR II

Whatever the relative paucity of interest both in building and collecting model automobiles as a serious hobby prior to World War II, there is no question that when the hobby burst forth with a vengeance immediately following the war, this out-

Fig. 127. Window and store displays of model automobiles around 1940. The cast-metal miniatures in these scenes are mostly Barclay and Manoil; in fact, their products form the entire battleground scene. The units in the third photograph are all Barclay, except for the large tractor and truck that are molded of rubber.

"Playthings"
F. W. Woolworth & Co.

Fig. 128. A. J. Koveleski of Hudson Miniatures, the man most responsible for the present-day model automobile building hobby as a result of the 3/4-inch-scale kits manufactured in the late 1940's and early 1950's. Also pictured is a 1952 stock advertising mat emphasizing the model car collecting theme.

"Craft, Model and Hobby Industry"

pouring of popularity represented not only a current interest in itself but contained many elements of long-pent-up and slowly maturing interest that had been building since well before the war. The racing of model cars powered by miniature internal-combustion reciprocating engines, which aroused great interest in the late 1940's both in America and in Great Britain and then suddenly suffered a most substantial falling off, must be considered a part of this overall model-automobile enthusiasm, even though it was essentially apart from the newly developed theme of building and collecting static model automobiles. While internal-combustion-engine model-car racing had had a considerable following prior to the war, the hobby of building and collecting static model cars was for the most part a postwar development. As a matter of fact, however, there were a number of signs of interest manifested even before conclusion of the war.

At the time, perhaps, especially in the United States, these signs were not generally regarded as a portent of great things to come. During and immediately after the war it seemed natural enough that a number of hobbyists would be interested in building models of military vehicles such as tanks and the newly famed Jeep general-purpose vehicle.* As far as Great Britain is con-

---

* Considerable controversy and litigation developed over both the origin of the name Jeep and the right to its ownership as a trade name applied to motor vehicles. The word Jeep appears to have originated as the name of a character in the "Thimble Theatre Starring Popeye" comic strip well before the war. When the first prototype of the vehicle was developed by the American Bantam Car Company of Butler, Pennsylvania, it was officially designated a GP, or General Purpose, vehicle in United States Army nomenclature. Popular usage among the soldiers quickly transferred "GP" to "Jeep." Following the war there was a suit to determine who owned the by then valuable name as applied to automobiles: American Bantam, who had created the design but whose production facilities had proven woefully inadequate even to begin to approach the demand; Willys-Overland, who had then become the first large prime contractor; or Ford, who also had manufactured the car in quantity during the war. The matter was adjudicated in favor of Willys as having been the first of the three actually to have used the name Jeep.

Fig. 129.   A group of 3/4-inch-scale models built from Hudson Miniatures kits. In this and the following two figures the models are arranged chronologically according to the age of their prototype, rather than in the sequence in which these kits of largely wood components were introduced by Hudson. The cars are the 1900 Packard, 1903 Rambler, 1903 Ford Model A, and 1904 Oldsmobile.

Polk's Model Craft Hobbies, Inc.

cerned, the interest not only in military vehicles but in racing cars as well can be dated to before the actual end of the war. Charles Woodland, a noted British model-car authority and hobbyist whose personal activity in model-automobile building dates back to the early 1930's, notes that not only can the real interest in the hobby in Great Britain be dated to 1945 "but almost to the month of May, Victory in Europe." At that time the first known book on model automobiles was published in England, *Model Race Cars* by D. A. Russell and D. B. M. Wright. The subject of its title was to be of primary interest among British model builders and model-car collectors for some time to come.

On the other hand, the first widespread commercialization of model-car kits occurred in the United States when some kits, being made of wood and other noncritical materials, came on the market prior to the actual ending of the war. By the end of 1945 there were approximately a dozen American manufacturers making such kits, mainly of military vehicles but including at least two racing cars, in 1/4-inch, 3/4-inch, 1-inch, and 1 1/2-inch scales.* Among these were at least six

---

*It is possible there still are additions to be made to the following list of wooden kits that were on the market by the end of 1945: All-Star, Jeep; Austin Craft, 1 1/2- and 2 1/2-ton trucks, Jeep; Cavacraft, bulldozer, amphibious truck; Megow, Jeep, Sherman tank, and two different racing cars; Mod-Ac, half-track, scout car, amphibious Jeep (also four-wheel army searchlight); Ready Cut, station wagon, 1 1/2-ton truck, Jeep, amphibious Jeep, trailer for truck or Jeep (also antitank gun); Rogers, Sherman tank, Weasel amphibious tank;

Fig. 130. Four more 3/4-inch-scale model cars built from the famous Hudson Miniatures kits of the late 1940's and early 1950's. In the earlier kits the wheels and small parts were die castings. Later molded plastic was employed for these components. The models illustrated here are the 1906 Locomobile, 1909 Stanley Steamer and Ford Model T touring car, and 1910 Ford Model T roadster.

Polk's Model Craft Hobbies, Inc.

kits for Jeeps, three for amphibious Jeeps, and three for Sherman tanks.

Most of these kits were in production for only a comparatively short time, although a very few carried over into the early 1950's. The demand for most of these miniature vehicles obviously was a result of the war. It is generally acknowledged that in the United States the first really substan-

Star, amphibious truck; Ting, Willett truck; West Craft, Jeep (a sort of superkit, and sometimes designated the Super Jeep—there were over 100 parts furnished to build this 1-inch scale model); Western, 1 1/2-ton truck, Jeep with antitank gun, Sherman tank. In addition there were the following additional kits whose manufacture or manufacturers have not yet been identified: Jeep, amphibious Jeep, and amphibious truck.

Ting is included in this list although to date the writer has been unable to ascertain anything further concerning this make through inquiries both in the United States and in Great Britain. Their Willett truck kit has been found so far cataloged only by an American jobber, but it seems most likely it was of British manufacture.

tial trend of interest and enthusiasm and the main point of departure for the modern hobby of building model automobiles was in the area of models of old cars. This in turn had much to do with prompting the modern enthusiast to collect both models of old cars and old model cars. The first of the 3/4-inch-scale "Old Timer" kits manufactured by Hudson Miniatures of Scranton, Pennsylvania, appeared in 1947 and became literally an overnight sensation in the toy and model trade. These were kits incorporating primarily wooden components. In the initial kits of the series the wheels and small fittings were made of die-cast metal, but molded plastic was employed for these parts in the later output. As additional kits were introduced gradually over five seasons, not all the kits were made or can exist today in two distinct versions according to which material was used for the wheels and small parts, the later models having been produced only with plastic

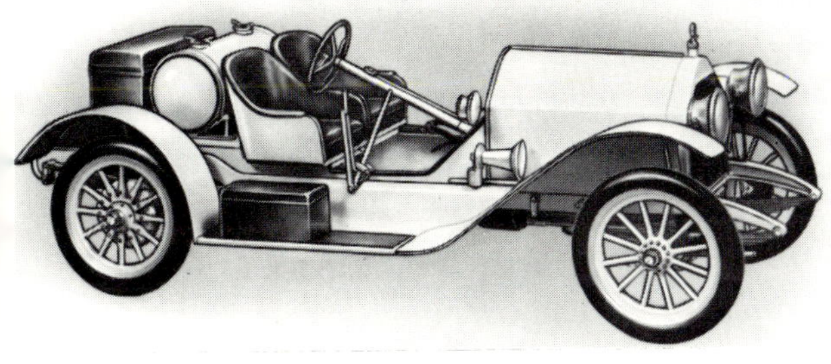

Fig. 131. Another representative group of 3/4-inch-scale wooden models constructed from the famous "Old Timers" kits manufactured by Hudson Miniatures in the late 1940's and early 1950's. The five models pictured here are the 1910 International, 1911 Maxwell and Buick "Bug," 1913 Mercer, and 1914 Stutz.

Polk's Model Craft Hobbies, Inc.

wheels and small accouterments.*

Both the kits themselves and completed models built up therefrom now are avidly collected, the kits being sought intact as collectors' items in their own right. It would, indeed, be a hardy soul who, securing a Hudson Miniatures wooden kit today, would have the temerity to build it up into a completed model car instead of keeping it intact as a historical model kit. The actual production of these wooden kits halted in

---

* Reference is made here only to the original Hudson Miniatures "Old Timer" kits with wooden parts. Aurora Plactics, Inc., somewhat later purchased the rights to the name and designs, and currently manufactures several of the same models in completely plastic form under the name "Old Timers."

1953 in the face of the by then rather wide availability of much lower-priced kits of molded plastic parts for both antique and current-type model automobiles produced by other manufacturers. While the sale of these wooden kits, which in the late 1940's had universally been considered one of the most sensationally successful lines of all time in the hobby trade, did fall off greatly in the face of the competition of kits of plastic parts, it would be far from correct to assert that the latter suddenly killed the demand for the wooden "Old Timers." The many enthusiasts who still sought them could be supplied from a very sizable remaining stock. What did write *finis* to the Hudson Miniature "Old Timer" kits was a disastrous

50 NATIONAL MAGAZINES carried the "Old Timer" message to 25 million readers throughout the year!

TELEVISION SHOWS featured "Old Timers" before audiences of 25 million viewers on coast-to-coast networks! Recently seen on James Melton's "Ford Festival" and on Sheriff Bob Dixon's Show!

MAGAZINE STORIES on old-time autos appeared in nearly every national magazine! Color cover story on the 1914 Stutz Bearcat in Mechanix Illustrated; also the 1903 Model A Ford article in Science and Mechanics.

RADIO PROGRAMS continued to feature scripts and comedy situations built around the old-time autos. The Maxwell continues to head the list on the top-ranking network show!

STUTZ BEARCAT TOUR. "Chicago or Bust" created hobby interest en route to Chicago at the World Hobby Exposition.

OLD-TIME AUTO MEETS and Hill Climbs were held in many sections of the country and kept antique autos at high pitch throughout the year!

NEWSPAPER PUBLICITY by the reams appeared throughout the country as old-time autos were featured in Anniversary celebrations, Glidden Tours, etc.

WINDOW DISPLAY CONTEST on "Old Timers" among hobby dealers created further interest in the Science and Mechanics tie-in story on the 1903 Model "A" Ford.

What A Year Our "OLD TIMERS" Chalked Up in 1951!

BRIEFLY on this page we've outlined a review of the 1951 promotions, advertising and publicity that have made "Old Timers" the most talked-about hobby in the industry! Everywhere you looked — on television, in magazine ads and in feature stories — you saw them publicized from coast-to-coast! In 1951 — more than ever before "Old Timers" reached into the hearts of millions of hobbyists—youngsters and oldsters—from the age of 9 to 90—and won their enthusiastic interest!

AS WE GO in to the Annual M.I.A. Trade Show in Chicago, we are getting ready to announce exciting new models to expand our line from the 16 antique auto kit models in our collection! Above we show the 1902 Air-Cooled Franklin that lists at $2.50. The other 15 models retail at $1.95 to $3.95.

SO FOR THIS YEAR in the hobby industry look to "Old Timers" for bigger and better promotions! We assure you that we will be in there "pitching for you in '52!"

VISIT US at Booths 37 and 38 At The M.I.A. TRADE SHOW Morrison Hotel, Chicago

DEALER HELP MATERIAL was furnished free! These included colorful Window Streamers for Father's Day, Model "A" Ford, Christmas, etc. Newspaper mats in two sizes as well as color folders and brochures were furnished to hobby stores free!

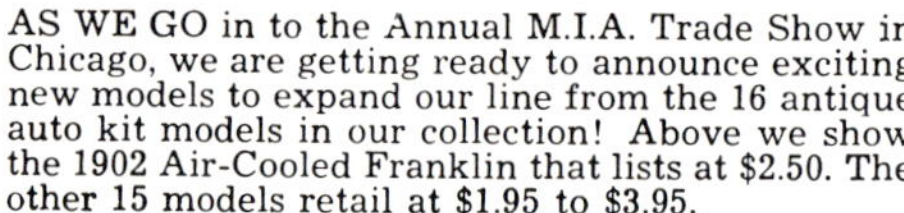

Fig. 132.   The 3/4-inch-scale "Old Timers" kits were the subject not only of an extensive magazine advertising campaign but of many forceful special promotions as indicated in the sketches around this 1952 trade advertisement. The model pictured in the center of the ad is the 1902 Franklin.

"Craft, Model and Hobby Industry"

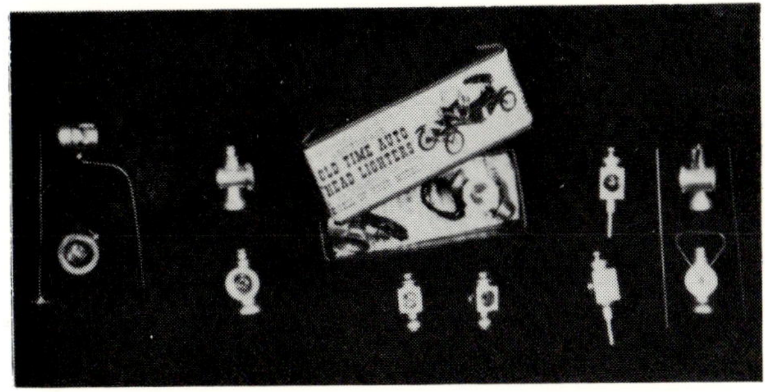

Fig. 133.   During the great years of the real Ford Model T, numerous manufacturers made accessories and extra equipment items for Ford owners. Somewhat similarly, in the heyday of the Hudson Miniatures, Aristo-Craft offered these battery-powered brass lamps for cars built from Hudson kits.

Aristo-Craft Distinctive Miniatures

fire that destroyed the entire warehouse stock in 1958, with the result that once readily obtainable merchandise immediately became scarce and much sought-after collectibles.

In all, there were twenty different 3/4-inch-scale Hudson Miniature "Old Timer" wooden kits produced. The complete list follows, no catalog numbers ever having been assigned to any of the kits by the manufacturer, and the order of the list is not that in which the kits were introduced but follows the rotation on the last Hudson Miniatures order form (the first kit was the 1911 Maxwell and the twentieth and last model brought out was the Ford Model-T fire engine): 1904 Stevens Duryea, 1904 Oldsmobile, 1911 Maxwell, 1903 Ford Model A, 1900 Packard, 1911 Buick Bug, 1903 Rambler, 1903 Cadillac, 1910 Ford Model T (roadster), 1902 Franklin, 1906 Columbia electric, 1914 Ford Model-T fire engine, 1909 Stanley steamer, 1910 International Harvester, 1909 Ford Model T (touring car), 1911 Brush delivery truck, 1914 Stutz Bearcat, 1913 Mercer Raceabout, 1906 "Old 16" Locomobile, and 1914 Regal underslung.* In addition, four 3/8-inch-

scale kits of plastic parts were introduced in 1951 and 1952 by Hudson Miniatures. Designated "Little Old Timers," they duplicated the prototypes of four of the 3/4-inch-scale wooden kits: 1904 Oldsmobile, 1911 Maxwell, 1913 Mercer Raceabout, and 1914 Regal underslung.† An additional series of four 3/8-inch plastic models was announced by Hudson Miniatures in 1953 but never put into production.

There appears no inclination even on the part of the most iconoclastic members of the model-hobby fraternity to dispute the fact that it was the Hudson Miniatures 3/4-inch scale "Old Timers" kits that really were responsible for the great boom and enthusiasm in model-automobile building, or that the entire model-automobile hobby and kit industry of today owes a tremendous debt to Hudson Miniatures and the pioneering and promotion of its proprietors, A. J. (Tony) Koveleski and Doris Hudson. It is interesting to note that Mr. Koveleski himself was—and is—a most zealous collector of both real old automobiles and of old model cars. A completely outgoing personality, he put a promotive effort behind the "Old Timers" kits of a fervor and compass never previously seen in the hobby business, including radio and television appearances, an enormous advertising campaign in some fifty national magazines, and, above all, his numerous personal appearances in one or another of his old automobiles, especially in his meticulously restored gleaming yellow 1914 Stutz Bearcat, probably the most famous antique automobile in America. Just one of his exploits, which garnered reams of publicity for model cars all along the way, was his famous "Chicago or Bust!" trip in the Stutz from Scranton to the World Hobby Exposition in Chicago in 1951. It is probably not too much to say that, apart from the role the Hudson Miniatures "Old

---

* Following the success of the initial Hudson Miniature "Old Timers" kits, somewhat similar wooden kits were brought out by others, most prominently the Fador Manufacturing Company of Elmira, New York, who made the following seven 3/4-inch scale "Smallster" automobile kits, the first types appearing in 1949: 1904 Cadillac, 1905 White Model-F touring car, 1905 Reo four-passenger runabout, 1908 Baker electric, 1909 Hupmobile roadster, 1909 EMF 30 racer, and a 1909 EMF "three-in-oner" kit that could optionally be built up either as a roadster, single rear seater (a type with a second seat for but one additional passenger), or a touring car. The Mod-Ac Manufacturing Company of Los Angeles, California, made kits for a 3/4-inch-scale 1902 Pierce and a 1/2-inch-scale replica of the 1877 Selden car, the scaling down being in relation to the full-sized Selden vehicle constructed on the 1877 design in the early 1900's. As accessory units primarily brought into being by the popularity of the Hudson Miniatures kits but suitable also for use on other makes, Aristo-Craft Distinctive Miniatures of Newark, New Jersey, brought out five types of brass head and sidelights fitted with miniature working bulbs for those who desired to add working lights to their display models of old-time automobiles.

---

† The molds for the four 3/8-inch-scale "Little Old Timers" kits subsequently were sold by Hudson Miniatures to Revell, Inc. Revell did not use these molds in the United States but sent them to England, where kits were produced from them.

Fig. 134.   Following the initial success of the Hudson Miniatures "Old Timers" 3/4-inch-scale wooden kits, several kits of a somewhat similar nature were produced by Fador. Pictured here are four of the Fador "Smallster" models, the 1904 Cadillac, 1905 Reo, 1905 White steamer, and 1909 Hupmobile.

Polk's Model Craft Hobbies

Timers" kits played in stimulating model-car building and collecting, they undoubtedly were one of the major factors in creating the widespread interest in real old automobiles and in automobile history in general that became increasingly notable in the late 1940's and 1950's.

The foregoing, however, has brought us well past World War II and into what most enthusiasts consider the modern, or current, era of model-car history and of the model-automobile-collecting hobby. Having thus circled back to this point, it is time to proceed with further information on the techniques and customs of the active side of model-car collecting as it is practiced today.*

---

* However, that the story of the kits of wooden parts made in the years immediately following World War II may be as complete as possible for collectors and enthusiasts interested in the subject, mention should be made here of the line of 1/2-inch-scale kits manufactured by Ace Products of Pasadena, California, in the late 1940's and early 1950's. These were models of contemporary cars, and the fully developed line consisted of seventeen numbers: No. 1R, pickup; No. 2R, jalopy; No. 3R "T" rod; No. 4R, dirt-track racer; No. 5R, midget

ARRANGEMENT, HOUSING, AND DISPLAY

The beginner collector invariably wants to be able to see all his model cars at any time the mood strikes him. This is understandable. But he is puzzled when he finds that many experienced collectors and owners of large collections rarely display more than a portion of their collections,

racer; No. 6R, midget racer; No. 7R, Jeepster; No. 8R, MG; No. 10R, deluxe midget racer (1-inch scale); No. 15R, convertible; No. 20R, hot rod; No. 25R, Jaguar; No. 30R, Corvette; No. 49R, club coupe (designed for optional use with a Supermite electric motor if desired, and could be built up either as a coupe or as a convertible); No. 146, roadster; No. 242, civilian Jeep, and No. 246, U.S. Army Jeep. (See Figs. 135 and 136.) In addition, in the early 1950's there was a line of 1/4-inch-scale kits of wooden parts manufactured by the Miniature Trucks Company of Benton Harbor, Michigan. One was a Mobilgas trailer tank truck, and there were at least six other kits, but information is not available as to whether some or all of these were distinctly different models or merely the trailer tank truck in other company names and colors. In all, there were well over seventy-five kits of wooden parts for building model automobiles and trucks manufactured in the United States between the end of World War II and 1953.

Fig. 135. In the late 1940's and early 1950's a line of kits of wooden components for building models of contemporary automobiles was manufactured by Ace Products. Illustrated here are five of the Ace models, the MG, roadster, civilian Jeep, Jeepster, and club coupe. The latter was designed to be powered by means of an electric motor if desired.
Ace Products

packing the rest away in boxes, chests of drawers, or other suitable containers.

However, having all the models in a collection on display, either on open shelves or in protective cases, enables the collector to see it expand in size. Another advantage is that of instantly checking whether an identical model or variation already is represented in a collection. This is an advantage that is of real value to all collectors, those with a few or those with many models. Collectors have excellent memories, and know exactly what they possess. Nevertheless, no matter how good a collectors' memory may be, or how detailed and accurate an inventory of his collection he may keep, there are times when points arise as to whether a model is an exact duplicate or not that can only be determined by a very careful physical examination of the speci-

mens themselves. Thus, being able to keep every model on display has a definite advantage even for owners of extremely large collections.

On the other hand there are good reasons why many collectors do not feel that they must keep every model out on display. Substantially there are two reasons involved here: space and deterioration. Both are closely linked. Many collectors simply do not have the available space properly to house all their model cars on display. The collector who feels he must do so eventually finds that instead of showing his model cars and trucks full-side view or at a slight angle, he is forced by additions to place them ever closer and closer together and at an ever greater angle until eventually many of his cars are crowded side by side on shelves with only the front ends visible. The next step invariably is to place some items

Fig. 136. Five more wooden car models constructed from kits manufactured by Ace. The models pictured are the 1/2-inch-scale jalopy, "T" rod, hot rod, midget racer, and dirt track racer. Except for their 1-inch-scale deluxe midget racer which is not illustrated, all Ace kits were 1/2-inch scale.

Ace Products

directly atop others, or add more shelves and display cabinets, until in time there remains no more available space. Long before this point is reached, most collectors give up, and accept the fact that a substantial portion of a collection should be packed away.

How much can or should be displayed depends, of course, on the individual collector's space situation, and also on the size or sizes of the models in a collection. Obviously, within a given space a great many more models in the miniature cast-metal range, where the average model size is around 4 inches in length, can be displayed than 15- or 20-inch-long stamped-metal vehicles. It is certainly true that a great many of the small cast-metal or plastic models in the 1/48th- to 1/42nd-size range can be displayed in a room that can be devoted to model automobiles; even a great many 1/25th- and 1/24th-size models. However, even in these cases there are

Fig. 137.   The great boom of kits of plastic parts for building model automobiles started in the early 1950's. These are five 3/8-inch-scale models built from Revell kits of the period, the 1914 Stutz, 1910 Cadillac, 1908 Buick, 1910 Studebaker electric, and 1915 Ford Model T sedan.
Revell, Inc.

practical limits for most collectors, as a few simple calculations will establish. Many collectors, far from being able to devote a room, or at least its walls, to a display of their models are hard pressed almost from the beginning to find adequate display space.

Fortunately, it is a characteristic of most model automobiles, and especially of models of

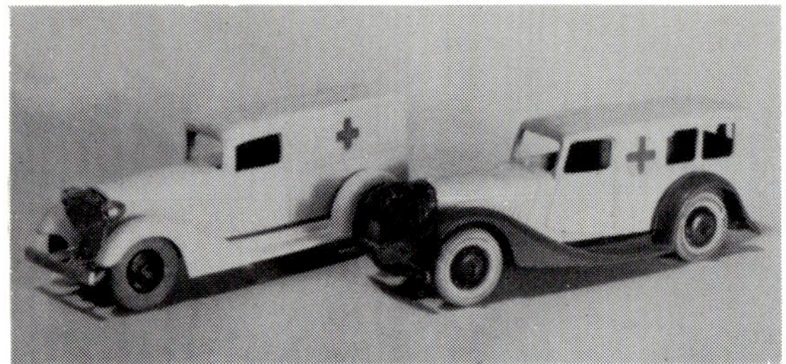

Fig. 138. The three-part-construction miniature cast-metal automobile with separate body, chassis, and grille castings was launched late in 1932 with the first of the Tootsietoy Grahams. The Tootsietoy Graham ambulance (left) appeared in 1935. At the right is a Dinky Toy ambulance introduced in 1934.

Dr. Clinton B. Seeley

old cars, that they possess a great deal of eye appeal and decorative value, and because of this displays may well be allowed to invade living and dining rooms. However, there usually are limits to the practicality of this type of display. A few large models or a few cases of small models may well be accepted in most families as adding to the décor of a room, but in most cases, regardless of their own interest in or enthusiasm for real or miniature cars, the distaff side of a household will feel that there is a point beyond which this definitely can be overdone. Fortunate indeed, then, is the hobbyist who wants to display a substantial part of his collection and can devote space in a bedroom, den, or family room to his hobby, or who has available space in the cellar or attic.

There are few collectors who are able successfully to display their models on open shelves with relatively little accumulation of dust and grime. Having to dust models at periodic intervals is not at all a task that the average collector approaches with enthusiasm. It is arduous, the more so because it must be done with great care lest delicate models be damaged in the handling. The condition of the models deteriorates under this repeated handling and cleaning. Much that may be found in ordinary dust acts as a fine abrasive during the cleaning process. In addition, having models out on open shelves is a temptation to

visitors to touch and handle the models, which is far from beneficial to them, especially in the case of particularly rare, detailed, old, or fragile ones. For these reasons, protective enclosures are highly desirable, though often far from practical.

Dustproof glass cases are the ideal means by which to display model cars. These are now available both in stock sizes or built to order. Some collectors may have the equipment and ability to construct them for themselves. The cost of purchasing such cases is not a light one, especially when it is equated with the cost of additional model cars that could be bought for the same investment. Furthermore, insofar as the stock cases are concerned, the cases usually are not of a size or a capacity to hold a really substantial number of miniature cars, with the result that a growing collection may well keep far out in front of the capacity of display room on hand. Despite all this, the careful consideration of securing one or a number of such cases is recommended to all collectors who desire to both display and protect their model cars. They should be substantially dustproof. This is rather difficult to attain with cases with double sliding doors, which are handier and neater than cases with wide and somewhat unwieldy hinged doors. However, when the latter are properly constructed they will be found to keep out dust much more satisfactorily than cases

Fig. 139. At the top left is a Tootsietoy die-cast Graham sedan; to the right what appears to be a Kilgore Graham in cast iron. The lower photograph shows a Tootsietoy four-part die-cast La Salle (left) and a similar cast-iron three-part vehicle manufactured by Dent. Note that in the Dent three-part construction the front bumper is part of the chassis casting.

Dr. Clinton B. Seeley

Fig. 140. As described in the text, Hubley employed three different forms of three-part construction for various cast-iron model automobiles. The coupe illustrated is of the second form. Note that whereas in Dent models (Fig. 139) the front bumper is part of the chassis casting, in Hubley models it is integral with the grille casting. See also Fig. 174.
Adam Pellicot, Jr.; William Dreyer photograph

Fig. 141. Slush-cast models of the 1920's and 1930's. All were manufactured by the Kansas Toy and Novelty Company except for the coupe at the lower right of the group of four. This latter model is marked PACKARD on its sides, and its manufacturer is as yet unidentified.
G. William Holland photograph
Adam Pellicot, Jr.; William Dreyer photographs

with double sliding doors. Most of the stock cases currently available are suitable only for housing the smaller-size model cars; they are in fact designed for cars in the 1/48th-to-1/42nd-size range.

For those who are deterred from purchasing such cases because of the cost, or who desire to display larger-sized models under glass but not go to the expense of having custom-made cases constructed, secondhand furniture shops may provide practical and acceptable substitutes in the form of glass-fronted bookcases, china cabinets, and similar units, which, if they are not dust-tight when secured, usually can be made substantially so with a little judicious application of felt stripping.

Cases can be purchased with lights already fitted, or lights can be installed in almost any cabinet when desired. Lighted cabinets naturally look extremely attractive, and beautifully show off the models housed within them. Glass shelves are mandatory when lights are used in the cabinets themselves. However, the excessive heat generated by lights in enclosed areas makes their use a far from unmixed blessing, and to most, their disadvantages far outweigh their advantages. In many instances, their heat may distort and ruin some of the early types of plastics used for entire model cars or car components. If fluorescent lights are used, they have a tendency to change or distort the precise appearance of color values. Exact colors and shades are of considerable importance to most model-car collectors, both from the standpoint of attaining the exact shade of the color of prototype and of minute variations in factory colors on the part of those whose collections are

oriented to the history of the model automobile itself. Therefore, fluorescent lighting of collections is avoided by most knowledgeable collectors. Any careful evaluation or comparison of model-automobile colors should be made in natural light or under conventional incandescent lights. Model automobiles should not, however, be exposed to direct sunlight for any sustained period of time, or serious deterioration may result.

Special cabinets and display boxes are available for those who find glass cases impractical. These are obtainable from hobby supply dealers. They are usually quite inexpensive, and are especially made for model automobiles of the smaller sizes. Usually they are molded of clear plastic and are relatively dust-tight. If not, they can be sealed with transparent tape, although this obviously precludes easy access to their contents. Some of the cases are in the form of shadow boxes that will hold perhaps a half a dozen of the small 1/48th-to-1/42nd size cars; others are designed for a single specimen. Some of the cases may readily be arranged in multiples on special racks that are available for use with them in wall mounting, and an extensive display of such individual cases can be very attractive. Another display-case device that is especially designed and suitable for somewhat larger models in the 1/32nd to 1/24th sizes is supplied as a kit that builds a complete enclosed automobile-carrying trailer with its body molded entirely in clear plastic. A single completed model car is placed on display inside the trailer. As a possible variation or "change of pace" display, several or even a long row of such trailer case display boxes can prove quite interesting and attractive, although its cost may be pro-

Fig. 142. Some additional interesting cast-metal miniatures of the 1930's: above, two as yet not definitely identified slush-cast cars, the coupe at the right having red centers painted on the wheels; left, a Barclay die-cast car carrier bearing slush-cast coupes, and three slush-cast Manoil military units.

G. William Holland photographs

hibitive for an entire collection of hundreds of model cars.

Another variation consists of scenic shadow boxes of varying size and elaboration. These shadow boxes may be only a few inches in depth, containing one or two small cars, and placed within an old-style picture frame, or may be of considerably larger size and provide display space for a dozen or two dozen models. Appropriate scenic backgrounds are used, either hand-painted or with printed scenic background sheets of the type sold in hobby shops for model railroads, or any suitable colored pictures clipped from magazines and other sources. Sometimes the background scene alone is considered sufficient furbishing in front of which to pose a model car. At other times three-dimensional foreground effects are added, using materials and accessories obtainable in most hobby shops and mainly intended for model-railroad use such as ground-work materials, shrubs, and trees, fences, lampposts, buildings, and miniature figures.

While such displays can be most attractive, they generally require more space than is practical for larger collections. The same thing applies to larger and more elaborate scenic displays of model cars where a good-sized table is used to house a complete miniature town or automotive scene, with streets and roads, model buildings, and natural scenic effects providing a display background for dozens of model cars, even as many as one hundred. Others model tabletop automobile shows or custom-car shows, and display quantities of their models in these settings,

while still others who collect models of old cars may build a miniature antique automobile museum without a roof or with a removable roof so that the contents readily may be viewed, of the type pictured in the frontispiece and in Figs. 19 and 148.

Another type of display is that of a collection of static model cars as part of the scenic background of an operating model railroad, raceway, or roadway system. Most builders of such operating model layouts ordinarily use model automobiles and trucks as part of the scenic picture, and the cars employed for this purpose may in many cases as readily as not be a segment of less important models from a model-car collection, since under these conditions they will continually be exposed to dust and dirt. Preferably, the model cars thus displayed should be of prototypes appropriate to the era that the model represents. Some care will be exercised in this direction by most hobbyists. For example, models of modern cars would hardly be appropriate on a model-railroad system that features a railroad of the early 1900's, but there are numerous model cars that would be proper for such a scene. On the other hand, in this era of old car preservation and driving, models of antique automobiles on a modern model railroad or raceway can always logically be accounted for, aside from the fact that it is always possible to fall back on the miniature antique automobile museum idea mentioned in the preceding paragraph.

The users of static model cars on such operating model systems usually prefer to use

Fig. 143. Two views of portions of collections. Left, a group of slush-cast miniatures temporarily shelved on a pegboard fixture in the collection of Dr. Clinton B. Seeley (*Dr. Clinton B. Seeley*). Right, a group of friction models as displayed in the home of Raymond L. Spong (*Raymond L. Spong*).

Fig. 144.   A group of foreign clockwork-powered stamped-metal model automobiles arranged as an attractive decorative effect in the home of G. William Holland. The first and fourth cars on the long shelf are Bing; the second and fifth are Gunthermann models. Below, left to right, are a CIJ Alfa-Romeo, a Hess, and a Japanese model bearing what is evidently intended to be a simulated Lehmann trademark.

G. William Holland Collection

model cars of a scale identical to or at least approximating the scale of the model trains or automobiles that are being operated. Younger hobbyists tend to select static models larger in scale than the operating models for their model-railroad layouts. Actually, it is not necessary to stick to static models of the same scale as the operating units. Varying smaller-scale static models can be used quite effectively if only a little thought and care are given to their placing so as both to establish a satisfactory-appearing arrangement in themselves and to provide a measure of realistic depth and perspective to the overall model scene. Thus, in the model raceway scene pictured in Fig. 149, the first row of cars parked immediately behind the track fence are of the same size, 1/32nd, as the operating race cars. They are deliberately backed by a road fronting the parking lot, to provide a break in the continuity of the display, and the cars carefully arranged in the parking lot to the rear of this road are all 1/42nd-size or even smaller models. This is a very acceptable model scene which achieves an effect of much greater depth and of possessing more area than there

actually is. Almost any type or age of motor vehicle can logically be worked into a scene on a modern model railroad, raceway, or roadway, including passenger cars, racing cars, safety and security vehicles, antique cars, commercial vehicles, trucks, construction vehicles and machines, and military vehicles.

A considerable latitude is also possible in the scales of the scenic vehicles involved, dependent both on their actual scale and on their arrangement in the scene, before the effect becomes grotesque. In considering the suitability of static car models for this purpose besides scale, bear in mind also that there are big cars, small cars, and compact cars, and that much the same thing applies to a certain extent with trucks and other vehicles. Thus, while a 3.5-mm.-scale model automobile might give a drastically undersized effect in the foreground of a 4-mm.-scale layout if placed side by side with a 4-mm.-scale model of the same car, the 3.5-mm.-scale model car may well pass muster if it is regarded—at least for the purpose of the overall layout display—as a compact instead of a large car.

Fig. 145. Two ideas for the display of individual model cars. Left, a 3/8-inch-scale model hot rod mounted on a wooden base intended to be covered with a glass or plastic dome (Pyro Plastics Corp.), and, right, a simple but effective scene suggestive of the racetrack employed to display a 1/2-inch-scale Bugatti (*Monogram Models, Inc.*).

There also is a general rule of thumb for static model cars used as scenic adjuncts to their layouts by model railroad, raceway, and roadway operators. While there are big cars and little cars, big trucks and little trucks, and so on, there is only one size of human being. Thus in considering a given model car or other vehicle, look at the doors and imagine them in comparison to a six-foot-tall man scaled down to the scale that has been selected for the layout in question. If such a miniature man could get in and out of the doors of the static model car used, well and good. But, if the doors obviously are too small or too large for the imaginary man, pass up this model.

Withal, most serious model-car collectors sooner or later come to the conclusion that it is best to display only a small part of their collections and store away the rest, if possible, in their original, individual boxes. There is, in fact, a double reason for retaining the individual boxes: protection, and the fact that a collector's model car always is more valuable in a collection or in terms of eventual trading or sale if it is accompanied by its original individual box (or, indeed, even by its original blister card in the case of models so packaged). There is no more desirable condition for a model car than to be labeled brand new in the original box. Everyone will agree that it certainly is far better to know about the potential value of boxes at the start of one's collecting career than to learn about it later, after dozens or hundreds of original boxes have haplessly been discarded. Any box has an added value, even when the car within it is in far from new condition. In the case of some of the first miniature cast-metal

cars that were packed in individual boxes in the late 1920's and early 1930's, such as the Tootsietoy Ford Model-A coupe and sedan and the Barclay Cord L29, the presence of such an original box would probably at least double the value of the car.

Reference should also be made here to the special collectors' boxes and carrying cases produced by certain manufacturers of miniature cast-metal automobiles themselves—another manifestation of the appreciation of the value of promoting the hobby on the part of the present-day industry. These usually are compartmented boxes or cases, sometimes arranged in multiples, and furnished either empty or at times containing a series of models. In the latter instances they become a form of set packaging. Each model car has its own individual compartment. A primary intention in the design of these cases is that the hobbyist conveniently can carry duplicates in them when going to the homes of other collectors for trading sessions or to model-car meets. They perform good service in this usage, although some of the cases are designed so as to accommodate smaller models only, and the compartments will not take the 1/48th- to 1/42nd-size models of the largest cars. These cases are good for storing and protecting a number of models (rubber-tired models should, of course, preferably be inserted in the compartments upside down), as well as providing a handy means of carrying unboxed models from place to place. Since they are an integral part of the lines of manufacturers of miniature cast-metal automobiles, the cases will inevitably be sought after as collectors' items themselves, especially the cases

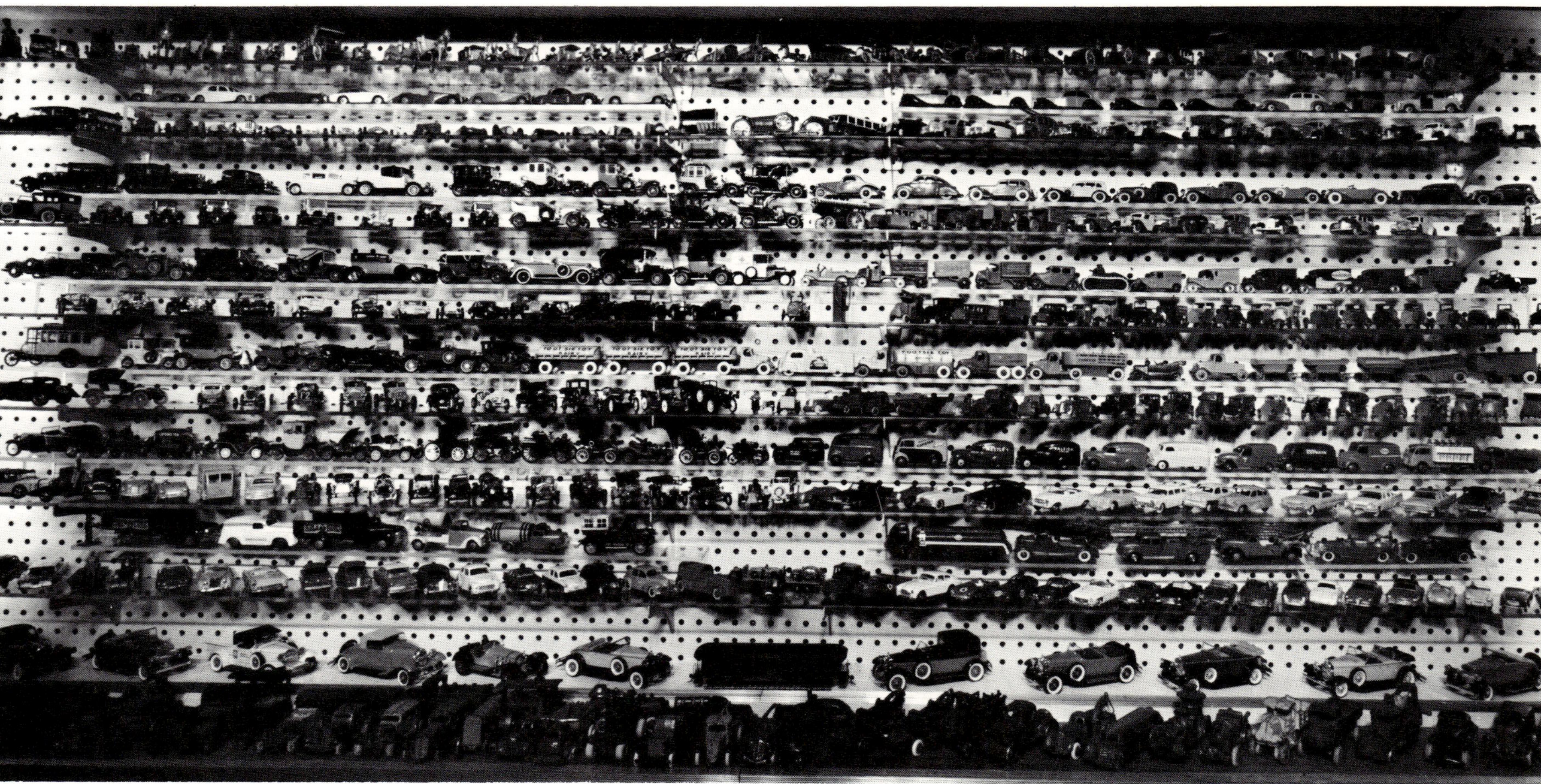

Fig. 146.   A section of the pegboard mounted shelving in the home of Adam Pellicot, Jr., displaying a part of his collection, in this case mainly old and modern cast-metal miniatures. A careful examination of this photograph will reveal that the specimens in the left half are mainly models of old cars, while those in the right half are mainly old model cars.

Adam Pellicot, Jr.; Walter Dreyer photograph

Fig. 147. Many of the old Tootsietoys in the historical collection owned by the manufacturers, the Strombecker Corporation, are sewn to sheets of cardboard to prevent any damage in handling, and are housed in drawers. The men examining the models are, left to right, Joseph, Allan, Myron, and Richard Shure.
Tootsietoy—Strombecker Corp.

(complete with the original contents) made up with special combinations of model cars and sometimes with the store name as an exclusive for a particular wholesale customer.

DETERIORATION

This may seem a surprising element of consideration for beginners, but the fact is that all rubber deteriorates. Many think in terms of rubber deteriorating only when oil or grease accidentally reaches its surface and of the importance of avoiding this condition. Oil or grease does hasten deterioration, but entirely apart from this, all rubber gradually hardens and to some extent deteriorates with time. It is quite true that there exist specimens of model cars made in the 1930's which, having been stored under ideal conditions, show virtually no deterioration of the rubber tires. Even after thirty or more years, they may be fairly resilient and show no external signs of cracking or of flatness. For the most part, however, the rubber on older model cars shows varying degrees of visible deterioration, from the most common flat spots to the vitrually complete breaking up of the tire. While care in modern manufacturing processes have supposedly given hobbyists reasonable assurance against deterioration of modern zinc die castings, as far as can be ascertained actual rubber, when it is employed as the material for miniature plastics, still retains within it the natural inherent characteristics that act over a period of time to harden and deteriorate. This is particularly true in the area of miniature tires acquiring flat spots when the wheel rests in one position for a length of time, just as the tires on a real automobile develop flat spots (which is, of course, something entirely different on a real car than a so-called "flat tire,"

which results from the air escaping from within) when left too long in the same position. When real automobiles are put in "dead storage" over the winter—by no means today so frequent a custom as it once was—one of the most important steps is to block up the axles so the tires will not rest in the same position on the garage floor all winter and develop flat spots. The weight of the average miniature car, slight as it may be, can cause noticeable flat spots to develop if the model is left resting on the tires, unmoved over a prolonged period of time. This is as true of a relatively light 4-inch-long die-cast model as of a heavy 15-inch-long cast-iron model since the ratio of car weight to tire support and resiliency is always about the same.

Once a miniature tire develops a flat spot, there is no way to correct it, although steps can be and should be taken to prevent further flattening. In the case of current or recent models for which replacement tires are available, a new tire can be installed if it is felt to be worth the effort and if this can be accomplished without having partially to dismantle the model, install new axles, or recrimp the old axles (all of which detract from the value of the model car as a collectors' item). While natural rubber hardening and deterioration cannot be prevented or retarded, there are two ways by which the development of flat spots can be prevented. One is to see to it that a model car never rests on the same positions on its tires for any prolonged period of time. This means that a collector must handle every rubber-tired model every few months and shift the position of the tires. New collectors very often scorn such advice until several years later, when they suddenly discover noticeable flat spots on most of their tires. Naturally, periodically shifting the position of all the tires on all the cars in an extensive collection

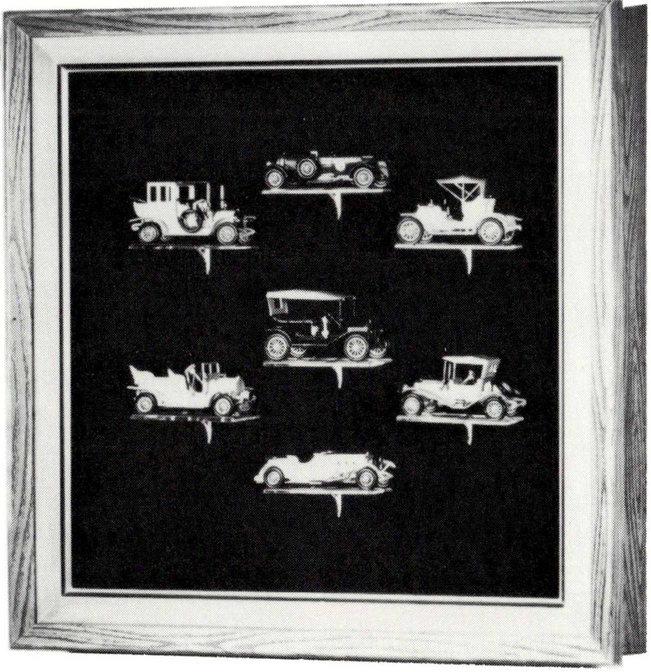

Fig. 148.   Display ideas for groups of model cars. All of the vehicles in these particular views are in or near 1/4-inch scale: Two additional pictures, one showing the construction of the removable roof of the museum building illustrated in the frontispiece (*Model Racing Buyers' Guide*); a twelve-foot-long parking structure with a capacity of 1,000 model cars (*Dinky Toys—Meccano Ltd., Lines Bros.*), and a glass-fronted museum-type wall case available either assembled or as a kit of plastic parts (*L. M. Cox Mfg. Co., Inc.*).

is a lot of work, more often honored in the breach than by performance. Relatively few collectors prove capable of carrying it through conscientiously year in and year out.

The second and most assured way of preventing flat spots from developing in miniature rubber tires is to display or store your models so that the weight of the car never rests upon the tires. One way to accomplish this and still keep the models on display is to make a special wooden base or lifting fixture for each model that will be concealed under the car and lift it just enough so that the tires are clear of the display shelf and the weight of the model car rests entirely on the base. Even if these bases are carved out of balsa wood with comparatively little effort, the number needed for an extensive collection of model automobiles would by no means be a simple task, and would involve a considerable amount of time. Furthermore, there are matters of the balance of the cars involved if the bases are to remain low and inconspicuous and at the same time keep all four wheels clear of the shelf. Hobbyists who have made such bases report that it is one of those jobs that sounds easy but proves a great deal more difficult in actual practice. At best, from a practical standpoint, they could be used for a few dozen selected models cars on permanent display, but not for displaying hundreds of cars.

The simplest and easiest solution to the problem of flat spots on tires is to pack and store the bulk of the rubber-tired models in a collection positioned so that the weight of the vehicle is not on the tires. This can be accomplished by using a layer of cushioning material, or, even simpler, an inverted position. And while some models in every extensive collection may no doubt have to be packed in this manner, the very easiest, most uncomplicated, safest, and historically sound method is merely to keep the models in the individual boxes in which they were purchased and to carefully store these boxes upside down. Depending on the type of packaging, this may not seem practical or advisable in the case of a few models with delicate roof racks or other exposed details. Laying models on their sides has not been suggested because in many cases this would transmit weight directly to the side rather than the tread of one or more of the tires, with resulting flat spots or distortion. However, many packages are so designed that such positioning is possible. If this is not the case, some other arrangement must be made to keep the weight off the tires and at the same time protect delicate roof detailing, but unquestionably the vast majority of model cars can safely be stored in the original boxes in an inverted position.

It must be admitted that there are a number of collectors who are quite aware of this problem of flat spots yet do not feel that the whole thing is worth the bother of paying any attention to it. Their attitude is that the harm already has been done to older model cars whose tires have developed substantial flat spots and that it hardly pays to worry about the current models which will inevitably develop flat spots over the years to come. They feel that it is more desirable to have the cars resting naturally on their tires in a display case than to build some sort of stand under each car to keep the tires out of contact with the shelf or to hide the models away where they cannot be seen. It is possible to quarrel with this outlook on the grounds that it is an extremely shortsighted one that will probably be regretted a decade or so hence when many of today's currently obtainable models have become scarce collectors' items in their own right, but no one can deny an individual enthusiast's right to pursue his hobby in the manner that he personally prefers.

The results of the weight of model cars resting on plastic tires, particularly soft types that closely resemble rubber in texture, have not as yet fully been determined. Certain of the early plastics are subject to deterioration of their own under conditions of heat, including strong sunlight. As for the more modern types, the safest bet would seem to be to take no chances and treat them as if they had the identical qualities of real rubber.

While it seems reasonably safe to assume that most model cars manufactured today have attained a relatively high degree of stability in regard to the quality of the cast metals or molded plastics used for their bodies, the paints by which they are decorated, and the materials employed for the wheels or tires, experience has taught knowledgeable collectors not to take chances and to preserve their specimens under the best possible conditions for their long-term preservation. Dampness of any kind obviously is in no wise beneficial for the storage of any artifact, regardless of its material, and extremes of heat or cold likewise should always be avoided. Strong direct sunlight will fade any paint in time, even though the fading may be imperceptible over a long period and finally be noticed only when a collector becomes aware that one side of a model has become a noticeably different shade than the unexposed side of the same vehicle. Sunlight, to a varying degree, is damaging to the finish of all types of model automobiles, and if only for this reason no model, even though constructed of metal, should ever be placed in a position where it is regularly exposed to direct sunlight. Sunlight not only will fade

Fig. 149.   Some ideas for the display and functional use of model automobiles: A 1/2-inch-scale model built from a kit of plastic parts set up in individual display unit with a miniature figure (*Monogram Models, Inc.*); a cast-metal miniature posed on a display base that is part of its packaging (*Dinky Toys—Meccano, Ltd., Lines Bros.*); a .48-inch scale car-hauling trailer molded of transparent plastic that can be used as an interesting individual display case (*Model Products Corp.*), and three cast-metal miniatures mounted on desk accessories ("*Matchbox*"—*Fred Bronner Corp.*).

colors but even in many instances change them, for example drawing the yellow out of a green lithography and changing the color to the less rapidly fading blue that in combination with the yellow made up the original green. Sunlight is in fact especially deadly to lithographed finishes, but it is damaging to all types of paint as well. This means that care must always be exercised in laying out model displays and positioning cases, or else the shades must be kept drawn or the cases curtained so as to assure that at no time during the day does direct sunlight fall on models. There is no way of reversing or compensating for damage of this type. Once the original finish of a model automobile has been impaired or altered in this manner, the value of the model is irrevocably reduced. Repainting simply reduces the value even more. All that a hobbyist who has unwittingly allowed his model cars to be exposed to sunlight can do is to prevent still further damage by moving or screening the models once he becomes aware of the situation.

The foregoing remarks apply particularly to model automobiles of the type secured in completely assembled form, wherein the presence and condition of the original factory paint is a major point affecting their value, as also is the particular color or shade in which the model originally was painted or lithographed. It does not apply so rigidly to models built by an individual hobbyist and painted by him, for, in case of sun damage, he can always repaint them. However, it seems pointless to allow one's models to deteriorate into such a state. If the models are made of wood, the effect of prolonged sunlight is bad enough, not only from the standpoint of the inevitable fading but also in drying out and shrinking the wood, and in drying out the glue in the joints and thereby at times reducing a model to its separate component parts. The effect of sunlight on plastic miniatures can, however, be completely devastating within a comparatively short period of time, as indeed can any heat on or even near them.

The first plastic material used for miniature automobiles in the late 1930's was Bakelite, a relatively stable but highly fragile material that soon fell into disuse because the latter factor made it unsatisfactory for the play use to which the models were put by children. There then followed a period during which most plastic model automobiles were molded of butyrate, which was less fragile and had the added advantage in that it could be molded in many different colors. However, it distorted rapidly under a very limited exposure to sunlight or moderate heat of any sort. Many readers who were youngsters in the late 1940's or early 1950's will recall an experience wherein a toy automobile molded of this substance was thoughtlessly left on a windowsill exposed to the summer sun, or on a working radiator during the winter. When the owner returned, the model was warped and distorted beyond all usefulness. The use of butyrate was followed in widespread use for model automobiles and for kits of parts by polystyrene and then by high-impact copolymer styrene, successively much stronger and far more stable materials. Many of the butyrate model automobiles are now, if only by reason of their age, fairly desirable collectors' items. Because of its low cost, butyrate still is employed as a material for a number of inexpensive model cars. Obviously any model made of butyrate or including butyrate parts must be kept out of the sun and away from heat at all costs in order to preserve it as a suitable collectors' item. But what of styrene and copolymer styrene models, the much more stable plastics? Sunlight and proximity to heat must be considered taboo for them as well. This does not necessarily mean that they will immediately warp under such conditions, but why take chances? If you happen to have the opportunity to see master packing cartons, the outer cartons that contain a dozen or so individual kits as shipped from the factory, you will find a warning printed on many of them to the effect that they should not be allowed to stand on the sidewalk in the sun after being delivered and unloaded but should immediately be taken indoors. This in itself tells the story.

Sunlight and heat will also speed up the deterioration of rubber by drying it out more rapidly than normally would be the case. In short, it is prudent and wise to refrain from exposing any model automobile to sun or heat if it can at all be avoided. This also means that a hot, unfinished attic may prove an unsuitable place in which to display or store many types of model automobiles.

There is a third type of deterioration, less understood by hobbyists, that may prove a problem; that is, the deterioration of metal, specifically zinc die castings. This subject is one that has proved puzzling for so long a time to so many hobbyists that a whole body of legend, folklore, half-truths, old wives' tales, and misinformation has grown up. These have circulated around the world to the point where relatively few hobbyists know the facts or, even having heard them, have recognized and accepted them.

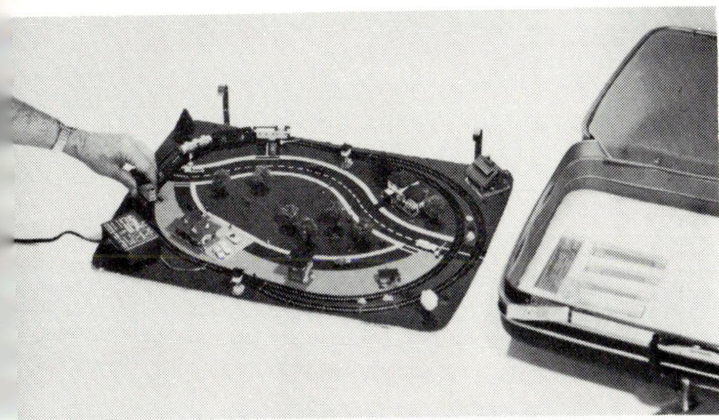

Fig. 150. The static model automobile as a contribution to the scenic realism of operating layouts: Two .48-inch-scale models alongside a raceway track (*American Russkit Co.*); a group of units of varying scales carefully arranged with the smaller scale models in the rear so as to give an effect of distance and perspective to a 3/8-inch-scale slot-car system (*Scolextric—Lines Bros.*); road vehicles completing the picture on an N gauge model railroad so diminutive that its 18-inch width packs into a suitcase (*Hobby Industry Association of America, Inc.*), and on a large permanent HO gauge model railroad (*Samuel Podell*).

THE FACTS CONCERNING DIE CASTINGS

One of the most curious and widely accepted results of this situation is the widespread belief that lead alloy castings are weak and go bad, while zinc alloy castings do not, and the consequent undeserved reputation for fragility recently accorded lead alloy or white-metal alloy castings. This is a distortion obviously based on a misunderstanding of the reason why zinc die castings sometimes go bad. The fact is that lead alloy castings are absolutely stable. Zinc alloy castings when poured from pure and properly alloyed mixes also are stable. They are two entirely different alloys. However, when a zinc alloy casting mix contains more than a microscopic proportion of lead (or tin or cadmium) the castings will go bad. Thus, many collectors erroneously equate bad castings with lead and good castings with zinc. If an old model car starts to deteriorate and to break up, these collectors knowingly nod and say, Ah, a weak casting made of lead, whereas the fact is that if the casting in question had been made of lead or tin alloys it would, barring exposure to heat somewhere in excess of 400 degrees Fahrenheit * or deliberate mutilation, most likely have remained in perfect condition. What actually has happened in the case of the casting breakup in question is that a zinc alloy casting was contaminated by a tiny amount of lead or tin or cadmium, or even in some cases too much copper, in the mix.

---

* There are tin-based alloys that have a melting point of 400 degrees Fahrenheit, but such alloys have not been used in model cars for many decades and probably never were deliberately so used owing to the relatively high cost of tin, although there is no absolute guarantee as to what mix may at times have been poured by some small manufacturers using scrap metals or in cases where model cars were cast by home workers. In the 1930's much publicity was accorded the availability of various bismuth-based alloys to hobbyists and home-workshop owners, some of these having a melting point actually below the 212 degrees Fahrenheit boiling point of water, one in fact having a melting point of only 117 degrees Fahrenheit. It is not impossible that some home craftsmen did pour some model automobiles from these extremely low-melting-point bismuth-based alloys in the 1930's or even later. Also, it is understood that some modern replacement castings for old model automobile parts have been cast in such alloys. Conceivably, strong sunlight under certain conditions could generate heat sufficient to exceed the 117-degree-Fahrenheit melting point of the lowest-melting-point alloy of this type. Most if not all lead-based alloys have a melting point of at least 450 degrees Fahrenheit. Pure lead alone has a melting point of 627 degrees Fahrenheit. However, an alloy of 88 percent lead and 12 percent antimony has a melting point of about 500 degrees Fahrenheit, and varying other combinations of lead, antimony, and tin can produce an alloy with an even lower melting point.

Fig. 151. Two cast-iron models of the mid-1930's, a Kenton cement truck and an Arcade bus (compare the latter with the model in Fig. 119). The cement truck has a filler cap, seen facing the viewer, in the body, and a chain-drive mechanism that revolves the tank body as the vehicle is pulled or pushed along the floor.

G. William Holland photographs

It is quite true that a casting poured from a white-metal alloy (as all lead-, tin-, and bismuth-based alloys are termed) will have a much lower tensile strength and Brinell hardness than a casting made from a purely compounded zinc alloy. When Dowst made the changeover in the early 1930's from using a white-metal alloy for Tootsietoys to a zinc alloy, they variously claimed in trade advertisements and catalogs that the new alloy was 33 1/3 or 40 percent lighter and of four to five times greater tensile strength. Probably three times the tensile strength would have been closer, but indisputably there was an enormous increase in strength.* This certainly resulted in a vastly stronger toy, notwithstanding which the white-metal-alloy automobiles are utterly undeserving of the reputation for weakness and fragility that has wrongly been pinned on them by many collectors in recent years.

Another widely held misconception is that white-metal alloys always were used for hand-poured or gravity castings, including slush castings, and never used for pressure die castings, whereas zinc alloy invariably is used in making pressure die castings but never for gravity casting. This belief carries with it the implication that one can invariably tell the type of metal used in a model simply by examining a given model and determin-

ing the type of casting method employed. This is quite incorrect. White-metal alloys were and at times still are used for pressure die-cast model automobiles. In fact, prior to the Dowst changeover to zinc alloy in the early 1930's all their castings from the inception of the Dowst casting business in the 1890's had been white-metal-alloy pressure die castings. Other manufacturers, both in the United States and in Europe, have made die-cast model cars of white metal alloys both before and since the early 1930's. Conversely, there are examples of slush-cast gravity-molded model automobiles made both before and after World War II of zinc, not white-metal, alloys. Why zinc-based alloys were used for such castings is not readily understandable, as zinc normally is more costly than lead and has a higher melting point. The logical explanation would appear to be that at certain times supplies of scrap zinc were more readily or more cheaply available to the particular manufacturers in question than was lead.

THE MENACE OF DIE-CASTING CONTAMINATION

Now let us examine in detail exactly why so many zinc-alloy pressure die castings, particularly but not necessarily entirely confined to early ones (that is, those made prior to World War II), deteriorate with varying rapidity to the point where they usually break up completely, or at least to the point where a model car may become so fragile that a collector scarcely dares to touch it and just hopes that if he can leave it alone it will continue to retain its form.

The basic fact concerning zinc die castings is this: If the original metal mix was pure, the resulting castings from that mix will remain sound virtually indefinitely. If the original metal mix was contaminated with certain metals in quantities over very, very tiny maximum limitations, the castings will go bad. The chief contaminating metals are lead, tin, and cadmium; it would be

---

* The change was announced early in 1933. The March 1933 advertisement reproduced in Fig. 161 says 33 1/3 percent lighter and 400 percent greater tensile strength. The 1933 catalog that appeared at about the same time states 40 percent lighter and four to five times greater tensile strength. The actual date of the change is uncertain, and may have been in 1932. If it were not actually made until 1933, then an extremely interesting point arises concerning the first Tootsietoy Graham passenger cars that were in production late in 1932 and that, in the event the alloy was not changed until 1933, were made of lead, not zinc alloy. The writer has not yet had opportunity to subject sufficient Tootsietoy Graham passenger cars to weight-comparison tests to establish this point. Just prior to the suspension of production because of World War II, some Tootsietoys, including Graham ambulances, are reported to have been run in white metal alloy, due to the unavailability of zinc.

158

Fig. 152.   This group of photographs illustrates the concept of collecting model cars on the basis of prototype make, in this case Studebaker. The first photograph shows two cast-iron models of the 1930's (*Adam Pellicot, Jr.; William Dreyer photograph*). The second and third photographs are of cast-metal miniatures of the 1930's to the 1960's, and the fourth picture, a larger metal 1948 model and a plastic 1950 model (*G. William Holland photographs*).

159

highly desirable if it were possible from a practical standpoint to eliminate them completely from zinc casting alloys. A little copper customarily is called for to perform certain functions, but too much copper also is a contaminant. The standard zinc die-casting alloy in the United States and a number of other countries is what is known as Zamak No. 3. There actually are several Zamak alloys, designated by numbers, but Zamak No. 3 is the one universally employed for toys and models. Where the Zamak No. 3 alloy is not used, very similar alloys are employed, and for success the formulas and purity must be regulated as carefully as with Zamak No. 3. Zamak No. 3 alloy consists of 3.90 to 4.30 percent of aluminum, 0.03 to 0.06 percent of magnesium, a maximum of 0.03 percent of copper, and the balance of the purest (99.99 plus percent) zinc. It is impossible commercially to refine zinc so as to eliminate all impurities; if the zinc is 99.99 plus percent pure, it is pure enough so that any remaining lead, tin, or cadmium is too slight to contaminate the mix, although the amount of any of these materials that will be sufficient to contaminate any given batch of mix would seem to anyone not conversant with the die-casting art to be minute indeed. If the original metal mix is contaminated with tin or lead, generally in amounts over .005 percent of the total original batch, the castings eventually will go bad. This will be indicated first by disturbing surface manifestations that may be followed immediately by disintegration or during which the casting has become so fragile that only a slight jar or drop will break it. Or there may be an intermediate stage wherein the casting expands—actually grows while still retaining its form—then followed by disintegration. In some cases the original stages of deterioration, including even the expansion, pass unnoticed and a superficially perfect-appearing model one day simply breaks up when it is handled or shipped. The deterioration is due entirely to contamination in the original mix. It is not caused, as some believe, by dampness or by extremes of heat or cold, although humidity and heat do hasten the deterioration process if the original metal mix is contaminated. There are many instances of two seemingly identical models stored together for a number of years when, upon unpacking the specimens, one was found to be as good as the day it was made and the other had reached so advanced a stage of disintegration as to be completely worthless. One model of the two had been cast from a pure zinc alloy mix and the other from a contaminated mix.

The process by which even very small excesses of lead, tin, or cadmium work to destroy zinc die castings is known as "subsurface network corrosion" or "intergranular corrosion" or "intercrystalline corrosion." The reason for including a small amount of magnesium in the mix is to reduce this intergranular corrosion. The aluminum, which is present in the alloy in a greater quantity than any material other than zinc, performs several useful purposes, including making the alloy stronger, reducing shrinkage, increasing the fluidity of the molten metal, and restraining the zinc from having a galvanizing effect on the steel dies and the steel and iron parts of the die-casting machine. Copper is added to achieve

Fig. 153. A collection group made up of models of Ford Model T's only, and all in 1/4-inch or closely related scales. Included here will be found old and recent models, models of metal and wood, and models originally sold both in assembled form and, in at least one instance, as a kit.
Dr. Clinton B. Seeley

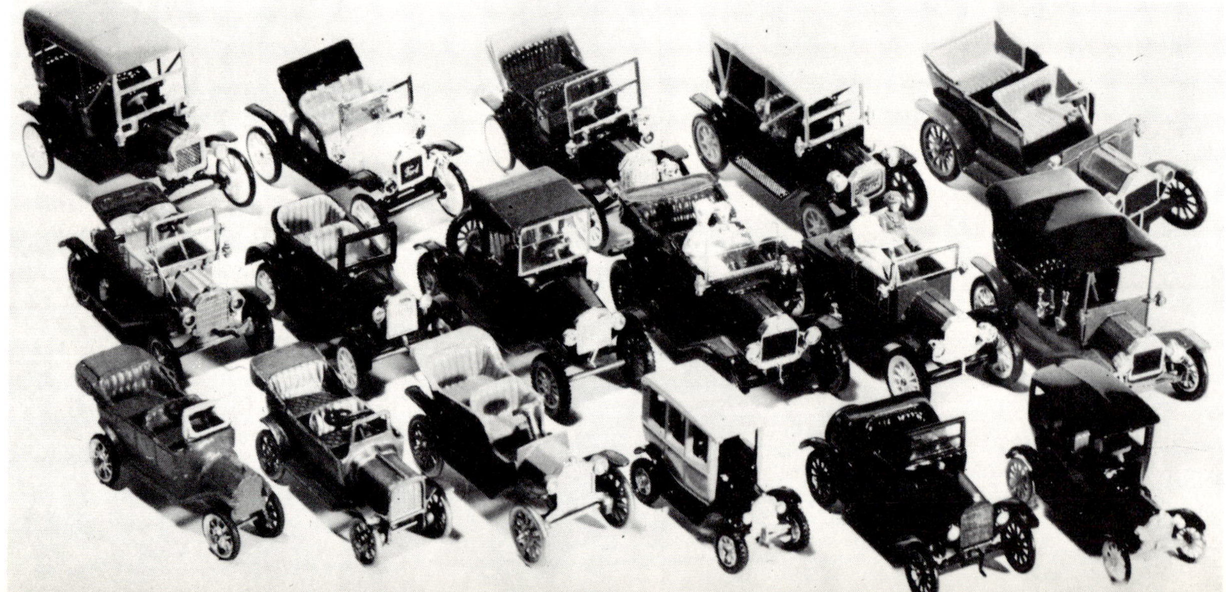

greater strength and hardness and also because it acts like magnesium in reducing or counteracting the intergranular corrosion. However, copper in excess can itself be a contaminant inasmuch as, entirely aside from the deterioration resulting from intergranual corrosion, it has the effect of promoting the expansion of castings as they age. Thus, while care must be taken to eliminate completely any traces of lead, tin, and cadmium, and though copper is not in exactly the same category, great pains must be taken to precisely control the copper content of the alloy.

All zinc die castings appear sound when they come from the molds. It is usually only with the passing of some years that the results of any contamination manifest themselves. While early die casters of zinc were unaware of the causes of deterioration in their castings—many of which broke up fairly rapidly, especially when used in warm or humid climates—the facts concerning the dangers of lead, tin, and cadmium contamination were fully established in the early 1920's and well known to die-casting engineers. As much contamination was the inevitable result of using zinc that contained a substantial percentage of one or more of these materials, it was obvious that a vital step was to develop processes by which far purer grades of zinc could be refined. Eventually the New Jersey Zinc Company was successful in producing commercially a zinc that was better than 99.99 percent pure, known as Horse Head "Special" zinc, the horse's head being the ancient symbol of the state and before that the colony of New Jersey. Thus satisfactorily pure zinc was available prior to the time that zinc alloy first was employed for the manufacture of miniature cast-metal automobiles. That, however, was only half the battle, because even when the pure zinc was available, casters at times employed cheaper and less pure grades, or melted old scrap zinc, or scrap aluminum that might contain lead. Even this was still not the whole story because zinc die-casting operations often were carried on on the same premises and with the same equipment that previously had been used for lead die casting, and much accidental contamination was inevitable Today, proper die-casting shop practice calls for completely separating the departments where zinc is melted and cast and where lead or tin are worked, even to the extent of separate buildings. In the old days, however, there always was a certain danger of contamination through accident or ignorance, for in many cases the workmen who did the actual casting were unaware of the vital importance of avoiding lead and tin contamination. A workman might toss a single chewing-gum wrap-

per into a pot of molten metal to dispose of it, not realizing that it contained enough tin to "poison" the mix!

It must also be admitted that there probably were times where the matter of a possibly contaminated mixture was not considered of real import in relation to inexpensive toys and that regardless of contamination it was expected that the alloy would stand up perfectly over the normal play life of a ten-cent model automobile and beyond. No one thought of future collectors, and the quickest and cheapest production methods were often the order of the day, even at the hands of experts who knew better. This is all a thing of the past, at least in properly operated die-casting facilities, and there is little need for the purchaser of modern zinc die-cast model automobiles to worry about contamination with the great pains now being taken to assure that the casting mixes are uncontaminated. This is certainly the case in American and British establishments, and presumably in continental European ones as well. And yet in all candor it must be mentioned that occasionally reports are heard that this or that model or series appears to have been made from batches of contaminated alloy. One can only hope that such reports are untrue; there certainly is nothing that could more quickly give a line a bad name than if such an instance were to be established as factual. These remarks do not apply to certain German models made immediately following World War II which proved notoriously unstable owing to the necessity of using whatever materials, including scrap, were available in order to get back into production as rapidly as possible. The inherent situation was of course realized at the time and reportedly corrected as rapidly as possible. Fortunately for collectors, as a group there is probably less collectors' interest in these particular models than in any others.

It would appear, then, that model-car collectors may feel secure in the purchase of any modern die-cast models. But what of the older models, especially the much sought-after collectors' items made prior to World War II in a period where there was without question a considerable amount of accidental contamination? It can be fairly said that if a model made during this period has stood up and remained in perfect shape this long, it undoubtedly was cast from uncontaminated metal and will remain in good shape. This leaves the older models that show various degrees of deterioration. The hobbyist must judge for himself how far advanced this may be and whether such models should be acquired. Certainly they must always be treated with the proverbial kid

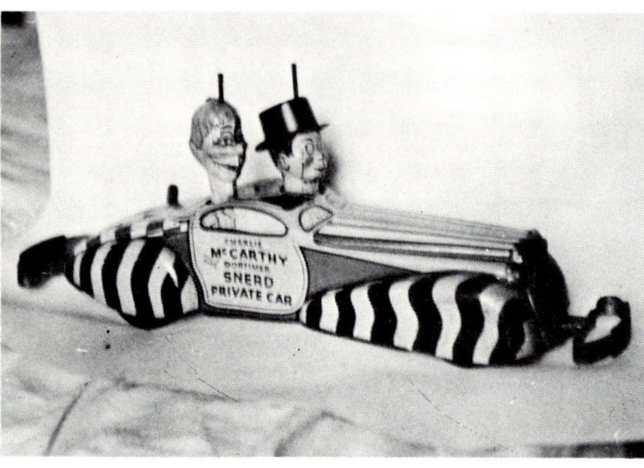

Fig. 154. Two Marx clockwork-powered lithographed stamped-metal novelty automobiles. Top, the Amos 'n' Andy "Fresh Air Taxicab" of the early 1930's, a model on which an enormous amount of promotion effort was expended but which substantially "flopped" (*Ward Kimball*). Bottom, the later Charlie McCarthy and Mortimer Snerd automobile (*Henry Kuell*).

B-96—Hill Climbing Automobile, 12½ in. long, $1.00

B-3—Hill Climbing Fire Engine, 11¾ in. long, $1.00

B-25—Hill Climbing Automobile, 9 in. long, 50c

B-2—Hill Climbing Automobile, 10½ in. long, $1.00

B-10—Hill Climbing Automobile, 8 in. long, 50c

B-107—Mechanical Hook and Ladder, 18 in. long, $1.75

B-20—Hill Climbing Patrol, 10 in. long, 50c

B-4—Hill Climbing Hook and Ladder, 19¼ in. long, $1.00

B-375—Mechanical Mail Wagon, 7 in. long, $1.00

B-210—Mechanical Automobile, 7½ in. long, 50c.

B-1—Hill Climbing Locomotive, 18½ in. long, $1.00

B-121—Butterfly Push Toy, 25c

B-132—Iron Hook and Ladder, 28 in. long, $1.00. Others, 25c, 50c

B-777—Iron Fire Patrol, 17 in. long, $1.00

B-856—Iron Ice Wagon, 15 in. long, $1.00, 12 in. long, 50c

B-115—Mechanical Fire Engine, 9¼ in. long, $1.00

B-701—Steel Trolley Car, 15 in. long, with clock work, $1.75

B-104 Mechanical Hook and Ladder, 13¾ in. long, $1.00

Fig. 155. An interesting page from a 1904 John Wanamaker Christmas catalog, which includes a selection of contemporary Clark friction automobiles (first five in column one and first two in column two), and Wilkins clockwork models (the remaining automotive vehicles). Note that both lines featured an automatic aerial ladder truck, although employing greatly differing forms of ladders.

gloves and handled or moved as little as possible. The writer personally would under no circumstances deliver or receive such a model by any means other than by hand. No matter how carefully it may seem they are packed, such models are likely to break up during shipment by mail or express. If a small piece or pieces break off such a model, they can be carefully cemented back into place. Some collectors try to save models that are showing signs of deterioration by painting the insides with various substances. Inasmuch as the deterioration is actually internal, this is rather a pointless stopgap, unless one assumes a coat of paint or bonding agent of sufficient strength could hold together a number of expanding parts in their original form. The best advice that can be given a collector is to either avoid or at least never pay more than a very nominal price for any old zinc die-cast model that is showing signs of deterioration.

Soldering, it should be noted, is never a satisfactory means of repair for any miniature cast-metal car, whether it is of white metal or zinc castings. White-metal alloys seldom can be satisfactorily soldered owing to the fact that their melting points are close to or at times even under that of the solder. It is sometimes asserted that zinc alloys cannot be soldered. This is not true, but for practical reasons it is advisable not to attempt such operations on model cars. For one thing the heat has a deteriorating effect on the casting, although it may be so slight as to seem of no consequence at the moment. However, it is virtually impossible to solder a small model car without blistering the paint near the point of applying the solder. In view of the availability of modern adhesives that can be applied cold, it is obviously pointless to attempt to make soldered repairs on any sort of cast-metal model cars.

Certain differences in terminology between American and British practice that cause confusion when describing miniature cast-metal automobiles for informational or trading purposes should be mentioned here. In the United States the use of the term "die casting" invariably refers to a casting made in a permanent mold into which the molten metal is forced under pressure. In Great Britain this process frequently is designated "pressure die casting," and the term "die casting" itself is applied to all types of permanent mold castings or else solely to methods of casting other than the injection of the metal into the die under pressure. Thus, British collectors frequently have described models as die cast which in the United States and Canada would be called slush cast. In a slush-cast model the molten metal is poured into a metal mold or die and flows in solely by the action of gravity. The mold then is inverted so that the hotter metal in the center of the mass pours out again, leaving a comparatively thin layer of more rapidly cooling metal adhering to the surfaces of the mold, producing a hollow casting.

Slush castings may be designated either as "permanent mold castings" (as contrasted to sand castings, a process in which a new and thereby obviously impermanent mold is made in sand for each pouring) or "gravity castings." Sand castings also are poured by gravity, but the term "gravity castings" is always taken to refer to the use of some form of mold of sufficient permanence to permit of varying and successive castings being made in the same mold. Such molds invariably are made of metal. In the United States, at least, the term "permanent mold castings" generally is applied to castings poured by gravity but not thereafter dumped while the central mass of metal still is molten to produce hollow castings, as is the case with slush castings. Occasionally, in the belief that any use of the term "die casting" must in itself seem to add a supposition of added appeal, such terms as "hand-poured die castings" or "gravity die castings" have been used in reference to permanent mold castings, but they are rather superfluous and misleading. The production of hollow castings is not necessarily confined to the die-casting or slush-casting process, and the assumption that permanent mold castings must of necessity be solid is erroneous. Hollow permanent-mold castings may be produced by means of a removable core piece, and there are a few instances of miniature cast-metal automobiles having been produced by this method. Cores may also be used with other casting methods as well; they were and are frequently used with die-cast model cars, and at times have also been employed in conjunction with slush-cast models, as for example to produce a smoothly finished interior of the open truck body cast from the slush-mold pictures in Fig. 162.

There are two other methods of casting that should be noted in connection with miniature cast-metal automobiles. One, lost wax or investment molding has, as far as is known, been used for only one model automobile, the cast-brass (and the only cast model car commercially made in this material) 3.5-mm.-scale 1915 touring car manufactured by Kemtron Products Company in the 1950's. This actually was a motorized HO-gauge model-railroad item, an electrically powered replica of an automobile fitted with flanged wheels to run on railroad track, as a number of early automobiles were fitted either for use as inspection cars or on out-of-the-way lines where passenger traffic requirements were so minimal as not to warrant more conventional rolling stock.* In the lost-wax casting method, which in fact is almost two thousand years old, undercuts in the finished casting that would be quite difficult to obtain with permanent-mold casting methods, even where complicated coring is employed, are extremely simple of achievement. A wax pattern of the part to be cast, furnished with a suitable stem or pattern for a pouring mouth, is surrounded with a casing of plaster of Paris through which the stem protrudes. When the plaster has hardened, the wax is melted out, leaving a hollow cavity provided with a pouring mouth through which molten metal is poured into the mold. When the metal has cooled, the mold is broken away, and the casting removed. In actual production work it is necessary first to provide a number of identical wax patterns, as obviously with this process a pattern is needed for making the mold for each casting; lost-wax casting definitely is not a permanent-mold casting process.

The second casting method alluded to above is that of centrifugal casting. In this method molten metal is poured into a mold that is then spun at high speed so that the molten metal is forced by centrifugal force into all the small crevices or runners that have been cut in the die. Molds for centrifugal castings may be made of metal, but in miniature automobile components manufactured

---

* Red Ball Models manufactured a similar HO-gauge motorized automobile in the 1950's, but it was built up of sheet brass, not cast. It also is, of course, a model-automobile collectors' item today, but it is not a miniature cast-metal car.

MODELLED MINIATURES No. 22
MOTOR VEHICLES

This very attractive die-cast set consists of two Motor Cars, two commercial Vehicles, one Tractor and one Army Tank.   **Price**, per set, **4/–**

The items in the above set may be purchased separately.

Fig. 156. Early days of the Meccano Dinky Toys, a British line of cast-metal miniatures with widespread collector popularity. Left, the original six automotive models, introduced in 1933 and not yet designated as Dinky Toys. A measure of the subsequent development of the line may be gleaned from the three catalog pages of the mid-1930's, also reproduced.

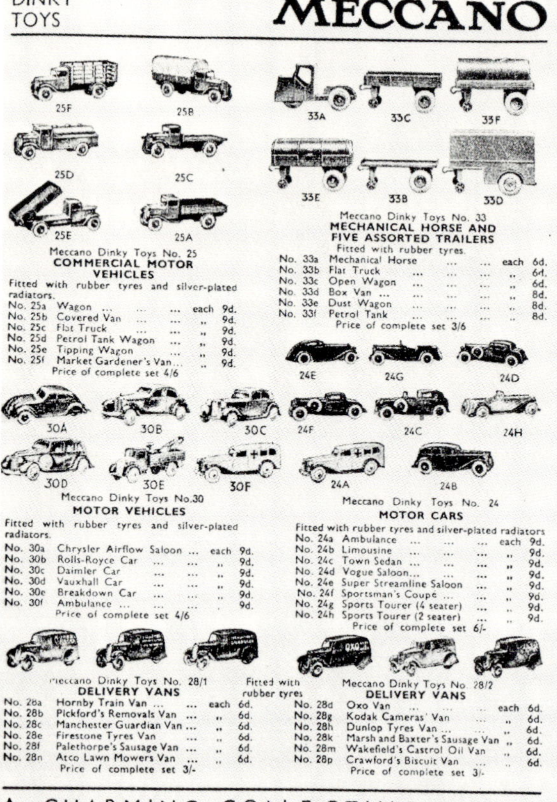

DINKY TOYS   **MECCANO**

25F   25B   25D   25C   25E   25A

Meccano Dinky Toys No. 25
COMMERCIAL MOTOR VEHICLES
Fitted with rubber tyres and silver-plated radiators.

No. 25a	Wagon	each	9d.
No. 25b	Covered Van	,,	9d.
No. 25c	Flat Truck	,,	9d.
No. 25d	Petrol Tank Wagon	,,	9d.
No. 25e	Tipping Wagon	,,	9d.
No. 25f	Market Gardener's Van	,,	9d.
	Price of complete set 4/6		

33A   33C   33F   33E   33B   33D

Meccano Dinky Toys No. 33
MECHANICAL HORSE AND FIVE ASSORTED TRAILERS
Fitted with rubber tyres.

No. 33a	Mechanical Horse	each	6d.
No. 33b	Flat Truck	,,	6d.
No. 33c	Open Wagon	,,	6d.
No. 33d	Box Van	,,	8d.
No. 33e	Dust Wagon	,,	8d.
No. 33f	Petrol Tank	,,	8d.
	Price of complete set 3/6		

30A   30B   30C   30D   30E   30F

Meccano Dinky Toys No.30
MOTOR VEHICLES
Fitted with rubber tyres and silver-plated radiators.

No. 30a	Chrysler Airflow Saloon	each	9d.
No. 30b	Rolls-Royce Car	,,	9d.
No. 30c	Daimler Car	,,	9d.
No. 30d	Vauxhall Car	,,	9d.
No. 30e	Breakdown Car	,,	9d.
No. 30f	Ambulance	,,	9d.
	Price of complete set 4/6		

24E   24G   24D   24F   24C   24H   24A   24B

Meccano Dinky Toys No. 24
MOTOR CARS
Fitted with rubber tyres and silver-plated radiators

No. 24a	Ambulance	each	9d.
No. 24b	Limousine	,,	9d.
No. 24c	Town Sedan	,,	9d.
No. 24d	Vogue Saloon	,,	9d.
No. 24e	Super Streamline Saloon	,,	9d.
No. 24f	Sportsman's Coupé	,,	9d.
No. 24g	Sports Tourer (4 seater)	,,	9d.
No. 24h	Sports Tourer (2 seater)	,,	9d.
	Price of complete set 6/-		

Meccano Dinky Toys No. 28/1
DELIVERY VANS

No. 28a	Hornby Train Van	each	6d.
No. 28b	Pickford's Removals Van	,,	6d.
No. 28c	Manchester Guardian Van	,,	6d.
No. 28e	Firestone Tyres Van	,,	6d.
No. 28f	Palethorpe's Sausage Van	,,	6d.
No. 28n	Atco Lawn Mowers Van	,,	6d.
	Price of complete set 3/-		

Fitted with rubber tyres

Meccano Dinky Toys No. 28/2
DELIVERY VANS

No. 28d	Oxo Van	each	6d.
No. 28g	Kodak Cameras' Van	,,	6d.
No. 28h	Dunlop Tyres Van	,,	6d.
No. 28k	Marsh and Baxter's Sausage Van	,,	6d.
No. 28m	Wakefield's Castrol Oil Van	,,	6d.
No. 28p	Crawford's Biscuit Van	,,	6d.
	Price of complete set 3/-		

A CHARMING COLLECTING HOBBY

MECCANO   DINKY TOYS

Meccano Dinky Toys No. 22e
TRACTOR
Assorted Colours.
Price 9d. each

Meccano Dinky Toys No. 23a. **RACING CAR**
Assorted Colours. Fitted with rubber tyres.
Price 6d. each

Meccano Dinky Toys No. 22h
STREAMLINE SALOON
Fitted with rubber tyres.
Price 6d.

Meccano Dinky Toys No. 22f
TANK
Assorted Colours. Price 9d. each

Meccano Dinky Toys No. 23b
HOTCHKISS RACING CAR
Assorted Colours. Fitted with rubber tyres. Price 6d. each

Meccano Dinky Toys No. 22g
STREAMLINE TOURER
Fitted with rubber tyres.
Price 6d. each

Meccano Dinky Toys No. 31
HOLLAND COACHCRAFT VAN
Assorted Colours. Fitted with rubber tyres. Price 6d. each

Meccano Dinky Toys No. 25g
TRAILER for use with No. 25 Series. Fitted with rubber tyres. Price 7d. each

Meccano Dinky Toys No. 22c
MOTOR TRUCK.
Fitted with rubber tyres.
Price 6d. each

Meccano Dinky Toys No. 26
G.W.R. RAIL CAR
Assorted Colours. Price 6d. each

Meccano Dinky Toys No. 17
PASSENGER TRAIN SET

No. 17a	Locomotive	each	9d.
No. 17b	Tender	,,	5d.
No. 20a	Coach	,,	7d.
No. 20b	Guard's Van	,,	7d.
	Price of complete set 2/3		

Meccano Dinky Toys No. 19
MIXED GOODS TRAIN SET

No. 21a	Tank Locomotive	each	9d.
No. 21b	Wagon	,,	4d.
No. 21d	Petrol Tank Wagon	,,	6d.
No. 21e	Lumber Wagon	,,	5d.
	Price of complete set 1/11		

Meccano Dinky Toys No. 18
GOODS TRAIN SET

No. 21a	Tank Locomotive	each	9d.
No. 21b	Wagons (3)	,,	4d.
	Price of complete set 1/9		

Meccano Dinky Toys No. 20
PASSENGER TRAIN SET

No. 21a	Tank Locomotive	each	9d.
No. 20a	Coaches (2)	,,	7d.
No. 20b	Guard's Van	,,	7d.
	Price of complete set 2/6		

REALISTIC MODELLED MINIATURES

by this method rubber molds customarily have been employed. The centrifugal casting method has been used for making metal wheels and parts for basically wooden kits, such as some of the first Hudson Miniatures "Old Timers," and, more recently, for various reproduction parts for old miniature cast-metal automobiles.* Relatively low-

* The writer must confess his lack of personal knowledge of the centrifugal casting method being employed for any cars or kits in toto as current regular merchandise at the time they were made. However, in the book *Model Car Collecting*, F. Brian Jewell cites centrifugal casting along with pressure die casting as the two main methods of manufacturing cast-metal model cars, and it would seem likely that he wrote from some specific knowledge on this point concerning its employment for this purpose in Europe. The descriptions accompanying Mr. Jewell's useful checklist of some 175 model-car manufacturers of the world through 1963 unfortunately is not clear on this point; most makes of cast-metal model cars are cited as "die-cast," a few simply as "metal." The writer has been unable so far to obtain clarification from Mr. Jewell concerning this matter.

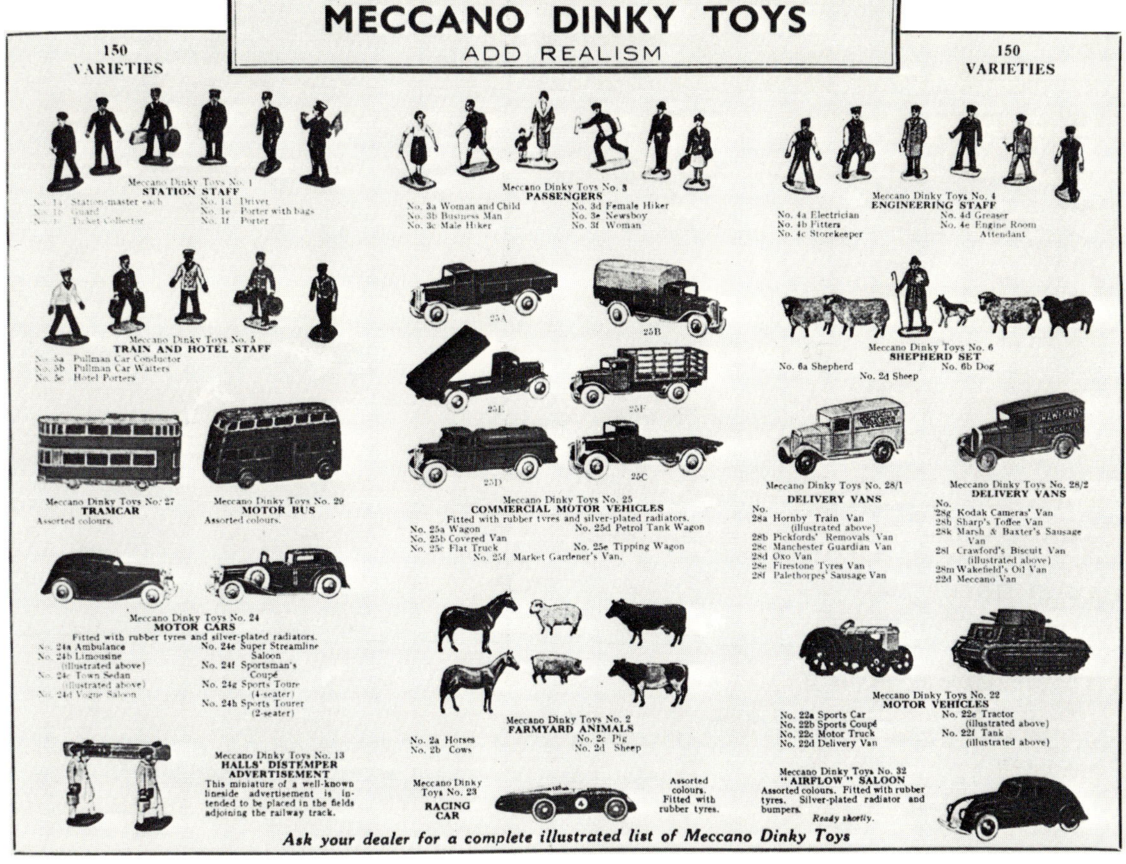

melting-point white-metal alloys are employed for these castings.

Many model-automobile collectors are puzzled by the small round markings or indentations found in various positions on die-cast and permanent-mold-cast miniature automobiles. These marks are caused by the action of the round knock-out or ejection pins or rods that kick a finished casting out of a die when it is opened after the metal has been poured into it. Depending on circumstances, such as the force employed to operate the ejection pins, the alloy used, and just how rapidly the surface of the casting has cooled, these marks may be only the slightest of surface markings, often unnoted under a coat of paint unless especially sought, or they may be depressions of some depth. Modern dies are designed so that the ejection pins are in such a position that they will not act upon the outer surfaces of the castings. On some older models, however, the traces of these pins will be found quite prominently placed on the exterior of a model vehicle. Not all permanent molds were fitted with ejection pins; in some small-run production efforts the still-hot castings were removed from the opened mold by the hand use of a pair of pliers.

As has been seen, model-automobile casting types can be classified according to the method of casting—die cast, slush, sand, and so on—or by the type of metal or alloy used—white metal, zinc, iron, and so on. By far the most important basic divisions are those of casting method, with the material of the casting secondary, if it can be ascertained. Although aluminum can be die-cast, its use in small model automobiles has been confined to sand castings, and a reference to the sand-casting method automatically implies that the material involved either is aluminum or iron, the latter by far the more predominant. There remains one other term to be discussed in this connection, "pot metal." "Pot metal" as a term has long been established in our language; among model builders and collectors it has become accepted rather as a term of disparagement; actually, it has become rather meaningless.

Some collectors are under the impression that "pot metal" specifically refers to a method of casting, equating it with slush casting and sometimes employing it as an identical substitute—some never having heard the term "slush casting" at all. What "pot metal" meant originally, if it ever meant anything really specific, was a metal mix used in castings that was compounded of any sort of pure metal or scrap that was thrown into the melting pot and would melt down at whatever temperature was being employed. For years many casters of toys, regardless of what name they applied to the metal employed—pewter, Britannia metal, lead, tin—simply melted down any usable scrap they could get, not excluding, after they had come into widespread use, old collapsible tubes that often added some residues of toothpaste, shaving cream, vaseline, and similar products to the mix. In fact, during the depression, home casters often were outspokenly advised that such old tubes were an ideal source of inexpensive scrap metal to melt down, and in many cases the continuing casting schedule of children with toy casting sets was dependent on how often the tubes in their household and those of their neighbors became available.* At the opposite extreme from manufacturers who relied on whatever scrap metals were available at the time, there were certain large manufacturers, such as Dowst, whose white-metal alloy always was carefully compounded of definite proportions of lead, tin, and antimony. To many hobbyists, however, "pot metal" became a term of denigration applied according to their variable personal beliefs in recent years to white-metal alloys by some and to zinc die-casting alloys by others. Or some would, and do, apply it to zinc die castings that have deteriorated, but not to all zinc die castings. In short, in popular usage among hobbyists the term has become quite confused and meaningless.

MODEL-CAR COLLECTORS' NOMENCLATURE

The confusion regarding "pot metal" is typical of a number of widely used but often meaningless terms. Perhaps the most notable and confusing error of this type is the relatively recent usage of "tin plate," "tin-plate," or "tinplate" either as a specific synonym for lithographed sheet metal, or, on a wider basis, as a designation for all stamped sheet-metal (as opposed to cast-metal) miniature automobiles. Both usages are so manifestly incorrect and confusing that most collectors have been hard put to understand how they could have originated of late in Great Britain. The answer is that some enthusiasts, evidently out of touch with the toy- and model-collecting hobby as a whole, were reaching for a vaguely recalled word, "tin printed," and came up instead with the somewhat similar and much more common word of entirely different meaning, "tinplate." From the use of "tinplate" instead of "tin printed" for lithographed sheet-metal automobiles there developed among some in turn a concept that "tinplate" referred to all stamped metal toys.

"Tin plate" or "tin-plate" means one thing, and "tinplate" another. "Tin plate" or "tin-plate" refers to a specific material, sheet metal plated with a thin coating of tin that inhibits rust and that also permits the material readily to be soldered. The great era of toys made of tin-plate was prior to the twentieth century, save for the employment of the material for toy train track. Consequently there were comparatively few types of miniature automobiles ever manufactured out of the material tin-plate, and thereby in this sense literally tin-plate toys. In short, all model automobiles fabricated of tin-plate are sheet-metal toys, but far from all sheet-metal model automobiles are tin-plate in this meaning. In the other application, where the word is spelled "tinplate," it refers, not to a material, but rather to commercial mass production, deriving from tinplate trains—mass-production toy trains, and at times extended as applicable to all sorts of mass-produced toys. In this context, "tinplate," however, is not limited to articles wholly or partially fabricated of sheet metal, but also includes cast iron, white metal and zinc alloys, and other materials; so this variation of spelling is also wholly inapplicable to denote sheet-metal miniatures.

Lithography, as applied to toys and models, is the process of printing a design in color on sheet metal in the flat, after which the material is blanked out, pierced, and formed on press tools and the components then assembled into the completed toy. Lithography is a method of printing, although completely different from letterpress printing. In lithography the colors and designs are transferred to the sheet metal either directly from a lithograph stone or by an offset process. Lithography was and is always referred to by that name in the United States and also to a predominant extent in Great Britain. However, there was another and exclusively British name applied to the process of lithographing on sheet metal (much lithography, of course, also is done on paper or cardboard). This was "tin printing," and it was for this term that British hobbyists were reaching when unhappily they came up with the word "tinplate" instead.

---

* Hence the designations, still heard from time to time, for toy soldiers home-cast in the 1930's as the Colgate Army, the Ipana Army, the Burma Shave Army, and so on.

Fig. 157. More British-made models, in this instance clockwork-powered stamped-metal ones. Pictured are a Ranlite ad of 1931 showing substantial models that could be purchased in kit form if desired, including a replica of the "Golden Arrow." All the model automobiles shown on the page from the 1937 catalog were manufactured by Wells, except for the dump truck in the center column, which was manufactured in the British Marx factory.

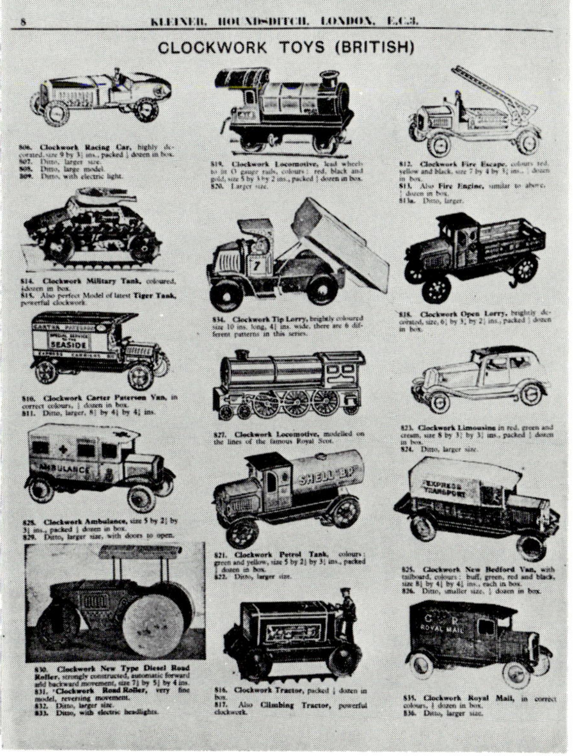

The first lithographed toy automobiles were introduced in the 1890's. Most but far from all of these lithographed automobiles were relatively inexpensive because in mass production the relatively low cost of lithography, as opposed to painting and hand-lining and decorating, permits large economies in manufacturing costs. Another economy of lithography is that in most instances soldering is eliminated in assembly, the various units being stamped with little metal fingers and corresponding slots, the fingers easily being passed through the slots by relatively unskilled workers and then bent over or twisted to complete the joint. Caution—these joints are more than adequate in sturdiness as originally assembled, but once opened for repair or examination purposes, the fingers or lugs frequently break off when bent down again. The foregoing applies to any joints of this type, whether in lithographed, painted, or plated sheet metal. Although lithography was used in many inexpensive toys, including automobiles, a great number of lithographed cars were extremely beautiful and some quite large, costly, and handsome, as a survey of the overall model automobile field will reveal. Despite this and the generally well-established knowledge of the many meritorious possibilities and actual production uses of lithography, some individuals disparage this method as a cheap finish applied only to small, flimsy, and inexpensive models. This prejudice is entirely unjustified. The fact that lithographed automobiles may be inexpensive does not mean they are crude or unattractive.

To sum up:

"Tin plate" or "tin-plate" refers to sheet metal plated with a protective coating of tin; "tin plate" or "tin-plate" are properly used as adjectives only in referring to toys actually fabricated of this material.

"Tinplate" refers to the factor of commercial mass production, most generally of toy trains (the word itself has become a noun synonymous with mass-production toy trains), regardless of the materials of which they are constructed, and by extension—although now seldom employed in this sense—may be used to describe any mass-production toy, including automobiles, whether made of stamped metal, cast iron, or other materials.

Lithographed models are those assembled from sheet metal that was printed with colors and designs while in the flat. "Lithographed" is the same as "tin-printed," although the former word is by far the more widely used, and is preferable today.

"Sheet metal" or "stamped metal" or "pressed metal" are correct all-embracive or generic designations for all types of sheet-metal toys and models as a group, whether they are fabricated from tin-plate, steel, or other materials, and whether they are finished by painting or lithography.

Apropos of all this, to avoid confusion and permit sufficient identification, where rubber wheels and tires are concerned, collectors should be careful to denote whether a vehicle has a wheel of cast metal, wood, or other material with a separate rubber tire, generally referred to as a rubber-tired wheel, or whether a one-piece molding combining both wheel and tire is involved. Naturally if the tire or the wheel and tire combination is made of a material other than rubber, this material should be specified, and especially in the cases of model cars made prior to World War II, it is always important to give the color of the rubber tires or wheel-and-tire combination. In fact, it would probably be well if this were adopted as a standard procedure in describing all model automobiles. Not only is such information of the utmost importance in connection with many models in determining whether or not they are variations the collector has or lacks, but also in distinguishing between models with original tires or wheels and replacements.

Not as consequential, although judging from collectors' comments quite annoying and confusing to many, is a matter that relates to the continental European custom of identifying models in a way that, when literally translated in correspondence or literature, fails to make much sense to English-speaking hobbyists, especially such usages as "factory reference" or "referenced as." Actually, these are merely typical examples of what all too often happens when a translation is direct and literal rather than properly idiomatic. For instance, the most frequently heard, the French *référence du fabricant* translates literally into English as *manufacturer's reference* or *factory reference,* or perhaps a little more idiomatically as *manufacturer's number* or *factory number.* If it can be remembered that the proper idiomatic English translation of *référence du fabricant* is "catalog number" (in Great Britain it would be spelled "catalogue") or "model number," or, indeed, simply "number," * any confusion would immediately

---

* In the United States and Canada, at least, the word "number" alone generally is employed throughout the trade and hobby, and is understood to be the equivalent of "catalog number" or "model number." In fact this usage is so well established in the vernacular that the word "number" has become synonymous with the physical object it identifies, thus "Here is a new number," that is, a picture, handmade sample, or actual specimen of an item, or "That was a good number last season." In the American idiom the word "number" often is used as a slang reference to a girl, as in "some number."

be eliminated; similarly, when a French correspondent writing in English says "referenced," bear in mind that he means "cataloged."

COUNTING THE PIECES

The novice collector frequently is confused by references on the part of more experienced hobbyists to the construction of miniature cast-metal automobiles in terms of the number of parts or pieces in a unit, particularly when they may count the parts in a similar unit and come up with a different number. This confusion is understandable, and at the outset it should be stated that some collectors interpret the parts count to refer specifically to certain types and series of Dowst pre–World War II models, others to any models of generally similar construction, while still others make and cite a parts count, rather ingenuously, simply on a literal basis of the precise number of separate units involved in the makeup of a given model automobile. The latter enthusiasts follow this procedure without, of course, realizing that in this overall rather airy circumstance of model-car collecting some components customarily are included in such a parts count while others are not, or that to many hobbyists the specification of a model by a parts-number designation automatically implies a certain definite constructional arrangement of the parts adduced. As hobby knowledge has increased, and with it the realization that there often was more

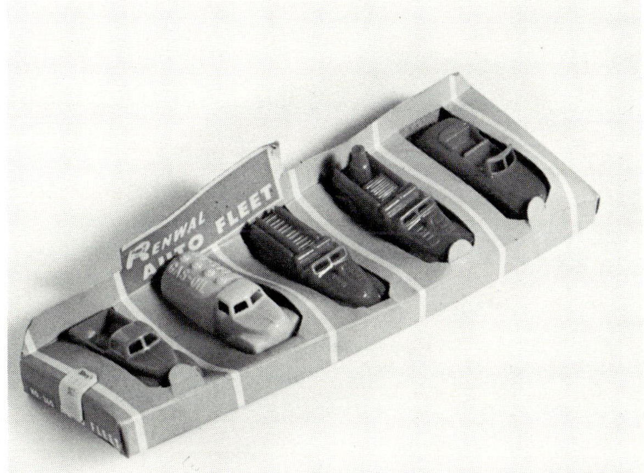

Fig. 158. Model automobiles in new or like-new condition, and with their original boxes if possible, are, of course, always particularly prized by collectors. Pictured here are three brand-new sets of about 1950: Renwal plastic miniatures, a Hubley die-cast taxicab set, and a die-cast Manoil set.

G. William Holland photographs

Fig. 159   Another brand-new boxed set, a Williams cast-iron set of the 1930's. This particular set provided three interchangeable bodies—stake truck, sedan, and roadster—for optional mounting on the single chassis provided. The set is shown completely boxed at the left, and, right, with the sedan made up. See also Fig. 173.

Dr. Clinton B. Seeley

than one method of construction employed involving the same number of counted parts, the situation has become more confusing, and the designations, except when modified by a reference to a specific make, series, or model, ever more meaningless. Nevertheless, as the designations, if not agreement on their interpretation, appear rather firmly established, it would seem that the model-automobile-collecting hobby will have to live with them for some time to come, and it is best for the beginner to acquaint himself with the intricacies of the situation.

If three parts were sufficient for Caesar into which to divide all Gaul, no less than four have been felt to be required by those hobbyists who would divide all miniature cast-metal automobile construction. Thereby we get the now famous—or, as some would prefer, infamous—designations of one-part, two-part, three-part, and four-part construction, sometimes rendered as one-piece, two-piece, and so on.

First, to understand the system, if it can be dignified by such a name, it must be appreciated that wheels, separate tires, or axles never count as parts or pieces (neither, in case any one may think to involve them in the application of some variation of the system to cast-iron models, do rivets, screws, or nuts), although curiously enough the only time that a pre–World War II model-car manufacturer ever made reference to the number of parts involved constructionally, he did include wheels and axles in the count. This was in connection with the Tootsietoy Bild-A-Car sets made from 1933 to 1938 which were cataloged as containing "60 pieces." Each set built 5 vehicles of the now memorable Tootsietoy Graham series, and the 60 parts in each set broke down to 5 bodies with radiators already fitted, 5 chassis, 20 wheels with tires, 20 half-axles (4 on each car), and 10 axle joiners. Inasmuch as the separately cast radiator with headlights and front bumper was supplied already fitted to a car body, the unit thus created was counted as one part in this instance. However, the most commonly accepted constructional definition of a three-part model is primarily based on the design of the Tootsietoy Grahams, the three parts thereby accounted for being the body, radiator, and castings. It should also be noted that the parts-count system cannot be reduced and systematized to counting the *castings* used in the body and chassis, as some have attempted, because in the case of certain British models, counted parts that usually are castings in American models are provided in the form of sheet-metal stampings.

The generally understood constructional parts-count interpretations are as follows:

One-part model: The entire vehicle body is a single casting.

Two-part model: The body is one casting and the chassis is another; it is usually taken in the sense of the design of the Tootsietoy General Motors series that appeared in 1928.

Three-part model: This description is customarily taken to relate to the aforementioned Tootsietoy Graham series, the first of which, but not the Bild-A-Car sets, appeared late in 1932 with separate body, chassis, and radiator castings.

Four-part model. This usually is accepted as referring to the Tootsietoy La Salle method of construction first used late in 1934 on models made for the Cadillac Motor Division of General Motors, but not placed on regular sale until 1935. The parts are the body, chassis, and radiator, with the fourth part being the rear-bumper casting. However, the constructional method by which these four parts are assembled into a completed model was entirely different from those employed on the three-part Graham series, and was used only on the four Tootsietoy La Salle models.

These designations are at times inept and at times incorrect and inaccurate. A further point of potential confusion not already mentioned is the fact that frequently beginners count parts more accurately or at least more literally than some of those who brought the system into being. For example, the construction of the original Dowst Ford Model-T touring car, introduced in 1914 or 1915, and the Ford Model-T pickup truck, which came out in 1917, although usually accounted one-part cars, actually have two-part bodies. The second part is the windshield, firewall, steering column, and steering-wheel casting that is tightly crimped into position. A similar casting that likewise may pass either unnoticed or be, at the other extreme, over counted, is employed on cars of the Tootsietoy General Motors and Graham series on which the driver's seat is not roofed over, that is to say, on the General Motors roadsters and on the Graham roadsters and town cars. There are many other possibilities for vagueness, inaccuracy, or variable interpretations of the parts-count system, but sufficient already has been mentioned to caution the beginner as to the potential confusions and misunderstandings inherent in this area, and further pitfalls will become apparent upon the actual examination of the models comprising a typical collection of old miniature cast-metal cars.

It may, indeed, appear to more experienced collector-readers that perhaps undue emphasis is being put upon what may in some cases be minor points of potential confusion and misunderstanding. However, it would be well to bear in mind that all too often information and interpretations that have become second nature to established hobbyist all too often appear forbidding and inexplicable to the newcomer to any hobby. This is especially true in the case of a worldwide hobby where important differences in usage or in spelling, applicable both to models and to prototypes, frequently occur even in countries that reputedly speak the same language. For instance, what in the United States and Canada is termed the "hood" of an automobile becomes the "bonnet" in Great Britain, while the American "top" is known as the "hood" in the mother country. Some of the most common of these points that suggest it is not really as common a language as some may believe are set forth in Appendix III.

SEEKING AND RELATING INFORMATION

Sounding curiously strange and inaccurate to the ears of most model-car collectors is the use of such words as "issue," "issued," "reissue," "reissued," "make" (not in the sense of identifying a manufacturer but rather as a synonym for issue), and "remake," terms that seem to be limited in use to certain British hobby circles. Automobiles, real or model, or other similar fabricated productions are never properly spoken of as issued or any of these variations. The customary accepted and immediately understood expressions for real and model automobiles are such terms as "made in," "brought out," "put into production," "placed on the market," or, in the case of "reissue" or "remake," "returned to production," "put into production again," "brought back," and the like. Actually, except in the instances where the production of a model was interrupted by a wartime cessation of production, there are very few cases where the terms of the second grouping would apply to model cars, and virtually none where they would pertain to real automobiles.*

---

* The last real cars made in the United States prior to World War II were designated as 1942 models; when production was resumed after the war with virtually the same cars, they were designated 1946 models. No such differentiation was offered in connection with model cars returned to production at that time, although collectors in many and probably most cases can distinguish between prewar and postwar specimens by differences in the colors of the bodies or tires. There are a few instances, however, where production of a model car or set of model cars was discontinued for a year or so and the unit then returned to the line. An example is the Tootsietoy Raceway outfit whose mutations already have been discussed.

"Issue" is in fact a word deriving from book- and stamp-collecting usage, and can be correctly applied only to articles made of paper.* From stamp collecing, too, comes the word, sometimes applied to model automobiles, "mint," although oddly enough its origin obviously derives from coinage. "Mint" also has wormed its way into some references to books, although collectors and dealers have battled, in the main successfully, to publicize its impropriety. "Proof," which on occasion also is applied in an equally lugubriously sounding manner to model cars, is a word that has validity, although entirely different meanings, in relation to coins and to stamps or other printed matter, but never to models and toys. It should also be noted that the proper designation of the time a model car was made is strictly regulated by the years it was cataloged or known to be in actual production, not on some nebulous accounting that, either from personal recollection or mere probability, a model may have continued to be available in some store stocks until a certain time. Either cataloging or actual production may be the operative determiner, and they are not necessarily always exactly the same thing. In some cases a miscalculation as to the salability of a model in one year may have been made, and sufficient quantities remain on hand to warrant it being cataloged as part of the following year's line although no further actual production is undertaken. Contrawise, at times a model may be dropped from the cataloged line but continued in or returned to production for some special promotional purposes. If this fact is ascertainable it must be taken into consideration in accounting the time span during which a model was manufactured. For example, five of the models of old American automobiles of the Tootsietoy Classic series of the early 1960's, the No. 3101 1912 Ford Model T, the No. 3102 1929 Model A, the No. 3107 1906 Cadillac, the No. 3108 1919 Stutz, and the No. 3109 Stanley Steamer were dropped from the cataloged line after 1963 but continued in production for several years for use as premiums by a soup-mix manufacturer. Their companion sixth piece, the No. 3111 1922 Mack truck was, however, discontinued at the time the models were taken out of the cataloged line. Continued uncataloged production need not, however, necessarily imply the models were made only for one particular customer, as in this instance. At times models removed from the cataloged line (or never

included in the cataloged line) may be in production and available as special promotional items to any accounts.

The ascertainment of information concerning catalog dates can obviously apply only to those manufacturers who issued trade or consumer catalogs or where information of compatible validity can be secured from their advertising or from the catalogs of jobbers or large retailers. Fortunately, in the case of pre–World War II models, such precise information is available concerning some of the most important manufacturers. Actually, in the case of these companies there appears to have been comparatively little production of uncataloged specials, inexpensive miniature cast-metal automobiles not adapting themselves quite so easily to this sort of merchandising as some more expensive types of toys such as electric trains. In any case, when dates are specified for an item the figures given properly embrace the first and last years the model is known to have been cataloged or made. Thus, 1932–1937 is understood to specify that the item in question was first cataloged or made in 1932 and last cataloged or made in 1937. To say that the imaginary model used here as an example was discontinued in 1938 should also be readily understandable. The foregoing assumes that any given model was made when it was cataloged, although this may not always be the case. There may be some instances where a model was cataloged in one year but, owing to unexpected and unavoidable delays, actually was not put into production until a year or more later; there may also conceivably be instances where a model was cataloged but never actually put into production. (Or, conversely, instances where a model was made but never cataloged.) There also are a few known cases where models actually appeared on the market in the year prior to which they were included in the catalog. For example, it is known that some of the Tootsietoy Graham passenger cars (but evidently none of the Graham trucks) were actually made, delivered, and on sale late in 1932, although none of the Grahams were cataloged until 1933.

Another point the collector must take into account in perusing catalogs for information to date the span of models is that certain models were at times dropped from separate listing but continued in production for inclusion in sets and that some models never were cataloged separately but were listed only as a part of a set or sets. Among such Tootsietoy items in the 1930's, for example, were the Ford Model-A mail truck, the Graham taxicab, and the Graham tire truck. Similarly, the Tootsietoy Coppertoys and Silvertoys

---

* In stamp collecting the word "issue" usually is used in the sense of "a new issue" or "the issue of 1869." In the case of magazines, each successive number is, of course, referred to as an "issue."

were cataloged only in sets.* This does not mean absolutely that none of the foregoing or similar items were ever sold separately at the wholesale and thence at the retail levels, either on a specific order or through the dispersal of overstocks. Unless, however, such information definitely is obtainable, the only logical approach in considering such matters is to assume the validity of the data presented in the catalogs. Regardless of this, it is almost certain that some such models were sold separately across the retail counter. This no doubt occurred when sets had to be broken up because of pilferage or damage to boxes, or simply because the merchant felt the goods could be more readily

---

* In addition there were at times Tootsietoys with various plated finishes that were distributed as souvenirs, either alone or mounted on bases as paperweights or penholders. Also, the first Tootsietoy La Salles delivered to Cadillac in the fall of 1934 were plated. None of these models should be confused with the Coppertoys and Silvertoys of the late 1930's that were mass-produced in imitation plated finishes and always regarded as part of the regular line. It seems likely, however, that many individuals who were presented with samples of the Coppertoys and Silvertoys initially took them to be specially plated souvenir pieces.

moved in this manner, or when some youngster desiring a specific unit induced a friendly storekeeper to remove it from a set and substitute an unplated vehicle in its place in the set box.

While make (as equated with the word "issue") and remake can readily be dismissed, there is one matter in connection with this usage that possesses a certain merit of implication that may have been behind its initial use. "Issue," as a stamp-collecting term, implies a certain cachet of authority, authenticity, and originality which qualifies an item as possessing merit as a collectible. Exactly the same interpretation applies to model-car collecting from the viewpoint of the model car and its history itself, and, indeed, invariably to all forms of toy and model collecting. It is no accident that in explaining the accepted customs and practices of toy and model collecting the parallel is almost always drawn to stamp collecting. In many ways the recognized principles of the hobbies are the same insofar as obvious variations permit, and so many individuals have at one time or another collected stamps that the situation in regard to toys and models is more easily explained in this manner. In the case of model cars the manufac-

Fig. 160.   Three more boxed items, cast-metal miniatures from the mid-1920's to the early 1930's. Pictured are a Tootsietoy interchangeable truck set with three different bodies; a Tootsietoy farm tractor set in the "Akana" ("a can of") packaging; and a Barclay L-29 Cord.
Adam Pellicot, Jr.; Walter Dreyer photographs

Fig. 161. A Tootsietoy advertisement to the trade in March 1933, announcing their use of a new metal (zinc alloy) and their new model automobiles. Although not identified by name, the models described were the Grahams, some of which had already been in production in late 1932.
George H. Hartman

turer, say Tootsietoy, stands in the same position to the miniature automobiles of their production as does the government of a country stand in relation to the stamps it issues. Whatever variations of stamps, whether deliberate or accidental, that come into circulation are validly collectible. Similarly, the factory-production variations of model cars, whether deliberate or accidental, are validly collectible. Any private changes, variations, or so-call restorations are meaningless.

THE NEED AND RATIONALE FOR STANDARDS

Those who are familiar with the collecting of other types of toys and models, or of toys and models in general, have heard and understood all this before, but it must be reiterated for each new group or type of specialized collector, all the more so be-

cause there always are a few lone-wolf individuals or those with a commercial interest in varying from normally accepted standards who will attempt to speak differently. The rationale and logic behind the customary standards is so basic, obvious, and elementary that the experienced hobbyist invariably is hard put to understand the need to spell it out repeatedly. It is the same rationale that informs a stamp collector that because a certain stamp is common in red and scarce in green he is deceiving only himself if he dips a red specimen in green dye and then hinges it into a blank space in his album. Yet most particularly in a field that often links interest in actual automobiles with model automobiles, and especially that often links interest in actual antique automobiles with old model automobiles, the point must be all the more emphasized. The reason for this is that the collecting of real automobiles is one of the very few hobbies involving manufactured collectibles where repainting or restoration is considered needful or acceptable and does not detract materially from the value of the articles collected. As a result, the collecting of real automobiles invariably is cited as the shining example by the limited number of model-car collectors who for one reason or another advocate repainting or so-called restoration. The universal rule in any field of collectibles, whether old furniture, books, models, or whatever, is that original condition, no matter how poor, always is the desideratum and that restoration, in whole or in part, is permissible only when necessary to make serviceable an old article that is to be used actively. By coincidence, considering the context of this book, those who disagree with this rule almost invariably cite the hobby of collecting actual old automobiles as evidence that repainting or so-called restoration does not detract from but rather may enhance the value of a collectible. This is utter casuistry. Those who use this example in an attempt to prove the acceptability or even the desirability of repainting or restoration always fail to point out that such work usually is a necessity in order that full-size antique automobiles may safely be operated. The same principle also would apply to antique real, not model, airplanes, boats, or railroad equipment. However, only a rather limited number of enthusiasts can or do collect old airplanes or boats, and only an extremely small number can be the fortunate owners of real locomotives, whereas the number of enthusiasts actively interested in old automobiles is legion. Hence the totally false assumptions sometimes offered toy and model collectors based on the practices of real automobile collecting, and the particular pitfall that yawns in this direction for the collector of old model automobiles because of the obvious links between real and model automobiles.

All this does not mean that the collector of old model automobiles does not want his specimens in the best condition possible. Most collectors constantly endeavor to upgrade their specimens. A few who would like to do repaint work for others or who, to their regret, have unwittingly repainted many of their models in the past, occasionally attempt to becloud the issue by implying that the established collectors' standards are a reflection of a ridiculous attitude on the part of hobbyists to the effect that something that is old or antique should look battered and tattered. Nothing, of course, could be further from the truth. Every collector would prefer his specimens, regardless of age, to be in as near new condition as possible. But on the other hand he operates under no compulsion that any or all of his specimens should look new to the uninitiated observer when this must be accomplished by repainting. The fact is that the average collector feels that the better and more authentic looking a repaint or a restoration, the greater the menace it represents, because it may someday, either innocently or deliberately, be offered to a novice as an original in premium condition.

Manifestly, inasmuch as old model automobiles are not going to be used as a means of personal transportation, there is no safety factor involved, and there is no justification for repainting or restoration. This does not mean that under proper conditions a collector should not or will not repair a damaged specimen or replace missing parts. Neither should it ever be taken to mean that the average collector will never accept and add to his collection a repainted model, although only until such time as he can replace it with an original, and in full awareness of the fact that the customary rule is that any repaint, regardless of the caliber of the workmanship, is worth no more than half of the value of a specimen in original paint, no matter how poor the condition of that paint job may be. Fortunately, by far the overall proportion of old model automobiles that have survived remain in their original paint, although a regrettable number of the largest pieces, juvenile automobiles and to a somewhat lesser extent steel trucks, because they so often were played with or left outdoors and suffered fading and rust, were repainted

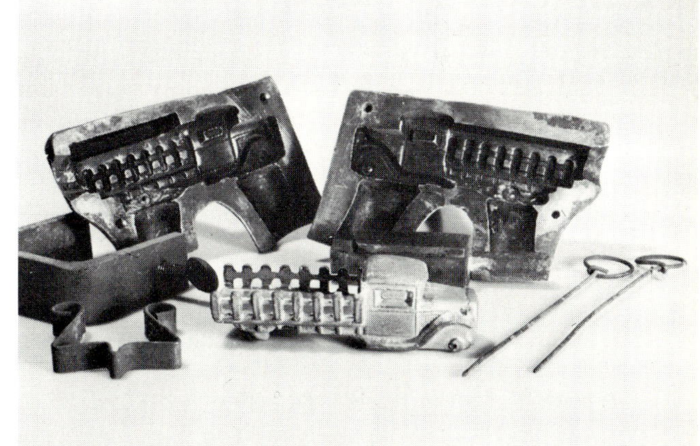

Fig. 162. An actual stock mold for hand slush-casting a miniature stake truck, manufactured by Metal Cast in the 1930's and 1940's. The first photograph shows the mold closed with a truck cast from it in the foreground; the second picture shows the mold open, with a truck casting in the cavity; and the third picture shows the casting removed from the cavity.

Dr. Clinton B. Seeley

when they passed from one generation to the next. On the other hand, comparatively few miniature cast-metal automobiles were repainted for or by the youngsters who played with them. Occasionally a youngster would accidentally drop paint on a car or deliberately repaint it or perhaps attempt to paint over scratches (something that never should be undertaken regardless of how close a color match may be the new paint). Some children were on occasion given to scratching names or initials into the relatively soft surfaces of white-metal alloy castings—there is no cure for models that have thus suffered, the collector can only wait and hope eventually to replace them with better specimens. Some collectors will not accept a repainted or otherwise poor specimen under any circumstances. This is a matter of personal preference, and, of course, results in a collection comprising only first-class examples, although inevitably a smaller one. Most collectors would not care to limit themselves in this manner, preferring to take whatever is obtainable with the hope eventually of replacing repaints and other poor specimens. Midway between these patterns are hobbyists who will take anything in original condition, regardless of how poor, but who absolutely eschew repaints or so-called restorations.

For all of these outlooks, there is one important word of caution. At one time a number of miniature cast-metal cars were put out in unpainted form in painting sets and the young owner painted the cars himself. The best known of these sets were made by Barclay in the mid-1930's and included vehicles that also were at the same time factory-painted and sold as completely finished model automobiles in the usual manner. Collectors coming across the usually poorly painted specimens, and not being aware of the facts, often refuse them as repaints or erroneously discard them as inferior duplicates of similar and obviously factory-painted models of the same cars. Such home-painted models definitely do not rate as repaints but are a desirable and eminently collectible special classification of old model automobiles. Nor should such models be cleaned of paint in an effort to restore them to the bare metal in which they were sold, a sort of repainting in reverse. The number of such sets left in the original state must at best be extremely minute, but ideally a collector would welcome having each such model in factory-painted and assembled form, in home-painted form, and in unpainted form either separately or as a part of a complete set.*

---

* The following vehicles, all with red wooden wheels and separate white rubber tires, are known to have been included in such Barclay 1934 sets, but there

The above vehicles are the exception to the rule about repainting, and are not in any sense repaints.

COLOR VARIATIONS

It is when the serious collector reaches the stage where variations become of serious significance to him that color and the originality of that color become matters of illimitable importance in model-automobile collecting. Bear in mind always that insofar as old model cars and the history of the model-car industry is concerned, variations of any sort occurring in the manufacturer's production procedure are vital, valid, and collectible; variations created privately at any length of time after the model leaves the manufacturer's premises have no standing or desirability, but detract from the desirability and value of any item. Assume a certain model car is known to have been made in either red or blue, and assume also that you posses two red, or perhaps even ten red specimens, but none in blue. This ratio might be pure coincidence but it might also imply that the car is common in red but scarce in blue. Assume, then, that you paint one of your red cars blue and place it in your collection. Do you now have a blue specimen of the miniature automobile in question? The answer is, Of course not! You simply now have a repaint—a "fake" many forthright individuals would not hesitate to call it—and have despoiled and depreciated the value of one specimen. In short, long as it may take and difficult as the search may be, to fill in the series you need a specimen in original blue paint. Of course, if you happen to be the type of individual who does not mind self-deception or who actually manages to receive some sort of pleasure from the mere act of successfully deceiving his fellow hobbyists, there

---

may also have been others: in the five-cent toy size, averaging 3-inches or a little longer, were: coupe, sedan, tank truck, bakery truck, Mack U.S. Army canvas-covered truck, and antiaircraft gun truck; in the ten-cent toy size, averaging about 4 1/4-inches, were: coupe, roadster, stake truck, wrecking truck, Mack dump truck, and Mack side dump truck. Some sets also included a monoplane, dirigible, and figures of soldiers, cowboys, and Indians. There also is a later series of larger proportioned cars averaging about 4 1/2-inches in length and fitted with Bakelite wheels that reputedly were supplied in painting sets just prior to or after World War II. These usually are found unpainted, although sometimes bearing traces of paint. The series includes a steam fire engine, hook and ladder, teardrop racing car, and what have been identified as a model of a Chrysler coupe of the early 1930's and a streamlined Hupmobile coupe of the later 1930's. It is possible these and other models were included in painting sets, but the matter still is uncertain, and it is possible these cars were made from stock molds and simply sold in the unpainted bare metal finish.

is no law or anything else to stop you from turning the red car into a blue one. If you carry this a step further, and knowingly offer your creation as a rare genuine original blue one and sell it as such, you may well launch yourself upon a career that eventually will bring the postal inspectors or a representative of the district attorney to your door. However, if such endeavors be your inclination, it seems highly unlikely that anything that might be said here will deter you from your chosen path.

Still, assuming that a particular car is known to have been made in red or in blue, suppose a specimen eventually turned up in still another color, say yellow or green or purple? If the new find were a genuine original factory paint job, it would most certainly be regarded by collectors as an extremely rare and highly desirable color variation, as well as an important enhancement of the model-car-collecting hobby's ever-increasing store of detailed knowledge. On the other hand, if the new color variation simply had been created by repainting a red or blue specimen, it would merely be another almost worthless repaint, of interest and value solely for its structural form in the collection of someone who had not yet managed to obtain any original specimen. Obviously, when repainting is expertly done, it requires considerable knowledge, including familarity with genuine shades of comparable colors to unmask such a specimen or even to expose its authenticity to doubt. This is why it so frequently is remarked that the better or more expert a repaint or restoration, the more dangerous it is. It should be observed that repainting does not merely mean carefully painting one color over another, a process that usually is fairly easy to detect. If a model is cleaned of all its old paint down to the bare metal and then painted, it still is just as certainly classed as a repaint and rated just as undesirable, although models processed in this manner may be considerably more difficult to detect because all possible giveaway traces of the original paint have been expunged.

At the present time, the hobby of model-car collecting is in a state where considerable knowledge concerning authentic colors has been gained and codified, but much research remains to be done. It always is possible for scarce and previously unknown color variations to turn up; in fact, there will always be a possibility of this, and as more and more collectors become active and bring large quantities of new specimens to light undoubtedly many rare color variations are likely to become known. At the present time, however, much information definitely is known concerning the colors and combinations employed in the pre–World War II production of the two largest makers of miniature cast-metal automobiles, Dowst in the United States and Meccano in Great Britain. It often is said in the toy- and model-collecting hobby that one must learn to read a catalog. Part of this conveys the thought that catalogs are not always necessarily accurate either in their color illustrations or in printed specifications regarding colors and variations. Their use must be leavened with caution and supplemented by other sources of data, especially personal examination of as many actual specimens as possible. The data resulting from such research and proper correlation can provide highly reliable collector information. In the field of the color and other variations of the Meccano British Dinky Toys, the collector should refer to Dr. Cecil Gibson's book, listed in Appendix II. A detailed checklist of the known Dowst and Tootsietoy models, with color information, is currently in the course of preparation by the present writer.

Authenticity and originality of color variations apply not only to the colors themselves but also to the combinations in which they are applied to the model vehicles finished in more than one color, usually by combining two or three castings painted in different colors to make up a completed automobile, and at times by masking castings during painting. While there always exists the possibility of unusual authentic color combinations turning up, the proper color combinations usually were strictly planned and regulated by the larger manufacturers. Models that have been made up by collectors in combinations that are not authentic, even though the individual components are in original paint, are regarded as of little value and in a certain sense hardly better than repaints. This is one reason why a number of hobbyists insist that the cars accepted for their collections have the original axles and axle-end crimpings to assure that models have not been tampered with. Unfortunately, it is not always easy to detect such meddling, especially if the original axles have been put back and recrimped. In some cases this condition may be revealed by the fact that the axles are slightly shorter than they should be, the wheels lack sufficient room for free play, or the axle ends are scarred and show traces of bright metal. Completely new axles usually can be detected by their brightness. On the other hand, original axles customarily reveal the light rust, or the patina, that is the normal result of the passing of several decades. These are not always sure signs, however, for certain individuals have been quoted as boasting that they are quite capable of arti-

WHEEL TOY SPECIALS

Four selected items of proven selling power. An assortment which, by themselves, will keep even a good sized manufacturer busy.

Rubber wheels, supplied at $3.50 per thousand are easily assembled by simply slipping over axle nails. No spreading of axles necessary.

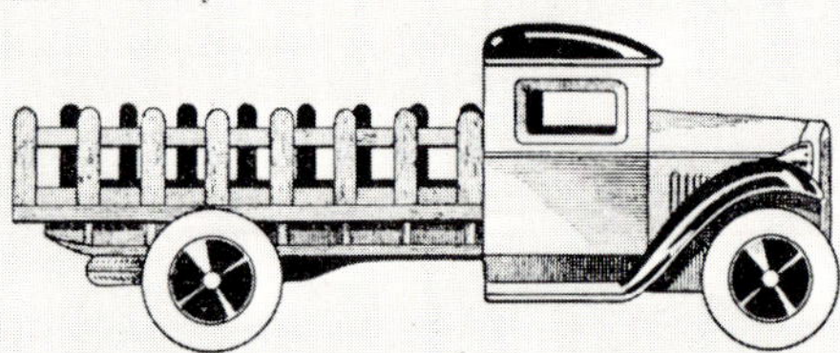

No. 64—TRUCK

4¼ inches long

Bronze Castingform
for hollow casting $45.00

No. 61—HOOK AND LADDER

4½ inches long

Bronze Castingform
for hollow casting $40.00

This hollow Frog is easily cast with opening in mouth, ready for use. Finished green with a few spots for added color. An ideal chain store item.

Bronze Castingform $50.00

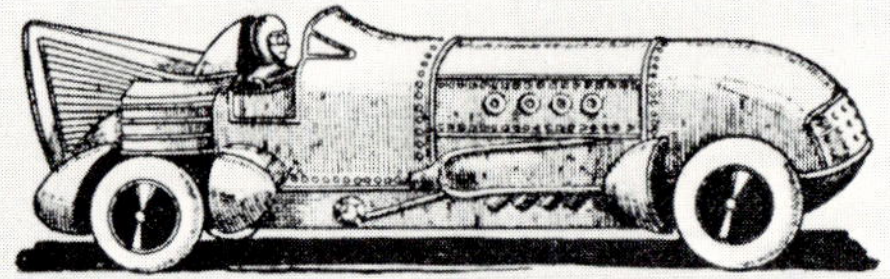

No. 62—RACER

4½ inches long

Bronze Castingform
for hollow casting $40.00

No. 66—AEROPLANE

4½ inch wing-spread

Bronze Castingforms
for Plane and Propellers $55.00

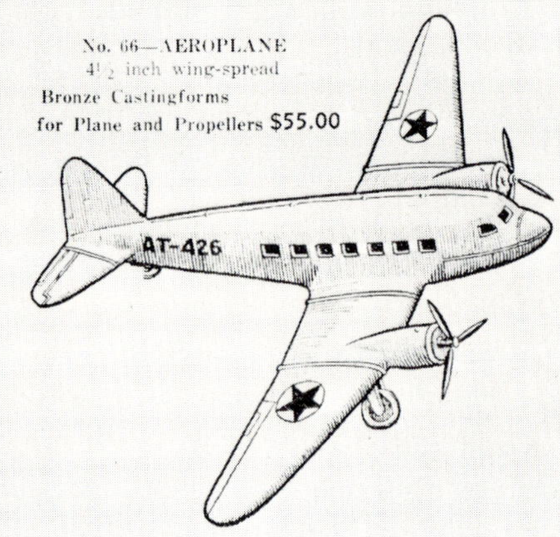

Fig. 163.   The stock mold shown in Fig. 163 was but one of a number of types offered to small manufacturers in the 1930's and 1940's by Metal Cast, as indicated by catalog listings of some of the molds available in the 1930's and, in the case of those pictured, carried over into the post-World War II era of the late 1940's. It is not certain if the Nos. 40, 41, and 42 molds were introduced just before or just after the war, but the trailer trucks and tank molds evidently did not appear until after the conflict. Also pictured is a dealer price list on finished toys from these latter molds.

John L. Davis

DEALERS PRICE LIST SERIES "O" TOYS		
	Retail Each	Wholesale per gross (144 pieces)
TRAILER TRUCKS		
Tractor Unit and Van (Nos. 01-02)	.50	$43.20
Tractor Unit and Tank (Nos. 01-03)	.50	43.20
Tractor Unit and Rack Body (Nos. 01-04)	.50	43.20
TRAILER TRUCK SETS		
Consisting of one each:		
Tractor - Van - Tank and Rack Body Trailers	1.00	86.40
WAR TANK	.40	34.56
METAL CAST PRODUCTS CO.	**New York 60, N. Y.**	

ficially "aging" an axle or other components so as virtually to assure that they will pass inspection. The reader may be left to draw his own conclusions as to the motivations involved. It would appear that the best advice that could be given is always to proceed with caution in contemplating any multicolored model whose color combination is not well established as authentic and whose axles excite any suspicion.

It should not be assumed that all spurious combinations of components with original paint were by any means deliberately made up to deceive. In the past, a number of collectors, quite unaware of the fact that the specific combinations of colors on such series as the Tootsietoy General Motors models and Grahams were strictly planned and regulated at the factory, have innocently but regrettably made up many models in an unauthentic manner. It often seemed both proper and simple to take the body from a car with a broken chassis and a good chassis from a model with a broken body and make up a "complete" car, using the two sound components. Were these combinations actually made up at the factory and capable of authentication as such, some, if not all, would rate as indisputably rare and desirable variations. Unfortunately, this cannot be the case and, rather, collectors must inevitably regard such specimens somewhat dubiously and of lesser value than models in known authentic combinations. This is regrettable, for, undoubtedly, only in few cases did bad intent enter into the picture. A few enthusiasts who evidently were more prototype- than model-oriented have conceded that at times they deliberately transposed various color Tootsietoy or Dinky Toy bodies and chassis to secure what they regarded as a more personally pleasing color combination or a more authentic (from the standpoint of real automobile coloring) color combination. Although such actions may horrify serious collectors, it certainly cannot be said that these actions, lamentable as they may be, were conceived with dubious motivation. However, all this serves

to point up again the absolute importance of maintaining original color combinations. Whatever their prompting, unauthentic combinations, most particularly once out of the hands of their creators, can only serve to confuse and confound serious hobbyists for years to come.

There is one situation that must be excepted from the general remarks concerning factory-determined color combinations. This relates to the Tootsietoy Bild-A-Car sets of the 1930's already mentioned. Five chassis and five bodies were included, and the possibilities of varying the color combinations was one of the features of the sets. As the catalog stated, a boy could enjoy changing "body and color combinations as often as he wishes." Five differently colored bodies and five differently colored chassis in each set meant that, regardless of color variations in the overall makeup of sets themselves, any given set permitted the construction of twenty-five different body and chassis combinations. In view of this, in the case of cars built from the Tootsietoy Bild-A-Car sets, any body and chassis color combination is considered authentic and collectible. The cars built from these sets can be recognized from the fact that half-axles connected with special axle joiners are used instead of the conventional full one-piece axles used on factory-assembled models. Of course, there actually is no physical barrier to preclude any individual, either sometime in the past or today, from using the split axles to reassemble vehicles other than those whose bodies were furnished in the Bild-A-Car sets,* namely, the Graham coupe, sedan, roadster, and tire truck. Consequently, barring the uncover-

---

* There were three Tootsietoy Bild-A-Car sets, the No. 05360 of 1933–1936, the No. 5360 of 1937, and the No. 5360 of 1938. The first two each contained bodies for a roadster, two coupes, and two sedans. The 1938 set substituted the tire truck body for that of the roadster. The tire truck body was a little less expensive to manufacture than that of the roadster, the latter requiring the additional steps of making, painting, and inserting the separate windshield casting.

ing of proper evidence contradictory to the foregoing, the acceptance as authentic of vehicles employing the half axles logically must be limited to these four types. Theoretically, there should be no Bild-A-Car versions of the Graham convertible coupe, convertible sedan, town car, ambulance, milk truck, and wrecking truck. Probably this should also apply to the Graham taxicab, which used the sedan body. However, the latter is a point that cannot be stated with absolute certainty at this writing. The Tootsietoy Graham taxicab bodies were painted in a single color and did not bear any special legend identifying them as taxicabs.

Another point in regard to color variations is well demonstrated by the Tootsietoy Graham and La Salle convertible coupes and sedans. It is obviously the determination made by the manufacturer at the time of production whether a given unit is to be regarded as a distinctly different by collectors or merely as a color or other variation of a model. This point is of especial importance to collectors who have not yet reached the point of collecting color variations but simply are seeking to obtain a single example of each model regardless of color. Inasmuch as most collectors eventually start collecting color variations, at least of old model cars, the foregoing limited procedure may eventually be regretted at a later date when a collector actively seeks all possible color variations and looks back with dismay at the recollection of those he has passed by. At any rate, the Tootsietoy Graham and La Salle convertibles were not mere color variations of the corresponding regular coupes and sedans, as most collectors erroneously have regarded them. The convertibles were distinctly separate models, each version (four in the Grahams, two in the La Salles) with its own catalog number. Structurally the convertibles were identical with the respective regular versions of the coupes and sedans, the bodies being cast in the same dies, and the only physical difference in the convertible models being that after the bodies were given their initial overall basic coat of paint the convertible bodies were masked and tan paint applied to simulate cloth tops. Again, there was a definite pattern of color combinations, and in many instances attempts to fake convertibles by applying tan paint to the roofs of regular coupes and sedans will immediately give themselves away.

A somewhat similar example exists in the case of the Erie-painted and chromium-plated Packard roadsters and Lincoln Zephyr sedans of the 1930's. These were not merely different colors or finishes of the same models, although units of. the same size and type were molded in the same dies, but definitely different models, selling at dif-ferent prices, even though catalog numbers never were assigned to any of the Erie models. In the smaller-size cars the painted versions were five-cent sellers and the chromium-plated versions were ten-cent sellers. In the larger-size models the painted cars retailed for ten cents and the plated models for twenty-five cents.

Collectors of certain miniature cast-metal automobiles have discovered still another, if rather uncertain, type of collectible paint variation. These are found on modern models painted entirely by automation, the machinery being regulated in an attempt to apply the absolute minimum amount of paint required to cover the exposed portions of the castings. As a result, perceptible variations sometimes can be found on the exposed surfaces of various models, at times appearing as slight unpainted areas, at other times presenting upon close scrutiny a sort of mottled paint effect, the result of a pattern of tiny bare metal spots showing through the paint. Even more interesting to some collectors is the degree of paint found on the underside of these models. Theoretically the undersides are to be left bare and not painted at all, no provision being made in the setting up of the machinery for intentionally painting these surfaces. However, at times the paint has a tendency to "lift" under and within the model. The result is that in some cases the lower undersurfaces—for example, the bottom of a truckbed as compared to the inside of the roof of the cab—will be found to have received a virtually covering coat of paint, while other, identical, models will be found to be, as intended, almost totally devoid of any traces of paint underneath. Naturally, there often are found all sorts of intermediate stages. The customary objective in collecting this sort of variation is to find two specimens of the same vehicle in the same color, one with as little and one with as much underpaint as possible. This form of collecting may, in truth, appear somewhat farfetched and even perhaps a little grotesque, especially to persons not yet really thoroughly immersed in the lore and lure of miniature cars. It is, however, nonetheless a quite valid and legitimate species of collecting based on the long-accepted principle of the importance of factory-production variations.

With the exception of the paragraph immediately preceding, all the foregoing remarks concerning color variations have been directed primarily to pre–World War II models, and the examples cited have all been from this period. However, the same customs, principles, practices, rules, or whatever term an individual may prefer, apply equally to model cars of somewhat more recent date, to those being manufactured at the present time, and to those that will be made in the future, whenever the collector's outlook is directed toward these models in terms of the history of the miniature automobile itself. Similarly, regardless of the date of manufacture of the particular models that may be described as examples, the comments following this section pertaining to other types of variations apply equally to models regardless of the period of their actual production. In regard to color, the present-day purchaser who seeks to secure such variations of current model cars often operates at a disadvantage. A number of models, mainly of the less costly types, still are sold in open stock in counter bins or are packaged transparently so that the prospective buyer immediately can discern the colors available. Some of the more costly models also are packaged so as to reveal the color. A good many model cars, however, are packed in such a manner that there is no way to ascertain differences in color—or other possible variations of interest to a collector —without actually opening the package. It readily is understandable that this is not something that the average merchant, no matter how friendly or cooperative he may be, is apt to look upon with favor. It would be highly desirable if all such packages could be stamped with a notation of the color of the model within, as was widely done on toy locomotive and railroad car boxes in the 1920's and 1930's. Unquestionably, the adoption of such a practice would result in some increase in sales, although whether this gain would be sufficient to compensate for the overall added costs involved is something that cannot be asserted with accuracy. Parenthetically, it would appear to be to the advantage of all model-car manufacturers in every way possible. Although conceivably the average total an individual hobbyist would spend on a given line might not increase as might be anticipated, many collectors would spend no more but perhaps would purchase one specific model in several different colors rather than several different models. Nevertheless, the implications of the matter are worth the attention of manufacturers interested in encouraging serious model-car collecting, following established historical lines. It would, of course, be most unfortunate and self-defeating if attempts were made by current manufacturers to exploit this collector interest by offering special "limited edition" runs of unusual colors especially for collectors.

In the meantime, whatever innovations in packaging and coloring are considered, it should be kept in mind that many of the collectors of the more expensive modern models are oriented toward the prototype-automobile outlook, and while some may at times prefer a model car in a certain color if a choice is available, these hobbyists are not as interested in collecting color variations as such as is the hobbyist who collects from a primary interest in the history of the model car and the model-car industry. Regardless of the precise outlook on model-car collecting as a whole, and more specifically on the matter of color variations, it would appear that the collector seeking color variations of current miniature automobiles must continue to rely largely on chance to learn of the existence of specimen variations of this type.

MORE CONCERNING COLOR VARIATIONS

Collecting color variations may be based on different colors, such as red as opposed to blue; on definite changes in colors; and on comparatively minor variations in shading of the same color. In the latter case the collector need always be especially acute, both to detect these shades—usually possible only when two models are compared side by side—and to avoid accepting and classifying as variations differences caused by fading rather than by an actual slight change in the factory paint or the factory painting process. It is surprising even today, when colors are far more rigidly controlled, what disitnctly different shadings can be found on similar models, even in some cases within the same lot at a local store. Even more noticeable, when actually seen, of course, are color variations resulting from a definite change in colors. Unfortunately, the hobby has not yet reached a stage of properly codifying even the most obvious of these changes. In fact, many collectors are not yet aware of the nuances of the situation. As a result, many hobbyists buying or trading through correspondence may pass up a model that actually is a completely different color than one they already own because the description of color simply is given as "green" or "red" and they already have the model in *a* green or *a* red.

In the early 1930's Tootsietoy made a complete change in the colors of their basic spectrum. The four basic colors remained, as in the 1920's, red, yellow, blue, and green, but the new colors were a brighter, richer red, yellow, blue, and green. Some of the new colors probably were used late in 1932; certainly they were being employed in 1933, although this does not necessarily mean that every car made and painted in 1933 took the new colors, if only because logically whenever the change was made there must have been certain stocks of some of the old colors re-

Fig. 164. Three 1/2-inch-scale military vehicles constructed from Austin-Craft kits containing primarily wooden components that were popular in the years following World War II, a 2 1/2-ton truck with tarpaulin; a Jeep, and a Jeep trailer with tarpaulin.

Austin-Craft Co.

maining on hand to be used up. However, it seems fairly safe to say that most if not all of the Tootsietoy models originally made in the 1920's or in the very early 1930's that carried over into the 1933 line or beyond exist in two definite and complete (insofar as the four basic colors are concerned) color series. Tootsietoy, in fact, brightened and broadened their array of colors considerably after 1932. Specifically, these included new light and dark blue, light and dark green, light and dark brown, white and cream, salmon, silver, orange, red, and yellow. The black also seems to have become glossier, and a change may also have been made in the khaki. In any event it is important to distinguish between the Tootsietoy khaki, light brown, and dark brown, which were three entirely different colors. Similarly, the white and the cream of the 1930's, while each may exist in minor shading variations, were two completely different colors, and were so intended and designated by the factory.

When separate numbers of Tootsietoys (as contrasted to boxed sets of assorted models) were sold, the standard factory packing was one or two dozen to a box. In many cases these were color-assorted equally, three or six of a given color or combination of colors in each dozen or two dozen respectively. In some cases, in the 1930's, however, the assortment to a dozen might be four, four, four; or four, three, three, two; or four, four, two, two colors; or some other combination. By the mid-1930's Dowst, as well as most other toy manufacturers, were acutely aware of the importance of bright and attractive colors and color combinations, and also of prorating the number of each color in a standard package in accordance with the relative popularity of the colors at the retail counter. Color variations were as vital to the manufacturers at the time the old models were in current production as they are vital to the collector today.

Color selectivity and assorting evidently reached a particular peak in the depths of the depression when every manufacturer of cast-iron, white-metal, or zinc miniature automobiles was competing desperately for the nickel, dime, and fifteen-cent trade. It is most interesting to read the introductory remarks concerning "Color Assortment" in the 1935 Tootsietoy catalog, the catalog, of course, being directed to the wholesale trade:

"The following is the current schedule of colors in which the dozen-packed items shown on pages one, two, three, and four are packed at the present time. Occasionally, the desires of the buying public for certain colors change. We attempt, to the best of our ability, to keep abreast of these color desires. We truly believe that we are in the best position to know what the public really does want and will always govern our color assortments accordingly. We request that you do not ask for special color assortments as it only causes confusion *in all departments* of the factory *and slows up production.*"

Other manufacturers of miniature cast-metal cars were equally concerned with color selection and assortment. The original 1934 Manoil boxing for their then new cars was five red, two green, two gray, two silver, and one orange to a dozen—these refer to body colors, all of the chassis being black. Other manufacturers also sought brighter colors and carefully planned packing combinations. One important result of all this is that in the case of the models manufactured in the 1930's, there is much greater disparity in the relative rarity and collectors' desirability of different color variations than with the model cars made in the 1920's when the colors almost always were equal quantities of red, yellow, blue, and green assorted in equal quantities to the dozen. It is self-evident that, in the case of the first series of Manoil models of 1934 (assuming, as seems logical, that the survival ratio was just about the same for all five colors), an orange specimen today, as at the time it was made, should be five times as scarce as a red one and twice as scarce as a green, gray, or silver specimen. Similarly, a green, gray, or silver specimen should be two and a half times as scarce as a red one. Unfortunately, lacking such definite information on the makeup of the color assortments, determinations even to a partial extent of in what colors a given model car may originally have been made and of the relative scarcity of the color variations can in many instances be made only tentatively, and even then only after considerable studying of a great many models in a great many collections. Whether an orange first-series Manoil car would be regarded by most collectors as actually worth five times as much in cash or trade as a red one is something else again, and these matters will be discussed a little later in this chapter.

Regarding the Tootsietoy standard four colors of the 1920's, it is not quite certain what actually constituted "yellow." There was a color that was a typical yellow, as used on the body of the No. 4653 water tower (red chassis, yellow body, and red tower) which appeared in 1927, but this color is not found on any of the one-piece cars of the 1920's, all of which came in equal assortments of red, yellow, blue, and green. (The water tower was one of the few units that came only in one color combination at a time.) The standard yellow on most of these cars evidently was really an orange yellow or a yellow orange, the former term being used in some of the catalogs as a color specified for railroad cars but not automotive vehicles. In addition, there was a true rich orange color that sometimes appears, as, for example, on bodies and chassis for the Mack trucks but differs from the orange used in the mid-1930's, the earlier orange being in fact a richer, brighter orange than that used later, for instance, on the No. 0804 "City Fuel Company" coal truck. It would appear that the orange yellow was indeed the basic "yellow" of the Tootsietoys in the 1920's, although all that can be said with absolute certainty at this point is that each of the so-called one-part cars were made and sold in equal quantities of red, blue, green, and *a* "yellow" and that, with the exception of the General Motors series, this condition was paralleled on at least most of the other Tootsietoy cars of the 1920's.* In fact, this assorting probably applies to the General Motors cars made in 1928 that had variously colored bodies on chassis that uniformly were black. However, after 1928 the Tootsietoy General Motor chassis were painted in various colors; the overall number of colors became broader, and there were many combinations of body and chassis colors. One model, the coupe supplied as an army scout car in the No. 5061 Aerial Defense set of 1931–1933, appears never to have been supplied in two-tone, but to have been made up for this particular use with both body and chassis painted khaki.

Presumably in the 1920's the four assorted standard colors sold out evenly when they reached the store counters, an assumption confirmed by the overall survival ratio, the four colors being found today with just about equal ease. When the cars were sold in most sets, barring a special case such as the Aerial Defense set, an effort was made to assort the colors of the various units within a given set as far as possible, and presumably in the long run all color quantities more or less balanced out on the basis of original produc-

---

* There was, in fact, considerable confusion and disparity concerning yellow in this period, both within and outside the toy business. In the 1920's and 1930's, for instance, the Lionel Corporation made numerous locomotives and cars finished in a beautiful orange but which they officially referred to as "yellow" and which they so stamped on every box. Similarly, the Yellow Cabs and other commercial vehicles of the Yellow fleet were, much to the confusion of youngsters at the time, uniformly painted in what indisputably was not yellow but orange.

tion in identical quantities of each color. However, in the 1930's many of the Tootsietoy color packing assortments on individual models began to emphasize the brighter colors and to decrease the relative quantities of blues and greens. There may, in fact, have been a definite if temporary antipathy to green in the late 1950's. At any rate the following quotation from an interview with Myron B. Shure of Tootsietoy which appeared in the Chicago of September 27, 1958, provides an interesting commentary on matters of color preference from the manufacturer's standpoint: " 'We've discovered that kids like any car as long as it's red.' . . . Bright yellow and royal blue are two other regular colors among the Tootsietoy set, Mike added. But the kids won't touch a green one for some unknown reasons." It cannot dogmatically be stated on the basis of this that any green Tootsietoy circa 1958 must perforce be a scarce color variation, although such a suggestion obviously is implicit in the statement. However, given two specimens of a Tootsietoy model from this period, one painted red and the other green, it would seem a reasonable enough deduction to regard the latter as the considerably rarer of the pair.

VARIATIONS IN LETTERING AND DECORATION

Closely allied to color variations are variations in lettering and decoration on miniature automobiles. In the earliest period a number of models were decorated by means of hand lining; a few were finished with stencil decorations. Hand lining mainly disappeared about World War I, but some vestiges of it remained in the 1920's, particularly on some American friction automobiles, and well beyond the 1920's on some of the more elaborate European clockwork and live-steam models. Another form of hand-painting treatment that endured on larger models through the 1920's and even a little beyond was the practice of picking out lettering or insignia by hand in a contrasting color on cast-iron models. In the case of two models, both identical structurally and in the basic color or combination of colors, the fact that one has been striped in gold and the other in red automatically in itself constitutes a color variation. Similarly, two otherwise identical models striped in the same color but in an obviously intentionally different manner, perhaps one with a single broad stripe along the top of the hood and the other with two narrow parallel stripes in the same position, also is an obvious factory variation; and to the

advanced or specialized collector, at least, it is a specimen to be retained rather than regarded as a duplicate, the more so because such a variation presumably represents a point in production procedures where it was realized it was easier and quicker—and consequently cheaper—to have a single wide line instead of two narrow ones painted on a model. Or perhaps, conversely, a competitor was doing a better job of striping, and it was felt necessary to enhance the decorative quality of a line. However, in most such cases, it may be assumed that changes of this type tend to the downgrading, rather than the upgrading, of a product, in an effort to cut costs. Sometimes the change is made simply because there is too much spoilage with the more elaborate or more delicate scheme of things, which is, in effect, another way of cutting costs.

The individual collector who has been saving two such slightly different versions of the same model vehicle has to decide for himself whether to exchange one if he is offered a specimen of an entirely different miniature automobile of comparable value that he does not yet possess. To some, particularly novices, it may seem self-evident to exchange what merely is a variation of another piece in the collection for something that is entirely different. But for the experienced collector, on the contrary, there probably would be a fifty-fifty chance that he would reject the trade. His reasoning would be: One, the variation between two otherwise identical models illustrates an important and interesting change in production procedures; and, two, the chances of replacing the precise variation with an identical specimen are considerably less than the chances of coming across any representative specimen of the model offered in exchange, even though the cash values of the two items involved are approximately the same.

At the other extreme, every hand-decorated specimen is likely minutely to differ from every other even though the same person may have striped many thousands. It is possible for the over-punctilious collector to get so bogged down in scrutinizing every line as to its precise thickness, length, regularity, and placement in relation to similar lines on other specimens that he may never declare any specimen a duplicate.

Many of the older automotive models are unmarked as to manufacturer; some may be identified as to make by structural comparisons or by tracing down patent numbers or dates. Stenciled lettering, opaque ink rubber stamping, lettering raised or impressed in the metal, or paper labels may at times be used to indicate patent informa-

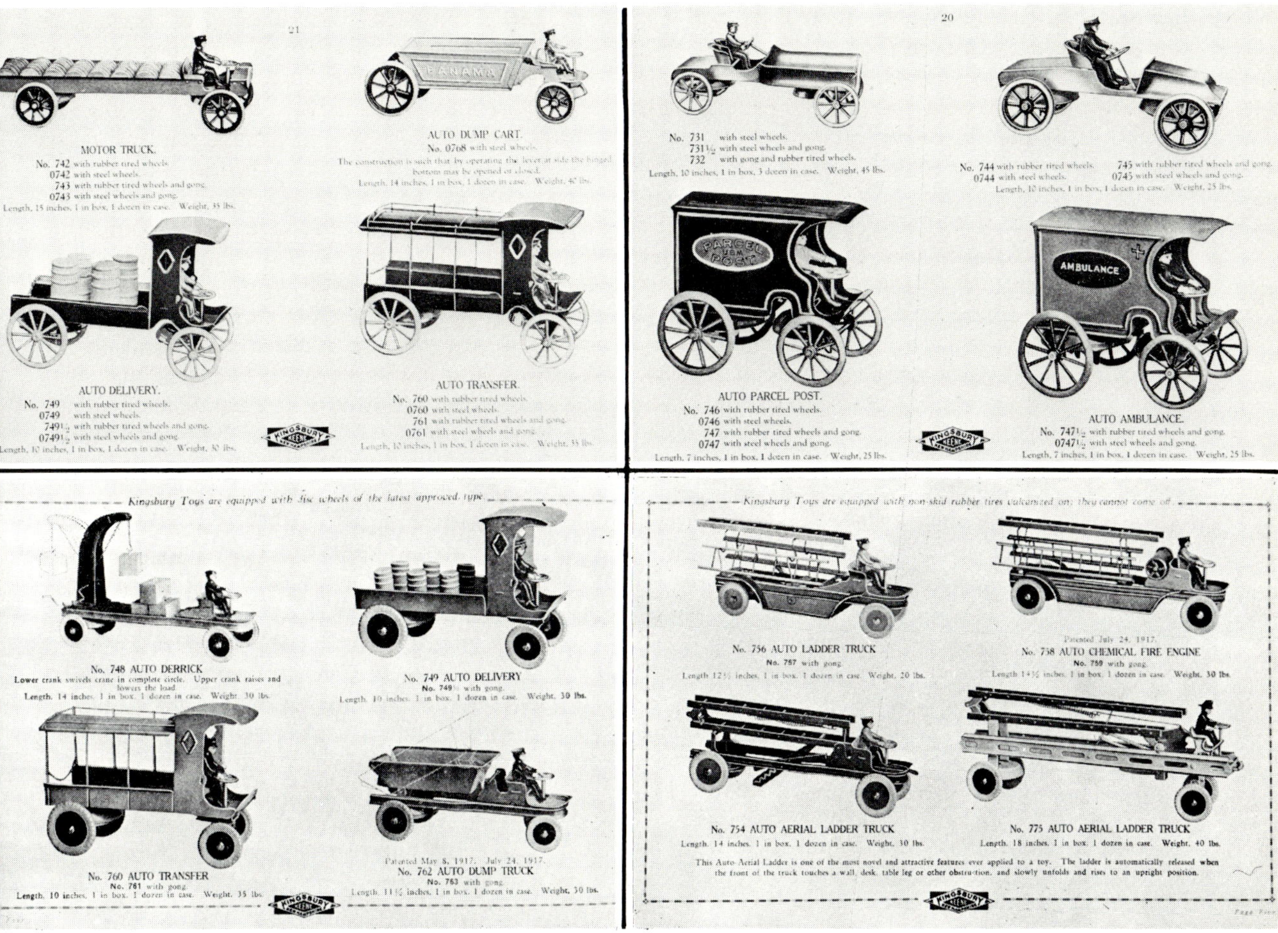

Fig. 165. Representatives of the ever-popular Kingsbury line of stamped-metal, clockwork-powered vehicles as offered in two of the manufacturer's catalogs of the 1920's. Note the change in design between the earlier trucks and the later versions of the "Auto Delivery" and "Auto Transfer," eliminating the crane neck under the driver's seat.

tion, and variations in otherwise identical pieces can occur with the change of form from patent applied for or patent pending to the statement that a patent has been granted. Lithographed models almost always carry any or all decoration, manufacturers' names, trademarks or identifying initials,* and patent information incorporated into the lithographed finish itself. Occasionally there are interesting exceptions that provide unique variations. For example, the Lehman "Naughty Boy," a small comical clockwork lithographed toy portraying a man and a boy seated facing each other in an open automobile (Fig. 172) exists in at least three variations of the patent markings: (1) notation of European patents but with no reference to a United States patent lithographed on the back; (2) the lithographed notation cov-

* A comprehensive list of toy manufacturers' trademarks and identifications will be found in the book *The Toy Collector* by the present writer.

ered with a printed paper label pasted over it, advising that a United States patent had been applied for; (3) revised lithographed legend, including the United States patent. Naturally, the paper-label version is the rarest and most desirable, but a set of all three types is regarded as an extremely interesting and noteworthy series in any collection.

In short, apart from the potential value in helping to ascertain the make of an otherwise unidentified piece, patent and other information should always be compared on two seemingly identical specimens in order to make certain that they do not represent distinct variations of lettering. If the latter proves to be the case, then it is up to the individual collector to decide if he wishes to retain both in his collection and, if not, of which one he will dispose.

Although by the time the model automotive era had fully arrived, the use on metal toys of paper, either for identifying labels or decorative purposes, had largely passed, there was still an occasional vestige. Collectors should not assume, as some do, that such a decorative application of paper invariably has been done by a child, although usually this proves to be so. At least some of the smaller Arcade Checker Cabs in the 1920's had the checker pattern applied to the cast-iron taxis by means of a gummed paper band.

The usual means of applying such decorations, labels, and information to many steel or cast-iron toy automobiles in the 1920's and thereafter, however, was decalcomanias or transfers. Most often in America decalcomanias were employed on medium- and larger-sized pieces. The usual way of incorporating lettering, including that making up part of the external design of the unit itself, used on pre–World War II miniature cars cast of zinc or white-metal alloy, was to incorporate it into the castings themselves. Parenthetically it might be said that any such model bearing in raised cast lettering the name of any actual prototype make of automobile—the Tootsietoy General Motors series is probably the best known and most extensive group—is considered by a substantial body of collectors as a fairly desirable model. Prior to World War II, decalcomanias seem to have been employed in the United States on models especially lettered with the names of, and sold only to, individual stores and chains. This is a particularly interesting and desirable group of models, the more so because some of them, especially those lettered with decalcomanias instead of raised cast lettering or lithographed inserts, may originally have been made in quantities as small as only a few thousand.

In Great Britain, however, decalcomanias were very extensively used during the 1930's to apply prototype lettering and insignia to small cars and trucks cast of nonferrous metals. Often the same castings, or several progressive variations of similar castings, were used for whole groups of models differing only in their lettering, for example the Dinky Toy 28-series of delivery trucks. Each model was identified by a letter—28a, 28b, 28c, and so on—and the series ran through the alphabet except for a few letters that were omitted, and then a 280-series was begun. In some cases a specific model was changed from one insignia to another, while retaining the same catalog number. At other times a new number was assigned to a new model. The particular time at which models were added or dropped probably determined if a model were assigned an existing or a new number, but the matter does not seem ever to have been completely systematized. In any event, although colors for specific truck names

were fairly consistent, barring changes in castings —there were three basic types, some trucks being made in all three, some in two, and some only in one style—there are at least thirty-four different names appearing in the regular or cataloged series. In addition, as in the United States, some trucks were made up as specials for the use of a particular customer, such as the Bentalls truck.* One point is that in the cataloging system the same number may at times stand for different colors and lettering at different times, but it may also stand for different models made at the same time, for instance the Dinky Toy No. 33R mechanical horse and trailer combinations that appeared in 1935 in the colors and lettering of the four major British railroads of the day, the London, Midland & Scottish, the London & North Eastern Railway, the Great Western Railway, and the Southern Railway. Possibly there was some subtle distinction in the numbering system between the use of small or capital letters employed by Dinky, with the lowercase referring to a model available at a given time with a specific marking—or no marking at all—and the uppercase denoting assorted items sold simultaneously under the same number.

However, the point is that all decalcomanias may exist in major or minor variations of style, color, or lettering, particularly when used over a sustained period of time where new lots must be made up periodically. Not all these changes are as noticeable, and obviously deliberate, as are the changes in the decoration on the Dinky Toy No. 280d Bisto (a British breakfast food) truck of the late 1930's where the entire design changes substantially as illustrated in the two specimens shown on page 27 of the Gibson book on Dinky Toys (see Appendix II). Changes may be very slight and even subtle, perhaps merely a substitution of a slightly different style of letter, either by accident or design when a new type setting must be made for a new batch

---

* There were American Dinky Toys in this sense, although none ever were cast or assembled in the United States or Canada. During the early 1960's, vehicles such as the No. 919 Guy Van would be lettered in the New York workrooms of Lines Brothers with decalcomanias with the name of a store; then these specials would be repacked and shipped out to the account. Also, the writer is certain he remembers seeing in the later 1930's a truck specially lettered for Morgan, a Montreal, Canada, department store. It may be that the latter vehicle and others of its type were completely fabricated at the Liverpool factory and shipped overseas in completed form, although at that time Meccano had an office in Toronto. Possibly at all times the fact whether such specials were lettered in Great Britain or in the United States or Canada was dependent on the quantity involved.

of decalcomanias. A change of this sort often can be detected by collectors only upon very careful comparison of two seemingly identical specimens. How many such variations exist cannot be said here; all that can be pointed out is that experience has shown that some such changes almost always accompany a widespread use of decalcomanias over a period of years. There may also be variations stemming from differences in the placing of decalcomanias or other forms of lettering. Here, as in the case of hand striping, the too zealous collector may let his enthusiasm carry him too far; but in the cases of vehicles where the lettering or insignia on one obviously has been placed perceptibly high or low, or in another position completely, the result obviously is a collectible minor variation.

Major or minor changes in the style or size of lettering are not confined to the use of decalcomanias, but may at times be found with various other forms, such as stenciling, lithography, rubber stamping, and so on. Again, they usually come to the notice of the collecting fraternity only when someone carefully compares two or more specimens. However, the wise hobbyist always keeps on the alert for such obvious differences as serif and sans-serif type faces. The Barclay Radio Police car of the late 1930's, for instance, not only has the words RADIO POLICE cast in raised letters on each side of the vehicle but also carries the word POLICE rubber-stamped on top of the hood. There were at least two rubber stamps —or two styles of rubber stamps—used for this lettering at the Barclay factory, one with serif and one with sans-serif lettering, the serif style also employing slightly larger letters, although the overall length of the legend is the same or so close to it that it would require finer measuring instruments than the average model-automobile collector has at hand to determine a difference in this direction. It is possible that there even was a third stamp or type of stamp for applying this lettering at the factory. In all such matters, and probabilities and possibilities (an astute hobbyist would seem especially well-advised to seek minor styling changes in the lettering applied to models whose production was interrupted by war), the best advice that can be given to the collector is— *compare!* *

---

* It should be pointed out, apropos of this admonition, that the difference in the rubber stamping cited above is by no means the only variation that occurs on the RADIO POLICE cars. There are at the very least no less than four distinctly different castings! Making no attempt to cite them in the order of their manufacture, on three of them the word POLICE is directly under RADIO; they also carry the legends BARCLAY and

Because reference has been made to identification through patent dates or numbers in the case of models that do not bear the manufacturer's name or trademark, it would be appropriate to supply certain pertinent information here, before moving on to further types of variations, which may save the reader the necessity of visiting a large library and consulting the United States patent records usually to be found in such an institution. Furthermore, many such models may not actually carry a patent date or number, whereas in all cases possession of the following information will afford the collector instant identification. The references all are to cast-iron model automobiles whereby the body and chassis, or at least the grille, could be readily made in two distinct colors or finishes, or where a series of bodies were provided to be interchanged upon a single chassis. It is obvious that seeking some such means to provide an interlocking two-color construction that would not infringe upon the Dowst patent became a matter of some importance to many of the manufacturers of cast-iron toy automobiles following the great success that attended the appearance on the market of the Tootsietoy General Motors series in 1928 and, subsequently, the Tootsietoy Grahams with their separate plated grille, headlight, and front-bumper assemblies. This led to a great flurry of competitive excitement manifested by the following methods:

Dent employed a mode of construction somewhat similar to the one used by Hubley (the second in the enumeration of Hubley systems in the following paragraph), and for clarity both will be described in detail here. Both methods made use of three-part construction, incorporating a body casting, a chassis casting, and a grille casting, with the body and chassis castings interlocking at the rear and the entire assembly permanently locked together by the insertion of the front axle.

MADE USA in smaller cast lettering; the windshields are cast solid, and the headlights and spotlights have flat surfaces. The specific variations are that one type (the version pictured in Fig. 177) has a one-bar front bumper. The second type has a two-bar bumper, and the inner edges of the headlights almost touch the grille. The third type has a similar bumper, but the headlights are noticeably away from the grille. The fourth type is slightly larger, the only cast-in lettering is RADIO POLICE on both sides, and the two words are not aligned, the P being set back so as to be almost directly under the A and with the E correspondingly moved to the right so that nothing is over it. Furthermore, in this model the windshield is cast open; there are two vertical bumper guards, and the headlight and spotlight surfaces are deeply indented. In addition there are color variations, and it is, of course, possible that there exist even more than these four types.

In both systems a small segment of the grille casting engaged the top of the hood at the front of the car. On Dent models, the nickel-plated grille casting consisted only of the grille and headlights, and the front bumper was part of the chassis casting. On Hubley models, the front bumper was part of the same nickel-plated casting as the grille and headlights. On Dent models, a spreading V-shaped rearward projection at the bottom of the grille casting provided the two axle bearings for the front axle, there being no closed bearings in the chassis itself. On Hubley models, the front-axle bearings were in the chassis, and the rearward projection at the bottom of the grille assembly was simply a keeper element running back to and under the front axle. It should be observed that the Hubley element is also somewhat V-shaped, although solid and not as spreading as the two distinctly divided wings of the Dent V. On Dent cars the base of the V is toward the front of the vehicles; on Hubley cars, the base is toward the rear.

Hubley had three systems. First, a wire wrapped around the axles and running under the center of the car and passing through a hook cast on the body, which provided for a differently colored body and chassis, but no separate grille. Second, the rear of the body interlocking to the rear of the chassis, a separate nickeled grille assembly in front connecting the body and chassis, and the insertion of the front axle serving to lock the entire vehicle together, as described in detail in the paragraph about Dent, above. Third, the body, fenders, and running boards are cast in one piece, while a second casting, in practice nickel plated, includes the grille, headlights, front and rear bumpers, rare spare-tire mount, and the axle bearings. The body interlocks to the chassis at the front, and the entire assembly is completed and locked by placing a rubber tire in position on the rear mount or dummy spare wheel. If this spare tire is removed, the chassis readily can be removed from the body. It is suggested that this information be taken as sufficient and that no hobbyist attempt to demonstrate the principle involved by actually removing the spare tire from one of these vehicles, the condition of the rubber likely being such that the tire will break up in the process and thereby preclude the possibility of reassembling the car, at least using the original spare. This method of assembly is illustrated in Fig. 173.

Kilgore models may be recognized by a strip of wire running the length of the car on each side of the chassis. There are several variations to this system, in one of which the strips of

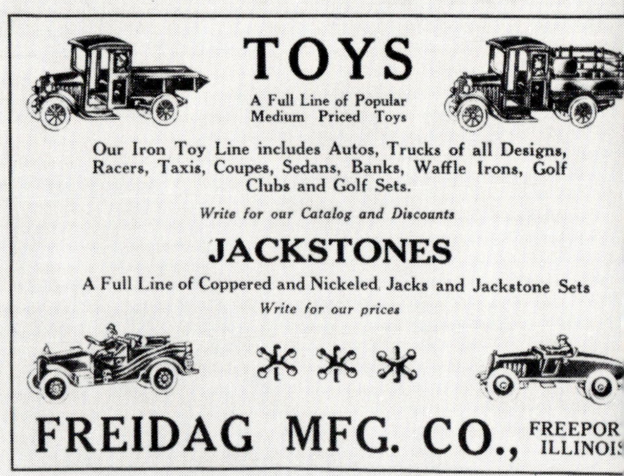

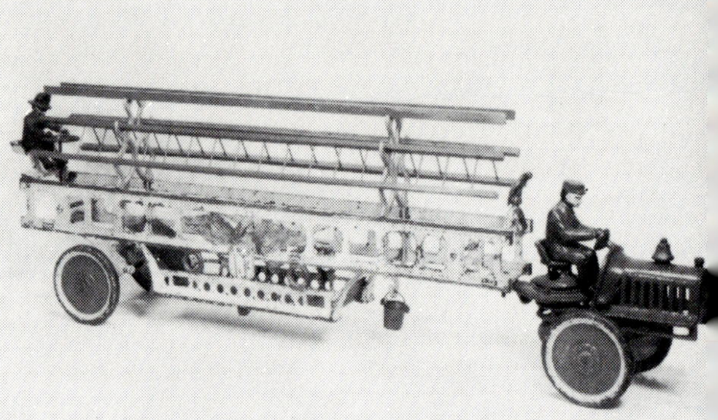

Fig. 166. A Freidag ad of 1925 showing four of their cast-iron models, including their famous American La France pumper at the lower left ("*Playthings*"). Also pictured is a 28-inch-long cast-iron Hubley hook and ladder from the series that emulated originally horse-drawn prototypes that had been motorized, and a Kenton 12-inch-long cast-iron steam pumper (*Lloyd W. Ralston*).

wire are not continuous but are broken at lugs about midway between the two axles. However, the view of a piece of heavy wire at each side of a chassis will be sufficient to identify the model as a Kilgore.

Williams made use of a flat spring hook on the body that locked around a cross member cast in the chassis. Unlike the other methods described, which were intended essentially as permanent factory assemblies, the hook could readily be released by a young user so as to permit the repeated easy substitution of different bodies on the same chassis. This construction is pictured in Figs. 159 and 173, and was employed not only on models sold in sets with several bodies and a single chassis but also on complete cars sold separately. At times on the larger models, as pictured in Fig. 173, a separate nickeled grille casting was used, but it played no part in the attaching of the body to the chassis. Similarly, at times, other manufacturers used separate nickeled grilles or complete fronts or other components that played no part in the joining of the body and chassis but were simply employed as decorative structural components and were variously interlocked, bolted, or riveted in position.

Incidentally, although most collectors refer to the process of closing the free end of any axle so that the wheel will not escape as crimping, there actually are two processes, and each has its technically correct designation. When a small area of the protruding portion of an axle is flattened so as to hold the wheel, this is known as "crimping." When the actual end of a protruding axle is hit by a punch so as to expand the end sufficiently to keep it from sliding back through the wheel, it is said to have been "upset," and the process is known as "upsetting." It is also sometimes referred to as "heading." In most cases the axles of the small car models cast of nonferrous metal were crimped, while those of cast-iron cars and larger model vehicles in general were upset, although in some cases other methods might be used to secure the axles of larger models, and even in a few instances very small ones, as for instance employing a forced fit with the wheels themselves to hold the axles. Customarily the axles that were fastened by crimping or upsetting already had a head at one end, much like the head of a nail, and in fact actual nails often were employed for the axles of small white-metal alloy cars. If for any good reason an axle should be removed and reused, always open the crimped or upset end. This will not only prove easier, and in some cases permit recrimping or reupsetting, but

will also always leave the axle ends on one side of the vehicle at least in their original state of factory closing. Always make a note which side of the body carried the headed axle ends and which side the crimped or upset ends, as collectible variations can occur when the sole difference between two models is that on one the axles was inserted from the right-hand side and on the other from the left. So too do important variations occur, depending on whether a rivet or rivets holding together the two halves of a cast-iron miniature vehicle were originally inserted from the right-hand or left-hand side. There are, as a matter of fact, some specialized collectors who have devoted considerable time to the investigation of the relative incidence of right-hand or left-hand rivet insertion on certain specific models in an effort to ascertain whether one form noticeably is scarcer than the other. Such devotion to minutiae many seem to be carrying things to an extreme, but this is a quite legitimate and often a rewarding facet in the study and reconstruction of factory methods and procedures.

It must remain the decision of each collector whether he is to permit himself to become enthralled to such an extent by what may properly be called "minor variations." This much more must be said—and in all good spirit concerning such things: Were too many collectors to engage in such specialization, the limiting effects of the lack of availability of various models might well become perceptible to the hobby as a whole. This would especially be so if a substantial number of collectors happened to hit upon the selfsame specialty. Fortunately, this is seldom true. For the most part a collector interested in this sort of study tends to limit himself to one or two specific models or series as specialties for studying in depth, and furthermore usually selects an area that has not yet been plumbed in depth and wherein he can make a basically new and worthwhile contribution to the hobby. Nevertheless, certain specialties already are overcrowded, such as the Tootsietoy Graham series. Insofar as this interest may be based on an inquisitive interest in ascertaining through the acquisition of multiple specimens precisely what variations exist in this series, it is possible that the material on this series to be presented shortly will serve to alleviate this particular log jam, for the Grahams have been the subject of a prodigious amount of mythmaking, guesswork, and misinformation, especially from the standpoint of structural variations and of exactly what models were made.

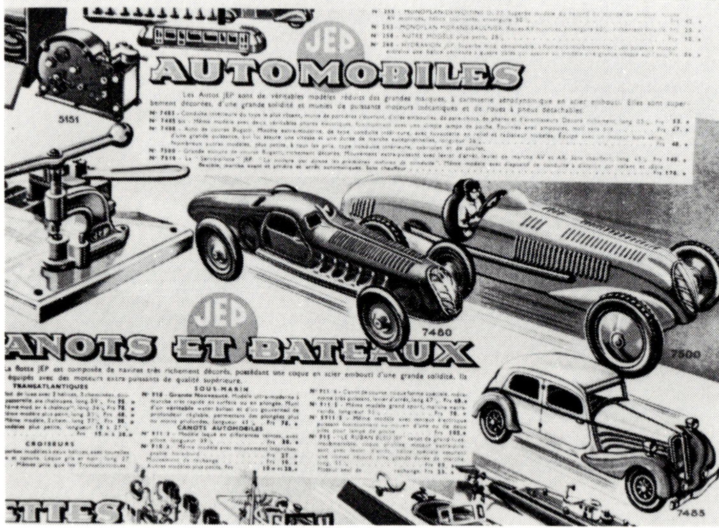

Fig. 167. French stamped-metal clockwork-powered models. Pictured are the C.I.J. Alfa-Romeo P-2 (*G. William Holland Collection*), a Citroën roadster (*C. W. Frey*), and a large (22-inch-long) Citroën taxicab, the latter fitted with battery-powered working electric headlights (*Adam Pellicot, Jr.; William Dreyer photograph*). Also shown is a section of a page from a 1938 JEP catalog.

OTHER FORMS OF VARIATIONS

Color variation, although a most important topic in itself, often is conveniently grouped with variations of lettering and decoration under the general heading "graphic variations" or sometimes "decorative variations," in an effort to distinguish them from structural variations. If considered, as often is the case, as a separate and distinct major form of variation, wheel and tire variations may be looked upon as being somewhere midway between graphic and structural variations. Wheel and tire variations are an important category that is of prime importance to most collectors. The wheel variation may occur merely in the coloring of the wheels, such as in the case of the change in the standard Tootsietoy wheel in the late 1920's from gold-colored or gilt wheels to black ones. This change was not made all at once to all models; and a few types of vehicles, such as the No. 4651 safety coach, 4652 hook and ladder, and No. 4653 water tower, deliberately were continued to the end of their production runs in the early 1930's with the gilt wheels. (This fact should militate against the practice of some collectors who seek to "create" for their displays variations that they think "must exist" but that they have not yet been able to obtain.) Barclay made some very pretty color combinations by using varied colored wheels in combination with different body colors in the early 1930's. Here again the patterning was deliberate, not haphazard, even in occasional instances where the same color was employed on both the wheels and the body of the same vehicle.

The Kansas Toy and Novelty Company in the 1920's and perhaps even early 1930's employed a wheel casting that represented a spoked wheel on one side and a plain disk wheel on the other. Depending upon which side of the wheel was mounted facing outward, a given vehicle appeared to have either dummy spoked wheels or disk wheels. As it appears now, some types of cars deliberately were produced with one or the other wheel face showing, while a few types were made, probably progressively, with both forms of assembly. Sufficient already has been said to make further detailed comment concerning the advent and development of rubber tires and wheels unnecessary here. Obviously this progression makes for important wheel variations and distinctly different vehicles even when the designs and colors of the bodies remain identical. A number of model cars went through two, three, or even more wheel and tire variations. In most cases the elapsed time required to cover such changes would probably in itself bring forth changes in body color so that the collectible variation would not depend solely on the wheel and tire changes; but on occasion this proves not to have been so. In any event, wheel and tire variations constitute an important classification, whether on miniature cast-metal cars or on any other category up to and including the large steel trucks and perhaps even the juvenile automobiles.

One point should be brought out, namely, that many collectors erroneously believe that rubber tires for model automobiles first came into use in the 1920's or 1930's and that vehicles with such tires cannot date from before the 1920's, in the case of larger steel and cast-iron cars, or from before the 1930's in the case of the miniature cast-metal models. The latter assumption is correct—the first ten-cent toy automobile with real rubber tires was marketed in 1932—but the former is erroneous. Miniature automobiles with rubber tires were manufactured in the 1890's, and thenceforth in varying degrees. Eliminating the rubber tire or imitating its presence by painting, lithography, or shaping made for a less-expensive product. Even in the first decade of the twentieth century, most Wilkins automobiles and trucks were optionally offered, under individual numbers as distinct models—they are not in this case variations—either with or without rubber tires. However, the extensive advertising campaigns featuring their rubber tires in the 1920's by Wilkins's successor, Kingsbury, have led many people to believe, then and more recently, that rubber tires were an innovation of that era.

In any event, wheel and tire variations are an obvious and wholly external variation, except perhaps in the case of a Kansas Toy & Novelty Company model vehicle where the collector undoubtedly not only will want to observe whether a wheel is of the disk type but also whether it is the dummy spoked-wheel casting mounted in reverse. The other forms of variations are structural and are divided by some collectors into the obvious and the unobvious; by other enthusiasts into external, internal, and metallurgical. Basically, by obvious variations, collectors refer to a difference that theoretically can be seen without lifting the model from an ordinary position resting on its wheels and having to look underneath or peer inside. In actual usage, except for the most obvious variations, it is almost invariably necessary for the collector to pick up and peer at a model closely, and likewise with a similar model, in order to detect even these so-called obvious variations. However, by an unobvious variation is meant one that can be detected only by examining surfaces not visible when the model is in repose or by weighing the miniature!

Assuredly, "external," "internal," and "metallurgical" are much more precise and desirable descriptions. Some collectors, in fact, carry their search for and retention of variations only to the external, feeling (although wrongly in the views of many and probably most of their fellows) that a line should be drawn at this point. Certainly a line can be drawn at this point, although whether it should be so strong is a highly debateable point. Much of the fun of collecting can stem from discovering, recording, and preserving internal and metallurgical variations; and certainly an infinite amount of knowledge concerning model-car production techniques and history, and in many cases the definite or probable sequence of similar models, can be learned only by studying such variations. This choice is, again, a matter to be determined by the preference of the individual collector. In any event, regardless of how far he extends his interest in and scrutiny of variations, a major point always to be kept in mind is the necessity of distinguishing between two specimens that actually represent two distinct models and those that properly represent variations of the same model, the model in most cases being determined by the fact that a car originally was made, offered, and sold as a distinct model, usually under a specific individual catalog number.

Fig. 175 presents a series of pictures of four pairs of models that serve graphically to introduce the hobbyist to some of the possibilities of external and internal variations. Furthermore, the vehicles pictured are of comparatively recent make, and demonstrate that the possibilities for this interesting sort of investigation need not by any means be confined to models of the past and that examples can be found in current production at any time if a hobbyist knows what to look for and how to look for it. The demonstration is, however, valid for models of all ages, although it is interesting to note that the eight models pictured were all purchased in the same shop and all within several weeks during 1967. In all cases the models are arranged in the same positions in both views, with what appears to be the original or earlier form at the left and the second form to the right. It should also be pointed out that whether any model is the first form or the second, or even a third, does not in itself imply that one form is rarer or more desirable than the other. The toy- and model-collecting hobby as a whole has unfortunately been encumbered with a great amount of nonsense concerning variations. Depending on the circumstances in each individual case, the greater rarity and desirability may lie with the first or with the second or any subsequent version. However, when the presumption is that the first version was initially made alone and then in company with a second version, the first version almost certainly is commoner. When one version is completely replaced by another, their relative rarity is far less easy to determine. Admittedly, some collectors always prefer a model they can establish as being the first version on the principle

that this mirrors the initial type made, even though a given specimen may not necessarily be any older than a later version. These are variables, and the average collector, barring some definite knowledge concerning a particular model, would probably prefer simply to acquire an example of each version of a basic model and let it go at that.

Only one of the four pairs in Fig. 175 is intended to illustrate an external variation, that of the Jeeps, although the sharp-eyed reader may quite possibly detect both external and internal variations that have so far escaped notice on any of these models. In the case of the Jeeps, the model at the left has a smooth floor below the front seats, but a cross-hatch floor pattern has been placed in the die of the second version. Inverting the two models, it is found that the second version carries the name Jeep under the hood, the die cavity number, 2, in the center, and the trade-name and manufacturer's address above the rear wheels. Although color variations do not enter the present discussion, which is confined to structural or die variations, it might be noted incidentally that the two Jeeps are slightly but perceptibly different shades of red, the second being a little darker.

The second pair consists of two tank trucks, externally identical. Looking into the interior of the castings reveals that the first type, at the left, has three round indentations corresponding to the three external filler caps. In the second version this strip has been filled in completely and carries the tradename; the word "Chicago" and letters "U.S.A." are added one on each side, and the cavity number, 2, has been set into the interior of the cab roof. Again, as with the Jeeps, the tank trucks are two slightly different shades of red, but in this instance the darker red is on the first rather than on the second version.

The third pair consists of two wrecking trucks. In the first version, to the left, a slot is cast within the boom, and extends backward into the main casting to the rear axle. In the second version this slot is filled in, the transverse oblong opening under the winch is a little larger, the transverse lip at the rear is a little narrower, and the cavity number, 2, appears. Equally interesting and important is the fact that in the second version the locations of the two rear knockout pins have been moved. In the second version the left-hand rear knockout pin has been moved slightly forward, while the right-hand rear pin has been moved farther back and to the right (the right in the photograph of the undersides; this corresponds to a move toward the left were the vehicle sitting on its wheels) so that its impression now plainly shows in the photograph behind rather than partially next to the axle mount. The first version carries the number C421 inside the cab roof. This is also present on the second version, but in addition the tradename and manufacturer's address are cast on the underside of the hood in the later type.

It must be admitted that "first and second version" or "type" may not be absolutely correct in its application to the foregoing models, "early or later version," or "type" or "die" might well be more preferable, as there really is no guarantee that each pair specifically represents the first or second version. What has been termed the "first version" here might indeed prove to be a second type, and the second the third. It is here possible to speak with relative assurance because of the recent date of these models and the opportunity to secure confirmation from a manufacturer who happens to be interested in the hobby. However, in most cases the hobbyist must proceed from a purely deductive standpoint on his own and without the availability of confirmatory evidence, and it is best to rely wholly on what can be deduced from an examination of the models themselves.

The fourth pair of photographs in Fig. 175 show two shuttle trucks that evidently are identical in every way except for the die cavity numbers that can be seen just below the rear axles, "1" on the truck on the left and "2" on the truck on the right. The numbers are somewhat larger than those on the other models shown in Fig. 175 when a cavity number was employed in the later version. Both of the shuttle trucks carry the manufacturer's trademark and address, as well as the name of the type of vehicle and a copyright notice in identical styles and positions. Inasmuch as in the previously described three pairs neither the name of the vehicle nor the manufacturers' identity appears on the earlier types, but the latter or both have been added in the castings identified by the numeral "2," it would appear a valid assumption that in this instance both cavities were prepared at the same time, that there exists no earlier version, and that the only variation between the two trucks is that of the different cavity numbers.

Years ago the dies employed for miniature cast-metal automobiles were relatively small and contained only one cavity. As the industry developed, larger dies and die-casting machines evolved, and a greater number of cavities might be placed in a single die. The practical number, of course, varied and still varies, depending on the size of the die and of the size of the vehicles or parts to be cast. Today, however, in the case of the smaller vehicles of the type illustrated in Fig. 175, averaging about 2 1/2 inches in length, thirty or more cavities may be put into a single die and as many vehicle bodies cast at a single "shot." That is not to say that in such instances thirty or so identical vehicles are cast at once, for the cavities are assorted, usually one or two for a specific type of model. Until the die is completely filled, additional cavities may be added, either of new models or duplicating popular earlier designs.

The purpose of cavity numbers in cavities for the same model is to permit the easy and immediate identification of any cavity that might at any time somehow show up as having developed a defect as reflected in an imperfect casting picked out during the inspection process. For the most part, when a die initially contained only one cavity, it was not numbered, but additional cavities, either in the same or in separate dies, were numbered. However, when two or more cavities are prepared at the same time, they are numbered by starting with "1." At times in the past a number of duplicate cavities may have been used for some miniature cast-metal automobiles without identifying numbers having been used. However, in seeking variations a collector should always check very carefully to ascertain if a model carries a die cavity number. These are invariably placed underneath or inside on a die-cast model, although in some instances it is possible that they may be concealed during the assembly process. However, inasmuch as lettering or numbering obviously cannot be placed inside a slush-molded model, cavity numbers when used on such models must appear cast somewhere on the outside of the vehicle. They should not be confused with model numbers so cast on Kansas Toy and Novelty Company vehicles. Usually the cavity designating number is a "2." In no case, so far as is presently known, does a cavity number higher than 4 appear on any pre–World War II model.

The numbers frequently found cast into sand-cast models are not cavity numbers but rather pattern numbers. These may, or may not, be identical with the model's catalog number, followed by identifying letters such as "R" for right, "L" for left, or "B" for base, or numbers. In some cases additional markings identify a particular pattern among a varying number of otherwise identical ones, and pattern numbers and pattern-number combinations can be and are collected as definite variations just as are die-casting cavity numbers. Most sand-cast vehicles were cast in two halves; accordingly, if more than one pattern was used, it is possible to find specimens with various combina-

Fig. 168.   Repainting is of course utterly taboo among all knowledgeable collectors, enormously reducing the value of any such model. In the case of the two Dinky Studebakers, the model in original paint, at the left, is worth at least twice that of the repainted specimen at the right. The two Kenton fire engines were touched up but not completely repainted. Their value is therefore impaired, but not as much as if they had been completely repainted.

G. William Holland photographs

tions of pattern numbers. Thus, if there were two right-hand and two-left hand patterns involved in the production of a particular model, there should exist four combinations: "A-A," "B-B," "A-B," and "B-A." If there were six patterns for each side, there could be thirty-six possible combinations. Certainly only a most-devoted specialist in a certain model would seek to assemble a complete group of thirty-six different pattern combinations; nevertheless, there are a few such hobbyists known who are attempting to do precisely that. The greatest difficulty in such an operation is not merely to have to locate and examine an almost endless line of specimens but also that such pattern combinations can occur only by chance. Theoretically there should exist approximately equal quantities of every possible combination. However, it is also possible, purely through chance during the assembling process, that one or more possible combinations of pattern letters or numerals never happened to come together. Most collector-students content themselves with ascertaining how many duplicate working patterns were used during the production of a given model, or perhaps with collecting sufficient models to include at least one specimen of each, and let it go at that without trying to secure every possible combination.

A question frequently asked is whether defects in castings or in assembly should be regarded as constituting legitimate variations. To a certain extent this is something that every collector must determine for himself, but generally it would seem proper to say that if a defect were of sufficient importance to cause it to be rejected during the inspection process if it had not passed unnoticed, then it certainly represents a properly collectible and often quite interesting and desirable variation. The difficulty lies in determining which defects would have been rejected in inspection and which

would not have been considered important enough. This naturally varied with the different manufacturers. In the case of cheaper goods there would be less incentive and need to weed out models with minor defects than when more expensive models were involved. A casting wherein the molten metal had not completely filled a crevice or corner of the mold but where the defect would hardly be noticeable when the model was painted might well be passed on a ten-cent toy but rejected on a toy retailing for a dollar or more.

THE IMMORTAL BULLDOG MACK

A good example of this sort of thing may be found from time to time in the case of the radiator caps on the original Tootsietoy Bulldog Mack truck series. Original, that is, in that it was the first series of Tootsietoy Macks, the initial models in the series being produced in 1925, but actually the longest lived of the famous Tootsietoy Macks, some models on the basic design surviving in the line until World War II and thereby outlasting both the arrival and departure of all the later Tootsietoy prewar Mack trucks. The chassis in question is the one perhaps best described as having a cab (unlike the little Tootsietoy Macks of the 1930's) but no windshield (unlike the largest series of Tootsietoy Macks of the 1930's). The chassis measures 2 3/4 inches in length, and with slight variations was employed as the chassis for stake, coal, tank, and mail trucks, for army searchlights and antiaircraft guns, and as a tractor for American Railway Express and A&P and car carrier trailers. It was deservedly popular, for it accurately caught the lines and spirit of one of the most popular and powerful-appearing of all truck types. The prototype appeared in 1922, and versions were made by Mack well into the 1930's, the name deriving from the unmistakable resemblance of the hood contours to that of a jutting countenance of a bulldog. It was a much-favored prototype among all sorts of model-automobile manufacturers, and there are countless men now living who will assure you that their image of a really good and powerful truck is a Bulldog Mack of the 1920's.

All the Tootsietoy Macks of this series, even the first ones of 1925 and 1926 that lacked the "MT" insignia on the front and the chain drive detail, were made with a detailed radiator cap. (On a proper Bulldog Mack the radiator is *behind* the hood, just ahead of the firewall and the driver's seat.) The radiator cap was the most difficult detail to cast. From time to time specimens will be found with a truncated radiator cap, even occasionally to the extent that there appears to be no radiator cap at all. In such models the cavity in the die that cast the radiator cap either failed to fill completely with molten metal or perhaps at times the fragile caps would break off during handling in bins at the factory. In any case, the imperfection of the radiator cap was not considered sufficient grounds for discarding a Mack chassis at the Tootsietoy factory. They were simply painted and sent out into the world in this condition.

A similar situation appears to have occurred sometimes with some of the slush-molded cars of the 1920's that carried a radiator cap intended to delineate a cap incorporating a Boyce MotoMeter, or a projecting roundhead casting just below the radiator that evidently was intended to represent either a crank handle or a tow hook. The Boyce MotoMeter was a popular piece of automotive equipment in the second and third decades of the twentieth century, sometimes supplied as standard original equipment, more often purchased subsequently by a car owner. It consisted of a thermometer set in a round frame with glass sides atop the radiator cap and facing the driver so that he could read it while driving. Because of casting difficulties, when reproduced on slush-cast models it was represented with its faces parallel to the sides of the car which evidently was considered by the manufacturers as good enough for the purpose. At times the MotoMeter radiator-cap assembly or the front crank/tow hook castings, or both, were molded imperfectly, but this usually seems to have been considered of insufficient importance to reject the castings. Most collectors probably would prefer a Tootsietoy Mack truck with complete radiator cap, and a car with complete MotoMeter or crank, but whether specimens on which these appurtenances are incomplete —and, from the state of the original paint, obviously so from factory days—should be regarded as collectible variations would seem to be a matter that must be decided by the individual hobbyist. In a sense such models probably are definite factory variations, but how is one to measure exactly what degree of imperfection of such a casting properly constitutes a separate variation?

At times an important structural imperfection goes on sale through faulty assembly and imperfect inspection. Such items must necessarily be considered unusual variations because in most cases they are caught at the factory. There is a collector who recently acquired an awaited specimen of a current model automobile. Upon unpacking it, he found that because of a fault in the assembling process it was forever destined to sit lopsided because one wheel firmly was positioned lower than the other three. It might have been possible to repair it, although this would have involved the risk of breaking a casting. Naturally, the collector preferred to leave it exactly as it was. A visiting friend, a novice model car collector, assured him that it would be a very simple matter merely to return it to the dealer and secure a perfect specimen in exchange. "Not on your tintype," exclaimed the first hobbyist, "this could be a one-in-a-million piece to get out of the factory, and I can assure you that it is going to stay right here in my collection exactly the way it is!"

But to return to the original type of Tootsietoy Mack truck chassis as an example of variations. There are three basic types of castings, each fitted with the two holes near the ends of the truck bed to receive, either permanently or interchangeably, the various bodies or for use as tractors with the early trailers, although the latter did not appear until 1928 and the mail-truck body until 1930:

Type I has no chain drive, no arch cast in the front bumper, no "MT" insignia, no handles and hinges on the doors, no Tootsietoy name, and was fitted with gilt wheels. 1925–1926.

Type II has the chain drive, a wide arch in the front, door handles and hinges, no Tootsietoy name, and was fitted with gilt wheels. 1927–1928.

Type III has the chain drive, a wide arch in the front, door handles and hinges, carries the Tootsietoy name cast underneath the truck bed, and was fitted with black wheels. 1929–1933. It was also used with the new wheels with rubber tires in 1933 and possibly in late 1932.

There also are two specialized types of chassis that present some intriguing points. One is the chassis used for the army-searchlight and antiaircraft-gun trucks. It has the chain drive, a narrow arch in the front, no door handles or hinges, carries the Tootsietoy name cast inside the cab roof, has one hole toward the rear of center in the truck bed, and a strengthening rib cast in the underside of the truck bed from the back of the cab almost to the hole. It occurs with four types of wheels, the standard black wheels 1931–1933, on occasion the wheel cast without bolt heads, the rubber-tired wheel from 1933 or late 1932, and finally, in the years immediately prior to the suspension of production in World War II, with an all-rubber one-piece wheel and tire molding.

The second is the chassis used as a tractor for car carriers. It has the chain drive, a narrow arch in the front, no door handles or hinges, carries the Tootsietoy name cast inside the cab roof, no strengthening rib or hole, but has a stud cast facing upward on the truck bed to receive the body of the car carrier trailer, and was made with black wheels 1932–1933 and with rubber tires 1933–1936.

Now, two interesting questions will arise in the minds of readers who have followed the discussion up to this point. One concerns the narrow arch in front, which also is accompanied by narrower fenders and running boards and which may perhaps be put down simply as a seemingly desirable die modification. The second presents a definite mystery as to why the door hinges and handles that were added to the basic models in 1927 and seemingly continued on all subsequent castings through 1933 should have been omitted from models tooled up for 1931 and 1932. Several possible explanations occur, but none seems particularly likely to hold up, the more particularly as the dies then employed by Dowst were good for approximately 800,000 castings when used with white-metal alloy (and about 600,000 when run with zinc alloy), and the basic 1927 design must have had to undergo retooling several times during the five years it was in use for the trucks. As a matter of fact, it is possible to weave considerable speculation concerning the presence or absence of door handles and other detail on several of the Tootsietoys of this period. Why, for instance, did the first model in the sequence, the No. 4629 sedan, have both door handles and bolts cast into the spare wheel in exact imitation of the arrangement on the actual wheels, the No. 4636 coupe have neither door handles or bolts in the spares, and the No. 4641 touring car have door handles but no detail in the spare? Economy? The savings would have been very slight in the face of the overall cost of the dies, and the added metal per casting would have been microscopic. Oversight? Possibly, although certainly Dowst was obviously con-

scious of door-handle detail off and on during this period. Rugged individualism on the part of individual designers and toolmakers? Even more unlikely. One possible explanation is that when Dowst was faced with fairly strong competition on an item, as they are known to have been on the Mack truck in 1926–1927, they moved to improve their product and add detail; when they were not so faced they did not bother. But even this is not a wholly satisfactory answer for all situations. It is inexplicable minor points such as this that add much of the interest to the game.

It is easy enough to spot such obvious variations as the presence or absence of such things as door handles, chain drives, or the manufacturers' name. Much of the search for differences and variations is more difficult, and requires the most careful inspection in order to determine whether or not two given models came from the same or different dies. There are, for example, at least three slush-cast 2 1/8-inch-long Ford Model-A coupes made in the late 1920's or early 1930's. Seemingly at first—and even at second glance—identical, a vigilant examination reveals that all three are from different dies. The differences show up in the thickness and number of louvres and of horizontal lines in the radiators, and in the thickness and placing of the headlights and fenders. At least one of these models is a Barclay; or, to be even more scrupulously precise, Barclay is known to have made at least one car of this type. Perhaps all three are Barclay variations or perhaps they represent three different manufacturers, although specimens have been found seemingly all in the same red and with the same black wheels. Comparing models where one or more is badly scratched or even largely or entirely devoid of paint, especially when the comparison must be made to a specimen with its paint in reasonably good condition, can be even more difficult. The presence or lack of paint can very often make the same casting seem somewhat different, and it is difficult to determine whether a detail appears sharper or deeper or otherwise varies because it actually is so, or simply because it is not softened in appearance by the coat of paint. It is surprising how much difference in the appearance of a model or part of one a full or partial coat of paint can make. The collector can only check and recheck and compare, and endeavor to come up with valid answers based on acute observation.

In the slush-casting process varying amounts of metal may cling to the edges of the openings in the bottom of a vehicle through which the excess internal molten metal is dumped, and these edges often show disparities in relative smoothness or roughness. In fact it is probable that every model would reveal some tiny difference in the final casting at these points. With the possible exception of models showing a really major exception to the normal in these cases—a substantial area not filled completely with metal or perhaps a gross excess of metal clinging to the edges—it seems hardly probable that any collector would regard such differences as constituting collectible variations.

THE GRANDIOSE GRAHAMS

Grandiose here, at least, not because of their popularity among collectors or their admitted beauty —some of the passenger-vehicle color combinations make for extremely pretty little models—but because of the intricacy and extent of their variations. The Tootsietoy Grahams, in fact, constitute a rather advanced course in variations, and provide the best possible example of the subject of structural differences, even without taking into account at this time either secondary or minor variations, or their multitudinous color combinations. It would, in fact, be not too difficult to write a rather lengthy treatise devoted entirely to the Tootsietoy Grahams of the 1930's and their variations. Indeed, it may very well be that someday someone will do exactly that, for such a study would be precisely the type to be both of interest and of substantial practical value to a great many serious-minded students and collectors of model automobiles.

In any event, suffice it to observe that there is no doubt but that the Tootsietoy Grahams are at once the bane and the delight of most collectors of old cast-metal miniature automobiles.

The Graham passenger cars, with their cataloged range of six body-styles and each type optionally available under a separate number with one spare wheel and tire mounted at the rear or two spare wheels and tires mounted in fender wells, plus still other types, could in a certain measure aptly be described as a manufacturer's and merchants' nightmare—a good idea seemingly gone wild. The range was called into being by a very dangerous competitive situation that suddenly erupted early in 1932 when Kilgore brought out ten-cent cast-iron model cars equipped with real rubber tires, models that for the moment virtually eclipsed the Tootsietoys and every other line of ten-cent toy automobiles. The Tootsietoy Grahams evidently served their intended purpose by blanketing the market with such a variety of models of then-modern passenger automobiles fitted with rubber tires as to a large extent to re-

claim Dowst's threatened leadership in the ten-cent car field. There were, as already mentioned, six Tootsietoy Graham passenger-car body-styles: roadster, coupe, convertible coupe, sedan, convertible sedan, and town car. Each of these was available with rear spare-tire mount (RM) or with side spare-tire mounts (SM). There was also a taxicab, which was a sedan without any spare tire at all. Three styles, roadster, coupe, and sedan, also without spare tires, were used in the Bild-A-Car sets and can be identified by the half or split axles connected by a joiner that are employed in cars assembled from these sets. There were also four Graham commercial or service vehicles—the wrecking car, the milk truck (marked "Tootsietoy Dairy" and also variously textually described as a milk-delivery car or a milk-delivery truck), the ambulance, and a tire truck lettered "Commercial Tire & Supply Co." The tire truck was never cataloged for sale as an individual item, but was supplied only as a component of sets, first in the 1935 Tootsietoy Motors sets No. 05300 and No. 0530X, and later as part of the second and last form of the Bild-A-Car sets, replacing the roadster; and hence, the tire truck exists with both one-piece and split axles. The four commercial vehicles carried no spare tires and made use of the same frames without fender wells, as did the passenger cars with rear-mount spares, and the taxicab. The milk truck, ambulance, and tire truck were identical in basic design and varied only in their lettering or insignia and in their colors (although white or cream were evidently always the favored colors for the wrecking car, milk truck, and ambulance, and, as far as is known, all tire trucks had orange bodies). When sold as a factory-assembled vehicle, the tire truck had a brown chassis. The Bild-A-Car version could, of course, be made up using any one of five differently colored chassis furnished in the set, there being one matching body color for each of the chassis colors. Thus there was always an orange chassis in these later Bild-A-Car sets which in a certain sense nominally belonged to the tire truck. Accordingly, some collectors regard an orange chassis as proper for the second type of tire truck. Others reason that inasmuch as one feature of the Bild-A-Car sets was to permit the assembling of two-color cars, and the factory-assembled tire trucks appear always to have come with a chassis a different color from the body, then a tire truck of the second type, assembled from Bild-A-Car components, should properly have a chassis *any color that was provided in the corresponding Bild-A-Car sets except orange!*

Leaving this point for personal and perhaps futile debate among Graham aficionados, we come to what is of far more general interest and importance: the vital differences in the frame castings employed for the Graham series, far beyond the obvious distinction between frames with and without fender wells. There are, in fact, nine distinct Graham frame castings in all, or five, if we count frames otherwise identical that were made for both rear mounts and side mounts as single basic types. In the list below, Roman numerals have been applied to the five basic casting types, and letters indicate further variations: RM for rear mounts, SM for side mounts, and B for frames that are sufficiently recessed to receive the split axle joiner used on the Bild-A-Car models: *

I-RM. The openings inside the frame have square corners; there is no small opening immediately behind the front axle like that found on all other eight types; the frame is lettered TOOTSIETOY/U.S.A., whereas all other eight types are lettered TOOTSIETOY/MADE IN/ U.S.A.; the underside of the back of the casting is flat and smooth; and there are eight treads cast in each running board.

II-RM. Identical to I-RM except for the opening behind the front axle and the change in lettering.

III-RM. Identical to II-RM except that there is a ridge cast across the underside of the back of the casting.

III-RMB. Identical to III-RM except that room has been provided to accept the split axle joiners of the Bild-A-Car construction.

IV-SM. The corners of the openings inside the frame have more rounded corners; there is no provision for using Bild-A-Car axles; the underside of the back of the casting is plain, neither flattened nor ridged (all following types are identical to IV-SM in this respect), and there are seven treads cast in each running board (again, all subsequent types are identical to IV-SM on this point).

IV-SMB. Identical to IV-SM except that room has been provided to accept the split axle joiners of the Bild-A-Car construction.

IV-RMB. Identical to IV-SMB except that there are no fender wells.

V-RMB. The openings inside the frame have distinctly rounded corners and there is a wide, flaring lip behind both the front and rear axles to receive the impact of the knockout

pins, whereas on previous models the front knockout pin hit in front of the front axle and there was only a small round lip behind the rear axle, approximately the size of the knockout pin itself.

V-SMB. Identical to V-RMB but with fender wells for side-mounted spare wheels and tires.

It will be observed that in one measure the Graham frames may be divided into two basic styles, the eight-tread and the seven-tread running boards. The fenders are also wider on the eight-tread running-board frames than on the seven-tread frames. The tread count should always be made at the *front* of a running board because the innermost tread is never a complete one, being intercepted by the outward curve of the back of the running board that conforms to the curve of the body of a passenger car. Sometimes the body of a passenger car that was made from contaminated metal will expand outward sufficiently to partially cover an additional tread. (The Graham trucks have narrower bodies and never seem to present this problem.) However, an accurate count of the running-board treads can always be made at the point where they start just behind a front fender, and seven or eight treads will be found here, according to the die.

It will be noticed that the seven-tread frame comes into existence coincidental with the first of the frames for side mounts (Type IV). However, as the Grahams with side mounts presumably came on the market in 1933, it seems unlikely that frame types I, II, and III could all have been used and abandoned by the end of 1933, although it is not entirely impossible, considering the enormous demand for Grahams between the end of 1932 and the end of 1933. The Type I frame undoubtedly is the first one, and dates from late 1932. The use of some of the eight-tread dies for frames for cars with rear mounts and without spares may have continued well past 1933. In the case of dies for cars with side mounts, they actually were identical with the corresponding dies for rear mounts, for the dies were fitted with removable inserts to permit their use for the optional casting of fenders with or without wells. As a result, the solid fenders on frame Types IV-RMB and V-RMB reveal, on close examination, the outlines of the well openings on the front fenders.

Another cursory mode of dividing the Graham frames into two types is to group those with the small round seat for the knockout pin at the rear (I, II, III, and IV), and those with the wide, flaring lips at the front and the rear (V).

* The writer wishes to express his special appreciation to Gates Willard for working with him on this compilation and for making a special last-minute before-publication trip so that we could be absolutely certain of our findings.

Although this is a very obvious distinction, the classification is not very satisfactory from any but a most superficial standpoint. The later two-lip Graham frame evidently derives from the La Salle frame, for the La Salles have a somewhat similar lip at the rear. The La Salle frames were tooled up in 1934. It therefore seems a logical assumption that the final revision in the Graham frame design was not made until—and probably in—1935, which helps somewhat in dating cars with V-RMB and V-SMB frames. The matter is also of passing interest, for it is probably the reason why there were not infrequent early pronouncements among collectors that there were three types of Graham frames. The three types of "Graham" frames mentioned here probably were the obviously different frames without lips (I, II, III, and IV); the frames with lips (V); and the La Salle frame, which was confused with those of the Grahams.

There also are several distinct variations of the Graham grille-headlights-front-bumper casting. They have not yet been satisfactorily codified. Presumably, each time a new frame die was tooled up, there was also need for a new grille casting, if only to keep up with the supply of frames. Quite possibly the grille cavities were included in the same dies as the frames themselves, and continuing research may eventually establish that the number of grille types corresponds to the number of frame types, although this need not necessarily prove to be the case. In any event, there undoubtedly was considerable overlapping of grille types, providing variations in assembled vehicles that certainly are collectible, yet there was no dogmatically "proper" grille for a given type of frame.

In addition, there exists a number of variations in the body castings, with consequent overlappings and collectible combinations. Some of these take the form of reinforcing ribs cast inside the bodies—for instance, behind the window pillars of the sedan (which, curiously, appear to occur only on the earliest sedan bodies) or inside the cab roofs of trucks. Another variation is found in the presence or absence of patent numbers cast inside the car hoods or roofs. The patent numbers, when they appear, actually are not those of the Graham patent itself (No. 1,984,258, issued to Ted Dowst, December 11, 1934), but those of the earlier patents that covered features of the interchangeable Mack truck bodies (No. 1,690,217, issued November 6, 1928), and of the construction used on the General Motors series (No. 1,728,725, issued September 17, 1929). Both of the earlier patents included claims under which the Grahams were manufactured. These patent markings were placed on the cars on the advice of

Fig. 169. The Tootsietoy General Motors series of the late 1920's and early 1930's. A two-part construction—body and chassis—was employed. All six body styles and all five radiator styles (blank, Chevrolet, Cadillac, Oldsmobile, and Buick) are pictured here.

Dr. Clinton B. Seeley

the Dowst attorneys in connection with legal action then being brought against Manoil for infringement of the Dowst patents covering their two-part construction. An urgent memorandum from Ted Dowst, dated October 27, 1934, instructed the factory to place these two patent numbers "as rapidly as possible" in the dies of all cars manufactured under them "with particular reference to the Graham Paige and LaSalle line." At the same time, in another memorandum, he instructed that all printing plates for box labels and box covers "for all items that contain any of the Graham Paige cars" be changed so that the two existing patent numbers as well as the words "other patents pending" appeared, and that new rubber stamps with the patent numbers be made immediately for use on all boxes containing the individual packing of the Grahams.)

In view of the above, it is safe to assume that the Graham dies were changed to include the two earlier patent numbers between the end of October, 1934, and mid-December, 1934, when Dowst would have become aware that patent No. 1,984,258 had been granted. Thus, all Tootsietoy Graham vehicles *not* bearing the two patent numbers would have been made up from parts fabricated between late 1932 and late 1934, although collectors should bear in mind that it is quite possible and even probable that some of the unmarked bodies were not assembled into complete vehicles until after 1934.

The most important and noticeable variation in Graham bodies—what collectors usually term an external rather than an internal variation (the reinforcing ribs and patent numbers are both internal variations)—occurs on the Graham convertible. There are two types of rumble seats. In all cases the rumble-seat top is open, revealing the surface of the seat itself. In the earlier castings, the vertical areas in front of and to the sides of the surface of the seat are not filled in with metal. This type of rumble-seat arrangement is sometimes rather confusingly referred to by collectors as the "open" rumble seat. In the later type of the Tootsietoy Graham convertible body, there are walls cast in front and to the sides of the seat, a form on occasion also confusingly termed the "closed" or "enclosed" rumble seat. As the rumble-seat lid is always cast in a raised position, revealing the seat or simulating what most people would call an open rumble seat, the use of the words "open" or "closed" to indicate the absence or presence of the cast-in walls can be very misleading. Hopefully, the terms "without internal walls around seat" and "with internal walls around seat" will in the future commend themselves to collectors as a more acceptable means of designation in the interest of clarity.

With such a plethora of potential frame, body, and grille combinations, and without taking into consideration color variations, much less certain minor variations not even mentioned here, how many different Tootsietoy Grahams are there? This is a question countless collectors have asked, and, not to beg the issue, what with the multiplicity of frames alone, it is one that seems virtually impossible to answer with any hope of precision—at least within the scope of our present state of knowledge. Some frames can exist only on certain models. Obviously, cars with side mounts must

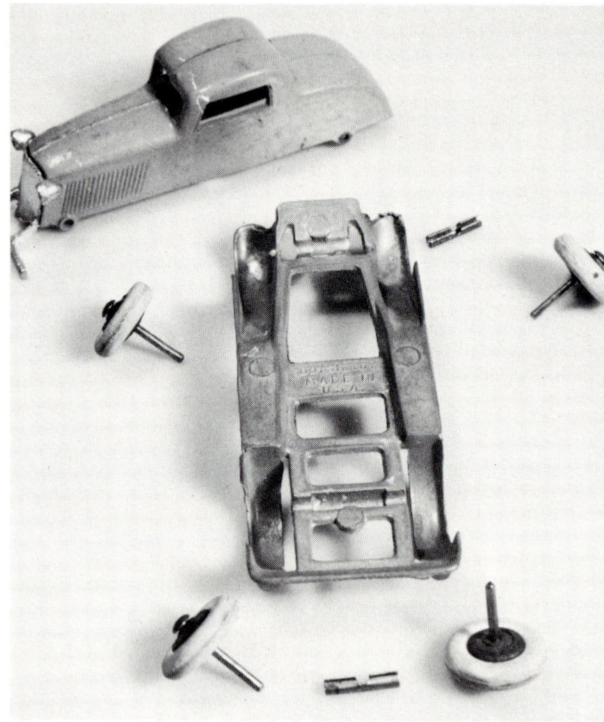

Fig. 170. The method of assembly employed in the Tootsietoy Bild-A-Car construction sets of the 1930's is clearly delineated in this photograph. The car is a Graham coupe. The photograph also demonstrates the three-part construction of these cars—body, radiator, and chassis, whether sold in assembled or knocked-down form.
Dr. Clinton B. Seeley

have frames with fender wells, and it is unlikely that cars with rear mounts or without spares were ever put out on side-mount frames. On the other hand, while vehicles in Bild-A-Car sets had to have the frames with provision to accept the axle joiners, cars assembled at the factory with one-piece axles certainly at times were put out on frames that would accommodate the Bild-A-Car mode of assembly (this is obviously true of, but by no means necessarily confined to, cars using frames of the basic Type V design). There exists, therefore, no mathematical way in which the number of basic types can be computed, even by taking into consideration just frame and body types and ignoring grille variations.

The beginner—and, indeed, many advanced collectors—naturally is anxious for some guide to what justly can be considered the basic *structural* variations of the Tootsietoy Grahams. Such a guide can be provided—and is provided below—by ignoring frame-type variations other than the manifestly basic ones: that is, that cars with side mounts have frames with fender wells, and that cars constructed from Bild-A-Car sets reveal themselves by their split-axle construction and frames without fender wells arranged to accept the Bild-A-Car axle joiners. (Side-mount frames Types IV-SMB and V-SMB will accommodate the split-axle joiners but were not used in Bild-A-Car sets.) Here then is the complete, basic, and most pruned-down possible list of Tootsietoy Grahams—twenty-one types in all:

Sedan with rear mount
Sedan with side mounts
Sedan, no spare, Bild-A-Car
Taxicab (sedan, no spare, one-piece axles)
Convertible sedan with rear mount
Convertible sedan with side mounts
Coupe with rear mounts
Coupe with side mounts
Coupe, no spare, Bild-A-Car
Convertible coupe with rear mount
Convertible coupe with side mounts
Town car with rear mount
Town car with side mounts
Roadster with rear mount
Roadster with side mounts
Roadster, no spare, Bild-A-Car
Wrecking car
Milk truck
Ambulance
Tire truck, one-piece axles
Tire truck, split axles, Bild-A-Car

Of course, a further consideration does arise from the change in the catalog numbers of the Grahams surviving in the line after 1936. For example, the wrecking truck, No. 0806, became No. 806 in 1937, and so on. This was merely a token acknowledgment of the fact that by 1937 all Tootsietoy cars had rubber tires, and it was no longer necessary to distinguish the cars so equipped by numbers with the prefix 0. The models thus renumbered, if some physical indication of this change can be ascertained, would probably be collected as two distinct models by most aware and conscientious collectors, thus raising the number of basic types to more than the twenty-one enumerated above. The one vehicle that would provide no problem of identification between its two numbers is the tire truck, which is, as a matter of fact, included in the list separately in each of its two numbers, albeit in this case not because of the number change but because of the structural differences. Although never cataloged separately, the tire truck with solid axles was No. 0807, and the Bild-A-Car tire truck would, of necessity, rate as No. 807.

Somewhat similarly, although not exactly parallel, a Graham ambulance in camouflage colors would definitely be a No. 809, not a No. 0809. But not all solid-color Graham ambulances would be No. 0809's. To attempt to go into these matters further, however, would lead to innumerable complexities that justly may be considered beyond the scope of this volume.

As has been seen, the convertible sedan, convertible coupe, and town car do not properly in any form exist without spares, either with one-piece or two-piece axles. In fact, the roadster and coupe should not exist without spares unless fitted with the split axles that identify them as deriving from Bild-A-Car sets. Nevertheless, there are a few reports of cars other than the sedan (taxicab) without any spare tire and with solid axles. In the course of customary factory production procedures, it is always within the realm of possibility for a mistake to have been made, or for some uncataloged substitution deliberately to have been made at times. However, the most likely explanations for the cars in question would be either that the bodies and frames were improperly mixed by unthinking early collectors, or that, in a number of cases, youngsters at play in the 1930's removed the rear-mount spares, which were not subsequently restored to the vehicles. When a little thought is given to the matter, it will be seen that nothing would be more logical or tempting to many children than to pry off a rear-mounted spare tire and to play at changing tires. (It would have been much more difficult, although not impossible, for a youngster to remove side-mounted spares, as they were held in place by an axle passing through the car body.) Prudent collectors will view with great suspicion any variation without a spare tire that is not included in the twenty-one basic Graham types listed above.

WEIGHTY MATTERS METALLURGICAL

Within the realm of cast-metal-automobile collecting there exists an important type of collectible variation that is unique to this field and those closely allied to it, that of variations of weight, or, rather, more properly, variations in the metal used in the casting process, of which relative weight serves as the means of identification. In the sand-cast models, by far the majority of which were made of cast iron, the distinction is merely between similar models cast in iron or in aluminum. The difference in weight between two such models is quite apparent, in addition to which the aluminum models produced by a few manufacturers, such as Dent and Freidag, customarily were not painted but were put out in a polished finish, sometimes trimmed in red or paint of some other color. Furthermore, these manufacturers usually identified designs made in both metals by separate catalog numbers, and accordingly iron and aluminum vehicles in most if not all cases represent actual separate and distinct models and not metallurgical variations of the same item. Aside from the lighter weight, and the attractiveness to some of the polished finish, the cast-aluminum toys were less fragile and were regarded as less liable to breakage. They were, however, more expensive than corresponding cast-iron pieces, and their popularity seems to have been of a relatively limited nature; as far as toy automobiles were concerned, they were largely confined to the 1920's and early 1930's. The novice collector should learn, as he invariably quickly does, to distinguish between articles actually cast of aluminum (which in some instances may have been repainted to resemble the full-paint job customarily accorded cast-iron units) and models cast of iron but painted or repainted in aluminum or silver paint.

The situation is different in the case of the miniature die-cast and slush-cast cars, as here the model numbers had no relation to the composition of the metal mix, and a change in alloy might be a major one from white-metal to zinc alloy, or a minor one in the composition of, in most cases, a lead-based alloy. In any event, the variation cannot be detected by appearance but only by the comparative weights of various specimens. Just the same, in the model-car field these can be just as valid, important, and collectible variations as any of the visible kinds, most particularly in the case of programmed changeovers from white-metal to zinc alloys in certain major lines.

Throughout their white-metal casting activities, from the 1890's onward, Dowst always employed exactly the same formula for their lead-based alloy. The fact that their automobiles and other toys were always of uniform weight was featured in their advertising and literature, especially in the 1920's, as well as in jobbers' catalog listings of their products. From this alone it is obvious that at least some other manufacturers' goods might vary in weight and also that the fact of uniform weight was a most definite selling feature to the trade. As has been noted, some manufacturers, and possibly not only very small ones, often threw whatever low-melting-point scrap metal that was readily and most cheaply obtainable into their pots. At first thought the value of uniform weight may not seem of any great importance, and it scarcely was to the ultimate consumer, but it most definitely was of material consequence to the trade, for it affected both the predictability

and the actual amount of shipping costs where large quantities were involved. An increase of, say, half an ounce in the weight of each individual unit might mean nothing in itself, but it signified hundreds of pounds' additional freight weight and charges when an order for a hundred gross was involved, and this was a matter of some moment in the case of toys retailing for ten cents where the profits all down the line were measured in pennies and fractions of pennies.

With only some exceptions, the variations of weight indicating a decided change in the makeup of the alloy in slush-cast models can be detected only on a fairly delicate if relatively inexpensive scale of the laboratory type similar to that pictured in Fig. 191. In a few instances such differences in weight between two seemingly identical models are so extreme that a collector instantly can detect them merely by hefting them, but a scale that provides readings—not a mere balance—really is necessary for a proper examination. As an exercise in higher alchemy, a number of apparently absolutely identical slush-cast models in quantities of from two to four of a kind were weighed in this manner. In each case differentials of weight varying from less than half a gram to over six grams were noted. Now half a gram difference is, admittedly scarcely anything to get excited over, but five grams already is slightly more than 1/6th ounce, and often the differential in weight between specimens came to as much as 10 percent of the total weight of an average specimen. Put it this way: a freight bill 10 percent higher than the previous one on an identical shipment was more than enough to give an alert toy buyer not a little discomfort. Although all the experiments were conducted with old slush-cast models of the 1920's and 1930's, the possibility that such similar variations conceivably can occur even in some current die-cast miniatures cannot be discounted. Where all this may be carried from this point depends, of course, on the inclinations of each collector. Discussing the matter with a number of leading collectors brought reactions ranging from the thought that the matter really appeared too minor to take into account in collecting variations through to the thought that if a weight differential could be detected by merely handling the models, they would consider it a variation worth retaining, to the expression of an intention immediately to procure a scale and that every collector now would have to have one.

In the more important and obviously major collectible weight variation between identical models, one cast in white-metal alloy and one in zinc, there is hardly any area of debate that the really interested collector will seek and retain both the lead and zinc versions of a given vehicle even though they are otherwise absolutely identical both structurally and as to color. This variation in material seemingly can and probably does occur on all Tootsietoys originally made of the heavier white-metal alloy that carry over through the 1932 and 1933 lines. It is possible that some models brought out in 1932 may have been made in the zinc-alloy only; this seems especially probable in the case of the first Grahams that appeared late in 1932, but it cannot be regarded as absolutely certain. It is also likely that some models were still run in 1933 using white-metal alloy. Dowst no doubt had a variable supply on hand and would use it up. Also, castings may have been made in the old alloy but not yet painted and assembled into complete vehicles, which were finally made up in 1933 or even perhaps a little later. To repeat, the possibility exists for all Tootsietoys originally made in lead that span the 1932–1933 line to have been made in both alloys, although examples of all types have not yet been observed.

When the change has been made from lead to zinc, the difference in weight readily is apparent when holding two models, and the collector rapidly becomes so accustomed to the differential in these cases that he usually can tell if any single specimen is cast in one or the other alloy without having to have a second car for comparison. The series the collector is most likely to encounter to any extent that demonstrates this is that of the little five-cent cars, of which the Buick sedan and coupe were used as the cargo on the early Tootsietoy car carriers. The first three models in this series,

Fig. 171. Four die-cast Erie vehicles of the 1930's including three more truck types than those shown in Fig. 109. As nearly as can be ascertained, six different truck types were manufactured in each of the two size series made by this concern, one of the few firms to make pressure die-cast miniature cars prior to World War II.

New Jersey Zinc Co.

selling for ten cents with a garage,* were the sedan, coupe, and Mack fire engine. These, without the garages, became five-cent toys in 1932, and at that time the remainder of the series was added: roadster, stake truck, tank truck, racing car, and tractor. The 1931 productions were, of course, lead, so were all those in 1932 and quite possibly even in 1933. The series was last made in 1935, except for the coupe and sedan, which still carried over in 1936 as the cargo of a car carrier. Therefore, regardless of colors, all eight models exist in both white-metal and zinc castings although the white-metal ones seem more plentiful, which suggests that Dowst used up their remaining supply of this alloy on these their smallest and cheapest cars.

However, from the structural standpoint there is another point of variation interest as represented by the presence or absence of the name TOOTSIETOY inside or underneath the castings. The first models do not have it, but many that do are of lead, and the wording evidently was added to the dies late in 1932 or in 1933. It appears that all the zinc-alloy models have the name, and therefore, each of these eight vehicles exists in three progressive variations, quite apart from the potential color variations:

Type I, no name, white-metal alloy casting.

Type II, with TOOTSIETOY, white-metal alloy casting.

Type III, with TOOTSIETOY, zinc-alloy casting.

There is a very interesting further complication on at least the sedan. This exists with the TOOTSIETOY reading from the back to the front, and, in slightly smaller lettering, with the word cast into the inside of the car roof so that it reads from the front of the vehicle to the rear. On other vehicles in the series the lettering has been found facing in one direction or the other, but so far the writer has not seen it facing both ways on the same type of car other than the sedan. The implication is, of course, that all the models may be found with both placings of the trade name. Furthermore, both the sedan and the coupe (which would have been required in greater quantities because of their use on car carriers) may exist with both styles of lettering and with each style facing in either direc-

---

* It is still described as a garage even when sold with the Mack fire engine, and is so cataloged by Dowst. In fact, the Mack is not truly a fire engine as such but, as designated in the catalogs, an insurance patrol. The later ten-cent No. 1042 also was a patrol and was so designated, but the five-cent No. 237 that Dowst identified by the same name actually is a model pumper, not a fire patrol. Also, in each series two vehicles (Nos. 1041 and 238) were called hose carts, although both were pumpers with deck nozzles. These variations in terminology have led to much confusion among collectors.

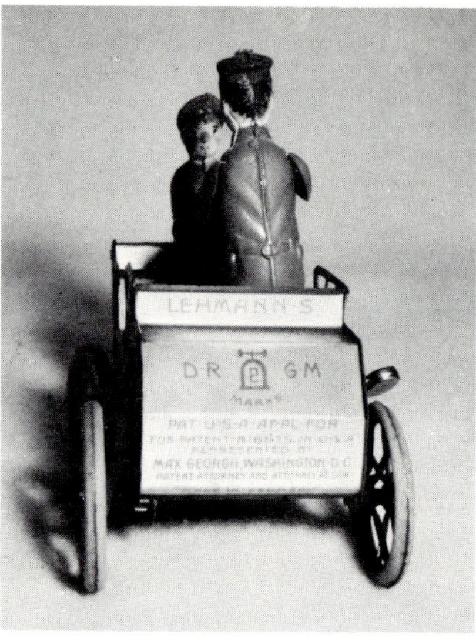

Fig. 172. An interesting variation in patent markings on a Lehmann clockwork automobile. The specimen of the model known as "Naughty Boy" (at the left) has the European patent markings incorporated into the lithography below the trademark behind the man (*C. W. Frey*). The specimen at the right has this area covered with a special paper label noting that a United States patent has been applied for (*Robert A. Ahlers*).

tion. Or, again, this may not prove to be so. But these are points to look for and compare.

In any event, in the late 1920's and early 1930's most, and likely all, of the existing Tootsietoy vehicles underwent the alteration to the dies whereby the trade name was applied to previously unmarked models. Not all models were changed at the same time, and as has been seen in the case of the small series introduced in 1931 and 1932, as late as the latter year some models were still being introduced without the trade name. However, some models evidently were retooled as early as 1927 or 1928. They therefore exist, entirely apart from color or alloy or other variations, in most cases both with and without the trade name. It is possible that a few models were made only with the trade name. But here is an interesting point for collectors to keep checking as the hobby and its research progresses: the form of spelling of the trade name was not always consistent—it usually appears as TOOTSIETOY, but may alternately appear on some models as TOOTSIE TOY. This may even occur at a time when the name seemingly was added more or less simultaneously to an existing series. For example, on the five-cent series of 1931–1932, the form is that of a single word on all the vehicles except the tank truck, where it is the two-word form.

This looseness is all the more curious when it is observed that the trademark always was registered and renewed at the United States Patent Office from 1921 on in one-word form and that in the mid-1920's Dowst evidently went to particular lengths to assure that it was looked upon as one word. One of only three changes between the 1925 and 1926 Tootsietoy catalogs was to reset a paragraph in the introduction where the Tootsietoy name was divided between two lines from "TOOTSIE-TOY" in 1925 to the division "TOOT-SIETOY" in 1926. The point is that up to now the spelling of the name has been noted in one form or the other on various models, but so far no variation has been observed whereby the name appears in both forms on otherwise identical models. Such a variation or variations, although seemingly unlikely in the cumulative light of present observations, may conceivably exist in the case of one or more models.

Unfortunately, the date at which Meccano, Ltd., changed the composition of the Dinky Toys from a lead-based alloy to zinc does not, unlike the Tootsietoys, appear accurately to have been ascertained. Presumably, however, there was such a definite date sometime in the mid-1930's, although possibly not the same date for both the British and French factories, so that otherwise identical Dinky Toy models overlapping this date exist in definite and importantly collectible variations that differ only in the metal and that can be identified only by the perceptible difference in weight.

Enough has been said now concerning variations to convey the sweep, scope, and fascination of these to the model-car collector. For the most part these remarks have applied to model automobiles sold in assembled form, for in the main it is only when such variations occur, either deliberately or accidentally, in the course of normal factory production that they assume any historical value and thereby are matters of moment to a collector. For the most part the builder and collector of cars supplied in kit form, or built from scratch, and the customizer do not encounter these same combined problems and enchantments, for any changes, additions, or modifications they make are on a basis of individual craftsmanship and creativity, and lack the historical foundation of factory changes. This is not true in every case. For example, there was introduced in 1968 a line of kits of plastic parts for building 7-mm.-scale models. Each kit contains major components molded in two distinct colors of plastic. The major differences in color may occur between a body and chassis or body and top or between a body and an interior. However—and this is the key to the situation—ten different colors are employed in molding the various parts, and any kit for any specific model will always include two different color moldings but far from the same two colors. A kit with a red body will include a top in any one of nine colors other than red. This means that there are eighty-one possible factory color combinations for each car model. (As the series develops, it appears there must be a few exceptions arising, as for example in the case of a United States mail truck that, logically, can come in but one set of colors.) Among the initial eight kits in the series there can be no less than 648 color combinations!

Of course, the thinking behind such a series is to enhance sales by creating a new form of model-car collecting. This aspect certainly is no more deserving of criticism by self-anointed ultra-purists among collectors than is the present-day promotion of the collecting of their models by manufacturers of miniature cars sold in assembled form. Securing, assembling, and preserving these models in their various color variations is a new but obviously legitimate form of model-car collecting because the color variations are factory created. It must be admitted that the number of legitimate potential color variations for a given model is a little staggering, particularly as they can be secured only on a hit-or-miss basis unless a hobbyist is to be permitted to look inside a number of boxes before making his purchases. In the absence of a kit that, say, builds a car with a green body and a red top, there will no doubt arise a question as to whether it is to be considered proper collectors' procedure to take a green body from one kit with a top whose color duplicates one already in the collection, and a red top from a second kit, and assemble the desired green body and red top combination? It must be admitted that there seems no way to preclude this practice, that the most stringent injunctions against it will go unheeded, and that once a hobbyist grows enthused over the potentialities of this type of collecting it is going to be the same as the old World War I song that wondered "How are you going to keep 'em down on the farm after they've seen Paree?"

Nor is this all, for each kit includes an assortment of decalcomanias, and it can be seen that by applying different decalcomanias, or even using the same decalcomanias but varying the position in which they are placed on a similar color-combination model, the number of potential variations becomes literally endless. However, as the decalcomanias are to be applied by the individual hobbyist, their selection and placing cannot be considered factory variations (although, it is true, the entire sheet of decalcomanias is in a sense factory work, and the potential of then acceptable variations thereupon simply staggers the imagination). It would seem that eighty-one variations of color combinations alone would be more than enough at which the average hobbyist would want to aim, if he does indeed so choose to aim. Furthermore, although the individual kits are quite inexpensive, the cost of eighty-one kits adds up to a substantial amount, and many collectors will no doubt decide to stop well short of eighty-one. Yet, in years to come, possession of even one favored model in a complete selection of eighty-one color combinations conceivably might become a possession well worth having, and certainly the display value impact of such an aggregation would be far from slight. If the series should be found to embrace one particular prototype that an individual greatly favors for one reason or another, such as a car he owns or has owned, a number of enthusiasts may be inspired to try for eighty-one.

FACTORS THAT AFFECT VALUES

The factors that affect the value of any model automobile are somewhat diverse, but nonetheless rather definite and universally understood and accepted. In the main they are concerned, as is the collecting of old model cars on the whole, with the mass-production manufactured models.

From time to time the question arises as to what would happen if by chance someone should uncover an early miniature replica of a prototype car or an early experimental model, fully authenticated as having personally been built by a real automobile pioneer such as Charles E. Duryea, or Ransom E. Olds (he whose name provided the appellations for two of the most famous of American makes, Oldsmobile and Reo), or Elwood Haynes, or some such automotive notable, or even a model commissioned by their companies and built either within or outside their factories. The question usually is asked as if it were automatically assumed to be self-evident by its propounders that the results would cause worldwide excitement among model-car collectors. On the contrary, and perhaps rather saddeningly so to some, the truth is that the discovery of such a model would cause very faint ripples indeed among the model-automobile collecting fraternity. If the model were offered for sale there would, in fact, probably be only an extremely limited number of model-car collectors who would display even a limited interest or enthusiasm. The model would probably be evaluated and sold at a price consistent with its admitted historical association value and its intrinsic value as a piece of—presumably—relatively good modelmaking, but, in truth, even this conjecture is by no means an absolute certainty. In all probability such a model would be sold, not to a model-car collector, but to a collector of or enthusiast for actual full-size old automobiles. Such individuals undoubtedly would express a higher degree of interest in a miniature of this type than the average conventional model-automobile collector. The reason the impact of such a model would be so slight among model-car collectors, contrary to what many people, and particularly noncollectors of models, might assume at first thought, is that as repeatedly observed in these pages the vast majority of model-automobile collectors simply are not oriented to patterns of collecting that take such models into account. The probably quite estimable creation of the famous Mr. Duryea or Mr. Olds or Mr. Haynes simply would not carry a fraction of the meaning and attraction to the great majority of model-car collectors as does the (to some) conceivably far less prepossessing—but only when falsely measured in terms of pure modelmaking art alone—mass-produced creation of, say, Mr. Theodore Samuel Dowst (Tootsietoy), Mr. Harry T. Kingsbury, Herr Ignatz Bing, Mr. Frederick A. Lundahl (Buddy "L"), or dozens of other makers and shakers of the toy and model-automobile world that as readily could be named. Much the same thing applies to the interesting, ofttimes elaborate, and usually highly decorative silver or gold model automobiles—frequently trophies presented in important bygone real automotive competitions—that do appear upon the market from time to time with what seem to those offering them justifiably high asking prices. These, however, are not articles that have much or any appeal to most model-car collectors, and the demand for such items usually is very limited.

Nor for that matter does the fact that in a few cases mass-production toy or model automobiles were manufactured or distributed by a maker of prototype cars by any means automatically in itself establish a greater desirability for such miniatures on the part of model-car collectors. When a real automobile manufacturer does on rare occasions enter the toy and model business, either as a sideline or merely as a promotion, their efforts in this direction are judged essentially on the basis of their activities in the established trade in little cars, not big ones. American collectors in particular have long been somewhat at once amused and nonplused by the obvious and rather strident efforts of some European collectors and dealers strenuously to establish as many models as possible as "works models"—that is, a miniature manufactured by and at the same factory as its prototype—and bemusedly to attach special importance and high values to such miniatures on this basis alone. As a result they have tended, if anything, to become oversuspicious and dubious of such attributions and in most cases justly so. The so-called "works model" and supposedly very limited production clockwork replica of the Alfa-Romeo P2 racing car (Figs. 144 and 157) upon relatively slight proper investigation was found not to have been manufactured by the Alfa-Romeo factory in Italy but to be the product of a French toy company, made in large quantities, and widely sold in the late 1920's and early 1930's, the price being the equivalent of about six dollars on the Continent and in Great Britain. The original price of a model is, of course, absolutely no criterion of present-day collectors' values, except within certain limits insofar as it may provide a clue to the original quantities produced. This particular Alfa P2 model is without question a nice miniature, and would stand as a welcome addition to the collection of any model-car enthusiast whose interests embrace this type of model, but as such things go it is not a rare model but a comparatively common one. This, however, is probably not what you will be told if you should happen to saunter through the marts of Paris on a model-car-hunting expedition. Facts similar to those relating to the P2 have easily been established in regard to a number of models of Citroëns, Delages, Packards, Sunbeams, and other prototype makes that some had freely designated "works models" either in a deliberate attempt to delude or in overenthusiastic naïveté.

It does appear definitely established that the Citroën company of France did manufacture or cause to be manufactured for them in the 1920's and 1930's a number of mass-produced models of various disparate sizes and types: juvenile automobiles, clockwork models, and cast-metal and molded-composition miniatures—the pros and cons of the "situation Citroën" are discussed later. Although in the uncritical viewpoint of some enthusiasts such activities automatically invest themselves with a certain aura, they most definitely do not by their mere existence make the models involved unusually desirable or valuable on this basis alone, the discourses of some European antique-shop sales personnel notwithstanding.

In any event, the proved "works models" are indeed few and far between, although there are a number of instances of toy and model automobiles licensed by the manufacturer of the prototypes or permitted to carry some such designation as "approved" or "official" model in connection with the name of the maker of the actual vehicle. Insofar as American models are concerned, there would seem actually to be no cases where this designation truly would apply to miniature automotive vehicles. The Carlisle & Finch electric model automobiles appeared in the same year, 1899, that the company built a real electric automobile of a presumably similar pattern, but they constructed only one such full-sized car, and their main business, at least as it developed, was not real automobiles but toys and models and various other electrical goods. The model dump trucks made by the White Company prior to 1924 may have been "works models" in a certain sense, but if so, it was before the fact, as they were promotional pieces, never offered for actual public sale, and their chief interest would lie in the fact that they were the direct forerunners of the Kelmet toy trucks. Oddly enough, the only American "works model" manufactured by a real automobile company, and completely substantiated to everyone's satisfaction as having been mass-produced and regularly offered for sale to the public, is not an automobile at all. It is the toy Studebaker Wagon, big enough for a child or two to ride on, produced by the Studebaker Company around 1910.

Models approved or actually licensed by the manufacturers, creators, or users of the prototypes have a certain interest of their own, although no more particularized value because of this fact than exists in the case of the "works models." They usually are far better substantiated at any rate as being what they purport to be. The pieces associated with distinct real automotive personalities are particularly interesting to a number of model-car enthusiasts. In the late 1920's and early 1930's Major H. O. D. Segrave, Sir Malcolm Campbell, and other notables evidently made a fairly good thing out of licensing toy manufacturers in Great Britain and the United States to make "approved" models of their cars. The Kingsbury clockwork replicas of Campbell's Bluebird and Segrave's Sunbeam and Golden Arrow * are

* A curious sentiment-inspired legend, or perhaps more properly an insistence, widely persists among toy

Fig. 173. Top and bottom views of a Hubley Airflow sedan and a Williams coupe, showing the method of assembly used to hold the models together. In the Hubley—this was one of three methods employed by this company—removing the spare tire allows the body and frame to be separated. In the Williams model (see also Fig. 159) the body is held to the chassis by means of a spring clip on the cross member.

G. William Holland photographs

particularly well known. Of course, in many instances unapproved models also were produced by other manufacturers, or obvious substitutes resorted to such as Red Arrow instead of Golden Arrow. In 1932 Tootsietoy introduced both five- and ten-cent miniature cast-metal versions (Nos.

and model collectors, particularly among those who were themselves boys in the late 1920's and early 1930's, to the effect that Segrave's 1929 record of 231.362 mph never was exceeded, although what proportion actually believe this and what proportion merely profess to believe is uncertain. As one enthusiast put it recently, "If anyone ever did go faster in an automobile than Major Segrave, he should not have been permitted to do so." In any case, this posture is an interesting overamplification of the aura that surrounds Ives toys to whom Segrave lent the use of his name for promotional purposes in 1929. A number of fans also will insist, straightfaced, that Segrave was knighted, not for his speed run, but in recognition of his service to Ives. Dr. G. A. Robinson, himself a true believer, who was much in Daytona Beach at this time, provides the interesting detail that Campbell and Segrave kept their cars at the local Ford Agency, this being the largest garage in town, but adds that, at least in the case of Segrave, this was only because there was no Ives showroom nearby.

110 and 4666) of Campbell's new record car, the Bluebird II, although without any reference to the name either of the car or of the driver, simply noting that the larger one was "an exact reproduction of the 'World's Fastest Racer.'" Similar obviously derivative models of this and other noteworthy record cars were produced by other manufacturers in the United States and Great Britain in the 1930's. They evidently proved good sellers, and at least one such model was virtually considered a requisite in even the shortest lines of slush-cast model automobiles.

The old Tootsietoy files contain some enlightening correspondence on such matters, albeit the surviving papers relate to airplanes, not automobiles. This does not, however, materially diminish its pertinence or interest in providing an inside look as to how this sort of thing might be carried out from either side of the fence, or a uniquely achieved insight into the workings of the toy and model business as a whole. In fact, in the following information in connection with what already has been said regarding the Campbell and Segrave licenses as to why in 1932 Dowst did not even consider using actual names in connection with the models of Bluebird II, it is not even necessary to essay the customary "reading between the lines":

At the Toy Fair in 1928 the Dowst Manufacturing Company displayed a sample of a new Tootsietoy airplane, an obvious replica of the Spirit of St. Louis, which had achieved fame the previous May. As Ted Dowst—and it is as well here to commence using this familiar form *— related the process in his own words, "We showed this number from a sample at the Toy Fair in New York and were successful in obtaining many large orders." The Tootsietoy model No. 4660 was, however, not named Spirit of St. Louis partially because of what were felt to be difficulties in securing permission for its use, but even more because Ted Dowst had created what he considered an even better name for the model, Aero-Dawn. As the catalog explains, "*Aero-Dawn*—doesn't the name alone tell a story? Isn't the present day but the dawn of air travel? And when that is combined with worthwhile merchandise of educational value to sell at a popular price and thru any channel of distribution, you have an item that moves, and moves rapidly." By chance the photographs of the original sample of Aero-Dawn, without any markings, and the handmade mockups of the individual carton and counter display box have survived and

are reproduced in Fig. 194. This was a new type of individual packaging and display carton for Dowst, and similar in concept to that for the Ford Model-A coupe, also introduced in 1928 (Fig. 195). A unique feature of this particular style of packaging, and one that many enthusiasts would much like to see adopted by present-day manufacturers, was that each box was in the color of the model packed within. You got a red Ford coupe or Aero-Dawn in a red box, a green model in a green box, and so on.*

Somewhere between the Toy Fair and the beginning of May, 1928, Ted Dowst was struck with the possibility that Aero-Dawn might be made even more popular and salable if it could carry the actual number of the Spirit of St. Louis, NX211, or, failing that, a very similar number. Accordingly, on May 3, 1928, he wrote to his patent attorneys, Duell, Dunn & Anderson in New York:

"Please advise me at the earliest possible moment if we have the right to use the lettering NX211 on either the fuselage or wings of a new aeroplane we are producing in our 10¢ class of merchandise.

---

* The standard color assortments for the models packed in this manner did not coincide with those of the rest of the line. In 1929, for example, the colors and packing on Aero-Dawn were six silver, three red, and three green to the dozen, and on the new 1929 biplane No. 4675 the same but with blue substituted for silver. The Ford-A coupe came in equal quantities of red, black, green, and tan, and on the Ford-A sedan equal quantities of red, black, green, and yellow. The new biplane, which was named Wings, should not be confused with a slightly earlier biplane, No. 4650, introduced in 1926. Wings also happened to be the name of a popular motion picture dealing with World War I aviation. However, the 1929 catolog does not point out this rather self-evident fact but merely notes, "The enormous demand for Aero-Dawn confronted us with the necessity of preparing additional equipment to fill the orders. We chose instead to produce another plane of a different type. Here it is—WINGS." Just in case anyone missed the point, however, the display carton for Wings portrayed biplanes flying over a trench filled with doughboys. Dowst ran into a threat of trouble over Wings, not from the motion-picture company, but from Parker Brothers, Inc., of Salem, Massachusetts, who had introduced and registered a trademark on a card game also named Wings (subtitle, "The Air Mail Game"), and showing biplanes on its box cover. Ted Dowst wrote (May 3, 1929), "You can see for yourself there is no possibility of similarity between the two items, theirs being a game and ours a toy. It is perhaps unfortunate that we both struck on the name 'Wings' at about the same time, but I think this can be easily adjusted." The matter evidently was so adjusted, perhaps the more readily because Dowst was supplying Parker with the miniature cast-metal playing pieces for many of their games, and Wings remained in the Tootsietoy line under that name until 1936, being fitted with rubber tires in its last version as No. 04675.

---

* Theodore Samuel Dowst's business cards (Fig. 193) proffered his name as Theodore S. Dowst; he appears always to have signed himself as T. S. Dowst, and he was, of course, known to his friends and associates as Ted.

Fig. 174. Another type of Hubley construction method is represented by the cars shown in this catalog listing of 1934; the bodies interlock at the rear of the chassis and the front axle holds together the final assembly of body, chassis, grille, and bumper. See also Fig. 140.

A. E. Moredock

"It is my recollection that this is the number of the famous 'Lindy' plane or at least it is so close to it that the average layman would recognize it as such.

"If there is any objection to using the actual number of the 'Lindy' plane for the toy, please advise me if it is possible to use any such serial number.

"Your kind attention to this will be greatly appreciated."

Upon receipt of Ted Dowst's letter the attorneys instituted a search of the United States Patent Office trademark records to ascertain if NX211 might be registered as a trademark. This search revealed that an application had been filed on July 26, 1927, for "N-X-211 Spirit of St. Louis" by R. Richard Spira of New York, New York, for use on a mechanical toy airplane and claiming as the date of its first use as May 21, 1927, which was pretty good considering that the flight to Paris that endowed the marking with its potential value itself took place on May 20 and 21 of that year. The trademark had not been issued, however. Further investigation showed that this was due to the fact that it had been placed in interference on September 15, 1927, with an application for a similar trademark by J. Chein & Company of Harrison, New Jersey. As a result of these findings, his attorneys advised Ted Dowst that they believed it best that he abandon any plans for using NX211, although

there would be no objection to using another serial number. Accordingly the number *214* was cut into the dies, *4* being regarded as the numeral most closely physically resembling *1*, especially in the style employed in this instance, and the vast fleets of Tootsietoy Aero-Dawns took off numbered in this manner.

A decade later a somewhat converse situation arose when "Wrong Way" Corrigan sought to sell his name and story for use in connection with a Tootsietoy airplane. On June 18, 1938, Douglas G. Corrigan achieved aeronautical immortality when he took off from Floyd Bennett Field in Brooklyn, New York, in his nine-year-old, nine-hundred-dollar monoplane, supposedly cleared for a flight to California, after he had been refused permission to make a trans-Atlantic flight because of the condition of the aircraft. Twenty-eight hours and thirteen minutes later he set down safely instead in Dublin, Ireland, claiming that through an error he had flown the wrong way. Corrigan returned to be acclaimed a hero, admired both for his courage and his excuse—for he was, of course, a pilot of great competence—received the greatest ticker-tape welcome New York had given up to that time, and prepared to take advantage of his achievement and go the usual route of selling his endorsement, photograph, signature, story, and whatever else was by accepted custom properly negotiable under such circumstances. Naturally, this might include " 'Wrong Way' Corrigan" toy airplanes, and Dowst was approached in the evident anticipation that they would jump at the opportunity. Instead, Ted Dowst showed very little interest, for one reason because with the exception of the Buck Rogers rocket ships that Tootsietoy had secured a license to manufacture in 1937, Dowst was used to having people pay them for duplicating their prototypes in miniature and placing their name thereon. R. R. Ballenger, in charge of Tootsietoy's East Coast office and sales, is quoted as having said early in September, 1938, when the matter was brought to his attention, that in his opinion "Corrigan would be dead as a public figure before you could get on the market and that he would be laughed at by buyers if he were to offer a Corrigan ship."

The negotiations slowed down. Corrigan's asking price for commemoration on a Tootsietoy evidently was something in excess of the $500 advance against royalties that it was stated he had turned down from another firm. Finally it was suggested that instead of having to undergo the delay and expense of tooling up an exact model of Corrigan's own plane, the good old Aero-Dawn, which was still in the line although now

Fig. 175. Inexpensive modern cast-metal miniatures, sold separately or in sets, such as the one pictured (*Tootsietoy—Strombecker Corp.*), used to demonstrate interesting variations such as alert and aware collectors look for, study, and preserve on all types of model automobiles. Complete details of the points of difference between the cars in each pair is given in the text (*G. William Holland photographs*).

equipped with rubber wheels (it would remain in production until World War II), simply be repackaged in a box bearing Corrigan's photograph, signature, and story of his flight so that a quick and profitable turnover might be achieved at a cost only of the cartons. There was, in fact, a certain grim if perhaps unintentional humor in this particular suggestion, for in the eyes of many the nature and apparent ease of Corrigan's achievement had to some extent shed a slightly ridiculous light on those of some of his predecessors. Nor, at the moment, could it be foretold that September, 1938, was to be the month of Munich and that subsequent events were to keep Corrigan's name and fame established longer and more firmly than might have seemed likely that summer when America was deriving a hearty laugh out of the "wrong-way" flight. But in any event, Tootsietoy did not respond favorably to the overtures.

One major operative factor on Dowst's lack of enthusiasm may well be that their two great adventures into this sort of arrangement, although both dealt with fictional characters, not real celebrities, had by no means proved as successful as they had anticipated. The first of these, the Tootsietoy Funnies, vehicles driven by comic-strip characters, had remained in the line but two years, 1932 and 1933. The second, Buck Rogers Rocket Ships, were at the very time of the Corrigan business showing an approximately equal failure to live up to perhaps overoptimistic expectations. Their season, both as separate items and boxed as a set with the dirigible Los Angeles, with twenty feet of cable cord on which the craft

would "sail through the air on their concealed pulleys," and statuettes of Buck and Wilma, lasted out only the 1937 and 1938 lines. Rather inexplicably, however, seemingly the sole surviving original colored wash drawing of a proposed new Tootsietoy item of the pre–World War II era is that of the No. 1031 Buck Rogers Battle Cruiser, the TSD M-3030 (Fig. 194). Minor details and the placing of the lettering differ somewhat between the drawing and the final production models, but both carry the same initials and number. This appears to have been the only Tootsietoy ever to bear the initials of Ted Dowst, and perhaps this accounts for his retention of the original wash drawing. Both the Tootsietoy Funnies and the Buck Rogers Rocket Ships were manufactured under license and royalty agreements similar to those proposed for the "Wrong Way" Corrigan airplane.*

It was one of Ted Dowst's well-remembered characteristics that he never wasted worry on or mourned over slack sellers. If anything, his attitude in this direction was considered perhaps just a little overly ruthless or precipitate by some of his associates. Upon making up the new Tootsietoy line each season, he would inquire in turn how many each existing item had sold the previous year, and if the quantity cited did not measure up to what he deemed properly requisite for a Tootsietoy, although it might be a figure that some of his staff considered quite satisfactory, he would command, almost eagerly, "Throw it out of the line this year!" As R. R. Ballenger recalls, "Ted Dowst always liked to get rid of an old number."

---

* Tootsietoy also paid a royalty of thirty-five cents per gross on toys retailing for ten or fifteen cents, and twelve and one-half cents per gross on toys retailing for five cents, to Louis Marx & Company of New York under a license to manufacture toys such as tanks and tractors employing a continuous molded rubber tread, the No. 108 and the larger No. 4646 tractors, and the No. 4647 army tank, all of which came out in 1932, under patent No. 1,334,539. Dowst evidently had shown samples of these to some of their largest accounts, as early as the fall of 1929, as something that would be in the 1930 line, for in November, 1929, they were contacted concerning the matter by Marx. The introduction of the Tootsietoy tractors and tank with rubber treads consequently was held up until Ted Dowst became convinced he had no other recourse, and then by negotiations until the signing of the licensing agreement on January 16, 1932, gave the company the go-ahead signal for including them in that year's line. The patent in question was issued on March 21, 1920, to W. H. Huth, and at that time was assigned to the Wolverine Supply & Manufacturing Company of Pittsburgh, Pennsylvania, so that when the agreement was executed between Dowst and Marx it still had approximately five more years to run. The royalties were payable on the fifteenth of every month, covering the shipments made by Dowst the previous month, and Dowst was required to submit samples of each type of toy that it proposed to manufacture under the license to Marx for their approval. Two samples of each, initialed by Dowst were sent to Marx, and, if approved, one sample was likewise initialed by Marx and returned to Dowst. Marx also had previously licensed the Kilgore Manufacturing Company of Westervelt, Ohio, to make cast-iron toys under the patent, and the agreement with Dowst included a clause to the effect that the Kilgore agreement would not be altered to permit them to manufacture toys under the patent in any metal other than the cast-iron stipulated in their original license. Presumably the patent, originally employed by Wolverine to cover the treads of their famous Sandy Andy Tank, covered all toy use of a continuous rubber piece especially molded to represent a tractor tread. Ted Dowst originally had endeavored to argue that the patent covered only mechanical toys and was therefore not applicable to Tootsietoys. The patent evidently did not affect manufacturers of miniature cast-metal vehicles such as the Kansas Toy & Novelty Company that simply employed ordinary rubber bands to represent the treads on their slush-cast tractors, such as their somewhat curiously named "Caterpiller Whoopee" tractor No. 47.

Much of this, of course, was standard procedure for any toy manufacturer, and with low-priced Tootsietoys the sales of given items had to be in tremendous quantities to permit economical production, but it would appear that at times Ted Dowst may have carried the principle to an unnecessary extreme. However, it is quite apparent that in the 1930's a Tootsietoy that had proved a very profitable staple could quickly become a dead issue and leave the factory holding a considerable stock on hand. The Bild-A-Car sets, for example, after six highly successful years, suddenly went sour in 1939 and were dropped, leaving a considerable inventory in the stock room, and they are found listed in jobbers' catalogs as late as 1941. One reason for this falling off could have been that by 1939 models of 1932 Grahams may have struck many youngsters as rather unattractively obsolete in style, but the failure to substitute a Bild-A-Car set with newer designs suggests that, for the moment at least, the whole concept had paled greatly.

Generally speaking, as time wears on, although the actual comparative production quantities of given items may well increase greatly, the length of time over which any model vehicle sells well tends to diminsh. This is in part due to more rapid general changes in broad prototype styles and in part to an increase in the market tempo, with ever-greater emphasis on something being new. Some of the first Dowst miniature automobiles enjoyed a production life-span of fifteen years or more. Most of their automobiles introduced in the early 1920's remained in the line until the early 1930's. However, for the most part the Tootsietoys brought out in the later 1920's had even shorter runs of popularity, and as the years of the 1930's passed there was for the most part an even greater speeding up of introductions and dismissals. Much the same process may be observed in all lines of all types of toy and model automobiles. In seeking clues to relative rarity, it should, however, be borne in mind that, as mentioned, production quantities often rose, and there may have been many more made of a three-year model in the 1930's than of a six-year model in the 1920's. But this must always be taken as a variable and not as a hard-and-fast rule. As a matter of fact, the greatest quantity in which any one model automobile ever was produced undoubtedly is that of the Dowst—later Tootsietoy —No. 4570 Ford Model-T touring car. Some 50,000,000 of these were manufactured between 1914–1915 and 1928, a record that may well never be equaled. Yet it must also be remarked that for much of this period it was one model

Fig. 176.   Generally speaking, white rubber tires on model automobiles indicate pre–World War II production, and black tires indicate postwar, as indicated by this pair of Barclay army trucks, and by the postwar version of the Manoil car whose prewar counterpart is seen in Fig. 109. However, the color of the tires is not an absolutely infallible indication, as a few manufacturers did use black rubber tires prior to World War II. For example, note the tires on the two specimens of the Arcade cast-iron stake truck.

G. William Holland photographs

among but a few available, whereas in the mid-1930's the Tootsietoy line offered on the average between forty and fifty different automobiles and related vehicles. This figure could probably be multiplied by several times in reaching a grand total of all makes that would represent the potential variety that might be found on store counters during this period.

RARITY AND DESIRABILITY

It is now axiomatic among collectors that rarity and desirability—and therefore value—are not by any means the same thing at all. Relative rarity is, of course, always most satisfying to know, but unless a rare model is attended by a high degree of desirability, it will probably not attain a spectacularly high collectors' value in terms either of buying or trading. Incidentally, in discussing the factors that affect values in old model automobiles, intrinsic worth, either at the time a model was made or today, can for the most part be dismissed from consideration. A 20-inch-long steel truck may look far more impressive and prepossessing to noncollectors or even to novices than a 4-inch cast-metal miniature, and undoubtedly the former sold for a great deal more than the latter at the time the two were in current production,* but measured in practical collectors' terms, the little vehicle may be worth as much or even more than the large unit. But then, again, very frequently it may not. No generalities are possible, for in the final consideration every model automobile must rest on its own particular individual relative rarity and desirability, with desirability by far the more important. What the noncollector, and so far very often the professional dealer, and even the novice collector so often fail to realize is that because one model of a certain size, material, and type readily brings a certain price, seemingly high or low, it does not follow that another model of generally similar or even almost identical appearance is worth the same price or anything near it. It may be worth much more or it may be worth much less to the knowledgeable collector. Lack of awareness of the broad implications of the situation, much less the infinitely complex detailed ramifications, is the reason why some invariably price any old model car high for fear they inadvertently sell something too cheaply; thereby, in effect, they are dealing in futures. As in any field of collecting, any individual who expects to become a collector, buyer, seller, or trader must acquire at least a start on a particularized knowledge of the subject. It always is possible to forgive a lack of knowledge, but not a lack of a desire to obtain knowledge. Speaking broadly, the most that can be said of model cars in a general way is that any old model automobile now does possess a certain definite collectors' value but that such value may be nowhere so high or nowhere so low as some would like to believe, or which might seem indicated by actual transactions involving either closely or vaguely similar specimens.

Furthermore, while certain broad principles concerning the relative desirability of model

automobiles can be enunciated today with a fair degree of accuracy, there almost always are exceptions both in terms of specific models and of an individual collectors' outlooks and preferences. To a collector who has assembled all but a few models of a particular series, for example, any of the specimens still missing from the series automatically becomes, in his eyes at least, a most desirable model even if, on the whole, it is no more and no less desirable than many of those he already possesses. Similarly, to a collector who specializes in some category that is not too widely collected, models of this sort take on a greater desirability, accompanied by a willingness to pay or trade more if necessary, than such models are likely to possess in the overall collective viewpoint of the hobby as a whole. It should also be remarked that novices very frequently manifest the proverbial beginners' luck that early puts them in possession of a highly desirable model or models. They must then almost always face up to the problem of whether at this time they desire quantity or quality; whether they should retain the desirable specimen or specimens or exchange them for a greater quantity of lesser models although of a similar or even greater total value. When collecting first begins, there is always a strong temptation to prefer as great a number of models, even if of lesser desirability, as can rapidly be attained. So long as the novice is aware of all the aspects of the situation, this is one more matter that can satisfactorily be resolved only on a basis of personal preference. However, it can truly be said—and must be said in an effort to caution the novice to consider such matters carefully—that experienced collectors in any field almost invariably believe that quality is ever to be preferred over mere quantity.

In any case, where value and desirability are concerned what is one collectors' meat may well turn out to be quite a different dish from that of his fellows. Also, hobby trends invariably expand in various directions in the course of time, particularly when faced with a noticeable drying up of the availability of certain initially more popular categories. Nor should sight ever be lost of the fact that in every widely established hobby there always are certain individuals whose interests to a large extent at least are inclined toward monetary considerations and who, in order the more readily and the more gainfully to "merchandise" specimens or whole categories of specimens that are comparatively easily obtainable, do not hesitate deliberately to attempt to manipulate or reverse established patterns of desirability for their own ends. There also exists among many

---

* But some amazing things were done, as regards production, in the realm of stamped light-metal automobiles, particularly in the 1920's when such companies as Chein, Girard, Marx, and Strauss got into their stride, and there were a number of *clockwork-driven* cars and trucks up to perhaps 9 inches or so in length that retailed for only twenty-five cents, and nonmotorized units that could be purchased for the same ten-cent cost as a standard miniature cast-metal vehicle.

model-car collectors, as among all collectors, a certain feeling that the grass always is greener on the other side of the fence; they look upon models made in another country or on another continent as automatically extremely rare and desirable. They lose sight of the fact that a model or a make that was not regularly imported into their own country at the time of original production is inevitably likely to be fairly scarce within their own country for this reason alone, but by the same token is likely to be comparatively common within the country where it was made or the countries where it was regularly widely distributed and sold. It is, in truth, all too easy for a collector, and most especially a comparative beginner, to become bemused by the obvious differences in "feel" or in design and production techniques that are difficult to describe precisely in words—quite apart from the factor of foreign prototypes—of foreign models. Nor, no matter how wordly and unbiased an individual is, or at least thinks himself, is it ever quite possible on the other hand entirely to free oneself of a certain unavoidable natural predilection for the designs and products of his own country. In fact, some collectors who are aware of this fact quite apparently subconsciously attempt to compensate for it by overrating the relative desirability of goods from other lands.

Nevertheless, and taking the entire foregoing into account in making the following statements, the average American collector has a primary interest in, and assigns an overall higher national rating of desirability to, models produced in the United States and Canada,* and, for the most part, a definite second preference to British models, with the remaining scale of national desirability (and it must be remembered that the country of origin is only one of several types of the judging of desirability) somewhat uncertain and not agreed upon, although in all probability French models would come third in order. The average collector in the United States also admittedly takes pride in the fact that, generally speaking, American model cars are considered extremely highly desirable and are widely sought in most other countries. In Great Britain the national preference naturally is for British models

in the miniature cast-metal category, with American products of this type a close second. It would appear that to a large extent British collectors are only now gradually discovering their own heritage in old model cars of various other types, although American collectors have been aware of it for some time. The primary interest in British model cars understandably extends outside Great Britain itself to collectors in most of the lands within or formerly within the empire. In most other countries in which there exists active model-car collecting, however, it is evident that, regardless of what may at times be said under the influence of national pride, there exists an extraordinary demand and preference for American models of all categories.

Why?

A consciousness of what already has been said concerning natural preferences for the products of his own country must in itself give an American who is about to attempt to supply an answer pause. Yet it appears that the following can be said without fear that the writer may seem to be motivated by any of the lesser or baser motives that may impinge upon such observations, and, indeed, should and must be said: For the most part, as an inspection of the numerous photographs and reproductions of catalog pages suggest, and as their histories reveal, American manufacturers generally have led the way or played the most vital roles in the development of the most important categories of model automobiles. The cast-metal miniature, the cast-iron model, friction cars, steel vehicles, clockwork models, and so on, were mainly or totally American developments, and for the most part the most desirable old models consequently are American products. As is the case with most American toys and models, in the case of miniature automotive vehicles the manufacturers of the United States were on the whole able to strike an ideal balance between constructional and mechanical merit and stability, and esthetic and external considerations. The miniature cast-metal car, although evidently originating in Great Britain and being further refined in France, was little more than a petty trifle until the advent on the scene of the Dowst family of Chicago, Illinois. The cast-iron model automobile was, as far as can be ascertained, strictly an American innovation and product.†

---

* The details of Canadian-made model automobiles are still somewhat uncertain, and such facts as have been established are not widely known. It is, however, certain that miniature cast-metal vehicles have been manufactured in the Dominion by London Toys of London, Ontario. It also seems very likely that at least some cast-iron model automobiles were made in Canada, at least by the New Market Manufacturing Company of New Market, Ontario, if not by others, too. It is possible that other types also were made in that country.

---

† A number of excellent cast-iron toys were manufactured in Great Britain in the early years of the twentieth century, mainly banks but including some other types and at least one train, but the records indicate that no automobiles were produced. A few iron banks were offered by French manufacturers, but there is ample evidence that if these were not actually entirely fabricated

The friction vehicle was another minor type, little more than a form of top attached to a chassis and running gear, until the City of Dayton, Ohio, gave birth to a substantial form of the general concept. The steel automobile and truck, in all its grandeur, was strictly an American creation, although subsequently taken up in Europe; and the clockwork model automobile originated in the United States and there underwent its greatest flowering on a mechanical and structural basis, although it unquestionably also thrived and flourished in Europe. Both the juvenile automobile and the electric model automobile may have originated in the United States, although at this point these matters cannot be considered certain, and it certainly is preferable to leave the matter open for now rather than to attempt dogmatic and perhaps unduly nationalistic claims. The steam model automobile indisputably was a European creation, and to be absolutely fair all around, on an absolute basis it probably would be proper also to allot a similar standing to the full-bodied miniature cast-metal car with movable wheels and to the friction vehicle.

The fact is that between about 1855 and 1875 the center of fine production toymaking had to a large extent shifted from continental Europe to the United States, and from that point on much of what was done on the Continent was essentially derivative, and found its basis either in copying or cheapening. By the time the automobile arrived on the scene as an important factor in real life and in miniatures, in the 1890's, this cheapening process had reached a height. Cheapness is, of course, comparative, but its meaning is fairly well understood within the context of any particular era or type of merchandise. Seemingly unable for the moment to compete with cheap European hand labor, American manufacturers of model automobiles in this initial period concentrated on quality and sought a middle ground of caliber and substance combined wherever possible with the true economies that mass-production manufacturing made possible. As a result American miniature automobiles on the whole largely (and in many eyes entirely) escaped the paltriness and tawdriness so widely associated with European model cars of this period, including even many that were in the lower portions of the lines of those manufacturers who also made quality goods. All this has served to imbue the

old American model automobile as a whole with an air of quality and desirability all its own.

All this is by now too well established historically to merit debate at this late date. It is really only necessary to look at the pictures of the American models of the later 1890's and early 1900's to appreciate the fact, keeping in mind that while some models of similar or approachable caliber were made in Europe at this time, these were the only types of miniature automotive vehicles made in the United States, whereas European productions spanned an entire spectrum, largely downward. This is another reason why old American toy automobiles have become a byword of desirability among collectors; there virtually was no such thing among them as a cheap, tawdry model. The attitude of the few who would uncritically accept a derogation of the American product is therefore inexplicable. It is quite true that not a little propaganda has been expanded in behalf of such an outlook, at times from strange and unexpected quarters, and on occasion not uneffectively, both at the time the old models were being made and more recently in a collectors' frame of reference,* but it is quite some time since knowledgeable persons were taken in by this sort of thing. All this, of course, is not to say that there are not valid and generally accepted standards of desirability wherein certain European model cars and makes figure highly in the scales.

An important measure of desirability can and is often based on the make of a model. Correctly or not, there are favorite makes almost any of whose products are considered highly desirable by most collectors, and there are makes from which collectors as a whole have turned their faces, perhaps in some instances unfairly, and which rank very low in overall desirability. This collector favoritism for makes may be sentimental, intuitive, based on hard fact, or on the result of combinations thereof. Sometimes it may even appear illogical to beginners or noncollectors, and it certainly may and often does greatly annoy speculators who prefer a climate where they more readily can "merchandise" models or makes of lesser desirability. It is somewhat difficult to analyze why certain makes definitely have the mystique that makes them highly desirable, while others do not. It often helps if a manufacturer is no longer in business, or at least no longer making model cars. However, this is by no means a requisite. In the field of miniature cast-metal

---

in the United States, the patternwork for them at least was produced in Connecticut. German claims to have made cast-iron toys are quite specious; the catalog illustrations adduced in support are quite manifestly stamped metal toys copied from American cast-iron designs.

---

* These matters are discussed in somewhat greater detail in the writer's book *The Toy Collector,* and there is no point in repetition here.

automobiles, old Tootsietoys and Dinky Toys obviously are considered highly desirable overall makes, yet both are still producing vehicles of this type. It also helps if somewhere along the way a particular manufacturer has produced at least one model that is particularly outstanding because of its quality, design, uniqueness, or special associations. For instance, Lindstrom's very high status as a desirable make rests to a large extent, if not entirely, on their *U.S.A.-A.E.F.* truck, a memento of the days of General Pershing and the American Expeditionary Force.† This is not by any means a large or prepossessing model, but, make aside, on a basis of comparative desirability of individual specimens, it has an extremely high rating of desirability. Because of its extraordinary historical connotations some collectors in fact look upon it as the most desirable of all model automobiles. However, lacking the specifically indicated relation of this truck, the contemporary Lindstrom and Gilbert ambulances, both World War I toys, do not carry a particularly high ratio of desirability. One thing at least is definite concerning desirable makes of model autos; the products or at least most of the products of such makes must definitely be known and recognizable. Unless a model car possesses some particularly outstanding feature, such as being steam-propelled, specimens that cannot definitely be attributed to a specific make usually never are considered as possessing a particularly high degree of desirability.

In any event, regardless of whether or not some or all of the precise reasons for the circumstances can be ascribed, these preferences as to the desirability of various makes more or less *in toto* assuredly exist and are held by a majority of aware collectors. For reasons already described, most of the early American makes are rated as highly desirable. Some, such as Carlisle & Finch, Hafner, and Knapp, manufactured only a few or even only one type of model automobile. Others, such as Converse and Wilkins, had larger lines. Ives is, of course, universally recognized in toy- and model-collecting fields as the leading manufacturer, occupying a sort of solitary position of preeminence.* Any model that can be at-

tributed to Ives automatically becomes highly desirable for this reason alone. However, it must be noted with regret that there is definitely known to be only one model of Ives manufacture, the 6 1/2-inch-long clockwork-powered cast-iron vehicle pictured in Fig. 42 of *The Complete Book of Model Raceways and Roadways*. Also, new collectors must be cautioned that there now exists a considerable and widely ranging trade in fake Ives models, toys of other makes, often, although not in all cases, necessarily limited to very cheap and generally undesirable specimens, doctored up with fake "Ives" rubber stamps to entice the uninformed. This little game now appears to be practiced both in the United States and in Europe. Among American cast-iron model automobiles, Champion, Freidag, Ives, and Kenton probably are considered, as makes, the most desirable. The other three names produced much more extensive lines in this field than did Ives.

Almost any pre-World War II British clockwork model automobile, other than the fairly common small-size Minic cars, such as Burnett, Wells, and the products of the British fac-

---

† This model is illustrated in color in *The Toy Collector*.

* In sum, from 1868 to 1930, in fine toys in general and in such particularly favored categories, both among contemporary youngsters and modern-day collectors, as clockwork toys, cast-iron vehicles, and mechanical and electric trains, Ives in most cases made it first or made it best (and if they could not successfully sell the best they would not make it at all, rather than to cheapen an article or a line merely in order to meet low-priced competition), surrounding the whole enterprise with an infinite air of pride and joy in inventing, designing, manufacturing, cataloging, advertising, merchandising, and, above all, interest in the ultimate consumer, that has never been approached. See *Messrs. Ives of Bridgeport* and *The Toy Collector*. Why, then, some model-automobile enthusiasts have been moved to inquire, did Ives, famous for mirroring each great new innovation, especially in vehicles, in toys, fail to follow up the horseless carriage more extensively after briefly commemorating its initial arrival? The answer probably is twofold, although the importance of the second should not be underestimated: (1) In the early 1900's Ives found it increasingly difficult to merchandise their fine iron toys in the face of rising costs and competition from cheaper brands, and eventually they discontinued this line entirely rather than lower its quality; (2) Edward R. Ives, the founder of the company and in this period still its active head, was a great lover of horses and trains, and not only always looked with disfavor upon automobiles but indisputably, following an episode in a topless car during a rainstorm, as related in *Messrs. Ives of Bridgeport,* became prejudiced against them. On at least one remembered subsequent occasion he absolutely refused to ride in an automobile, and insisted on waiting until a horse and buggy could be procured. His son, Harry C. Ives, on the other hand, was a great automobile enthusiast, but by the time Harry assumed full charge of the company, following his father's death in 1918, other manufacturers had solidly entrenched themselves in the toy-automobile business. Furthermore, in the 1920's, the company was suffering from want of capital sufficient to back up properly the ever-expanding demand for their famous toy trains. They did, as described in *The Complete Book of Model Raceways and Roadways,* on occasion experiment with model automobiles running on a track system, but never put anything of this kind into actual production.

Fig. 177.   Variations of painting and lettering. The first photograph shows a Barclay slush-cast ambulance and police car of the later 1930's; the police car exists with at least two types of lettering used to stamp the word POLICE on the hood. Next, the two basic forms in which the 1948 Studebaker Starlight coupe was put out by National Products for the Studebaker Corp., with and without lettering on roof. There are numerous colors of each type. The third photograph shows how the two original finishes of the Dinky Toys No. 179 Studebaker President were put out: blue with dark blue trim, and yellow with blue trim.
G. William Holland photographs

Fig. 178.   Not an incomplete cast-metal miniature, as it might seem at first glance, but an interesting variation of the Tootsietoy Mack coal truck of the mid-1930's at the time the transition was made from a three-axle model to two axles. This is an early two-axle truck that uses leftover frame castings with provision for the third axle immediately under the "L" of FUEL.
G. William Holland photograph

tory of Louis Marx & Company,* is considered very desirable either in itself or as a make. Among German manufacturers the most desirable makes undoubtedly are Bing, Carette, and Hess. Bear in mind that when we say, "makes," it means over-all makes. A given model of some other make can be and often is regarded as far more desirable than a number of models of a so-called desirable make. French model automobiles, unfortunately, have not as yet been sufficiently categorized and studied to enable a definite rating to be established as in the case of the German companies. It seems probable in any event that Rossignal and JEP will have to be included in any eventual list of desirable French makes. Nor can anything really be said at this time concerning the makes of other countries, although it seems likely that in the future, as today, in the case of Japanese makes there always will be a considerable measure of desirability attached to the manufacturer who adorned at least some of his cars with an imitation of the familiar handpress trademark of the prolific German manufacturer, Ernst Paul Lehmann.

THE LEGEND OF USA

Model-automobile collectors recently have revived, if only to question, the old story of the town of Usa, Japan. During the 1930's, when there was considerable agitation against the cheap Japanese products, including toys, that were reaching the United States in large quantities, and amid many injunctions to protect the American workman by examining goods before purchase to ascertain where they were made and to buy only American goods, the name of Usa was widely publicized. According to the story, finding their export business handicapped by Americans scrutinizing goods for the citations of the country of origin, the Japanese had founded an industrial town which

---

* An interesting example of the interplay of rarity, the lure of distant fields, the instance of a transoceanic branch of an American factory, and, perhaps, plain snobbishness, among model-car collectors in the United States, where, of course, the British-made models never regularly were sold, the British-made Marx models are considered much more desirable than similar or identical units manufactured in the United States. But bear in mind that rarity, desirability, and actual value are three different things operating in varying relationship to one another, and the aforementioned does not mean that any British-made Marx vehicle by that fact alone automatically commands a high price among American collectors. Incidentally, although Marx is the only American company to have established an actual factory in Great Britain, in the 1920's and 1930's many American makes of model vehicles, such as Kingsbury, Structo, Tootsietoy, and Wolverine, were extensively sold in Great Britain.

they named Usa, so that instead of being marked MADE IN JAPAN goods could be brought into the United States reading MADE IN USA, which at once would be technically accurate and yet would be taken to mean "made in the United States of America." The Japanese deny there ever was a Usa; the name is unknown to cartographers, and what is in itself more than sufficient and to the point, United States Customs regulations require that foreign goods be marked with the name of the *country* of origin. Accordingly, any shipment of goods from Japan marked, not with that country's name, but, instead, MADE IN USA, never would have been permitted entry. It was undeniably a good story, however, and widely believed at the time and still, to some extent, today. A number of collectors, therefore, continue to search hopefully for what they regard as the potentially highly desirable MADE IN USA model automobiles. Such models do not exist. What collectors occasionally do find, to their initial elation and subsequent deflation, are American-made products that for one reason or another have been marked MADE IN USA but with the periods between the initials omitted. There was no prescribed form for this marking; sometimes the periods were left out through happenstance, or, in the case of miniature cast-metal cars, it was not considered worth the bother. At times the periods may be present but almost obliterated by the coat of paint. Some Barclay models of the later 1930's, for example, are unmarked. In some cases variations of the same unit exist with a marking; sometimes the legend may read MADE U.S.A.; sometimes it reads MADE USA. Models with the latter definitely are not, as some would like to believe, rare and desirable copies made in the legendary Usa, Japan! It is true that there is a connection between these marked models and the economic and political affairs of the time. It is simply this: As the 1930's wore on and more and more Americans fell into the habit of examining goods to see where they had been made before purchasing them, more American manufacturers were inspired to add this information to their own products as a means of increasing sales.

There also exist some miniature cast-metal military vehicles simply and prominently marked USA. This obviously stands for "United States Army." Nevertheless, they are still on occasion thought by collectors to represent, entirely because of the omission of the periods, rare and desirable imitations made in jolly old Usa, Japan! When of pre–World War II origin, these vehicles were manufactured in the United States. Since World War II, a number of types of American military vehicles have been manufactured abroad by various manufacturers; they all bear markings attesting the country of their origin. There may, of course, be occasional exceptions to this today, but in general the modern custom is for manufacturers to incorporate the name of the country of origin in all mass-produced models as a matter of course. Earlier in the century a number of toys and models were not so marked except in the case of units specifically intended for export to the United States or some other country requiring such markings. As a result, examples purchased abroad were brought home by travelers, or, more recently, through exchanges and purchases on the part of model-car collectors. Thus, the fact that a given specimen is not marked as to having been made in a foreign country does not absolutely establish that this was not the case. However, most collectors very rapidly become attuned to recognizing through definite if only slight nuances of style, construction, and workmanship whether or not a particular model is of native or foreign manufacture, and even to a considerable extent accurately judging in which specific country it was made in the latter instances. In any event, as far as can be ascertained, there were no miniature cast-metal automobiles manufactured in Japan prior to World War II, although there was a very considerable activity in the making of lithographed stamped metal cars of a similar small size, as well as of larger-size model automobiles. Model-car collectors may safely be advised to stop looking for the famous Usa cars or reading things that do not exist into specimens in their possession.

TO MARKET, TO MARKET

Relative rarity can usually be ascertained by careful research and study, sometimes assisted to a varying degree by the prudent exercise of existing compatible information, and even to some extent through intelligent intuition. Desirability is somewhat more difficult to define. In all cases involving considerations of rarity and desirability, the end result, actual collectors' value, is something that usually requires considerable experience, seasoning, and, perhaps most important, a wide exchange of outlooks and customs within the hobby. Perhaps no model, or, more properly, series of models can better serve to sum up all the factors involved as an ideal example than the Tootsietoy No. 4630 delivery van of the early 1920's to 1933, and its rubber-tire counterpart of 1933 alone, the No. 04630. Originally there were six different numbers, each covering the van in one of its six standard forms of lettering: Grocery, Bakery, Market, Laundry, Milk, and Florist.

Precisely how they were sold is not quite certain. In the mid-1920's the catalogs illustrated all six types, and noted that they were packed one dozen in a box in "assorted colors and letterings." From the late 1920's on, only the Grocery truck was illustrated in the catalogs, and reference was made only to the assortments of colors, not of letterings. However, it is reasonably certain that the trucks to the end of their production run continued to be made and packed in assorted styles, although it is not absolutely sure that all six forms of lettering were continued to the end. An assorted dozen or so would naturally be the ideal form of packing for the average small store owner who would sell out more or less evenly. Presumably, regardless of colors, he would receive two of each type in a box. As for color, the boxes might also be assorted so that, regardless of lettering style, he would receive three each in red, yellow, blue, and green in each box. However, larger accounts and chain stores who bought Tootsietoys in more substantial quantities could vary the relative quantities of each type they desired according to their experience with the relative rate of sale across their counters. An experienced buyer might thus order ten gross of some types, five gross of others, and perhaps even none of one or more models. This is not only self-evident but is made plain by the fact that there now exist sufficient specimens in model-car collections or that have passed through the hands of some of the more active collectors to indicate that there was and is a considerable difference as to the relative quantities that were made of the six types and that all six are by no means equally rare or equally common. This might also be affected by which trucks customarily were packed in sets of Tootsietoys wherein one of the delivery vans was included. It may be that the division of such trucks always was equal among the six types, or it may also be that, at times at least, certain of the then known to be more popular types were regularly packed in sets while others were not. But the incidence in sets might even be somewhat determined on the opposite basis, the sets receiving trucks on which the factory found itself overstocked. Probably the exact details of these procedures are forever lost in the vanished mists of Tootsietoy history.* In any event, the important

---

* There could also be a certain definite geographic distribution of truck types at the time they were

Fig. 179.   Marx clockwork Ford Model T's. The pair are a model of the 1920's with slogans lithographed over it, with solid wheels, and, right, a similar updated model made after World War II (*Ward Kimball*). The third model is another type of the 1920's, with plain body and cut-out wheel spokes (*G. William Holland Collection*).

fact is clear today that not all six types are to be found today in equal quantities.

A survey of a number of well-established model-car collectors indicated that there is indeed a considerable variation in the incidence, and thereby in the rarity, of the six different delivery vans. While there exist some expected differences of opinion about some of the types, it was made very clear that there is general agreement that the Milk truck is the commonest and the Florist truck the rarest, with the other four types variously placed in between. (One collector rated the Market truck as on a level of equal scarcity of the Florist truck, and another placed the Laundry truck as the second commonest, noting that the Bakery, Grocery, and Market trucks appeared just a little easier to find than the Florist truck. In any case there is sufficient agreement to name unquestionably the Milk truck as the commonest by far and to place the Florist truck as the scarcest.) That the Florist truck should be the rarest and the Milk truck the commonest is, in fact, precisely what previous deduction, or, if you will, intuition, would have predicted. Of the six trades represented by the trucks, that of Florist would be that least met with in rural areas and many small towns in the 1920's, or in any event least likely to impress itself upon little boys of the age for Tootsietoys no matter where they resided. On the other hand, Milk trucks would be the vehicle most frequently and regularly seen by children and those most closely connected with the routines of a greater number of households. Furthermore and by no means of lesser importance, milk obviously carries strong psychological implications and attractions both for youngsters and for their mothers, who did much of the buying of toys of this type. Confronted with a counter of variously lettered vehicles, and desiring to take home a toy, a mother would almost invariably select the Milk truck.

As a matter of fact, looking backward, it may well be that Ted Dowst was guilty of one of his few important tactical lapses when in the

overhauling of the Tootsietoy line in 1933 the word MILK was omitted from the new vehicles. The established great salability of Milk trucks was recognized with three new models, the No. 0808 Graham delivery truck, the No. 0805 Mack tractor with one milk tank trailer, and the No. 0192 Mack tractor with three milk tank trailers. However, although the catalogs designated them all as milk haulers, the miniature vehicles themselves all were lettered TOOTSIETOY DAIRY. They sold fairly well, but undoubtedly would have sold much better if they had, as was the old No. 4630 truck, actually been lettered MILK. This was a mistake that was not committed by Michael Levy, the head of Dowst's leading competitor, Barclay. In the 1930's Barclay manufactured at least three —perhaps four *—successive or overlapping Milk trucks, on each of which they were careful to inscribe the word MILK, and these proved to be among their most popular sellers. Considering the continual great popularity of toy Milk trucks of all kinds and the factors involved, it can only be suspected that Ted Dowst allowed himself to doze when he yielded to the temptation to introduce vehicles marked TOOTSIETOY DAIRY. Many real milk trucks, of course, carry a firm name that includes "Dairy," but the word is by no means as conducive to toy sales as is the straightforward word "milk."

Incidentally, these Milk trucks are the only pre–World War II Tootsietoy automotive vehicles † on which the brand name externally appears in full. Thus publicizing the Tootsietoy name may possibly have been a motivating force in their creation, although if this were the case it is difficult to see why the name was not then employed more extensively. When subsidized lettering was not available, it was the firm's custom to use some sort of generic lettering such as CITY FUEL COMPANY, EXPRESS, and LONG DISTANCE

---

made, and as a result a correlated finding of models today, through this chance packing in sets. If, for instance, on one day nothing but Bakery trucks were being put into sets, and later a large order happened to be filled from the stockroom by picking up entirely from this batch of sets and shipping to a jobber in, say, Minneapolis, then this might show up among collectors now in a perceptibly greater incidence of Bakery trucks turning up in Minnesota and surrounding states. Of course, this might well be balanced out by subsequent shipments. In any event, the overall ratio of the various types for the country as a whole currently would rest on the total quantities of each type originally manufactured.

* There is a 5-inch-long Milk truck with its body contoured in the form of a horizontal milk bottle, a design of truck favored by some real milk companies in the 1930's, that appears to be a Barclay model, but the attribution is not absolutely definite as yet. Barclay may, of course, have manufactured still further types of Milk trucks in this period. Without question they were well aware of their appeal, and Milk trucks may be considered a sort of specialty of theirs. Among all American manufacturers in the 1930's, there were at least thirteen different miniature Milk trucks produced, and very possibly there are still others that have not yet come to light. On the other hand, European manufacturers do not appear to have gone in for miniature cast-metal Milk trucks.

† The freight cars—boxcar, gondola car, and caboose—brought out in the late 1920's and made until 1938, are lettered TOOTSIETOY RR.

Fig. 180.   Structural variations, actual and probably accidental. Two versions of a Dayton Friction touring car. There are important structural variations in the presence or absence of the toolbox on the running board, headlight, and so on (*G. William Holland photographs*). On the other hand, both of the Schieble mail trucks should probably look like the specimen at the left (*Robert A. Ahlers*); the rear-fender line probably having been accidentally bent upward on the example at the right (*C. W. Frey*); although, of course, if it should be ascertained that any were ever actually turned out with this contour, it would then constitute a legitimate collectible variation.

MOVING such as appeared on three of the other vehicles in the new 1933 Mack series, or COMMERCIAL TIRE & SUPPLY CO., which appeared on a Graham truck. The fifth new Mack vehicle that came out in 1933 was a tank trailer; it used the same stamped-metal tank as the milk trailers but on a different chassis, and was lithographed DOMACO GASOLINE AND OILS.* The mistake on the new milk trucks and trailers, of course, was not in use of the name "Tootsie-

____

* With one exception, all of the big Mack trucks of the series initiated in 1933 come in two basic styles, first, with dual rear wheels, making ten wheels to a vehicle but changed in 1936 to single rear wheels, making six wheels on the trailer rigs and four on the "City Fuel Company" truck, except for the "Long Distance Hauling" trailer, which was dropped after 1935. An ex-

tremely interesting variation occurs on the coal truck as a result of the transition, old frames with openings for two rear axles being used up with an axle only through the rear pair of bearings, as pictured in Fig. 178. The American Railway Express truck never was made in a dual rear-wheel version, having been introduced as a four-wheel vehicle in 1935. Also, dual wheels never were used on the No. 0192 triple-unit milk tank trailer rig. The numbers—0801 for the express trailer, 0802 for the oil tank trailer, 0804 for the coal truck, and 0805 for the milk tank trailer—were not changed at the time the reduction was made in the number of wheels, but the prefix *0* was dropped from these and the No. 0810 American Railway Express truck and the No. 0192 triple-unit milk tank in 1937. It is not certain if there is any means by which collectors can with certainty distinguish between most four-digit numbered vehicles with single rear wheels and the three-digit numbered models. There is a definite change in the shade of green on the American Railway Express trucks somewhere along the line, but whether it was coincident with the change in toy" but in employing "Dairy" instead of "Milk." In any event it is interesting and perhaps to some degree pertinent that these are the only automotive vehicles of the era on which the full name "Tootsietoy" appears externally.

While by this time the name appeared on the underside of virtually all the models, there were very few attempts at even an indication externally on any automobiles or trucks. Where there is such an indication it is in the form of an initial or initials. The No. 109 five-cent stake truck is lettered TT, and the ten-cent No. 4646 tractor, described as a Caterpillar Tractor in the catalogs (as is the five-cent No. 108), carries a T inside a diamond on the side. This undoubtedly stands for Tootsietoy, not Diamond T, for the Diamond T Motor Car Company manufactured trucks, not tractors, at the time. At the same time it is obvious that there was no connection with the actual Caterpillar Tractor Company involved at the time, Caterpillar being used generically. On the other hand, Ted Dowst was indeed capable of considerable subtlety, and it is quite possible that such markings and models (the No. 109 represented a departure in the series from unmarked Mack prototypes in the case of the No. 104 insurance partol and No. 105 tank truck, and it would have been somewhat cheaper, as regards production, to have based the No. 109 stake truck on the existing drawings rather than making it, as was done, a General Motors prototype) were all to some extent concerned with Dowst's extremely active endeavors at this period to secure subsidies from real automobile and truck manufacturers for new dies. There are sufficient surviving recollections to suggest that something like this indeed was rather artfully taking place in the depression years of the early 1930's, and Mack indisputably did come back into the fold in 1933 with the new truck line, although it was Graham, not General Motors, who finally responded to Dowst's desire for a subsidy for their new passenger cars. It might even be possible that Ted Dowst may have conceived some sort of what would today be called a subliminal campaign to bring about an association in children's minds of Tootsietoy and milk. It was at approximately this time that André Citroën supposedly made his often (and in the views of many model-car collectors, tediously) quoted statement to the effect that the first three words a child should learn should be "Mama, Papa, and Citroën" as the alleged reason for his manufacturing model cars. Ted Dowst would certainly have thought of, and may have consciously undertaken, action toward this end via the milk route, so that the child's first three words should be "Mama, Papa, and Tootsietoy."

To revert specifically to the No. 4630 delivery vans as an ideal example of the workings of rarity and desirability, from a standpoint of rarity alone, there is no question that the Florist would rate as the most desirable. It unquestionably is regarded by many collectors who are aware of the ratio of incidence of the six types as the most desirable, and by all aware collectors as *one* of the most desirable. Why this seeming discrepancy? The answer acutely demonstrates the fact that rarity and desirability are by no means synonymous. A considerable and growing number of collectors rate the Laundry van as of equal or even greater desirability than the Florist truck. Yet, as has been seen, the Laundry is by no means so rare as the Florist, and in fact one leading collector who probably has had as many models pass through his hands as anyone actually reckons the Laundry truck to be the commonest after the Milk truck. Here, rarity and desirability most definitely part company. The workings of the collector mind are sometimes obscure to the noncollector, but seldom are they actually arbitrary or irrational. In the world of the collector of old miniature cast-metal vehicles, the name Dowst (whether as a company name, the name of Ted Dowst, or as a triumvirate of Ted and his father and uncle), or the virtually synonymous word Tootsietoy, are, figuratively speaking, on a pedestal. In short, within this particular collecting realm the name Dowst stands much in the same position of eminence as does that of Ives in toys in general, or Stiegel in glass or Chippendale in furniture or Paul Revere in silverware. Anything pertaining to Dowst is of extraordinary interest. The Dowst business started with the publishing of a laundry trade journal, and their die-casting process itself was developed in order to make collar buttons, which they sold to laundries. Hence the Laundry truck is considered a

---

numbers cannot be said. Any coal truck with the earlier frame and only four wheels is surely a No. 0804, but a vehicle with the later frame could be a No. 0804 or a No. 804. Barring some pertinent research development, collectors probably always will have to use their own discretion in differentiating—or even whether to attempt to differentiate—between the 0800 series and the 800 series of Macks. Color variations seem to be the only possible likely clue. Incidentally, the No. 0192 triple-unit milk tank rig always was pictured in the catalogs without lettering. This was because only one hand-lettered sample tank (on the sample of the No. 0805) was made up for the 1933 Toy Fair. The artist who prepared the catalog drawings worked from these samples and showed the lettering only on the No. 0805. This oversight never was corrected for later catalogs. All the tanks on all the No. 0192 and No. 192 rigs, however, carried the TOOT-SIETOY DAIRY lettering.

most Dowstian item. Some collectors believe it must have been Ted Dowst's favorite of the six and that it was included in the series because of the family's laundry business connections and background.

Numerous collectors of old miniature cast-metal cars look upon the Laundry truck as being as desirable as the Florist van, if indeed not more so. Such is the manner of the workings of the desirability factor among collectors.

Actual value now enters into the picture. Value to a large extent naturally hinges on desirability, but the ratio of the one to the other is not always equal. In the overall picture, the Florist and Laundry trucks undoubtedly will be rated the highest in value of this particular system. It is even quite possible that as time passes the Laundry truck will take on an even greater amount of desirability, and conceivably could surpass the Florist van in actual value. However, there are other considerations involved here. If it could be said with certainty that the Florist truck or the Laundry truck had three times the desirability of the Milk truck, then logically it would follow that they would have an actual worth three times that of the Milk truck. Or perhaps it would be six times. On the other hand, a collector who had five of the series would probably gladly pay or trade more for the sixth, even if the missing specimen were the Milk truck, than for another of the types he already had. Nor does this mean that in every instance a collector would gladly trade three—or whatever the actual ratio of desirability may appear properly to be—of the other trucks for a single Florist or Laundry truck.

The foregoing discussion of desirability as applied to the No. 4630 Tootsietoy trucks has been limited to the six standard stock designs.* There are, too, the special proprietary vans bearing the names of department and chain stores. These stand apart from the regular series both because of their special interest and because of their comparatively small production. All are considered highly desirable, much more desirable in fact than any of the standard models. At present all the specials are rated as more or less equally desirable, although already there are indications that

certain of them were made in smaller quantities than others, and in time a pattern may become sufficiently clear to provide a recognizable scale of comparative desirability and value based on the relative incidence of different ones or other factors. In fact, there undoubtedly are many types that are as yet unknown, as specimens have not yet turned up.

In point of fact, there also remains to be precisely determined their contemporary mode of use. It is possible that occasionally when a special truck was made up for a store, only the special design would be sold in that store, or at least that more of them would be placed on the counters than of one or several of the standard designs. Obviously, it was extremely good advertising to have a boy playing with a van lettered, not anonymously MARKET or MILK, but, rather, BAMBERGER or BOGGS & BUHL. (In the 1930's two major oil companies competed for the privilege of paying Lionel a subsidy for placing their name on toy tank cars, not only for current promotion but also in the expectation that when a boy grew up he would thereby be likely to use their brand of gasoline in his automobile.) Some collectors believe that these proprietary trucks were simply given away as souvenirs to children who entered the stores with their parents. Though it is possible that this happened on occasion, it is generally unlikely, as the cost of these vehicles was too high for widespread use in this manner in the 1920's. Free store souvenirs in this period usually were lithographed cricket noisemakers and the like, on which the cost to a store was perhaps a tenth, or even much less, that of a Tootsietoy. It is possible, however, that in some instances a major use for these special trucks was to be given as a gift to boys who paid a visit near Christmas to the store's resident Santa Claus to tell him what they hoped he would bring. Santa would listen solemnly, promise to remember and do his best, and then give each child a peppermint cane or an inexpensive present appropriate to the child's sex. A truck of this type would have made an ideal gift under these circumstances for the boys.

Unlike the standard models of the No. 4630 van, all six forms of which came in the usual Tootsietoy assortment of red, yellow, blue, and green, all the specially lettered trucks seem to have been made in but one color form only, and that one presumably reflecting the livery of the actual delivery trucks of the particular store for which they were lettered. For example, blue for Boggs & Buhl, red for Pomeroy's, yellow for the J. C. Penney Stores, yellow and black for Hochschild,

---

* Just prior to this book's going to press, Dr. Clinton B. Seeley reported the existence of a Tootsietoy No. 4630 delivery van lettered U.S. Mail—an item never cataloged separately, although possibly included in some of the first No. 5041 Air Mail sets prior to the readying of the Ford Model-A mail trucks usually provided in these sets. In any event, the appearance of this seventh form of the No. 4630 obviously complicates the matter of the relative rarity and desirability of the vehicles in this group.

Kohn, and so on.* So far, all these models that have turned up, with the exception of the latter, carry the store name cast in raised lettering on the sides, and are painted in a single color. The Hochschild, Kohn van, however, is cast with smooth sides, painted in a handsome and comparatively elaborate combination (secured by masking the basic yellow and then spraying with black), and lettered in black with decalcomanias or a rubber stamp. It is quite possibly to be accounted of somewhat greater desirability than the others because of these points. It was not necessary for a store desiring such models to pay Dowst for the cost of a complete special truck die. One of the original six dies was constructed so that a matrix bearing any wanted special lettering could be inserted in place of the standard lettering. It is not known at this time, and perhaps never will be known, which of the six dies was selected, although it is possible that eventually extremely close scrutinizing of standard trucks will reveal some sign indicating which standard die or dies (there may have been more than one over the long run) was used. It is, in fact, not impossible that the original die was constructed in this manner and that initially the six standard forms of lettering also were varied in the die by means of matrices. However, the best recollections available on this point are that there originally were six different dies and that only one of these was arranged for matrices. It would appear, as evidenced by the Hochschild, Kohn truck, that there also was available some arrangement whereby unlettered smooth-side castings could be had. Unlike standard Tootsietoys, which always were packed and sold in multiples of dozens and grosses, and priced accordingly, these specials were sold by the thousand. The price to stores in the 1920's was $60 per thousand, with a minimum order of 10,000 reputedly required but

perhaps not always insisted upon. Owing to the extra labor involved in the two-color finish, Hochschild, Kohn probably paid a little more for their trucks or else ordered in such quantities as to secure the basic price. The wholesale price charged by jobbers for the assorted six standard vans was $0.79 a dozen and $9 a gross in the 1920's. This figures out to $.0641 cents and $.0625 cents per unit respectively. On this basis it would appear that the specially lettered proprietary trucks actually cost their purchasers less than the standard trucks. However, such large accounts customarily purchased their Tootsietoys direct from Dowst, not through jobbers, and probably actually paid somewhere around $.05 per unit for the standard trucks in the quantities they customarily used. The specials did therefore cost them somewhat more per piece than would have the ordinary Milk, Market, Laundry, and so on. Evidently they felt the approximately extra penny on each vehicle was well worth the cost for the additional advertising value thereby derived.

As will have been seen, the Tootsietoy No. 4630 trucks provide perhaps the most ideal example possible by means of which to demonstrate the workings of those so-often misunderstood factors, rarity and desirability. The Dowst policy of providing delivery trucks in the name and colors of a particular store was revived in the late 1930's, using the No. 123 Ford light delivery truck that was included in the cataloged line only from 1937 to 1939. It was a five-cent number. Presumably there was a hiatus during the depression when no one felt it was worthwhile paying extra to obtain proprietary vans.† The No. 123 was regularly made with only one form of lettering, SPECIAL DELIVERY, from which many boys thought the vehicle was intended to represent a special-delivery mail truck. As in the case of the No. 4630 trucks,

---

* Special trucks bearing actual store names are not only to be found among the miniature cast-metal vehicles but also among other types of models. Whatever their size and construction, trucks specially lettered for stores are considered highly desirable by model-car collectors. Hochschild, Kohn and Company, a Baltimore, Maryland, department store, evidently regarded the advertising potential of such models quite highly, and went into them relatively heavily. There also exists a Tipp and Company clockwork lithographed truck identical to the model lithographed for Strawbridge and Clothier, a Philadelphia, Pennsylvania, department store, pictured in Fig. 102, but finished in the Hochschild, Kohn colors and lettering. Identical or somewhat similar vehicles have been reported in collections or recalled from childhood memories as having been made for Kauffman Brothers of Pittsburgh, Pennsylvania; R. H. Macy of New York, New York; John Wanamaker of New York, New York, and Philadelphia, Pennsylvania, and other department stores.

† The fact that the No. 4630 was dropped from the line after 1933 does not, of course, preclude the possibility that special proprietary versions were not ordered and made up after that date, especially in the case of stores that previously had purchased them. No known proprietary specimens of the No. 04630 rubber-tired van of 1933 are yet known to have turned up. Proprietary versions of the No. 123 may well have been made after it was dropped from the cataloged line after 1939. Apropos of this situation as applied to standard vehicles, it should be noted that from time to time, even to the present day, Tootsietoy on occasion receives inquiries as to the availability of discontinued items, usually for premium purposes. If the dies are still on hand and in good condition, and if the quantities involved are sufficient, orders may be accepted and the toys made up. But it should hastily be added that the dies for the "classic" vehicles of the 1920's and the 1930's, as well as the die-casting machines capable of accommodating them, have all been scrapped.

Fig. 181.   An interesting group of cast-iron models: an Arcade delivery truck and a stake truck (*Joseph N. Imler*); an Arcade tank truck, a Champion roadster, and a Kenton ditcher (*Lloyd W. Ralston*); and a Hubley street cleaner (*Joseph N. Imler*).

the No. 123 is considered much more desirable an item when lettered for a store than in the standard "Special Delivery," but it also serves to illustrate a final point concerning rarity and desirability. The standard version had the lettering cast in raised lettering on its sides. The specials exist in two forms, lettered with decalcomanias on a smooth recessed side or with inserted lithographed sheet-metal nameplate filling the recesses. More versions with the former style of lettering are known than with the latter, which is considered more desirable. Yet, theoretically, it would seem likely that of any given version of either type, there would be less originally made and, accordingly, less surviving, of a model using decalcomanias than of a model employing the lithographed insert. It was more expensive to prepare the lithographed metal sheets, and a great quantity would have to be made up to warrant the outlay in any event, and their employment also required press operations to blank and form them. In other words, of the two examples illustrated in Fig. 198, it would seem likely that the Miller & Rhoads truck, lettered with decalcomanias, was initially manufactured in smaller quantities and is today scarcer than the Shepherd's truck that makes use of lithographed inserts. However, the Shepherd's van is considered a more desirable item because it seems probable that fewer stores bought No. 123 truck specials with lithographed inserts than purchased them with decalcomania lettering. The point demonstrated, if by still another type of example, is once again that rarity and desirability never can be regarded as synonymous.

CONDITION

Condition is, of course, a paramount factor in determining the value of any individual specimen of a model car, once the vehicle has been evaluated as to rarity and desirability. Obviously, with any model, the closer it resembles its original condition when new, the more the model is worth. First, however, it must be rated on rarity and desirability. A common model in superb condition willl be worth considerably less than a scarce or highly desirable model in very poor condition. A perfectly equitable and mutually satisfactory trade may be effected involving a prepossessing-looking specimen for a rather dilapidated-looking model, or even of two, three, five, or even more items in good condition for a single piece in poor condition. Of course, such trading should be done only between two individuals who are sufficiently versed in model automobile collecting to know precisely what they are doing. Also, it should be noted in passing that the current feeling, especially among novices, is that trades should be conducted on a one-for-one basis, the theory evidently being that in this manner each participant adds to his collection the same number of models that he did not previously possess. This view is not held by experienced collectors. In a book such as this, it is impractical to attempt to cite specific cash values because they rapidly become obsolete and thus misleading. Collectors, dealers, and others, being human, invariably tend to make such quotations for their own ends, citing the low prices as authoritative examples when they want to buy, and the exceptionally high prices when they want to sell. Until the hobby has grown to such size as to warrant the publication of a comprehensive price catalog, or at least a graded list providing the comparative rarity and desirability of each model, prudence dictates that specific references to cash values be omitted. Suffice it to say that some old models still command prices that are by any standard quite low, while some others bring prices that seem almost unbelievable to most enthusiasts. Most tend toward the lower price levels.

To find old models today in brand-new condition is not easy, but it is also not impossible. There still are old model automobiles to be found in old store stocks or even in the hands of individual purchasers, although naturally the number of such as yet undiscovered specimens diminishes with each passing year. The enthusiast can only search and hope. At the time they were manufactured, model automobiles, especially cast-metal models, were commonly sold in many outlets other than hobby and toy shops. Just as today the number and variety of stores that regularly handle one or more of the current lines of lower-priced miniature automobiles appears almost endless, so in the 1920's and 1930's there were an amazing number of outlets for the products of that era. Miniature automobiles were sold in drugstores, hardware stores, novelty stores, notion stores, five-, ten-, twenty-five, and thirty-nine cent stores (thirty-nine cents being a favorite price limit in the 1920's, although at that time most stores of this type still retained the traditional famous five- and ten-cent price limits), general stores, souvenir stores, variety stores, and "Racket Stores." The latter name, which excites much curiosity when mentioned today, did not in any sense imply there was anything dubious about their activities or merchandise; it was a standard and accepted description for a type of variety store in the United States during the first three decades of the twentieth century and into the 1930's, although no one today seems able to account for its origin.* The miniature cast-metal automobiles and related toys were the most widely sold type of all. One computation placed the number of potential retail outlets in the United States in the mid-1920's at approximately 140,000. In

---

* Older mercantile men will remember the term, but no one so far has been able to furnish any explanation of its origin or meaning; all agree, however, that there was no connotation of anything dishonest. The writer has therefore come to the conclusion that "Racket" must therefore refer to a supposed high level of noise in these establishments. Inasmuch as the usual reference is to "Variety and Racket Stores," it is obvious that the two terms were not synonymous but that there was a definite distinction. Possibly the original distinction was between fully staffed stores (which in the early 1900's implied not only clerks but a cashier and, in the absence of an overhead conveyer system for making change, a cash boy or boys), and small more or less one-man operations, by necessity and not intent early forms of semi-self-service stores, wherein the customers supposedly noisily picked over the pots and pans and crockery by themselves. Probably "Racket Store" was coined as a term of opprobrium for such establishments by the proprietors of more prepossessing variety stores, the implication being that a person of breeding would not care to patronize a noisy and improperly staffed shop.

addition, virtually every newspaper store, stationery store, school-supply and candy store, as well as many cigar stores, had their counter boxes of ten-cent cast-metal automobiles. Remnant brand-new Tootsietoy, Dinky Toy, and other makes of automobiles of this type from the 1930's have been found in surviving outlets by assiduous collectors as recently as 1967, and no doubt on occasion will continue to be found.

After brand-new specimens the model-car collector grades his choices as follows: "like new," "almost like new," "excellent," "very good," "good," "fair," "poor," and perhaps may include a terminal gradation of "good only for parts." Beyond the first two or three gradations, many collectors may well have their own ideas of what properly constitutes each grade. One collector's honest conception of "very good" might be another's "good" or even "fair," for example. However, the system is generally recognized as workable and, except for minor differences of opinion as to interpretation, acceptable to most hobbyists. As certain models or categories become more widely collected, there is a tendency among many collectors to upgrade the application of the various designations. Thus, a model that twenty years ago would probably have been rated as only "fair" may today appear to a majority as "good." Even such designations as "junk" or "good only for parts" may today seem less appropriate to many. A number of models that might once unquestionably have been designated by such terms may now well seem worthy of a proud place on a collector's display shelves. Today a really rare or desirable model would scarcely be labeled "good only for parts." No matter how battered, dented, scratched, or incomplete such a model may be, there undoubtedly would be a number of collectors who would be happy to add it to their collections, while still, of course, hoping eventually to replace it with a better specimen.

The model-car collector is, in fact, likely to find himself placed in somewhat of a dilemma as to the condition of models. Particularly when a collection is first getting under way, many collectors are prone to lean too far either in one direction or the other concerning condition. Some collectors set their sights unduly high, seeking to acquire only models in very fine condition; others go to the opposite extreme, and eagerly accept anything and everything, even the most common models in the poorest condition imaginable. There is much to be said for the theory that anything that comes one's way should be retained. So long as the collector who follows this latter policy bears in mind that models can often be found in good condition, he is no doubt on safe ground. But he should never be led into feeling that condition is not important, or he may very likely then fall victim to the dangerous concept that repainting and the widespread employment of replacement parts is acceptable or that his models should all, by such ministrations, be made to look as "new" as possible.

The great majority of old model automobiles that have survived are in relatively good condition. Multitudes of models in fine shape were discarded, but when old models were kept for any reason, one of the major considerations for doing so was that they were in fairly good condition and it seemed a shame to throw them out. If worn or broken, they were usually thrown out as soon as they ceased to have any value as playthings. Of course, in the case of many early die-cast model cars, there were a number of specimens that seemed perfect when they were put away years ago, but because they were made of contaminated metal, they deteriorated badly over the intervening decades. Nevertheless, it seems reasonably safe to assert that probably 90 percent or better of the old model cars that have survived are found today in comparatively good shape. As far as pre–World War II specimens are concerned, the average knowledgeable collector will have some in relatively poor condition and some in unusually fine condition, but the bulk of any collection usually will run toward average good specimens, neither extremely good nor extremely poor, but just about in accord with the usual overall ratio in which old model cars as a whole are found.

As in the case of the collector who accepts almost anything, and exerts little or no effort to upgrade his specimens, the type of collector who sets his sights too high is also doomed to disappointment. All too often the beginner, particularly if he has had an early stroke of good fortune and secured some models in exceptionally fine condition, will repeatedly pass up specimens that most collectors would consider to be in quite good, or even better than just good, condition in a misguided effort to secure only models that are in new, like new, or other more or less optimum states of condition. In the course of pursuing such a policy, he will unquestionably pass up many opportunities that will never be repeated, and, regardless of how much time or money he may have available for his hobby, his collection will remain small, although choice. What the average collector continually endeavors to do is to upgrade the specimens he has whenever opportunity affords. A repainted specimen may be replaced by one in poor original condition; later, that in turn may be replaced by another in fair or good condition, and

Fig. 182. Two Barclay military models of the late 1930's, a slush-cast model at the left and a die-cast model at the right. Aside from two definite color variations (khaki and greenish), the truck at the left was produced both with and without the legend MADE U.S.A. cast in the side.
G. William Holland photograph

perhaps in time the latter will be replaced by one in very good condition, and so on. But arbitrarily to set for oneself unattainable standards is badly to restrict the growth of one's collection, and thereby the enjoyment that makes any hobby truly worthwhile. Lastly, the collector who unrealistically sets his sights too high as regards condition is also too prone to perform the ultimate heresy—repainting. All too often, failing to find sufficient old models in a condition that is new, like new, or almost like new, he feels he must try to make his poorer specimens look "new." He fools only himself, because most repaints, no matter how skillfully done, can be detected. It is now a long-established and well-accepted principle of toy and model collecting, including model cars, that a repaint, no matter how well done, is worth only about half as much as is the same model in the very poorest condition of original paint.

One further notation should be made here concerning the use of the terms "mint" or "proof." Obviously, these terms, if they have any valid meaning at all in connection with model cars, mean that any specimen so described is in a condition that is new or like new. However, it would be better not to use them at all. A number of model-car collectors, well aware of the importance of originality of finish, have curiously tended to adopt a usage wherein "mint" or "proof" mean not specifically "newness" (which, of course, automatically signifies original paint); rather, it is being synonymous with "original paint." This causes much misunderstanding and ill feeling, because the words are being improperly used. A model vehicle offered as "mint" or "proof" often turns out to be in very poor—although assuredly original condition—far removed from the condition of new or like new that the purchaser anticipates.

COMPLETENESS

The basic measurement of the condition of collectors' models relates to the state of their original finish. Naturally, if a given model is described as "fair" or "poor," such designations would indicate that the model is likely to have dents, bent parts, and other such defects. In describing a model that is badly afflicted with rust or some similar ravage, it is to be hoped that these conditions also will be specified.

There is also a secondary factor relating to condition, that of completeness. This refers to the model's original completeness and the need to specify any parts that have been replaced with reproductions. It must be obvious to any fair-minded individual that a model automobile can and should correctly be described, such as "like new, but one wheel missing," or "good, but one wheel missing," or "poor, one wheel missing," the "like new," "good," or "poor" indicating its over-all condition, with the reference to the missing wheel providing necessary information concerning completeness. Most model-car collectors quickly acquire the knack of properly describing their available duplicates or surplus items when exchanging or selling through the mail. Discrepancies and omissions usually are accidental, and any differences of opinion arising from them are as a rule amicably adjusted. To play it safe, it is always better to provide more detailed information than may actually be required. Whenever there is any doubt as to what description of general condition is most appropriate to a given specimen, select the lower designation. A collector who receives a model that has been described as "very good" but which he would rate only as "good" may well accept the specimen and say nothing about the matter, although making a mental note to be careful to allow for such discrepancies when dealing with the same source in the future. On the other hand, a collector who receives a model described to him as "good" which he finds "very good" is a happy and contented friend.

Of course, in all matters relating to descriptions of condition, allowances must at times be made for the fact that there is no universally accepted scale of definitions of descriptions relating

228

Fig. 183. To an enormous number of collectors, the contours of the Mack trucks of the 1920's are an eternal symbol of the apogee of truck design, and, ideally, what a powerful truck should look like. Macks were popular prototypes among model-vehicle manufacturers. The lines of the remembered Mack of a bygone day are perfectly caught in this 16-inch-long cast-iron Dent model.
Adam Pellicot, Jr.;
Walter Dreyer photograph

to model automobiles or to old toys and models in general. Thus, many individuals have their own personal and therefore variable conceptions of what should be meant by the different designations. This, however, has nothing whatsoever to do with accidentally or deliberately confusing condition with completeness.

The man who happens to run into an occasional collector whose personal frame of reference equates condition and completeness according to some arcane formula is likely to end up feeling much as he would during a dream wherein he is desperately bailing a leaky rowboat while the sharks circle around. Attempts to combine both condition and completeness are so obviously an entry into a *Through the Looking Glass* world that it naturally is quite incomprehensible to minds attuned to ordinary logic how anyone deliberately can adopt such a bizarre, inevitably grossly misleading, and patently ridiculous species of nomenclature.

At times collectors innocently misdescribe a specimen's completeness because they are unaware of exactly what a given model originally consisted, or overlook telltale clues that something is missing. The lack of a wheel from a model automobile would obviously make it incomplete. It could scarcely happen on a vehicle that originally had four wheels. Yet it is conceivable that the absence of one or more wheels could pass unnoticed on a model vehicle—and there were a few— that originally carried dual wheels. (Conversely, it is conceivable that a conscientious hobbyist might incorrectly describe a model such as the Tootsietoy truck variation illustrated in Fig. 178 as being incomplete and lacking wheels and axle, even though in this particular and rather unusual instance the seemingly "incomplete" model actually represents a "complete" specimen of an interesting authentic variation.) It is at times fairly easy, however, to overlook a missing top or windshield or spare wheel or some other component that originally was a separate part. In the case of some spare wheels they were originally deliberately

made detachable, and consequently frequently are separated from the vehicle and lost by the time it reaches the hands of a collector. Akin to this is the fact that at times additional fittings were progressively added to various models. The hobbyist should be aware of these developments, and be able to distinguish between cases where examples of similar models were made without these components. In such a case a proper description would note, for example, "model made without headlights." He should also know when the model was made with these parts that may be present ("model with headlights"), or a truly incomplete model that lacks some parts ("headlights missing"). Naturally, every collector cannot be expected to have at hand detailed information on the makeup of every model he may run across, either in the form of contemporary catalogs, pictures in books, or recollections of specimens actually seen. As a result a good many sins both of commission and omission innocently occur in describing models as to their completeness. These factors should be taken into consideration before too hastily condemning anyone for descriptive errors of this sort. Many dealers and novice collectors have no concept of the existence of variations and the depth to which serious hobbyists go in their studies and collecting activities concerning such things. If, for example, you are offered an old Buddy "L" truck that spans the period during which headlights and rubber tires were added but no reference is made to these accouterments in the description, and you already possess one type but not the other, it would be wise to write and seek clarification on these details. The model in question might prove to be a duplicate or it might turn out to be the variation you are seeking.

In old model vehicles the components most likely to be missing, if the unit originally was equipped with them, are rubber tires and separate parts such as the figures of drivers and passengers, ladders, and so on. Rubber tires often deteriorate over the years to the point where the tires simply break up. This certainly does not happen in every case, and old model automobiles going back to the turn of the century are still frequently found with the original rubber tires in relatively good condition. In the case of separate figures, more models probably are found with these missing than with them still in position if they are of the removable type. If the figures originally were permanently mounted, they are most likely still to be in place. The use of removable figures, or of figures of any type, was highly variable. In the case of at least some of the better-quality European toy automobiles, they often were sold as separate accessories to be purchased and added by the customer if desired. Such model vehicles are therefore not in any sense "incomplete" if there are no figures, although it might be said that they are "more complete" if such figures are present. Cheaper European models often had figures that were supplied with the vehicle itself, and if such models reveal holes, slots, or pins in the seats but have no figures with them, it can be safely assumed that the figures are missing and the models are therefore incomplete.

No pre–World War II American manufacturer ever offered figures as separate optional accessory items. American-made vehicles either came with figures as standard equipment—either permanently mounted or removable—or were supplied without figures.* In most cases when cars or trucks came with figures, this fact immediately is made apparent by the presence in one or more sets of slots (for stamped-metal figures) or holes (for cast-metal figures). Most of the Wilkins and Kingsbury vehicles reveal dual slots for each figure. A component that almost always is missing on old Wilkins and Kingsbury units is the steering wheel. This was a separate part with a hole that fit over the top of the steering column that was shouldered to receive it. A few cast-iron vehicles of the 1930's were made with removable figures that were contoured to fit into position without the use of pins on the figures and matching holes in the seat, as in the case of the driver and fireman on the

---

* In the late 1920's and early 1930's a German line of figures, each about six inches in height, were sold in the United States for use with the large steel trucks of the Buddy "L" type. These figures had jointed metal bodies that permitted them to be arranged in any desired pose, including sitting at a steering wheel; they had molded composition heads, hands, and feet, and were dressed in appropriate clothes actually made of cloth. The series comprised a fireman, a policeman, a hobo, and Mutt and Jeff. It is not certain whether these figures were especially created for use with the steel trucks or whether it was simply realized that they were ideally suited to this purpose. From the makeup of the series the latter seems most probable, although the fireman may have been added especially for use with model fire engines.

Hubley fire engine pictured in Fig. 93. For the most part, however, the use of figures on American models is revealed by the presence of slots or holes in the seat or seats, and in the main this is the only valid clue. There is no way of presenting any sort of hard-and-fast guide to the use of such figures according to the type of vehicle, although none of the large steel trucks of the 1920's and 1930's carried them. Generally their use was favored by manufacturers of friction models, larger cast-iron vehicles, and clockwork automobiles.

There are only a very few instances of removable figures on pre–World War II miniature cast-metal automobiles, and with only one possible exception all the presently known examples are of European manufacture. Probably the ultimate in models with separate figures among vehicles of this size is the Hill fire engine of the 1930's, pictured in Fig. 95, which carries a full complement of no less than six separate removable British firemen. To find anything to equal this galaxy of removable figures in quantity on a single vehicle it would probably be necessary to go to some of the fairly large-sized cast-iron fire and police patrols, at least insofar as pre–World War II model vehicles are concerned. Apropos of completeness and the very small model cars, it should be noted that in some cases among recent or current models, separate plastic figures or objects are included with such models, although the model cars themselves show no signs of provision for these units, as in the case of the seats of older models. The figures, in fact, often are not designed to sit in the cars themselves but may merely be essentially scenic accessories or adjuncts. Of course, in collecting such vehicles from the standpoint of the history of the model automobile, either at the time they are in production or at some future date when time has enhanced their interest, such extra figures and accessories will be necessary if the model is to be considered truly complete, just as are the figures supplied with a miniature vehicle made in the early 1900's. For example, although not included in the photographs reproduced in Fig. 152, both of the Studebaker Lark station wagons with sliding roofs shown in the center, the products of two different model manufacturers of the 1960's, include such adjuncts; the station wagon at the left, figures of a hunter and a dog, and the ambulance version at the right, a stretcher.

As remarked above, there is one known American pre–World War II miniature cast-metal model that included a separate removable figure, but perhaps it would be more accurate to say that there is one such model where the presence of a hole in the seat would seemingly give evidence that such a figure originally was supplied with it. The vehicle in question is one version of the Tootsietoy No. 23 racing car manufactured from 1926–1933 (and also, with rubber tires, as the No. 023 in 1933). This car has been found with a square hole in the seat, which was taken to indicate it originally came with a separate removable driver, and also in what generally is believed to be a later version, complete with a driver fitted with a square peg that matches the hole but with the bottom of the peg peened over so as to hold the figure permanently in place in the cockpit. The assumption is that so many of the loose drivers were lost when the cars were spread out in boxes or compartments on store counters that the figure was fastened permanently in place to obviate this.* It is possible that this is true, but there have been found no contemporary references to the feature of a separate driver as such, although from 1929 through 1933 the catalogs make much of the fact that the driver is painted a different color from the car. In the late 1920's Tootsietoy became very conscious of the added sales value of two-colored vehicles. Casting and painting the driver separately would have been the most economical mode of accomplishing this. It is quite probable that this was the only reason for the separate figure of the driver. The writer is very much inclined to believe that the specimens of the No. 23 racing car without the figure of the driver attached do not actually represent a separate early variation but merely are cars from which the figure subsequently either accidentally or deliberately was detached. It would be both easy and natural for many youthful owners to loosen the figure of the driver so that it could be removed and inserted at will; of course, almost invariably it became lost.

On the other hand there may still be two major variations of the No. 23. The writer feels extreme reluctance in suggesting the possible existence of a variation of which no specimen or other positive confirmatory evidence currently is known to him to have been found. All too often such a supposition results in placing an error in the permanency of print and setting collectors on a long search for a model that does not exist. With all due regard for what experience has taught of the dangers that surround such a situation, it seems

proper to note that the writer has a very strong suspicion amounting almost to a conviction that there were indeed two major variations of the No. 23 but that the first version was not the supposed one with a removable driver mentioned in the preceding paragraph, but, rather, one in which the figure of the driver instead of being a separate casting was cast integrally with the body of the racing car itself.† This type of No. 23 would have been manufactured in 1926, 1927, and possibly

---

* It may strike readers that a similar problem of frequent loss of separate components would occur on store counters in the case of the three ladders with which the No. 4652 hook and ladder or the ladders supplied with subsequent Tootsietoy hook and ladders. In the case of the hook and ladders, however, these were shipped from the factory with the ladders held to the vehicles with rubber bands and were put out on the store counters in this condition.

† The writer has several reasons for this supposition, some of which in themselves would not be of sufficient weight to be of any real importance. There are, however, two main reasons that suggest an integrally cast driver on the early Tootsietoy productions. One is the fact that there is no reference to the later definitely heralded feature of the driver being a different color than the car either in the Dowst 1926 catalog supplement when the No. 23 was introduced (Fig. 215), or in jobbers' catalog listings in 1927 or 1928. In fact, there is a definite implication that the entire vehicle is painted in one color inasmuch as specific reference is made in the description of the No. 4650 biplane introduced on the same page of the 1926 supplement to the fact that the wings are one color and the fuselage another; the copywriter obviously was aware of the importance of mentioning a two-color construction. (Of course, the decision to use a separate driver casting painted in a second color might have been made after the catalog supplement was printed and the sample shown, but before any actual production was undertaken.) The foregoing in itself would still not be sufficient to convince the writer, but there is, second, the material relating to the Dowst-Pressman legal action of 1927 in which the Tootsietoy No. 23 was one of the model cars that figured. There is no reference in any of the papers pertaining to this matter *to the effect that the Tootsietoy No. 23 and Pressman No. 114 were anything but virtually identical in appearance and construction.* In claiming that the latter was a copy of the former, it is conceivable that Dowst would have deemed it best not to make any reference to this point. However, had the Tootsietoy racing car so obviously differed from the Pressman vehicle in having a separately cast and painted figure of the driver, it would seem that this point unquestionably would have been brought out by Pressman's excellent attorney, J. George Silberstein, to bolster their contention that their model was not a copy of the Dowst and could not be mistaken for it. In the case of the Pressman No. 116 Ford Model-T touring car, this was precisely the argument successfully used by Mr. Silberstein; that, as reported by the Dowst attorney to Ted Dowst, the Pressman No. 116 was "so different that it could not be confused with yours" (the Tootsietoy No. 4570). Here, in fact, the major point of difference between the two Fords was that there were no figures in the Tootsietoy model, while the Pressman model carried the nonremovable integrally cast figures of a driver and a passenger. Inasmuch as nothing was said regarding any difference in the casting or painting of the driver, it seems reasonable to believe that both the Pressman No. 114 and the then current version of the Tootsietoy No. 23 were made with integrally cast drivers. Pressman was able to sustain their claim that their No. 114 was not a copy of the Tootsietoy No. 23 but that both were derived from an earlier miniature cast-metal racing car.

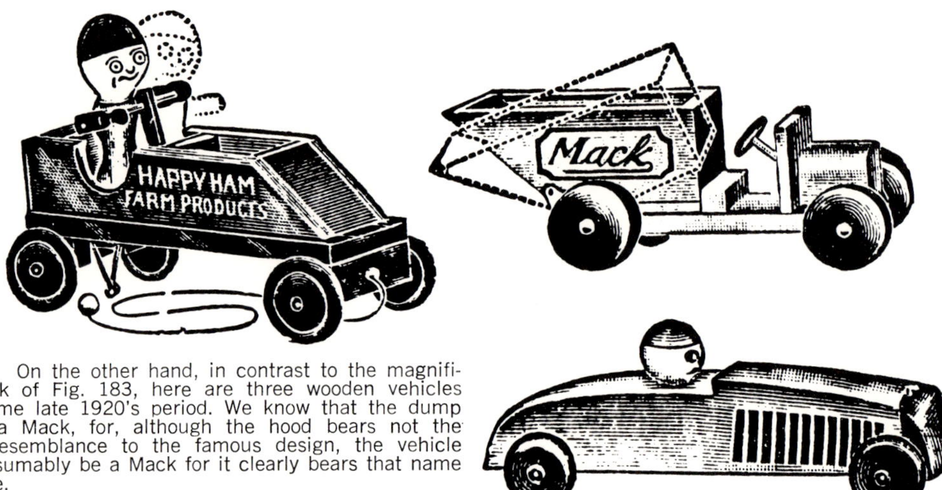

Fig. 184. On the other hand, in contrast to the magnificent Mack of Fig. 183, here are three wooden vehicles of the same late 1920's period. We know that the dump truck is a Mack, for, although the hood bears not the faintest resemblance to the famous design, the vehicle must presumably be a Mack for it clearly bears that name on its side.

A. E. Moredock

1928. Around 1928, at the time when Tootsietoy was paying particular attention to the appreciation and realization of the enormous sales values inherent in two-color vehicles, the No. 23 would have been redesigned with a separately cast and painted figure of the driver, assuming the supposition advanced here is correct.

Be this particular point as it may, it is safe to take the presence of holes or slots in the seats of miniature automotive vehicles as an indication that such models did originally come equipped with miniature human figures, usually designed to be freely removable but perhaps in a few cases designed to be permanently affixed to the seats, although in virtually all such cases fairly readily detachable if anyone were so minded.

Another important area of removable parts on model vehicles is that of the ladders on fire engines. This is somewhat more difficult to ascertain as to the number originally provided on a given model, as, unlike the holes or slots in the seats for figures, the vehicles themselves seldom if ever furnish a definite clue as to the original equipment. Usually the problem is one of missing ladders, although occasionally a model may come into the hands of a model-car collector that previously had been owned by a fire-engine buff who has furnished it with a number of ladders, either of varied but originally mass-produced types or homemade, that would be approximately correct for a prototype but which from the standpoint of toy or model original equipment amounts to a surfeit. The model-car collector naturally wants his specimens to be equipped with no more and no less than the number of ladders originally supplied with the vehicle by the manufacturer when it was new, and also, most importantly, that the ladders be the

authentic types. As a general rule, it may safely be assumed that in the case of any model vehicle representing an American hook and ladder, regardless of type and the material of which it is made, unless a comparatively small and inexpensive model in which ladders were made an integral part of the construction the truck originally carried at least two separate ladders, possibly three, or even more.

Sometimes the configuration of the vehicle itself will provide a definite clue as to the number of original ladders that should be present for completeness. This is not always certain, however, for on occasion an extension ladder that originally was fixed on the vehicle will be missing, and the collector may assume that its position was occupied by a separate ladder. At still other times separate but double ladders may have been furnished, although the ladder mounting brackets give no indication of this fact. In time the interested collector usually does become familiar with the various types of ladders—whether of wood, cast iron, or stamped metal—made and used by the different manufacturers, and can recognize them by make and period so as to be able to look for and eventually acquire the authentic ladders needed to complete a given vehicle. There are no hard-and-fast rules for these matters except to note that the large steel trucks of the type made by Buddy "L," Keystone, Structo, and so on, always came with stamped-metal ladders of heavy-gauge steel more or less complementing the material of the trucks themselves. Also, when wooden ladders were supplied with toy fire engines, as was the case with most of the Wilkins and Kingsbury clockwork-powered vehicles, and some other models, the rungs were always of metal, usually wire stock. If the collector secures a fire engine with wooden ladders with wooden rungs, he can safely take it that they are the work of a fire-engine buff. It should also be pointed out that it is quite common for dealers, and, regrettably, even at times some collectors, to replace the missing ladders on a truck with any ladders that may be at hand, including the ladders from modern toys, and fail to point out this substitution. A fire truck "complete with ladders" should, of course, mean not merely that it has ladders or even that it has ladders to the proper number, but that it has the original ladders, or at least that missing ladders have been replaced with duplicates of the authentic original type. Because ladders were so frequently lost, the value of any model fire engine that originally was equipped with separate ladders naturally is materially enhanced if it has the original ladders or authentic replacements.

In assigning designations to various types of fire engines, toy manufacturers often did not too closely follow precise prototype nomenclature, thus confusing anyone not versed in all its nuances. Many, perhaps most, people are prone to call any piece of fire apparatus a "fire engine" or a "fire truck," and any unit that prominently carries ladders usually will be termed a "hook and ladder" or a "ladder truck" as somewhat distinguishing options to the first two names. The nomenclature of the manufacturers of miniature trucks often reflected a similar lack of precision and certainty. Space does not permit a detailed discussion of this matter here. Suffice it to say that the model-car collector should be cautious regarding descriptions of miniature fire apparatus both in offering and in securing equipment by mail. One man's "fire truck" may be another man's "fire engine" and a third man's "hook and ladder," and all three may well be identical or just as readily they may be three entirely different vehicles. This is also true of the designations applied by the various original manufacturers, and owing to the relative paucity of catalogs of old model automobiles, the proper original designations may often be difficult or even impossible to come by. Apropos of this general situation, as well as that of the presence of original ladders, it should be observed that Keystone water towers, or, as they initially particularized them, water pump towers, and fire towers also carried short removable ladders mounted on their sides; Buddy "L" and Sturditoy water towers did not carry ladders.* The original distinction in the

1920's between a Keystone water pump tower and a fire tower was that the former actually was arranged to pump water through the tower nozzles, while the latter type of vehicle was merely a dummy water tower, although as if it really was a compensation, the catalogs observed that the fire towers possessed "a larger space in the body of the truck in which to put articles." In the 1930's, however, the Keystone fire towers were manufactured to pump water, and the distinction between a water tower and a fire tower was simply that the difference between the two vehicles was basically that the water towers were somewhat larger, more detailed, and more prepossessing vehicles.†

The proper equipment of one well-known steel vehicle, the Buddy "L" No. 205 fire truck, should specifically be enumerated, for not only is this one of the most frequently found models but also one concerning which in particular there has been much confusion and misunderstanding. This was an extremely popular model in the 1920's and early 1930's, and consequently a good many today

---

a definite voice and those when he was simply presented with an article that had been selected without his prior knowledge.) In the case of the Buddy "L" vehicles of the 1920's and 1930's, the aerial ladder and water tower rose from their base toward the front of the truck, just behind the driver's seat, as in typical American practice; so too did the Kelmet and the largest Kingsbury aerial ladders. The Keystone aerial ladders and water and fire towers, and the Sturditoy towers rose from the rear of these vehicles, and these designs constituted a great source of controversy and discussion among boys who regarded them as odd and alien. There were a few prototype water towers that were mounted at the rear of the truck; but in the main, pre–World War II American practice was to mount aerial ladders and water towers at the front, and these were the only types most boys ever saw. As a result, there was much fierce debate between owners of Buddy "L" trucks and those who possessed Keystone and Sturditoy vehicles over the relative realism and merits of their respective designs, and although no young owner of a rear-mounted aerial ladder or tower would admit to any dissatisfaction with their arrangements, this point played a definite part in sustaining the fame and popularity the Buddy "L" vehicles enjoyed. This does not mean that there were not individual vehicles of other makes that contemporary boys considered superior; among boys who were aware of its existence, for example, it was generally agreed that the Sturditoy American La France pumper was the best and most realistic of all the steel fire engines.

† Initially, in the 1920's, the Keystone No. 56 water pump tower (Fig. 200) and the No. 59 fire tower were substantially the same vehicle, except for the body compartment and the omission of the tank and pumping mechanism on the No. 59, with the same elaborately detailed 41-inch-high tower. In the later 1930's the No. 56A remained much the same as the No. 56, with the same 41-inch tower. However, the new No. 942 fire tower with working pumping mechanism carried a new ten-inch-shorter and rather stark tower without a controllable nozzle and other details.

---

* It is important never to underestimate the influence of the concepts and prejudices of contemporary children in the degree of favor accorded a model, or even, thereby, a complete line. (One must, of course, distinguish between purchases made wherein a child had

come into the hands of collectors. (It should not be confused with subsequently introduced Buddy "L" fire apparatus, all of which carried the basic number 205, but followed by identifying letters: 205A, 205AB, 205B, and so on.) All the No. 205's were originally equipped with four three-foot ladder sections and with a removable crane. The latter was intended to be employed to convert the vehicle into a wrecking truck by removing the ladders and inserting the crane. Much of the confusion regarding the No. 205 has been due to the fact that the earliest illustrations did not show the crane. After the crane had been abandoned many toy dealers and jobbers continued to use old cuts that did include the crane, and the manufacturer's stock cuts pictured the ladders mounted on the truck overlapping in such a manner that it was not clear how many ladder sections were mounted on each side. Finally, the catalog descriptions themselves in regard to the ladders seem confusing also at times. There initially were *four* ladder sections, which, when combined, formed a six-foot ladder, but the manufacturer counted the four sections initially as constituting *two* extension ladders. From 1928 on, the crane was abandoned and the truck supplied with *two* ladder sections, *one* on each side of the body. It is not impossible that some of the confusion regarding this vehicle was deliberately instigated or at least abetted by individuals with incomplete specimens who endeavored to pass them along to others as "complete," sometimes as the "early model without the crane." But there is no early model without a crane. Those not supplied with a crane are later models dating from about 1928. To be truly complete, a Buddy "L" No. 205 made prior to 1928 should have the crane and four ladder sections, its twenty feet of sash-cord "hose" with brass nozzle (which also carries over to later models), and, like all Buddy "L" trucks of the day, with the possible exception of the little Ford Model T's, its long loop of sash cord attached to the front for use in pulling the truck. The latter accouterment is in most cases missing today, owing to deterioration, accidental loss, or deliberate removal; a number of boys took them off themselves because they felt that the draw cord detracted from a vehicle's realism.

It always pays to be careful in ascertaining from old catalog illustrations and descriptions the original ladder equipment of any fire truck, for in instances other than the aforementioned Buddy "L" No. 205, ladder sections are shown overlapped or the manufacturers were seemingly inconsistent in their descriptions and especially in their outlook on what constituted an extension ladder or a ladder section. Thus, while Buddy "L" said their No. 205 truck came with *two* extension ladders, Keystone cataloged their more or less corresponding No. 49 fire truck as being furnished with *four* extension ladders. Yet actually both vehicles were supplied with four ladder sections of approximately the same length, any two of which when carried overlapped on the truck or used together as a continuous ladder formed a single "extension ladder." Keystone, in fact, complicated matters by at times showing a single ladder section thrown down on the ground in front of a fire truck in their catalogs and in the stock cuts furnished jobbers and dealers for use in their own catalogs, as shown in Fig. 200, so that upon cursory examination it has proved difficult for many hobbyists satisfactorily to determine how many ladder sections actually were supplied with the vehicle.

Nor is the number of ladder brackets on a truck any certain indication of how many ladders were carried in each position, for there may have been single or double sections. A rough rule of thumb, at least as far as the steel trucks of the 1920's are concerned, can only be one that is based on the seeming relative original retail price of the vehicle as well as its type. If the truck was a lower-priced model, or if side ladders were carried only as auxiliaries to an aerial ladder or a water tower, there probably was only a single ladder section on each side. But if the vehicle was somewhat more prepossessing and expensive, there probably were two ladder sections carried on each side. However, the Kelmet No. 504 fire engine, one of the most beautiful and realistic of all such vehicles, carried ladders only on one side, and a hose on the other. The Sturditoy No. 250/7 American La France working pumper (Fig. 209), a highly regarded model, was the only large steel fire engine that, while from a prototypical standpoint it might be expected to carry a ladder, was not furnished with a ladder at any time during its production as far as can be ascertained. Curiously, Sturditoy never made any fire truck with a ladder, their two pieces of apparatus being the No. 250/7 pumper and No. 250/9 water tower. The omission seems strange, and any really devoted young Sturditoy enthusiast who desired a ladder for his miniature fire department, much less a complete ladder truck, had to turn to the line of another steel toy manufacturer to obtain it. Presumably Sturditoy felt that the market was already too glutted with ladder trucks to warrant their producing one, although the omission of a ladder from their otherwise extraordinarily realistic and detailed No. 250/7 seems inexplicable, the more so because what with the cost of all the other tooling necessary for this vehicle, the dies for a ladder

Fig. 185. Notwithstanding the levity of the preceding caption, the famous old Mack design was no laughing matter to its admirers in the 1920's, nor is it to its countless aficionados today. Here it is in cast iron in two slightly different versions by Arcade, and in stamped steel as a hook and ladder by Turner (*Lloyd W. Ralston*), and as a dump truck by Chein (*Joseph N. Imler*).

would appear to have represented a nominal additional outlay.

In the more than four decades since the Sturditoy No. 250/7, which they designated as a "Chemical pumper," appeared, the absence of a ladder has represented a continuing mystery of almost Conan Doyle proportions among model-automobile enthusiasts. Numerous explanations have been proffered for the lack of so obvious and vital a piece of equipment which it seems safe to say was carried on every piece of American fire apparatus of its era with the exception of chiefs' cars and steam pumpers. The Sturditoy No. 250/7 appears to have been copied from an American La France vehicle of the type designated as a Combination Chemical and Hose Car with Junior Pump, which included as standard equipment a twenty-foot extension ladder and a twelve-foot roof ladder.* It has been suggested that the Fire Department of Pawtucket, Rhode Island, where the Sturditoy factory was located, possessed one of these vehicles, and at the time it was examined by the Sturditoy designers the ladders happened for some reason to be dismounted, but it seems in-

---

* A reproduction of an American La France catalog page picturing and describing the prototype appears in *100 Years of America's Fire Fighting Apparatus* by Phil Da Costa, Bonanza Books, New York. This book is an excellent source for model-car collectors seeking information on prototype automotive fire-engine designs.

credible that even if this were so, ladders would not be thought of by everyone concerned. Also, from their use of the American La France name and insignia on their models, it is evident that Sturditoy must have been in direct communication with the maker of the real thing and must have been supplied with a number of actual photographs or at least the catalog illustration. That the model was, indeed, designed from photographs and not from an actual vehicle is confirmed by the fact that the model has both a hose reel *and* a vestigial hose basket. On the Sturditoy model the latter is simply an upward extension, open at the back around the front half of the main hose compartment. This indicates the model was largely designed from side-view photographs of the prototype by men seemingly unaware of the actual function and construction of this appurtenance.

Actual full-size fire engines carried either a hose basket or a hose reel for the small-diameter hose attached to the chemical tank, usually a basket for 3/4-inch hose, of which 200 feet customarily would be carried, or a reel for a hose 1-inch in diameter, of which the usual length was 400 feet, although variations in this equipment and practice might at times be called for by the chief of the department or the purchasing committee. But *both* a hose basket and a hose reel seemingly would never be carried on the same truck. (Some ladder trucks carried baskets for either or both chemical hose and other equipment, and conceivably there may have been ladder trucks that carried a reel for chemical hose and a basket for general stowage, but not any pumpers or chemical trucks as such.) Probably American La France supplied Sturditoy with a number of illustrations of different vehicles, some fitted with hose baskets and others with hose reels, and Sturditoy more or less created a composite design including both features, the working reel being most practical for an actual miniature rubber hose, and the representation of the basket being included, as noted, under some sort of a misapprehension. The small-diameter chemical hose, carried in a basket or on a reel, should not, of course, be confused with the regular larger-diameter water hose used by pumpers, which was carried in the main hose compartment, or hose body as it usually was called by firemen, or pumpers and hose cars (or hose carts or hose wagons, if you prefer). And, of course, the even larger-diameter suction hose, employed to connect the pump with a hydrant or body of water, always was carried slung outside the truck body.

It also has been suggested that no ladder was included on the Sturditoy No. 250/7 because at the time Buddy "L" and Keystone were in some sort of contention over patents pertaining to the design of miniature steel extension ladders, but there is nothing to support this. Each steel truck manufacturer managed to create his own mode of locking together two or more ladder sections to form a longer ladder, and Sturditoy no doubt could have done the same, or simply included plain ladder sections if need be. However, in reviewing this perplexing situation again in recent years, the writer has come to the conclusion that there can be one partially logical explanation: At the same time that Sturditoy designed and tooled up the pumper, they also planned to bring out a separate ladder truck of some type, and reasoned that the inclusion of a ladder or ladders on the working-model pumper would to some extent serve to impede the sale of a companion ladder truck. However, the ladder truck was never put into production, presumably owing to the aforementioned plethora of ladder trucks being produced by other steel truck manufacturers. It must be admitted that this is a somewhat speculative and by no means authoritative or definitive answer to what may very well be the most puzzling conundrum in model automobile history.

The much-admired Sturditoy No. 250/7 pumper also had a rather curious effect on the recollections of prototype fire-engine design in the 1920's on the part of those who were boys at the time and who assumed that, except for the matter of the ladder, this model showed an extraordinary degree of fidelity to the prototype, a conception that in the main must be granted to have been correct. However, as a result of one point in its design, questions frequently arise concerning the tanks on real fire engines of the period. Fortunately, unlike the matter of the ladder, these questions can be answered precisely. Because of the Sturditoy design, older hobbyists insist that most fire engines, or at least all American La France pumpers of the 1920's, carried dual chemical tanks behind the driver's seat. Actually, what Sturditoy did on their model was to represent what on the prototype were two tanks entirely different in size and finish as what appears to be a pair of related tanks of identical diameter. (On the Sturditoy model the dual tank assembly actually contains the working hand-cranked pump, the tank which was filled with water preliminary to pumping being concealed within the body of the miniature.) On the prototype, and on most fire engines of the day, there was a single gasoline tank mounted either directly behind the driver or farther back. The gasoline tanks used by American La France and some other engine manufacturers had round ends; certain other makes employed tanks with oval ends. In all cases the gasoline tanks were painted the same color as the engine body, usually the traditional red, of course, although a surprising, though still small, number of American communities have regularly painted their fire engines white. The chemical tanks were somewhat larger, although in many cases not radically so, and were never painted; instead, they were nickel-plated, and might be carried in a number of varying positions on a vehicle. On some American La France engines, including the prototype of the Sturditoy No. 250/7, the single chemical tank was mounted directly behind the gasoline tank, giving the appearance upon a cursory first glance of a pair of matched tanks. This effect was, as it were, stabilized in design of the Sturditoy model, the seemingly dual tank assembly being painted red to match the rest of the truck.

Apropos of the foregoing notation on color, a survey of old toy fire engines reveals a surprising range. By far the great majority were, of course, red, as would be expected, but a few were white, and some were other colors, including the yellow used on certain Dayton Friction Toy Company ladder trucks. Most startling from the prototypal standpoint is the fact that blue was employed as widely as it was for toy fire vehicles in the first decades of the twentieth century. It seems most probable that this curiously colored toy fire apparatus represented more the manufacturers' ideal of varying colors for greater sales appeal on toy counters than attempts specifically to emulate the finish of any prototype. Following World War II, a very creditable hook and ladder was manufactured in molded plastic, with the components all manufactured in both red and in white, and parts then drawn from each color run to be combined in individual vehicles. That is, these were available with a red body and white aerial ladder and small trim, or with a white body and a red ladder and trim. Collectors are cautioned that at the time of its production a number of model railroaders purchased two or more of these vehicles in order to secure sufficient parts to make up all-red or all-white hook and ladders but that the authentic models as manufactured all combined both red and white moldings in a single truck. There were other plastic fire engines at the time that combined red and white or near-white moldings, but these always did so on a consistent basis, for every truck that was produced had a red body with ladders and trim in the second color.

Lastly, concerning ladders, note that a model fire engine may originally have been supplied with a ladder, but the structure of the truck itself provides absolutely no clue whatsoever to this fact in the form of ladder mounting brackets or other evidence. The Kenton cast-iron fire engine, shown to the right of its companion steam pumper in one of the photographs included in Fig. 168, is one such vehicle. It came boxed with the single cast-iron ladder intended to be carried inside the body, as shown in the photograph.

The subject of the completeness of model automobiles relates strongly to two other important matters. First, the potential sources of information that, in the absence of clues to obvious missing parts such as holes or slots in seats, or empty ladder-mounting brackets, can aid a collector in ascertaining just what may be missing from a given unit. This is taken up immediately following. The second is the matter of the hobby's outlook on and acceptance of reproduction parts as substitutes for missing pieces as alternatives to authentic replacements. In turn this leads to various other aspects of collecting model cars, some of them of necessity compelling even the most sanguine hobbyist to take, if only for his own self protection, a hard look at the other side of the model car collecting coin and seeing revealed thereon at least some rather dismal and less entrancing aspects of the game.

CATALOGS AND OTHER PRINTED MATERIAL

Obviously, for securing information concerning exactly what equipment and accouterments a model automobile originally carried, old catalogs are the best source of all. This is not to say that catalogs are infallible, for they must be read and interpreted with care. As already seen in discussing the matter of ladders, they may even at times be confusing or seemingly contradictory. A search for nonexistent variations may be inspired by the use of handmade samples rather than production models for illustrations, or merely by the particular retouching of a given picture; old cuts may be retained in use even after a model itself is modified, colors or color specifications may not always be accurate or at least current, and so on. Though actual errors may have occurred and passed unnoticed without doing any material harm at the time, they serve today to confuse the collectors that scrutinize them. For example, in the Hubley 1941 catalog, it will be observed that the cuts of the No. 472 die-cast fire engine on page 2 and the No. 528 cast-iron fire engine on page 5 obviously have been transposed, although the companion hook-and-ladder cuts are correct. The two engines, although the cast-iron model is four inches longer than the die-cast unit, were generally quite similar in appearance, although differing in some details and proportions; the printer evidently picked up the wrong cuts, and the error passed unnoticed in the proofreading. Another error occurs on one of the pages of the Kingsbury catalog of the early 1930's reproduced in Fig. 201. A slightly different description of the No. 362 dump truck is printed twice, but no description or catalog number—the latter a point of extreme interest to model-car collectors—is included for the covered truck in the center of the page. What occurred seems manifest; the revised copy and the small sketch of the No. 362 in dumping position were to replace the original copy for this toy at the lower right. Instead the copy for the covered truck at the left center was mistakenly knocked out and replaced by the sketch and new copy for the No. 362. The correct number for the covered truck is 360.

In short, at the time they were issued, catalogs were simply sales tools, made as accurate and as conducive to their purpose as possible, but also at times made up in haste and under pressure to have them ready for use in time for the forthcoming Toy Fair. They must be regarded and intelligently used for what they actually are; not looked upon as some sort of infal-

Fig. 186. Here are three small—about 8-inch-long—Chein lithographed stamped-metal pull-toy Macks, including two moving vans with most interesting decorations; one HERCULES, the trade name of the Chein steel truck line, an example of which is shown in Fig. 185, and the other reproducing "The Spirit of '76."

C. W. Frey

lible documentary evidence from on high. In fact most model car collectors, being devoted—but not to the point of being ridiculous—students of their subject, generally abhor and eschew ponderous and unappropriate references to their research and research materials. After all, the investigation of, say, Buddy "L" trucks, or Tootsietoys, or some similar specialty can hardly be equated to practical or historical matters that obviously are far more weighty. Only with a proper appreciation of this fact and guided by an appropriate sense of proportion can old model car catalogs and other printed material properly be employed and enjoyed.

A great deal of the interest in and use of old catalogs and reproductions of old catalogs or pages is as much nostalgic as investigatory.

Old catalogs thus have a value—and often a not insubstantial one—to collectors not only because of the pure factual material that can be recovered from them but also because it is simply fascinating to leaf through the literature employed some decades previous to describe and merchandise now collected models at the time they were in current production.

Yet while the rarity of old model automotive vehicle catalogs can be overestimated, it is equally faulty to underestimate it. The reason is that for the most part, prior to World War II, the catalogs and other literature put out by model automobile manufacturers was not designed for distribution to the ultimate potential consumers, but only for the use of the trade. The quantities printed, therefore, were infinitely smaller than those of the familiar and now widely collected toy train catalogs, which were printed and circulated in immense quantities each year. As a matter of fact, although they are by no means easily come by, and command fair and valid prices when available, such train catalogs as also included model automobiles are, in the main, the form of model-automobile catalogs easiest for the model-car collector to locate. The exposition of this fact is perhaps the greatest service that this book could perform for the model-car collector seeking catalogs: The American Flyer Manufacturing Company was for a number of years the distributors of Structo trucks. Consequently, American Flyer train catalogs from about the mid-1920's to the mid-1930's contain one or more pages illustrating and describing Structo trucks and related toys —if not the complete Structo line each year, at least of some of it. From their inception in 1933 through the 1936 issue, the complete line of Dinky Toy automobiles was included (and pictured in full color from 1934 through 1936) in the large British Hornby train catalogs, as well as in a number of other catalogs and folders put out by both the British and French companies. Even after 1936, and until after World War II, the full Dinky Toy line usually is found included in the smaller black-and-white condensed or pocket-edition catalogs of Hornby trains and other Meccano products.

The pre–World War II consumer catalogs or catalog folders issued by such continental European manufacturers as Bing, Bub, JEP, and Maerklin also customarily include their model automobile lines. All these catalogs have long been collected by toy-train collectors, and duplicates sometimes may be secured from such hobbyists, while numerous copies still remain in existence in attics and other odd spots awaiting discovery. Model-car collectors should, however, be cautioned about one type of literature in this connection that may be offered them and erroneously described as catalogs. These often turn out to be track-diagram booklets put out by such German manufacturers as Bing, Carette, and Maerklin. They sometimes include from one or two to a substantial number of pages illustrating additional articles of model train equipment, and thus can be considered a form of catalog in this sense, but automobiles or other types of toys virtually never are included in this sort of literature. Occasionally in the early Maerklin track-diagram booklets one or two automobiles may be found pictured on a final page or two of representative general toys. However, it would be prudent for the model-car collector to check on the amount of automobile material, if any, that may be found in any old toy train catalog he may run across or be offered.

There were, to be sure, some consumer catalogs and other literature devoted to model automobiles issued by certain manufacturers prior to World War II, although most of their literature was prepared for the use of the trade only and in relatively small quantities. By far the majority of the great number of small stores that regularly sold toy automobiles never saw a manufacturer's catalog; they selected and ordered their stocks from the catalogs issued by toy or general merchandise jobbers, concerning which catalogs more in a moment. A few model-car manufacturers printed and distributed consumer literature in relatively large quantities in the 1920's and 1930's, but it is not possible to particularize to any great extent concerning this. Some catalogs and folders were advertised in various magazines and mailed to those requesting them; some were included packed with the model vehicles themselves, and some were designed for counter distribution in stores. As a general thing, the more costly and elaborate were the toys in a manufacturer's line, the more likilihood that some consumer literature was published, but the situation is at best somewhat spotty, and the mere fact that a manufacturer issued such material one year, or for several years running, does not by any means indicate that such literature was put out over any long, sustained period of time. Some manufacturers evidently abandoned the practice when the depression came, while others who had not previously attempted it thought that it would be a worthwhile sale stimulant under such conditions. Buddy "L" and Keystone put out consumer catalogs for a while in the 1920's and early 1930's. Among iron-toy manufacturers, Arcade issued some sheets as well as booklets dealing with the adventures

Fig. 187. Marx clockwork Mack trucks of the 1920's and early 1930's. Note that the dump truck in the photograph is, with the exception of the driver, painted, not lithographed. The wheel spokes are cut out, but the hood detail is lost without the lithography. The catalog drawing shows a similar dump truck as it looked in lithograph.

C. W. Frey

of the "Tiny Arcadians" who supposedly made their toys. Tootsietoy put out a few types of folders and booklets in the early 1930's, of which the 1932 booklet already remarked upon and pictured in Fig. 118, was probably the most widely distributed.* Kingsbury advertised and circulated some very attractive consumer catalogs of their clockwork-model vehicles in the late 1920's and

---

* It is an interesting point that although Tootsietoy on occasion in the 1920's advertised their dollshouse furniture in consumer magazines, so far no consumer advertisements for the automobiles have been brought to light. Presumably the reason was that the individual sales of miniature furniture, then sold only in sets retailing for fifty cents and a dollar, appeared to warrant the expenditure for such advertising, while the individual ten-cent automobiles—although also available in sets—did not.

239

early 1930's that probably also served in these years as their advance or trade catalogs as well. Most of the Wilkins and Kingsbury catalogs that are found today are earlier trade editions.

A few manufacturers' consumer catalogs of or including miniature automobiles actually appeared before 1920. There were, for example, the Structo catalog from which some pages are reproduced in Fig. 103 and as early as 1915, even before the Mysto Manufacturing Company became the A. C. Gilbert Company, the Gilbert clockwork automobiles were cataloged in the back of Mysto Erector instruction manuals. This is a point to be kept in mind; catalog listings for model automobiles on occasion will be found included in the instruction books or sheets for both distantly and closely related toys; for an instance of the latter see Fig. 210, where the firehouse is included on the instruction sheet for the Kingsbury No. 275 aerial ladder truck of the late 1930's. Actually, of course, any instruction sheet or manual for any sort of model automobile is a collectors' item in its own right. Any sort of construction-set instruction manual that includes plans for building any kind of automotive vehicle —and the sets need not necessarily be only those comprising metal parts—is a model automobile item. Most especially, however, is every Erector or American Meccano manual or parts list that includes any of the components originally made for the Kelmet White trucks. Indeed, probably the most readily obtainable of all model-automobile literature would be an Erector instruction manual of the late 1920's or 1930's that illustrates the employment of these parts in an Erector truck model.

It cannot be ascertained if every manufacturer of miniature automobiles issued trade catalogs or, if issued, at what intervals, for while many put out a catalog annually, at least a few are known to have carried over the same catalog, either with or without supplements, for a varying number of years. A safe assumption, however, is that almost every manufacturer of models selling for a fairly respectable price issued catalogs. The difficulty is in interpreting what, in the context of the times, constituted a "respectable price," but a safe pre–World War II figure would seem to be fifty cents a unit at retail. There were a few exceptions, but for the most part it would be reasonable to state that every manufacturer of clockwork automobiles, friction automobiles, cast-iron automobiles, steam automobiles, pressed-steel vehicles, juvenile automobiles, and similar merchandise had their catalogs. A substantial number survive in the hands of collectors

or are as yet undiscovered, but obviously the original quantities printed were by no means large and, unhappily, all too many recipients carefully weeded out and discarded the older issues when new ones appeared. A point of special interest to collectors of miniature cast-metal cars is what manufacturers of this type of merchandise issued catalogs. Assuredly some manufacturers—and not by any means only the smallest—did not find it incumbent upon themselves to put out any sort of literature. In some instances their entire output might be bought from samples by a few accounts, or in other cases a single jobber or so would have the exclusive distribution of their line, and in turn take care of any listings that might be required. Dowst, whose Tootsietoy line of course makes their literature of particular interest among collectors of miniature cast-metal vehicles, did not issue catalogs each year until 1925, but there were substantial and most attractive annual catalogs or supplements covering their line from 1925 onward.*

Barclay and Manoil are known to have issued pre–World War II literature, although the frequency and regularity of their emission is uncertain. Actually, there has been found to date only one piece of printed matter from each firm that includes automobiles from this period (Fig. 211), although there is additional Barclay material covering soldiers and other miniature figures. The Manoil sheet is obviously a second version, to which the words PATENT PENDING

---

* There does not appear to have been any 1942 Tootsietoy catalog, and there were no catalogs during subsequent World War II years. No new models were brought out in 1942, and any reference to a catalog required at that time could be accomplished by consulting the 1941 issue. The problem in 1942 was not of selling more merchandise but of equitably allotting such merchandise as might still be available. The writer has not yet seen or heard of Tootsietoy 1927 and 1928 catalogs or supplements, but it would seem rather certain that there must have been at least supplements describing the new models for these years, and most particularly for 1928, when so much was added to the line, including the General Motors series. Nor have catalogs or supplements yet been found for 1922, 1923, or 1924, although the bench mark introduction in 1922 of the Tootsietoy line of dolls-house furniture would seem to have made the appearance of at least some sort of supplement or folder mandatory at that time, and presumably such literature also would have included such new model automobiles as were introduced in the years it was issued. The 1921 catalog includes only three cars: the No. 4528 limousine, the No. 4570 Ford Model-T touring car, and the No. 4610 Ford Model-T truck. It is the present absence of any literature for 1922, 1923, and 1924 that is responsible to a large extent for the difficulty of pinpointing the years in which several model vehicles definitely were introduced in the early 1920's.

have been added with a typewriter, which raises and exemplifies an interesting bibliographical point that will be discussed shortly. Barclay had a supply of electrotypes of their miniature cast-metal cars and other vehicles of the 1930's, which they supplied to various jobbers for use in their own catalogs but at present it is uncertain—although it would seem rather likely, if these also were employed in comprehensive Barclay catalogs themselves during these years. That such catalogs were not always considered necessary by even the largest manufacturers is evidenced by the case of Erie. This company, who was one of the most substantial and important factors in the miniature cast-metal car field for several years in the mid-1930's, never issued any catalogs, according to Fred W. Ziesenheim, who, as the head of the endeavor, presumably would be in the best position to know. Pressman is known to have included their cars in at least one catalog, 1927, and it would seem reasonably likely, although not by any means necessarily certain in view of the situation that applied to Erie, that catalogs or sheets of some sort were put out by at least some of the other American manufacturers of the 1920's and 1930's. There always exists the chance that something will come to light originating with these or other manufacturers of this era; such a continuing hope and possibility naturally adds much to the zest of studying these matters and searching for historical materials.

On the other hand, as suggested, it is quite conceivable that a number of manufacturers never issued catalogs or lists, and this would appear most likely in the case of the majority of the small home-basement or kitchen-table type of operations that cast miniature cars from stock molds. Yet the Metal Cast Products Company, the chief supplier of such standard molds in the 1930's, continually emphasized that they could supply the purchasers of their molds with circulars making use of their cuts if desired. Inasmuch as merely having such literature imprinted with his name might well in itself make the user of the molds feel he truly was "in business," aside from any potential sales-promotion value such circulars might have, the proposition might well have seemed sufficiently alluring for at least some such manufacturers to have issued printed material of this type. Some examples may therefore eventually surface.

Regarding pre–World War II catalogs of European manufacturers of miniature cast-metal autos, relatively little can be said with assurance. Meccano, of course, always gave complete catalog coverage to the Dinky Toys produced by both the British and the French factories, although not in the same catalogs, the French factory always issuing its own literature. So, too, did Britain and Maerklin each include their miniature cast-metal cars in their regular complete catalogs; the Maerklin catalogs of the 1930's incidentally exist printed in a number of language versions for use in different countries. Catalogs of at least some other British manufacturers of the 1930's have survived as evidence of their existence. In all likelihood most of the more substantial of the manufacturers in France and Great Britain issued catalogs or sheets, although some may not necessarily have been annual affairs. In the case of the smaller manufacturers, the situation was in all probability very similar to that suggested in the preceding paragraph as applying in the United States during the same period, although the incidence, if any, of the use of stock molds in Europe is uncertain.

Departing from the consideration of catalogs relating only to miniature cast-metal cars and returning to the overall spectrum of toy-automobile manufacture, ranging from these miniatures to the largest and most imposing pressed-steel trucks and juvenile automobiles, one of the best sources of information available may be found in the catalogs issued by toy and general merchandise jobbers. These catalogs, on occasion large and imposing volumes running to hundreds of pages, often were printed in far larger quantities than the catalogs of the individual manufacturers themselves. The jobbers' catalogs circulated widely among storekeepers, who usually never received the manufacturers' catalogs. As a consequence they are more readily obtainable than manufacturers' catalogs, and are literally fountains of information and illustrations on all types of old model automobiles; a number of pages from such catalogs are reproduced herein. It is true that jobbers' catalogs do not always include all the models made by a manufacturer in a given year, and when available the manufacturers' own catalogs are naturally preferable sources of data. On the other hand, the jobbers' catalogs at times include exclusive lines or special models not to be found listed in manufacturers' catalogs. As a consequence, neither type of catalog actually is a complete substitute for the other but, rather, both must, if available, be employed in a wide-ranging plan of research.

The larger jobbing houses issued catalogs at varying intervals throughout the year, seasonal, midseasonal, bimonthly, and so on. Collectors should thus be forewarned that the great bulk of miniature automobiles of all types will be found

Fig. 188. Strauss may have also aimed for a Mack truck in the 1920's, but does not seem ever to have approached the realism of some of their competitors. Pictured here are an open-sided van and a log truck (*Robert A. Ahlers*) and a SPEEDWAGON. Strauss possibly was endeavoring to suggest a Mack truck in this clockwork series of the 1920's, as some hobbyists believe, although if things are to be approached from a prototypical standpoint, it must be noted that "Speedwagon" was a trademark of Reo. At any rate, here are four Strauss trucks, the first two from the collection of Robert A. Ahlers and the second pair from that of Joseph N. Imler.

in the catalogs put out in the fall of the year by the general merchandise jobbers, as well, of course, in any specialized toy-jobbing catalogs. Some spring and summer catalogs will be found to be devoid of toys, although in many cases these issues carry certain goods suitable for outdoor play such as juvenile automobiles and stamped-steel vehicles, as well as a sprinking of other types of more or less staple sellers. To avoid disappointment, a collector who cannot examine an offered catalog in person should ascertain not only its year but also its season of issue. Any fall issue of a large jobbing catalog, such as a copy of one of the "Our Drummer" catalogs of Butler Brothers, will provide a treasure trove for any model-car enthusiast. It is perhaps unfair to particularize, but the immense New York house of Butler Brothers was probably the dominant jobbing firm in the 1920's and 1930's, with branches in Chicago, Illinois; Dallas, Texas; Minneapolis, Minnesota; and St. Louis, Missouri. In the late 1920's they also acquired the Baltimore Bargain House, and from that point on their catalogs each year were virtually identical with Butler's. There were, however, many other jobbers large and small, all of whose catalogs are well worth securing.

Jobbers' catalogs generally assign their own numbers to the merchandise, although in many instances the manufacturer's catalog number also is given as an identifying reference in parentheses. In the case of well-known standard makes, the manufacturers' names usually are given, although this does not always hold true, and a little detective work may be necessary. Unnamed merchandise may represent a special or regular product of a well-known factory that cannot be identified owing to a special price deal. Unfamiliar names but possibly heralded as "famous" may indicate special proprietary brands and merchandise made under this name by a regular manufacturer of similar goods (sometimes recognizable by the knowledgeable collector) or specially fabricated for the jobber by a factory not otherwise engaged in making similar merchandise under their own name. "Oh Boy" was such a line of steel trucks controlled by George Borgfeldt & Company; "Sampson" was a line of related toys such as derricks and steam shovels, which may also have included trucks, controlled by Butler Brothers, and there was also at least one other proprietary line of steel trucks, controlled by the Rieman, Seabrey Company.

There remains one other general class of

catalog that the model-car collector is likely to encounter. These are the retail catalogs issued by large toy stores, department stores, chain stores, and catalog service houses, such as the "Billy and Ruth" catalogs that were distributed by and imprinted with the names of various local toy stores, as well as premium lists and catalogs, and mail-order catalogs of all types, ranging from the large Charles Williams Stores, Sears, Roebuck, and Montgomery Ward issues to all sorts of small circulars and folders. All these that include automobiles possess considerable interest, nostalgic value, and usefulness to model-car collectors but at a somewhat lesser level than do the catalogs of the manufacturers themselves or of jobbers. For one thing, retail catalogs seldom show anything approaching any manufacturer's full line for a season, but usually only a limited selection. For another, and of particular interest to collectors of miniature cast-metal cars, the economics of producing such catalogs and of selling merchandise from them almost invariably precluded the separate listing of five- and ten-cent toys. Thus, the hobbyist may at times find boxed sets of Tootsietoys included in such catalogs, but not (unlike jobbers' catalogs that frequently listed each item separately for sale by the dozen or by the gross) illustrations and listings of separate low-priced articles of this type. However, in connection with this, it should be pointed out that the Christmas toy catalogs issued by some chain stores, a practice evidently started only shortly before World War II, at times include groups of inexpensive toys of this sort with a general notation that they have available a wide assortment of such items selling for five or ten cents. Thus, in such catalogs will be found illustrations of a number of miniature cast-metal cars and other inexpensive automotive vehicles, often including some not known to have been pictured elsewhere. Such groups often provide valuable help in dating old models.

At times the retail catalogs make use of the manufacturers' own numbers, but in many instances numbers may be omitted altogether, or the store or mail-order house's own numbers are used. The latter practice understandably was necessary in the case of catalogs where thousands and thousands of items were being offered and the use of the manufacturers' numbers would have created endless duplication and confusion. For inexplicable reasons a few stores reversed or juggled the order of the numerals in manufacturers' numbers in order to provide their own catalog numbers; possibly the rationale was that if Sears, Roebuck and Montgomery Ward created their

own catalog numbers, then they too should do it so as to keep apace. Thus a Buddy "L" No. 205 fire truck may appear in such a catalog as the store's No. 502, or a Schieble No. 110 bus may become No. 011. There must have been some hair-tearing at the points where a manufacturer's number such as 1 or 2, or 22 or 44, was encountered, and in any case duplication of numbers was never eliminated by this practice, which would seem to have been the only possible logical reason for its use. Be that as it may, the astute collector usually can decipher most of it fairly rapidly and accurately with a little detective work.

Certain points already mentioned in discussing jobbers' catalogs also apply with retail mail-order catalogs. Sears, Roebuck and similar concerns usually issued two general catalogs each year, a fall-winter issue, and a spring-summer issue.* It is in the former that the bulk of toy listings invariably will be found. However, even prior to World War II, in a number of instances special Christmas catalogs also were issued by such firms, and in many cases these special catalogs contain a wider selection of toys, including miniature automobiles, than the general catalogs. On occasion there will be substantial differences and relatively little overlapping between the toys in the general fall-winter catalog and the special toy or Christmas catalog for the same year. Mail-order catalogs, like jobbers' catalogs, may also contain specials or proprietary brands. For example, Sears, Roebuck's brand for the Steelcraft trucks made by the Murray Ohio Manufacturing Company was Boycraft. As a general rule, a great many of the items found included in mail-order catalogs will not be identified by the brand or manufacturer's name. The manufacturers had to walk a tightrope warily in an effort to sell as much merchandise as possible and yet not create discontent among the smaller retailers. Hence proprietary brand names at times were employed.

---

* There also were regional issues of each, the type and assortment of goods of greatest interest to, say, Massachusetts, not being identical to that of interest in Wyoming. The writer has not had sufficient opportunity to compare regional issues to comment on this point as far as miniature automobiles are concerned. It may be that the toy content was substantially the same in all catalogs. However, the suggestion has been raised that, given the limited opportunities for personal Christmas shopping from a widely assorted stock in the less densely populated areas, the catalogs destined for these regions may have contained more toys than the others. It is an interesting but moot point. All that can be said at this time by way of advice to collectors is that any old twentieth-century fall-winter issue reasonably can be expected to contain a good assortment of toys, including automobiles.

The mail-order houses were able to take full advantage of their immense buying power and consequent ability to offer goods at figures lower than the regular list price without the manufacturer of the merchandise finding he was losing sales to local stores. In most cases this method worked out fairly well and happily for all concerned. For example, apart from the overall and continuing irritation and resentment felt by a local merchant against the inroads of mail-order competition, there was really little tangible he could put his finger on, assuming he did become aware of the circumstances, when Sears, Roebuck offered for $2 as a Boycraft truck the same miniature vehicle that carried a $2.50 price tag in his store under the Steelcraft name. And, presumably, if a customer did raise a point concerning this, the dealer could assert that the $2 truck that a prospective customer had seen only as a picture in a Sears, Roebuck catalog did look pretty much like the $2.50 truck in his store, but the latter was a much finer and sturdier article and well worth fifty cents more.

There is one classic example of a mail-order proprietary toy deal going badly astray, although at the time it was arranged it was considered one of the greatest coups in the history of the mail-order business, and in retrospect it appears incredible that it was not foreseen that there could be no outcome other than that which did happen. In 1929 Montgomery Ward accomplished the astounding feat of securing and publishing in their fall and winter catalog a statement from A. C. Gilbert that the modified special Erector sets they were selling that year under the name of Steel-Tech actually was better than Erector; that Steel-Tech was his "idea of a perfect Construction Set based upon my experience in building ERECTOR and noting various points where improvements are possible, and that if he were to build ERECTOR over it would be exactly as STEEL-TECH is made!" *

---

* Despite his natural affection for the name Erector, which he introduced in 1913 as Mysto Erector, his company at the time being named the Mysto Manufacturing Company, it is apparent that A. C. Gilbert subsequently was greatly attracted by the sales potential of the use of the word "steel" within the name of a construction set. He made use of it in the 1920's for at least three brands of construction sets that were merchandised parallel to Erector. These were Steel Builder, Steel Engineering, and Steel-Tech. A. C. Gilbert is known to have regarded the Ives construction sets, Struktiron, introduced at the same time as Erector, 1913, as both the best designed and most felicitously named of all construction sets, the latter partially at least because the name itself made it evident that the set furnished metal components, and this no doubt inspired his latter affinity for construction-set names that incorporated the word "steel."

There must have been a substantial initial order involved, although at a price low enough to provide Wards with a very satisfactory mark-up, but regardless of how large it may have been, A. C. Gilbert must have been too sagacious not to have foreseen the type, if not the extent, of the inevitable reaction in the trade. Actually, the chief difference between Steel-Tech and Erector was the elimination of the standard-width latticed Erector girder (but not the wide-latticed girder) and the substitution of a basic girder of similar width, and with similarly channeled edges to permit four strips being bolted together into a so-called square girder, but pierced only with holes. (The Erector square girder was, of course, never really a mathematical square, one dimension always being slightly greater than the other owing to the method of assembly, but visually it was close enough to a square to justify the famous designation.) The same Kelmet parts for the White truck, including the hood, fenders, and dump truck body, and for the steam shovel, appeared in the larger Steel-Tech sets as they did in the corresponding 1929 Erector sets, and in fact the set numbers were identical. Presumably the two brands were so obviously similar and Erector so familiar to the public that Steel-Tech could only be justified and made salable by some explanation along the lines of the statement quoted above. Not surprisingly, regular toy dealers from coast to coast who were stocking Erector were incensed by the appearance of this statement, and figuratively blew their tops.

The reader may naturally be moved to inquire as to just what Sears, Roebuck was doing at this point, their great competitor, Montgomery Ward, having Steel-Tech and A. C. Gilbert's all-too-bountiful testimonial. The answer is that in 1929 Sears, Roebuck had their own proprietary brand of Erector-based construction set, Trumodel. Except for the name, Trumodel was identical with Steel-Tech, and by a strange coincidence the sets bore the same numbers (which were also identical to the 1929 Erector set numbers), and sold for exactly the same odd prices of from $.89 to $13.67. Trumodel had its own testimonial from A. C. Gilbert, although by no means as fulsome as Steel-Tech's, and it was printed without the benefit of Mr. Gilbert's portrait. For the promotion of Trumodel (a trademark incidentally that Gilbert had used previously and would use again; it was by no means as exclusively Sears' as Steel-Tech was Ward's), A. C. Gilbert allowed himself to be quoted to the effect that "If I were to start over again I surely would incorporate all Trumodel ideas into Erector." This was not quite as bad as his plug for

Steel-Tech but it was bad enough, particularly in the year when the appearance of the fall and winter issues of the Sears and Ward catalogs and the stock-market crash were almost coincidental, and from the viewpoint of local toy merchants the Steel-Tech and Trumodel affairs could not possibly have occurred at a worse moment.

There was a sequel to all this, and in the eyes of many local toy dealers, just retribution fell upon A. C. Gilbert, and he did penance by losing business, or at least so it seemed to many a small merchant trying to keep afloat in the early 1930's. The merchants' hearts, therefore, forgivingly softened toward Gilbert when they saw that from 1930 to 1932 Gilbert evidently had lost the Sears, Roebuck construction-toy account, with Erector vanishing from the Sears' catalogs. Sears was, instead, selling Meccano. Accordingly the heart of many a former friend and retailer of Erector softened toward Gilbert, and they again stocked Erector, albeit with a heavy heart for the lost greater turnover they might have enjoyed in the prosperous late 1920's. The Sears Erector-Meccano gambit was in point of fact a magnificent ploy to regain goodwill and cover up a boner by casting oneself in the role of an underdog; most and perhaps all of the small merchants being of course quite unaware that since 1928, the A. C. Gilbert Company had also been the secret owners of the Meccano Company of America, Inc.! In fact, it may have been the need to assist in the financing of the Meccano deal that originally had impelled Gilbert into the complexities and special arrangements that accompanied the creation of the Steel-Tech and Trumodel deals.*

Of course, during the sustained depression —and in some cases even before—many manufacturers of toys, including lines of model automobiles and trucks, were forced to submit to the

listing of their products under their own names at slightly or in many cases greatly reduced prices in such catalogs in order to secure the highly desirable—and at that period often absolutely essential for their survival—mail-order business, even though they were fully aware that the effects on the sales of their products to local stores would be, to say the least, deleterious.

UNBRANDED AND PROPRIETARY MODELS

The question naturally arises as to under what circumstances the unbranded or proprietary branded miniature vehicles are collectible as distinct specimens. The answer must be that if the models themselves show no physical difference, such as the omission of a name or the substitution of another, or a properly authenticated distinction in color, if, in short, they are identical with the unit as regularly manufactured and sold, then there is no distinction to be made *except in instances where packaging also enters the picture,* a situation that will be discussed in a moment. On the other hand, far from merely constituting a variation, there obviously is an absolute distinction between a model vehicle marked "Steelcraft" and an otherwise identical one marked "Boycraft"; between a dump truck body marked "Erector" and the same body marked "Steel-Tech." (William D. Perry, long a close and important associate of A. C. Gilbert's, advises that he believes in most cases and perhaps invariably it will be found that the "Steel-Tech" or "Trumodel" labels were placed over existing "Erector" markings.) In any such instances the model-car collector will, of course, almost always want versions of *all* divergent specimens that make up a given pair or more extensive sequence. Having to make a choice between acquiring a model marked with the basic factory brand or one carrying the markings of a proprietary brand, a collector almost certainly would prefer to possess the specimen marked with the proprietary brand as presumably being the most desirable.

Sometimes, however, evidence that a model car was sold under a proprietary brand name exists only when the model itself and the original packing are available to the collector, whereupon original boxes take on an even more important meaning and greater value than ordinarily is the case. These conditions are particularly likely to be operative in the case of miniature cast-metal cars, where it frequently was impractical to apply special markings to the models themselves or to remove standard markings from

---

* It is, of course, possible that the modified form of Erector was sold in 1929 under still other additional brand names than Steel-Tech and Trumodel, in which case there would be additional versions of the dump-truck body to be collected. Also, although the writer is not aware that the possibility previously has been raised, and Mr. Perry's comment reported on this page would appear to preclude it, it is not entirely impossible that the dump-truck bodies were supplied in some proprietary brand sets without any markings at all, in which case the brand of a given body could be ascertained and authenticated only by a collector securing the entire boxed set with manual, or at least the original accompanying box or manual. In point of fact, the 1929 Sears and Ward catalogs do not show any name on their proprietary dump-truck bodies. This is not too significant, however, as in their 1928 catalogs, when both offered Erector, Sears shows the dump-truck body bearing a name and Wards shows it without any markings.

the dies. For example, as far as can be ascertained, the only way that the models sold as Playtoy vehicles can be distinguished from contemporary regulation Tootsietoys is when a collector finds the Playtoys in and secures them with the original box. As far as anyone can remember, the Playtoys were made in the regular Tootsietoy dies and consequently carried the Tootsietoy name underneath, and were not painted in any distinguishing colors. Certainly to date no specimen actually marked "Playtoy" is known to have come to light. Playtoy was Woolworth's 1937 brand name for Tootsietoy sets. Similar sets may also have been made in a subsequent year or so, but no records confirming such a supposition yet have been found. The Playtoy brand grew out of the general situation already described, and was the result of considerable drawn-out negotiation between Dowst and Woolworth that spanned the first seven months of 1937. As finally settled, it represented a compromise between Woolworth's tremendous buying power (in the late 1920's and 1930's Woolworth accounted for approximately one-third of the total Dowst sales) and Ted Dowst's desire to protect his other accounts. As Ted Dowst himself put it just before rushing east after the Fourth of July to show the Playtoy label samples to S. R. Lewis, Woolworth's toy buyer, and conclude the deal, "This is being used at this time merely as a makeshift trade name to avoid using the usual trade name of TOOTSIETOY in a spot where it might cause trouble. It is nothing that we ever will attempt to popularize to any great extent and will probably be forgotten at the end of the current season."

"Trouble" of course meant that Woolworth was going to be able to sell the sets at slightly lower prices than currently obtained on similar sets under the regular Tootsietoy name in other stores—the "trouble" that would have erupted for Dowst from these other accounts had not the Woolworth sets been branded "Playtoy" instead of "Tootsietoy."

Any set of old Tootsietoys with the original box is a good collectors' item. But a boxed set with the PLAYTOY label obviously is somewhat of a prize, and the more so because only such a box containing some or all of its original contents can serve as a means of distinguishing a Playtoy from a Tootsietoy.

The Playtoy boxes, however, should not be confused with a standard type of Tootsietoy box of the late 1920's through 1937 (a modification, shown in Fig. 212, was employed through 1938 for the Tootsietoy Midgets) lettered TOOTSIETOY PLAYTIME TOYS and depicting a boy and a girl approaching a door lettered ENTRANCE TO PLAYTIME that was surrounded by such fairytale characters as Humpty Dumpty, Mother Goose, Simple Simon, and Little Red Riding Hood. Even after 1937 certain regular Tootsietoy sets, bearing modernized labels, were designated as Tootsietoy Playtime Sets. In 1931 new "Tootsietoy Playtime Toys" labels were developed for the Aerial Defense, Aerial Offense, and Field Battery Set (all of which used the same label design), and for the Air Mail Set (which had its own special label.) It is, of course, all too easy for an overenthusiastic collector who fails to bear the precise nomenclature in mind to come across one of the boxes with the PLAYTIME label and confuse it with the much scarcer and more desirable PLAYTOY label.

From 1932 on, special labels often were developed for individual sets. There were, for example, boxes for the Tootsietoy Speedway, Tootsietoy Motors, Tootsietoy Trucks, Tootsietoy Taxicabs, and so on. As a matter of fact, in 1934 and 1935, even prior to the Playtoy sets—which it should be remembered were definitely a proprietary brand for Woolworth—certain exigencies of the current sales situation induced Dowst to furnish certain sets in two styles of boxes. The sets known to have thus been produced were the No. 05300 Motor Set and the No. 05310 Truck Set. The variations were designated No. 0530X and No. 0531X respectively, and the situation was indicated in the catalogs as follows: "Exactly the same toy content as the above described set but packed in a cheaper kind of container. This set is especially designed for the jobbing trade for whose purposes the set in the above style can not be produced at right pricing." There were the two largest and heaviest sets in the line in 1934 and 1935, and the "right pricing" for jobbers meant not only a lower price on a cheaper box but also a substantial saving in weight and consequently in shipping costs. The regulation sets weighed thirty pounds per dozen, and the "X" sets weighed twenty-five pounds per dozen, another instance of the extreme importance of weight in the miniature cast-metal car field. Inasmuch as the weight of the actual toys was identical in both versions of a set, this means that there was a difference of approximately 6 1/2 ounces in the weight of each set box itself between the regular box and the "cheaper kind of container." It also means, of course, that for collectors who seek and are fortunate to find Tootsietoys in the original set boxes, there are two distinct variations each of Tootsietoy Motors and Tootsietoy Trucks for both 1934 and 1935, for the contents of the sets were changed

Fig. 189. Of course, no discussion or portrayal of the Mack truck in collectible models would be complete without reference to the famous Tootsietoy Macks of the 1920's and 1930's, and here is a selection of models based on the original type of cab and hood design. For an example of the later Mack brought out in the 1930's, see Figs. 178 and 192.

Dr. Clinton B. Seeley

from their 1934 makeup for the 1935 line.

As a matter of fact, there are two variations of composition for 1935 itself, as far as the No. 05310 and No. 0531X truck sets are concerned. Prior to 1933, when the first sets designated as Tootsietoy Motors and Tootsietoy Trucks appeared, most of the Tootsietoy Playtime Toys —assorted trucks, automobiles, and airplanes in various combinations—retailed for $0.50, $1.00, $1.50, $2.00, and $2.50, although there were a few specialized sets such as the fifty-cent Aces of the Air with four airplanes, and the farm set (actually called the Farm Tractor), which consisted of a tractor, box trailer, road scraper with additional rake arm, and the Ford Model-T pickup truck. Tootsietoy Trucks No. 05310, as introduced in 1933, was a dollar seller containing five Mack trucks, a Graham milk truck and wrecker, and a delivery motor cycle. In 1934 the contents of the set were changed by replacing the milk truck and delivery motorcycle with a trimotor airplane. For the 1935 line the contents were changed again, by substituting the new American Railway Express truck for the Mack van trailer (the No. 0803 lettered LONG DISTANCE HAULING). The No. 05310 and No. 0531X sets made in the first months of 1935 had this composition, but in sets packed after about May 1, 1935, the new No. 0717 TWA Douglas Airliner was substituted for the trimotor plane included in earlier sets; hence there were two 1935 versions of each of the No. 05310 and No. 0531X sets, and six versions in all spanning the 1934 and 1935 lines that a collector might seek as more or less complete boxed sets.

Now admittedly, the last remark is somewhat hypothetical, and is included primarily to demonstrate the point that though there survive far more boxed Tootsietoy sets from the 1920's

and 1930's than many might imagine, there assuredly is not such plethora as to make it likely that any one collector would deliberately set about hopefully searching for, much less anticipate securing, six variations of what essentially is the same basic set from two year's production. Furthermore, the composition of Tootsietoy Trucks, now called No. 05210, changed in 1936. It changed again (as No. 5210) in 1937, again in 1938, again in 1939 (then renamed the No. 5210 Tootsietoy Commercial Set), and so on. In short, in the 1930's Tootsietoy-set box labels, numbers, and compositions changed frequently, often each year. The changes in makeup were, in fact, considered a noteworthy selling feature that was emphasized in the catalogs. Invariably the changes were heralded as giving added value. Thus, the collector of boxed sets, if he considers matters from a practical standpoint, has relatively little chance of attaining anything like a comprehensive assortment. On the other hand, when offered a boxed set by name or number it is vitally important that the collector ascertain the exact type of label and the exact makeup of the set or its surviving pieces, because it is quite likely that the set offered, even though it carries the same name and number as a set he already possesses, actually is not a duplicate of the related set or sets in his collection.

In 1938, there was added to the Tootsietoy line still another type of packaging that should be kept in mind by the collector. This was the so-called Tootsietoy Gift Box, a chest into which any three standard fifty-cent Tootsietoy sets selected by the jobber or retailer could be slid like bureau drawers and delivered in this form as a complete unit, packed a dozen Gift Boxes (thirty-six sets) in a carton. (In 1939 the fifty-cent sets of Coppertoys and Silvertoys were excluded from inclusion in Gift Boxes.) Inasmuch as the makeup of the Gift Boxes was a matter that rested entirely with the individual jobber or large retailer, there were endless combinations, all of which in one sense may be regarded as "correct" or "official," yet none of which in another sense can rate as "official" in that, as combinations, they were a definite part of the 1938 or 1939 Tootsietoy line. The fact that the Gift Boxes were offered only in 1938 and 1939 may indicate that they achieved relatively little acceptance in the trade or it may indicate that they were withdrawn because a necessity for conserving packaging materials had already become evident by 1940. Naturally, any Tootsietoy Gift Boxes of this three-tier type that come the way of the hobbyist are avidly collected as is, and, in any event, the serious collector wants to know what was made and the status of anything he may come across and acquire.

A great deal of thought, energy, and artistic talent were devoted to the packaging and labeling of sets of miniature cast-metal automobiles and related toys in the 1930's. It is not too much to say that these sets led the way and played a disproportionate part in the modernization of toy packaging in this era. Erie won packaging prizes in the 1930's, and in an article on packaging for toys in September 1938 issue of *Playthings,* no less than four of the nine boxes pictured as outstanding examples of modern toy packaging were Tootsietoy products, including one of the Gift Boxes. There is no doubt that some very attractive labels were produced, albeit some of them perhaps go to extremes of modernism more acceptable in the later 1930's than to today's tastes, but already, only three decades later, there exists much the same rather pleasant and redeeming aura of "period" around the packages of the late 1930's as there does about those of the 1890's.

It should also be kept in mind that although enormous quantities of boxed sets of miniature cast-metal cars were sold in the 1920's and 1930's, by far the bulk of the sales of such vehicles was in the form of single unboxed pieces sold from open counter bins in five- and ten-cent purchase units. Not only did the vast majority of contemporary young model-vehicle enthusiasts never own boxed sets of the cars, but a very great number of them were in fact totally unaware even of the existence of such boxed sets and that their model automobiles might be purchased in this manner. Even among those who were cognizant of the sets and who might at times have been offered the opportunity to be given one may well have preferred to make their own individual selec-

Fig. 190.   Some of the most detailed, beautiful, and famous of all the Tootsietoys. Seen here are the six body styles of the Graham passenger cars, some with rear-mount and some with side-mount spare tires. The second photograph shows the No. 0715 La Salle convertible sedan and No. 0713 La Salle sedan.

G. William Holland photographs

tions of desired models and colors rather than accept the assortment offered in a boxed set. In any event the point to be made is that the ratio of complete or incomplete boxed sets to that of surviving individual vehicles is relatively small. Even when miniature cast-metal cars were originally purchased as boxed sets, the boxes were often disposed of at some point over the years, while the vehicles themselves were retained and preserved.

Any old model-car box has in itself a definite collectors' value, and any old model car or cars in the original box always, regardless of the condition of either or both box and vehicle, is worth more to collectors than the model alone. Presumably, as model-car collecting continues to expand and grow, the latter principle also will apply in the case of more recently manufactured specimens merchandised in newer forms of packaging, such as transparent blisters on cards. In fact, it seems safe to say that in years to come, a blister-packed model car of, say, the 1960's, will be worth most to collectors if it is in an intact original package, and somewhat less than this, but still more than merely the car alone, if it is accompanied by its original although opened blister package.

Within the history of model cars and the lore of collecting them, boxes and catalogs at times closely complement each other, in some cases one provoking mysteries that can perhaps be solved only by the other. This seems especially true in the case of miniature cast-metal cars. Two examples will suffice to demonstrate the point and the principles involved, but the serious collector may well come across a number of others, either

Fig. 191. This photograph vividly demonstrates the change in weight that occurred when Tootsietoy production was changed from white-metal-alloy castings to zinc-alloy castings in the early 1930's. Although the zinc-alloy Mack chassis at the right carries a stud for the car transport body mounting, it is actually much lighter than the older white-metal casting in the left-hand pan.
G. William Holland photograph

in the form of catalog listings or of physical specimens of curious and seemingly unaccountable sets themselves: The 1930 catalog of the large New York store F. A. O. Schwarz boxed a set designated as "Traffic Police," selling for the heady figure of $15 and including two 8-inch-high working traffic-light standards with red and green lights, figures of traffic policemen in various positions,* traffic signs, and "12 assorted automobiles." The automobiles appear quite clearly to be Tootsietoys, but the remainder of the set's components are unidentifiable and may well be European; the policemen are capped, not helmeted, "Bobbies," but might still be British or Continental. Unfortunately, the 1930 catalog does not even supply in regard to any of the listings such information subsequently deemed pertinent as to whether certain items are imports or exclusive with Schwarz, data that might provide pertinent clues concerning the set. Was the set some sort of uncataloged Dowst special, either made up for Schwarz or generally available to their customers? It seems improbable. Were the sets assembled by Schwarz themselves, using components from various sources? Were the sets made up in Europe, including Tootsietoys that in this case were first shipped abroad and then returned to the United States? Or is it possible the sets were an entirely European production? If the latter is correct, then the most important inference to be drawn is that the number of Tootsietoy copies made in Europe was much more extensive than has previously been imagined, for the sets include two of the Mack trucks, both early fire engines, the racer, the Overland Bus, the Ford Model-A coupe, the early truck, and four of the General Motors series. F. A. O. Schwarz not being in a

position to furnish any definite information on the matter, this evidently is a mystery that can be cleared up only when one of the "Traffic Police" sets comes into the hands of a model-car collector who is aware of the conundrum involved and can adjudicate the situation.

A somewhat less complex mystery, but one that hints at a possibly much broader base of pertinence to model-car collectors, is to be found in the fall and winter 1933 Sears, Roebuck catalog, where a "Complete 29-Piece Village" is offered for fifty-nine cents. This comprised "four 3-inch metal trucks with rubber tired wheels," twelve buildings, and a "village plan of streets and parks" that opened to 43 by 19 inches of lithographed cardboard, and twelve "tiny people," material unspecified, who might have been metal castings or might also have been lithographed cardboard. There is no specification of the vehicles being Tootsietoys, but from the illustration they would appear to be the sedan, hook and ladder, Mack stake truck, and Mack airmail truck. It was quite common practice in the 1930's for toy manufacturers to make up multipiece uncataloged specials by including a number of knocked-down cardboard buildings. Obviously Sears, Roebuck did not themselves go to the bother of making up these special sets; they obtained them from some supplier. The question is whether Dowst themselves had the carboard buildings made and used them in various special sets at the time, a thought that opens up endless possibilities, or whether some outside manufacturer purchased Tootsietoys and made up these sets as a more or less standard item. Again, the solution to the mystery awaits the location of one of these sets in more or less complete form, or at least, the discovery of one of the "village plan of streets and parks" that, hopefully, will bear some indication of its manufacturer.

A more informative listing, although by no

---

* The catalog description says "12 traffic police figures" and "a mounted police." The illustration of the set, however, shows thirteen standing policemen and a motorcycle policeman.

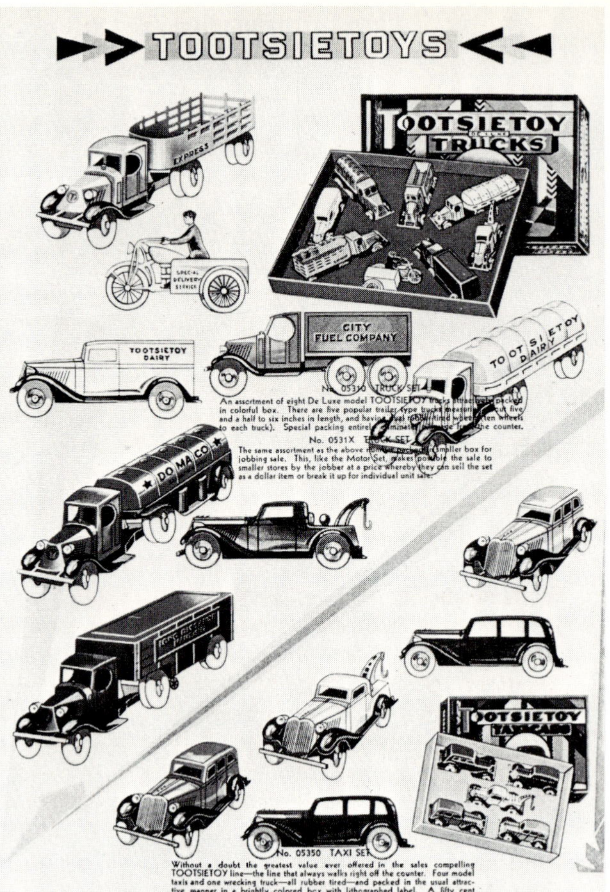

Fig. 192. Three pages from the 1933 Tootsietoy catalog, showing the complete new line of Grahams and Macks introduced to the trade at that time, including the Tootsietoy Dairy Graham and the Mack milk-truck trailers. Note the City Fuel Truck in its original three-axle form, and compare it with Fig. 178.

George H. Hartman

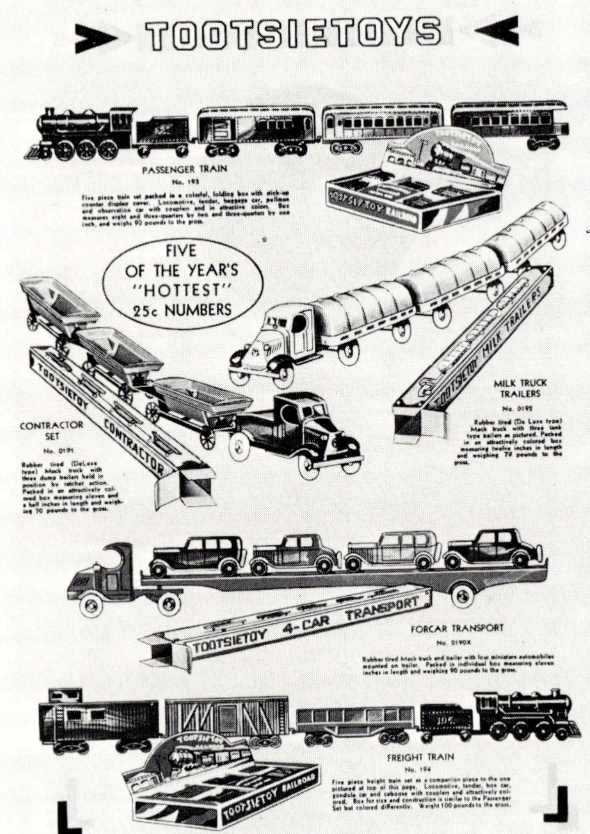

means parallel to the previously mentioned mysteries, may be found in the fall and winter 1934 Sears, Roebuck catalog, where there is a listing of a special sixty-nine-cent set of seven automobiles and a monoplane with rubber tires, a set about halfway between the usual five-piece fifty-cent Tootsietoy sets and the ten-piece dollar sets. It hints at the possibility of a number of uncataloged sets, some or all of which may have included supposedly discontinued numbers; the continuation in production for such specials of models dropped from the cataloged line being a device widely employed by toy manufacturers in the 1930's for justifying the cut-price basis of such specials. The 1934 Sears set comprises the airplane, Graham coupe, sedan, town car, and roadster (according to the illustration, the first two with side-mount spares and the latter two with rear mounts), Graham wrecker, and the No. 023 racing car and No. 04680 Overland Bus. The Grahams were, of course, current, but the last two vehicles were out of the cataloged line after 1933. Whether they represented leftover stock or, perhaps along with other uncataloged numbers, actually were produced in 1934 and perhaps even later for such sets cannot be said with certainty at this time, but again a catalog listing—and at first glance a seemingly minor and superficial one —opens up suggestions with broad potential implications to the serious model-car collector and researcher.

Truly, there is infinitely much more to the model-automobile hobby than might appear to many to be the case at first glance. Signposts, examples, and suggestions may be given here, but in the long run the accumulation of interesting and useful information depends on the combined efforts of many individual enthusiasts. How rapidly our store of knowledge grows depends on how many collectors are willing and able to observe, study, compare, and record. This applies to boxes and catalogs as surely as to the actual model cars themselves. In comparing boxes, both for individual vehicles when they were so packed, and for complete sets, great attention must be paid to all details, including the model or set number. As with the model cars themselves, both boxes and catalogs of or including model cars may exist in collectible major and minor variations. In the case of catalogs particularly, such variations may at times be highly informative. In any event, a collector should never assume from seemingly or actually identical covers that two catalogs are duplicates, but should carefully compare them, page by page and, preferably, word by word, as well as scrutinize the illustrations as minutely as he can.

Catalogs were, of course, made by fallible human beings, which is something that overenthusiastic beginners sometimes forget, and must be read and used with this in mind. They are, in effect, tools with which to build, and not, despite their intrinsic information value, the ultimate and completely authoritative last word. This is particularly true when, as so often happens, they are available singly and not in extensive sequence. At times errors creep in through verbal slips or misunderstanding of dictated copy. In some such way, for instance, by 1936 the Tootsietoy Aero-Dawn monoplane already mentioned had become, in the jobbing catalog of G. Sommers & Company of St. Paul, Minnesota, something called "Aerdon"; and the entire fallacious structure on which reports of the supposed existence of, and consequent world-wide search for, a Tootsietoy Oakland in the General Motors series evidently stems from a misprint of "Oakland" for "Oldsmobile" in the N. Shure & Company catalog for 1928, the year this famous series was introduced. Apparently someone in the Shure organization owned an Oakland or otherwise had Oakland on his mind when he jotted down or dictated the copy for this then newly

Fig. 193. Theodore (Ted) S. Dowst, the spark plug behind the development of the Tootsietoy line in the 1920's and 1930's ("*Playthings*"), his business card, and a scene in the assembly room of the Dowst factory in 1927 (*Tootsietoy— Strombecker Corp.*). The boxes are filled with Tootsietoys that the girls are putting together.

introduced series. The point has aroused so much interest in a negative sort of way that the present writer was moved to investigate whether Mr. Shure himself might have owned an Oakland at that time or was known to express an interest in one. It was ascertained that Mr. Shure owned a Franklin in 1928 and subsequently a Chevrolet in the early 1930's, and it is extremely improbable that, being a comparatively well-to-do man, he ever unsuccessfully coveted an Oakland. He drove a Chevrolet during the depression because he did not feel it was an appropriate time for ostentation in automobiles. But the model-car collector who seeks valid information from old catalogs must always be careful of the Aerdons and Oaklands of the world.

A prime example of the matter of catalogs differing although the covers are identical exists in the case of the Tootsietoy 1925 and 1926 catalogs, as well as providing one of the great mysteries of model-car industry history. Both the 1925 and 1926 use the identical covers, printed in black, red, and green, and lettered TOOTSIETOY/CATA-LOGUE/No. 46/DOWST BROS. CO./CHI-CAGO/ILL., as well as, twice, THE "ALL-THE-TIME" LINE, a reference to the fact that the toys were not merely seasonal but, rather, year-round sellers (see Fig. 214). The only changes and distinguishing features occur on pages 1, 2, 9. On page 1 two lines of type in the introduction were reset in 1926 so as to change the division of the name as broken at the end of one line from TOOTSIE-TOY in 1925 to TOOT-SIETOY in 1926. This change evidently was regarded as of extreme importance in relation to the use and protection of the trademark Tootsietoy, and peculiarly a reference to the "Bungalow" in the same line of type was not changed to "Doll House" in 1926, when the bungalow was replaced with the new dollhouse and the text and illustration on page 9 changed accordingly. The third change was an alteration from "Dowst Brothers Company" on page 2 in 1925 to "Dowst Manufacturing Company" in 1926. Presumably the need for a similar change on the cover was overlooked or was not deemed worthy of the effort—although actually, the name appearing in black letters against a white background, such a change would have been both simple and inexpensive, or, as may well be the case, the printer already had a substantial supply of excess covers made up and left over from 1925. There is no doubt of the dating of these two catalogs both from the makeup of the line and the style of the company name. The only possible alternative theory is that both catalogs are 1925, the version with the Dowst Manufacturing Company imprint and the dollhouse having been made up late in 1925.

In any event, from the standpoint of presently available knowledge, if a bibliography of Dowst catalogs were being prepared, the listing would likely read as follows: *

1925, Dowst Brothers Company imprint on page 2

1926, Type I, Dowst Manufacturing Company imprint on page 2

1926, Type II, as Type I but with eight-page 1926 supplement

Or, on the basis of the alternate theory suggested above, the bibliographical entries would read:

1925, Type I, Dowst Brothers Company imprint on page 2

1925, Type II, Dowst Manufacturing Company imprint on page 2

1926, same as 1925, Type II, but with eight-page 1926 supplement

But regardless of which of the above may eventually prove correct or at least be generally accepted as the correct sequence, a substantial mystery attaches to the designation of "No. 46" on the cover. Dowst did not issue a catalog every year; the closest catalog issue of the company yet brought to light preceding No. 46 is the 1921, and neither that nor any of the known earlier Dowst catalogs carry any issue numbers. Obviously the concept of an issue number and the number itself was pulled out of the air sometime between 1921 and 1926. "No. 46" must have some validity or at least meaningful inference. "No. 25," for example, would be readily understandable as indicating a 1925 catalog; other companies often used such a system, but what was used by Dowst was No. 46, and it must have related to something. The only thing pertinent that took place approximately forty-six years earlier was the establishment of the original predecessor firm, in 1878, and this no doubt was the basis for this number. But if the 1925 catalog is No. 46, then the theoretical catalog No. 1 would have been 1880, not 1878.

It is hardly likely that Ted Dowst could have made an error of this type in computing the number. The writer is therefore of the opinion that the plates for this No. 46 catalog cover originally were made up and used for a 1923 catalog, never changed thereafter, and that there probably were both 1923 and 1924 Dowst catalogs using this cover. This would provide an acceptable explanation not only for the mystery of the catalog-cover number itself but also for the seemingly inexplicable lack of catalogs between 1921 and 1925 alluded to earlier in this chapter. Akin to many other companies, Dowst did not make it a great

---

Fig. 194.   Tootsietoy samples and artwork. Unfortunately, no photographs could be located of similar material relating to automobiles, but here are the original samples of the Aero-Dawn monoplane, its individual box, and its counter display box (*George H. Hartman*). The only original colored wash drawing of a Tootsietoy that could be located at the factory was this one of a Buck Rogers rocket ship (*Tootsietoy—Strombecker Corp.*).

point to retain a comprehensive catalog file. Even with the best of intentions, catalogs once in ample supply dwindle away, copies are borrowed by various departments and not returned to a central file, and so on. While the differences in "No. 46" catalogs would probably have been well known to some at least in the mid-1920's—although perhaps even then not considered of any essential importance from the standpoint of a need to retain each type—in later years the fact that the covers were identical may well have led people to believe the catalogs were duplicates that might· as well be removed or discarded. It could even be that, annoyed at picking up earlier issues that did not include as much of the line as later ones because of the similarity of covers, someone deliberately threw out the older "No. 46" catalogs. Somewhere along the line, and perhaps even more tragic for overall miniature cast-metal car history, a fairly comprehensive file of pre–World War II competitors' catalogs evidently was blithely discarded as

of no possible interest or use during a tidying-up operation at the Tootsietoy factory; the present-day model car enthusiast may well grimace at the thought.

When the present owners of the business themselves became interested in its history and old catalogs, it was found that no such thing as a pre–World War II file even of Tootsietoy catalogs existed, and a fairly complete series eventually was built up from several sources. A 1926 issue was secured from a former executive, and later a general overturning of old records in an effort to locate material that might be of help in preparing the present book brought a copy of the 1925 catalog to light in the factory.* Manifestly the fact that

---

* In the course of the research for this book, the writer located another 1925 No. 46 and a 1926 supplement in another theoretically complete file. This would seem still further to confirm the theory that every "No. 46" catalog was generally looked upon as identical. Admittedly, it was a natural enough assumption.

a pre-1925 "No. 46" has not yet come to light does not preclude the possibility—which now seems a probability—that such issues existed. It is unfortunate that they have not yet turned up, for they would be most pertinent in definitely establishing the dates at which certain models were introduced between 1921 and 1925.

A rather curiously similar although by no means exactly parallel situation in regard to two different catalogs bearing the same covers and number is found in the case of two Sears, Roebuck cloth-bound catalogs both bearing the number 112 not only on the covers but also repeatedly at the head of many pages. One has 1,200 pages and the other 1,088 pages, overlapping pages being quite different. Undated as catalogs, the 1,200-page issue contains bank references dated October 1901, and the 1,088-page issue has new references dated October 1902. The situation actually involved here is uncertain and cannot be commented upon with any accuracy, except that in matters of interest to toy and model collectors the 1,200-page issue carries thirteen pages of toys and the 1,088-page issue but five pages of toys and may represent a spring catalog (spring 1903?). But to bring the point down specifically to the limits of interest of the model-car collector, the 1,200-page No. 112 illustrates and describes not only the first model Hafner automobile with straight dash—one of the all-time landmark models in miniature automobile history—but two cheap imported model automobiles as well. On the other hand, the 1,088-page No. 112 offers no model automobiles whatsoever.

Naturally, while any model-automobile collector would eagerly accept any Dowst "No. 46" catalog, or for that matter any old Dowst catalog whatsoever, caution must be exercised before making an investment in a Sears, Roebuck "No. 112," if model automobiles alone are one's interest, and quite possibly in other early-date or relatively low-number Sears catalogs. Later—presumably about 1913—the general Sears catalogs appear to have been standardized at a spring and summer and a fall and winter issue each year, and from that point on the spring issues bear *even* numbers and the *fall* issues, which are of primary interest to model-car collectors, carry *odd* numbers, 145, 147, 149, 151, and so on. Montgomery Ward fall catologs also carry *odd* numbers, although the numbers are somewhat lower than for corresponding year Sears, Roebuck catalogs. The number of the fall 1929 catalog, for example, is 159 for Sears and 111 for Ward. The numbering system of the Charles William Stores, Inc., catalogs is rather obscure, there evidently being two issues a year with the usual spring and summer or fall and winter designations,

but the numbers jump four between a given season for one year and the next. Thus the fall and winter catalogs for 1920, 1921, and 1922 are numbered 29, 33, and 37 respectively. Shortly thereafter the William catalogs drop numbers entirely and identify themselves only by season and date. Presumably the unusual numbering system originally was adopted in an effort eventually to catch up with or at least approach Sears and Ward numbers, thereby creating an impression of comparable longevity for William. Subsequently it was decided that it might look even better not to employ numbers at all, because someone computed that at the rate they were going it would take them until 1952 to catch up to Ward's numbers and until the year 2024 to come abreast of Sears' numbers! (The William catalogs usually appear almost as thick as Sears', but contain less pages and bulkier paper.) In any event, the result is that, apparently, *all* numbered William catalogs carry odd numbers that consequently do not have the immediate recognition value for collectors that an odd number on a Sears or Ward catalog for the same era possesses. There were a number of other substantial firms in the retail mail-order business prior to World War II who issued comprehensive catalogs. However, Sears, Ward, and William appear to have been the largest and best known, and their catalogs the most useful to the model-car collector and the most frequently available.

Informative and collectible variations can exist in otherwise identical catalogs not only through actual changes in the physical setting of the type itself, but also through additions by means of rubber stamping, as in the case of some of the Tootsietoy catalogs of the 1930's, or even—although it is admittedly rather unusual—by type-

Fig. 195. A substantial amount of mystery surrounds Tootsietoy's introduction of their replica of the new Ford Model A in 1928, shortly after the prototype was unveiled late in 1927. Pictures of the sample Tootsietoy used in early catalogs, such as this one, suggest that Dowst was working closely with Ford and was given information and drawings as Ford's work progressed. Compare this sample with the production models shown in Fig. 106. The car pictured on the counter box was the actual automobile, not a model.
A. E. Moredock

"Tootsietoy" New Ford Pewter Coupe

1F2441—2¾ in. long, bright asstd. colors, wire spoke wheels, each in box. 1 doz. in display carton.

Doz 75c

writing, as in the case of the second type of the 1934 Manoil catalog sheet on which the words PATENT PENDING have been typed. Any such changes in catalogs or other sales literature are obvious bibliographical variations and collectible as such. In addition, they may well provide important historical clues—sometimes to actual physical alterations in the models themselves; sometimes to happenings in product or company histories—to the discerning collector, and consequently may be equally if not even more important from this standpoint than merely because they expand a hobbyist's file of old catalogs.

Indeed, any sort of catalog that includes model automobiles is a collectible item in itself, and is also a source of varying value as a tool in identifying and dating models and, depending on the reader's interest in such things and his ability properly to interpret the information that is presented, in delving into the further reaches of model-car research. Also collectible and informative are all instruction sheets, advertisements, trade magazines (preferably in complete and intact form, of course), and any printed material that pertains to or in any way, if only by indirect association, touches upon the subject. Any such paper material should, naturally, be preserved carefully in its original state, unclipped and unmarked. It often baffles some observers that there are serious collectors who would, if given a choice, prefer the catalogs and other paper material to actual specimens of the models themselves, but to the serious student there is nothing more important than such historical literature. Any collector coming across such material who does not wish to keep it for himself can readily find others who will gladly trade models for paper.

As in parallel hobbies, the growth of model-car collecting has witnessed the making available of reproductions of old model-automobile catalogs and sheets, thereby allowing the flavor and information of the originals to be made available to a wide audience. Undoubtedly as the hobby of model-car collecting continues to expand, many more such reproductions will become available, although naturally such reproductions are never complete substitutes for the originals, and especially so when the originals were printed in full color, as was the case with a number of model-automobile catalogs in the 1920's and 1930's.

As for the type of printed material mentioned above that pertains indirectly or by association to model cars, specific reference should be made to copies of the *National Laundry Journal,* which, during the years it was owned and operated by the Dowst family, was (and still is) a very definite model-car collectors' item. So, too, if to a somewhat lesser extent, are copies of the *Confec-*

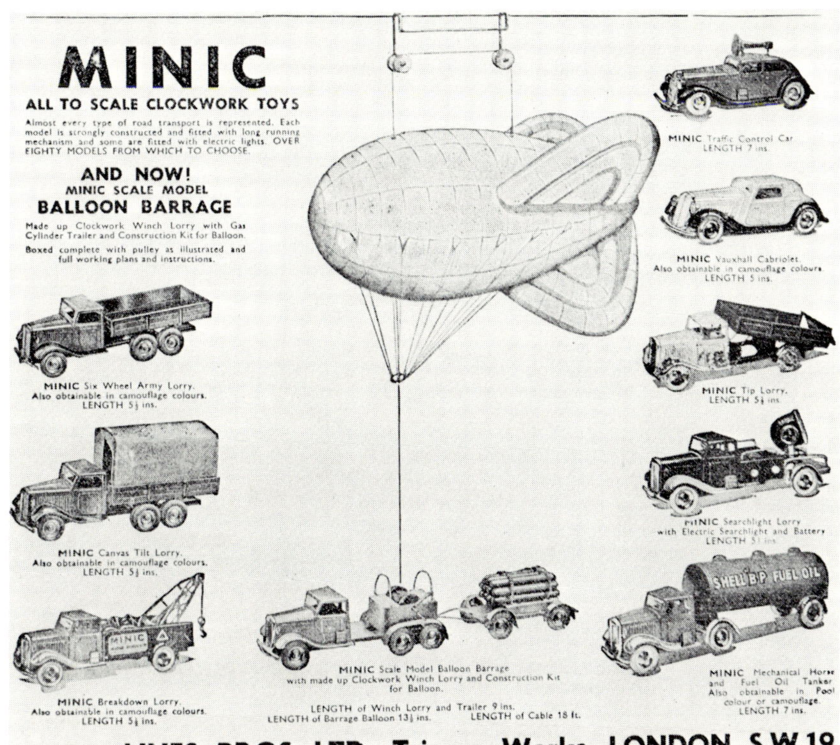

Fig. 196. An August 1940 advertisement showing an assortment of Minic clockwork stamped-metal miniature automobiles, including the unique balloon barrage with lorry, trailer, balloon, and overhead cable. The balloon was 13 1/2 inches in length. This outfit is one of the most unusual, historic, and sought-after of model-automobile collectibles.

tioners' Journal and similar trade magazines that contain advertisements of metal toys for packing with candy or for souvenir use of Dowst, Calumet, and other suppliers.

REPAIRS, RESTORATIONS, REPRODUCTIONS, AND FAKES

Yet as pleasant as it may be to discuss the many positive sides of collecting and their numerous entrancing variations, sooner or later today in attempting completely to cover any hobby we must inevitably come to the dark side of the moon, as it were. To attempt to deny or to gloss over the fact that everything is not quite perfect in paradise would be to eschew the honorable responsibilities that must lie upon anyone who essays a chronicle of this sort, and one can only add, by way of consolation to any who may become disheartened at having all the facts put before them, is that, although there are marked potential dangers, the good by far outweighs the bad, and predictably will continue to do so if newcomers to the hobby are staunch of heart and alert to pitfalls. The model-automobile collecting hobby is, as will be well recognized by those who have over the years participated in similar model-collecting activities, going through a period of rapid growth, transition, and eventual solidification. At such a period any hobby is likely to attract the attentions and participation of those who innocently can be led astray, as well as those few who will seek to gain personal return from it. Sometimes the line is very difficult to draw, for what may well start as a proper convenience and limited service to fellow hobbyists may in other hands burgeon into a definite menace to the hobby as a whole and most particularly to beginners.

Furthermore, the model-automobile collecting hobby is to some extent inevitably tied to the actual old-automobile hobby and to full-size automobile enthusiasm and interest in general. As a result—and it is necessary candidly to recognize this fact—there is within the model-automobile collecting hobby, or at least hanging on its periphery, what amounts to a definite subculture deriving its interest and mores, not from the history of the model automobile or of the model-automobile industry itself, but rather from the prototype automobile. To a large extent, with the best goodwill in the world, members of this group simply cannot understand or accept many of the normal, well-established, and quite rationally founded principles of model-car collecting as such or of the much more broadly based long-established general hobby of toy and model collecting from which they derive. Sufficient already has been said in this chapter to make clear many of the outlooks of and points of differences between these two groups, broadly identified as the approach to the model automobile from the standpoint of the history of the real automobile and from the standpoint of the history of the model automobile, to make it unnecessary to dwell upon these distinctions at any great length here. However, one other point should be noted, to be returned to again a little later, and that is that in some cases the prototype automotive group, through insufficient knowledge of the ins and outs of the model hobby, have to a considerable extent imposed upon themselves and adopted among themselves a somewhat rudimentary set of standards of rarity, desirability, and value that bears little or no relation to the realities of the situation as known and accepted by the vast majority of model-car collectors. This is unfortunate, for the beginner who happens first to fall among a prototype-oriented group is all too often prone to accept

Fig. 197.   The six standard body styles of the Tootsietoy No. 4630/5 delivery truck, lettered respectively, left to right, rear row: BAKERY, MARKET, and MILK, and, front row, FLORIST, LAUNDRY, and GROCERY.

Dr. Clinton B. Seeley

the collective exceptions for the mainstream, a natural-enough mistake but one that can provoke many subsequent difficulties, mistakes, and misunderstandings as he continues to pursue his model automobile collecting hobby activities.

In brief, the orientation and outlook of this group—and it certainly should immediately be emphasized that, for the most part, man for man, they are as pleasant, admirable, honorable, and sincere enthusiasts as are the members of any other hobby group—in regard to such things as repaints, restorations, and reproduction parts is utterly at variance with the accepted mores and standards of the vast majority of serious conventional old-model-car collectors and historians. They are certainly a far cry from the unprincipled and ignorant horde of all-destroying barbarians or shifty-eyed unprincipled moneygrubbers that some collectors imply. Nor, it should hastily be underlined, can the conventional model-car collectors justly claim any real or imagined superiority or justify any intolerant insistance on the acceptance of their views simply because they are part of an established majority, or apportion any sort of accolade as representing the only "true" profile of the model-car collecting hobbyist. Intolerance from one side is just as odious and unacceptable as from the other. Yet in all fairness one thing the model-automobile history-oriented group can and does properly point out is that all too often in their enthusiasm, in their particular pursuit of the hobby, the other group does irreversibly depreciate, mangle, or destroy that which they are interested in preserving, studying, and recording. Here it must be granted that they are understandably incensed at the great damage done both to the cause of serious historical investigation and of model-car collecting itself by unthinking, unknowing, or uncaring repainting, chopping, transpositions and combinations of parts, and so on. Here there can be no question that fact and history—in both the sense of past model-car history and in the sense of the long-range outlook on these acts themselves—are unquestionably on their side. An old and historical model car that has been repainted or subjected to the same process under the perhaps hopefully less blunt and seemingly more positive-thinking elision of "restored" has much of its historical as well as intrinsic value ruined forever, and all too often many an enthusiast has come in the course of time deeply to regret having done such deeds and to wish he could turn back the clock and possess these models once again in the original state in which he first obtained them.

To speak the truth plainly, because of this element of prototype-automobile-oriented interest where the hobbyist sees little or no difference between repainting or restoring an old actual automobile and an old model automobile, it must be admitted that there is probably a larger percentage of those who repaint among those who profess to be model-car collectors than among any other group of toy or model collectors. Some claims have estimated such enthusiasts as making up as much as 5 percent of collectors of old model cars, but this surely is an exaggeration, and even if it might once have been so, the percentage has of course greatly decreased and will continue to decrease as more and more hobbyists become fully aware of and aroused to its dangers and the opinions of other collectors regarding it.

Some, not fully realizing the implications of what they are saying, condemn repaints, not on the grounds that they are spurious, but because they never can truly duplicate the original factory finish—although there always seem to be artists of varying skill who can come close enough so that they can truly convince themselves and sometimes others that they can. Of course, the better a repaint, just so much the more dangerous it is. (But, fortunately, all too often there invariably is some detail on which the fakers slip up.) Some years back, collectors of toy trains began seriously to discuss the possibilities of subjecting questionable specimens that might be involved in fraud cases to spectroscopic and other laboratory tests. As it transpired, this has not to date proved necessary, despite the repeated claims of repainters that they could produce a finish that nobody could tell from the original. Obviously, however, while any repaint job destroys the original status of a specimen, the more closely the repaint approaches the original in appearance, the more dangerous it becomes and the more people that may be taken in by it, a vital consideration in a period when some old model cars command startlingly high prices. Unbelievable as it may sound to many, it is today possible to purchase on the open market supposed matching paint for the factory colors of model trains of the 1920's and 1930's, not to mention decalcomanias and rubber stamps reproducing their original lettering. Unless the burgeoning model-car-collecting hobby is ever vigilant and unrelaxing in its standards, the day may conceivably come when it similarly will find itself being offered tins of "authentic matching" Barclay, Dinky Toy, Tootsietoy, and other old colors of the pre–World War II era, accompanied by a barrage of propaganda emanating from those who have a stake in promoting their sale and use.

The essential point that is truly or professedly disbelieved by those who condone or practice repainting is that it destroys the histography of color variations and thereby the basic fiber of serious collecting of old model cars. That it de-

Fig. 198.   Three examples of Tootsietoy trucks especially lettered for stores. Pictured are the same van as in Fig. 197 but with "J. C. Penny Co. DEPARTMENT STORES" cast into the sides, a No. 123 Ford truck of the later 1930's with the lithographed metal insert "Shepard" (*G. William Holland photographs*), and a "Miller & Rhoads" No. 123 (*Adam Pellicot, Jr., William Dreyer photograph*). See also Fig. 225.

stroys the cash value of collectors' holdings also is obvious, although this point need not be stressed too much lest it seem too heavily to inject a consideration of fiscal matters into a hobby discussion, for what point is there in seeking a needed color or in studying color variations at all if it is permissible to repaint? It all comes back to the pathetic absurdity of the parallel of the stamp collector who dips a common stamp in dye to produce a scarce color to fill an empty album space, or the antique collector who wishes a two-hundred-year-old artifact to look as if it left the maker's atelier yesterday. Conversely at times, in recognition of the importance of originality to most collectors, modern reproductions of antiques sometimes are artfully artificially aged, including the creation of chips, worn surfaces, and the proverbial wormholes. Similarly, if again almost unbelievably to moderate minds, old models sometimes are repainted and then artificially aged so they can be purveyed to collectors as seemingly original specimens at higher prices but without awaking the suspicions that might be conjured up by bright, too perfect-seeming paint jobs. It has been reported but yet not fully verified that this has been done to miniature cast-metal cars, and it is definitely known already to have been done with cast-iron and pressed-steel model vehicles.

Nevertheless, it must somewhat sadly be admitted that, based on previous experiences of the wheelings and dealings, propaganda, and incipient commercialism that have surrounded the growth of other similar collecting hobbies, it is perhaps too much to hope that model-car collecting ever can entirely defend itself against or entirely purge itself of these practices, and all the more so because of its obvious close relationship to the hobby of collecting full-size antique auto-

mobiles, which, it should again be emphasized, is one of the very, very *few* antiquarian collecting hobbies where repainting and restoration is, although of admittedly detestable necessity for reasons of safety, accepted and capable of justification. On the other hand, the natural and perhaps never susceptible of complete separation—obviously a matter of debatable desirability in any case—of model-car hobbies from real car hobbies cuts both ways; and there is also to some extent an automatically suspicious association of ideas to the effect that an individual capable of repainting an old model car and suggesting straightfacedly that it is an acceptable or even a worthy act would be equally capable of setting back an odometer or putting sawdust in the transmission of a used real car he was trying to sell.

If a model has already been repainted by some youthful owner before it reaches the hands of a collector, or has been stripped of paint, which occasionally is found to be the case with miniature cast-metal cars, especially racing cars whose owners sought to give them a bright or pseudo-plated finish by scratching off all the paint, it can be said that it does no harm to repaint them. It also must be said that it does no good, either. Furthermore, in such instances care must be taken to assure that the supposed crude repaint does not actually represent a home-applied original paint job on one of the miniature cast-metal models sold in unpainted form in the painting sets already mentioned, or that the model was not originally manufactured and sold—as were some versions of the ubiquitous little racing car of the 1920's and later—with the bodies and sometimes the wheels unpainted. Also, when a model car is obtained in definitely repainted state, there always exists a possibility that the new paint can be removed

Fig. 199. An unusual miniature truck, a Marx milk truck of immediately before or immediately after World War II, although the black tires naturally suggest postwar production. It is made of heavy sheet metal and is lettered MILK with a rubber stamp. As observed in the text, milk trucks were always extremely popular toys.
G. William Holland photograph

without also taking off the original paint, and the model car therefore truly be restored—in the best and only proper meaning of the word—to its original although perhaps dulled and almost certainly scratched finish through the careful application of mild lacquer thinner on a clean cloth, usually accompanied by much patient and gentle rubbing. The possibilities of success in cleaning away a repainted coat by this method vary from specimen to specimen. If the repainting was done with a lacquer, considerable success often attends such efforts, but if enamel was used to repaint a model it seems almost impossible, given presently available solvents to remove it without removing the original coat of paint that lies beneath it as well. The surface character of the repainted model upon which an attempt is to be made to remove the repainting also plays a part in the relative success of the operation. Relatively smooth surfaces such as are found on stamped-metal and die-cast model automobiles often clean down to the original paint rather easily, whereas on rougher surfaces, such as those of cast-iron models, the high spots may clean down not only to the original coat of paint but to the bare metal itself, while traces of the repaint color still remain in the pits. In any case, great care must be exercised in such cleaning attempts and most particularly so with the small and often delicate miniature cast-metal models; there obviously is little point in cleaning off a repainted coat if it is done at the expense of breaking a windshield frame or bumper casting. Usually a brief test on a small area of any repainted model vehicle will reveal if there is much hope for the model cleaning down to its original paint or not. If the clean cloth with which the mild lacquer thinner is applied rapidly shows traces of the repaint color transferring to the cloth, then there is a very good chance that the cleaning can be performed successfully. Occasionally, the model-car collector is fortunate enough to find a repainted coat that almost literally washes off under the ap-

plication of lacquer thinner, but such instances are the exceptions.

Notice should be taken here that there exists an opening for the ready misunderstanding of nomenclature regarding the condition of original paint on a model in the descriptions of offerings of surplus models listed by some enthusiasts. Some collectors of miniature cast-metal cars have fallen into the habit of using "chipped" to indicate that the paint of a model is other than excellent, but in the case of cast-metal models of all types, to most hobbyists "chipped" implies that the casting is chipped. If paint is not baked onto any sort of metal model, or the bare metal is not properly primed in some manner, it is possible that the paint will not bond permanently to the metal surface and in later years it may literally fall off in flakes or chips. While the term "paint chips" is readily accepted and understood to refer to samples of paint colors, and although it may be technically correct to refer to defective paint on a model as "chipped" (even though in most instances it is a case of the paint being scratched or worn), the use of "chipped" in this sense often leads to much misunderstanding, leading the potential buyer to believe that the paint on the proffered models is in substantially poorer condition than actually is the case or that the castings themselves are chipped. Customarily the condition of the paint on a model is covered by such variable overall descriptions as "very good," "good," "fair," and so on, in the absence of anything being said to the contrary, it being fairly assumed that the paint in question is original. It would seem desirable, both to avoid any misunderstandings in general and to provide a detailed key to the condition of a model's paint if this system were adopted by all collectors, that "flaked" be reserved for such models as actually present this condition due to improper bonding, and that "chipped" be reserved as a term descriptive of the condition of castings, not paint. In any event, the collector must

Fig. 200.   Keystone steel trucks and a steam shovel of the 1920's and early 1930's. These trucks were based on Packard prototypes, a feature made much of by the company. Keystone made a particular point in the 1920's of distinguishing between what they designated a water tower (with working water-pumping action as shown here) and a fire tower (a dummy water tower).

be cautioned as to the potential variable use of "chipped."

The widespread disapproval of repainting has led even its most ardent advocates and apologists now to believe, or at least to profess to believe in order to maintain face, that all such items should in some manner be identified as repaints. The potential danger is, of course, that although such a specimen may be described as a repaint when it passes from the hands of an individual who has repainted it, in subsequent changes of ownership this fact may accidentally or deliberately be lost sight of, and eventually the model is acquired by someone under the impression that it is original, and for a price in cash or trade that an original properly would command. Various methods of marking repaints have been suggested, such as using rubber stamps or decalcomanias to indicate this information. However, these are so readily susceptible to removal or obliteration as to render them virtually worthless. There do appear to be three methods generally accepted by collectors of old toys and models of all kinds: to leave the undersurface of an article clear of all paint; to scratch the word "repaint" into a repainted undersurface; and to paint the word "repaint" in a contrasting color, *using the same type of paint as the basic body repaint color* on an undersurface. The latter method assures that the word "repaint" cannot be removed by the use of paint remover without also revealingly cutting into the basic body color as well. To date, it seems the most practical and trustworthy method of marking, as a lack of paint on an undersurface may not strike a novice as telling, and a scratched-in marking may escape notice. However, all three of these methods may be considered suitable for larger model automobiles. In the area of the miniature cast-metal vehicles, however, there are considerable difficulties to be encountered in proper identification of repaints; for one thing the models are so small as to make marking with the word "repaint" rather difficult. For another, a considerable number of the older models of this type originally were painted only on their exterior surfaces, so that leaving the underside or interiors in the bare metal is by no means in itself a telling indication, even to the most knowledgeable collector, that the specimen has been repainted. Furthermore, in at least a few instances some such models originally were sold with their bodies unpainted, for example, some versions of the ubiquitous little racing car of the 1920's and 1930's. Such models are obviously "original" only when unpainted!

A serious and unsolved problem exists in regard to identifying and marking repainted miniature cast-metal cars properly. Perhaps in lieu of room to write the word "repaint" with a contrasting color paint, conscientious repainters might employ the letter "R" or a circle of contrasting paint, but naturally there would be many beginners who were not familiar with such coding and its meaning. In any case, all that can be said here is that collectors and most particularly beginners will have to be extremely cautious regarding models of this type and size.

Much of what has been said here regarding the potential pitfalls of repaints applies in a general way to other areas of repairs or restoration or the completion of an incomplete model, or whatever designations an individual collector cares to employ. Much may be confused or concealed by seemingly innocent references to restorations or replacements, and there exists a wide area of differences among collectors as to what is acceptable, commendable, and desirable in these matters. There does exist general agreement among reputable collectors that any unauthentic replacements should be noted in selling or trading a model and that considerable danger is present that even when this is done, some eventual owner will not be aware of the circumstances. Structural repairs of broken models would seem to be straightforward and simple enough, so long as they can be accomplished without damaging equal or more important aspects of condition, such as scorching a substantial area of original paint by inept soldering. Fortunately, the availability of modern epoxy cements capable of bonding metals has made the satisfactory reuniting of broken castings rather easy, without the difficulties and side effects that formerly attended the brazing of broken cast-iron components and which often made it seem more desirable to leave the broken portion alone than to attempt to repair it. Ill-advised attempts to repair broken white-metal castings by soldering, of course, almost inevitably resulted in the destruction of the specimen. Today, providing it is a matter of a clean break between two pieces that have been retained, there is hardly ever any problem in making a sound cemented joint.

In the case of cast models where a part has been broken off and lost, there always exists the possibility of building up the missing portion from some suitable material, or of recasting the part by using a complete specimen as a pattern and fitting and securing the recast part into position. Repairs of both these types are, however, heavily frowned upon by most collectors on ethical grounds, and, fortunately, at least up to now, such repairs have tended to be so costly in proportion to the overall value of the models as to be impractical. As ex-

KINGSBURY TOYS *For Girls and Boys*

$1.00

INCLUDING POSTAGE

West of Mississippi 10 per cent more

Fire Engine No. 726

9 in. long. Bright red finish, blue wheels, gold bronzed boiler. Non-skid rubber tires. Spring motor. Automatic gong, 25c extra.

Auto Aerial Ladder No. 736

Ladders spring up automatically when toy strikes any obstruction. 9½ in. long. Dark blue finish, yellow ladders, red wheels, strong spring motor. Automatic gong, 25c extra.

Auto Truck No. 718

Open body truck, 9 in. long. Dark blue body, red wheels. Non-skid rubber tires. Powerful spring motor.

Auto Dump Cart No. 729

A lever tips the body to dumping position. Tail board removable. Bright red body, dark blue frame, red wheels, 9 in. long. Sturdy spring motor.

No 626 New York to Paris Monoplane

A Pull Plane with draw wire attached for the little tots. Propeller spins as plane is pulled along. Finished in bright silver with blue propellor and red rubber tired wheels. Length 12 inches.

Auto Roadster No. 733

Smart sport or racing type car. 9 in. long. Light blue body, red wheels, speedy spring motor. Big non-skid rubber tires.

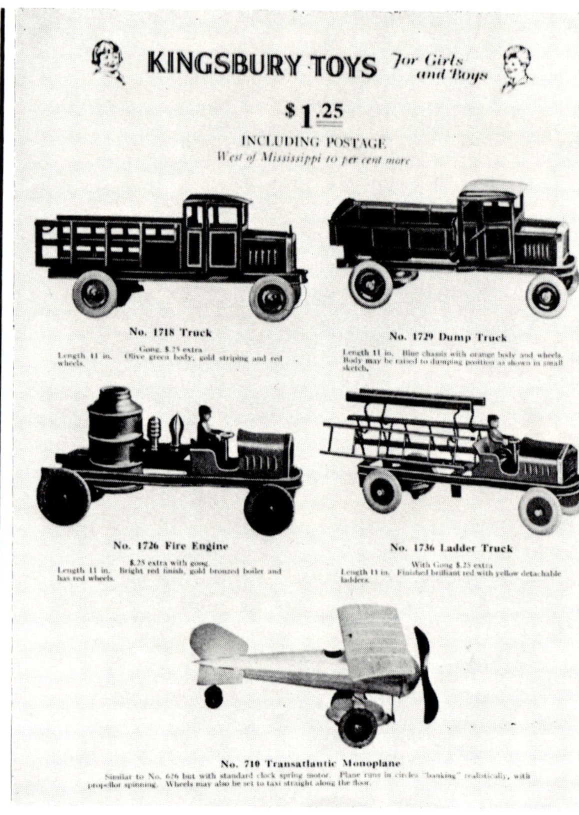

KINGSBURY TOYS *For Girls and Boys*

$1.25

INCLUDING POSTAGE

West of Mississippi 10 per cent more

No. 1718 Truck

Gong, $.25 extra

Length 11 in. Olive green body, gold striping and red wheels.

No. 1729 Dump Truck

Length 11 in. Blue chassis with orange body and wheels. Body may be raised to dumping position as shown in small sketch.

No. 1726 Fire Engine

$.25 extra with gong

Length 11 in. Bright red finish, gold bronzed boiler and has red wheels.

No. 1736 Ladder Truck

With Gong $.25 extra

Length 11 in. Finished brilliant red with yellow detachable ladders.

No. 710 Transatlantic Monoplane

Similar to No. 626 but with standard clock spring motor. Plane runs in circles "banking" realistically, with propellor spinning. Wheels may also be set to taxi straight along the floor.

KINGSBURY TOYS *For Girls and Boys*

$3.00

No. 343 Roadster

Length 13½ in. Snappy sport model roadster. Finished in several combinations of two-tones, providing a choice of colors, to duplicate practically all of the new sport roadsters of the large cars.

No. 340 Cabriolet

Length 13½ in. A perfect reproduction of the artistic models seen on Fifth Ave. Finished blue with orange striping and wheels. Rubber tires and motor.

No. 345 Sedan

Length 13½ in. A deluxe model with full equipment even to the trunk. Finished in several two-tone combinations.

No. 344 Coupe

Length 13½ in. The latest type with rumble seat. Finished gray with red stripe and red chassis, or choice of several colors.

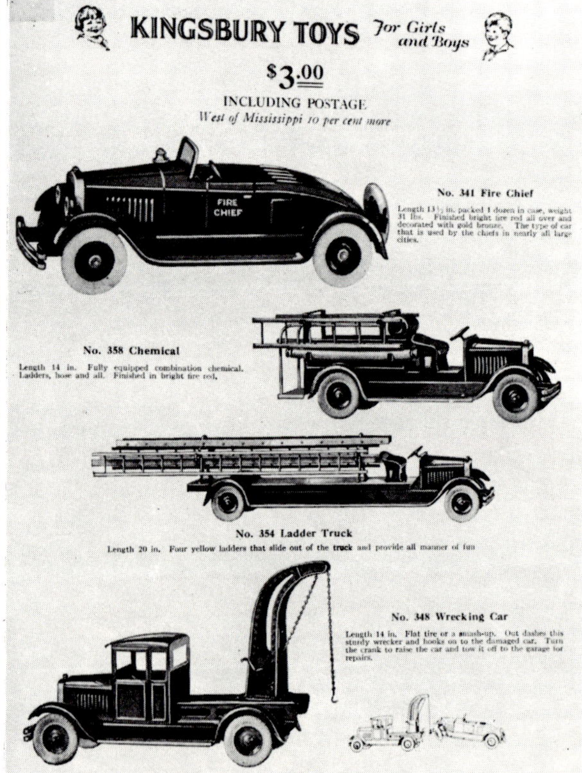

KINGSBURY TOYS *For Girls and Boys*

$3.00

INCLUDING POSTAGE

West of Mississippi 10 per cent more

No. 341 Fire Chief

Length 13½ in. packed 1 dozen in case, weight 31 lbs. Finished bright fire red all over and decorated with gold bronze. The type of car that is used by the chiefs in nearly all large cities.

No. 358 Chemical

Length 14 in. Fully equipped combination chemical. Ladders, hose and all. Finished in bright fire red.

No. 354 Ladder Truck

Length 20 in. Four yellow ladders that slide out of the truck and provide all manner of fun.

No. 348 Wrecking Car

Length 14 in. Flat tire or a smashup. Out dashes this sturdy wrecker and hooks on to the damaged car. Turn the crank to raise the car and tow it off to the garage for repairs.

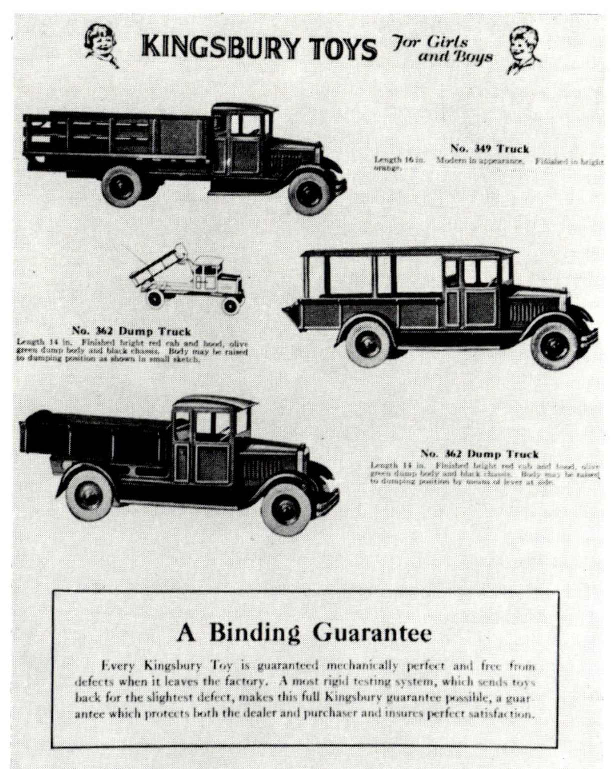

Fig. 201.   Six pages from the Kingsbury, 1929 catalog, showing typical examples of the evolving clockwork vehicle line of the day. Interesting comparisons may be made with other Kingsbury cars pictured in this book. Note the error on the fifth page reproduced, where the No. 362 dump truck is described twice; but no description is provided for the No. 360 covered truck.

perience in other related toy and model-collecting hobbies has shown, this may not always continue to be the case with model automobiles and future days may witness some strange doings accompanied by varyingly successful concealments being done in the oft-abused name of "restoration." The buyer, as always, will have to be aware. Some people will do these things, or have them done for them, because despite the fact that most knowledgeable collectors could not care less and, in fact, in most cases would prefer an incomplete original specimen to a fraudulently completed one, simply because it somehow salves their egos to be able to display seemingly "perfect" specimens: others will do it blatantly supposedly to add to the commercial value of models they intend to sell as "complete and original." Even in cases when it is done for the first reason named, such models may very well eventually be offered to others. It will not always be easy for the innocent to protect themselves.

In passing, it might be said that insofar as is known, sand-cast model automobiles have been produced by using two materials only, by far the majority in cast iron, a few in cast aluminum. This is in contrast to some other types of iron toys, where, on occasion, brass or white-metal castings have been employed for certain small parts. Because of its relatively high melting point, reproduction parts seldom are cast in iron; they are usually poured in white-metal alloys or sometimes in aluminum, or may, in fact, be fabricated from nonmetallic materials. It therefore seems reasonably safe to assume that any such replacement parts that have been incorporated into cast-iron model automobiles can be detected by going over the suspicious areas with a small magnet. The magnet will, of course, be attracted by iron, and a lack of such an attraction will reveal that a part or area has been replaced by some substitute and nonmagnetic material. The magnet test naturally will be useless in reference to cast aluminum, white-metal alloy, and zinc-alloy model automobiles. However, the chances are that the greater part of such fraudulent casting replacements will be made on cast-iron model automobiles, and the magnet will reveal the presence of such nonferrous substitutions.

There remains the problem of the use of already widely available reproduction replacement parts—reproductions or substitutions for components that are complete in themselves, such as tires, wheels, windshields, radiator grilles, and so

Fig. 202. Some aspects of prevailing collector customs. The original rubber tires on the European-made clockwork stamped-metal touring car of the early 1900's are somewhat the worse for wear, but they are the original tires, which is the important thing, and the sagacious owner would not think of replacing them with new rubber. Though the upper rear part of the body is missing on the friction car, neatly exposing the flywheel, it is a specimen a knowledgeable collector would keep, and keep as is, until a better one comes along.

Ward Kimball

on. This is a much more complex situation, although also involved in the potential of innocent or deliberate misrepresentation, and in many ways also closely allied to the repainting problem. When a part is missing from a model car, there is no inherent harm in itself in the act of replacing it with a reproduction or substitute component in the absence of an original, although in the view of many and probably most collectors there is somewhat of an air of futility and of the ridiculous in the act. Most want their specimens to be as complete as possible, but only insofar as this desired attribute can be attained with original and authentic components. Collectors see little point in installing a reproduction of a missing part or parts simply to make the model look "complete." They would rather wait until they can secure original parts to complete the model properly, or until they can upgrade an incomplete or damaged specimen by replacing it with one in better condition and disposing of the previous specimen. Thus any extensive investment in replacement parts appears, even when the use of such parts is viewed in the best light, rather wasteful and useless. In the main it is beginners who overworry about lack of completeness, and rush headlong into the futile use of reproduction replacement parts. The more experienced collector has learned not to let such things bother him. This is all natural enough, for the novice with a few model cars is likely to desire to display them all and to feel his individual specimens should appear "complete" and his whole display thereby the more impressive. The man with many model cars could not care less about this point but is more concerned with the overall ethical nuances of the matter and more particularly with his own standing in the hobby and the po-

tential harm it may have upon his disposal of duplicates if it becomes widely known that he is an extensive user of reproduction parts.

No one would particularly blame anyone if, upon acquiring a model car lacking its original rubber tires, he mounted reproduction tires, or upon securing a model car body without wheels he chose to make it into a viable, if somewhat less than authentic, model vehicle by adding a set of wheels of some type. The latter is precisely what occurred in the case of the car pictured in Fig. 203; a cast-iron coupe body in excellent original condition except that the wheels and axles were missing was made into a "complete car" by adding a set of fairly appropriately sized wheels and axles. Of course, the owner would prefer to have been able to add a set of the original wheels, or, even better, to have replaced the entire specimen with the same model with its original wheels and axles. Nevertheless, the specimen in Fig. 203 will do in the meantime. However, in the case of a collector holding dozens or even hundreds of such incomplete cars, what might seem logical in the case of a single model or even a few specimens would to most appear a gigantic exercise in futility, involving considerable labor and expense in the case of so large a number.

Be that as it may, the point is that when parts are missing there is no real harm in replacing them with either improper original units or reproductions except insofar as the point is reached where such replacements might mislead potential future owners. But it is even more important to avoid replacing any original components, no matter how poor their condition may be, with reproductions. Fig. 203 also illustrates this point. The Hubley cast-iron Airflow at the left is in somewhat poor original paint and still carries its four original tires, although the rubber has deteriorated to a point where these tires are in poor condition. Nevertheless, they are the original tires, and the aware collector knows that to replace them with readily obtainable reproductions, as someone did in the case of the tires on the Hubley cast-iron hook and ladder in the same photograph, would result in perceptibly lowering both the historical and actual value of the Airflow by impeaching its integrity just as much as would repainting its body. Someone replaced the tires on the hook and ladder. If it was done because the model came into the hands of an owner with the tires missing, it was permissible. If, however, the original tires were present, regardless of in how poor condition, and were discarded in the belief that to replace them with reproductions would improve the specimen or make it more desirable and valuable to a collector, the person who performed the deed acted under a gross misapprehension. As a matter of fact, the replacement tires all too obviously stand out as a visual awkwardness and ineptitude to any discerning collector. They will do for the moment, but the present owner of the specimen naturally hopes eventually either to secure an extra set of original tires, even if in as poor condition as those on the Airflow, and mount them on the hook and ladder in place of the reproductions, or, even better, to replace the entire hook and ladder with a specimen with original tires *and with the proper original ladders.*

The fact is that the hook and ladder pictured came into the hands of a collector without its original ladders. The ladders that have been added to it are original Hubley ladders from the same period but from a similar but slightly larger cast-iron hook and ladder; they are eight-rung ladders that came with a 6 1/2-inch vehicle, whereas the model in question is a 5-inch specimen and should properly carry a slightly shorter seven-rung ladder. Although the eight-rung ladders will "hang" on the 5-inch hook and ladder if brought forward to overlap the driver, as shown in the illustration, an experienced collector who has delved to any extent in the lore of models of this type and period would perceive at a glance that the ladders were not correct, although they might well pass muster as being the original equipment in the eyes of a novice. Admittedly, eight-rung Hubley ladders from the 1930's are just as close as anyone could get to seven-rung Hubley ladders from the same period, but still they are not the right ladders for this vehicle and, barring obtaining a complete specimen with the proper ladders in the meantime, the present owner of the hook and ladder is searching for two seven-rung Hubley ladders of the era.

Fig. 203. Further examples of collector practices. The cast-iron coupe was found without wheels. It was acceptable to make it into a complete vehicle with much later and entirely unrelated wheels, but doing so adds not a whit to its desirability or value. In the second photograph the Hubley cast-iron Airflow has poor rubber; but, again, as in the case of the touring car in Fig. 202, it is far more desirable to a collector in this form than if replacement tires of modern manufacture were installed. The Hubley cast-iron hook and ladder has a contemporary Hubley replacement ladder, but from a larger engine, and awaits the finding of two authentic ladders of the correct length.
G. William Holland photographs

Fig. 206 includes another example of the situations that arise in regard to replacement parts, repainting, and the principle of progressively upgrading the models in a collection. It shows two specimens of the M&L racing car made in the late 1940's, an especially interesting post–World War II miniature because of its continuation of a basic design originating in the 1920's. The first example acquired by the collector who owns these examples was the specimen at the left that was repainted and decorated with decalcomanias by some misguided racing-car enthusiast, an act all the more disheartening because the use of the decalcomanias indicate that the model had survived in original condition until fairly recently. This specimen, however, does have the original rubber wheels, and, regardless of this point, would serve any collector as an acceptable if by no means prime specimen until a better one came along. Somewhat later the same collector acquired the second specimen, at the right, which is in the original blue paint but has plastic replacement wheels. Obviously, the indicated procedure here is to transfer the original wheels and axles to the body in original condition, thereby quite properly and authentically creating an entirely original specimen—a perfect example of proper and legitimate "restoration." The replacement wheels and axles would then be transferred to the repainted specimen, and it would then presumably be passed along to some other collector who as yet possesses no example of this model, properly described, of

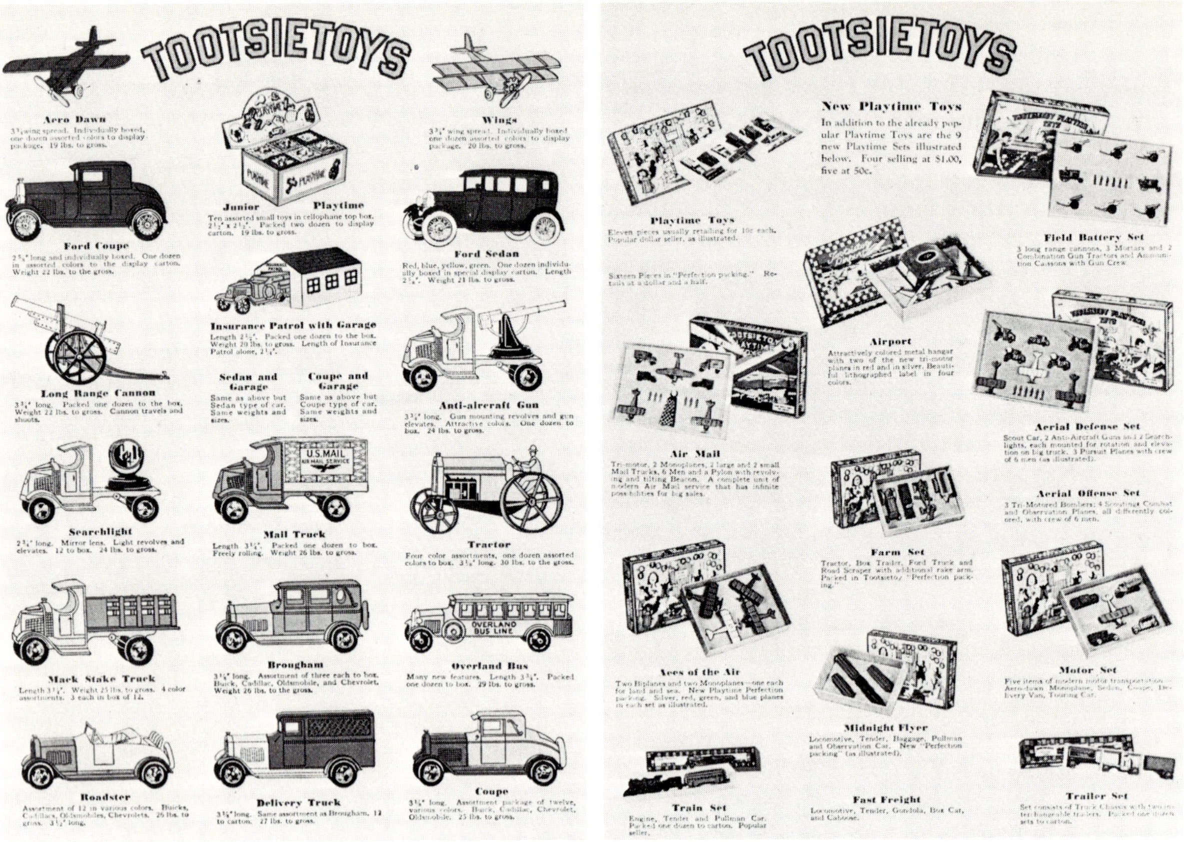

Fig. 204. Two pages from a Tootsietoy folder of 1931. One shows a number of separate vehicles, including the small fire engine or "Insurance Patrol" (also seen in Fig. 112) with garage. The garage was also furnished that year with the small-size coupe and sedan. The other page illustrates a number of sets.

George H. Hartman

Fig. 205. The ubiquitous cast-metal miniature racing car was a top favorite among manufacturers, and was copied, recopied, and slightly modified by a number of manufacturers in the 1920's and 1930's. The three models from the 1920's pictured here have noticeably different castings, and represent the products of three different and as yet not positively identified factories.

G. William Holland photograph

Fig. 206. The models derived from the popular racing car of the 1920's, illustrated in the proceding figure, were still going strong in the late 1940's, as evidenced by these two specimens of the M & L model of about 1948. The specimen at the left is repainted but has the original wheels; that at the right is in the original paint but has replacement wheels. The obviously desirable procedure, taken shortly after this photograph was made, was to switch the wheels so as to produce one specimen with all its components authentic and original.

G. William Holland photograph

course, as a repaint with replacement wheels and axles. However, the collector who is about to make the transfer of the original wheels and axles to the original body notes, "I think I can press the wheels past the crimped ends and off the axles without damaging them, and then back into position on the original body. If this doesn't work out, though, then I will still be on the lookout for still another specimen, with the original wheels factory-mounted on an original body, in order to upgrade still further."

The photograph in Fig. 207 further illustrates some of these basic principles as generally accepted by knowledgeable collectors. The model in question is a commendably stamped-metal clockwork model of a Rolls-Royce fitted with battery-operated headlights, made around 1930 by the French manufacturer JEP. Considerable of the original paint has flaked off, especially on the hood. This particular specimen, in fact, would appear to present a perfect example of the condition, mentioned a little earlier, that results when paint is not properly bonded or baked at the factory. In addition it will be observed that although the windshield for the passengers' compartment remains, the front windshield has disappeared and that the rear right wheel is not original to this specimen. Of the missing windshield, little can or need be said; the owner, of course, hopes that somehow an original replacement will turn up. Concerning the paint, the enthusiast who is oriented toward prototype automobiles might well think it self-evident that the model stands badly in need of being repainted, of so-called "restoration." The knowledgeable model-car collector, on the other hand, is aware that any such procedure would be an act of unthinkable destructiveness no matter how carefully and beautifully it was carried out—a "desecration," as one hobbyist put it. The model reached the hands of its present owner with the rear right-hand wheel missing. The wheel now mounted in this position is an identical original JEP wheel but in a different original color, either from a specimen of the same Rolls-Royce painted another color or from some other JEP model that made use of the same wheel. It is, barring the securing of the same wheel in the correct original color, the most authentic replacement of the missing wheel that could possibly be made. Of course, in the meantime, repainting this wheel to match the front wheel would be ridiculous, aside from rendering the wheel of far less value as an eventual spare part. At some future date when this model may be completed with a wheel in the proper original color, this extra wheel left in its original color may well serve toward the authentic completion of some other JEP model that requires the same wheel and perhaps in this particular original color.

Taking all things into consideration, it would seem that the objections raised by many collectors to such things as reproduction tires and the use of improper wheels to complete a model car are somewhat overdrawn, although understandably motivated by a fear that the availability of such things and their acceptance by collectors may prove a dangerous opening wedge for materials and practices of a much less salutary nature. In the ultimate run, it would unquestionably be highly desirable if the whole hobby of collecting old model cars could be kept to the bounds of the absolutely original and authentic. Notwithstanding, many hobbyists, and most particularly beginners, obviously are going to seek substitutions for missing wheels or tires, if only so that they can display a "complete" specimen in the upright position, foursquare on four wheels, that is indicated as the normal stance for a healthy motorcar, real or miniature. Indeed, without losing sight of the fact that in unscrupulous hands such replacements may be the subject of misrepresentations, it would appear that, on balance, the model-automobile hobby owes a debt of gratitude to William H. Hall

Fig. 207. A large JEP clock-work-powered model of a Rolls-Royce, and a prime piece despite the condition of the original paint, and, of course, far more valuable and desirable in this condition than if an attempt were made to touch up the bare spots or entirely repaint it. The rear wheel is a replacement from a contemporary JEP vehicle in another color.
Adam Pellicot, Jr.;
William Dreyer photograph

Fig. 208. While the collector who sets his standards of acceptable condition unreasonably high is likely to be doomed to disappointment, it is not impossible on occasion to find old model automobiles in new or like-new condition. Here are three such examples: a Kingsbury engine and firehouse, an Arcade cast-iron Ford (*Lloyd W. Ralston*), and a Buddy "L" fire engine (*B. J. Donnelly*).

for having managed to induce one of the large rubber companies to fabricate replacement tires in various diameters at a time when the potential demand could have, at best, seemed very slight to say the least.

However, the further one progresses from such basic things as wheels and tires, the greater the number of hobbyists that question the soundness and propriety of the availability and the use of various other reproduction components, both on the grounds of the dangers of misrepresentations by some concerning the originality of models incorporating such parts, and equally on the dan-

gers their use, even with the best of intentions, presents to serious historical research and the integrity of the models themselves. Certain such reproductions of small parts, particularly of parts for miniature cast-metal automobiles, cast in white-metal alloys and even in bronze, are presently known or reliably reported to be fabricated and freely offered for sale in the United States, France, and Great Britain. A number of such parts undoubtedly already have been incorporated into models that have changed hands, and their detection, while in most cases easy enough for an advanced collector, could be an extremely difficult matter for a beginner. That such parts are acceptable to the prototype-oriented model-car collectors is clear enough, just as they accept repainting; for their prime and in many cases only interest is in having a presentable-looking model, and it matters very little to them whether, say, a Tootsietoy Graham has the original headlight, grille, and bumper assembly. To most knowledgeable collectors of old model cars, such things, of course, matter greatly.

The greatest fear of collectors of old model cars is summed up in the question, "If small parts, why not then complete vehicles?" It is a nightmare to collectors that someone might produce all the reproduction parts required for the fabrication of complete reproduction specimens of desirable old models, particularly in the field of miniature cast-metal vehicles where the problems involved are far from insurmountable and detection of the fakes would be difficult for many. If this fear were ever realized, then the hobby of model-car collecting would suffer a drastic fall in values, not only of the specific models known to be reproduced, but of most models in general, for fear that they too would be reproduced. In time, as the means of detecting the fakes became widely known, the values of genuine models probably eventually would rise again, and perhaps even surpass their former values.

So far, fortunately, model-car collecting has not been subjected to many such situations either in terms of reproductions of components or of entire vehicles. This may not always remain true, as the hobby continues to grow. A number of reproductions and pseudo-reproductions already have arrived in the closely associated field of cast-iron toys such as horse-drawn vehicles and banks whose originals were in many cases contemporary with cast-iron toy automobiles. A few reproductions and pseudo-reproductions of old cast-iron toy automobiles undoubtedly already have been made. The term "pseudo-reproduction" is used here to distinguish an item that superficially appears to duplicate an old model but that actually was designed, tooled up, and manufactured—more or less by the same methods employed some decades earlier—in modern times. To the more knowledgeable collector they appear to be exactly what they are; to the less aware hobbyist they seem to be reproductions of specific older items, perhaps even made by using the original old patterns, and to the novice, all too often, they may appear the genuine old models they are, deliberately or innocently, represented to be. However, the currently or recently made old-style cast-iron model automobiles that the collector is most likely to encounter today are neither reproductions nor pseudo-reproductions, but the Ford Model T's manufactured by the Grey Iron Casting Company. Grey Iron has been manufacturing these Fords off and on since the 1920's, and although considerable quantities are bought today by decorators and others not engaged in the toy business, they are still legitimate articles of today's toy trade. The danger they present to new collectors is that they may be misrepresented either by unscrupulous or by unaware individuals as being genuine "old" cast-iron model cars from the 1920's, and it must be admitted that some less than reputable individuals have purchased these by the dozen for use in trades in furthering their own collections.

There are, of course, two types of misrepresentation. One is to describe or list such a model as old, taking one's chances on eventually receiving a call from Uncle Sam's or John Bull's postal inspectors, with the consequent unpleasantness. The second, which is safer and somewhat more insidious, is misrepresentation by implication. It is quite easy, for example, to set down a modern specimen amidst all sorts of assorted automobile parts and literature and other goods on the tailgate of one's station wagon at a real automobile meet and allow some novice excitedly to spot it and assume he has made a real find, telling him the truth if he inquires, but keeping silent if he does not. Some individuals indeed justify this procedure to themselves on the grounds that the unquestioning purchaser probably thinks he has found a sleeper of whose value its owner is unaware and that he is the one who is doing the outfoxing.

There are today, also, a considerable number of sheet-metal models of old automobiles on the market, many made abroad, that at times may be taken for genuine old models by beginners. There is even a curious psychology that works here; a novice collector may see such a model offered for sale on a modern toy counter, and not give it a second thought, but some months later, encountering the same item, perhaps in used con-

Fig. 209. The Sturditoy American La France fire engine is justly considered one of the most realistic and desirable of the big pressed-steel pull-toy trucks of the 1920's. It was equipped with a working water-pump action. There was also a companion water tower with pumping action in the Sturditoy line.

"Playthings"

dition, at an automobile meet or antique shop he may eagerly seize upon it as a genuine old specimen. Far more dangerous, however, is the transposition of such models into downright fakes. Most of the models of this type are rather gaudily lithographed. The faker picks out such models possessing the structural contours most suitable for his ends (usually open cars or closed vehicles with windows pierced out, not represented by lithographed surfaces), paints over the lithography in an imitation of dulled "old" paint, and applies a rubber stamp reading "Hafner" or "Wilkins" or some other famous early model manufacturers' name—most of whom, incidentally, did not actually stamp their name as an identification on their genuine products—and offers it to a gullible beginner at an appropriate price or plants it where some such novice is likely to run across it. It may even be sold to an antique-shop owner who actually believes it is a genuine article and sincerely offers it as such, for such dealers naturally, no matter how good their intentions, cannot possibly be infallible judges of the status and merits of everything that comes their way.

Another fake that often attracts beginners

because of its sheer size and the attraction of the prototypical concept is the trailer truck in the large pressed-steel-vehicle category. Here a home-brewed three-axle articulated vehicle is created by cutting up and grafting together components of two ordinary two-axle trucks.* The novice is then presented with what appears to him to be a large and quite appealing, although repainted, aerial-ladder truck, tank truck, moving van, or other trailer type supposedly manufactured by one of the heavy-steel model truckmakers of the 1920's. Collectors should bear in mind that virtually no such model vehicles were manufactured in the 1920's, and very few even in the 1930's. In fact, with the possible exception that the classic Turner No. 76, 36-inch-long articulated Mack hook and ladder, or some earlier version thereof, was introduced prior to 1930, which appears unlikely,† it seems safe to state that the only two such large all-metal units produced in the 1920's were the 24-inch Structo No. 420 motor transport and No. 421 U.S. Air Mail transport trucks which just barely qualify by having been brought out in 1929.‡ There were, categorically, no Buddy "L" or Keystone—to name the two makes whose components usually are employed for the creation of such fraudulent composites—trailer trucks manufactured in the 1920's.

Lastly, there are three miniature cast-metal models that must particularly be mentioned here, if only because so much already has been spoken concerning them in the model-car-collecting hobby

---

* Such three-axle articulated vehicles should not, of course, be confused with models achieving a three-axle count by having dual rear axles on a solid frame. A few such pressed-metal nonpowered vehicles were made by Turner, and there also were some Hill Climber and Turner friction models that would provide a similar axle count.

† As far as is known, all Turner No. 76 hook and ladders had working headlights, which would preclude its dating from before the early 1930's.

‡ The Structo No. 420 and No. 421 bear the round decalcomania reading "A.F. Lines Air Service" that has evoked so much curiosity. These decalcomanias originally were created in 1928 for use as wing insignia on American Flyer steel pull-toy and clockwork airplanes, and subsequently were employed to embellish the sides of the Structo trailer trucks when they came out in 1929, American Flyer then being the distributors of Structo toys. Subsequently, around 1933–1934, the remaining stock of these decalcomanias was thriftily used up on American Flyer railroad tank cars.

Fig. 210. Instruction sheets and manuals are also highly collectible. Illustrated here are the instruction sheets for the Buddy "L" No. 220-A steam shovel of the late 1920's (*Arthur B. Lundahl*) and the Kingsbury No. 275 aerial ladder truck of the late 1930's, which also pictures their large firehouse. The No. 275 was a greatly updated version of the ladder truck shown in Fig. 155, but with virtually the same action (*G. William Holland Collection*).

THIS Buddy "L" Improved Steam Shovel is made and operates just like the real steam shovels. It's mounted on a turntable so that it can be swung around to any desired position by turning the tiller wheel in the center of the machine.

Here's how to operate it: First of all notice the levers lettered A and B in the illustrations. When you move lever A forward it throws the necessary gears into place and by turning the crank C in a clockwise direction the dipper stick D moves downward or forward along the boom E. By turning the crank in a counter-clockwise direction the movement of the dipper stick is reversed.

Lever B simply raises the dipper F without moving the dipper stick. Move lever A back so that the clutch is disengaged and move lever B forward. Then by turning the crank in a clockwise direction the cable G is wound around the drum H, pulling the dipper up until it reaches the pulley at the end of the boom.

The dipper is emptied by tripping the bottom with the cable I, by hand or, with lever A in gear, by running the dipper stick to its full length and the bottom is tripped automatically.

A little practice and you'll be operating this improved steam shovel like a veteran engineer.

MOLINE PRESSED STEEL CO.
East Moline, Illinois, U. S. A.

CUT HERE

Dear Friend:

Now that you have this Buddy "L" Steam Shovel I'm sure you'd like to have some of the other Buddy "L" Quality Toys.

The newest one is the Buddy "L" Tool Chest—but it's really more than a toy, for it is a strong, sturdy chest filled with standard quality tools—the kind a real carpenter uses.

We've had some circulars printed showing a picture of the tool chest and telling all about it. If you'll write your name and address on the coupon, cut it out and mail it in an envelope to me, I'll send you one of these circulars.

Sincerely yours,
BUDDY "L"s DADDY.

Moline Pressed Steel Co.,
East Moline, Illinois.   Atten: Buddy "L"'s Daddy

Gentlemen:

Please send me the circular telling about the Buddy "L" Tool Chest.

Name ....

Street Number ....

City .... State ....

Another

KINGSBURY

Motor Driven Toy

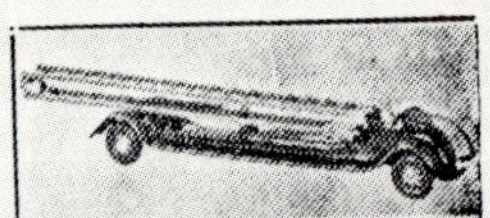

NO. 275.   AERIAL LADDER TRUCK

The action of this toy is entirely automatic. Wind the motor up and place toy on bare floor, allowing it to run toward wall or any obstruction. Upon hitting obstruction the ladder is released and will slowly raise to its full height. When folded back the ladder is held in down position by pushing the two black prongs over nearest rung.

If when ladder goes up it remains perpendicular instead of falling against wall, bend the back of the seat to which ladder wire is attached very slightly toward the driver.

Driver is held in position by bending the steel ears around his feet.

We picture below the No. 7 Firehouse which is an interesting accessory to the ladder truck. The truck may be wound up and placed inside. When ready for the "Fire", press a lever on the side which rings a bell and the truck will run out under its own power.

If your dealer does not stock it, it will be sent postpaid from Factory for 50c (60c west of Mississippi.)

KINGSBURY MANUFACTURING CO.
Keene, New Hampshire

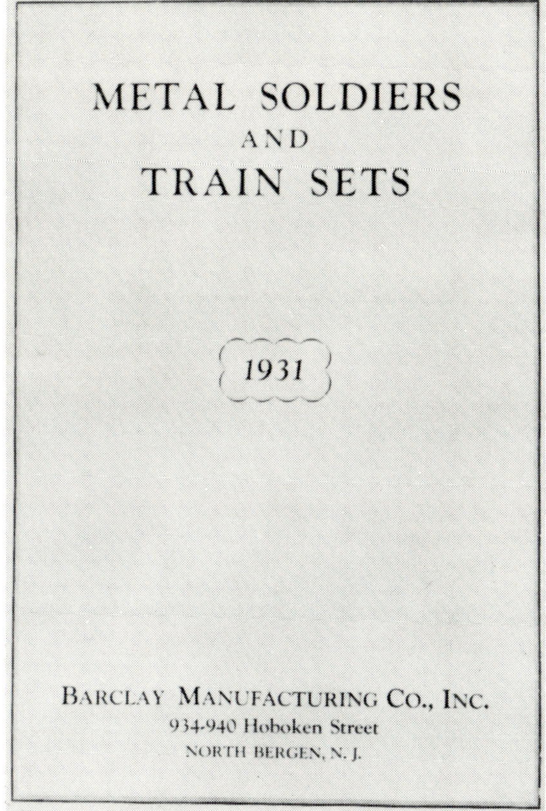

Fig. 211. The cover and the only page show-ing an automotive vehicle, the No. 53 antiair-craft car, from the Barclay 1931 catalog (*Bar-clay Mfg. Co. Inc.*), and the 1934 catalog sheet, printed in full colors, that introduced the Manoil line of automobiles (*Tootsietoy—Strombecker Corp.*).

and so much confusion has thereby arisen. The three models in question are the three vehicles in the Tootsietoy Classic Series of the early 1960's that reproduce prototypes similar to those on which three early Tootsietoys were based, models already mentioned in this section. The fact is that the vehicles of the 1960's do not reproduce the earlier Tootsietoys either in design or size; the only similarity is that the three later models vaguely mirror or parallel three Tootsietoys variously made between 1914 and 1933: the Ford Model-T touring car, the Ford Model-A coupe, and the Mack stake truck. The early No. 4570 Ford Model-T touring car is a model of a 1914 prototype with the driver's seat enclosed; the model of the 1960's (No. 3101) is based on a 1912 prototype with no doors on the driver's compartment. The early No. 4655 Ford Model-A coupe is the model most closely mirrored by the later model (No. 3102), but they are quite readily distinguishable even in a photograph, the model of the 1960's having plastic wheels, the spare being a fifth wheel instead of part of the body casting, and an open rumble seat in place of the closed rumble on the model manufactured from 1928 to 1933. The Mack truck of the 1960's, No. 3111, is undoubtedly the most interesting and scarcest of the three later models. For reasons that are not quite clear to the hobbyist, who can only regard this as a rather attractive miniature, the Tootsietoy factory was never quite satisfied with the diework for this model, and it was dropped from the line after a fairly short—by modern Tootsietoy standards—production run. The late No. 3111 is instantly distinguished from the old No. 4638 by having a plastic body with no openings going through between the stakes and sideboards, and spoked wheels. Furthermore, all the vehicles in the 1960 series were plainly marked "Tootsietoy Classic Series" underneath. There were both modern cars and other old-time models in the 1960 series, but as the latter were of prototypes never made by Tootsietoy at an earlier date, no confusion has arisen concerning them, as in the case of the two Fords and the Mack truck.

The whole matter of confusion has been a greatly inflated tempest in a teapot, no doubt immeasurably stirred by enthusiasts who had heard of but had never actually seen the earlier models either in themselves or even as catalog illustrations and who jumped to erroneous conclusions. However, this much must be said: Because of the rough mirrorings of the 1960's, it is quite possible for a person, either innocently or with deliberate intent, to defraud, to advertise or list for sale a "Tootsietoy Model-T touring car," a "Tootsietoy Model-A coupe," or a "Tootsietoy Mack stake truck" and live up to the letter, if not the impression created in the minds of many by such descriptions, of the offer of an example of the 1960 series. Already there have been misunderstandings and ill feelings as a result of these confusions, and undoubtedly they will long continue. Anyone responding to such offers will have to protect himself by ascertaining just *which* Model T, Model A, or Mack actually is being offered! Yet it must also be observed that these are three recent models that a great many enthusiasts who otherwise limit their collections to models made prior to World War II are rather prone to seek and preserve, although were it not for the confusions and publicity that have arisen concerning them they would in all probability blithely have ignored them.

Obviously, in the case of any dubious models, repaints, so-called "restorations," reproduction parts, and related matters, the danger is not so much in the existence of these units and practices but in the resulting loss to history and in the misrepresentations that they induce, misrepresentations often both as to the acceptance and propriety of such things and as to the specific supposed genuineness and value of the models themselves. It is unfortunate that each successive book that attempts to treat comprehensively, frankly, and impartially with any phase of collecting old toys and models must, in turn, once again set forth these pitfalls and problems, yet there is really no alternative if a broad picture is to be painted fairly and honestly. Nor, as experience sadly has shown, seldom can such situations adequately be held in hand and a desirable and healthy climate be fully maintained. In the long run, at best all that can be done is to place as many collectors as possible on their guard. There will always be novices away from the mainstream of thought that can be misled, and those who stand in some wise to profit by various departures from the norm will, it is to be feared, always find some means of doing so; channels of distribution are found or created; even supposedly disinterested organizations may be set up to provide a cover or give a seeming benign approval to the traffic, once it ceases to be merely representative of the personal inclinations of a few individuals and reveals itself as possessing minor commercial possibilities.

The model-automobile hobby can only wait and trust that it may be successful in maintaining certain standards, although experience has shown that all too often the minority who would overturn such standards are far more inclined to activity in their own interests than the greater but all too often listless number whose hope it is to be able to maintain some measure of ethical subvention amidst the hurly-burly and give-and-take of any active growing hobby. Alas, too, there are almost invariably to be encountered some wretches who find something inherently humorous or, reflecting their own less than admirable inner images of themselves, even suspicious in those who aspire to speak of ethics. Unfortunately, many hobbyists are all too shortsighted, think only of the moment and not of the long pull, and too easily allow themselves to be imposed upon by those who make scant efforts even to conceal their contempt for the average honorable but easygoing hobbyist. As surely as Gresham's law accurately foretells that bad money invariably drives out good money, so too must it be considered rather axiomatic that bad hobbyists drive out the good, and that bad hobby organizations drive out the good organizations. Only those who bear the honorable scars of battle, not so much against corruption and petty meanness themselves, but rather against what will be found to be the prime enemies, lassitude and indifference on the part of honorable men in determining the direction a hobby will take, will fully appreciate and believe the import of these thoughts. The model-automobile hobby can only be forewarned and its enthusiasts permitted to hope for the best.

Most collecting hobbies start honorably and on a high plateau because the first to become attracted usually are animated by the normal reasons of pleasure, knowledge, and relaxation. An occasional bad egg stands out, and generally is shunned. But as a hobby grows, and particularly when it becomes obvious that a stage has been reached where there is opportunity for less-admirable personal benefits, the potential dangers increase and become the greater menace to the innocent and naïve, particularly to those who mistakenly assume that because an individual is, or at least professes to be, interested in the same hobby as themselves he must perforce be as sincere and honorable as they are. It may well be that the hobby of model-car collecting is reaching its basic moment of truth and decision, its inevitable fork in the road that can lead either to a truly great future or to one marked with disappointments and bitterness at substantially the moment that this

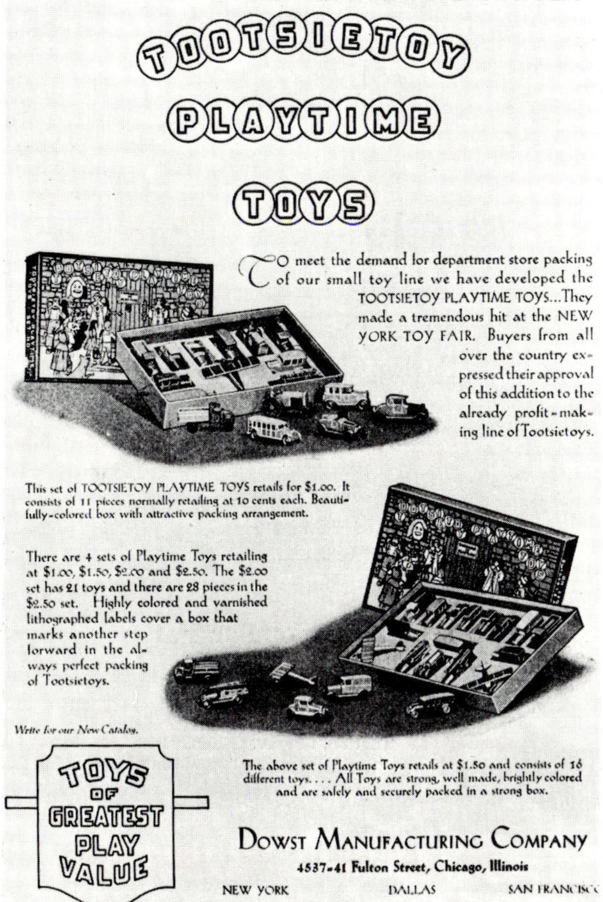

Fig. 212. Left, a 1929 advertisement featuring boxed sets of Tootsietoy "Playtime Toys"—standard-size vehicles—showing the label used in the late 1920's and early 1930's. Right, the set of Tootsietoy "Midgets" introduced in 1936—very small vehicles with fixed wheels—with their box employing a modified version of the same label.

George H. Hartman

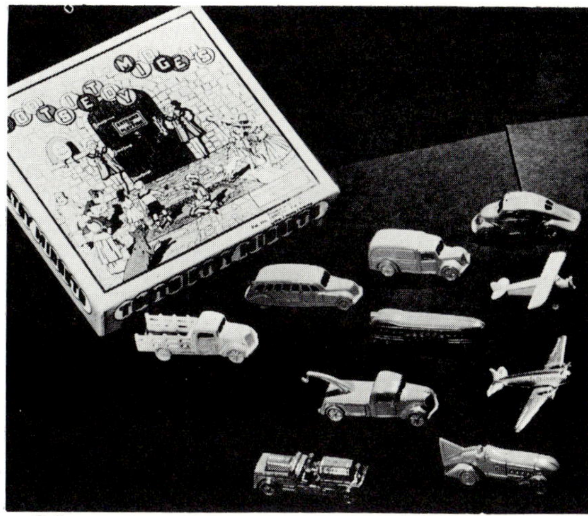

present volume is being prepared. Latter issues of the discontinued British journal *Model Car Collector* have found it necessary to carry a standing notice to the effect that the magazine "cannot be held responsible for any bad debts incurred because of contacts made through these pages," which in plain language must be interpreted as meaning that even among so seemingly mutually enthusiastic and strictly hobby-minded a group as its readership there have been cause for complaints. Not, we should hasten to add, that reference to this fact is to point a finger at any particular group of collectors; readership of *Model Car Collector* was worldwide. Among American collectors there are cases of model cars paid for but never delivered, of model cars delivered but never paid for—"pay" in both instances being represented either by actual cash amounts or models in supposed exchange—of models misdescribed and misrepresented, and all other imaginable trickery and ills. There also have arisen problems of what appear to the recipients obviously inadequate packing procedures resulting in damaged models, with the consequent recriminations and debates as to the fair and proper mode of concluding the transactions involving such cars. This is all too sadly familiar to those who have been active in other such hobby pursuits, and underlines the dangers of insisting on looking upon a hobby through rose-colored glasses simply because it is a hobby, or at least purportedly so—there are those who delightedly bring to every two-dollar hobby transaction the steel-trap manipulations that one might normally associate with a nineteenth-century attempt to secure control of the Erie Railroad! Mentioning these situations may well not appear to be the most salutary advertisement of a hobby to possible participants, and there will no doubt be those who would prefer that nothing be said concerning such things, but they are nonetheless properly a portion of the overall picture that both candor itself and hopeful aspirations for a sound future for the model-car-collecting hobby compel reference to here.

In reference to packing for shipment, most particularly of small, fragile die-cast models whose metal may well already be showing varying traces of deterioration owing to contamination of the original mix, one further thought should be added: Shipments that cross national frontiers are subject to being opened, examined, and repacked by Customs, a necessary and esteemed service in every land but one whose representatives may not always be attuned to the extraordinary delicacy of the die castings found in old miniature automobiles.

COLLECTORS' CHOICE

Withal, the fake as a physical entity, while its offering often in accompanied by the tender of a fallacious cover story, is not by any means synonymous with fakery as an unsavory but nevertheless indisputably practiced art. It is apparent that whatever jeopardy may be presented to model-car collectors today or in the future by out-and-out fakes themselves, the greatest potential source of danger is in various misrepresentations. Misrepresentations of what one has or will deliver, or of what one will pay, are obvious noxious acts; misrepresentation of such goods as may actually change hands, such as repaints and those incorporating reproduction parts, are tangible and not undecipherable pitfalls, but consderable if less obvious peril may also attach itself to misrepresentations of the whole sweep and scope of various divisions of collecting and to relative prices, rarity, and desirability. The price factor will be dealt with candidly in the following section. As for the mores and outlook of most knowledgeable collectors and of the model-car-collecting hobby as a whole, in the final analysis each collector must, of course, set and pursue his own pattern, but what is important is that the beginner not be misled and cajoled into paths of whose true overall importance and direction he is unaware.

It should be borne in mind that not everyone among those who do misrepresent may do so in conscious charlatanism, for honest error has a way of feeding upon itself, and those who have unwittingly acquired a wholly or partially false conception of things may quite innocently pass their concepts along to others, even perhaps thinking they are thereby providing a novice with a commendable service and partial education in the complexities of a fascinating hobby. In short, some people deliberately misrepresent because they seek to achieve some financial (or even, in a few odd cases, psychological) gain—if these individuals had not been attracted to the hobby of model automobiles as affording a potentially profitable field for their operations, they would be similarly active in other areas, whether they embraced clipping the perforations off postage stamps to sell them as rare imperforates or in offering to sell the toll concession on the New York Throughway, there being relatively few prospects left around these sophisticated days for the peddling of the Brooklyn Bridge. Furthermore, purely within a given hobby such as model-automobile collecting, some individuals deliberately misrepresent because, sadly, the profits from such acts, whether in model cars themselves or in cash, provide them with a means of expanding their own cherished collections that they otherwise would not possess, while some simply innocently misrepresent because they themselves have been the still-unawakened victims of misrepresentation. A peculiar and paradoxical side effect of the latter type of activity is that if there be sufficient innocent and unrecognized misrepresentation in the early days of a hobby, the erroneous conception may almost achieve the status of an accepted fact among many, and one only regretfully and perhaps never completely dissolved. It is incumbent upon us, or at least desirable, that all look with a certain measure of kindness and tolerance upon such matters, even while explaining them, and to emphasize again that not everyone who professes to believe and attempts to act upon these legends is by any means a deliberate deceiver.

Throughout the course of preparing this book it has been apparent that the good old "works model" enticement still continues unabated, that that boring old humbug concerning the supposed high virtues and great historical and collectors' value of handmade models marches ever onward, and that there is no diminution in the efforts to inculcate or nurture the tiresome conception that whatever must pass through a Customs barrier to reach a young automotive enthusiast at the time it was made or a collector today must automatically be immeasurably more desirable than something manufactured in one's own native land. In by far the great majority of cases not only is there present the general or particularized fallacy of the supposed or claimed virtues of the supposition involved, but also the fact that the proffered models—regardless of frequently present collectors' interest and value of their own when properly identified and not sailed under false colors—often turn out to be something quite different from their supposed attributions. While the work model imposition unquestionably, as the very name given them indicates, emanates from Europe, many native American impositions under this description have been observed of late: Structo clockwork roadsters called Stutz work models (admittedly a seeming most alluring combination of words for those likely to be attracted by such things), Keystone and Structo steel trucks termed Packard works models, and a number of Kingsbury models being called all sorts of works models as the mood of the moment seems to render appropriate. As for the handmade models, it is enough to judge such specimens as actually qualify for this description on their individual merits, although whether supposedly works models or simply the creation of an individual model

craftsman engaged in building such a miniature for his own satisfaction and enjoyment, such models actually possess interest for a very limited group of collectors. Lately it has become clear that a number of the humble workmen who supposedly toiled at their benches to lovingly handcraft a model car supposedly made highly desirable by the fact that it is an example of what British collectors designate as a "one off" model and Americans simply refer to as handmade, must have had access to substantial sand, slush, or centrifugal casting facilities. In short, of late it has only become necessary to show a novice collector something that is not even handmade but simply beyond his as yet limited experiences to pass it off—or at least to make the attempt with a reasonable expectation of success—as a handmade model of substantial worth! There is not always even logic in these manipulations—although to most collectors who are interested only in old mass-produced model cars there is little logic ever present in the collecting of handmade models at all—for some of the big cast-iron Arcade and Hubley and Kenton vehicles that have thus been offered as individual creations would be worth just as much to an aware collector if proffered as exactly what they, in truth, are.

As for such mass-produced models that have been to a varying degree "chopped," reworked, and repainted at some stage before they reach the point of being offered to beginner collectors, either by the perpetrator or by some subsequent owner, the less said, the better.

As for the lure of foreign models, whether for cash or in trade for the models of one's own country, the beginner can best be served by the injunction that he would do well carefully to consider all such propositions carefully before rushing into an acceptance. This does not mean that such situations are always disadvantageous or that the aware collector invariably wisely avoids such deals, but rather that many novices are all too prone to be unduly attracted by such proffers without thinking them through and evaluating them unemotionally. Admittedly, it adds a certain gloss to the act of showing off a collection to one's friends to point to certain models, particularly if they are large and showy and somewhat unusual in appearance, and denote them in turn by the country of their origin. However, the beginner is all too prone to accept that which is merely unusual or somewhat exotic in shape, construction, and finish as the equivalent of actual collectors' values, and there are too many ready and willing to take advantage of this well-known fact in every field of collecting. The result is that many a col-

Dowst's Catalogue 1921

Introduction

AFTER an interval of several years, during which time we issued no catalogue due to war conditions which prevented our doing so, we are pleased to once more present to you our 1921 catalogue of the DOWST line of metal novelties and small toys.

Our old friends will notice in addition to many new numbers presented, the absence of many of the old numbers. We have reduced our line as noted, to the best selling numbers for all classes of the trade in order that we might carry stock of all the numbers in the catalogue, thus eliminating delay and congestion in the factory caused by a line that had become unweildy.

For the toy trade we are packing all the small toys listed on pages eighteen to twenty-three in one gross boxes. For the candy trade and those who do not need the gross packing on these numbers we still pack them in bulk. Our price list which we are enclosing will give you the prices for both methods of packing. The articles listed on pages twenty-four to twenty-eight inclusive are not packed in gross boxes except as assortments, but are also

obtainable in bulk as individual numbers. Please specify in your orders which method of packing you desire.

We have endeavored to show in this catalogue under all the larger toys the method of packing. We also wish to add that unless otherwise stated the illustrations shown here are the exact size of the toys they represent.

On account of the extremely high prices of electrotypes that prevail at the present time we regret that we cannot furnish you cuts gratis for cataloguing and circularizing, but we will be pleased to furnish them at cost or loan them to you if you do not care to keep them permanently. With that understanding we offer you the use of any of the cuts illustrated in this catalogue.

Dowst Brothers Company
120-124 Ann Street
CHICAGO, ILL.

No. 4570. AUTOMOBILE

A perfect reproduction in miniature of the well known "Flivver." Undoubtedly one of the best selling small toys on the market and gaining in popularity each day. Body finished in enamels of different colors; windshield bronzed; steering gear black and movable wheels bronze finish. Packed one dozen to the box.

No. 4610. TRUCK

Companion piece to our famous No. 4570 Automobile. Finished and packed exactly the same as the above number.

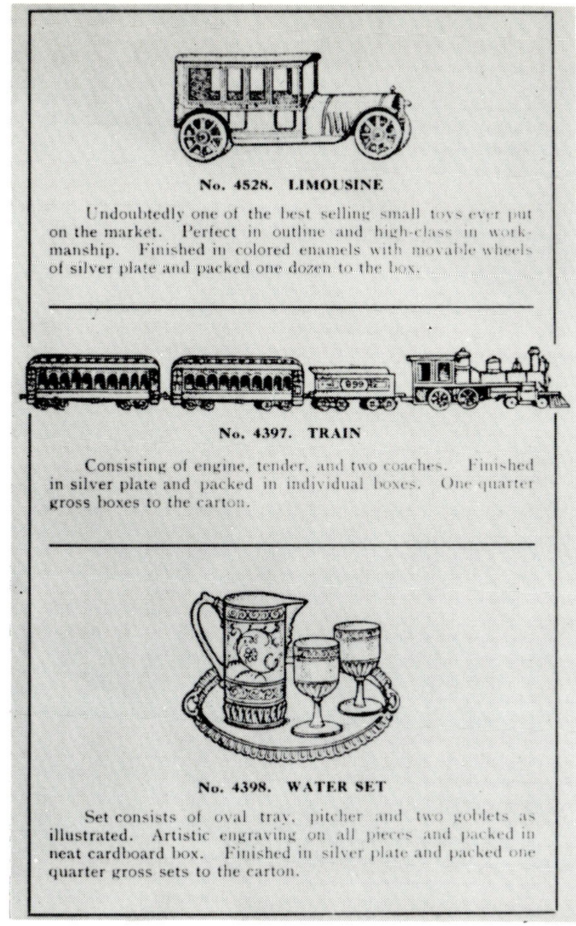

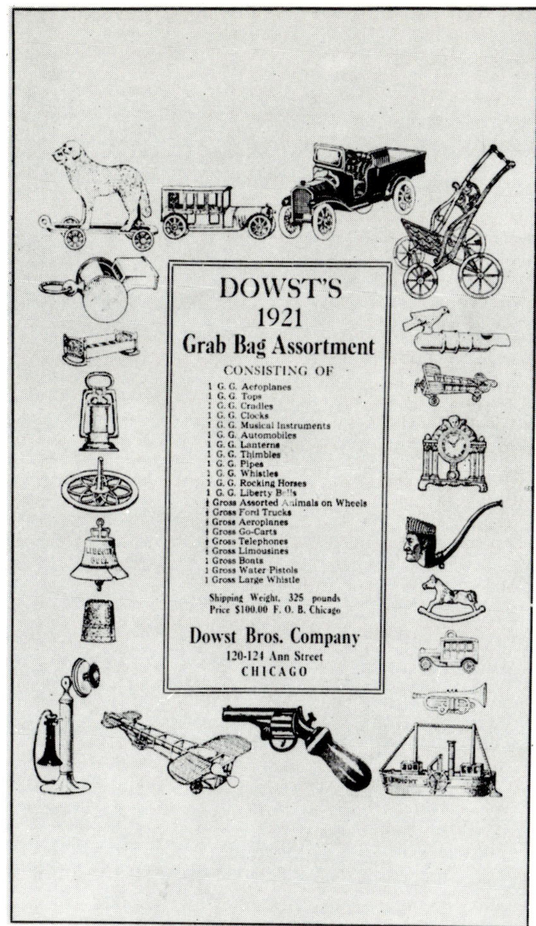

Fig. 213. The cover and introductory pages and pages relating to the three model automobiles with turnable wheels then being manufactured and which later became part of the Tootsietoy line from the Dowst 1921 catalog. The three vehicles are the No. 4528 limousine, No. 4570 Ford Model-T touring car, and No. 4610 Ford Model-T truck.

Tootsietoy—Strombecker Corp.

lector who, in his novitiate days, supposes he has either had the good fortune to encounter a most genial and generous fellow overseas, or that he has perhaps on his own initiative done a handsome piece of trading finds in time that his supposed prize or prizes are considered so much dross by the bulk of his more knowing fellows.

All this obviously merits some further explanation. Sincerely attempting to eschew both the overly chauvinistic and the near metaphysical, let the following be considered: When one holds in his hand a foreign model, no matter how elaborate and well crafted, its primary appeal is that of the strange or unusual; the hobbyist who holds it seldom distills from it any of the spirit of the prototypes of his native land, and never any of the spirit of its modelmaking craft. But when an American holds an old model car fabricated in the United States, he is grasping the essence of both the prototype American automotive industry and, even more important by far to the American model-car collector, the essence of the design and productive capacity of the American toy and model industry. And so too, in turn, it must ever be with a Briton and a British-made model; with a Frenchman and a French-made model, and so on. This is the basic reason why an alien model never can be as attractive, regardless of how elaborate, admirable, and accurate it may be, as one manufactured in one's own country, and all the stream of artificial and at times strenuously imposed forces of promotion, the lure of faraway places, and what you will, cannot alter or displace this fact.

In the particularized case of the American enthusiast, on the whole he operates in most matters on a conscious or subconscious basis of preference which begins, naturally enough, for things made in the United States, and then moves more or less progressively eastward, not without a salute in passing to the north. After American-made products—in this case, of course, model cars—his preference is next for Canadian and British, and thence easterly onto the Continent, with overall preferences next for the countries bordering the Atlantic, such as France, and then still farther easterly in turn. This may not be an entirely logical or commendable progression, at least from all viewpoints, but it nevertheless is a reality. If one questions its overall validity, one need only look to the extreme popularity among collectors of model cars made in more recent years for the products of certain relatively obscure Belgian and Dutch makes. There also are operative in the background of the American collector factors that hardly are present in the case of British or French collectors and many others; namely, that the fact is—and this point is so seldom consciously appreciated—that much of what comes from Central Europe is automatically rejected or found odious by most Americans as either overtly or obscurely representative of a narrow and circumscribed if not downright oppressive life from which his ancestors were fortunate enough to have escaped and which he now is sufficiently assured, mature, and secure to reject.*

Contemporary American children usually instinctively rejected the reflection of such things in toys and models even when they were thrust upon them as presents, and most American collectors even if only subconsciously reject them for similar reasons, even when these unspoken intuitions are, perforce, thrown into a balance against the all too blatantly obvious, if ofttimes unthinking, lure of the distant, the different, and the exotic, or what one nameless late nineteenth-century toy advertising copywriter called the "Kuaint, Kueer, and Kurious."

FOREIGN MODELS

In every field of model collecting—automobiles, trains, boats, airplanes—as in other areas quite apart from models, there evidently must always be a struggle between these elements: between the conscious, hard-to-deny pull of faraway places and the unaccustomed in designs, and the subconscious rejection of a barren past—and almost invariably the latter wins. There are two partial exceptions to this, one where promoters with an ample stock of foreign-feeling designs deliberately campaign to push them as something most desirable for collectors, and the other the comparative few occasions when foreign manufac-

turers did truly catch the lines, techniques, constructional methods, and spirit (of both prototype and model) that would make certain goods specifically produced for the export trade highly acceptable merchandise. The great German firm of Bing, for example, was and is one of the few companies famous for their success in doing this, thereby giving modern American model-car collectors certain items highly successful in their day and highly desirable by present-day collecting standards, such as their clockwork Checker and Yellow taxicabs † (Figs. 216 and 217) and in their famous series of five clockwork 6 1/4-inch Ford Model T's—sedan, touring car with roof up, coupe, roadster, and pickup truck. This was not the longest series of Ford Model T's; Buddy "L" had no less than nine nonpowered types, but unquestionably the longest series of inexpensive clockwork Model T's were the Bings, ranging from 37 to 50 cents, depending on when and where they were sold.

But the American manufacturers Marx and Strauss were able to put the prices on some of their comparable size Ford Model T's, certain of which included erratic action (Figs. 179 and 222) down to as little as 25 cents retail, which was quite a production triumph spelling the end of the great flurry of popularity of the Bings, the more particularly so because at the time of the tariff hearings in the early 1920's, while admitting to Harry T. Kingsbury that he acknowledged him king of the clockwork automobile manufacturers, John Bing, the head of Bing's agency in the United States, had boasted that he did not care what tariff was imposed on imported toys *so long as it was based on the factory price,* as indeed the 70 percent tariff instituted at that time was based. What Mr. Bing meant was that he could, if necessary, sell goods to himself at any price at the factory so that even after paying the 70 percent duty based on this cost the toys would be in a fine competitive position with American goods upon their landing and that Bing's profit could be

---

* An interesting psychological point: many American collectors equate Central European toys with some of the traditionally less pleasant aspects of immigration and refer to them by such terms as "rags and wooden shoes toys," "steerage toys," and so on.

† There were two sizes of Bing Yellow Taxi in the 1920's, 7 1/2-inch and 8 3/4-inch, and a Checker cab in the latter and possibly both lengths. The larger cabs had dummy taximeters, two doors that opened, dummy cowl lights, and a spare tire. Structurally the cabs appear to be rather close copies in lithographed sheet metal of Arcade cast-iron taxicabs; the Bing Checker cab at least has somewhat more detailed lettering and insignia than its Arcade counterpart, an enhancement made easy by the character of lithography. The Bing taximeters are externally mounted on the left sides of the cabs, a carryover from European practice, although the Bing and other continental-type miniature taxicabs (Figs. 32 and 167) carry their meters outboard on the right side. Prototype American taxicabs of the 1920's had interior taximeters.

gained in the United States, not at the factory. Not all European toy manufacturers of the day were in the same position as the Bings, of course, but even among the great majority who did not maintain American branches there was all sorts of opportunity for side deals and special manipulations on the basis of the factory price. What is surprising is not that great difficulties were imposed on American manufacturers because of this but that nevertheless American productive knowhow enabled domestic manufacturers of similar lines to compete successfully and remain in business.

Nevertheless, such desirable items must be accounted as being among the relatively few exceptions that prove the rule. Apropos of this general theme, some of the Tipp vehicles made for the British market, particularly their double-deck buses, appear to be similar examples of the spirit of one nation's vehicles being successfully emulated by a foreign manufacturer. However, the intricacies of such matters are so subtle that it is truly difficult to assess such things unless one has been born and bred in the specific country whose cars are being imitated. To an American, for example, the appearance of British advertising signs and tires marked "Dunlop" may make them appear British; to a Briton there may be nuances present that completely negate this impression, and this in a nutshell may well sum up all the difficulties attendant on such matters from the first moment that a manufacturer decides to produce a model or a series of models designed to sell in another country. In short, an American, no matter how capable, would be no more competent in most cases to design a toy car that would truly catch the spirit of a British vehicle than a German an American vehicle, or a Frenchman a German vehicle, and so on. Only in recent years, with line-for-line scale copies of prototypes of other lands has this inherent difficulty been overcome to a considerable extent; but the result is, of course, in effect a photograph rather than a painting, to use a now familiar simile in modeldom. On the other hand, most miniature cars of the type and era now so widely collected by enthusiasts of old model cars were, whatever else they may have been, and without trying to read into them any sort of snobbish inferences, truly creative, if multiply produced, works of art that in many instances grandly caught the spirit of the real thing, even if far from scale reproductions. Even many of the generally looked-down-upon early Lehmann automobiles from a purely artistic standpoint caught the spirit of the European automobile of the time, and the social outlook that attended it. The point is that the American in the days the old model cars were

Fig. 214. This cover and the following two pages relate to automobiles from the Dowst 1925 catalog. The cover and these pages were identical in the 1926 catalog. There is one set of four cars, the Interchangeable Truck set, and, counting the six different versions of the delivery truck as separate items, a total of fifteen different automotive vehicles.

Tootsietoy—Strombecker Corp.

Tootsietoy Auto and Garage

Packed in the famous
Tootsietoy Box

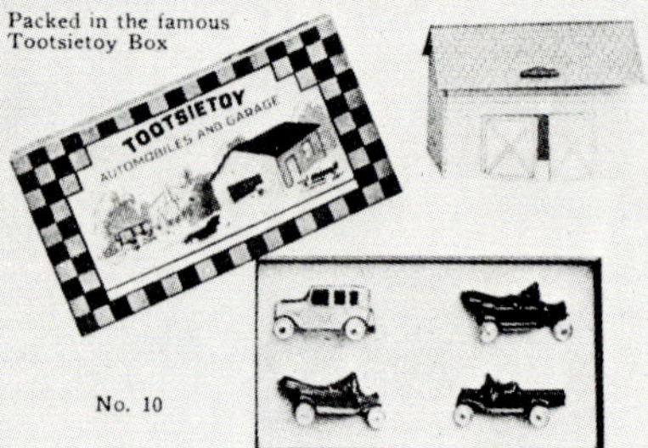

No. 10

A very fine set of four automobiles with a folding garage. The set includes a Sedan, Truck, Roadster and Touring Car. Each automobile is about 3¼ in. long, of late design and with movable wheels. The colors are realistic.

Tootsietoy Train and Station

Packed in the famous
Tootsietoy Box

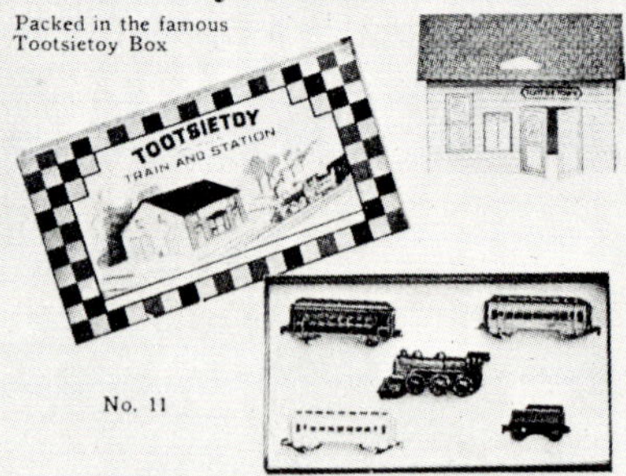

No. 11

A train set that is good for steady all-year round sales. Consists of Engine, Tender and three Pullman Coaches and Folding Station in handsome colors. Boys never tire of playing with trains and every boy is a prospect for this complete set. Movable wheels and coupling devices. In black and colored enamels.

TOOTSIETOY

Interchangeable Truck

No. 170

The very latest idea in toy trucks. The chassis is a copy of a well-known standard make, very solidly built and with movable disc wheels. Three separate bodies, tank, coal, and stake, fit into the chassis and make three different styles of trucks.
The chassis is enameled in black or red, the bodies in bright contrasting colors.

Packed one set to a box in the famous TOOTSIETOY box, and one dozen sets to the carton.

Mac Stake Truck

No. 4638

The Stake Truck Body on a sturdily built chassis. A fine selling item for all times of the year.
The chassis is finished in black and red, assorted, the bodies in bright, contrasting colors, and the disc wheels in gold bronze.
Packed one dozen to the box, assorted colors.

Mac Coal Truck

No. 4639

The truck chassis fitted with the coal truck or dump body. A heavy, powerful looking truck that is exactly like the "real thing." Same color scheme as above.
Packed one dozen to the box, assorted colors.

Mac Tank Truck

No. 4640

Tank Body on the famous Mac chassis. A perfect reproduction in all its parts of a heavy tank car. Freely moving disc wheels and the entire car finished in the same three color scheme as its two companion numbers.
Packed one dozen in a box, assorted colors.

No. 4610. TRUCK

General utility truck of the well-known "Flivver" brand. This is one of our best selling pieces and should be included in every stock. Movable wheels, windshield, steering wheel, etc. Body enameled in assorted colors. Disc wheels in gold bronze.
Packed one dozen in a box, assorted colors.

Tootsietoy Touring Car

No. 4641. TOURING CAR

Reproduction of one of the latest models of a popular make of Touring Car. An exact copy to even the most minor details. Easily turning disc wheels, windshield, "one-man-top," etc. The seats and upholstery are in a contrasting color to the body carrying out our new three color scheme.

Packed one dozen in a box, assorted colors.

Tootsietoy Coupe

No. 4636. COUPE

There is something about this Coupe that makes it tremendously popular. We present it as a "sure fire" seller. Notice the perfect reproduction of even the most minor details. Finished in bright enameled colors and packed one dozen assorted colors to the box.

Tootsietoy Sedan

No. 4629. SEDAN

A real masterpiece in miniature automobiles. We have tried to overlook no details and this Sedan is a car we are proud of. Bright color enameled finish on body and movable disc wheels in gold bronze. This number should be in every dealer's stock.

Packed one dozen in a box, assorted colors.

Tootsietoy Ford

No. 4570. FORD

You can't beat the "Flivver" for sales, and this is a reproduction of our old "Stand-by." Body finished in bright enameled colors with bronzed windshield and disc wheels.

Packed one dozen in a box, assorted colors.

Tootsietoy Delivery Vans

No. 4630/5. DELIVERY VANS

A whole fleet of Vans for delivery purposes. The large cut shows the actual size of the item and the small cuts show the different styles of lettering. The fleet includes "Grocery," "Bakery," "Market," "Laundry," "Milk," and "Florist" cars. They come packed one dozen in a box assorted colors and letterings.

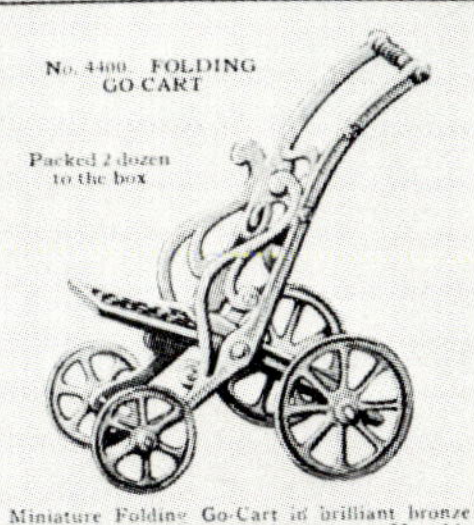

No. 4400. FOLDING GO-CART

Packed 2 dozen to the box

Miniature Folding Go-Cart in brilliant bronze finish. Folds like a real go-cart. Movable wheels.

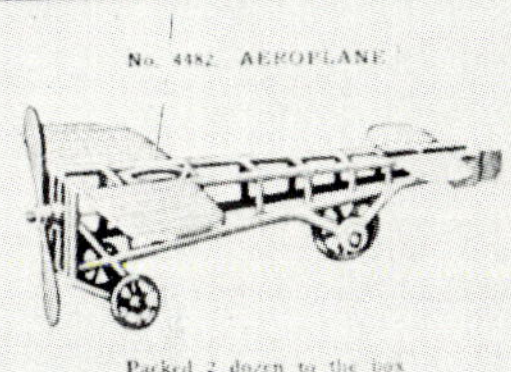

No. 4482. AEROPLANE

Packed 2 dozen to the box

Any boy will understand the fine points of this reproduction of a well-known make of monoplane. Propeller and wheels turn. Bright gilt finish with colored wheels. A sure sale to any boy who sees it.

No. 4528. LIMOUSINE

Simply can't be surpassed as a quick seller. Lines are perfect and everything about it stamps it as a high-class small toy. Colored enamel finishes and silver plated smooth running wheels.
Packed 1 dozen to the box.

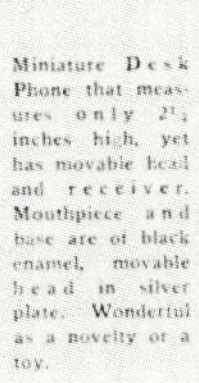

No. 4341. TELEPHONE

Miniature Desk Phone that measures only 2½ inches high, yet has movable head and receiver. Mouthpiece and base are of black enamel, movable head in silver plate. Wonderful as a novelty or a toy.

Packed 1 dozen to the box

Metal Animals

No. 4601. HORSE

Miniature horse on movable wheels. Realistic, natural colors and a spirited pose. Wheels bronze finish. Fine either as toy or a favor.

One Dozen to the Box

No. 4602. DOG

A husky St. Bernard on wheels that move. He's finished in black, dark and light brown. Be sure you have plenty.

One Dozen to the Box

No. 4603. LION

Faithful reproduction of a lion. He's the favorite animal of most children. On movable wheels. In dark and light brown.

made, and the American collector today, prize most the miniatures that successfully caught the American spirit, as do, for the sake of their own national mystiques, the British, French, German, Italian collectors, and so on.

Offering what one has a lot of or can readily obtain under the guise of great desirability is an old trick. Much of the promotion and pushing of foreign models that goes contrary to the aforementioned spirit is, although quite manifestly this is not obvious to many, because of the ready availability of such models. In a normal reputable course of events, sellers price their goods in cash or in trade in accord with their relative generally recognized rarity, desirability, and value, which certainly appears logical and proper. In various fields of model collecting, however, some acute individuals have conceived the enormous potentials inherent in a reverse scheme of things, paying little heed to good items and on the occasions they come their way actually playing and pricing them down, while pricing up and extolling beyond all conceivable relative merit the less desirable items that are much more readily acquired. While such schemes are, to say the least, grossly misleading and certainly a far cry from admirable, the potential for doing considerable profitable business, particularly among eager beginners, by such methods are all too apparent. Thus, in train collecting one frequently today finds the on the whole much more frequently encountered and less desirable American Flyer and Lionel items being pushed at the expense of the rarer and more desirable Ives; in model cars one finds numerous parallels to this situation, all the more readily carried through because of the comparative newness of model-car collecting and the lack of communications and as a result of as yet inadequately stratified, accurate conceptions of rarity and desirability. A great deal of what knowledgeable collectors look upon as more or less junk is avidly promoted with what appears to be a fair amount of success. In the end, of course, it is almost always the beginner who pays, not only in cash or trade, but also in frustration and disgust.

Furthermore, what also all too often is not fully understood—or perhaps even suspected by novices *—is that a trade may well represent an absolute equality of raw values as such, yet by no means be fair and equitable, particularly when a beginner is involved. This applies not only to the classic quantity for quality conundrum that so frequently confronts beginners (whether or not to accept a proposal to trade a single valuable item for equal or even greater values as represented by a tempting quantity of less desirable models), but also in trades where the seemingly unusual is offered for the familiar and seemingly commonplace. Before allowing himself to become involved in such transactions the novice would be well served if he has prepared for himself a definite pattern of what his proposed long-range collecting activities are to consist, and has familiarized himself to some extent at least with the actual situation that obtains in the hobby as to the general desirability and availability—for the latter also is an important factor here—of various classifications of model cars. Admittedly, this is not easy to learn, given the diversity of outlooks and opinions and of types and makes of old model cars, and while the newcomer to the hobby can, hopefully, perhaps learn much from what has been said throughout this chapter, it is virtually impossible to set everything down in definitive Yeas and Nays and all possible gradations in between.

That there are favored categories of models among most aware collectors becomes obvious to anyone who has investigated the hobby of model-car collecting even to a very limited extent. It would be nice if definite guidelines to all these favorites as to make, type, date, and so on, could be set down in black and white, but this is a practical impossibility. Also, it should never be forgotten that such things are even when most widely accepted customs rather than rules, and there is nothing to inhibit any collector from charting and following a course of his own. Within certain broad classifications of model cars, subheadings of popular favoritism are most generally based on make. The great importance of make is demonstrated by the fact that unidentified model cars are almost invariably regarded by most collectors as rather in the class of little better than petty nuisances and of comparatively little interest, but as soon as a model or series of models can be identified as to make, it automatically immediately takes on immeasurably greater collector interest, desirability, and value. This, of course, does not mean that every identifiable make is of equal over-all value and interest as a make within its particular broad category of, say, miniature cast-metal cars, cast-iron vehicles, clockwork models, and so on. However, within certain bounds of relative desirability, the more that definitely can be ascertained regarding the identity of a make and of its history, the more enhanced becomes the model car collectors' interest in and respect

---

* The assumption throughout this book is, of course, the idealistic one that the newcomer to the hobby is a cherubic innocent who needs protection against pitfalls. There are, of course, newcomers to this or any other growing hobby who are attracted by less than noble motives and who cannot wait until they can sink their fangs into some hapless victim.

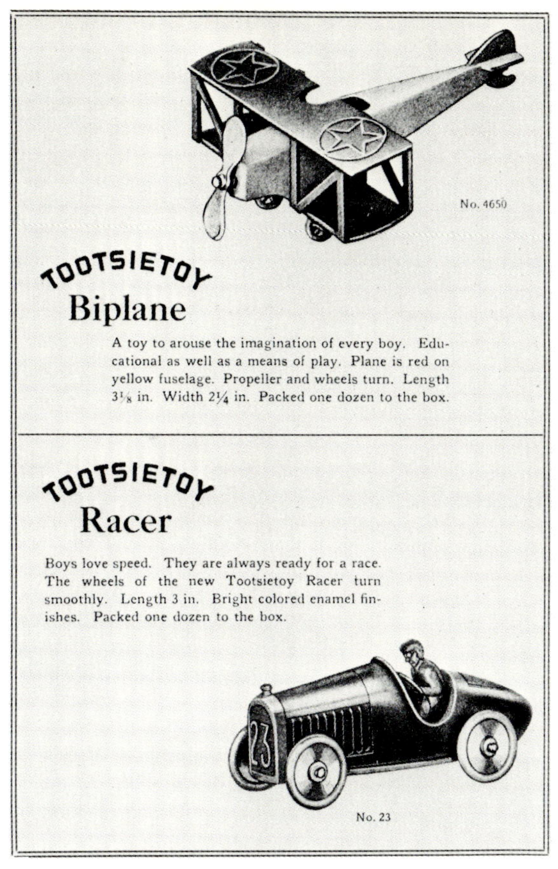

Fig. 215. The two pages relating to automotive vehicles from the Dowst 1926 catalog supplement. Two additional models were added that season, the No. 23 racing car, its odd low number deriving from the expression "Twenty-three—Skiddoo!" which was Tootsietoy's version of the type pictured in Fig. 205, and the No. 4651 bus.

George H. Hartman

for the model or models involved, and, indirectly, as a general thing, the more desirability and value is taken on by the model or models.

This favoritism based on make may at times variously be sentimental, intuitive, or based on hard fact, or combinations thereof. Sometimes it may even appear illogical to beginners or non-collectors who are more prone to base their favoritism on the appearance of models themselves rather than on usually more reasoned historical factors. Similarly it may even greatly annoy speculators where they can as readily if not even more readily "merchandise" more easily obtainable models. Regardless, these preferences exist and are held by a majority of aware collectors who feel their choices are based on solid ground indeed, albeit displaying an ever-ready willingness to add still additional names to the list of favorites at various levels as continuing research appears to warrant appropriate. For example, with the appearance of the present volume, a considerable number of new names undoubtedly will be added to the list of favorite makes among miniature cast-metal cars, if only because models previously unidentifiable now can be accorded positive attribu-

tions. Inasmuch as there was only recently a considerable outcry among California collectors when word got out that a particularly fine model had been sold out of that state to a new owner in Texas, the general burden of the excitement being that some means should have been found by loyal Californians to retain the specimen within the borders of that state, it should not be too surprising to report that there are those so chauvinistically minded, or so preduiced, as to indicate that they feel any listing of favored makes as such of model automobiles should be confined to those of American manufacturers only, with perhaps a possible exception being made for Canadian and British makes! This is, of course, an extreme reaction to or reflection of points already delineated. However, in all candor and fairness, it would seem quite impossible even to consider making any such list without including upon it the names of such truly highly favored continental European makes as Bing, Carette, Doll, Gunthermann, Hess, Rossignal, and so on.

The individual collector, and most especially the beginner, often is hard put to adjudicate many such matters, whether points of individual models, makes, geographic groupings, and so forth, either from what he hears or observes for himself, for there are endless variables and imponderables involved. Lines of demarcation of relative desirability cross and recross all other boundaries. It would undoubtedly be helpful if more of a definite nature by way of at least suggested guidelines could be presented here, but it is impossible, and in the end much must remain up to the collector himself. As a final contribution of some possible pertinence and help the following thoughts may be presented, although, regretfully, while there unquestionably is a valid and useful theme here, it has not been possible to harden the structure to any degree of real permanence, but hopefully each collector can draw some advantage from them or at least use them as a foundation for useful building:

Somewhere along the line of the close and intensive association with the subject that ac-

companied the preparation of this book, it was believed that there was dimly glimpsed the lineaments of a perhaps profound and pertinent social theme linking the popularity of model vehicle types to economic cycles and political developments, as well as the contemporary social picture. If such a concept could satisfactorily be codified and proved, then many matters of comparative rarity and desirability and value, now so personalized and at times seemingly inexplicable or illogical, could to a considerable extent be more or less scientifically determined—although perhaps too much science would take much of the pleasure out of the hobby. In short, given almost any particular model, one could determine a great deal about the present-day status of the model, as far as collectors are concerned, by examining the economic, political, and social situation obtaining at the time and place the model was manufactured. As first envisioned, the proper basic theory

Fig. 216.   A Bing advertisement of 1924 showing several of their vehicles, including a Yellow Taxi copied from an Arcade cast-iron model (*"Playthings"*), and two of the Bing series of clockwork Ford Model T's; the four-door sedan and touring car (*Ward Kimball*). Also illustrated is a Bing European prototype model (*G. William Holland Collection*).

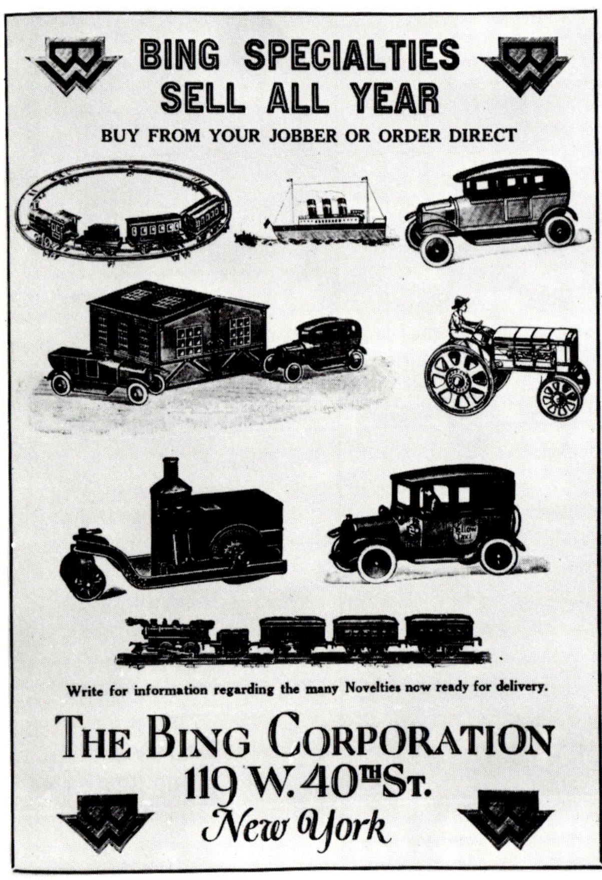

Fig. 217.   At the left of this photograph is an Arcade cast-iron Yellow Taxi from which the Bing illustrated in Fig. 216 was copied, while to its right is an actual specimen of the Bing clockwork stamped-metal lithographed taxi for comparison, but in this instance lithographed as a Checker taxicab.

C. W. Frey

Fig. 218.   Additional cast-iron taxicabs, an extremely popular type of model vehicle in the 1920's and early 1930's. Left, an 8-inch-long Hubley Yellow Taxi (*Ward Kimball*); right, a 9-inch Arcade Checker Cab with rubber tires (*C. W. Frey*). See also Figs. 123, 216, 217, and 219.

seemed to be that in good times models of pleasure and sports vehicles are most popular; in poor times models of commercial vehicles. Further reflection showed that such a thing cannot quite be true, for it was obvious that in good times trucks and related vehicles continue to enjoy an enormous popularity. Yet there seemed still some germ of truth in the general idea. Further thought suggested that what actually is the general case is that only in good times do models of pleasure vehicles attain any relative sustained popularity. Thus, only in such periods as the 1920's and in the years since World War II has the pleasure car in miniature held a noticeable popularity, which, hopefully, if this is any sort of a meaningful barometer, will continue. Yet, going further, even this theory cannot be quite valid, when it is recalled that large numbers of miniature cast-metal models of rather deluxe pleasure cars were sold during the 1930's. And, at the other extreme, in the 1930's, as always, replicas of pleasure cars were infinitely more popular than models of commercial vehicles among juvenile automobiles, the type of vehicle within which a child actually can ride and propel himself, usually by pedals. Further consideration evolved the theory to this point: Except for juvenile automobiles, a class of models

wherein the child actually places himself within "his automobile," inexpensive models of pleasure and sports cars always are popular, but only in good times do relatively more expensive models of pleasure cars attain popularity, whereas somewhat more costly models of commercial vehicles continually sustain their relative popularity but proportionately sell better than models of pleasure vehicles during bad times. This theory is still admittedly somewhat imperfect and not yet fully developed, yet it is felt there is some definite basis of validity to it.

There are obvious exceptions to it: Fire engines always have been enormously popular, and as for military vehicles, in periods approaching, during and following a war this type of miniature of course enjoys great popularity. Also, there has been, in the long run, a growing tendency toward models of pleasure cars. Perhaps the theory as a whole merely needs a little further thinking out to provide a really effective aid to model-car collectors. But much of what has been said can be established as correct, and there is some basis of truth in it all. For example, during much of the 1930's, with the expected exception of juvenile automobiles, it was extremely difficult on the whole successfully to merchandise in any

TOY YELLOW CABS—Nos. 1, 2, 3

This is the famous Toy Yellow Cab which has taken the country by storm. A beautiful and exact model of the Yellow Cab known everywhere in the United States as well as Canada and Mexico. New and novel, its appeal to children is strong and direct; kiddies prefer it to all other toys. Yellow Cabs have proved themselves quick turn-over insurance. Each cab is sturdily made from grey iron and is practically unbreakable; it has no clock work to get out of order. The different enamels are applied carefully insuring ⌐ fine finish. Top, hood, and fenders bright black enamel; body and discs, the familiar Yellow Cab yellow. We make Yellow Cabs in three sizes to meet all requirements. No. 1 and No. 2 cabs are furnished with a removable driver fastened firmly in place with bolt and nut. Rubber tires furnished on No. 1 and No. 2 cabs if desired.

No. 1. Size: Length 9 inches, wheel base 6 inches, height 5 inches, width 3½ inches.

No. 2. Size: Length 8 inches, wheel base 5¼ inches, height 4¼ inches, width 3⅛ inches.

No. 3. Size: Length 5¼ inches, wheel base 3½ inches, height 3 inches, width 2¼ inches.

PACKED:

No. 1 and No. 2 each in a paper carton, one dozen in a case.

No. 1. Case net 45 pounds, gross 55. Case measurements 21¼ x11¾x10¼ inches.

No. 2. Case net 31 pounds, gross 38. Case measurements 19¼ x10¾x9 inches.

No. 3. Each in a paper carton, ¼ gross in a case. Case net weight 39 pounds, gross 48. Case measurements 21x15 x6 inches.

TOY CHECKER CAB

For those who prefer a checker cab, we have just the thing. Same beautiful lines and sturdy construction as the Toy Yellow Cabs,—with or without rubber tires. You will find that they sell rapidly.

SPECIFICATIONS. No. 1. Length 9 inches, wheel base 6 inches, height 5 inches, width 3½ inches. Body deep green; checker finish with monogram (black, white, and gold) put on with a decalcomania transfer. No. 2. Length 8 inches, wheel base 5¼ inches, height 4½ inches, width 3⅛ inches. Plain two row checker, gum label band.

PACKED:

Each in a paper carton, weights and measurements same as the No. 1 and No. 2 Yellow Cab.

SPECIAL FINISH CABS

We can also furnish cabs in other popular finishes. The most attractive of these are Brown and White, Black and White, Blue Bird, and Red Top Cabs. Unusually striking, they add variety to a line of Yellow Cabs and never fail to sell rapidly.

Brown and White Cabs have a white enamel body and tires, with the remainder brown enamel. Black and White Cabs have the body and tires white enamel, while the rest of the car is a bright black. Red Top Cabs are brilliantly painted—the cream colored body is striped black, the top and window frames are a vivid red, and the hood and fenders are black enamel. Furnished with grey iron tires or rubber tires and the disk wheels are white with red hub caps. On orders of sufficient size we can furnish cabs painted to any desired color scheme. Specifications and packing same as No. 1 and No. 2 Yellow Cab.

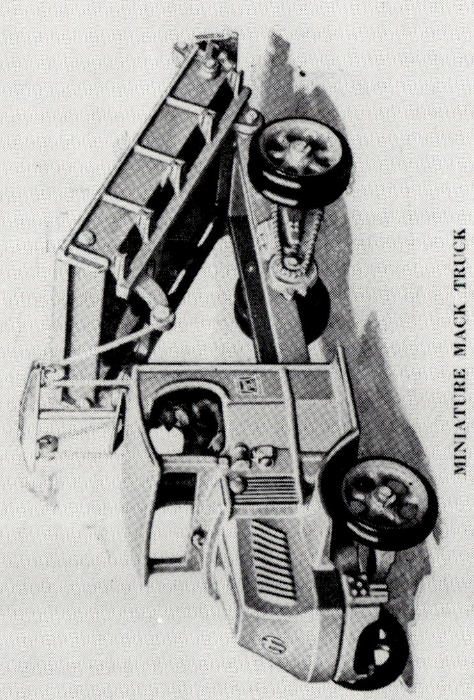

MINIATURE MACK TRUCK

TOY MACK TRUCK

Mack Truck (Body Hoisted)

The Husky Toy Mack Truck—just like the real ones—will stand rough treatment and won't wear out. Made of cast iron with steel frame. A **modern** toy that sells itself on sight. Dump body is raised by a clever but simple hoist—just press the spring on rear of cab which releases hoisting rod and the body raises in life-like motion by means of pulleys and ropes. Rear end-gate swings open when unlocked. Attractively painted in light grey or blue—gold trimmed—white tires—Mack monogram on front of radiator and trade mark on both sides of cab. Rubber Tire Disk Wheels at nominal extra charge. Length over all, 12 inches; height 5¾ inches; width of box, 4 inches.

No. 1. Mack Truck—Light Blue.
No. 2. Mack Truck—Grey.
No. 3. Mack Truck—Olive Green.

PACKED:

Each in a paper carton, one dozen in a case. Case net weight 57 pounds, gross 75. Case measurements 24x15x13 inches.

Mack Truck (Body Down)

TOY CHEVROLET LINE

CHEVROLET UTILITY COUPE

The popular Utility Coupe. Made to stand hard service and retain its attractive appearance.

Length 7 inches, height 3¾ inches.

PACKED:
Each in a paper carton, ¼ gross in a case. Case net weight 66 pounds, gross 80. Case measurements 26x20x8 inches.

UTILITY EXPRESS TRUCK

A popular solution to toy trucking problems.

Finish: Frame and chassis, black enamel, stake body grey and tires white.

PACKED:
Length 9¼ inches, height 4 inches, width of box 3⅛ in. Each in a paper carton, one dozen in a case. Case net weight 32 pounds, gross 40. Case measurements 19x11x10 inches.

All models supplied with rubber tires.

TOY CHEVROLET LINE

A complete set of miniature Chevrolet automobiles and the Utility Express Truck. New and popular sellers—they attract grown-ups and children alike. Sturdily built of quality grey iron. Perfectly cast to show every detail of the Chevrolet features. The automobiles are black enameled with white tires, gilded band around body and white Chevrolet monogram on radiator and rear spare tire carrier. All models will be furnished with rubber tires (another unusual Arcade feature) at a nominal extra charge.

CHEVROLET SUPERIOR TOURING

A good miniature, strong and well finished.
Length 7 inches, height 3¾ inches.

PACKED:
Each in a paper carton, ¼ gross in a case. Case net weight 80 pounds, gross 94. Case measurements 26x20x8 inches.

CHEVROLET SUPERIOR SEDAN

A very desirable model, certain to please.
Length 7 inches, height 3¾ inches.

PACKED:
Each in a paper carton, ¼ gross in a case. Case net weight 70 pounds, gross 84. Case measurements 26x20x8 inches.

CHEVROLET SUPERIOR ROADSTER

A handsome, well made toy.
Length 7 inches, height 3¾ inches.

PACKED:
Each in a paper carton, ¼ gross in a case. Case net weight 68 pounds, gross 82. Case measurements 26x20x8 inches.

ANDY GUMP AND OLD 348

Licensed by the Sidney Smith Corporation

No. 1 Andy Gump has a red tie, white shirt, blue suit, and brown sport hat with green hat-band. Old 348 has a bright red body with green trimmings, green disc wheels with red hub caps, white tires, and aluminum license plates. Size: Length over all 7¼ inches, wheel base 4⅞ inches, height 6 inches, width 4 inches.

No. 2 Andy Gump: Car, red; Andy and Wheels, full nickel plated; without license plate or front crank. Size, weight, packing: same as No. 1.

No. 3 Andy Gump: Car is red (only), wheels nickel plated with green disc and no license plate nor front crank. Andy is painted green with white collar and flesh colored face. Size, weight, packing: same as No. 1.

PACKED:
Each in a decorated paper carton, 12 in a case. Case net weight 36 pounds, gross 45 pounds. Case dimensions 19x12¼x8¼ inches.

Fig. 219. Some pages from an Arcade catalog of the 1920's including the listings of the Yellow, Checker, and "Special Finish" taxicabs. Three sizes of some taxicabs were manufactured. Other pages cover some of the trucks, Chevrolets, and Andy Gump, straight out of the comic strips in his famous old 348. Note that unlike the Yellow cabs, the three Andy Gump models were all the same size, the difference being in the finish and the presence or absence of the crank and license plate. For other model vehicles driven by comic-strip characters, see also Fig. 97.
Lloyd W. Ralston

quantity a model pleasure car retailing for, say, fifty cents or more, unless it was presented in the guise of a fire chief's or police car, or had some special promotional gimmick attached to it, such as a cartoon character—and even here there were difficulties once a product left the lower price brackets. One exception—that to some extent proves the rule—was the streamlined-car fever of the mid-1930's, and most particularly that of the Airflow. If Chrysler imagined the introduction of the 1934 Chrysler and De Soto Airflows was to give the real automobile business a needed shot in the arm, their expectations were no greater—and probably less fully realized—than those of the toy

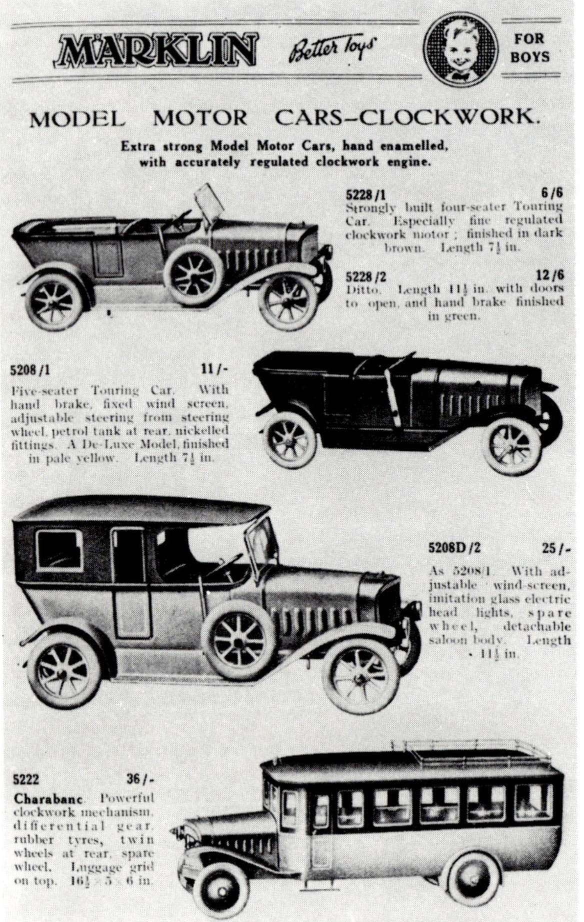

Fig. 220. Two pages from Maerklin catalogs. They produced a great many clockwork-powered model automobiles over the years, including the interesting clockwork fire engine with working pump of about 1911, of which two views are shown (*C. W. Frey*), and the four vehicles pictured from the 1920's. The second catalog page is from 1938, and shows their line of cast-metal miniatures.

and model-car industry. Around 1934–1936 the Airflow interest was everywhere felt in model cars of all types, from miniature cast-metal vehicles to juvenile automobiles, and even lapped over into such things as Airflow express wagons and Airflow baby rockers! In fact, a hobbyist can make quite a collection, as some have done, simply of toys and models that reflected the Airflows. The Airflow may have given the model automobile business a badly needed boost for a few years, although it appears that some manufacturers of miniature cars who had been as overly sanguine about the design as the makers of the real thing * were left with Airflow dies that had to be kept

in use almost up to World War II, but the interjection of the Airflow into the picture does not negate the validity of the overall model-automobile picture of the 1930's as drawn above or the theory advanced partially on that basis.

When one today speaks successively to a number of model-car collectors, especially to younger ones, he finds himself repeatedly informed, often not without some indication of at least a measure of snobbery, that they are only or primarily interested in models of pleasure and sports cars, although occasionally they will accept and retain trucks and tractors that come their

---

* There has, of course, been endless argument among automobile enthusiasts and historians about the stature of the Airflow design, its immediate impact, and long-range success. There are those who maintain its evident failure to live up to expectations was due to it being ahead of its time; others, perhaps speaking with the assurance of knowledge after the fact, that it was a poor design. It generally is acknowledged as the first of the streamlined automobiles, and as one who recalls from being there at the time, the writer can testify that in the mid-1930's the Airflow, while rather startling, generally was regarded as *the* modern automobile of the

moment, not as the grotesque and unwieldy abomination that some later critics have found it. The Pierce-Arrow Silver Arrow, unveiled at about the same time, is often acclaimed as the true forerunner of the modern automobile and a far better design than the Airflow, which may well be true. But the Silver Arrow, whatever its merits, was never put into mass production, whereas the Chrysler and De Soto Airflows indisputably were massproduction cars within the reach of many prospective automobile purchasers of the day. The Silver Arrow also was reproduced in model form, but by no means in the variety and range of the model Airflows.

Fig. 221. Buddy "L" produced a line of nine different stamped-steel pull-toy Ford Model-T cars and trucks in the 1920's, of which two examples are shown here, together with a head-on view of the truck. See also Fig. 89.

B. J. Donnelly

Fig. 222. The famous Strauss "Leaping Lizzie" erratic-action clockwork lithographed stamped-metal Model-T Ford of the 1920's, replete with slogans of the period. Strauss also subsequently produced an erratic-action Ford Model-T coupe. In operation, the hood and body being loosely connected, the cars would practically double up upon themselves.

G. William Holland photograph

way or collect commercial vehicles only because they are units in a specific series of recent or modern vehicles they are collecting in their entirety. Such hobbyists, having lived all or most of their lives in prosperous times, seem almost taken aback at a suggestion that there is something equally worthy and glamorous about trucks, tractors, steam shovels, and the like, although their somewhat older fellow hobbyists virtually without exception esteem such models, and there are, of course, many younger ones who are equally avid collectors of these types. But again there is in all this definite proof of the relationship of model popularity and the conditions of the times.

Many teen-agers today look forward to the time when they can drive a sports car; probably proportionately far more of their counterparts of the 1920's and 1930's looked forward to the day when they could get a job driving a coal or ice truck! * As to the repeated appeal of taxicabs in model vehicles—albeit it unquestionably was much stronger through the 1930's than it has been since World War II—this is a somewhat more complicated matter relating both to prototype propinquity and commercial aspirations, as well as other factors. It should also be noted that there was, almost from the very beginning of the availability of model automobiles, a very strong taxicab tradition. Initially the real automobile revealed itself to a great many turn-of-the-century youngsters in the form of the Columbia electric hansom cabs operated in the large cities, and, in miniature form, in the guise of popular toy renderings of these cabs such as will be found illustrated in Figs. 6 and 90. Although these models have, on occasion, seemed somewhat unusual and puzzling to modern collectors, some of whom have even questioned their prototypical authenticity, they were instantly recognized as comparatively accurate renditions of familiar and popular prototypes by contemporary youths.

It is not impossible that the extreme popularity among the earlier model-car collectors of the Tootsietoy Graham and La Salle series has in itself also had something to do with this noted attraction of many collectors to pleasure vehicles.

---

* It is interesting to note that some highly admired and now vanishing trades were once widely represented by rather popular model vehicles, such as the coal truck, ice truck, open baggage or transfer truck (the latter extensively used to convey baggage from one railroad station to another in the days when many towns had more than one depot). The still-universal model dump truck may, of course, be taken for and used as a coal truck, as indeed it always has been, boys usually making their own coal chutes out of cardboard, but at one time there were a number of types of specialized model coal trucks manufactured.

Fig. 223. Another group of cast-iron models, including an early Kenton touring car and the famous Kenton sightseeing bus bearing five comic-strip characters, including Happy Hooligan and Mama Katzenjammer (*Lloyd W. Ralston*), and a Kilgore car transport loaded with three American Bantam cars, one of which is shown separately in the close-up shot (*C. W. Frey*).

A number of model-car collectors, in fact, seem almost instinctively to have sensed something of the outline and principles of the theory being advanced here, as witness the widespread belief that the Tootsietoy Graham town car is the scarcest and most desirable body type of the Graham series, although it sold for no more than any of the others, and an impression that investigation confirms is but slightly if at all based on the fact that the town car body did not appear in any of the Bild-A-Car sets, a fact unknown to most collectors. These collectors have evidently largely based their belief on a sense, perhaps wholly intuitive, of the social and economic scene of the 1930's. The town car was associated with great wealth, with what many people of the day termed "economic royalists," whom many imagined in at least some measure to be responsible for the depression. The collectors' instincts regarding the Graham town cars were sound, for photographs of contemporary store displays of Tootsietoys indicate that some of their outlets at least did not, at times, handle the town cars. A photograph of the standard suggested arrangement for the Woolworth Tootsietoy counter in 1935 or 1936 shows the ten-cent passenger-vehicle stock made up entirely of roadsters, coupes, and sedans, with not a town car in sight, which it would seem may safely be taken as proof that that season at least Woolworth's massive order for Tootsietoys did not include town cars, which in turn must be taken to indicate that their experience was that the town car was not readily salable to their trade, undoubtedly because of the reasons already indicated. In point of fact, the Tootsietoy Graham convertible coupe and convertible sedan are scarcer body types than the town car, but of course up to now very few collectors have been aware of the definite distinction in models between these and the regular coupe and sedan.*

---

* The convertible coupe and sedan, of course, complicate matters substantially and open to question all previous attempts to survey the relative scarcity of the Tootsietoy Graham styles. Some collectors are of the opinion that, counting both passenger and commercial vehicles, the tire truck is the scarcest of the Graham body types. One enthusiast, who took into consideration variations in spare tires and kept careful records of a considerable number of Grahams that passed through his hands over a number of years, computed that the scarcest type was the roadster without spare tire—that is, the roadster from the Bild-A-Car sets, with the tire truck second. Unfortunately, in his survey he did not distinguish between regular and convertible coupes and sedans. What is required in order to shed some definite light on the whole matter is to compile records regarding the particulars of *all* the Grahams in a substantial number of collections. No doubt this eventually will be done. Rarity and desirability being what they are, it is quite possible

Thus, then, the outlines of a broad theory that, while it almost certainly needs further development and polishing, may prove of considerable practical value to model-car collectors in the future. It is to be hoped that collectors can successfully flesh out the images and principles here submitted in somewhat bare form.

THE FACTOR OF PRICE

One thing that is certain to impress the new collector of model automobiles who attends any gathering of collectors, whether an informal get-together of a few enthusiasts in a home or an organized public meet, is that so little of what he sees offered is priced or can be purchased for cash. Time and again he will be told that the duplicate models brought by other collectors that tempt him so are "for trade only." Superficially this is done in the feeling that, quite properly, duplicates available for trading are valuable property and often the only coin that will enable a collector to obtain additional specimens that he himself lacks, most especially when the general climate among collectors is that of trading only and not selling. It must be added at once that such a climate, no matter how logical and advantageous to a somewhat limited group of established collectors, is anything but conducive to inspiring the interest and enthusiasm of beginners, much less potential collectors, and most certainly has an inhibiting effect on the growth of the hobby. If additional models are not available except by trading, how then is the beginner to build a collection of his own of model cars other than those contemporary productions currently on general sale in hobby shops and other outlets? In short, the "trade only" prospect is likely to so limit the beginner that in all too many cases he grows disgusted and forsakes what would probably prove a most enjoyable hobby before he hardly begins. This certainly is far from the intent of the collectors who insist only on trading their duplicates, but it is to some extent at least an inevitable concomitant of that policy. Some obsolete models that a beginner might well want may, it is true, be purchased for cash at meets, and sometimes as the day wears on, some collectors, seeing that nothing has turned up for which they are particularly looking, may relax their rigid "trade only" rule and sell some specimens. However, by and large, it is reasonably safe to say that at such

---

that, regardless of the eventual findings of such a detailed study, a number of collectors will continue to look upon the town car as the most desirable body type of the Tootsietoy Grahams.

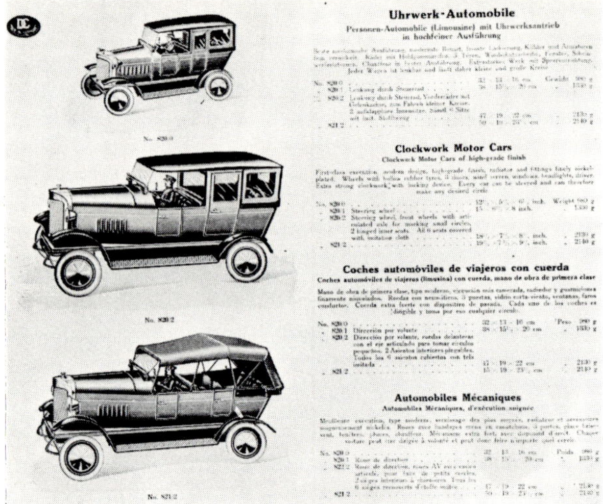

Fig. 224. A selection of catalog pages of the 1920's and 1930's showing representative examples of clockwork stamped-metal automobiles from the lines of five German manufacturers: Doll, Bing, Tipp, Bub, and Distler. A tremendous quantity and variety of such models were turned out by these and other manufacturers. A few of the lines, such as Bing and Doll, possess a high overall collectors' interest as makes, but a great many of the models manufactured by numerous other continental firms still attract relatively little interest among knowledgeable collectors.

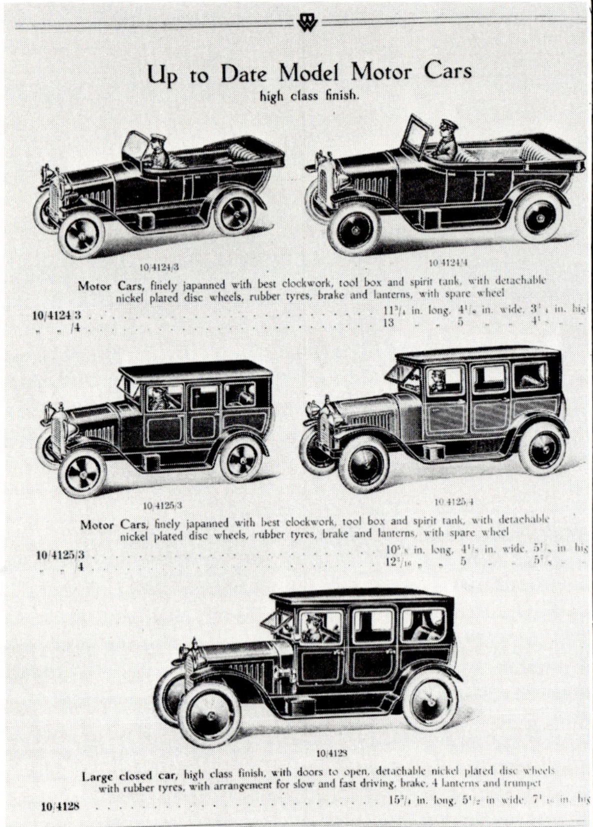

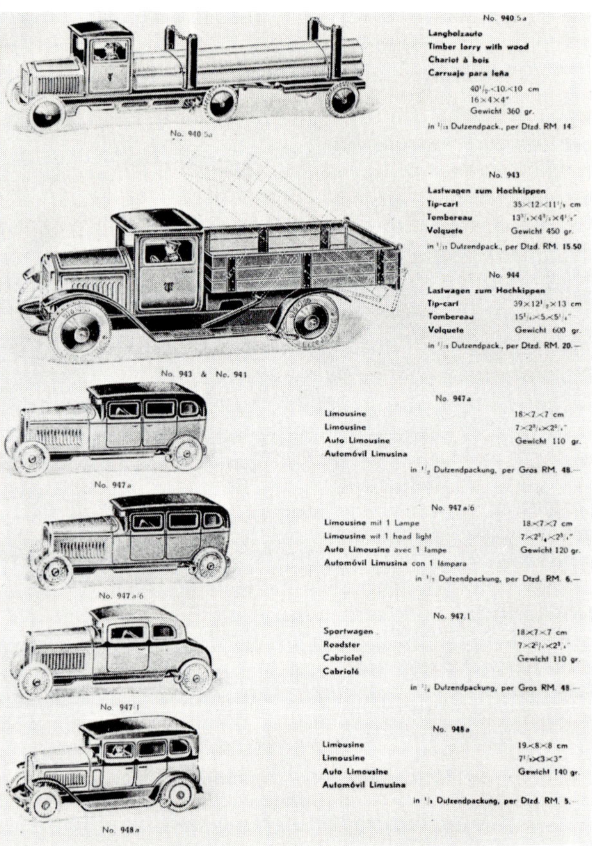

gatherings and also in the cases of lists of duplicates offered by mail, the rarest and most desirable duplicates can only be secured from many hobbyists by trading for them.

There is a widespread feeling that the beginner can and should acquire models through his own efforts, eventually owning a store sufficient to enable him fully to enter into the trading give-and-take of more established collectors. There is indeed much that most collectors can do on this score. As will be seen shortly, there are actually far greater opportunities for this sort of thing than many presently imagine. Yet the overriding point should be that this "trade only" policy, no matter how meritorious it may seem to its practitioners, most definitely discourages many beginners at the start and turns them, if not from collecting model automobiles in some form, at least from its most interesting path of collecting old model automobiles. Also, it should be noted

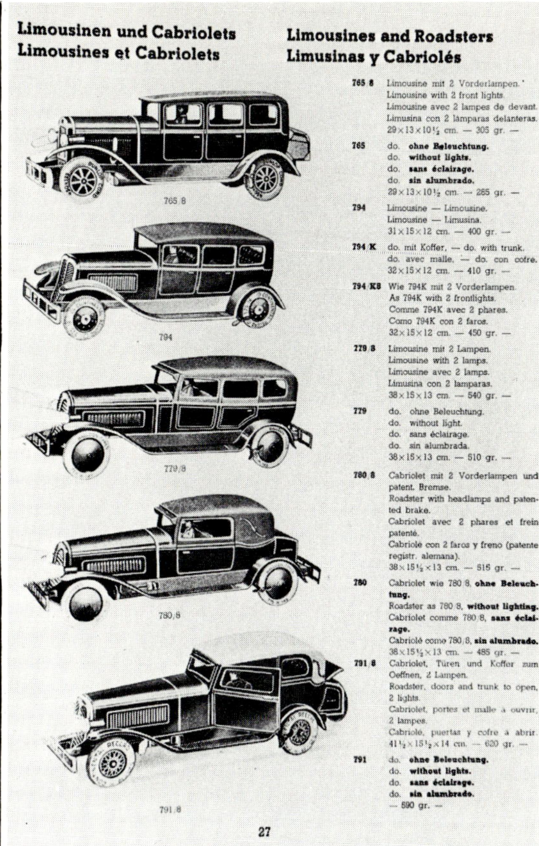

that many regard the policy as shortsighted and self-defeating; for a beginner encouraged by being permitted to purchase a few interesting models at such a time, in all probability will be so enthused by their possession as to set purposefully about searching for additional models, and in time will bring to light and to the hobby innumerable pieces that even the owners of the largest collections will greatly desire, and in turn may acquire in a reciprocation of past favors. Experience has shown that the more collectors continually are seeking specimens of anything, so much the more will be uncovered, often to the amazement of long-established hobbyists who feel the field already has long since been stripped bare by their efforts. Of course, it would probably not be desirable for an individual whose chief potential contribution to an overall hobby would be the availability of a large sum of money suddenly to sweep up everything in sight because a multitude of specimens could readily be purchased. On the other hand the policy widely followed probably does even more harm by discouraging many novices and thereby impeding the fruitful growth of the hobby. However, it would appear that this situation must be accepted for the present.

Two others factors appear to influence this "trade only" situation. One is a feeling that money should not be permitted to enter into the picture and that a hobby should be practiced on an amateur basis. Every collecting hobby goes through the same stage at one time or another; the concept sometimes is advanced for disinterested reasons; sometimes for personally productive ones—at one time individuals who fell so low as actually to purchase specimens from dealers instead of building up their collections entirely from stamps they or their friends received in the mail or by swapping with other hobbyists were considered by many as utter wretches unworthy of the name of stamp collector! In the early stages of any hobby there always are efforts, often well-intended, to keep it a "pure" or strictly amateur endeavor. All such efforts, however, fall by the wayside as any hobby grows in popularity. On the other hand, there always are those, particularly those who cannot or will not pay the current going prices for collectibles who are all too ready to point a finger of scorn at anyone who sells specimens at their market value, rather than invariably trading them to the individuals in question for whatever they may have available or choose to give, and raise great and seemingly horrendous cries of "dealer" and "speculator." There are accordingly in the early days of a hobby often many who adhere to a "trade only" policy because they fear having such cries directed at them.

On the other hand, after all these things are taken into account, a detailed survey of the situation leads to an inevitable conclusion that a great deal of the reluctance to sell duplicate models displayed by many model-car collectors is not primarily based on any of the foregoing reasons, but rather is due to the fact that most model-car collectors, no matter how comparatively experienced, are extremely unsure of the actual current fair cash values of their specimens. They feel safe when trading because trading values usually are relative and for the most part fair and mutually satisfactory. But cash transactions are an entirely different matter. If one sells too high he may well be cheating the purchaser; if he sells too low he may well be cheating himself. Both fears are unquestionably present; for some individuals the latter fear, although obviously far less commendable, may well be by far the greater one. There is indeed a terrible effect in the thought that one might sell something for half or a quarter of what it properly should bring, and not only once but repeatedly, in ignorance.

The plain fact—and this is at least firmly suspected by many hobbyists, even though they lack the credentials or proof openly to dispute it —is that a great many model automobiles of all types that do change hands for cash are today grossly overpriced when viewed—as such situations must be viewed—in relation to relative rarity and desirability, and of supply and demand. No one would make such a statement lightly, for one inevitable comeback is that anyone who would so state is very likely trying to deflate or manipulate the market for his own designs. Of course, the average collector actually is in a position where, if values go down, he can afford to purchase more specimens; if values go up, then his equity in his collection increases. Inasmuch as for most collectors, the hobby, despite the inevitable interjection of the topic of values, would still be an avocation and not a business, anyone who suggests to such collectors that many current prices might be, to say the least, somewhat watered, naturally risks being accused either of a lack of any real grasp on reality or of hoping to depress prices so that he can thereby acquire more model automobiles. This is a danger that candor must run. The present writer would emphasize that in some decades of participation in or observance of a great number of different collecting hobbies, some closely akin to model-car collecting, he no longer feels any sense of shock

at any price no matter how high at which any collectible changes hands, or arbitrarily feels that actual current value may not be represented in such a sale simply because the price involved seems startlingly high. Furthermore, the writer would readily state that he believes that the prices he feels much too high today very probably will represent fair values for the same articles at some future date if the hobby of model-car collecting continues to grow and spread at the same rate of progression that it has displayed in recent years, and, similarly, eventually somewhere in the future these same prices may appear absurdly low for the same goods. But the essential point is, unless one is knowingly and willingly dealing in model-car futures with these expectations in view, rather than in fair current values, then many of today's prices are grossly out of line with the facts of the situation.

How, it may justly and naturally be asked, did such a situation ever come about? There were two reasons, one that will be found almost automatically to accompany the rise of any new collecting hobby, and one that is perhaps uniquely peculiar to model-car collecting. The first is that before any collecting hobby of this sort starts, the objects to be collected are usually almost universally literally considered junk, and of no worth except for sentimental value or scrap. A few collectors start gathering specimens, often unknown to each other; in time, as the hobby slowly grows, enthusiasts come into contact with each other, and their hobby activities also become obvious to their families and friends; the collectors require some justification or seeming justification for their activities. Accordingly—and this is an invariable pattern—ideas and specific figures are bandied around to establish that their collectibles are not the junk they appear to others and whose perhaps better status the collectors themselves, despite their protestations, often are rather unsure of. "Gee, that's a rare one"; "Trash? Why Joe would give me X for that!"; "Why there are at least three men I could name who'd be glad to buy the whole collection anytime I would sell," and similar phrases are bandied around. So-called actual values adumbrated at this early stage the discussions of specific values seldom have any permanent meaning or validity because no one really knows enough about the objects being collected or the paths along which the hobby will develop. No one really knows what may really prove rare and desirable; quite often time and varied developments may completely reverse or obliterate early judgments. But at such times talk is good, and eventually the day comes when what once seemed fantastic suggestions of values may actually seem within the realm of possibility, although proper studies in the interim may result in their being assigned to entirely different specimens. In any case, the growth of the hobby and of knowledge concerning the collectibles results in the acceptance of an often somewhat different and far more valid scene.

The second reason, rather peculiar to model-car collecting, has been the frequent interjection of real automobile interest into the old model car picture. And here, for the last time in this book, we may encounter the hobbyist who is oriented toward the prototype automobile. It certainly cannot be denied that such enthusiasts have played a worthwhile role in the developing of the model-automobile hobby to the position it occupies today. However, they usually look upon old model cars from an entirely different viewpoint than that of the collector of old model cars themselves, and thereby unquestionably did much to implant many particularized and wholly false concepts of rarity, values, and desirability. What was good as a model of a specific prototype automobile they prized unduly; what was poor or had no recognizable prototype they downgraded. They had no concept of the quantities of the various models that were originally manufactured or that might logically still survive. Neither had they any knowledge of the comparatively large quantities of model automobiles of all types that were quietly, and for some years almost as an afterthought, being gathered up by hundreds, if indeed not thousands, of general toy collectors of whose operations and even of whose very existence they were totally unaware. Accordingly their scales of judgment and standards of values had little relation to the facts, and they were frequently astounded when upon meeting an occasional experienced toy or model collector it was found that he considered many of their sincerely conceived values ludicrous, quite apart from the usually concomitant fact that he found their repainting and "restoration" practices shocking.

What is the proper scale by which logical and valid values can be established? The answer depends upon several things: the quantity of an item originally made, the probable survival rate, the number of possible interested collectors, and the relative accepted desirability of the item in question.

Most people have little idea of the enormous quantities involved in the manufacture of many items. Nor can they easily conceive how such quantities can be absorbed by the population at any given time. Even model-car collectors

Fig. 225. Four more interesting examples of the Tootsie-toy No. 4630/5 delivery truck as specially produced bearing the names and delivery-truck color schemes of specific actual stores. (See also Fig. 198.)
Adam Pellicot, Jr.; William Dreyer photographs

think of really "big" production as something numbering in the thousands of pieces. But the facts of mass production of model automobiles are these: Depending somewhat on the relative retail prices of the miniatures—even in the period prior to World War II, the output of most model automobiles must be counted in the tens of thousands, the hundreds of thousands, and in some cases millions of units! For example, consider the original quantities made of many cast-iron model automobiles. Surviving inventories and production records of the Kenton Hardware Manufacturing Company alone provide many specific figures. Kenton, for instance, made 12,493 No. 1495 Yellow Taxis in 1923. In 1912 when the popularity of miniature automobiles was just getting under way, Kenton manufactured 8,274 of the small No. 1914 hook and ladders. Inasmuch as this was a popular item for more than a dozen years, it seems reasonably safe to put the total production of this number at over 100,000 pieces.

Or consider pressed-steel trucks. In July 1922, Buddy "L" advertised that they were producing one hundred No. 200 express trucks an hour and a total of 1,000 pieces a day of all types, with even larger production schedules for August. Now, while one naturally tends to trim down manufacturers' announced production claims somewhat, the facts are these: At that time Buddy "L" was using for toy production the entire 80,000 square feet of what had previously been a plant making real automobile parts, and the entire 1922 line consisted of only seven numbers: three trucks, two derricks, a steam shovel, and a miniature schoolroom. The plant could not have been kept going if sales and the resulting production required were not very high. All factors considered, it is safe to say that in 1922 Buddy "L" alone turned out some tens of thousands of No. 200 express trucks. Subsequently there were, of course, many more models in the line, and much competition on similar goods from other manufacturers. It seems, therefore, a safe bet, based on the incidence in which surviving specimens turn up today, that for the decade of the 1920's as a whole certain of the most popular Buddy "L" vehicles, such as the No. 200 express truck, No. 201 dump truck, No. 205 fire truck, No. 205B aerial ladder truck, and so on, were produced in totals exceeding 100,000 each.

Fred W. Ziesenheim reports that in the early 1920's the usual production run on a clockwork stamped-metal lithographed model automobile at the Girard Model Works would run about 1,000 gross—that is, about 144,000 units!

By no means at all unexpectedly, it is when we turn to the miniature cast-metal cars that we find records of the greatest productivity, although there unquestionably were a few home manufacturers using stock dies who felt well pleased with the production and sale of only a few thousand pieces. But the figures for established operations such as Tootsietoy, Barclay, Dinky Toy, and others ran into the millions annually, often into the millions on a single type of model if such production data as does survive is any indication.

In regard to production quantities, the two most overrated series are the Tootsietoy Grahams and La Salles. Not underestimated, assuredly, as beautiful models and accurate reproductions of their prototypes, for both series are without doubt among the most attractive of miniature cars, and the La Salles, with their unique four-part construction are probably the most detailed of pre–World War II miniature cast-metal vehicles, but grossly overrated as far as their supposed rarity is concerned, even when allowances are made for the fact that many of both series were unwittingly molded in contaminated metal. Well over 4,200,-000 Tootsietoy Grahams were made, and well over 1,100,000 La Salles! These figures are, if anything, low because of incomplete data. It is true that they are based on known chassis production, and in each case must be subdivided by a necessarily uncertain process into the various body types for each series. However, it is obvious that in any case the quantities of each specific body type that were made probably averaged around several hundred thousand each.

Now what is the survival rate on these and various other old model automobiles? Obviously it was highly variable, and can only be guessed at. Model cars were destroyed for a number of reasons. Probably the highest attrition rate would be found in the case of the large juvenile automobiles whose sheer size would often make it inconvenient to retain them indefinitely. With the smaller models there was a better chance of their surviving unnoticed, or of being considered not worth disposing of. On the other hand, the factor of contamination of metal causing many of the earliest die-cast models to break up must also be taken into consideration. Obviously, almost every day that passes some old model cars come to light somewhere, and instead of falling into the hands of collectors who will preserve them, are discarded. But equally obviously, the great bulk of surviving models still await discovery and, hopefully, recovery by a collector. Regardless of the great quantity of old model cars now in collections, the great bulk of surviving specimens have still to be found. It is safe to say that, as the hobby grows, the number of specimens now in collections will appear small indeed compared to the numbers that will eventually be found.

The attrition or survival rate at any given time can only be guessed at. Is the attrition rate on a given type of model vehicle now 90 percent? 95? 98? It would be very easy to guess too high or too low. However, if, say, only 5 percent of all examples originally made of a given model of which, say, 100,000 originally were made, still survive, that would mean 5,000 specimens; if only 2 percent, then that would be 2,000 pieces. Even if on some models the survival rate is less than 1 percent, say one-tenth of 1 percent even, then on an original production run of 100,000 pieces that would be 100 units. But it would appear merely on the basis of known surviving specimens of many specific models in existing collections today that any survival rate of less than 1 percent with the possible exception of juvenile automobiles would be much too low in most instances. Regardless of what considerations can be made and are made for various tangible and intangible factors, the writer would most respectfully submit that, given the present status of model-car collecting, widespread and favorably and enthusiastically looked upon as the hobby is today, no specimen of which hundreds or thousands in all probability survive at the present time is worth some of the high prices currently asked unless, to be sure, someone is consciously willing to deal in futures. If one desires to engage himself in trading in futures, it would candidly appear that speculation in grain futures would likely provide a more promising, or at least more conventional, medium than model-car futures, but manifestly if anyone wishes to go into the latter field, hopefully with his eyes open, there is, of course, no one to gainsay him.

In truth, and to give the full picture, there are at this time at least some individuals active in consciously trading in what can only candidly be described as old toy and model futures. Although sales of specimens are sometimes quite openly made on this basis, it is patently a highly speculative course and one that cannot be recommended to beginners. It is a hazardous game, based on the expectation that prices will rise. In an overall sense, this seems true of almost everything, including old models, but that specific models or categories of models will rise in the anticipated measure, is highly uncertain at best. The fact is that, at present, as far as model automobiles go, the collecting hobby in most instances possesses utterly insufficient knowledge of relative rarity and desirability even on today's basis, much

less in the future, properly to evaluate likely future trends. In the main, there is no guarantee whatsoever that the seeming "glamour" models of today will necessarily retain their aura a decade or several decades hence. Consequently this sort of buying is not only in itself perilous but also presents the danger that those who get themselves too deeply involved may well be tempted to essay less than admirable manipulations of tastes and trends in order to protect their efforts and, in a sense, to confirm the accuracy of their present intuitions.

Even if the aspect of trading in futures is eliminated and consideration is given to what some model-car collectors like to regard and call investment buying, the path is lined with pitfalls. Experience has shown that in most collecting fields such attempts seldom prove up to expectations. If a great number of hobbyists stock up on certain models in the expectation that, for one reason or another and often based on considerable study, they will prove "good," the very fact (which can hardly indefinitely be kept a secret) that such holdings are being preserved for this purpose usually is in itself sufficient to make the future of such models rather uncertain. Either the better elements in the hobby reject them simply because they are known to have been selected for speculative and manipulative purposes, or, contrawise, so many people attempt to get on the seeming bandwagon by stocking up on their own that the particular models in question show in the course of time a relative increment in value and demand far less than would have otherwise been the case if the river had been allowed to take its course. Investment buying is best left to more conventional modes; time has shown it is extraordinarily difficult, if not impossible, in the long run to manipulate collectible hobby items. There is, in fact, in the interpretations of most enthusiasts, something absolutely antithetical, if not also downright abominable, in any linking of an activity properly designated as a hobby and investment buying. Natural increments in values are welcome additions to the general fun, to be sure, but the prime motives for a collecting hobby are pleasure and relaxation, not profit. While some speculators and manipulators may, indeed, enjoy a transitory success, almost invariably, overall, events will catch up with them and their pretty bubbles have a way of bursting. Keep a hobby reasonably clean and it will prosper; allow it to become a tool of manipulation and there is no telling how it will falter and fail. Aside from the natural historical step in time provided by World War II, an additional reason why so many collectors employ it as their

Fig. 226. Here are two more of the much-regarded Kingsbury clockwork cars, similar to, but later versions of, two illustrated in the catalog in Fig. 201. The truck has dummy headlights, initially applied only to passenger cars (*William A. Hall*), and the roadster has several modifications, including battery-powered working headlights and taillight (*Joseph G. Collins*).

cut-off date is that, while there may be fakes and attempted manipulations of relative desirability, it is quite impossible for collecting-conscious speculators at this late date to attempt to rig things by acquiring and hoarding large quantities of likely looking specimens, while on the other hand, with the concurrent growth of model car collecting since the war, there is an ever increasing temptation and ever present opportunity to do precisely this in the case of currently produced models.

To reduce all that has been said on this point to a specific example: here is a particularly obvious and appropriate instance: The Tootsietoys Funnies series of 1932 and 1933 obviously proved by no means the great popular success that was anticipated for it at the time it was introduced; if not precisely an utter failure, it was by no means a sensation. Possibly the reason was that children young enough to have applauded recognizable nursery-rhyme characters in miniature automobiles were too young to read the comics themselves, while those old enough to read the comics and be familiar with the characters portrayed were by the same token old enough for the most part to prefer more realistic miniature vehicles for their play and to leave Moon Mullins and his fellows on the printed pages. As a result, the vehicles that today make up the Tootsietoy Funnies series are fairly scarce, and are regarded by most model-car collectors as relatively highly desirable. However, if in 1932 and 1933 numerous foresighted collectors had stocked up on a number of sets of these cars and held them for speculative purposes, events would probably not by any means have worked out as they did, and the models in question would today have a considerably lower status of rarity and desirability than they do today.

Following up the theme, in recent years a considerable number of prototype-oriented model-car collectors who regularly collect the cars of certain makes and series have disdainfully ignored the vehicles from time to time included in these series that are based on the supposed special vehicles used by certain fictitious characters such as the heroes of various television shows. If this situation were simply left as it is, the inevitable result will be that, some years hence, when today's current series have attained the status of old model cars, these will be the very models most sought and most difficult to find in order to complete the various series in which they originally appeared. Some decades hence these particular models probably will repeat the performance of the Tootsietoy Funnies. If, upon reading this, most collectors of these series purchase examples of these missing links, these models will then probably have little special stature one way or another. But if numerous readers of these lines immediately rush out and stock up on the model cars modeled on the vehicles allegedly employed by Batman, Agent 007, and their like, the probable result, contrary to the expectations that motivated such "investments," will be that in future days these models will possess not a higher but a much lower relative rarity and desirability among model-car collectors.

It is apparent that the model-car collectors' real problem today is not that few specimens of old models survive, but to locate the innumerable old model cars that do exist. This task, in truth, has merely just begun, and what can and will be found in the years immediately ahead will no doubt amaze and astound an enormous number of collectors.

APPENDIX I
MODEL AUTOMOBILE BUILDERS'
and
COLLECTORS' ORGANIZATIONS

The hobby of building primarily static model automobiles is naturally a rather loosely organized one, as also is the hobby of model car collecting. Unlike certain other model-building hobbies, where operation of the models is of equal or even greater import to enthusiasts than construction, there has been no need for governing bodies to establish standards of interchangeability, as in the case of model raceways, model roadways, and model railroads, much less for actual licensing authorities such as must enter into the picture where radio-controlled models are involved. Model automobile organizations consequently devote their activities primarily to encouraging model building, exchanging information, promoting fellowship, putting on model automobile shows, and similar activities. There are, of course, a number of local clubs, and your hobby shop can advise you on the existence of such activities in your area and the proper person to contact. Listed below are the major national organizations in the United States and Great Britain whose activities deal with building and collecting model automobiles:

COLLECTORS' AUTOMOTIVE REPLICA SOCIETY, P.O. Box 297, San Carlos, California 94070, U.S.A.

INTERNATIONAL ASSOCIATION OF AUTOMOTIVE MODELERS, 2725 West 43rd Street, Chicago, Illinois, U.S.A.

INTERNATIONAL CAR MODELERS ASSOCIATION, 615 Ridge Road, Arlington, New Jersey 07032, U.S.A.

INTERNATIONAL PLASTIC MODELERS SOCIETY (primarily model airplane oriented), P.O. Box 163, Ben Franklin Station, Washington, D.C. 20044, U.S.A.; in Great Britain, care of the Secretary, Cpl. R. J. Holland, Station Medical Centre, RAF North Luddenham, Oakham, Rutland, England

In addition there are clubs that are sponsored by manufacturers of model automobiles. In such cases, club activities are, of course, centered on the product of the sponsor. Information on club activities, membership requirements, and dues—almost always very nominal—usually will be found in the catalogs or packaging of the lines of model automobiles in question.

The following supplementary list of presumptively independent model automobile clubs in countries other than in the United States and Great Britain has been supplied through the courtesy of F. Brian Jewell:

ASSOCIAZIONE AUTO MODELLISTI, Brescia, Italy

CLUB DELLE QUATTROROUTINE, Via Monte di Pietl 15, Milan, Italy

CLUB INTERNATIONAL DES AUTOMOBILES MINIATURE, La Garde Freinet, Var, France

JAPANESE MINIATURE COLLECTORS CLUB, 22, 3-Chome, Asakusa, Kuramae, Taito-ko, Tokyo, Japan

MINI-AUTO CLUB, 94 Boulevard de Sebastopol, Paris 5, France

APPENDIX II
THE LITERATURE OF THE MODEL
AUTOMOBILE HOBBY

In other model hobbies, the initial and ever-continuing bulk of available books has always been concentrated on the building and operating aspects, with volumes including, much less devoted to the collecting and historical areas, coming along slowly and much later. For example, there were a substantial number of books devoted to model railroading published in the United States and Great Britain in the 1920's and 1930's, with some even earlier, but nothing specifically directed to the collector-historian until *Riding the Tinplate Rails* appeared in 1944. In the case of the model automobile, however, the situation has been, if not completely reversed, at least more substantially different, and the beginner may well be surprised at the amount of material that already exists in the English language on model automobile history and collecting. Indeed, it would appear correct to say that in this field of books the model automobile collector fairs much better than does his fellow hobbyist, the model automobile builder, a state of affairs that is in itself an adequate symbol of the whole development and makeup of the model automobile hobby as a whole.

It seems only fitting then, that the works of interest primarily to the collector be enumerated first in this list of suggested books for further reading. However, it should be noted at this point that a list of available books of interest to the model automobile hobbyist, both collector and builder, as well as reproductions of old catalogs, may be secured by sending a large stamped, self-addressed envelope to Mark Haber & Co., Box 121, Wethersfield, Connecticut, U.S.A. Books may, of course, in many instances be obtained from local hobby shops, bookstores, mail-order dealers specializing in model automobiles, or some of the model automobile magazines listed at the end of this section.

For the collector, then, there is *Model Car Collecting,* by F. Brian Jewell, which makes more than interesting reading in itself, more particularly since this 1964 volume was the pioneer in the field in the English language (it was preceded by a French emission), entirely apart from the fact that it contains a good deal of information, as well as checklists on an arrangement not duplicated anywhere else. In contrast to the general format of Mr. Jewell's book, *A History of British Dinky Toys 1934–1964* by Cecil Gibson is an outstanding example of a treatment in depth of a single manufacturer's line, covering such matters of pertinence to the devoted collector as colors and structural variations.

Many collectors of Dinky Toys, particularly in Great Britain, are still unaware of the fact that a biography of Frank Hornby, the inventor of Meccano and founder of the company that was to manufacture the Dinky Toys, was published in the United States—but not in Hornby's native England —as long ago as 1915, but such is the case. *Frank Hornby, the Boy Who Made a $1,000,000 with a Toy,* by M. P. Gould, is, of course, long out of print and a scarce collectors' item in its own right today. Obviously not published as a model automobile item (although it does include a drawing of a World War I armored car constructed with Meccano parts), it has now through subsequent company developments perforce become one, and may shortly be reprinted.

For what may well long remain the ultimate in checklists, there is the massive *Catalogue of Model Cars of the World,* by Jacques Greilsamer and Bertrand Azema, which lists some 7,000 model automobiles in two sections, one covering cars—mainly cast-metal miniatures—sold in assembled form, and one devoted to kits. While the first section is, understandably, weak on American models and further inhibited by the authors' announced program of omitting most items that are not good replicas of identifiable prototypes, the kit section appears to be rather comprehensive.

Several other books by the present writer contain model automobile illustrations and information that may serve to supplement the present volume. These are *The Toy Collector, The Handbook of Old American Toys,* and *The Complete Book of Model Raceways and Roadways,* the latter containing an historical chapter on the subject, including forerunners. *The Toy Collector* includes a lengthy checklist of manufacturers' identification marks. While Ives is known to have made but one miniature automobile, this company is, of course, the keystone of all toy and model history and collecting, and those interested in pursuing the saga will find it set down in *Messrs. Ives of Bridgeport.*

For those satisfied with pictorial values only, some magnificent ones relating to old model automobiles will be found in the opulent volume, *The Golden Age of Toys* by Jac Remise and Jean Fondin.

As already indicated, in the field of books catering to his specialty, the model car collector seems somewhat better served than the model car builder, although the latter is not without recourse to certain excellent volumes, and in addition has available a plethora of material appearing regularly in the model automobile magazines. In any event, for the builder from scratch, there is *Motor Modelling* by Rex Hays, and *Scale Model Cars* by Harold Pratley. The scope of *Plastic Model Cars,* by Cecil Gibson, is hardly adequately conveyed by its title; it is a thoroughgoing idea book. In this connection it should be observed that there is also much of interest and value to the model car builder to be found in *Model Car Collecting,* by F. Brian Jewell, already mentioned in connection with the subject of its title, particularly in the way of modifying standard models of racing cars to the exact state in which they participated in a given race.

In fact, all four of the titles listed in the preceding paragraph are not without interest and usefulness to the model automobile customizing enthusiast. His particular interests are specifically catered to in several manuals, however: *How to Wire and Detail a Model Car Engine* by Mike Doughty; *Car Model Custom Annual,* and *Building Customs from Wood and Scrap Parts.* In addition, there have been several other publications in the past sponsored by manufacturers of model car kits or paints, and far from devoid of practical interest and value to the model automobile builder and customizer.

The following is a list of magazines currently published in the United States and Great Britain that regularly carry material of interest to either or both the model automobile builder or collector:

CAR MODEL, 615 Ridge Street, North Arlington, New Jersey 07032, U.S.A.

ENGINE COLLECTORS' JOURNAL, P.O. Box 15162, Lakewood, Colorado 80215, U.S.A.

MECCANO MAGAZINE, 13–35 Bridge Street, Hemel Hempstead, Hertfordshire, England

MODEL CAR SCIENCE, Delta Magazines, Inc., 171 South Barrington Place, West Los Angeles, California 90043, U.S.A.

MODEL CARS, 13–35 Bridge Street, Hemel Hempstead, Hertfordshire, England

SCALE MODELER MAGAZINE, Challenge Publications, Inc., 7376 Greenbush Avenue, North Hollywood, California 91605, U.S.A.

TOY COLLECTORS' NEWS, 285 Auburn Road, West Hartford, Connecticut 06119, U.S.A.

In addition, those interested in building radio-controlled model automobiles will from time to time find material on this topic in the model airplane and radio control magazines, a list of which will be found in Appendix III of *The Complete Book of Model Aircraft, Spacecraft, and Rockets,* one of the companion volumes to this book.

APPENDIX III

AMERICAN AND BRITISH AUTOMOTIVE TERMINOLOGY

While the writer always feels it highly desirable to attempt to avoid repeating material found in one of his books, the following reprise of Appendix IV of *The Complete Book of Model Raceways and Roadways* appears justified here as a worthwhile aid in the use of the present volume as well as in further delving into the varied American and British books and periodicals listed in Appendix II.

Aside from such obvious spelling preferences as *tire* and *tyre,* the reader of automotive literature, both real and model, is quickly aware of a number of variations in terminology on the two sides of the Atlantic. The following lists, while far from making any pretensions to being exhaustive, include the terms which most often puzzle hobbyists. In the first list, the American term is given first, followed by the Brtish equivalent. In the second list, this procedure is reversed, with the British term first.

AMERICAN–BRITISH

cowl—*scuttle*
dashboard—*facia panel*
fender—*wing*
gasoline—*petrol*
generator—*dynamo*
rocker panel—*valance*
skirt—*apron*
tread—*track*
top—*hood*
trunk—*boot*
hood—*bonnet*
muffler—*exhaust silencer*
parking light—*side lamp*
windshield—*windscreen*
wrench—*spanner*

BRITISH–AMERICAN

apron—*skirt*
bonnet—*hood*
boot—*trunk*
dynamo—*generator*
exhaust silencer—*muffler*
facia panel—*dashboard*
hood—*top*
valance—*rocker panel*
petrol—*gasoline*
scuttle—*cowl*
side lamp—*parking light*
spanner—*wrench*
track—*tread*
windscreen—*windshield*
wing—*fender*

INDEX